TROLLOPE

'Trollope's definitive portrait . . . For the first time, Trollope emerges as a fully-fledged, living and breathing personality . . . Hall knows both Trollope's life and his work so well that he can integrate them with a smoothness rare among literary biographies and unprecedented in Trollope's case.'

Walter Kendrick, *Boston Sunday Globe*

'Hall has clearly demonstrated his devotion to Trollope's art. His expansive, thoughtfully constructed biography gives us a rounded portrait of an immensely energetic, vulnerable, difficult and generous man, and of a brilliant, dedicated artist.'

Deborah Denenholz Morse, *Chicago Tribune*

'Hall is ever the deferential, efficient servant of Trollope, who would doubtless have warmed to his latest chronicler's modesty, industry and common sense.'

Donald Lyons, *The American Spectator*

'[Hall] manages to persuade us to his view that Trollope is one of the great writers, and one whose genius was essentially comic.'

Richard Eder, *Los Angeles Times*

'a splendid, vivacious biography, Trollopian in its genially ironic spirit'

Publishers Weekly

'extraordinarily impressive as a composite record and impression of a complex personality . . . other biographers will be hard put to it to improve on this life'

Juliet McMaster, *Nineteenth-Century Literature*

'Like all great biographies, this one leaves the reader feeling he/she knows the subject almost as well as the biographer does . . . As much a page-turner as one of Trollope's own tales. Hall's is the best life of the novelist this generation is likely to see.'

John Halperin, *Biography*

N. JOHN HALL is Distinguished Professor of English at Bronx Community College and the Graduate Center of the City University of New York. He is editor of the sixty-two-volume *Selected Works of Anthony Trollope* and of *The Letters of Anthony Trollope*. He has been called by *The Times* 'arguably the world's leading Trollope scholar'.

TROLLOPE

A Biography

N. JOHN HALL

Oxford   New York
OXFORD UNIVERSITY PRESS
1993

Oxford University Press, Walton Street, Oxford OX2 6DP

Oxford New York Toronto
Delhi Bombay Calcutta Madras Karachi
Kuala Lumpur Singapore Hong Kong Tokyo
Nairobi Dar es Salaam Cape Town
Melbourne Auckland Madrid

and associated companies in
Berlin Ibadan

Oxford is a trade mark of Oxford University Press

First published 1991
First issued as an Oxford University Press paperback 1993

British Library Cataloguing in Publication Data
Data available

Library of Congress Cataloging in Publication Data
Hall, N. John.
Trollope : a biography / N. John Hall.
p. cm.
Includes bibliographical references and index.
1. Trollope, Anthony, 1815–1882—Biography. 2. Novelists,
English—19th century—Biography.
I. Title. PR5686.H26 1993 823'.8—dc20 92-34889
ISBN 0-19-283071-6 (pbk. : alk. paper)

1 3 5 7 9 10 8 6 4 2

Printed in Great Britain
on acid-free paper by
Butler and Tanner Ltd.
Frome and London

FOR

MARIANNE AND JONATHAN

ACKNOWLEDGEMENTS

I WISH to thank the following people for assistance: John Adamson, Alan S. Bell, J. E. H. Blackie, Robert S. Call, Angela Carter, Robert A. Cecil, Mary Ciebert, Nancy M. Coffin, Morton N. Cohen, Robert Colby, Desmond Corcoran, Nigel Cross, Marsha Cummins, Caroline Dakers, C. Justin Davies, Janet E. Dunleavy, Samuel Ehrenpreis, Elizabeth Epperly, Lady Faber, Mark Farrell, Lydia Fillingham, Mortimer H. Frank, Regenia Gagnier, Edward Gaposchkin, Stephen Gill, Vincent Giroud, John Glavin, Albert H. Gordon, David J. Gordon, Charles Green, David Greetham, Richard Gustafson, P. J. Gwyn, Katherine Haramundanis, Edgar F. Harden, W. Speed Hill, Kathleen Houghton, Harriet C. Jameson, Brian Johnson, William R. Johnson, Gerhard Joseph, William L. Joyce, Lynn Kadison, Fred Kaplan, Norman Kelvin, Coral Lansbury, Mark Samuels Lasner, Katharine M. Longley, Daniel K. Lowenthal, Bernard Mandelbaum, Amy Mandelker, Mario Materassi, H. H. Mathews, Laura V. Monti, Ira Nadel, John Nicoll, G. W. Pigman III, Gerald Pindar, Robert M. Polhemus, Norris Pope, Evelyn Schweidel, James N. Settle, Raymond Shapiro, S. M. Shepard, J. C. Simons, David Skilton, Patricia Thomas Srebrnik, Donald D. Stone, R. C. Terry, Duncan Thomson, James E. Tierney, Michael Timko, Chester W. Topp MD, Frank Walker, James E. Walsh, Malcolm Warner, J. G. Weir MD, Mark K. Wilson, Joseph Wittreich, Andrew Wright, Marjorie G. Wynne, David Zimmerman MD.

I owe very special gratitude to the late Gordon N. Ray, who first aroused my interest in Trollope and who guided my earliest Trollope projects; to the late Robert H. Taylor, who generously shared much of his knowledge of Trollope with me; and to Alexander D. Wainwright, who has tirelessly helped me in searching out the riches of the Taylor Collection and the Parrish Collection at Princeton University Library.

I am grateful to the CUNY Graduate School for providing me with graduate assistants, Sarah Paul, Bennett Graff, and Robert Timm, and for their patient work.

Parts of the book were read in manuscript, to my great advantage, by John Halperin, James R. Kincaid, Ruth apRoberts, Robert Tracy, S. M.

Acknowledgements

Grover, P. D. Edwards; and by John Sutherland, who, with his customary generosity, read the entire thing.

At Oxford University Press, I wish to thank the staff and particularly Kim Scott Walwyn, Frances Whistler, Elizabeth Stratford, and Mary Worthington.

My largest debt of thanks is to Nina Burgis, who assisted in various phases of this work, from library research and fact checking to manuscript reading and proof-reading.

I am grateful for assistance from the PSC-CUNY Research Award Program of the City University of New York, and, at Bronx Community College, the support of President Roscoe C. Brown, Jr., Dean Carl J. Polowczyk, and English Department Chairman Irwin Berger.

I acknowledge with gratitude fellowships from the American Council of Learned Societies and the John Simon Guggenheim Memorial Foundation.

Still other thanks are indicated in my dedication.

My debt to past and present scholars and authors is documented in the Notes. I wish here, however, to single out a few books that have been especially helpful. First is R. H. Super's *Trollope in the Post Office* (1981). Super first 'cracked' the difficult Post Office archives, and his findings helped me in annotating Trollope's *Letters* and were of much service in writing this biography. I am indebted to the original research in Helen Heineman's *Mrs. Trollope: The Triumphant Feminine in the Nineteenth Century* (1979), a work that greatly enlarged our knowledge of Anthony's mother. Patricia Thomas Srebrnik's *Alexander Strahan: Victorian Publisher* (1986) threw new light on Trollope's dealings with Strahan, and with another publisher, James Virtue.

As to other biographies: T. H. S. Escott's life of Trollope, published in 1913, though frequently inaccurate, is valuable as the product of a man who knew Trollope personally. Modern Trollope studies are still in debt to Michael Sadleir's *Trollope: A Commentary* (1927) – and also to his *Trollope: A Bibliography* (1928). The work by Lucy and Richard Stebbins (1946) contained some new research but was marred by an irresponsible use of Freudian psychoanalysis and an unexplained dislike of Trollope. James Pope Hennessy's *Anthony Trollope* (1971), while helpful on Trollope in Ireland, was inadequate in serious ways, including its utter lack of annotation. C. P. Snow's brief *Anthony Trollope: His Life and Art* (1975) is really a fine appreciative essay, enhanced by many illustrations. At the end of 1988 Robert Super's *The Chronicler of Barset: A Life of Anthony*

Acknowledgements

Trollope appeared, and I decided not to read the book. My own was nearly completed, and I did not wish to be 'answering' his. Professor Super and I have been in correspondence about Trollope for more than a decade, and he has always generously responded to my questions; he was willing to share information other scholars might have kept to themselves. In 1990, as my book was going through the press, Richard Mullen's *Anthony Trollope: A Victorian in his World* was published; again I did not read the book, but looked into it, and was impressed with its archival research; two or three of Mr Mullen's findings, including Rose Trollope's birthdate, I have incorporated into this book, with due credit in the Notes. Finally, I am looking forward to a biography of Trollope by Victoria Glendinning, whose work I admire. There will thus have been four biographies of Trollope within five years. But Trollope is a huge and complex subject, and I am confident the books will all be quite different.

New York City   N.J.H.
Great Barrington, Mass

CONTENTS

———◦◦◦◦◦———

Contents

MONTAGU SQUARE

SOUTH HARTING

ILLUSTRATIONS

Illustrations

ACKNOWLEDGEMENTS

Photographs and illustrations are supplied by, or are reproduced by kind permission of the following: Bodleian Library, Oxford, p. 193; Boston Public Library, Mass., 8, 19, 22, 23; British Library, 16, 18; British Museum, 14; Cheshunt Public Library, 10; Lady Faber, 25; Morris L. Parrish Collection, Princeton University Library, NJ, 6, 12, 15, 20, 26, p. 132; National Portrait Gallery, 3, 9, 11, 13; Orley Farm School, 2; Private collectors, 1, 4, 21, 24; Oxford University Press, 5, 7; Scottish National Portrait Gallery, 17; Robert H. Taylor collection, Princeton University Library, NJ, 27, p. 99, p. 492.

INTRODUCTION

TROLLOPE once said, 'The man of letters is, in truth, ever writing his own biography.' That notion underlies much of this book, in which I frequently quote his own words, not only from his letters and posthumously published autobiography but also from his fiction, as well as his travel books and essays. But which quotations? It has become a commonplace that the biographer himself is present in the biography, that the very quotations he selects tend to build up the image he already has of his subject, that anything approaching objectivity is illusory. In the course of writing this book, I have often been asked whether I have a particular slant or angle on Trollope. I have always answered that no, mine was not a 'thesis' biography. On the other hand, I do have leading ideas about Trollope, which, while not straining to solve all the mysteries of the man, inform this work: I think that Trollope was more of an intellect than is usually recognized; that his genius, while capable of depicting tragic figures, was essentially a comic one; that he was a writer of care and judgement—in spite of the fact that he seldom had to rewrite a line. And I think that he himself, for all the satiric self-depreciation he practised, knew he was one of the giants of English fiction.

Moreover, he was a prolific giant, who wrote nearly seventy books. They are all discussed here, but not, obviously, at length. I have chosen not to give plot summaries except in instances where they contribute to the narrative. For critical comment on the books I have drawn much from reviews contemporaneous with Trollope himself: these reviews are, so to speak, part of the record, part of the story; they are writings that Trollope himself watched closely and which to some extent influenced his work; they are, many of them, shrewd; others are good fun for their very wrong-headedness. I have also given prominence to Trollope's travel books, since they are so revealing of the man who wrote them. And I have treated the last decade of Trollope's life—which some would think relatively uneventful—with attention equal to that allotted to the previous grand decade. He went on writing and developing as a writer during these latter years, and it is as a writer that he is chiefly of interest to us.

HARROW AND LONDON

—◦•◦×◦•◦—

. . . the first twenty-six years of my life,—years of
suffering, disgrace, and inward remorse.

An Autobiography, ch. 4

1

Gentle Origins

ANTHONY TROLLOPE was born on 24 April 1815 at 16 Keppel Street, Russell Square, London. He was the fourth surviving child of Thomas Anthony Trollope and his wife Frances Milton Trollope.

He grew up in a society where, as he himself remarked at the opening of *The Prime Minister*, 'It is certainly of service to a man to know who were his grandfathers and who were his grandmothers' and 'to be able to speak of them as of persons who were themselves somebodies in their time'.[1] Such grandparents gave standing in the middle-class English world and the confidence that went with it; through them land and property might also be inherited; and they implied a network of relations able to assist young members seeking to rise in the learned professions (church and law), politics, army and navy, and the growing Civil Service. Trollope's grandfathers were both country clergymen, and he was connected to old baronetcies and the landed gentry through his paternal grandfather and—more distantly—through his maternal grandmother.

On his father's side Trollope was descended from a family that could be traced back to John Trowlope or Trolope of Thornlaw, Co. Durham, in the fourteenth century. The elder branch was ruined in the Civil Wars, but a second branch was established in Lincolnshire, and a baronetcy was conferred on the head of the family, Sir Thomas (of Casewick, Thursby and Bourne), in 1642. Anthony's grandfather and namesake was the fifth son of the fourth baronet. He was educated at Wakefield School and Pembroke College, Cambridge, took holy orders in 1762, and settled in Hertfordshire as rector of Cottered and Broadfield, two small villages near Baldock and Royston.[2] In 1767 he married Penelope Meetkerke, second daughter of Adolphus Meetkerke, owner of the fine house called Julians in the neighbouring village of Rushden; Meetkerke purchased the manor of Rushden in 1779. The Meetkerkes were a Flemish family who had settled in England in the sixteenth century, and acquired Julians in 1699 through marriage to the heiress Penelope Stone, after whom her granddaughter, the Revd Anthony Trollope's wife, was named; this Penelope's brother Adolphus, who inherited Julians and the manor of Rushden, was married but childless.[3] Anthony and Penelope Trollope had three daughters and one son, Thomas Anthony, father of the novelist, born on 23 May 1774. The eldest daughter, Penelope, married Thomas Partington, squire of Offam, Sussex (whose lavish hospitality her nephew Thomas Adolphus recalled in his reminiscences), Diana married her cousin Henry Trollope, rector of Harrington, Lincolnshire (she also remained close to her brother), and the youngest also married a clergyman. Thomas Anthony, whose mother died when he was 14, was educated at Winchester and proceeded (after first matriculating at St John's College, Cambridge) to the sister foundation, New College, Oxford in 1794. He was elected Fellow of New College in 1796 and became Bachelor of Civil Law in 1801. He adopted the legal profession, being admitted to the Middle Temple in 1799 and called to the Bar in 1804; two years later he migrated to Lincoln's Inn and became a barrister practising in the Chancery Court, with chambers at 23 Old Square, Lincoln's Inn.[4] In that year his father died at the age of 72, leaving his son a modest inheritance of about £1,700. By 1808, when he met his future wife, he was professionally successful, earning £700 a year at the Bar, with his income brought up to £900 by the New College fellowship; he had also invested in property valued at £6,000, including a leasehold in Keppel Street and freehold in Lincoln's Inn.[5] Moreover he was looked on as the heir of his childless uncle, Adolphus Meetkerke, and future owner of Julians.

Thomas Anthony was an intelligent, careful barrister, industrious to the point of laboriousness. His only liability, though in his youth it hardly appeared anywhere as calamitous as it would become, was a fierce temper that especially manifested itself in an unwillingness to suffer gladly anyone he considered a fool. A colleague once remarked that Thomas Anthony 'never came into contact with a blockhead without insisting on irrefutably demonstrating to him that he was such. . . . He was a disputatious man; and he was almost invariably—at least on a point of law—right. But the world differed from him in the opinion that being so gave him the right of rolling his antagonist in the dust and executing an intellectual dance of triumph on his prostrate form.' Even at recreation, Thomas Anthony's contentiousness and captiousness came out: he loved whist, but was not popular with his fellow players, as he continually scolded his partners. He was a respected man, but not a popular or well-liked one.[6]

If Anthony's great-grandfather Trollope was a baronet, his great-grandfather John Milton was a prosperous Bristol saddler, said to have lived to be 99. But his only son, William, born in Bristol in 1743, achieved a status in life quite comparable to that of the vicar of Cottered, for he was educated at Winchester College, and on 31 March 1762 matriculated at St John's College, Oxford; two years later he became, like his future son-in-law, a Fellow of New College. He was vicar of Heckfield in Hampshire (a New College living), from 1773 until his death in 1824, although it was not until 1801 that he became permanently resident there.[7] His only sister, Mary, married in 1773 George Bent, a member of an old Devon family, who held livings in Devon and Cornwall; George's father (also named George), educated at Oxford and St Catharine's College, Cambridge, where he took a medical degree, was an Exeter physician. Two of the Revd George Bent's children, John, an army officer, and Frances (always known as Fanny), a spinster who lived in Exeter until her death in 1860, maintained a lifelong friendship with their much younger second cousin, Anthony Trollope. (Fanny Bent was the original for Jemima Stanbury, the benign despot in *He Knew He Was Right*.) William himself married on 23 June 1774, at St Thomas's Church, Bristol, Mary Gresley (Anthony would use the name in his fiction),[8] daughter of Francis and Cecilia Gresley; her father was a remote connection of the Gresleys of Derbyshire and Leicestershire, holders of an old baronetcy. The Gresley family in the west of England was related to the rich Bristol merchant Joseph Hellicar, and William and Mary Milton's children visited and corresponded with their Hellicar cousins.[9] The couple had four children, Mary, born in 1776, Cecilia, who died in infancy in 1778, Frances ('Fanny'), born in 1779, and Henry, born in 1784. Their mother died shortly after the birth of Henry. Mary was to marry, at the relatively late age of 42, Captain Charles Clyde of the Royal Navy. Henry Milton attended Winchester and New College and had a considerable career in the War Office. Frances was to become the mother of Anthony Trollope; she would also become, at the age of 53, a celebrated author.

More is known of the Revd William Milton than of the Revd Anthony Trollope, partly because the former got into print, and partly because he lived so much longer and came accordingly to be written of by one of the family of writing Trollopes, his daughter's eldest son, Thomas Adolphus Trollope. By the time Thomas Adolphus Trollope knew him, William Milton had settled into an apparently jovial if somewhat eccentric old age as vicar of Heckfield. He had long been an amateur scientist, inventor, and mathematician. In 1792, still resident at Bristol, he had submitted plans for the improvement and enlargement of Bristol Port and Harbour; his plans were rejected with thanks by the city fathers, but he continued to advocate his scheme, and as late as 1812 he was still going into print on his original suggestion about making the Port a 'Floating Harbour'. His later years were given chiefly to inventing a stage-coach that would not upset, a subject on which he published a number of articles, including a pamphlet, 'The Danger of Travelling in Stage Coaches etc., A Remedy Proposed' (1810). Prototype models for these uncapsizeable, low-slung, huge-wheeled vehicles filled the coach-house attached to his vicarage. Another of his inventions was in a more personal line: the old man disliked the sound of a knife cutting on porcelain, and he devised dinnerware with a recessed, two-inch circular silver disk in the centre on which to cut one's meat. His inventions cost him much in time and money. Thomas Adolphus described him as a parish priest 'after the fashion of his day': kindly, liberal to the poor, liked by his neighbours; a charming old man, gentlemanlike, suave, and 'unquestionably [clever] in a queer, crotchety sort of way. . . . But he would have had no more idea of attempting anything of the nature of active parochial work . . . than he would have had of scheming to pay the national debt. Indeed, the latter would have been the more likely to occupy his mind.'[10] William Milton was in fact the kind of worldly clergyman of whom his grandson Anthony was so fond and delighted to delineate in fiction. He also possessed a lively sense of humour, one of his legacies to his daughter Frances. Her penchant for writing seems to have come to her through his example also. Certainly from him she took a love of reading and learning, for William Milton had more to do with the shaping of his daughter's life than did most fathers. On the early death of his first wife he had undertaken not merely to tutor his daughter but in effect to bring her up himself. She developed into a clever, lively, good-humoured girl. She learned quickly, read French and Italian, relished Molière and Dante, and knew contemporary English letters. It was not until 1801, when Frances was past 20, that her father remarried, this time to a distant relation Sarah Partington, and moved to Heckfield, taking up residence there. The Norman church and Tudor vicarage commanded a lovely view of the Hampshire countryside, and for a while Frances relished her new surroundings. She continued her literary interests, but soon grew somewhat restless in the country. There was little social life and few would-be husbands about. She apparently was never very close to her stepmother, whom she always called Mrs Milton.[11]

In 1803 there came to Frances a chance for a life different from that in a quiet rural vicarage. Her brother Henry had accepted a clerkship in the

War Office, and leased or rented one of the small houses in the recently built Keppel Street, Russell Square, Bloomsbury, an area forming part of the Bedford Estate. It was a neighbourhood popular with lawyers because of its nearness to the lawcourts; the move to the West End of judges and leading barristers had not yet begun. Frances and her sister Mary set up house with their brother at 27 Keppel Street, an arrangement made possible by an annual allowance of £50 to each of them by their father. Frances took immediately to London, especially to its theatres and galleries, and to the society of other young people with artistic and intellectual interests into which Henry brought her.

In the summer of 1808 Henry introduced his sisters to Thomas Anthony Trollope, who lived in one of the larger Keppel Street houses, No. 16, of which he owned the lease.[12] The young barrister's courtship of Frances began almost immediately, and its course can be followed closely because their letters for this period have survived. Thomas Anthony's to her were apparently kept among her own papers, and came down to posterity through her son Thomas Adolphus. Those from Frances to Thomas Anthony Trollope were sent by a stranger to Anthony in the late 1860s.[13] That love letters to Thomas Anthony from his future wife should have strayed into the hands of a stranger is perhaps emblematic of the disordered later life of the family, or at least of his own disorderliness.

Anthony, who contrived seemingly countless proposals in his fiction, and who gave letter writing such prominence in his novels, must have read his father's letter of proposal with intense interest. Written on 1 November 1808, and addressing her 'My dear Madam', it begins by mentioning a debating society discussion of whether a man ought to declare his attachment to a lady 'viva voce . . . or by epistolary correspondence'. He trusts Frances is 'not entirely unaware that my chief delight has long since had its source in your society and conversation' and if her feelings included 'the slightest degree of mutuality' she could perhaps give him an answer within three weeks. He then launches into a description of his financial status, £900 per annum, of which £200 would be cut off were he to marry and thereby surrender his New College fellowship. This lengthy letter he himself characterized as 'perhaps chiefly to be remarked by its singularity, and particularly in its manner and style being so little adapted to its subject'.[14]

She, ever spontaneous, answered immediately: 'It does not require three weeks consideration Mr. Trollope, to enable me to tell you that the letter you left with me last night was most flattering and gratifying to me.' She agreed that it was best to talk over financial matters at the very outset:

her income was an annual allowance of £50; she would receive a fortune of £1,300 on marrying.[15]

By December, writing from Heckfield, she again addresses money matters directly, confirming her relatively modest prospects—nothing beyond what she had told him of except one third of her father's estate upon his death and one third of £2,000 upon her stepmother's death. 'Ought not [her relative lack of money] to make a difference as to the *time* at which you mean to burden yourself with a poor wife?' He of course replies that he will hear of no delay, and he even tries to make a joke of her omitting to mention her secret snug 'pin money' from her one-eighth share of the profits to be derived from her father's uncapsizeable coach.

'And so you have found me out!' she answers. '*I did hope* that *my share* of the patent coach would have supplied all my little private extravagances and you have been never the wiser.' And later, 'I really think I must engage, if you behave well, to allow you a thousand a year or so, out of my coach-receipts. I know this is a trifling compared with what I shall receive.' But whatever the subject, she—like so many women in her son's novels— is recognizably wittier, quicker, more satiric than her man. In connection with some slight misunderstanding she writes, 'Would Easter were come, and then we could quarrel comfortably at our leisure.'[16]

Thomas Anthony already suffered from the headaches that were to be the curse of his life; he also complained of back pain, bad colds, and eye inflammation. At the same time he pesters her with questions as to her health, and she replies, '*I am perpetually well I thank you.*' She chides him jokingly about going to a ball in London without her: 'Do not, *if you can help it*, fall in love with Miss Foot.' She herself has been called aside from writing by a male visitor but she has returned to the letter: 'Do you not marvel how I could tear myself [away] to write to you? Even now I hear the sweet sound of his voice in the next room—and yet I stir not—Oh wonderful power of constancy! Remember this when you see Miss Foot.'[17]

Three weeks before the wedding, she writes with unusual seriousness: 'Does not the near approach of it almost frighten you? I tremble lest you should love me less a twelve-month hence than you do now. I sometimes fear you may be disappointed in me, that you will find me less informed, less capable of being a companion to you, than you expect.'[18]

He answers that perhaps her doubts have arisen from his 'cold and flegmatic manner of telling you how anxious I always am of knowing you are well. . . . but, my dearest love, are you still to learn my character and sentiments? still to be made acquainted with my lifeless manners, my stone-like disposition? Are you yet to be informed in what detestation I hold all ardent professions, & in what admiration actions that want not the aid of declamation but boldly speak for themselves?'[19]

'You are an odd mortal,' she replies, 'but you call *yourself* so many names . . . that I *forbear*. . . . What you say of professions, is very just,' yet she believes that women, at least, cannot help but be pleased with '*expressions* as well as *proofs*, of tenderness'. But such serious talk is short-lived with her, and five days before the wedding she is asking, 'How did *your* heart stand Miss Foot's attractions all Sunday?'[20] The letters reveal the differences in character and temperament between the two writers: his can never shake off a certain stiffness and reserve; hers are lively, easy, and informal. Anthony said of her letters, 'In no novel of Richardson's or Miss Burney's have I seen a correspondence at the same time so sweet, so graceful, and so well expressed.'[21]

Thomas Anthony Trollope and Frances Milton were married on his thirty-fifth birthday, 23 May 1809. She was 30. All Heckfield is said to have attended the wedding. Parson Milton decided not to perform the ceremony but to take the role of father.[22] The couple settled immediately into their newly refurnished home at 16 Keppel Street. Their years there seem to have been as happy—though socially and intellectually more lively—as those of the Thomas Furnivals, a Lincoln's Inn barrister and his wife, in *Orley Farm*, who also began their married life in Keppel Street. Letters written when Thomas Anthony and Frances were apart (he on circuit, she on country visits) show their mutual devotion, touchingly expressed in one she wrote from Julians in July 1809, responding to his plea that she take care of herself: 'As long as I am valuable to you, you need not fear my doing otherwise. . . . Love me half as well as I love you, and I will be contented. . . . if you were with me I should be very happy.'[23] They entertained a stream of interesting visitors, including many from Winchester College and Winchester Close, Lady Dyer, and Italian exiles—of whom the most distinguished was General Guglielmo Pepe, who was subsequently hero of the hopeless defence of Venice against Austria.[24] Anthony remarked of his mother: 'An Italian marquis who had escaped with only a second shirt from the clutches of some archduke whom he wished to exterminate, or a French *prolétaire* with distant ideas of sacrificing himself to the cause of liberty, were always welcome to the modest hospitality of her house.'[25]

On 29 April 1810 their first child was born; he was christened Thomas Adolphus Trollope, the middle name signalling his expected inheritance of Julians in Hertfordshire. Other children followed quickly, and during the Keppel Street days, four more were born: Henry in 1811, Arthur William in 1812, Emily, who died the day of her birth, in late 1813, and Anthony on 24 April 1815. Anthony was baptized in St George's Church, Bloomsbury, on 18 May 1815.[26]

The year of Anthony's birth also brought the end of the war with Napoleon and the consequent beginning of a protracted agricultural depression, when the artificially high price of corn plummeted as normal trade resumed. That depression gradually brought about the financial ruin of the modestly prosperous Trollopes, for Thomas Anthony had decided in 1810 that a country house and farm would be a good investment. The farm would provide extra income and give his growing family the benefit of summers in the country; his involvement in its management would prepare him for taking over the Julians estate after his uncle's death. Fanny, however, presciently remarked when the search for a suitable farm began in 1810, 'The profit of such a purchase must I should think be precarious.'[27] And looking back, many years later, Anthony would call the scheme 'the grave of all my father's hopes, ambition, and prosperity, the cause of my mother's sufferings, and of those of her children, and perhaps the director of her destiny and of ours'.[28]

2

Harrow Day Boy

In 1813 Thomas Anthony found what seemed the ideal farm, conveniently near to London, part of Lord Northwick's estate at Harrow. Ilotts Farm (the name went back to the late sixteenth century) consisted of more than 160 acres, with hay as the main crop, and included a small but pleasant farmhouse, gardens, an orchard, and outbuildings. Trollope took the farm on a twenty-one-year lease (with an option for renewal) at a rent of £600 a year, not an excessive price when corn and hay were fetching high prices. The Trollopes spent the following summer there, Mr Trollope making the hour's journey by gig to his Lincoln's Inn law chambers when his law practice required it. This summer residence replaced Fanny's former visits to Heckfield, from which her father and stepmother had retired to a smaller house at Reading. After Anthony's birth in 1815, Thomas Anthony moved his wife and four boys to the Harrow farmhouse and let 16 Keppel Street.[1] At Harrow two more children were born, Cecilia in 1816 and Emily in 1818.

One great advantage of their Harrow residence was that it made the boys eligible for virtually free education as day boys at the famous public school, where three members of the Drury family, all friends of the Trollopes, were housemasters and tutors. Thomas Anthony intended his sons to follow him at Winchester and New College; he would use Harrow as a preparatory school while they waited for places to become vacant at Winchester. Presumably the Drurys had encouraged him in this course; the Trollope boys entered Harrow School more as private pupils than as regular scholars as they were too young to attend in the schoolroom.[2]

By 1817 the family were outgrowing the farmhouse, and Mr Trollope gladly accepted Lord Northwick's proposal that Trollope should build a suitable house on the land (a possibility provided for in the lease), which would at some date revert to the estate; in return, rent would be reduced by £240 a year to cover a construction mortgage of £3,000. The house was completed during the following year, at a cost exceeding the intended

£3,000. Trollope persuaded Northwick to purchase additional acreage to accommodate improvements to the land surrounding it, these to be superintended by Fanny: relocation of roads, the planting of shrubbery, draining of ponds. These projects alone cost a further £1,000.[3] One of the fields purchased was known locally as 'Julians', the very name of the still-to-be-inherited place in Hertfordshire, and the Trollopes, remarking the curious coincidence, named their new home Julians.[4] An impressive red brick structure of two high storeys, with tall windows and a bowed out drawing-room, it still stands today.

The inevitable inheritance of the Hertfordshire Julians was a major consideration in building the new house: there was no question that during the present or extended lease of the Harrow property at a reduced rate either Thomas Anthony or his son Thomas Adolphus would inherit the fine country estate of Uncle Meetkerke. The Trollopes continued to visit the Meetkerkes, and young Thomas Adolphus was even 'shown to the tenantry' as the eventual heir. Tom later recalled how these visits contrasted with those to old grandpa Milton; the son of the saddler was highly cultivated, whereas Uncle Adolphus, for all his much grander establishment, had in him more than a touch of Squire Western. He was 'a good landlord, a kindly-natured man, a good sportsman', but a man of 'clownish rusticity'. At the parish church, the vicar, a bachelor named Skinner, would preach on Sundays a short sermon, after which the squire would sing out, as the preacher was descending the pulpit, 'Come up to dinner, Skinner!' Old Mrs Meetkerke, 'an admirable specimen of a squiress', was very active in helping the poor of the parish; she came down to breakfast every day dressed in a green riding habit, and 'passed most of her life on horseback'.[5] When she died, on 28 July 1817, the Trollopes, planning their new house, could have had no misgivings; after all, the widower was well past 60. However, in October 1818 Meetkerke married a young wife (Matilda Jane Wilkinson, daughter of R. Johnson Wilkinson, of Portman Square, London), and on 22 December 1819 was born the first of their six children, Adolphus, a son and heir to Julians.[6] (Many years later, Cecilia Meetkerke, the second wife of the new heir, became a 'dear Friend' of Anthony, who assisted her in publishing poetry.) It was asserted in various quarters that Thomas Anthony had brought the catastrophe on himself by arguing about politics so strenuously with the old-fashioned Tory. Uncle was no intellectual match for the liberal nephew, and Thomas Anthony had become almost *persona non grata* with the squire.[7] How much more pleasant must Meetkerke have found the company of the young woman who became his wife.

Thomas Anthony bore up under his disappointment, but now that the future was altered so drastically, he had to make adjustments. The new house, which seemed so sensible an arrangement when first built, was now an extravagance, especially as the farm had failed to turn a profit every year since he had purchased it. The family had been living in the new house scarcely more than a year when it was determined that the place must be let and the family return to the old farmhouse. Thereupon Trollope spent £500 enlarging the old house, which he and Frances with some courage named 'Julian Hill'. After renovations it would have the two storeys bowed out as did the new Julians. Anthony was to use the farmhouse for the original 'Orley Farm' in the novel of that name, in which the central figure's life is controlled and undone by her efforts to have her son inherit the house. Orley Farm/Julian Hill is described in the opening chapter as 'commodious, irregular, picturesque, and straggling . . . three buildings of various heights, attached to each other, and standing in a row.'*8

This 'pretty cottage', as Mrs Trollope called it, became a pleasant home, and the Trollope family had good moments within its irregular walls. Fanny soon had the house fixed up nicely, and the first five years of the 1820s were relatively happy ones. Here at Julian Hill she created a happy social life for herself and her children. She entertained friends and neighbours, including her closest Harrow friends, her immediate neighbours, the Grant family, some of whom lived on to be 'the oldest and dearest friends' of Anthony's life.9 Other neighbours on visiting terms were the Drurys and their relations the Merivales, whose boys were at Harrow School, and Lady Milman and her sons (Sir William, and the poet, the Revd Henry Milman), who lived near Pinner. London friends were also frequent visitors: Fanny's lifelong friends the Garnett sisters; the German *savant* Dr Pertz (whose courtship of Julia Garnett Fanny Trollope assisted); Mary Russell Mitford, George Hayter, the painter—in 1824 Thomas Anthony sat for one of the lawyers in Hayter's picture of Lord Russell's trial. 10 Fanny entertained her own and neighbours' children with charades and other games; she taught her children French and Italian, succeeding fairly well with Thomas Adolphus and Henry; she gave at-home theatricals in French and English. Some of the dramas were her own creations. Her love for Dante and Italian set even Mr Trollope studying Italian. And from Julian Hill she attended London theatres and museums, sometimes with her children. Anthony, in later life an avid, almost

* John Everett Millais drew Julian Hill for the first illustration and frontispiece of the novel. The house itself was torn down about 1905.

passionate, museum-goer, recalled being taken in 1824—he was 9—to the newly opened National Gallery at 100 Pall Mall, that 'dingy, dull, narrow house, ill-adapted for the exhibition of the treasures it held . . . but the spot is one which I shall always regard with warm affection, for there I conceived my first ideas of the nature of a picture'.[11]

The nursery at Julian Hill, as in the Keppel Street days, was ruled over by an ageing woman called 'Farmer'. An austere, somewhat grim person, she 'inspired more awe than affection', part of the awe arising obscurely from the fact that she was an Anabaptist. (Young Tom once told a visitor, Dr George Frederick Nott, one of the prebendaries of Winchester, that if the children were not always good it was because their nurse was an Anabaptist.) According to Tom, always his mother's special favourite, the children's happiness came from their mother: 'My mother's disposition . . . was of the most genial, cheerful, happy *enjoué* nature imaginable. All our happiest hours were spent with her . . . a *tête-à-tête* with her was preferable to any other disposal of a holiday hour.' But even Mrs Trollope's good nature could not compensate for her husband's irascibility, which increased as his health declined and his financial situation worsened. Tom wrote that their father was 'not popular' in his own home, that although he never whipped or caned the children, 'No one of all the family circle was happy in his presence.' Thomas Anthony sought alleviation from the 'bilious headaches' that plagued him through constant recourse to calomel, a drug widely used, chiefly as a cathartic. According to Thomas Adolphus, his father's continual use of calomel made him so irritable that 'unconsciously, we sought to avoid his presence, and to consider as hours of enjoyment only those that could be passed away from it.' Tom related how his father was inordinately fond of reading aloud to his assembled family in the evenings, how they would have escaped 'at almost any cost'; he said his father's nightly renderings throughout one winter of *Sir Charles Grandison* occasioned in him 'loathing disgust' for that work.[12]

Thomas Anthony's domestic efforts focused obsessively on his sons' education, which for him meant a grounding in the ancient classics. Anthony recorded, 'From my very babyhood . . . I had had to take my place alongside of him as he shaved at six o'clock in the morning, and say my early rules from the Latin Grammar, or repeat the Greek alphabet; and was obliged at these early lessons to hold my head inclined towards him, so that in the event of guilty fault, he might be able to pull my hair without stopping his razor or dropping his shaving-brush. No father was ever more anxious for the education of his children, though I think none ever knew less how to go about the work.'[13] Tom also wrote of how the hair pulling put Mr Trollope's small pupils in a nervous state of expectancy little calculated to increase learning. Then too, 'There was also a strange sort of asceticism about [Thomas Anthony], which seemed to make enjoyment, or any employment of the hours save work distasteful and offensive to him. Lessons for us boys were never over and done with.'[14]

Anthony grew up in a family only nominally religious, and sharply intolerant of evangelicalism in its various forms. Thomas Adolphus wrote, 'I think there was a perfunctory saying of some portion of the catechism on a Sunday morning. . . . But . . . in our own minds, and apparently in those of all concerned, the vastly superior importance of the Virgil lesson admitted of no moment's doubt.' All was 'respectability and propriety', and Tom never remembered seeing his father the worse from drink. But both parents abhorred 'evangelical tendencies', and any inclination to stress religious instruction would have been interpreted as such: 'I grew into boyhood with the notion that "evangelicalism" or "low churchism" was a note of vulgarity—a sort of thing that might be be expected to be met with in tradesmen's back parlours, and "academies," where the youths who came from such places were instructed in English grammar and arith-metic, but was not to be met with, and was utterly out of place, among gentlemen and in gentlemanlike places of education.'[15]

Evangelicalism at Harrow was embodied in the person of the Revd John William Cunningham, the low-church vicar of Harrow, formerly curate at Clapham under John Venn of the so-called Clapham sect. He suffered under the nickname 'Velvet Cunningham' for his authorship of *The Velvet Cushion*, a book so pious, prejudiced, and narrow-minded that some reviewers accused him of satirically attacking the Church of England. He had many followers in Harrow, but he was fiercely opposed by the Harrow School Drurys, themselves all clerics. According to Thomas Adolphus, the antagonism between Cunningham and the Drurys was '*the* leading fea-ture, of the social life of Harrow in those days'.[16] The Drurys, all of them enormous in size, included Mark Drury, the under master, who had nearly succeeded his brother Dr Joseph Drury as headmaster in 1805 but who had lost out to Dr Butler. It was Mark Drury who became Tom's first tutor in 1818. Because of his extreme obesity he had ceased 'going up', that is, ascending the hill to the school proper, and conducted all his teaching at his boarding house. Mark's son William was fifth master. But the unques-tioned leader of the Drury faction and most important Harrow master of his day—and the man who was to be young Anthony's tutor—was Harry Drury, assistant master, Joseph Drury's son. 'Old Harry' was outspoken, frank, and learned; he was rumoured to have all of Virgil and Horace by heart. And as Byron's former tutor and continuing friend, he was Harrow's one contact with Europe's most famous living poet. Charles Merivale, who was at Harrow with the Trollope boys, remembered Harry Drury as a 'big, stalwart man . . . genial but terrible; no other man has ever so elated, no other has ever so dismayed and confounded me.'[17] Anthony, at 19, would say Harry's 'frankness is bearishness—but he is a good natured fellow—though he has often nearly plagued my life out'.[18]

Trollope's father had long opposed evangelicalism, so he would have sided with the Drurys even had they not been old friends. But his wife became even more militantly opposed to Cunningham. (That Cunningham eventually came to live in the house they had built did not help endear him to her.[19]) Outwardly she did not quarrel with him, and she even invited him to some of her 'At Homes'. But she never lost an opportunity to have fun at Cunningham's expense. When the pretty 18-year-old daughter of a neighbour defended the vicar to Mrs Trollope, she told her to beware of Cunningham—a man with eleven children—lest his kiss of peace 'change its quality if repeated'.[20] She loved to tell the story of how Cunningham asked her one day whether she thought the games of charades with which she entertained young people at parties were a 'suitable diversion for young ladies':

'Why not, Mr. Cunningham?' demanded [Mrs Trollope]. 'Mrs. Cunningham has evening parties to which we are always glad to go to hear your daughters play upon the piano.'

'Ah, yes,' replied the Vicar, 'but my daughters always have their backs to the audience.'[21]

When Cunningham asked her why she continued to amuse herself by repeating this story, she told him, 'Because you deserved it, sir.'[22]

It was an event involving Cunningham that brought Mrs Trollope to write a privately circulated mock epic poem, an effort which in some ways presaged aspects of her literary career. In 1822, Allegra, Lord Byron's 5-year-old illegitimate daughter by Claire Clairmont, died at a convent in Italy. When the poet requested that a memorial tablet be erected in Harrow church where she was to be buried, the vestry, which included Cunningham, the clerical faction of the school, and important laymen of the parish, denied the tablet on the grounds that it would, as Anthony later said, 'teach the boys to get bastards'. The whole proceeding had an irresistible attraction for Mrs Trollope, who idolized Byron, to an extent that would eventually amuse Anthony. When he was 19, he copied out the poem, adding notes of his own, sharply critical of his mother's effort, from her metre to her politics. And Cunningham provoked a note from the future chronicler of England's clergymen: '[He was] a man almost worshipped by the low church at Harrow, very unpopular with the gentry, and much feared by the poor—a most despicable hypocrite—a gentleman like man with very pleasing manners and a sweet voice. I used to talk to Cunningham a good deal at one time, and recall he always used to be very civil to me, but he is a cringing hypocrite and a most confounded liar, and would give his eyes to be a bishop.'[23]

Mrs Trollope did not let up on Cunningham; in her fierce attack upon evangelicalism, *The Vicar of Wrexhill*, the story of a rich widow beguiled by an unctuous, dishonest, and licentious low-church cleric, it is obvious—although of course she denied the identification—that the model for the Revd W. J. Cartwright of the novel was J. W. Cunningham. Undoubtedly the family view of Cunningham and Anthony's own observation of the contest between him and the 'high and dry' clerical masters at Harrow School contributed largely to his fictional clergy and gave him an early interest in church politics. Cunningham/Cartwright influenced his portrayal of such evangelicals as Obadiah Slope, the Proudies, Jeremiah Maguire, and Samuel Prong, far though they are from the savage caricature in Mrs Trollope's *Vicar of Wrexhill*. On the other hand, his many worldly, broadminded clerics, from Archdeacon Grantly onwards, owe something to the Drurys and to George Butler and Charles Longley, successive headmasters of Harrow.

Anthony's earliest days were pleasant enough, with elder brothers and younger sisters, under the eye of Old Farmer, who seems to have been a benign tyrant. The worst part of his day was the early-morning classical lessons with his father (had Thomas Anthony not had to travel almost daily to London for his law work, he himself would have undertaken the entire early education of his sons); otherwise, the sympathetic and cheerful presence of his mother prevailed. But in early 1823 he entered Harrow School, together with his brother Arthur, a sickly boy who would die the following year. School records show Anthony and Arthur 'unplaced', that is, only informally enrolled because they were too young for the school proper. (Tom and Henry had entered on the same terms, in 1818.[24]) With this beginning of his formal schooling, Anthony entered that aspect of his boyhood that he later called 'as unhappy as that of a young gentleman could well be, my misfortunes arising from a mixture of poverty and gentle standing on the part of my father, and from an utter want on my own part of that juvenile manhood which enables some boys to hold up their heads even among the distresses which such a position is sure to produce'.[25]

Anthony's tutor, to whose house—the largest boarding house* of the school—he would trudge daily, was the formidable Harry Drury, Mr Trollope's closest friend among the Harrow masters. But the Trollope–Drury connection was of little help to the Trollope boys. Both Tom and Anthony recalled with bitterness their status as 'home boarders', that is, as day students or 'village boys', which actually meant 'charity boys' at a school for the sons of the nobility and the rich. Their standing made them, Thomas Adolphus said, 'pariahs'. Their situation was made even worse by a recent history of disturbance over the question of home boarders. Some parishioners had tried in court to have the school returned to a more local institution, in keeping with the intentions of the school's founder in Elizabethan days; they charged that at Harrow School as it had come to be operated the boarders or 'foreigners' were squeezing out free students, and that the latter, the village children, were in danger of imbibing 'the extravagant and expensive Ideas as well as the pernicious Habits of the young men of Fortune'; they complained also that village youngsters were 'scoffed at and ill-treated by the other Boys; and their lives not only rendered uncomfortable but often in great Danger; insomuch that Parents of such children have been obliged to take them away from the School.' The school authorities, somewhat lamely, protested that they used 'all the means in their power' to 'repress such conduct'. But the Master of Rolls, Chancery Court, ruled in favour of the School Governors, and very little changed. The entry of Tom and Henry brought the number of day scholars at the school, among a total of nearly three hundred boys, to a mere ten.[26] Tom, who suffered far fewer scars, emotional or otherwise, from his public school education than did Anthony, said that bullying at Harrow School was 'brutal', partly because at Harrow, unlike most other public schools, there was no official, and therefore somewhat controlled, system of fagging; rather the bigger and stronger boys simply '*assumed* an authority supported by sheer violence over the smaller and weaker'.[27]

There were critics of the anarchic freedom and bullying in eighteenth- and early nineteenth-century public schools; Sydney Smith, a near contemporary of Thomas Anthony Trollope at Winchester, characterized the

---

* All three Drurys, like the other masters, took in as many boarders as possible, a system that made them, in Thomas Adolphus's words, 'far more dependent on their trade as victuallers than on their profession as teachers'.[28] The Drurys were sadly unsuccessful in money matters: in 1826 Mark and William fled from their creditors to the continent, allegedly leaving behind debts to tradesmen of some £40,000.[29] The following year Harry Drury went bankrupt, probably because of his mania for collecting expensive books.

public school regimen as one of 'abuse, neglect and vice', resulting in 'premature debauchery that only prevents men from being corrupted by the world by corrupting them before they enter the world'.[30] Thomas Hughes's *Tom Brown's Schooldays* has made familiar the brutality of Rugby before Dr Arnold's reforms. Leslie Stephen, later a friend of Trollope's, said sarcastically, 'Nobody could have guessed that an ideal education would be provided by bringing together a few hundred lads and requesting them to govern themselves.'[31] On the other hand, the detractors were far outnumbered by advocates of public schools, who maintained that self-government by boys fostered a spirit of independence, freedom, and manliness. William Gregory, who was at Harrow during Anthony's later stint at the school, thought it a 'fine, manly place . . . a little world in itself and boys were the arbiters of their own happiness or unhappiness in it.'[32] Reminiscences and biographies of men who had been at Harrow in the 1820s—Cardinal Manning, Bishop Christopher Wordsworth, Sidney Herbert, Francis Trench—claim that they avoided the idle and 'low' sets, enjoyed friendships with other able boys, and got a good classical education. Certainly Mr Trollope, himself the product of a public school, thought that a rough-and-ready public school was the best preparation for later life.

Tom and Henry had gone to Harrow School from the 'big house', but Anthony, starting later, did so from the farmhouse, and he thought this might have made his position as home boarder even worse. He was barely 8 and 'never spared' by the older boys of the school. He was lonely—Tom and Henry had moved on to Winchester in 1820 and 1821 respectively, and Arthur was usually absent from school—and running to and from the school was a 'daily purgatory'.[33] One of his tormentors, G. F. Duckett (who entered the school in 1820 at the age of 9), later recorded that Anthony was 'pounced upon by boys to repeat his "pedigree," whenever they met him, and usually after each repetition [he] received a kick, more or less innocent, more or less severe. For a little defenceless boy this state of existence must have been a sore trial.' Duckett, who was once 'caught in the act' of kicking his victim by Mrs Trollope, claimed to remember the *ipsissima verba* that young Anthony was called upon to recite before being kicked: he had to say that his pedigree 'was derived Tally-Ho Sha the Norman (*who*) came over with William the Conqueror' and whose 'descendant a little time after killed three wolves. *Trois* being the French for three, and *loup* the French for wolf, the name was called "Trois loups" and after many contractions, our name became Trollope.'[34] Anthony's clothes were, by his own admission, always messy and dirty (he seems to have

been a messy, crumpled sort of dresser all his life). He recalled being met
by the headmaster, the awesome (and, if Byron is to be believed,
pompous) Dr George Butler, who asked him if it were possible that
Harrow School could be disgraced by so dirty a little boy: 'Oh, what I felt at
that moment! But I could not look my feelings. I do not doubt that I was
dirty. . . . He must have known me had he seen me as he was wont to see
me, for he was in the habit of flogging me constantly. Perhaps he did not
recognise me by my face.'35

After two miserable years at Harrow School, Anthony, not making any
progress academically, and still 'lag' or 'junior boy', that is, the youngest in
the school,36 was sent in early 1825 on the advice of Henry Drury to a
private school at Sunbury, kept by his cousin Arthur Drury. At Sunbury,
for two years, Anthony was somewhat better off, for though he had no
pocket money, he boarded at the school and accordingly lived 'more
nearly on terms of equality with other boys'. On one occasion four boys
were accused of 'some nameless horror', and Anthony, innocent not only
of the deed but probably of the very notion of the deed (some kind of
homosexual practice is hinted at), was punished along with the other
three, the 'curled darlings of the school', who Trollope well knew would
never have invited him to share their wickedness. Punishment consisted
in part of being served last at meals for an entire term and having to write
out a long sermon before being admitted to the playground, which task in
Anthony's case took him until two days before holidays. He eventually
learned that Arthur Drury condemned him because 'having come from a
public school, [he] might be supposed to be the leader of wickedness.' At
the start of the next term, Drury whispered to him that he may have been
wrong, and Anthony, with 'all a stupid boy's slowness', said nothing. Fifty
years later, writing his *Autobiography*, Trollope said the affair 'burns me
now as though it were yesterday. What lily-livered curs those boys must
have been not to have told the truth—at any rate as far as I was concerned.
I remember their names well, and almost wish to write them here.'37

In 1823, in spite of growing financial problems, Mrs Trollope induced
Thomas Anthony to take her on holiday to Paris. Her wanderlust was
beginning to show itself. In the French capital they were to meet up with
old Bristol friends of the Milton family, the Garnetts. John Garnett had
taken his family to America, living in New Brunswick, New Jersey, on the
banks of the Raritan River; but upon Garnett's death in 1820, his widow
and three daughters, Julia, Harriet, and Fanny, returned to England and
then settled in Paris. The Garnetts moved in intellectual circles, and

their friends, whom the Trollopes met on this and subsequent visits, included Washington Irving, Benjamin Constant, Jean Charles Sismondi, Stendhal, Prosper Mérimée, and Fenimore Cooper. Through the Garnetts Mrs Trollope renewed her friendship with the young Scottish reformer Frances Wright, whom she had met through her brother Henry.[38] Frances Wright, after visiting America in 1818, had become enamoured of the New World and republicanism; she now found England by comparison 'retrograde'; the one glaring fault of America was of course slavery, which she militantly opposed. By 1821 she had published *Views of Society and Manners in America*, a book that brought her some celebrity; she attracted the attention of General Lafayette, and subsequently became virtually a daughter to him, although nasty tongues unfairly linked the aged General and the wealthy young woman romantically.[39] Mrs Trollope's friendship with the Garnetts and Frances Wright led to an introduction to Lafayette, who invited the Trollopes for a lengthy stay at his country estate, La Grange. In her journal Mrs Trollope described in rhapsodic terms almost everything she saw, from the six manservants who waited on table to the handsome apartments. Of Lafayette himself, she wrote: 'Never did I meet with a being so every way perfect.'[40] The General was flatteringly attentive throughout their stay at La Grange, and he dined with the Trollopes on their last night in Paris at a dinner given them by Frances Wright.

In the summer of 1824 Arthur, the Trollope's third son, and the closest to Anthony in age, died before his twelfth birthday while visiting his grandfather at Reading. He apparently had always been frail and had been but one year at Harrow School, having spent much of his life at his grandfather's.[41] Then old William Milton himself died. Mrs Trollope, not looking back, attended to her family and friends. Not long afterward she took into her home an impoverished young French artist—then about 30, some fifteen years her junior—Auguste Hervieu, who had had to flee France for his revolutionary anti-monarchical politics. Mrs Trollope considered him an artist of exceptional but unrecognized talent—'*a man of genius*', she told Mary Russell Mitford, who was forced to struggle for enough food to eat.[42] She engaged Hervieu to tutor the children at Julian Hill; he moved in, and soon became practically a member of the family.

At Winchester, Tom was winning honours, while his brother Henry, a bright but irascible young man, was reportedly idle and not doing well in his studies. Mr Trollope's care-laden letters to his sons at Winchester touched every aspect of their progress and standing at school; he continually worried the boys, anxiously urged them onwards, doing more harm than good with Henry.[43] By late 1826, dismayed at Henry's poor showing, Mr Trollope determined to remove him from school and place him in a counting house. The dream of New College for one son, at least, had ended. At Mrs Trollope's insistence, the 15-year-old Henry was sent to a Paris counting house, so that he might develop his French and see more of the world. Anthony would later voice many times the complaint that he had been left alone in London—at 19—and urged by his mother to stay in during the evenings drinking tea and reading good books.

3

Wykehamist

IN the late summer of 1826, just prior to Henry's removal from school, Anthony was elected to Winchester College. But he had still to await a vacancy, and for months Mr Trollope fretted and troubled Tom for details about every boy who might possibly resign, making room for Anthony. On 14 April 1827 he was finally admitted.[1] On 11 April Mrs Trollope had written to Tom, commending Anthony to Tom's care: 'I dare say you will often find him idle and plaguing enough. But . . . [he] is a good-hearted fellow, and clings so to the idea of being Tom's pupil, and sleeping in Tom's chamber, that I think you will find advice and remonstrance better taken by him than by poor Henry. Greatly comforted am I to know that Tony has a praefect brother.'[2]

In spite of Anthony's bright hopes, he found Winchester more painful than Sunbury. A large part of the problem, ironically, was his brother, who as his prefect was in effect his tutor. Tom took his responsibility seriously, and perhaps understandably practised instruction in the fashion of actual masters of his own experience. If anything the young man worked harder than the schoolmasters in his effort to beat learning into his younger brother. According to Anthony, Tom's methods were positively draconian: 'Hang a little boy for stealing apples, he used to say, and other little boys will not steal apples. . . . as a part of his daily exercise, he thrashed me with a big stick.' Tom became 'of all my foes, the worst'.[3] And then too Tom did well scholastically. In *The Bertrams*, written thirty years later, Trollope has two cousins, brought up in the same household, attend Winchester from the age of 12 onwards; one of the boys takes honours, the other none, and the narrator soliloquizes:

I believe masters but seldom recognize the agony of spirit with which boys endure being beaten in these contests. Boys on such subjects are very reticent; they hardly understand their own feelings enough to speak them, and are too much accustomed both to ridicule and censure to look anywhere for sympathy. A favourite sister may perhaps be told of the hard struggle and the bitter failure, but not a word is said to any one else. His father, so thinks the boy, is angry at his failure; and even his mother's kisses will hardly be warmed by such a subject. We are too apt to think that if our children eat pudding and make a noise they require no sympathy. A boy may fail at school, and afterwards eat much pudding, and make much noise; but, ah! how his young heart may sigh for some one to grieve with him over his failures!4

Other hardships of daily life at Winchester were recalled by Trollope in an article on public schools written for the *Fortnightly Review* in 1865: beer was the only beverage permitted at breakfast, lunch, or dinner; the boys received daily a fatty, pound-size lump of mutton; neither knives nor forks were provided, only wooden trenchers; during dinner the younger boys were continually waiting on the older ones, and in the 'scramble' often lost their lump of mutton. The boys slept in dormitories of ten, each ruled by two or three 'kings' or prefects:

To furnish some prefect with candlestick, snuffers, and extinguisher was the great trouble of my early years. How often have I wandered in my nightshirt, on a winter night, out under the buttresses of the chapel, looking for snuffers, where I might as well have looked for a crock of gold;—have wandered searching where no finding was possible, have returned hopeless, snufferless, and suppliant, and have then been sent out again to wander, and again to search.

Solace came to him during worship services—some twenty times a week—for in chapel he could rest for half an hour with no fear of prefects calling for snuffers. The services themselves were hurried through by 'old-fashioned' chaplains, who served also as minor canons at the cathedral, and had livings in the city; Trollope remembered one protesting vehemently as he walked up the chapel nave, 'I have read the Litany thrice this day; and I'm d——d if I'll read it again.'5 (Tom Trollope recalled a chaplain who was 'ready to give any man to "Pontius Pilate" in the Creed [more than half-way through], and arrive at the end before him.'6)

Nothing but Latin and Greek was taught, and no real effort was made at teaching. The masters would hear the boys 'say' their lessons; the only tuition was done by big boys who for a fee would see to it that younger ones were made to memorize portions of Latin verse. The masters did nothing else except scourge the boys, and, Trollope wrote, 'in the performance of that task only, was my acquaintance with them ripened into intimacy.'7 In *An Autobiography* Trollope said, 'I feel convinced in my mind that I have been flogged oftener than any human being alive. It was just possible to obtain five scourgings in one day at Winchester, and I have often boasted that I obtained them all.'8 The severity of floggings or 'birchings' administered by masters at public schools is much disputed; some maintain that the beatings were more ritual charade than punishment. Doubtless practice differed from occasion to occasion, master to master, school to school. Tom Trollope, partly in reply to his brother's *Autobiography*, insisted that at Winchester (where the floggings were called 'scourgings'), a boy's bottom was bared only to the space equal to the diameter of a crown piece, and that a master inflicted three cuts with a 'rod' made up of four long slender apple-tree twigs (specially sent up from Herefordshire) attached to a yard-long stick that served as handle; that the three 'swishes' took about 20 seconds, that it was 'quite as likely as not that no one of the four twigs, at either of the three cuts, touched the narrow bare part', that 'the pain was really not worth speaking of, and that nobody cared the least about it,' that the whole business was 'mere form and farce. It caused neither pain nor disgrace, and assuredly morally degraded nobody'; when he himself managed to be scourged five times in one day he felt 'rather proud' of this 'rare *tour de force*'.[9] Anthony's matter-of-fact account leaves room for the inference that he for one perceived the punishment as physically and emotionally painful.

As Anthony was settling into his unhappy situation at Winchester, his parents were getting into deeper financial trouble at home. In 1825 Mrs Trollope had told Tom at Winchester, 'All the world are poor as Job,—and rather poorer, for Job put none of his sons to public schools, and had no clients who did not pay him. Next year I fear we shall be poorer still, for assuredly there will be *no hay*.'[10] Moreover, Thomas Anthony's law practice declined steadily, as his bad temper, made worse by steadily declining health, grew more violent, and he alienated solicitors who were to bring him clients. Household economies at Julian Hill became stringent; there were fewer entertainments; the Trollope women and faithful old Farmer made garments; old shoes were repaired rather than new ones purchased. Then, more drastically, Thomas Anthony in early 1827—as Anthony was sent to Winchester—determined that Julian Hill would have to be let and the family moved to Harrow Weald, three miles away, where he had taken still another farm. Anthony described the Harrow Weald house as 'not only no more than a farmhouse, but . . . one of those farmhouses which seem always to be in danger of falling into the neighbouring horse-pond. As it crept downwards from house to stables, from stables to barns, from barns to cowsheds, and from cowsheds to dungheaps, one could hardly tell where one began and the other ended!'[11] It was a terrible come-down from Julian Hill. But for Mrs Trollope the house itself was not the worst of the newly proposed arrangement; that lay in the prospect of isolated exile away from the immediate society of the Grant family and other Harrow neighbours. What would life be like for her and her two young daughters, alone in Harrow Weald with Thomas Anthony, whose temper so frequently made his company unbearable?

Mrs Trollope's answer was altogether unexpected. In September 1827 she had visited the lonely and unhappy Henry in Paris. While there she also saw, at La Grange, a recuperating Frances Wright. The young reformer was recently back from another visit to America, where, inspired in part by Robert Owen's socialistic New Harmony settlement in Indiana, she had founded—to Lafayette's horror—her own experiment in communal living, for the purpose of developing and freeing black people. She established her settlement at Nashoba, Tennessee, and purchased about twenty slaves, who were to be educated, freed, and then relocated in another country. Her Nashoba community had been the subject of unpleasant rumours not only about free thinking in religious matters but about free love, and Frances Wright was seeking a suitable female companion to allay some of the scandal. She had tried Mrs Shelley, who, while professing esteem for Frances, declined. And now Frances Wright suggested that Mrs Trollope be her travelling companion and that Henry become a teacher at her settlement in Tennessee.[12] Whereupon Mrs Trollope returned to Harrow to convince her husband of the feasibility of the plan. Her determination to go to the New World with Frances Wright was influenced by her admiration for that enthusiastic young woman and the hope that Henry might find a suitable profession there. Her chief motivation, however, was more probably a desire to avoid having to live in the dingy Harrow Weald farmhouse with her bad-tempered husband. For Thomas Anthony's physical and emotional condition had deteriorated greatly. Although he still kept up a semblance of a law practice in London, by now virtually all his clients had deserted him. His 'bilious headaches' became ever more severe; his disposition grew so soured that at times he seemed almost mentally unhinged.

But when Mrs Trollope argued her plan, her strongest point was money: by removing herself, Emily, Cecilia, and Henry to America, where expenses in no way matched those of England, she might by residence of a year or two there help considerably toward repairing the family finances. Thomas Anthony consented. Mrs Trollope tried to keep the move quiet, explaining vaguely to those who had to know something that she was visiting friends in America and placing her children in schools there.[13] Her plan shocked friends and neighbours. Lafayette thought it madness.

Harriet Garnett wrote that such a step once taken into the scandal-ridden Tennessee experiment would admit of 'no return' for Mrs Trollope to decent society. [14] To make matters more scandalous still, Auguste Hervieu was to accompany them, the plan being that he should board the ship at the last moment.

Mrs Trollope set sail for America on 4 November 1827. She knew about the talk she was causing: 'I have left the people making great eyes at me—but I care but little for this. I expect to be very happy, and very free from care at Nashoba, and this will more than repay me for being the object of a few "dear me's".' [15] She was not happy, but appalled, at Nashoba: it was, she wrote, a place 'infinitely more dreadful than I ever imagined possible'. Food was scanty and unwholesome. Hervieu, who was to teach art, found the 'school' consisted of '3 yellow children running wild in the swamps'. [16] There was nothing for Henry to do, either. Mrs Trollope left after ten days. Rather surprisingly still optimistic about experimental communities, she sent Henry off to New Harmony, Indiana, and then took her daughters and Hervieu to Cincinnati, Ohio, a prospering frontier town of some 20,000 people, where she arrived on 10 February 1828. [17]

She wrote continually to her husband, asking for money, and when nine letters had gone unanswered by May (they may have been lost in the post), she wrote in desperation to Tom and Anthony at Winchester, inquiring whether their father was ill or even dead. Without Hervieu's kindness they would have had nothing to eat. Tom must write her immediately. 'How are you both,' she closed, 'my darling boys? Oh, what could I do—alas, I have nothing to *give*, but what would I not give, to have you both for half an hour! Dear Tom, dear Anthony, do not forget us!' [18]

Mrs Trollope could not be idle while waiting for her husband's arrival to fetch them home. Henry was again with her; he had managed to endure only about a month in New Harmony, and now Mrs Trollope advertised his services as a tutor of Latin, boasting that he had a 'completely classical education at the Royal College of Winchester, (England),' and would give lessons, for 50 cents an hour, 'by an improved method of teaching, now getting into general use in Europe'. [19] Not one pupil applied. By April Hervieu had opened a drawing school in his lodgings, and through him Mrs Trollope met Joseph Dorfeuille, director of the Western Museum at Cincinnati. To attract customers to the museum, Mrs Trollope suggested constructing a show of an Oracle, the 'Invisible Girl', whose voice would answer in foreign languages questions put to it from the audience. The room was decorated in Egyptian style by Hervieu, with a witches' cauldron (from *Macbeth*) in the centre, from which an arm projected. The 'female voice' that answered in Latin, French, German, and Italian, was Henry Trollope's, and for a while the oracle was a tremendous success. Mrs Trollope then devised another project for Dorfeuille, a representation from Dante called 'The Infernal Regions' put together with the assistance of the young sculptor Hiram Powers and the indefatigable Hervieu.[20]

In September 1828 Mr Trollope and Tom (who had finished his course at Winchester and was hoping for a New College vacancy) sailed for America. At Cincinnati Mr Trollope allowed his wife to talk him into the idea of erecting a building for cultural and commercial activities, her famous 'bazaar'. The money was to come from what remained of her inheritance from her father; she probably hoped to keep her husband from losing it on the farm. A stronger motivation seems to have been her unwillingness to return to Harrow. She wrote to a friend, 'I will not deny that this scheme is the more agreeable to me because it promises me frequent intervals of tranquillity in the absence of Mr. Trollope. He is a good honourable man—but his temper is dreadful—every year increases his irritability— and also, its lamentable effect upon the children.'[21] She herself and three children in Cincinnati would be spared for a few years the pain of living with Thomas Anthony; Tom would soon be going to Oxford and was old enough to hold his own. Anthony was at Winchester, though he would be alone with his father during his holidays. Anthony seems to have been the one member of the family Frances could not or did not bother to protect. Perhaps his good physical health and bodily strength hid from her his mental sufferings. In any case, it would be Anthony who for three years, those of his early teens, had to bear the largest burden of coping with Mr Trollope.

Mrs Trollope's 'bazaar' was not chiefly a market for selling European trinkets to the natives, as has been frequently suggested. It was to be a cultural centre, a place for galleries, a music concert-hall, a coffee-house, a saloon for ices, a bar, private party rooms. The building itself was an exotic collage of Arabian, Grecian, Gothic, and Egyptian styles, complete with columns, tower, rotunda, and balconies.*

Mr Trollope was to advance $6,000 for erecting the building; the idea of a commercial bazaar for selling imported European goods was his. When it was objected that people having never seen such things might not want to

---

* The building became known as 'Trollope's Folly' and inspired many denunciations: Harriet Martineau called it 'the great deformity of the city'; C. D. Arfwedson said it was an 'absurd compound of every species of architecture'; Frederick Marryat labelled it '*preposterous*'; Thomas Hamilton said the effect of its 'Graeco-Moresco-Gothic-Chinese' architecture was 'eminently grotesque'.[22]

buy them, he replied that he would '*teach them*' by selecting the wares himself. Mrs Trollope implored him to spend no more than £150 on stock for the bazaar. He went home, sent $2,000 towards the building and then sent her '4000 dollars worth of the most trumpery goods that probably ever were shipped'.[23] (Anthony believed the merchandise consisted of 'little goods, such as pin-cushions, pepper-boxes, and pocket-knives'.[24]) Mr Charles Wilkes, a New York banker and friend, who handled the consignment, said such articles would never sell for as much as the import duties imposed on them. Mr Trollope had no more money; he had thought that profits from sales would cover the remaining cost of the building. Mrs Trollope went ahead on credit; the workmen clamoured for payment; she took ill with fever, spending eleven weeks in her room, often delirious. Henry was obliged to sell off the goods at auction. The rooms did not rent, and within half a year the building was put into receivership; everything, even Mrs Trollope's own belongings, was seized. Had it not been for Hervieu, she said, they would have starved. Henry, overworked, took ill. When he was again on his feet, Mrs Trollope contrived to have him sent, with Hervieu's help, back to England. He arrived at Harrow on 19 April 1830, having had to walk the last sixteen miles from London because he had no money whatsoever.[25] Mr Trollope could not understand why Henry had come home, and why they had been dependent on Hervieu when he had sent out so much merchandise. 'Is it not strange,' Mrs Trollope wrote to Tom, 'that he does not yet know that these goods never brought *one penny* into my hands. The proceeds of those we sold, went to the workmen and servants, and the *rest were seized*. . . . I would have you recall it to his memory.'[26]

Anthony, his brother having left school, was in the meanwhile pursuing his unhappy career at Winchester alone. For half a year he was the only member of his family in England. At this time, 'another and different horror fell to my fate'. His college bills had not been paid, and the tradesmen were told not to extend credit to him: 'Boots, waistcoats, and pocket-handkerchiefs, which, with some slight superveillance, were at the command of other scholars, were closed luxuries to me. My schoolfellows of course knew that it was so, and I became a Pariah.' Some boys, Anthony noted, do not seem to suffer much from the natural cruelty of other boys, but, as he remembered:

I suffered horribly! I could make no stand against it. I had no friend to whom I could pour out my sorrows. I was big, and awkward, and ugly, and, I have no doubt, skulked about in a most unattractive manner. Of course I was ill-dressed and dirty. But, ah! how well I remember all the agonies of my young heart; how I considered whether I should always be alone; whether I could not find my way up to the top of that college tower, and from thence put an end to everything?

Then his 'battels', the shilling-a-week pocket money paid out by the second master to the boys, were stopped because his father had not reimbursed the master for the last half-year paid. The worst of the situation was that the other boys learned of the stoppage. Then too he was unable to give the quarterly tip to the servants, and he 'never saw any one of those servants without feeling that I had picked his pocket'.[27]

At about this time (according to information Trollope is said to have given Escott in 1882) Anthony began to keep a diary: 'My mother was much from home or too busy to be bothered. My father was not exactly the man to invite confidence. I tried to relieve myself by confiding my boyish sorrows to a diary that I have kept since the age of twelve, which I have just destroyed, and which, on reference to it for my autobiography some time since, I found full of a heart-sick, friendless little chap's exaggerations of his woes.'[28]

At Winchester Anthony also developed the habit of escaping from his discomforts, failures, and lack of companionship, into the creation of an imaginary world. As a boy, and even as a child, he had been often thrown upon himself. Other boys had not much played with him, and he had had to 'form my plays within myself'. Now, the practice became continuous, almost systematic:

Study was not my bent, and I could not please myself by being all idle. Thus it came to pass that I was always going about with some castle in the air firmly built within my mind. Nor were these efforts in architecture spasmodic, or subject to constant change from day to day. For weeks, for months, if I remember rightly, from year to year, I would carry on the same tale, binding myself down to certain laws, to certain proportions, and proprieties, and unities. Nothing impossible was ever introduced,—nor even anything which, from outward circumstances, would seem to be violently improbable. I myself was of course my own hero. Such is a necessity of castle-building. But I never became a king, or a duke,—much less when my height and personal appearance were fixed could I be an Antinous, or six feet high. I never was a learned man, nor even a philosopher. But I was a very clever person, and beautiful young women used to be fond of me. And I strove to be kind of heart, and open of hand, and noble in thought, despising mean things; and altogether I was a very much better fellow than I have ever succeeded in being since.[29]

The seed for Anthony's disposition as novelist had begun to grow.

4

Harrow Weald

IN the summer of 1830, Anthony, having been two and a half years at Winchester, was withdrawn from the school by his father. He never knew whether the change was made because of the expense or because his hopes for New College were so slight. Ironically, he might have won his way to New College, as it happened that an exceptional number of vacancies occurred in his year.[1] On the other hand, there would not have been money enough for Oxford. Tom had won two Winchester exhibitions to Oxford, and there being no vacancy at New College, he matriculated at Alban Hall, in October 1829. (Mr Trollope chose Alban Hall because of the reputation for liberalism of its new principal, Richard Whately; Tom's Oxford career went satisfactorily until Mr Trollope detained him at home a day after a vacation, and when Whately tried to exact the payment of a fine—to his servant—Mr Trollope objected so strongly that Tom had to be withdrawn, and was lucky to be taken up by Magdalen Hall, then 'a general refuge for the destitute'.[2]) There was always the problem of the money needed to maintain Tom at university. Henry won a sizarship to Caius College, Cambridge in the autumn of 1830, but, because of lack of money, he remained there only a year.[3]

And so Anthony came to live alone with his father at Harrow Weald. He had done so before on his vacations from Winchester: 'There was often a difficulty', he recorded, 'about the holidays,—as to what should be done with me.' On one occasion he had passed the midsummer holidays in his father's chambers at 23 Old Square, Lincoln's Inn. He amused himself wandering about old deserted buildings and by reading a bi-columned Shakespeare ('It was not that I had chosen Shakespeare, but that there was nothing else'). Mr Trollope's chambers were depressing and alienating: they were, Anthony wrote, 'dingy, almost suicidal chambers . . . which on one melancholy occasion did become absolutely suicidal', when a pupil of his father committed suicide in them.[4] Trollope's fiction has a generous share of gloomy legal chambers, almost invariably located in the Lincoln's

Inn neighbourhood. In *Orley Farm*, the room in which the barrister Thomas Furnival sits, in a 'very dingy edifice in Old Square, Lincoln's Inn', is, the narrators says, 'of all the rooms in which I ever sat . . . the most gloomy'.5 But by the time of Anthony's removal from Winchester, Thomas Anthony had altogether given up his law practice and retired entirely into the gloom of Harrow Weald. Here Anthony suffered from the unrelieved presence of his father, his mental and physical health worsening, his farming as ineffectual as ever, and when able, engrossed in his last sad effort, the writing of an *Ecclesiastical Encyclopedia*, a huge catalogue of all ecclesiastical terms (a curious undertaking for a man of no particular religious bent). 'Under crushing disadvantages,' Anthony wrote of him, 'with few or no books of reference, with immediate access to no library, he worked at his most ungrateful task with unflagging industry.'6 Thomas Anthony was to labour away the remaining years of his life on this project, the first and only volume of which appeared over the imprint of John Murray in 1834. (Thomas Adolphus, explaining that the book was published by subscription, remarked, 'I do not suppose that any human being purchased the book because they wished to possess it.'7) The *Ecclesiastical Encyclopedia* became, as Anthony said, 'buried in the midst of that huge pile of futile literature, the building up of which has broken so many hearts'.8

Thomas Anthony, though engaged on his encyclopedia, and ill in bed half the time, still fought valiantly to keep the farm going. The landlord's agent clamoured for money, as did tradesmen. 'Of self-indulgence no one could accuse him,' Trollope wrote. 'Our table was poorer, I think, than that of the bailiff who still hung on to our shattered fortunes.' Anthony was compelled to go into the hay fields and help with the digging and planting. The only relief came in a few 'jocund hours in the kitchen, making innocent love to the bailiff's daughter'.9 Tom recorded at least one other pleasant distraction when he and Anthony determined to spend an evening seeing the illuminations and fireworks at Vauxhall Gardens at a specially advertised reduced price of a one-shilling entrance. The two brothers, impecunious as usual, had exactly that amount, and so they walked the fourteen miles from Harrow Weald to Vauxhall, timing themselves so as to arrive at nine p.m.; while Tom looked at the fireworks, 'Anthony danced all night. . . . Then at about 1 A.M. we set off and walked back our fourteen miles home again without having touched bite or sup! Did anybody else ever purchase the delight of an evening at Vauxhall at so high a price?'10

During the Harrow Weald days Thomas Anthony was not actively 'teaching' his youngest son, but he still kept a constant eye on his 'scholastic improvement'. He made him sit at table with the Greek and Latin books before him, Anthony remaining stubbornly idle during these sessions. His father rarely punished him at this time, though once, grieved at Anthony's idleness, he knocked him down with a great folio Bible.[11] (Thomas Anthony was said to have been a man of great physical strength. Tom recorded how, when he was a child riding with his parents in a buggy, the horse took fright and got itself half-way over a low stone wall that protected the road at a precipice: 'my father, with one bound to the horse's head, caught him by the bridle, and, by the sheer strength of his remarkably powerful frame, forced him back into the road.'[12]) Anthony's only reading was from the first two volumes of James Fenimore Cooper's *The Prairie*, this incomplete book being the only thing he could find in the farmhouse to his liking, a work he read over and over. The book was probably a 'dishonest relic' from Hookham's Library.[13]

Although it was Henry who had the greatest battles with his father, Anthony certainly had his share. When he came to write his first novel, it was to concern an Irish landowner whom adversity and debt had crushed into feeble-mindedness, and a son who in a clumsy, inept way tries vainly to save his family from ruin. Father and son are utterly unable to talk to each other; old Larry Macdermot simply cannot understand what his son Thaddy is about. Trollope's first story was his most tragic. Its power derived from a frightening awareness of his own miseries and of his father's near madness; expressing these things exorcised such unrelieved blackness from his fiction. Anthony came frequently to draw partial self-portraits in his male characters and, though they are always done with irony and frequently with satire, he never again created a young man so pitiable, inept, helpless, or bungling as Thaddy Macdermot. Thereafter he is more gentle with his young men, and nothing like *The Macdermots* ever came from his pen again. Still, another novel, *John Caldigate*, written in 1877, strikingly recalls its author's own early situation, saying on the very first page that John Caldigate and his father Daniel 'could not live together in comfort in the days of the young man's early youth'; their inability to get along 'was so great as to bring crushing troubles upon each of them':

There were but the two of which to make a household. When John was fifteen, and had been about a year at Harrow, he lost his mother and his two little sisters almost at a blow. . . . Then Daniel Caldigate had been alone. And he was a man who knew how to live alone,—a just, hard, unsympathetic man,—of whom his neighbours said, with something of implied reproach, that he bore up strangely when he lost his wife and girls. . . . It was rumoured of him, too, that he was as constant with his books as before. . . . When the boy came home for his holidays, the father would sometimes walk with him, and discourse on certain chosen subjects,—on the politics of the day, in regard to which Mr. Caldigate was an advanced Liberal. . . . Early in life . . . he quarrelled with his father,—as he had with almost everyone else.

John Caldigate 'felt sure that his father had no special regard for him;—in which he was, of course, altogether wrong, and the old man was equally wrong in supposing that his son was unnaturally deficient in filial affection. But they had never known each other, and were so different that neither had understood the other.'[14]

Other examples of disharmony between fathers and sons abound in Trollope's fiction. Old Mr Scarborough is at terrible odds with his two sons, one of whom, the younger, wishes for nothing so much as that his father would 'die out of the way'.[15] The Revd Dr Vesey Stanhope, in *Barchester Towers*, is in a constant state of comic but real acrimony with his son Bertie; in *The Last Chronicle of Barset*, Archdeacon Grantly threatens to disinherit his son Henry; in *The Bertrams*, Lord Stanmore 'might more probably be found under any roof in the country than that of his father';[16] in *The Small House at Allington*, Lord De Courcy and his eldest son hate each other 'as only such fathers and such sons can hate';[17] in *The Way We Live Now*, Dolly Longestaffe and his father quarrel continually, and 'it went altogether against the grain with [Dolly] that he should be engaged in any matter respecting the family property in agreement with his father';[18] in *The American Senator*, Lord Mistletoe, 'who had a large family of his own, lived twenty miles off,—so that the father and son could meet pleasantly without fear of quarrelling';[19] in *The Duke's Children*, Lord Grex hates his son 'worse than any one else in the world', and believes the son 'would do anything he could lay his hand on to oppose me'.[20] Sly little remarks catch at the reader: in *The Prime Minister*, Everett Wharton, when he becomes heir to Wharton Hall, 'found himself to be possessed of a thousand graces, even in his father's eyesight'.[21] The father need not even be still living to be worth mentioning in this regard: in *Can You Forgive Her?*, for example, it is said of Burgo Fitzgerald that 'for many years he had not been on speaking terms' with his father, who died aparently long before the novel opens and has nothing to do with the story.[22] As Madame Max Goesler remarks (in *Phineas Finn*), 'How odd it is how often you English fathers quarrel with your sons.'[23] It is only in a late, mellow story, *The Duke's Children*, that reconciliation reigns, as Plantagenet Palliser, Trollope's most elaborated character, comes slowly to terms of understanding and regard for his two sons. This novel Anthony would write nearly half a century after his worst times with his father, and immediately after finishing the *Autobiography*, the work in which he had put on paper the revelations about his childhood and youth.

Trollope would draw most extensively, and tenderly, upon his own father for the creation of the Revd Josiah Crawley, arguably the novelist's supreme achievement. Crawley—who appears in *Framley Parsonage* and plays the central role in *The Last Chronicle of Barset*—a strange, stubborn, proud, learned, self-pitying impoverished man, has few characters to match him in Trollope or in all of Victorian fiction. Always poor, Crawley cannot forgive those who relieve his poverty; he is most anxious about his children's education, taking it upon himself to teach them, with great energy, Greek and Latin; yet, he has no way with children, and though he loved his offspring, he 'was not gifted with the knack of making children fond of him'.[24] Crawley is moody, and frequently will not talk with his wife; he cannot help being distressed by 'the success of other men who had been his compeers, and, as he too often told himself, intellectually his inferiors'. Another character says of him, 'He is one of those men who always think themselves to be ill-used.' At times Crawley is close to madness: 'The intellect of the man was as clear as running water in all things not appertaining to his daily life and its difficulties. He could be logical to a vengeance,—so logical as to cause infinite trouble to his wife. . . . [She] knew well that he was not mad; but yet she knew that there were dark moments with him, in which his mind was so much astray.' Crawley, like Thomas Anthony, would never have been a pleasant man to live with, but had he not been continually crushed by money worries, the lot of those around him would have been infinitely more enjoyable. The narrator's discourse on genteel poverty clearly recalls Trollope's Harrow years:

None but they who have themselves been poor gentry,—gentry so poor as not to know how to raise a shilling,—can understand the peculiar bitterness of the trials which such poverty produces. The poverty of the normal poor does not approach it; or, rather, the pangs arising from such poverty are altogether of a different sort. To be hungry and have no food, to be cold and have no fuel, to be threatened with distraint for one's few chairs and tables, and with the loss of the roof over one's head,—all these miseries . . . so frequently near to reaching the normal poor are, no doubt, the severest of the trials to which humanity is subjected. . . . But there are pangs to which, at the time, starvation itself would seem to be preferable. The angry eyes of unpaid tradesmen, savage with an anger which one knows to be justifiable; the taunt of the poor servant who wants her wages; the gradual relinquishment of habits which the soft nurture of earlier, kinder years had made second nature; the wan cheeks of the wife whose malady demands wine; the rags of the husband whose outward occupations demand decency; the neglected children, who are learning not to be the children of gentlefolk; and, worse than all, the alms and doles of half-generous friends, the waning pride, the growing doubt whether it be not better to bow the head, and acknowledge to all the world that nothing of the pride of station is left.[25]

Still more painful than solitary life with his father at Harrow Weald was Anthony's second attendance at Harrow School. This time the walk to and from school, twice daily, added twelve miles of drudgery to his school miseries:

Perhaps the eighteen months which I passed in this condition, walking to and fro on those miserably dirty lanes, was the worst period of my life. I was now over fifteen, and had come to an age at which I could appreciate at its full the misery of expulsion from all social intercourse. I had not only no friends, but was despised by all my companions. . . . What right had a wretched farmer's boy, reeking from a dunghill, to sit next to the sons of peers,—or much worse still, next to the sons of big tradesmen who had made their ten thousand a-year? The indignities I endured are not to be described. As I look back it seems to me that all hands were turned against me,—those of masters as well as boys. I was allowed to join in no plays. Nor did I learn anything,—for I was taught nothing.[26]

One of the masters, his new tutor, remitted his normal ten guineas (the only expense for a day-scholar, apart from books), but Trollope was humiliated when he heard the man declare the fact before the boys assembled in the pupil room. The tutor was very likely William Mills, the sixth master, who taught the 'shell' (described by William Gregory as 'a kind of limbo between the fourth and fifth forms', itself divided into lower and upper shell, of which the latter 'was composed of extremely big and extremely ignorant boys').[27] Anthony—when 19 and out of Harrow—said, 'I used always to stick up for Mills—I don't know why—for he is a weak, quarrelsome, conceited ass—not to speak of his absolute vulgarity and ignorance. He has always a most laughable mode of keeping up his dignity, and walks with his nose ludicrously in the air. He had the upper shell when I was in that part—he used constantly to make bad puns on the boys' names.'[28] The bad pun on Trollope's name was the obvious one.

Trollope believed that he was never a coward and that he took his thrashings with as little care as any other boy, but that he had not the 'moral courage' to stand up to the 'acerbities of three hundred tyrants'. One witness to what was going on was Thomas Henry Baylis (later a judge), who attended Harrow from 1825, when he was 8, to 1834. He said Anthony used sometimes to call for him on the way to school, that they sat next to each other in the sixth form, and that he thought Anthony exaggerated his sufferings at Harrow: he was persecuted 'less than other home-boarders who went young to school: they were often sadly bullied and pursued with stones on their way home. Trollope was a strongly-built, powerful fellow, and could in a measure hold his own.' Of course Trollope had had his share of that sort of bullying during his first stay when he was small. The sufferings when he was bigger were more subtle, centring chiefly in exclusion and ridicule. Then there was also a rumour current at the school that Anthony's father, 'old Trollope', was an outlaw. Anthony was at last—in his words—'driven to rebellion' and had a great fight with another boy, after which his opponent, apparently James Lewis, the son of a well-known London book-binder, 'had to be taken home for a while'. Baylis confirms that the two fought 'in the fighting-ground for nearly an hour, until separated by Mills the master. Lewis had to go home, so severely was he punished.' Trollope called this victory the 'solitary glory of my school days'.[29] From Baylis's reference to 'the fighting-ground', it would seem that the fight was an arranged encounter—rather than a spontaneous brawl—that is, one involving 'seconds' and, in the custom of the day, divided into rounds by knockdowns, each knockdown followed by a one-minute rest, with the contest ending only when one fighter could not go on. Such fights, common at Harrow and other public schools, were sometimes terrible combats lasting for hours. (At Eton, in 1825, a two-hour fight ended in the death of Francis Ashley, youngest son of the Earl of Shaftesbury, a 13-year-old boy.[30]) One of Tom's anecdotes, excerpted from his diaries of the early 1830s, shows Anthony relishing physical combat: 'Went to town yesterday [from Harrow], and among other commissions bought a couple of single-sticks with strong basket handles. Anthony much approves of them, and this morning we had a bout with them. One of the sticks bought yesterday soon broke, and we supplied its place by a tremendous blackthorn. Neither of us left the arena without a fair share of rather severe wales; but Anthony is far my superior in quickness and adroitness, and perhaps in bearing pain too.'[31]

5

A Famous Mother

In early 1830 Mrs Trollope, with Hervieu's help, left Cincinnati for Washington where the artist hoped to have his work exhibited and to paint portraits. She and her daughters stayed in Stonington, Virginia, with Anna Maria Stone, one of the Garnett sisters and Fanny's 'oldest friend . . . in the world'.[1] She considered living with her girls in Germany with Lady Dyer, or in France with the Garnetts, because for a time at least she did not want to return to Harrow 'among the people who used to see us under different circumstances'.[2] Her great hope now was to make money by publishing a book on her travels in America. She explained to Tom that she wanted to get to Niagara, as her book would be 'very imperfect' without a description of the Falls, but could not do so unless Hervieu could supply the money: 'Sometimes my heart sinks when I think of our present dependence. Poor Cecilia is literally without shoes . . . I sit still and write, write, write,—so old shoes last me a long time. . . . Your dear sisters . . . mend,—and mend,—and mend. . . . Hope—that quits us the last, perhaps, of all our friends—tells me that it is *possible* my book may succeed. It will have great advantages from Hervieu's drawings. . . . My poor dear Anthony will have outgrown our recollection! Tell him not to outgrow his affection for us. No day passes,—hardly an hour—without our talking of you all.'[3] Hervieu did in fact make enough money by portrait painting to take Mrs Trollope to Niagara. When she had gathered sufficient materials for the book, she importuned Mr Trollope to send money for their return, but he said that he did not have it. Mrs Trollope then told him that she was '*determined*' to return and that if he did not send the means, she would 'apply to his family for them'. This threat brought eighty pounds from him.[4] Before sailing for home she entreated Mary Russell Mitford for a letter of introduction to her publisher, George Whittaker.[5]

Mrs Trollope arrived at Woolwich on 5 August 1831 and was soon reunited with her family at Harrow Weald. Financial affairs were worse than ever. The hay market had suffered disastrously in 1830 and many farmers throughout the country went bankrupt.[6] In December Thomas Anthony petitioned Lord Northwick to reduce his rent and that of a number of other tenants; this he did in language too strong for his own good. He asked, for example, whether Northwick wished 'to continue to put large sums of money into [his] own pocket, which have never been the produce of [his] own prosperity, and which can only be raised, not only at the expense, but by occasioning the ultimate ruin of [his] tenants'.[7] Northwick later granted a 15 per cent reduction, but excluded Trollope, whom he accused of being the leader of a conspiracy against him; he put a distraint on Trollope's crops and very nearly seized his goods.[8] Thomas Anthony was more depressed than ever.

But Mary Russell Mitford's introduction to Whittaker had resulted in Mrs Trollope's manuscript for *Domestic Manners of the Americans* being consigned to a reader, Basil Hall, author of *Travels in North America*, published two years earlier. Hall recommended publication, Whittaker accepted the book, and Hall himself proved helpful in seeing it through the press. Mrs Trollope was to receive half-profits on the first 1,250 copies, with the prospect of £270 if all sold.[9] She immediately set to work on another book, *The Refugee in America*, a novel drawing still further on her experiences in the States. For her writing, a room was set apart that came to be called 'The Sacred Den'. While she was working on the novel, the faithful retainer Hervieu fell ill of suspected cholera, and Mrs Trollope nursed him back to health.[10]

A worse distraction was the angry scenes Mr Trollope made, especially with Henry. The young man was now reading law with a Mr Lovat at his chambers in London, and Henry and his father had endless bitter arguments as to allowances for his upkeep. Frances Eleanor Trollope—who got her information from Tom—said that although Thomas Anthony loved to dispense hospitality and could be generous to his friends, 'he seems to have been absolutely a prey to a sort of monomania on the subject of allowing his sons any money.' Mrs Trollope, attempting to mediate between them, had sometimes to take a dose of laudanum to get a night's rest.[11] It was at this time that what his eldest son called 'the terrible irritability of [his father's] temper . . . reached a pitch that made one fear his reason was, or would become, unhinged.' Mr Trollope's anger took one particular form: 'simple assent to his utterances of an argumentative nature did not satisfy him, he *would* be argued with. Yet argument produced irritability leading to scenes of painful violence.'[12] Only when writing his *Ecclesiastical Encyclopedia* did he channel his morbid mental energies and become bearable to live with; the encyclopedia became a safety-valve for his mind. Mrs Trollope reported, 'I cannot express my delight at his having found an occupation. He really seems quite another being; and so am I too, in consequence.' Thomas Anthony did manage at least one remarkably good deed in these days: he displayed swift and sure competence in handling the plight of an old friend of his, a Mr Smith (perhaps an alias), who had unjustly been committed to a private mad-house in Salisbury. The patient smuggled out a letter to Mr Trollope, who immediately set off for Salisbury and managed, with the help of a local clergyman, to rescue the man, take him for some time to Harrow, and then leave him to live peaceably with his sisters. Thomas Anthony also at this time applied for a vacant London magistracy. His old Uncle Meetkerke (still hale, and destined to outlive by six years the quarrelsome nephew who was to have been his heir) had connections with the Whig party, and he called on Lord Melbourne, the Home Secretary in Lord Grey's administration, who seemed—at least to Mr Trollope—to have promised the post to him, but nothing came of it. [13]

Then, almost simultaneously with the disappointment about the magistracy, came encouraging words about his *Ecclesiastical Encyclopedia*; the first portion of the manuscript, submitted to John Murray of Albemarle Street, the famous publisher of Byron and Jane Austen, had been read and 'much approved' by the publisher's reader. But the real hope for the family lay in Mrs Trollope's *Domestic Manners of the Americans*. She described to Tom at Oxford how Mr Trollope, up at Albermarle Street to discuss his encyclopedia, was asked by Murray,

'By the bye!—*Trollope*—who the devil *is* Mrs. Trollope? Her book is the cleverest thing I ever read. I have read it through. So spirited!'
'The lady is my wife.'
'Why did she not bring it to me? It will sell like wildfire!'

(Might she not, she asked Tom, wake one morning like Byron to find herself famous?) That conversation took place in February 1832; copies had gone out for review and the book was so much talked about that she wrote nervously to Tom: 'I am afraid it is being over-puffed beforehand, *and that it will fall sadly flat afterwards.*' The Milman family had recognized its quality in the autumn of 1831, when she submitted the manuscript to Henry Milman for his opinion of the religious passages (which he found not at all 'too strong'). As publication drew near, the Milmans delightedly passed on news of the interest excited: in London it was 'spoken of in several places' and young Lady Milman's friend Lockhart, editor of the *Quarterly Review*, had read the first volume and said it was 'the cleverest woman's book he had read for a long time'; even Dr Longley, headmaster of Harrow, 'understood that it was very entertaining'.[14]

When *Domestic Manners of the Americans* was published on 19 March 1832—shortly after Mrs Trollope's fifty-third birthday—expectations were not disappointed. Reviewers and public were sharply divided, mainly along political lines, on the fairness of her picture of the Americans, and the controversy stimulated sales. *Domestic Manners* became the most talked about travel book of its day. The timing was fortunate, the book arriving at the height of the intense debate over the Reform Bill. Her lively criticism of the great experiment in democracy across the Atlantic de-lighted Conservatives at home and outraged Liberals. The Conservative *Quarterly*, owned by Murray, devoted forty pages to favourable commen-tary and extensive excerpts. The ever-helpful Basil Hall was the anony-mous reviewer, and he described the book as 'clever and amusing' and praised the author for her discussion of almost every aspect of American life. The chapters on religion are warmly recommended for 'those in any way distrustful of the benefits of the established church'; especially effective is her 'lively description' exposing a prayer meeting as an 'e?traordinary exhibition of hypocrisy, folly, fanaticism . . . and gross licentiousness'. On the other hand, the Whig *Edinburgh Review* roundly condemned *Domestic Manners* as 'a spiteful, ill-considered and mischief making book', the reviewer charging Mrs Trollope with drawing 'an indictment against a whole nation' from limited observations. Her preface was 'an express advertisement against the Reform Bill'. Moreover, the *Edinburgh*, like many other reviews, contained a generous dose of character assassination: the review began with a direct reference to her 'irregular' personal life and the presence of 'a Mr. H[ervieu]'. The *Athenaeum* reprinted her account of the camp meeting and said, 'Oh Mrs. Trollope! Mrs. Trollope! We hope that when this was going on that you remembered that you were *an old woman*.'[15] In America she was even more reviled; jokes circulated about the name Trollope, and her infamy spread throughout the land. When thirty years later Anthony visited America to write his own book on the New World—partly intending to present a more balanced view of America than had his mother—her name was still a term of reproach. Friends too were shocked, equally with the sexual frankness and her anti-democratic stance. Washington Irving, according to John Murray, claimed the book was fabricated in London by someone who had never been to America. The Garnetts disliked it; General Lafayette was so offended that he would no longer receive her.[16]

Mrs Trollope cared little for the abuse of reviewers, however sorry she might have been at the reactions of the Garnetts and Lafayette. She received many letters praising the book from friends, including Miss Mitford, the Gabells, Captain Kater, and Captain Hamilton—the last telling her that 'his two neighbours on the Lakes, Southey and Wordsworth, are both *delighted*' with the work. Mrs Basil Hall told her that Theodore Hook said the book was 'too clever to have been written by a woman'. ('Saucy, that,' was Mrs Trollope's reaction. [17]) She was soon taken triumphant to London, Captain Hall managing her progress among social lights and literary people.

Moreover, she had written *Domestic Manners* chiefly for money, not fame. The book, its sales helped by the outraged and slanderous reviews, went through four English editions and four American editions in the first year, making a profit to her of perhaps £600 in all. Her next book was immediately bought up by Whittaker, who offered £400 for the first 1,250 copies. The money went quickly; she paid rent and taxes, bought furniture, a cow, malt for brewing. She gave the faithful Hervieu, who was still living with the family, £100. Next she prevailed upon Thomas Anthony to cancel the sublease of Julian Hill and move the family back to their old Harrow home, and by September 1832 they were again ensconced in her 'pretty cottage'. [18]

Julian Hill, Anthony wrote, was 'an Eden as compared to our abode at Harrow Weald'. The presence of his mother and sisters and their pleasant neighbours the Grants helped bring some happiness into his life; improvement was made in his 'wardrobe', and the walk to school lessened to half a mile. But for Anthony Harrow School remained a torture. He still could not fit in: 'I was never able to overcome—or even to attempt to overcome—the absolute isolation of my school position. Of the cricket-ground, or racket-court, I was allowed to know nothing. And yet I longed for these things with an exceeding longing. I coveted popularity with a coveting which was almost mean. It seemed to me that there would be an Elysium in the intimacy of those very boys whom I was bound to hate because they hated me.' [19] William Gregory, who entered Harrow School in 1831 at the age of 14, and who in later life became Trollope's friend, corroborated Anthony's story:

I became intimate with Anthony Trollope, who sat next to me. He was a big boy, older than the rest of the form, and without exception the most slovenly and dirty boy I ever met. He was not only slovenly in person and in dress, but his work was equally dirty. His exercises were a mass of blots and smudges. These peculiarities created a great prejudice against him, and the poor fellow was generally avoided.

It is pitiable to read in his autobiography . . . how bitter were his feelings at that time, and how he longed for the friendship and companionship of his comrades, but in vain. . . . I had plenty of opportunities of judging Anthony, and I am bound to say, though my heart smites me sorely for my unkindness, that I did not dislike him. I avoided him, for he was rude and uncouth, but I thought him an honest, brave fellow. He was no sneak. His faults were all external; all the rest of him was right enough. But . . . poor Trollope was tabooed, and had not, so far as I am aware, a single friend. . . . He gave no sign of promise whatsoever, was always in the lowest part of the form, and was regarded by masters and by boys as an incorrigible dunce.[20]

Trollope never forgot or forgave the students or masters of Harrow School (the bitterness towards Harrow was greater than that towards Winchester): 'Something of the disgrace of my school-days has clung to me all through my life. . . . when I have been claimed as schoolfellow by some of those many hundreds who were with me either at Harrow or at Winchester, I have felt that I had no right to talk of things from most of which I was kept in estrangement.'[21]

Anthony had been at school nearly twelve years, and claimed, with some exaggeration, to have learned nothing except Latin and Greek, and very little of those languages. (Of Sunbury he said that he supposed he must have been in the writing master's class, but that oddly enough he could call to mind the man but not his ferule—usually 'It was by their ferules that I always knew [the masters], and they me.'[22]) In the *Fortnightly* article Trollope described his schooling in his last years at Harrow, his sixth-form days under Headmaster Charles Longley (who at the time of the article was Archbishop of Canterbury and having his difficulties with the Bishop Colenso case). The headmaster delighted in calling on the lads who knew their Thucydides:

That he very rarely,—almost never,—called upon me, who was certain to fail, I impute to him as no blame. When I failed, what could he do? What he did do was to undergo a look of irrepressible, unutterable misery at the disgrace which I brought to his sixth form, and bid me to sit down with a face of woe! How well I remember his face when he was thus woful! How I reverenced him and loved him,—though he could never have loved me! . . . I wonder whether the calling up of bishops who won't believe the Old Testament is pleasanter work than was the calling up of boys who wouldn't get up their Thucydides?[23]

One of Trollope's Greek school texts filled with his annotations survives. His copy of Plato's *Hippias Major*, in an edition intended for advanced classes,[24] inscribed with his name and dated 1833, shows him working diligently and steadily, doing roughly ten pages a day (its calendar of activity curiously prefigures the working diaries for his novels). He filled up the blank pages facing the text with observations and questions that show at best an elementary grasp of the language: he could certainly not be described as a fair Greek scholar. He found the latter part of the content baffling, but this comes as no surprise, as it has troubled scholars too.[25]

In maturity Trollope was an able reader of Latin, but that had been the effort of his later years, although he was willing to grant that at school he had received 'that groundwork of the language which will in the process of years make its way slowly, even through the skin'. When he left Harrow, very nearly 19, he was a monitor, and seventh boy, a position achieved 'by gravitation upwards'. He said that he had never won any of the prizes that were 'showered about', but Lord Bessborough, who had been a school-mate of his, wrote later that Trollope must have forgotten about the weekly English themes and how he, Bessborough, hoping for some small prize for an essay of his own, had gone to Dr Longley who said, 'You did well, but, you see, Trollope writes better English than you do, at present.'[26] In fact there is evidence that Anthony was a competent young man when he took pen into hand, even though he was in many respects a late bloomer.

Probably Trollope was deliberately uncooperative at school, but at home he wrote contributions in prose and verse for a family manuscript journal, 'The Magpie: A Weekly Magazine of Literature, Politics, Science, and Art', edited by Henry.[27] Nothing of the short-lived 'Magpie' has survived, but a copy exists of Edmund Burke's *Philosophical Enquiry into the Origins of our Ideas of the Sublime and the Beautiful* into which Trollope in 1833 entered, on facing pages, combative, irreverent commentaries on Burke's words. Young Trollope sounds like a budding if untried intellectual; he appears self-confident to the point of quarrelsomeness; he relishes attempting to deflate philosophical generalizations of Burke with down-to-earth particularities. When Burke writes that 'smallness is an attribute of beauty,' that the expression 'a great beautiful thing' is scarcely ever used, but that of 'a great ugly thing' very common, Trollope suggests 'Beautiful large eyes'. When Burke claims that in the passion of grief, 'pleasure is still uppermost,' Trollope replies, 'A man may be fond of the romance of grief—he may think himself overwhelmed with grief and have a kind of pleasure in pitying himself—but it is the romance he likes. NO ONE CAN LIKE GRIEF.' When Burke asserts that the three principal links in society are sympathy, imitation, and ambition, Trollope asks, 'Why not avarice, vanity, & others?' When Burke doubts whether any man could be found 'who would earn a life of the most perfect satisfaction, at the price of ending it in torments', Trollope replies, 'I would.' Anthony in his 1833 notes appears a more hopeful, optimistic youth than one would have thought possible from the account of his younger years as given in *An Autobiography*. One can hardly imagine the boy and young man pictured there writing, 'Is it not a pleasure to live, breathe, love and be loved—to exert the faculty of reason, to feel ourselves Lords of Gods earth &c?'[28]

Anthony did not win a sizarship to Clare Hall, Cambridge, for which he twice tried, nor the scholarship at Trinity College, Oxford, for which he also competed.[29] The family had planned that Anthony should stay on at Harrow School until the midsummer holidays of 1834, but in March it was decided that he should leave immediately, probably subsequent on the disappointed hopes of the two scholarships. In some other respects, life at Julian Hill had gone well. Mrs Trollope, setting an example Anthony would eventually follow, rose early every morning, at about four, and wrote at prodigious speed, having by this time completed a third book, *The Abbess* (a Gothic romance, complete with a pregnant nun). In May 1833—ever given to wanderlust and doubtless glad to be free of Thomas Anthony for a period—she left with Hervieu and Henry for a four-month tour of the Rhine in preparation for a book about Germany for John Murray. The venture was somewhat reckless, for she would have to pay her own costs out of any money realized on the book. Then, in the winter of 1833–4 influenza struck. Mrs Trollope wrote to a friend, 'For about ten days we were very seriously alarmed for Anthony—and since that more seriously still for my poor Henry who has been, and yet is, very ill—He is grown pale and thin beyond what you can imagine and has a cough that tears him to pieces.'[30] And money troubles returned, more severe than ever. Mr Trollope had been in arrears on his rents; calamitous farm conditions, together with high Poor Law rates, which as Lord Northwick himself said, 'spread ruin and desolation throughout the land, reducing industrious inhabitants of all classes . . . to a mass of insolvent debtors', oppressed Thomas Anthony. Towards the close of 1833 he had not money to cover a personal draft, and Lord Northwick threatened to take him to law.[31] Mr Trollope had kept the true state of things from his wife. 'We had no idea', she later explained, 'that a year's rent of the *pernicious* farm, which for twenty years has been so losing a concern for him, was due to Lord Northwick. . . . *I* could have paid this at almost any other period since my first publication, but now it was impossible. My last summer's tour was very costly and my five children's private expenses as well as my own have swallowed the rest of what remained from furnishing Julian Hill.'[32] She had not been cautious with her new-found money, which, she said, had been 'oozing fast'. As Anthony remarked, 'she was extravagant, and liked to have money to spend.'[33]

By April 1834 Mr Trollope was some £500 in arrears for rent, and Northwick's agent, a man named Quilton, urged legal action. As the situation became desperate, Mrs Trollope's brother Henry tried to intervene, but could do nothing beyond arranging a separate account for his sister so that some of her money might be safe from her husband's creditors. Mrs Trollope moved her furniture into Colonel Grant's house (under cover of selling it to him), and Mr Trollope told the agent he was going to Cheltenham to recover his health. Anthony was summoned to drive his father, who still kept a horse and gig, to London: 'He had been ill, and must still have been very ill indeed when he submitted to be driven by any one.' Only after they were en route did Thomas Anthony tell him of their destination, the Ostend boat, and 'to the last he never told me why he was going to Ostend.' Hitherto Anthony had heard something vague of a 'general flitting abroad' and realized what was happening only when he arrived back at Harrow to find the house and what was left of the furniture in the hands of bailiffs (one thinks of the bailiffs in Mark Robarts's house in *Framley Parsonage*). The gardener motioned him away lest the horse, gig, and harness should also be seized. Anthony took the gig into the village where the ironmonger bought the entire equipage for £17 but then claimed that was the amount owing to him anyway.[34] At Julian Hill Anthony joined his sisters and the Grant girls rescuing some of Mrs Trollope's 'pretty pretties'—china, glass, household silver, and a few books—and sneaking them over to the Grants' house. (Some of the books thus purloined were in his possession till his death.) At one point Lord Northwick's agent had the marauding stopped, thinking, as he later wrote to Lord Northwick, that Mrs Trollope and Colonel Grant 'had robbed your lordship sufficiently by so clandestinely taking away to his house that portion of furniture that should have come to the Hammer'. Quilton had an auctioneer appraise the goods, and after £12 had been paid, the children were permitted to continue their operations.[35]

The Trollope family sheltered a few days with the hospitable Grants, and then Anthony and Cecilia were sent to join their father in Ostend, where lodgings had been found for him by Mrs Fauche, wife of the British consul, who had been devoted to Mrs Trollope since her girlhood.[36] Mrs Trollope took Henry, whose health was bad, to Fanny Bent at Exeter before joining the rest of the family. Tom, still at Oxford, studying for exams, was not immediately told of the goings on. Mrs Trollope then settled her family in Bruges in a spacious old house called Château d'Hondt just outside the city walls. It was here that Frances Trollope's extraordinary powers of work under adversity manifested themselves more strongly than ever. Anthony recorded:

There were six of us went into this new banishment. My brother Henry . . . was ill. My younger sister was ill. And though as yet we hardly told each other that it was so, we began to feel that that desolating fiend, consumption, was among us. My father was broken-hearted as well as ill, but whenever he could sit at his table he still worked at his ecclesiastical records. My elder sister and I were in good health. . . . Now and again there would arise a feeling that it was hard upon my mother that she should have to do so much for us, that we should be idle while she was forced to work so constantly; but we should probably have thought more of that had she not taken to work as though it were the recognised condition of life for an old lady of fifty five.

The dreadful word had been pronounced; Henry had no longer a 'delicate chest', but consumption. Mrs Trollope tended the two sick men and kept writing her novels. 'The doctor's vials and the ink-bottle', Anthony said, 'held equal places in my mother's rooms. I have written many novels under many circumstances, but I doubt much whether I could write one when my whole heart was by the bedside of a dying son. Her power of dividing herself into two parts . . . I never saw equalled.'[37]

As for Anthony, he admitted to being 'an idle, desolate hanger-on, that most hopeless of human beings, a hobbledehoy of nineteen, without any idea of a career, a profession, or a trade'. But he was fairly happy: the misery of school was behind him, and there were pretty girls in Bruges, 'with whom I could fancy that I was in love'.[38] During the summer an offer came, doubtless through his mother's connections, to get him a commission in an Austrian cavalry regiment. He would first have to learn German and French; and it was arranged that he would do so while working as classical usher in William Drury's school in Brussels (established after Drury and his father had run away from their creditors at Harrow). Anthony said he hoped the thirty boys entrusted to him were there chiefly to learn French. His outings with them resulted in their clothes being so dirtied that Mrs Drury put a stop to such excursions. He never got around to the French or German studies, for when he had been at the school about six weeks, a position of clerk at the London General Post Office headquarters was as good as offered to him. A close friend of his mother, Mrs Clayton Freeling, wife of Clayton Freeling, Secretary of the Stamp Office, had prevailed upon her father-in-law, Sir Francis Freeling, Secretary of the Post Office—the highest permanent position in the service—to give Anthony a place in his own office. The Freeling family, which, like Mrs

Trollope's, came from Bristol, practically ran the Post Office (another son, Sir Francis's eldest, Henry, was Assistant Secretary, the second highest position in the service). Escott says that Mrs Freeling urged upon the Postmaster-General the claims of the Trollope family on the Whig government: Admiral Sir Henry Trollope had been meanly rewarded for his war service, and Anthony's father had been denied the London magistracy that Lord Melbourne had encouraged him to hope for. In any case, Sir Francis Freeling, as Secretary, had the appointment in his gift. Mrs Trollope told Tom that in the midst of all her anxieties the news of Anthony's clerkship made her happier 'than I thought anything just now could make me'. Her brother Henry Milton, in sending congratulations to his 'brother clerk', cheered him by recalling that he had himself begun as a clerk in the War Office at £90 a year. [39]

Anthony, on his way to London, stopped at Bruges. There he found that not only was his father very ill and Henry dying of consumption, but his younger sister Emily, who had previously been considered 'delicate', was now admitted to have the same dreaded disease. The elder daughter, Cecilia, had been sent to Uncle Henry Milton in Fulham, out of contagion's way, and Mrs Trollope was left alone in the house, assisted by two part-time Belgian servants, caring for three invalids. Anthony wrote: 'A sadder household never was held together. They were all dying,—except my mother, who would sit up night after night nursing the dying ones and writing novels the while,—so that there might be a decent roof for them to die under.' [40] Anthony would never see either his father or Henry again.

6

St Martin's-le-Grand

ON leaving Bruges for London, Trollope was grateful that at last he would no longer be a burden, or so he thought, to his parents. Now at least he would be out of the way, and on his own. His salary was to be £90 a year, and to a young man who practically speaking had never had as much as pocket money, it must have seemed, at first, a decent prospect. On that sum he was expected 'to live in London, keep up my character as a gentleman, and be happy'. He, at 19, supposed it possible, but was later astonished to think that others, especially his mother, had thought it possible.[1]

Trollope began his London career by moving into lodgings with his brother. Tom, who had left Oxford with a pass degree, was supporting himself by tutoring in Latin and Greek; the rooms were in Little Marlborough Street, off Regent Street, south of Oxford Circus. Tom described this residence as 'a queer house', a survival of an earlier period, situated apart in its own court. Their landlords were a tailor and his mother. Tom and Anthony were the only lodgers. The rooms were 'very cheap', probably because most young men would not have tolerated 'the despotic rule of our old landlady': 'She made us very comfortable; but her laws were many, and of the nature of those of the Medes and Persians.'[2] When Phineas Finn comes to London he stays in lodgings in Great Marlborough Street, in rooms let by Mr Bunce, himself a lodger there, the actual tenant being a tailor who occupies the ground-floor shop. Anthony began one essay, 'Welcome . . . mine ancient friend, my tailor',[3] and those 'ancient friends', first encountered in Little Marlborough Street, often feature in his fiction.

Anthony went to his friend Clayton Freeling, who accompanied him to the stately new General Post Office headquarters, recently completed in St Martin's-le-Grand in the neighbourhood of St Paul's Cathedral. Trollope was to be examined, not by the Secretary, Sir Francis, Clayton's father, but by Sir Francis's other son Henry, the Assistant Secretary. As a clerk's duties consisted largely of copying letters into letter books and minutes into minute books, handwriting was the chief matter for examination.[4] Anthony was asked to copy some lines from *The Times* and made a series of blots and misspellings. 'That won't do, you know,' Henry Freeling told his brother. But Clayton urged that Trollope was nervous, and should be allowed to prepare a sample of his handwriting and bring it in the next day. Trollope was then asked about his proficiency in arithmetic. 'I know a little of it,' he replied, although he later insisted—doubtless with some exaggeration—that at the time he did not even know the multiplication table. He was sternly admonished that, should his handwriting prove satisfactory, he must tomorrow be examined in arithmetic. On the way out of the building Trollope felt like returning to Brussels, but Clayton, who knew the ways of the Post Office, encouraged him.[5]

That night, in Little Marlborough Street, Anthony, under Tom's tutelage, made a beautiful transcript of a few pages from Gibbon. (Trollope had a decent hand when he took his time.) The next day, he was immediately seated at his desk, in a room with six other clerks. No one looked at his calligraphy, and no one examined his arithmetic.[6] Trollope said that he gave an accurate account of this 'examination' process in *The Three Clerks*, when Charley Tudor is initiated into the Internal Navigation Department. The only extra detail—certainly fictional—is that Charley Tudor did not know what a *Times* 'leader' was when asked to copy one. Sir Francis signed Trollope's appointment on 4 November, noting that 'Mr. Trollope has been well educated and will be subject to the usual probation as to competency' (a three-month period).[7]

Trollope entered the Post Office without any examination, and he later waged a continuous battle against the competitive examinations that were introduced as reforms in the 1850s. In his view no test could select the best candidates; the lads who won the competition, he maintained, were those who had best learned how to take the tests, those who had been best prepared by the tutors who had sprung up for the purpose. Basically, Trollope's argument came down to a class one: certain places 'can hardly be well filled except by "Gentlemen"'. But even among young gentlemen he would have fared poorly. In 1834 Trollope would, he thought, have done very poorly on any exam in 'things to be learned by lessons'. He could not read Greek, Latin, or French (he never learned to speak French, he said, beyond being able to order his dinner or buy a railway ticket; in later life he read French books with ease). He knew nothing of the rudiments of the sciences; his spelling was poor, his handwriting usually wretched. And yet, in his view, he knew at 19 more than most young gentlemen of his class:

I could have given a fuller list of the names of the poets of all countries, with their subjects and periods,—and probably of historians,—than many others; and had, perhaps, a more accurate idea of the manner in which my own country was governed. I knew the names of all the Bishops, all the Judges, all the Heads of Colleges, and all the Cabinet Ministers,—not a very useful knowledge, indeed, but one that had not been acquired without other matter which was more useful. I had read Shakespeare and Byron and Scott, and could talk about them. The music of the Miltonic line was familiar to me. I had already made up my mind that *Pride and Prejudice* was the best novel in the English language,—a palm which I only partially withdrew after a second reading of *Ivanhoe*, and did not completely bestow elsewhere till *Esmond* was written. And, though I would occasionally break down in my spelling, I could write a letter.[8]

(T. H. S. Escott claimed that Thomas Anthony had taught Anthony how to write a letter, emphasizing 'clearness, conciseness, abstinence from the repetition of words or ideas, and the non-introduction of any unnecessary or irrelevant matter'.[9]) In fact he thought himself overqualified for his clerkship. He wanted to become an author. He continued to keep a voluminous journal, the 'dangerous practice' he began at Winchester. His 'Salmagundi' manuscript, put together shortly after his arrival in London and consisting chiefly of a fair copy of his mother's poem about Allegra Byron's burial at Harrow, is further evidence of his desire for the literary life. The most striking aspect of the manuscript is the lofty, knowing, almost condescending tone of the notes he appends to his mother's writing: he finds fault with her matter ('This is vast nonsense—his Lordship [Byron] was certainly a clever man—but as selfish a bonvivant as ever lived and no more worthy of the etherial character so often given him than I am') and manner ('perspicuity of style is by no means one of the merits of this poem').[10]

And so, with little enthusiasm, dreaming of higher things, buoyed up only by a feeling that perhaps he would no longer be a burden to his family, Anthony entered into his work at the Post Office. It seemed largely a continuation of his unhappy and unproductive school days:

In my boyhood, when I would be crawling up to school with dirty boots and trousers through muddy lanes, I was always telling myself that the misery of the hour was not the worst of it; but that the mud and solitude and poverty of the time would insure me mud and solitude and poverty through life. Those lads about me would go into Parliament, or become rectors and deans, or squires of parishes, or advocates thundering at the Bar. They would not live with me now,—but neither should I be able to live with them in after years. . . . When, at the age in which others go to the Universities, I became a clerk in the Post Office, I felt that my old visions were being realised. I did not think it a high calling. [11]

From the first he failed to do well at the Post Office. He was supposed to be at work by ten every morning, but he was seldom on time, having, as he said, a watch that was 'always ten minutes late'.. He quickly 'achieved a character for irregularity'. His work was judged unsatisfactory. Dismissal was hinted at, and was not altogether an impossibility—the place Trollope held had become available when a certain Frederick Diggle had been allowed to resign in lieu of being dismissed. Mrs Clayton Freeling, Trollope later wrote, besought him with tears in her eyes to think of his mother. And the old Secretary, Sir Francis, who remained in office only a little more than one year after Trollope's appointment, 'showed me signs of almost affectionate kindness, writing to me with his own hand more than once from his death-bed'. Trollope apparently made friends fairly quickly with the other clerks, a fact hinted at in *An Autobiography* and supported by his fictional versions of Civil Service camaraderie. At headquarters, a comfortable sitting-room upstairs was kept for the clerk whose turn it was to remain on duty all night. Here the clerks would play écarté for an hour or two after lunch; and here they would be joined in the evenings by clerks from the foreign mails division, who actually lived in the building, and together they would have suppers and card parties at night—'great symposiums'. Trollope became friendly with this 'somewhat fast set' of foreign mail clerks, who were much given to tobacco and 'spirits and water in preference to tea'. During one of Trollope's evenings on duty, a Queen—of Saxony he thought it was—wished to be shown the departure of the night mails and, as no official 'pundit' could be summoned on short notice, he had to play host. Trollope accompanied the Queen around the building, 'walking backwards, as I conceived to be proper, and often in great peril as I did so, up and down the stairs'. At the departure one of the old barons escorting her majesty handed him, after some hesitation, half-a-crown. [12] It was the kind of story his fellow clerks enjoyed over their drink and tobacco. The companionship with his peers must have been pleasant enough, but as his superiors found his work unreliable, Trollope made no promising beginning in the department he was later to serve so ably.

While Anthony was becoming acquainted with the Post Office and London life, his mother was struggling on alone in Bruges with Henry in his last days. She sent brave letters to Tom, explaining how she went on scribbling at night as Henry, never an easy-going young man, became ever more '*exigeant*' on her. But Tom was told not to pity her or worry, for when she had not fortified herself with strong coffee for her nightly writing, she slept—approximately every other night—'like a top'. Finally, on 23 December, she wrote: 'It is over. My poor Henry breathed his last about nine o'clock this morning.' She asked that Tom, together with Cecilia, return immediately. Anothony was not summoned to Bruges for the funeral; Mrs Trollope told Tom, 'Give our most affectionate love to dear, dear Anthony. Tell him I will write to him in a day or two, but *cannot* do it now.' Henry was buried just outside the Catherine Gate at Bruges. Mrs Trollope, momentarily prostrated, nevertheless soon displayed her customary 'elasticity of spirit', and by February 1835 was in London arranging with Bentley for a book on Paris. By May she was in Paris with her husband, Tom, and Cecilia. A French physician, consulted about Mr Trollope's health, said that he saw no immediate danger, but that he had supposed the man to be past 80, when he was in fact just past 60.[13]

Tom had left London for Henry's funeral with no immediate plans for returning to the capital, and Anthony, probably soon after the start of the new year, moved into single lodgings in Northumberland Street (later renamed Luxborough Street) near Regent's Park. The previous September Tom had arranged for lodgings there for his mother, Henry, and Cecilia when Mrs Trollope had come to consult specialists about Henry. Anthony called his lodgings in Northumberland Street, where his room looked out on the back door of the Marylebone Workhouse, a 'most dreary abode',[14] and the place helped fix in his mind the depressing picture of London lodgings so prevalent in his novels. In *The Last Chronicle of Barset*, for example, the narrator observes that such rooms are 'always gloomy'; lodgings keepers seem to believe that dinginess adds to respectability, that any attempt at cheerfulness would suggest 'ideas of burglars and improper persons'; even rooms for well-to-do persons are 'as brown, and as gloomy and as ill-suited for comforts of ordinary life as though they had been prepared for . . . prisoners'.[15] In *Phineas Redux* the wretched Mr Emilius lodges in 'that somewhat obscure neighbourhood' of Northumberland Street and the Marylebone Workhouse, where Mrs Meager and her daughter endeavoured to live by letting rooms: 'The task was difficult, for it is not everybody who likes to look out upon the dead wall of a workhouse, and they who do are disposed to think that their willingness that way should be considered in the rent.'[16] Mrs Roper's boarding house in Burton Crescent, where, in *The Small House at Allington*, Johnny

Eames gets involved with the landlady's daughter, may well be modelled on Trollope's lodgings in Northumberland Street.

Trollope said that in Northumberland Street he 'must have almost ruined the goodnatured lodging-house keeper by my continued inability to pay her'. For after a few months in London, money problems began to be serious. Perhaps, he wrote, had he been under proper parental control he might have succeeded. If his money had been strictly budgeted, so that essentials of lodging, board, clothes, and washing were taken care of first, with a pittance left for pocket money, he might have made ends meet. But 'no such calculation was made for me or by me.' He sometimes had to go hungry, since the only meal provided at his lodgings was breakfast, and he might be deprived even of that when his credit ran out: 'Every day I had to find myself with the day's food. . . . after breakfast I had to pay day by day; and at your eating-house credit is not given.' He had not friends on whom he could 'sponge' regularly. Occasionally he would eat at his uncle Henry Milton's house out in the Fulham Road, but it was four miles away, and Trollope was at once too shy and too proud to seek out this refuge frequently. 'Then there came borrowing of money, sometimes absolute want, and almost constant misery.'[17]

As his financial worries multiplied, Trollope gave an acceptance of some £12 to a tailor, which found its way into the hands of a money-lender, who lived in a little street near Mecklenburgh Square. With this man, from whom he remembered receiving £4 and the original tailor's bill, and to whom he eventually paid over £200, Trollope formed 'a most heart-rending but a most intimate acquaintance'. He said, dramatizing for effect, that the money-lender became so 'attached' to him as to visit him 'every day' at the office. He would come and stand behind Trollope's chair, whispering always the same words, 'Now I wish you would be punctual. If you only would be punctual, I would like you to have anything you want.' He was 'a little, clean, old man, who always wore a high starched white cravat, inside which he had a habit of twisting his chin as he uttered his caution. . . . Those visits were very terrible.'[18] This Mecklenburgh Square money-lender had various incarnations in the novels, but most notably in the avowedly autobiographical *Three Clerks*, where Jabesh M'Ruen, a little man who lived near Mecklenburgh Square, visits Charley Tudor at his office, continually telling him: 'Only be punctual, Mr. Tudor; only be punctual, and I will do anything for you.'[19] In *Phineas Finn* the money-lender is called Clarkson, 'a little man with grey hair and a white cravat, some sixty years of age, dressed in black', who is forever telling Phineas, 'Do be punctual.'[20] Not the least part of Trollope's discomfort was that his indebtedness to a money-lender 'crept into official view' at the Post Office and served to give him a still worse character with his superiors. Years later he lobbied that government clerks be not subject to dismissal for non-payment of bills but might be allowed to seek the usual route of the bankruptcy court. Trollope insists that during the whole of his seven years in London he was 'hopelessly in debt'. It is not surprising that money, and especially indebtedness, plays so prominent a part in his fiction. Almost invariably, leading characters—and many lesser ones— are introduced with an account of their income and their prospects. 'No other novelist', the *Saturday Review* remarked in 1865, 'has made the various worries connected with the want of money so prominent a feature in most of his stories—and this not from the comic, but from the serious point of view.'*²¹

Living alone in London lodgings, Trollope also felt keenly his exile from the company of women of his own class. Young men in his situation, he said, were advised to go home after work and 'spend the long hours of the evening in reading good books and drinking tea', hard advice to follow for one whose mother had always surrounded herself with a bevy of pretty girls. Now, according to *An Autobiography*, 'There was no house in which I could habitually see a lady's face and hear a lady's voice. No allurements to decent respectability came in my way,' and 'the temptations of loose life' prevailed with him. He was, he writes, 'entirely without control,— without the influences of any decent household around me'. He asserts that he asked himself continually whether there was any escape from such 'dirt'.²² According to Escott, who talked with Trollope about his early life, much of the difficulty was Trollope's own awkwardness, shyness, and pride: the drawing-rooms of his women relatives were open to him; he shunned them all. Mrs Clayton Freeling, his early benefactress, who had a wide circle of friends, wrote letters inviting him; but he seldom came. John Forster and Henry Taylor are both said to have told Escott that they sent unavailing invitations to Anthony during his clerking days.²³ But whatever the case, all the talk in *An Autobiography* about 'dirt' and debauchery and the temptations of a loose life surely meant more than smoking cigars and drinking gin and bitters. Trollope would have thought it unbecoming to go into further details, but he gives obvious hints that he was involved with loose women; perhaps, when he could afford it, he went with prostitutes. That he was left so poor and so socially disadvantaged

---

* W. H. Auden wrote, 'Of all novelists in any country, Trollope best understands the role of money.'²⁴

became a lifelong grievance, and frequently he would insert in his work a few sentences admonishing parents—mothers most often—about the pitfalls of letting their children loose in London, especially as government clerks, without proper guidance. In *The Small House at Allington*, he wrote in connection with his surrogate Johnny Eames, 'Can it be that any mother really expects her son to sit alone evening after evening in a dingy room drinking bad tea and reading good books?' Mothers are concerned about their sons' flannel shirting and tooth powder, when they should try to provide them with amusement, dancing, parties, and 'the excitement and comfort of women's society', by getting them admitted to houses full of nice girls in order that they 'might do their flirting in good company'.[25]

Trollope did his flirting in other than what he termed 'good company'. In *An Autobiography* he recounts how a young woman down in the country had 'taken it into her head' to marry him. He says coyly that 'no young man in such a position was ever much less to blame than I had been in this.' The 'invitation' had been hers, and he had 'lacked the pluck to give it a decided negative'. But he did, he avers, leave her house within half an hour. Letters followed him to London, unanswered. Then the girl's mother visited St Martin's-le-Grand: 'My hair almost stands on my head now as I remember the figure of the woman walking into the big room in which I sat with six or seven other clerks, having a large basket on her arm and an immense bonnet on her head. The messenger had vainly endeavoured to persuade her to remain in the ante-room. She followed the man in, and walking up the centre of the room addressed me in a loud voice: "Anthony Trollope, when are you going to marry my daughter?"' Such 'little incidents', Trollope notes, 'were all against me in the office'.[26] In *The Three Clerks* Charley Tudor has not been in London six months before he had his favourite beer shop in a lane between Essex Street and Norfolk Street, where he spends much time consorting with Norah Geraghty, the barmaid, 'to whom he had sworn all manner of undying love, and for whom in some sort of fashion he really had an affection. . . . There had even been talk between them of marriage, and who can say what in his softer moments, when his brain had been too weak or the toddy too strong, Charley may not have promised?' Mrs Davis, landlady of the Cat and Whistle where Norah works, comes to his clerks' office and demands 'What are you a-going to do about that poor girl there?' But Charley, like Trollope, would not marry beneath his station; he was a (mildly) 'dissipated, dissolute rake' and in some sense had 'degraded himself', but he 'dreamt of other things and of a better life' and of a 'lovely wife; a love whose hair should not be redolent of smoke, nor her hands reeking with gin, nor her services at the demand of every libertine who wanted a screw of tobacco or a glass of "cold without"'. He wanted something 'poles away' from Norfolk Street.[27]

Other flirtations Trollope doubtless had, although little detail is available. One letter of this period shows him writing to a Miss Dancers, sending her a pair of gloves, the pay-off of a bet, asking her to thank another girl, Ellen, for her flowers, which are 'blooming on my desk the envy of all the Clerks in the Office', and teasing about yet a third girl, Miss Dancers' 'cousin Emma', in connection with the loss of a gingerbread man: she should not allow grief to prey long upon her spirits as 'it is very bad for the complexion'.[28] But for the most part Trollope's behaviour with young women must be inferred from the admitted partial self-portraits in the novels. Johnny Eames of *The Small House at Allington* is amorously entangled with Amelia Roper, the daughter of his boarding-house keeper. He is sexually drawn to the girl, but, like Charley Tudor, will not succumb: 'Nothing on earth shall make me marry her, not if they bring a dozen actions against me.'[29] At the same time Eames is deeply in love with his idealized woman, Lily Dale, who cannot love him because she has first loved someone else, someone who jilts her. Whether there was ever a Lily Dale in Trollope's early life, a woman he worshipped for years but, for whatever reason, could never win, is beyond discovery.

In Charley Tudor and Johnny Eames, we are presented with a less lugubrious picture of Trollope as hobbledehoy than that provided in *An Autobiography*. Tudor, with his 'infernal friends, and pot-house love, with his debts and idleness and low associations, his saloons of Seville, his Elysium in Fleet Street, and his Paradise near Surrey Gardens', is, in spite of his rough exterior, a young man of promise. He wishes to pursue a career as novelist while still a lowly clerk in the Navigation Office, and like his creator, 'he had often walked about the street, with his hands in his empty pockets, building delicious castles in the air.'[30] But the descriptions of Johnny Eames's slow rise from hobbledehoyhood, telescoping the early and early-middle stages of Trollope's postal career, come closer to Trollope himself, or at least to Trollope as he saw his own mental and psychological growth. (Mrs Oliphant remarked in 1874 that she could not read Trollope's book on Caesar without laughing, 'it is so like Johnny Eames.'[31]) Some of the paragraphs in *The Small House at Allington* on Eames are almost word for word those used later in *An Autobiography*. Eames's father, dead before the story commences, is described as a clever man who began in the world 'almost with affluence' and ended in poverty. 'A very good man he was,' Johnny is told, 'only he shouldn't have taken to farming.' Young Eames begins his London clerk's career at a salary of under £100. Like Trollope as a young man, he 'never gets petted', never 'shines', is awkward, ungainly, and shy. Social appearances are a 'penance' to him; he blushes when women speak to him; he is much alone, takes long walks, and is given to 'castle building'; in his day-dreams he shows great eloquence with women and is in fact a regular Don Juan with the ladies— although a kind-hearted one. Like Trollope, Eames matures slowly. People who knew Johnny could predict no great success for the young man; they saw him as gay-hearted, reckless, and open to temptation; above all they wrongly counted him thoughtless. But Eames, in fact, 'was ever thinking'; he feeds 'an imagination for which those who know him give him but scanty credit, and unconsciously prepares himself for that later ripening'. Moreover, 'he could read and understand Shakespeare. He knew much,—by far too much,—of Byron's poetry by heart. He was a deep critic, often writing down his criticisms in a lengthy journal which he kept. He could write quickly, and with understanding.' Men at his office begin to realize he is no fool.[32] Trollope's growth was if anything slower than Eames's.

When Anthony had been one year in the Post Office, his father died in Bruges on 23 October 1835, after a week's critical illness. Though in poor health for many years, he had not been thought to be in any immediate danger. Thomas Anthony was buried close to his son Henry in the cemetery at Bruges.[33] Anthony was again not summoned to the funeral. His father's death must have been a welcome release to the entire family. Mrs Trollope seems seldom to have complained of his temper, though in 1840 she published a novel called *One Fault* in which a marriage deteriorates into unhappiness: for the wife joy was 'for ever a stranger to her heart' and peace was 'unknown to her . . . solely because her husband was an ill-tempered man'.[34] When Anthony came in *An Autobiography* to write of his father's death (giving the date as February 1835, confusing it with the date of another family death still to come), he said that he sometimes looked back, 'meditating for hours' on his father's adverse fate: when he started in the world, everything seemed in his favour, 'But everything went wrong with him. The touch of his hand seemed to create failure. . . . But the worst curse to him of all was a temper so irritable that even those whom he loved the best could not endure it. We were all estranged from him. . . . His life as I knew it was one long tragedy.'[35]

Shortly after Mr Trollope's death, Mrs Trollope left Bruges and returned to England. She took lodgings in London, and planned a trip to

Italy in order to write another travel book. But Emily was failing in health, and the Italian journey had to be postponed. By January 1836 Mrs Trollope had rented what her son Tom called 'a pleasant house with a good garden' on the Common at Hadley, near Barnet, a few miles north of London.[36] Emily's tuberculosis grew quickly worse, and once more Mrs Trollope was nursing a dying child. Emily died on 12 February. Anthony wrote to Tom:

It is all over! Poor Emily breathed her last this morning. She died without any pain, and without a struggle. Her little strength had been gradually declining, and her breath left her without the slightest convulsion. . . . Were it not for the ashy colour, I should think she was sleeping. I never saw anything more beautifully placid and composed. . . . It is much better that it is now, than that her life should have been prolonged only to undergo the agonies which Henry suffered. Cecilia was at Pinner when it happened, and she has not heard of it yet. I shall go for her to-morrow. You went to the same house to fetch her when Henry died.[37]

Anthony placed parts of his 1859 novel *The Bertrams* in Hadley, where, when the parish church rings marriage bells, the narrator solemnly interjects: 'I know full well the tone with which they toll when the soul is ushered to its last long rest. I have stood in that green church-yard when earth has been laid to earth, ashes to ashes, dust to dust—the ashes and the dust that were loved so well.'[38] And in a late novel, *Marion Fay*, a story in which Post Office clerks play leading roles, the relatively placid early death of the heroine by consumption, 'the terrible curse of the family', is a fictional version of Emily's illness and death.

Emily, who was 17 when she died, had been Mrs Trollope's youngest child, the pet of the family, 'a very bright *espiègle* child, full of fun and high spirits'. But once again Mrs Trollope exercised what Tom called her 'innate faculty . . . to throw sorrow off when the cause of it had passed'.[39] She soon had a very pleasant household for Cecilia, her remaining daughter, for Tom when he was in town, and where Anthony would often spend two days a week. Anthony brought to Hadley one of his fellow clerks, John Tilley, five years his senior in the service, and the most promising young man of the lot as far as the Post Office authorities were concerned. Young Tilley soon fell in love with Cecilia Trollope. Mrs Trollope, as in the old Harrow days, gathered round her a knot of friendly young women; in some ways the household resembled that of the widowed Mrs Woodward and her three daughters in *The Three Clerks*. But Mrs Woodward was no match for Mrs Trollope, who before long, as of old, was organizing dinners, parties, charades, picnics, theatricals. Nothing is known of Anthony's participation in this social life, but if there were any Lily Dale-style romance in young years, Hadley seems the likely setting for it. In the nostalgic story *The Bertrams*, the narrator keeps interrupting an account of two lovers at Hadley: he says that for a man of his age country walks with a young woman are a thing of the past: 'We can still walk with our wives—and that is pleasant, too, very—of course. But there was more animation in it when we walked with the same ladies under other names. . . . for the full cup of joy, for the brimming spring-tide of human bliss, oh! give me back, give me back—Well, well, well, it is nonsense, I know it; but may not a man dream now and then in his evening nap, and yet do no harm?' He returns to the story, but again breaks in, 'There is, or was, a pretty woodland lane, running from the back of Hadley church, through the last remnants of what once was Enfield Chase. How many lovers' feet have crushed the leaves that used to lie in autumn along that pretty lane! Well, well, there shall not be another word in that strain.' But almost immediately he says, 'See how he opens the gate that stands by the churchyard paling! Does it stand there yet, I wonder? Well, well, we will say it does.'[40] The words sound too personal, too melancholy, to have lacked some basis in experience.

But by July Mrs Trollope, ever restless, left for the continent on another jaunt, together with Tom, Cecilia, and Hervieu; she was going, by way of Paris and Vienna, to Italy, the planned subject of her next travel book. In the Austrian capital, she came to know Metternich—and to idolize him—and his Princess; she determined to write about Vienna, postponing the Italian book. She did not return to England until a year later, and Anthony was again in London without any of his immediate family. But the terrible loneliness suggested in *An Autobiography* is exaggerated. A young man in his twenties need not rely on his mother and brother for companionship, and Trollope plainly did not do so. *An Autobiography* speaks mutedly about camaraderie with his fellow clerks and openly about some close friendships. One of the foremost of these was with John Tilley. Another friend was Peregrine Birch, a clerk in the House of Lords, who married one of the Grant daughters, the young ladies who had helped in purloining some of Mrs Trollope's furniture and books from the bailiffs' hands at Harrow.[41]

Anthony's closest friends were John Merivale and Walter Awdry. Merivale, youngest son of John Herman Merivale and the nephew of Trollope's Harrow School tutor Henry Drury, had been with Trollope at Sunbury and Harrow and was his 'earliest friend in life'. Merivale, a convivial and somewhat eccentric man, became a barrister and later a

Commissioner of Bankruptcy. Merivale too was 'impecunious', but not in the degree that Trollope was, and Merivale had a family home in London. Walter Awdry, educated at Winchester and Oxford, became a school usher, took Holy Orders late in life, never advanced beyond curacies, and died in poverty. In *An Autobiography* Trollope speaks of him only as 'W——A——' because of his misfortunes, and describes him as 'perverse': 'bashful to very fear of the rustle of a lady's dress; unable to restrain himself in anything, but yet with a conscience that was always stinging him; a loving friend, though very quarrelsome; and, perhaps, of all men I have known, the most humorous.' With Merivale and Awdry, Trollope formed a 'Tramp society' which took excursions into the countryside, usually Hertfordshire and Buckinghamshire, once as far as Southampton. They determined by rule never to pay for conveyances and never to spend over five shillings a day. They practised loud mirth and boyish pranks, such as pretending that Awdry was an escaped lunatic, with Trollope and Merivale his pursuing keepers. Such times were, Trollope said, 'the happiest hours of my then life—and perhaps not the least innocent'.[42] He must have had these adventures in mind while writing, in the mid-1860s, one of his 'Travelling Sketches' where he defends young Englishmen in small groups seeking out fun and larks, youths 'who have hardly as yet learned to think, and are still enjoying the irresponsible delights of boyhood at a time of life at which others less fortunate are already immersed in the grievous cares of earning their bread'.[43] Trollope later saw his early years at least partially in this light; he had remained a youth unusually long, in spite of his own immersion in the 'grievous cares' of earning his bread.

Mrs Trollope arrived back at Hadley in June 1837, and Anthony was able to come over and spend some of his nights there.[44] By January 1838 she determined to move from Hadley to London proper, explaining to a friend that it would be 'a change which both Anthony's occupations and mine renders very desirable, albeit I love my pretty cottage. . . . four hours out of every day is too much for Anthony to pass in, or on, a coach'. And she herself determined to live in the capital 'among clever literary people'.[45] The move took some time, one cause of delay being the influenza epidemic of that spring, which afflicted Mrs Trollope, Cecilia, and Anthony. Cecilia fainted on trying to stand up; and Anthony was so weak he was unable to lift his sister on to her bed after she had swooned. But by the autumn of 1838 Mrs Trollope, along with Cecilia, Tom, and Anthony, moved to 20 York Street, Portman Square. From this house Cecilia Trollope married John Tilley on 11 February 1839 in St Mary's

Church, Bryanstone Square, the ceremony being performed by the famous bibliophile, the Reverend T. F. Dibdin. Tilley, who had been named Surveyor of the northern district of England, carried his bride off to Penrith in Cumberland (where their nearest neighbour was seventeen miles away).[46]

Another important change in the family's way of life took place at about the same time. After Tom had joined his mother at Hadley in June 1838 they decided that he should not return to King Edward's School, Birmingham, where he had been a master since January 1837, and where he found the boys undisciplined and deceitful, and the lack of congenial society stultifying. Instead he would become Mrs Trollope's 'companion and squire', at home and on expeditions abroad. In the winter of 1838–9 Tom accompanied his mother to Manchester to assist in collecting materials for her *Michael Armstrong, the Factory Boy,* and in March settled the details of payment for the novel with Colburn. Meanwhile he succeeded in having articles of his own (on 'all sorts of subjects') printed and paid for, and in 1840 published his first full-length work, a travel book on Normandy and Brittany.[47] He was on his way towards a writing career, and Frances had acquired a lifelong companion, for her favourite son remained at her side until her death many years later.

By the end of 1839 Mrs Trollope fulfilled a long-standing promise and took Anthony to Paris (Tom went ahead first, and they joined him in early December). She may have sensed Anthony's deep dissatisfaction with his London life and thought the holiday would help him. In Paris that winter Mrs Trollope was her usual active and popular self, and went to 'so many good parties'; Frances Trollope always had, wherever she went, a collection of eminent friends and high connections—here they included Madame Recamier, Miss Clark (later Madame Mohl), Lord and Lady Granville, the British Ambassador and his wife in Paris; she was presented to Louis Philippe and the French royal family in the Tuileries.[48] It is not known how long Anthony stayed with her in Paris; it may have been the two months she hoped for; she had written earlier that she herself planned a long stay and hoped Anthony could stay a few weeks or even a couple of months; this visit 'will give him, perhaps, the only opportunity he may have of seeing la belle ville'. Nor do we know how many glittering parties Anthony attended with her. (Escott says only 'once or twice' did he accompany his mother to 'the great houses which opened their doors for her reception at Paris'.[49])

On his return from Paris Anthony took up lodgings in 3 Wyndham

Street, Bryanston Square. Mrs Trollope, in 'solemn audit' with Tom, had determined that the York Street house would be given up: London living had become too expensive; potatoes, she said, had become 'quite exceptionally dear'.⁵⁰ Of course her usual wanderlust was the real cause. She liked Cumberland, where Cecilia was settled, and would build a house near her daughter at Penrith. But on returning to London in May she found Anthony in the grip of a mysterious and nearly fatal illness. She wrote to the eccentric Lady Bulwer, estranged wife of Sir Edward Bulwer, whom she had befriended in Paris:

My poor darling lies in a state that defies the views of his physicians as effectually as it puzzles my ignorance. It is asthma from which he chiefly suffers now; but they say this can only be a symptom, and not the disease. He is frightfully reduced in size and strength; sure am I that could you see him, you would not find even a distant resemblance to the being who, exactly three months ago, left us in all the pride of youth, health and strength. Day by day I lose hope, and so, I am quite sure, do his physicians.

Anthony's illness, as his mother's letter implies, may have been psycho-somatic in origin. His condition remained bad in May and June and early July; Mrs Trollope wrote to Lady Bulwer, on 3 July, 'My poor Anthony is . . . very nearly in the same state as when I last wrote.'⁵¹ One of the specialists she called in—probably in an informal capacity—was Dr John Elliotson, who had become a friend of Mrs Trollope after he had treated her for inflammation of the trachea the previous year. Elliotson had done pioneering work in the use of 'animal magnetism' (mesmerism) in the treatment of disease, especially mental disorders. In spite of his some-times theatrical methods of demonstration, he was an able physician (Thackeray in 1849 was to credit Elliotson's (non-mesmeric) ministrations with saving his life, and to dedicate *Pendennis* to him). Elliotson was deeply involved in the celebrated case at University College Hospital of the Okey sisters, two young girls then about 13 and 14, who, as Thomas Adolphus Trollope expressed it, after a 'prolonged course of magnetizing' were found to have an eerie talent for predicting the deaths of patients at whose bedside they 'saw Jack'. Elliotson was forced to resign his post at the hospital after it banned the use of mesmerism; the *Lancet* denounced the Okey sisters as impostors, and the the hospital, which naturally enough found the presence of such 'prophetesses' undesirable, dismissed them. When Anthony became seriously ill, Tom records, 'the Okey girls, especially one of them (Jane, I think, her name was), were very frequently in the lodgings occupied by my brother at the time, during the period of his greatest danger, and used constantly to say that they "saw Jack by his side, but only up to his knee" and therefore they thought he would recover—as he did! I am almost ashamed to write what seems such childish absurdity. But the facts are certain.' Two decades later, also according to Tom, the daughter of one of the Okey girls lived as housemaid for some years at the Anthony Trollopes' home at Waltham Cross.[52]

By 9 July Mrs Trollope was writing to Lady Bulwer that Anthony 'goes on decidedly improving, but so slowly as to make every morning's inquiry one of fear and trembling. Still I DO hope and believe that we shall be able to leave England early in September.'[53] As it happened, she could manage only a trip to Penrith in the autumn to see her daughter and granddaughter—Frances Trollope Tilley. (Mrs Trollope called the child's name 'of all my honours and glories, the one I like best'.[54]) Cecilia was already pregnant with her next child by the time Mrs Trollope saw her first granddaughter. Mrs Trollope, who loved Cumberland, after superintending plans for her new home there, soon undertook the delayed trip to Italy for yet another travel book. Anthony was again on his own in London.

All in all Trollope estimated that during his London clerkship days he had stayed under his mother's roof for nearly two years; during that time he had lived 'in comfort'. His indebtedness was lessened, though not done away with, through her efforts: She 'paid all that I asked her to pay, and all that she could find out that I owed. But who in such a condition ever tells all and makes a clean breast of it?' He later wondered how he lived and even 'sometimes . . . enjoyed life' under such a burden of duns: 'Sheriffs' officers with uncanny documents, of which I never understood anything, were common attendants on me.' He was never 'locked up', but was taken 'prisoner' twice until someone—probably his mother or his uncle—paid his debt.[55] And during his stays with his mother he was able to enjoy the company of refined ladies.

Anthony's postal career had not prospered: for one thing, his patron and friend, Sir Francis Freeling, had not lived much more than a year after Trollope had entered the service. Sir Francis was followed in the position of Secretary by Lt.-Col. William Maberly, a former army officer who had married an Irish heiress, and whose 'chief characteristic' in the position, according to Edmund Yates, was 'indifference'; he did his Post Office work, but he was more concerned with his Irish landholdings and his wife's extravagances.[56] Maberly, Trollope said, apparently with some exaggeration, was decidedly not his friend, having formed very early a low opinion of his junior clerk and treating him as if he were 'unfit for any useful work'. Trollope struggled, somewhat half-heartedly, to do better, but his bad character stuck to him. That he could himself compose letters did not seem to be held in his favour. Punctuality was the desideratum in clerks, and he continued to be late. More serious sins were also laid to him, and he was 'always on the eve of being dismissed'.[57] In December 1838 he had got himself into grave trouble for failing to copy and post letters pertaining to postal arrangements with the railway companies; the Assistant Secretary recorded, 'I have observed with much regret an habitual carelessness on the part of this Officer, in the performance of his duties.' A week of his salary was docked, and he was admonished by the Postmaster-General 'that unless there is a great alteration in his attention to his duties, I shall be under the necessity of removing him from the service.' The following April he was again threatened with a suspension of pay for returning late from weekend leave; in May he was discovered to be so far in arrears in his work as to be made to stay after hours and penalized with a loss of seniority (which seniority would have put him in line for the next available promotion). Maberly wrote: 'I regret to be compelled to make such a proposition but Mr. Trollope is without excuse, as he has good abilities & as this neglect, which has undoubtedly brought the Dept into discredit (for some of the Cases are most gross) is entirely produced by want of proper attention to his duty.' And in November 1840, when all the clerks were found to be at fault for not properly reporting expenditures, Trollope was found to be especially guilty.[58] One contretemps with Maberly, heightened in the telling in the *Autobiography*, probably did him less harm than many of his other faults: after a letter containing banknotes disappeared from the Secretary's desk, he angrily turned to Trollope: 'The letter had been taken, and, by G—! there has been nobody in the room but you and I,' and he banged his fist down on the table. 'Then By G—! you have taken it,' Trollope fired back, bringing his own fist down on a movable desk containing a large bottle of ink which flew all over the colonel's face and shirt-front. The senior clerk rushed up with blotting-paper, when the Colonel's private secretary entered with the money, and Trollope was desired to leave the room.[59]

In *Marion Fay* Trollope, late in life, drew a cheerful picture of clerks in the London General Post Office; his hero, George Roden, lives with his mother in the suburbs, as for a while did Trollope, and eventually, again like Trollope, turns out to be more than he appears (in Roden's case, the son of an Italian duke). Two other junior clerks in the story, Bobbin and Geraghty, pleasant and good-natured, resemble Trollope in that they are 'as not yet very useful to the Queen', apt as they are to come late to their office and impatient to leave it at four every evening: 'Minutes would be written and rumours spread about, punishments would be inflicted, and it would be given to be understood that now one and then the other would certainly have to return to his disconsolate family.' Another clerk, Crocker, is altogether too ineffectual and mean-spirited, too much of a tuft-hunter for Trollope to have patterned him on himself; and yet Crocker's relations with his postal superiors reflect to some extent his author's situation. The narrator muses over the question of whether such a clerk, whom it would apparently be better to pay for staying away from the office, ought not, in the interest of saving public money, to be dismissed: 'But there is a necessity,—almost a necessity,—that the Crockers of this world should live. They have mothers, perhaps even wives, with backs to be clothed and stomachs to be fed, or perhaps with hearts to be broken. There is, at any rate, a dislike to proceed to the ultimate resort of what may be called the capital punishment of the Civil Service.' Rather than fire a clerk like Crocker, his superior can only bring himself 'to threaten, to frown, to scold, to make a young man's life a burden to him'. The official who will not invoke the ultimate sanction, Sir Boreas Bodkin, nicknamed Aeolus, i.e. Windbag, and described as 'a violent and imperious martinet ["Secretary" in the manuscript], but not in the main ill-natured' is plainly drawn upon Maberly.[60] The remarkably lax Post Office discipline portrayed in *Marion Fay* seems of a piece with a story Trollope recounted in an 1855 article on the Civil Service in which he wrote of a junior clerk who was told by his superior that 'if he, the clerk himself, could read any one line of his own writing' in copies he had made of letters, he would not be dismissed. This the lad could not do, and so was discharged.[61]

7

Aspirations

ALL through the years of his London clerking days, while unhappily putting in his time, Trollope hankered after authorship. He had always before him the example of his mother's successful career. Her books were very much in the public eye, constantly being attacked by reviewers, most notably for their 'vulgarity' and 'licentiousness'. She was also criticized for meddling in social and religious matters: *Jonathan Jefferson Whitlaw*, published in 1836, had been one of the first anti-slavery novels published in England, and *Michael Armstrong*, 1840, the first exposure in fiction of the evils of child labour in factories. That both such pioneering works of social criticism were from the pen of a devoted Tory added to the controversy they provoked. *The Vicar of Wrexhill*, 1837, a heavy-handed attack upon evangelicals, brought the greatest notoriety. Her vicar, W. Jacob Cartwright—modelled on her old Harrow antagonist, J. W. Cunningham—exercises his greed and hypocrisy through his extraordinary sexual hold on women. Reviewers were shocked. Thackeray, for example, writing in *Fraser's Magazine*, decried scenes that were a 'display of licentiousness, overt and covert, such as no woman conceived before' and called much of the book 'as improbable as it is rankly indecent'; Mrs Trollope would have done better had she 'remained at home, pudding-making and stocking-making'.[1] Such reviews, however, brought her so many readers that the *New Monthly* could assert in 1839, 'Certainly no other author of the present day has been at once so much read, so much admired, and so much abused.'[2] Anthony himself never thought highly of his mother's writings. He considered her plots unrealistic, her pathos melodramatic, and her characters deficient in human nature. In the *Autobiography* his criticism is muted but unmistakable: of her most successful work, *Domestic Manners of the Americans*, he says she shows herself utterly unqualified as a judge of a young nation: 'What though people had plenty to eat and clothes to wear, if they put their feet up on the tables and did not reverence their betters? The Americans were to her

[67]

rough, uncouth, and vulgar,—and she told them so.' As for social issues, 'with her, politics were always an affair of the heart,—as, indeed, were all her convictions. Of reasoning from causes, I think that she knew nothing.'3 On the other hand, he could not help but be impressed by the financial rewards.

Had Mrs Trollope known Anthony's reservations about her work she might jokingly have half-agreed. While she lived at York Street she was invited to meet Samuel Rogers at the house of a mutual friend; Rogers, who earlier had not caught her name, turned to her at table and observed, '"They told me Mrs. Trollope was to be here. She has written a great deal of rubbish, hasn't she?" "Well," [Mrs Trollope] immediately replied, "she has made it answer!"'4 But as for encouraging Anthony's literary aspirations—of which she probably knew next to nothing—she would not go beyond setting an almost unwilling example. It is true that when he had been in the Post Office only two months, she had written to John Murray on his behalf, asking if Anthony might be given some extra employment in correcting for the press ('He is a good scholar, and, as I believe your friend Henry Drury will allow, has very good abilities').5 But what she had in mind for him was after-hours work, not the perils of authorship; she regarded with horror any ambition on his part that might have jeopardized his Post Office career. For a long time she warned Tom, whom she considered immeasurably more gifted than Anthony in this and every other line, against the temptation of leaving teaching for the uncertainties of the literary life. In any case, Murray offered him no work of any kind. And Trollope was discouraged with what should have been the predictable outcome of his own first faltering approach to a publisher, recorded in his earliest surviving letter, dated 24 May 1835 and written to Richard Bentley: after disposing of business on his mother's behalf, Trollope asked the publisher, 'Is it in your power to lend me any assistance in procuring the insertion of lucubrations of my own in any of the numerous periodical magazines &c which come out in such monthly swarms. . . . My object of course is that of turning my time to any account that I am able.'6 Nothing came of his request. It would be twelve years before one word of Anthony's 'lucubrations' would appear in print.

And so Anthony went on secretly confiding his aspirations to his journal. In those pages he convinced himself that he must be an author; he also decided that he had not the talent for poetry or drama, nor the erudition for history or biography: 'But I thought it possible that I might write a novel.' He came to this determination before he had been at the Post Office two years. And still months, years went on and he never made the attempt, all the while suffering his own private mental disgrace for not making the attempt. He continued the day-dreaming that had begun at Winchester, carrying on a story in his mind for months or longer; it was an admittedly 'dangerous mental practice', but this 'castle-building' taught him how 'to maintain an interest in a fictitious story, to dwell on a work created by my own imagination, and to live in a world altogether outside the world of my own material life'. He would later believe that had it not been for this practice he would never have written a novel.[7]

Still, he was not as idle as *An Autobiography* suggests. For all his talk about being unable to stay at home in the evening, he seems, by his own testimony, to have done considerable studying. Trollope asserts that while in London he learned 'to read French and Latin' and made himself familiar with Horace, and with the great poets of England. He had his own 'strong enthusiasms', and once, while living in Northumberland Street, threw Johnson's *Lives of the Poets* out of the window because Johnson spoke sneeringly of *Lycidas* (Milton was his favourite poet after Shakespeare).[8] During 1840, according to Escott, Trollope discovered to his happiness that he could read Cicero and Horace, in the original, with pleasure.[9] His father would have been pleased.

Trollope kept in desultory fashion a commonplace-book for the years 1835 to 1840, and entered there under alphabetical headings some of his reading and literary interests. Most of the twenty-two entries are bare references to Italian and Spanish writers of the past: Alfieri, Boccaccio, Camoens, Cervantes, Calderón, Calsabigi, Dante, Ercilla, Lope de Vega, Metastasio, Petrarch, and others. It is not that he had read these authors, only read about them, in either Sismondi's *Literature of the South* or Schlegel's *Dramatic Art and Literature*, which works are cited with the entries. But a handful of other entries are substantial, most notably those on contemporary fiction; he finds himself generally dissatisfied with novels, but when he reads anything more 'abstruse' he gets fatigued and leaves off; moreover, 'when reading, I long to be writing,—& attempting to write, I become weary of the labor, & do nothing.' In a lengthy discussion of Bulwer, dated 19 December 1840, he complains that he was unable to finish the *Last Days of Pompeii* and *Godolphin*: he can 'get up no interest in the characters'. Trollope is convinced 'how wrong [Bulwer] is in his ideas on life & human nature—how false his philosophy is, & to what little purpose he has worked his brain.' Bulwer has conceived a character 'made up of Alcibiades & Sardanapalus—& has put the mixture on eternal stilts. The man is the same whether he is a murderer—success-full Democrat—an English nobleman—or a highway Robber. Ernest Maltravers, & Pelham. Rienzi and Eugene Aram. Godolphin & Glaucus—Devereux & Paul Clifford—are all the same person—all damned gentlemanlike—decidedly clever—very distingué—chivalrous & courageous in the extreme—successful in their amours & perfectly unnatural.' For Trollope, this last was absolutely damning. Bulwer's novels are also dangerous in that they might mislead a young man by making him think he could 'be every thing at once' and lead him instead to be nothing. Nevertheless, Bulwer's novels are the most amusing since Scott's day, and Trollope ranks only Galt's works and Lockhart's *Adam Blair* as their superior. Dickens, whom one can pretty safely presume he had read, is not mentioned. In another entry he comes down hard on the enormously prolific G. P. R. James's *Corse de Leon*, calling it an 'improbable string of adventures very badly put forth in bad writing'; this book, he asserts, will be the 'last of the modern adventurous class of novels I shall be tempted to read—for nothing gives me so great an idea of wasting my time—no not even idleness and castle building'.

In George Sand's *L'Uscoque* he finds nothing that the 'most careful mother need fear to put into the hands of her daughter. It might have been written by an archbishop without leaving any stain on his cloth.' He sees it as a version of Byron's *Corsair*, but one that makes vice ugly and virtue beautiful. On the other hand, although the first half of the book is written in a 'lively & very taking manner', the second half lags, and the end is 'a melange of extraordinary circumstances put together by way of conclusion with no other regard, than that of clinging still to possibilities'. In his commonplace-book, long before he had written any fiction, Trollope spelled out the norms he would follow throughout his career as writer and critic of fiction: 'morality', lifelike and natural characters, realistic behaviour and dialogue, believable, unsensational plots.

The commonplace-book also displays Trollope's interest in contemporary drama: Fanny Kemble, Sheridan Knowles, Henry Taylor, Joanna Baillie, Sergeant Talfourd. He thinks there might be 'room' for a dramatic poem, a filling in, as it were, of Shakespeare's *Richard II* and *Henry IV*— dealing, for example, with the time of Henry's usurpation.

Johnson's *Life of Cowley*, Trollope says, is written with the same 'unmeaning pomposity of . . . style' as Johnson's other works; moreover, Trollope, like most readers throughout the nineteenth century, did not appreciate the poets Johnson calls metaphysical (and this, he writes, is not the proper word to describe their 'tortuous ingenuity'). He found them 'more learned than enthusiastic & more witty than sublime or pathetic'.

In an early entry, dated 29 August 1836, Trollope attacks Pope's *Essay on Man*, holding the poet guilty of 'presumption' in trying to justify the ways of God to man and then at the very outset casting 'an imputation on his client [God] by sneering at those pursuits . . . which God has ordained' for men. Pope is 'a sort of metaphysical Calvinist—a rational pre-destinarian' who denies man free will, making him a 'puppet' to a system: 'And I fleece my brother that the chain of a preordained system might not be broken.' Trollope then half-apologizes for 'pitching on so beautiful—so popular—so deep—and so powerful a poem'. Three years previously, while still at Harrow, he had thought that he understood the *Essay on Man*, but can hardly do so now because through 'idleness—dissipation—& riot of my mind I have lost in a measure the power of thinking and reflecting'. Trying to put together his ideas brings only faint shadowy results: 'My poor would-be thoughts could not have been of good—for they were a product of that love of opposing which always affects me read what I will. I should read nothing but bad books. I love to disagree—to cavil—to oppose—to attack—to condemne—countermine—& argue—but have never store of argument to carry on the battle.'

Under the one non-literary entry in his commonplace-book, 'Order—Method', Trollope says, 'I am myself in all the pursuits (God help them) & practices of my life most disorderly & unmethodical.' This failing has brought him near to 'utter ruin'. Some of the blame he shifts to his parents: 'The first impression which a parent should fix on the mind of a child, is I think love of order. It is the reins by which all virtues are kept in their proper places—& the vices, with whom the virtues run in one team, are controlled.' Order is especially vital in religion, studies, accounts, diet, and cleanliness. In regard to accounts, he elaborates: 'A man entering life wd make no bad bargain in dividing half his last shilling to buying a red book with blue perpendicular lines. Those blue lines so hated by the young gentry of small fortunes, would fill themselves with figures on the right sheet, were they properly attended to in every monetary transaction.'[10] The concern for order and method and for the keeping of accounts accords perfectly with the practice of Trollope's mature years, evidenced most spectacularly in the 'working diaries' of his books, the meticulous daily summaries of pages written, intended to keep him on his mettle and at his desk every day. But evidently only the inclination for and little of the practice of such orderliness was in Trollope as a young man.

He also put together, in 1840 or 1841, an outline proposal for a 'History of World Literature', an undertaking that would have had staggering proportions. It was a project more ambitious than even his father's *Ecclesiastical Encyclopedia*. He divided world literature into nineteen chronological divisions (including five before Christ) and twelve main subjects encompassing every kind of writing from poetry and history to theology and the fine arts. Trollope appended a list of 'bibliographical books' from which he would work, including Müller, Hallam, Coleridge, Tooke, Harris, Johnson, Sismondi, Schlegel, and Roscoe. Trollope's 'History' would in fact be a lengthy compendium of such works. His purpose would be 'to give the opinion of those best capable of judging in different branches of literature, & not the authors own. It should be a collectanea of the criticism of the world—an abridgement of universal literary opinion.' He optimistically states that the whole thing need not be published at once, but could come out a volume or two at a time.[11] Trollope never began the work, merely condemned himself for failing to get started.

Hand in hand with such ambitions came a hopeless scheme, also probably about 1840–1, to found or be part of the founding group of a periodical, an account of which effort is given in fictional form in 'The Panjandrum', a short story Trollope wrote as editor of his own magazine in 1870. In the story six impoverished people determine to bring out a magazine that will be 'the great future lever of the age'. The narrator, plainly meant to represent Trollope himself, was chosen editor, in spite of his youth. At the time he is 'green' and 'ardent' in politics and considered a democrat because he opposes the Corn Laws. One colleague had as his speciality 'to be an unbeliever and a German scholar', who used to talk of Comte and 'prove that Coleridge was very shallow'. Another was an Irish barrister who wrote verse; another later went into business in the States, became a millionaire and was 'said to have erected Omaha out of his own pocket'. Another died young and was laid to rest in Kensal Green. At their meeting the projectors vote not to include novels, even though the young editor had volunteered to try one. It later transpires that each of the group is entirely dissatisfied with all the others' contributions, including the editor's short story, and they break up, the plan of founding a magazine abandoned. The editor and his closest friend part from two others 'under the walls of the Marylebone Workhouse' and console themselves over a pint of beer and a baked potato at a modest restaurant in Leicester Square. However much fictionalized, the story, as we are assured in the *Autobiography*, had been suggested by a struggle 'in my own early days . . .

over an abortive periodical which was intended to be the best thing ever done'.[12]

'The Panjandrum' is most remarkable for its detailed account of how the practice of 'castle-building' led Trollope into fiction. One cannot determine whether he actually wrote a short story at this time; the account in 'The Panjandrum' may simply reflect his later method, show how his daydreaming came to materialize on paper. The young would-be writer, while walking in Regent's Park on a harsh, rainy day, sees a middle-aged servant woman leading a girl of 10 or 11 with mud all over her stockings. As he passes them the girl says, 'Oh, Anne, I do so wonder what he's like!' 'You'll see,' Anne tells her. The narrator begins to think about who it is that the girl comes 'tripping along through the rain and mud to see, and kiss, and love, and wonder at? And why hadn't she been taken in a cab? Would she be allowed to take off those dirty stockings before she was introduced to her new-found brother, or wrapped in the arms of her stranger father?' The aspiring novelist saw no more of the girl and servant, but 'thought a great deal of the girl'. 'Gradually,' we are told, 'as the unforced imagination came to play upon the matter, a little picture fashioned itself in my mind.' Walking the whole round of Regent's Park, he builds his castle in the air, a story called 'The New Inmate': 'The girl was my own sister,—a sister whom I had never seen till she was thus brought to me for protection and love; but she was older, just budding into womanhood.' He furnishes a little white-curtained sitting-room, provides her with books, a piano, a low sofa, and 'all little feminine belongings'. He sells his horse—'the horse of my imagination, the reader will understand, for I had never in truth possessed such an animal'—resigns from his club, and devotes himself to taking care of his sister. But she soon falls in love and is given in marriage to his friend Walker. The narrator, returning home out of the rain, cannot wait to take up his pen. For five days he works on the story. When not writing, while 'walking, eating, or reading', he still thinks of the story. He dreams of it, weeps over it. The story becomes 'a matter that admitted of no doubt': the little girl with the muddy stockings is but a 'blessed memory'; his new-found sister is 'palpably' real: 'All her sweetnesses were present to me, as though I had her there, in the little street turning out of Theobald's Road. To this moment I can distinguish the voice in which she spoke to me that little whispered word, when I asked her whether she cared for Walker. When one thinks of it, the reality of it all is appalling. What need is there of a sister or a friend in the flesh . . . when by a little exercise of the mind they may be there at your elbow, faultless?'[13] When in *An Autobiography* Trollope described himself as 'living with his characters', as 'weeping with them, laughing with them', when he says he lived much with the ghost of Mrs Proudie after killing her off in *The Last Chronicle*, he is not speaking altogether figuratively. The fictional characters of his day-dreams came to have an 'appalling reality' for him. But as a London clerk, he still put off the day of writing a novel, contented—or discontented—himself with his castle-building and with chimerical schemes such as a history of world literature.

But day-dreams and ambitions were not enough, especially when they seemed so unlikely to come to fruition. Trollope was still unhappy, idle, often oppressed with loneliness, deeply troubled over his poverty and debts and (if we are to believe him) filled with remorse and guilt about the conduct of his life. The wretchedness of his boyhood had extended through his young manhood. Little evidence exists to corroborate or deny the story he gives us in the first three chapters of *An Autobiography*. In that work he had determined to write a straightforward account of his life, though he had no illusion about its telling 'everything of himself' or giving a record of his 'inner life'.[14] He wanted to avoid what he saw as the self-aggrandizing and self-serving aspects of many memoirs; he also hoped to avoid any untoward family revelations. But Trollope's story of his wretched childhood and youth presented, perhaps unwittingly, an account glaringly harsh towards his father and implicitly critical of his mother.

No valid reason exists for doubting the essential fidelity to the facts of Trollope's early life as he perceived them. If a child feels lonely, persecuted, bullied, neglected, and at times abandoned by his parents, it does no good to say that, looked at from another viewpoint, things were really not so bad, or that other children, including an older brother, seemed happy enough in similar circumstances. Of course autobiography has to use fictional forms; has to provide a narrative, give shape and direction and purpose where in real life there had been none of these. Trollope himself was aware that he was telling a 'story', that he was throwing his 'matter' into a 'recognised and intelligible form'.[15] A practised novelist (and one to whom his fictional world was 'appallingly' real), he could not resist the temptation to dramatize, to highlight events that would carry forward his story. And, writing half a century after the events, he would commit some factual inaccuracies and confuse some dates. But all this does not mean that he made the story up, that it was essentially fictional, or a bundle of lies. When judging the 'truth' or accuracy of *An Autobiography* one ought also to bear in mind the probity of its author (even persons who disliked Trollope admitted his almost quixotic honesty). Moreover, the writing, which no one was to see until he was dead, has about it a quiet passion, an intensity that bespeaks a man unburdening himself at last.

The exaggerations in *An Autobiography* embellish rather than create the story it tells. For example, the 'debauchery' and 'dirt', his associations with barmaids and loose women, his near escapes from what he saw as utterly unsuitable marriages, these experiences were probably not as painful and remorse-engendering as he claims in *An Autobiography*. He found he could not stay away from women, and when thrown in with those of a lower social rank, he felt some guilt at his conduct; he may have been tempted to marriage, had a few close scrapes; he sowed some wild oats. He believed that a good marriage could save him, but he felt as yet unfit for marriage. One of his somewhat autobiographical heroes, Jonathan Stubbs of *Ayala's Angel*, says, 'I regard matrimony as . . . the only remedy for that consciousness of disreputable debauchery, a savour of which always clings . . . to unmarried men in our rank of life. The chimes must be heard at midnight, let a young man be ever so well given to the proprieties, and he must have just a touch of the swingebuckler about him, or he will seem to himself to be deficient in virility. There is no getting out of it until a man marry.'[16] It was only later that Trollope could see his early London career as a kind of extended apprenticeship for life. Trollope's fear as a young man was that his disreputable state would go on indefinitely.

It is also true that Trollope in his *Autobiography* left unsaid some qualifications he himself probably would have admitted to. For one thing, he came to realize later that some men mature slowly, and that the slower process is not altogether bad. As he wrote in *Orley Farm*, 'The chief fault in the character of young Peregrine Orme was that he was so young. There are men who are old at one-and-twenty,—are quite fit for Parliament, the magistrate's bench, the care of a wife, and even for that much sterner duty, the care of a balance at the bankers; but there are others who at that age are still boys,—whose inner persons and characters have not begun to clothe themselves with the "toga virilis". I am not sure that those whose boyhoods are so protracted have the worst of it, if in this hurrying and competitive age they can be saved from being absolutely trampled in the dust before they are able to do a little trampling on their own account.'[17] In *Framley Parsonage* we read, 'there are men of twenty-six as fit to stand alone as ever they will be,—fit to be prime ministers, heads of schools, judges on the bench,—almost fit to be bishops'; but Mark Robarts, like Trollope himself, 'had not been one of them. He had within him many aptitudes for good, but not the strengthened courage of a man to act up to them. The stuff of which his manhood was to be formed had been slow of growth.'[18] Trollope believed that Englishmen generally 'are boys for a more protracted period of their life, and remain longer in a state of hobbledehoyhood, than the youths probably of any other nation'. Some of these boys, like himself, 'are nurtured on the cold side of the wall, and come slowly to maturity; but the fruit, which is only half ripe by the end of summer, is the fruit that we keep for our winter use. I do not know that much has been lost in life by him who, having been a boy at twenty, is still a young man at forty.'[19]

Nevertheless, such insights came only later, and one must credit Trollope's *Autobiography* when he sums up his first twenty-six years as a period of 'suffering, disgrace, and inward remorse'. He says that his 'mode of telling will have left an idea simply of their absurdities; but in truth I was wretched,—sometimes almost unto death, and have often cursed the hour in which I was born. There had clung to me a feeling that I had been looked upon always as an evil, an encumbrance, a useless thing,—as a creature of whom those connected with him had to be ashamed. . . . Even my few friends . . . were half afraid of me. I acknowledge the weakness of a great desire to be loved,—of a strong wish to be popular with my associates. No child, no boy, no lad, no young man, had ever been less so. And I had been so poor; and so little able to bear poverty.'[20]

In July 1841, when he had been seven years in the Post Office, there appeared a way out of his London 'miseries'. A new position in the service had been recently created, that of clerk to the postal surveyors. Surveyors, seven in England, two in Scotland, three in Ireland, lived in their various districts and superintended all postal arrangements. Their clerks travelled about the country under orders from the surveyors. These assistants had been all appointed, but word came to headquarters that the one for the Central District of Ireland, George L. Turner, was, in Trollope's words, 'absurdly incapable'. Trollope was the first to read the report when it arrived at St Martin's-le-Grand. Whereupon he went boldly to Colonel Maberly and asked for the position. Maberly sent him, Trollope's belief always being that Maberly was glad to be rid of him. The Postmaster-General, Lord Lichfield, approved Maberly's decision on 29 July. Even with departure pending Trollope could not stay out of trouble. He quarrelled violently with a fellow clerk named Adolphus Shelley and was instructed by the Postmaster-General, who was acting on Maberly's advice, that he must write Shelley an apology. Trollope did so, as non-compliance would have been, the Postmaster-General wrote, 'at his peril'.[21]

Anthony had not had time to discuss the move to Ireland with his mother or Tom, who were abroad. He consulted no one, except a 'dear old cousin', the family lawyer, who with pitying eyes lent him £200 to settle his debts and get out of England. His fellow clerks thought the move foolish. Rumour had it that surveyors' clerks were being made errand boys, sent out for beer and taking the linen to the wash.[22] And then to leave the capital for Ireland, of all places, seemed especially foolhardy. But Trollope, 26, in debt, in bad odour with Secretary Maberly, and still filled with deepening dissatisfaction and self-pity, still nursing his grievances at the world in general, saw allurements in any kind of change.

IRELAND

But from the day on which I set my foot in Ireland all these evils went away from me. Since that time, who has had a happier life than mine?

An Autobiography, ch. 4

8

Banagher and Good Fortune

IRELAND indeed brought change. Writing years later, Trollope called the move to Ireland 'the first good fortune of my life'. His London salary had risen to £180; a surveyor's clerk received only £100 in base pay, but this sum was greatly augmented by travel expenses: fifteen shillings a day while away from home and sixpence for every mile travelled. Trollope said in *An Autobiography* that his salary jumped 'at once' to £400; in fact it came, by his arithmetic, after expenses to precisely £313. 4s. 2d.[1] But the rise was still enormous, and living was less expensive in Ireland than in England. He never again had serious money troubles, and was able within a few years to pay back the £200 to the family lawyer. But the 'good fortune' went deeper. All the evils of his life—the feeling of uselessness, and shame, the failure to be popular, to be liked and respected, to do something with his life, all these evils 'went away', he said, the moment he set foot in Ireland.[2] Ireland was to transform him, and he later maintained that, from his Irish days onwards, few individuals led more enjoyable lives than he. Among the Irish, among people frequently worse off than he, the hobbledehoy emerged into a man, flawed certainly, and idiosyncratic in his extraordinary forcefulness and combativeness. To him it was a miraculous metamorphosis.

On 15 September 1841, however, when he disembarked at Kingstown and made his way to Dublin, such developments seemed less than likely. He was stepping into unknown territory, where nobody—friends, colleagues, the kind elderly cousin, even Trollope himself—thought he was right to go. To be a surveyor's clerk in Ireland at the age of 26 was not regarded as a likely route to professional success or congenial life. The country was seen as a backwater, economically and politically, with a native population living mostly on subsistence agriculture, and their landlords, English and Irish, often in scarcely much better condition; lack of investment and poor communications meant that little change could be hoped for. Moreover, the Irish were supposed to be a lawless and thriftless people, alienated from their English rulers and Protestant Ascendancy landlords by their Catholic religion and bitter memories of conquest and occupation. In this unpromising environment Trollope was to take on duties quite different from those at Post Office headquarters, including the investigation of postmasters' accounts, a task for which he felt quite unqualified, seeing that he had 'never learned the multiplication table, or done a sum in long division'. Small wonder that he recalled himself on the first evening, drinking whiskey punch in a dirty hotel, as solitary and filled with misgivings; he knew no one, and had with him only two or three letters of introduction from a fellow clerk. The next morning he took himself to the Secretary of the Irish Post Office and discovered that Maberly had sent a very bad character of him—hinting that he 'must in all probability be dismissed'. But the Irish Secretary said he would judge him on his own merits.3

After three days in Dublin, and having been posted first on business to Parsonstown, he arrived at Banagher, his headquarters, on Sunday, 19 September. Banagher, a town of some 1,800 on the River Shannon, situated in a corn-growing district in the dead centre of Ireland, in Kings County (today County Offaly), boasted one of the largest corn markets in the country. The town, its prosperity owing something to the opening of the Grand Canal, also had a distillery, a brewery, two tanyards, a malthouse, and corn mills. Trollope arrived in the midst of the September *aonach* or fair, lively with games, music, and dancing; nearby were the impressive, sombre ruins of Garry Castle, Clonony Castle, and Moystown Castle. Everything was very Irish and very different.4

Here Trollope met his superior, the surveyor James Drought (Trollope later gave the name Drought to an unlikeable, self-serving politician who helps bring down the Duke of Omnium's government in *The Prime Minister*). Drought was apparently an indolent worker; consequently, many of his duties and considerably more than usual responsibilities fell to his clerk.* Trollope, who still doubted his own ability, especially in accounts, was to be a 'deputy inspector' of country post office books; he was to investigate complaints from the public about mail service; he was to arrange delivery to distant locations within his district, which comprised roughly the ancient province of Connaught. Trollope, who had chafed at

---

* In 1855 Drought was forced to resign from the Post Office because of frequent 'misconduct', the Secretary of the Irish Post Office saying that Drought was 'unfitted to be retained in the public service' because of his 'systematic obstruction to my orders, and for insubordination'.5

the day-long sedentary work of a London clerk, sitting at a desk copying or writing letters all day, took immediately to the physical labour of travelling. A man of far above average physical strength and of seemingly indefatigable energies, he found himself at last. He had to keep careful accounts of his travels and expenses so as to be reimbursed, and six travel diaries survive that testify to the continual movement his work entailed. (Through these journals one can find Trollope's exact whereabouts on almost every working day from 1841 until his retirement twenty-six years later.) Having spent five days in Banagher, his first movements, as entered in his travel diary, were as follows:

Saturday 25	Sept	to Athlone
Sunday 26	"	to Longford
Monday 27	"	at Longford
Tuesday 28	"	Went to Drumsna, Mohill & Carrygallen
		Ballynamore & Carrick on Shannon
Wednesday 29	"	to Frenchpark & Ballina
Thursday 30	"	to Castlebar
Friday 1	Oct	to Headford
Saturday 2	Oct	to Banagher
Monday 4	October	to Ballinasloe
Tuesday 5	Oct	to Tuam

The entries show that during his first three weeks he spent sixteen days away from home, which added up to £12, and travelled 316 miles, which came to £17. 18s., leaving him, after expenses, a 'profit' of £13. 10s. ½d. It must have seemed a gold-mine. He learned his work quickly. Headford, where he returned for a week on 6 October, was probably the place from which he visited 'a little town in the far west of county Galway'—almost certainly Oranmore—and where, as recounted in *An Autobiography*, he was sent to investigate the accounts of a defaulting postmaster. He made the postmaster teach him the forms and then reported him unable to pay his debt. The postmaster was dismissed. Scarcely a few weeks into the job Trollope was developing a name for efficiency and tough-mindedness.[6]

Even more common than problems of defaulting postmasters were the complaints of the public, which surveyors or their clerks had to attend to. Trollope told of one such investigation he had to make that he deemed 'emblematic of many': a squire in Co. Cavan—not Trollope's district, but he had been 'borrowed' for the investigation because he was 'young and strong'—had incessantly and wrathfully found fault with the mail service in his neighbourhood. Trollope arrived at the complainant's country home, cold and wet, in a mid-winter snowstorm. The squire immediately got him hot brandy and water, insisted he stay the night, provided dinner, refused to discuss business over wine, and had his daughter sing for entertainment. Early the next morning the host confessed that he actually had no complaint, just nothing to do but write letters. What was Trollope to write in his report? 'Anything you please,' the man answered. 'Don't spare me, if you want an excuse for yourself.' Trollope merely reported that the gentleman was now satisfied with the postal arrangements.[7]

In 'Father Giles of Ballymoy', a story recounting the narrator's stay in the small town near Lough Corrib in Co. Galway, Trollope reveals some of his own feelings about his early days in Ireland: 'On this my first visit into Connaught, I own that I was somewhat scared lest I should be made a victim to the wild lawlessness and general savagery of the people; and I fancied, as in the wet, windy gloom of the night, I could see the crowd of natives standing round the doors of the inn, and just discern their naked legs and old battered hats, that Ballymoy was probably one of those places so far removed from civilisation and law, as to be an unsafe residence for an English Protestant.' He is shown up to his room and vaguely instructed that a Father Giles will call. His mother had warned him against the machinations of Irish priests: 'Was it possible that my trousers might be refused me till I had taken mass?' In the middle of the night he wakes to find a man in his room brushing his clothes and preparing, on his own admission, to go to bed. After some verbal altercation, the Englishman throws the intruder's shoes down the stairs and then the newcomer himself, only to discover that he has nearly killed the parish priest, who, unknown to the Englishman had agreed to share half his room—there were two beds—with the 'Saxon visitor'. A doctor, the police, and, it appeared, all the town were summoned, and vengeance against the assailant looked imminent. The Englishman is carried off to police head-quarters, for his own protection; and on the next day he becomes fast friends with the priest.[8] Trollope in *An Autobiography* said that the 'main purport' of the story actually happened to him.[9]

Trollope's romance with Ireland had begun; he came to regard the Irish with a real and lasting affection. With his incessant travel and observant eye he came to know Ireland and her inhabitants as few Englishmen did (he would eventually serve in all the country's postal districts). His embracing of the Irish extended to their priests—in spite of a caution given him by a hospitable Protestant shortly after his arrival in Banagher that he should have to choose one party or the other.[10] Trollope in his writings never fell prey to the customary English prejudices against Catholicism—as did, in varying degrees, such contemporary novelists as

Dickens, Thackeray, and Charlotte Brontë. In his very first nov
to draw a Father John McGrath who, as he told a corresponde
was 'as thoroughly good and fine a man as I know how to depict
developed a special liking for the Irish working man: 'The Irish people are
not murder me,' he wrote in *An Autobiography*, 'nor did they even break
my head. I soon found them to be good humoured, clever—the working
classes very much more intelligent than those in England—œconomical,
and hospitable.'[12] When, in 1862, Trollope had been three years out of
Ireland and was returning to England after eight months in America, his
ship touched briefly at Queenstown (now Cobh), Co. Cork, where he went
ashore, happy to be again in Ireland and in a place where in 'the good old
days' he had had such pleasant times: 'And when the people came around
me as they did, I seemed to know every face and to be familiar with every
voice. . . . when I meet an Irishman abroad, I always recognize in him
more of a kinsman than I do in an Englishman.' He admitted even to being
fond of Irish beggars—'an acquired taste,—which comes upon one as does
that for smoked whisky, or Limerick tobacco.'[13]

In Ireland Trollope learned to like his work; he also found his play. James
Drought kept a pack of hounds; he himself did not hunt, but Trollope took
up the sport. Drought was not happy about this but, according to Trollope,
'could not well complain'. So enamoured of hunting did Trollope become,
and so quickly, that he postponed repayment of some of his English debts
to buy a horse. It is not clear whether he hunted his very first season, but
An Autobiography implies as much. Although he was not a very good
horseman, being too heavy and extremely near-sighted, the sport soon
became not simply a healthy recreation but the object of a passionate
devotion. Until he was forced by age to give it up thirty-five years later,
'neither the writing of books, nor the work of the Post Office, nor other
pleasures' were allowed to stand in the way of hunting. It became as much
a 'duty' as his work for the Post Office. He loved the sport with 'an affection
which I cannot myself fathom or understand'. Hunting was difficult of
access for him—from the first it had to be fitted around his onerous duties
in the service, and soon also around the labour of writing books. He often
had to travel 'all night outside a mail-coach' in order to hunt the next day.[14]
Postal authorities soon learned that Trollope was a hunting man, and no
objection seems to have been made.
   Sociability was a large part of the hunt, and the sport opened doors for
Trollope. That he was an unmarried Englishman of some status made him
all the more welcome in certain homes. In the short story 'The O'Conors of

Castle Conor', which Trollope again claimed was largely autobiographical, the narrator is an 'erratic' fox-hunter, having only one horse, and 'whose lot it has been to wander about from one pack of hounds to another', subject often to the melancholy business of intruding himself on an entirely new set of sportsmen. He knows the painful journey home: 'When a man is alone, when his horse toes at every ten steps, when the night is dark and the rain pouring, and there are yet eight miles of road to be conquered,—at such times a man is almost apt to swear that he will give up hunting.' But in the story he is invited by an Irish squire to Castle Conor where a dance is planned for that evening: 'Now in those days I was very fond of dancing—and very fond of young ladies too, and therefore glad enough to learn that Tom O'Conor had daughters as well as sons.' A mix-up about his dancing pumps provides matter for the slim plot, but the narrator's infatuation with one of the daughters is of biographical interest: he finds her so fetching that he begins to think how pleasant a wife she would make: 'Where does one find girls so pretty, so easy, so sweet, so talkative, as the Irish girls? And then with all their talking and all their ease, who ever hears of their misbehaving? They certainly love flirting as they also love dancing. But they flirt without mischief and without malice.' His stay at Castle Conor is protracted; but for the interference of a maiden aunt, he would have made the daughter an offer in marriage.[15] In *Framley Parsonage* Trollope wrote, 'It is my belief that few young men settle themselves down to the work of the world, the begetting of children . . . without having first been in love with four or five possible mothers for them, and probably with two or three at the same time.'[16] That some of these 'possible mothers' of Trollope's own children were Irish cannot be doubted.

But in this matter Ireland was not to prevail. Trollope had been in the country scarcely a year when he met his future wife at Kingstown (today Dun Laoghaire), the watering place near Dublin. (His travel accounts show him in Kingstown from July to August 1842.) She was there taking a holiday with her father and sisters. Nothing else is known of the circumstances of their meeting or any of the details of their attraction for each other.

Rose Heseltine was the daughter of Edward John Heseltine, of Rotherham, Yorkshire. Heseltine, born in Hull, Yorkshire, in 1782 or 1783, was manager of the Rotherham office of the Sheffield and Rotherham Joint Stock Company. This position he had held since 1836, when the earlier privately owned bank—for which Heseltine had been manager for eight years—became a joint stock bank. He was permitted by the directors to run the Rotherham office pretty much as an independent bank, discounting bills and keeping separate accounts with London banks and only vaguely accountable to the Company's directors. He enjoyed the reputation of being a very able banker and was himself one of the directors of the Sheffield and Rotherham Railway, which opened in 1838. A fellow townsman later recalled Heseltine 'sunning himself on fine days . . . with his blue coat and gilt buttons, a chevalier of the old school'. [17] In 1854, after his retirement for reasons of health the previous year, he was discovered to have tampered with the books to the extent of some £4,000 or £5,000. Heseltine fled to France to avoid prosecution and died at Le Havre on 15 September 1855. [18] Of Heseltine's first wife Martha little is known except that she had been born about 1790, that she was not a native of Yorkshire, and that she presented her husband with four daughters, of whom Rose, born in 1820, was the youngest. Heseltine, although of Church of England background, had his youngest daughter, unlike the others, baptized in a Unitarian chapel. [19] The family lived in a fine old house above the bank on the High Street, the house where both Mary Queen of Scots and Charles I were alleged to have stayed while being escorted as prisoners to London. Martha Heseltine died on 21 November 1841, after severe suffering from an accident that occurred in September on the North Midland Railway, near Amber Gate. The Sheffield *Mercury* spoke glowingly of the deceased's 'many excellencies as a wife, a mother, and a friend' and of her 'high and various talents'. [20] By the time Trollope had met Rose and won her hand, his future father-in-law was evidently himself engaged to remarry. For on 13 December 1842, at the Cross-street Chapel, Manchester, Edward Heseltine married a second time. His new wife was Charlotte Platts, the third daughter of John Platts, a well-known Unitarian divine (1775–1837). [21] So Rose had no mother or even stepmother at the time of her meeting and quick engagement to Trollope; she was 21 when she met and accepted him. Few pictures of her survive; one from her middle years shows a robust, slightly stout woman, with her hair—which turned white prematurely—becomingly arranged; she is known to have been interested in dress, taking pains with her appearance (and, at least according to one observer, had 'beautiful feet'). [22] She remains the great unknown in Trollope's life; very little testimony about her personality exists. She apparently stayed somewhat in the background on social occasions: when George Henry Lewes dined and slept overnight at Trollope's house in 1861, he remarked in his journal that 'Mrs. Trollope did not make any decided impression on me, one way or the other.' [23] W. Lucas Collins, who first met the Trollopes when they visited his rectory for two days in 1870, wrote to a friend, 'What I like best in Mrs. T is her honest and hearty appreciation of her husband.'[24] It is known that she was the only person allowed to read Trollope's books in manuscript, and he said her doing so was 'to my very great advantage in matters of taste'. The sure touch his novels show in their references to female dress must have owed something to Rose. She came to relish foreign travel almost as much as he did, and in later years would go abroad on holidays by herself when Trollope was out of the country. Rose lived well into her nineties, having survived her husband by thirty-five years. Anthony and Rose were a good match, with Trollope's origins a bit higher on the social scale, with his college-educated barrister father and his now famous mother, poverty and calamity notwithstanding. On the other hand, Edward Heseltine's position was sufficiently high, and, although Trollope said that his future wife 'had no fortune',[25] Heseltine probably gave some small sum to Rose on her marriage, whether ill-gained or not we shall never know. In any case the marriage was no *mésalliance* such as had threatened Trollope in London.

Trollope eventually devised for his novels literally hundreds of marriage proposals. As for Trollope's own proposal to Rose Heseltine, he seems, remarkably enough, to have recounted it almost literally, in a passage in *Doctor Thorne* that amounts to a disquisition on the language used in marriage proposals. The Trollopian narrator admits that the novelist 'cannot well describe that which he has never seen nor heard', but insists that 'the absolute words and acts of one such scene did once come to the author's knowledge'. The couple are gently satirized as 'by no means plebeian, or below the proper standard of high bearing and high breeding'; they are a 'handsome pair, living among educated people, sufficiently given to mental pursuits, and in every way what a pair of polite lovers ought to be'. The scene takes place at the sea-shore, where they are walking:

Gentleman. 'Well Miss——, the long and short of it is this: here I am; you can take me or leave me.'

Lady—scratching a gutter on the sand with her parasol, so as to allow a little salt water to run out of one hole into another. 'Of course, I know that's all nonsense.'

Gentleman. 'Nonsense! By Jove, it isn't nonsense at all: come, Jane; here I am: come, at any rate you can say something.'

Lady. 'Yes, I suppose I can say something.'

Gentleman. 'Well, which is it to be; take me or leave me?'

Lady—very slowly, and with a voice perhaps hardly articulate, carrying on, at the same time, her engineering works on a wider scale. 'Well, I don't exactly want to leave you.'

And so the matter was settled.[26]

(*Doctor Thorne*, written in 1857–8, was one of the few of her husband's works for which Rose was called upon to make a fair copy; she must have smiled as she came across this passage.[27])

That engagement came so quickly upon meeting is indicative not only of Rose's attractiveness to him, but of his own new-found confidence in himself as civil servant and bread-winner. Moreover, he was 27, and had long yearned, like Charley Tudor, for someone 'poles apart' from barmaids, his 'pot house loves', or the daughters of London lodgings keepers. Impetuous in everything, Trollope was not one to pine away searching for the perfect partner. In *Orley Farm*, with reference to Felix Graham's scheme to 'mould' the ideal future wife, the narrator says that he prefers the old way: 'Dance with a girl three times, and if you like the light of her eye and the tone of voice with which she, breathless, answers your little questions about horseflesh and music—about affairs masculine and feminine,—then take the leap in the dark.'[28] In *Can You Forgive Her?*, the narrator remarks that 'leisurely repentance' follows leisurely marriages as often as it does hasty ones.[29] In *Ralph the Heir* the narrator muses, 'It takes years to make a friendship, but a marriage may be settled in a week,—in an hour.'[30] Marriage was a serious enough step for Trollope—but not all important. In *An Eye For An Eye* we read that a girl is taught to 'presume that it was her destiny to be married. . . . a young man generally regards it as his destiny either to succeed or fail in the world, and he thinks about that. To him marriage, when it comes, is an accident to which he has hardly as yet given much thought.'[31] These comments, some of them coming as many as thirty years after his engagement, represent fairly well Trollope's modestly satisfied verdict on his own engagement and marriage. In 1861 he told a friend, 'I have daily to wonder at the continued run of domestic & worldly happiness which has been granted me. . . . no pain or misery has as yet come to me since the day I married; & if any man should speak well of the married state, I should do so.'[32]

In the midst of his courting of Rose Heseltine, Trollope took time off to visit his mother and brother at Mrs Trollope's new home, Carlton Hill, near Penrith. The Tilleys lived nearby, and it was the first family reunion since Anthony had gone to Ireland. The two brothers took long rambles in the Lake District, and Tom thought Anthony was 'already a very different man from what he had been in London'. When Anthony returned to Ireland, Tom went along for a holiday. He met James Drought, and though mildly shocked at the slatternly bare-legged servant girl who opened the door, found the surveyor hospitable and his wife and sister pleasant women. Anthony, he discovered, stood high in Drought's good graces because he had taken the 'whole work and affairs of the postal district on his shoulders'. Tom was sent sight-seeing to the Killaries (the Harbour and Bay, on the Mayo–Galway border), where Anthony joined him when work permitted; Tom recalled a walk they took over the mountains and witnessing spectacular changes of rain and sun against a background of mountains and sea: 'We returned wet to the skin to "Joyce's Inn," and dined on roast goose and whisky punch, wrapped in our blankets like Roman senators!' On the same trip they attended an election, where the hustings collapsed, heaping together two or three hundred people. Tom and Anthony, 'tolerably stout fellows', extricated some of their neighbours, including a priest, a little man who had been pinned under others, roaring piteously. The priest in his gratitude kept shouting 'Tell me your names, that I'll pray for ye!' When told it would be no use as they were heretics, he shouted, 'I'll pray for ye all the more!'[33] But for all the late developing camaraderie between the brothers, Anthony kept quiet about Rose.

And if he did not tell Tom or his mother about his engagement, he certainly did not tell his Irish associates and friends. For one thing, he was intensely private; for another, he was prepared for a long engagement, two years as it turned out. Rose had no fortune, and Trollope still owed the £200 to the family lawyer; moreover, as he said only half-jokingly, the marriage would have come earlier had it not been for hunting expenses. But in truth Trollope welcomed the long engagement. Had he married quickly, he would have had to forfeit much enjoyable social life. As it was, the pleasant evenings, and the dances, continued, with Trollope doubtless regarding with some sighs the Irish colleens who beguiled him. When he did bring Rose to Banagher, he was made to feel that he had 'behaved badly' towards Ireland: when a young resident Englishman had been received so hospitably into an Irish circle, though he was not absolutely expected to marry a young woman of that society, it was 'certainly . . . expected of him that he . . . not marry any young lady out of it'.[34]

9

Marriage and Authorship

TROLLOPE had three 'jolly years' as bachelor in Banagher: 'The hunting, the whisky punch, the rattling Irish life' were a joy. He had become, almost overnight it seemed, a respected servant of the Post Office; now instead of himself always 'trembling' as in his London clerking days, he made others tremble; instead of loneliness and lack of decent female companionship, he had an active social life, saw much of pretty girls, and was in fact engaged. Only one satisfaction was lacking: his very successes were 'continually driving from my mind the still cherished determination to become a writer of novels'. He did not doubt his intellectual capacity, but doubted his industry. Until recently he had not had vigour for one profession, much less two simultaneously.[1] Now, in September 1843, a year into his engagement, exactly two years resident in Ireland, he made a beginning. Doubtless he had told Rose his aspirations, and perhaps, engaged now, he felt all the more bound to make the attempt.

He had been sent to investigate money problems of the post office at the village of Drumsna. While taking a walk with John Merivale, who was visiting him, he stumbled upon the ruins of a country house:* 'It was one of the most melancholy spots I ever visited. . . . We wandered about the place, suggesting to each other causes for the misery we saw there, and while I was still among the ruined walls and decayed beams I fabricated the plot of *The Macdermots of Ballycloran*. . . . When my friend left me, I set to work and wrote the first chapter or two.'[2]

At last the castle-building, which had continued apace, began translating itself on to paper. The first words which Trollope was to publish, although they were not to reach the dignity of print until nearly four years later, were these matter-of-fact sentences:

In the autumn, 184—, business took me into the West of Ireland, and, amongst other places, to the quiet little village of Drumsna, which is in the province of

---

* Said to have been Headfort Castle—still standing—once the seat of a family named Jones, and then of the Johnstones, who married into the Jones family.[3]

Connaught, county of Leitrim, about 72 miles W.N.W. of Dublin, on the Mail Coach Road to Sligo. I reached the little inn there in the morning by the said Mail; my purpose being to leave it late in the evening by the Day Coach, and as my business was but of short duration, I was left, after an early dinner, to amuse myself.

The narrator then tells of his exploration into the ruined house, its roof off, the rotting joists and beams showing, parts of the floor removed for firewood, window frames gone, the door half-destroyed, its iron knocker still in place. He then lights a cigar and sits meditating 'this characteristic specimen of Irish life': 'The sun was now setting beautifully behind the trees, and its imperfect light through the foliage gave the unnatural ruin a still more singular appearance, and brought into my mind thoughts of the wrong, oppression, misery and despair, to which some one had been subjected, by what I saw before me.' When one considers the nearly 12 million words that Trollope was to publish, these first words give his reader pause. Did he agonize over them, rewrite, rearrange his sentences and paragraphs? The evidence has not survived. Trollope's earliest extant manuscript, that of *The New Zealander*, dates from 1855–6; the earliest for a novel, *Framley Parsonage*, from 1859–60. But it seems unlikely that, even at the beginning, Trollope ever did much revision. His written words, generally the product of day-dreaming, streamed on to the paper as though dictated to a secretary. (A friend later recorded that Trollope used as a 'favourite expression' the words 'told himself' to describe his novel writing.[4]) The many manuscripts that survive from 1860 onwards, those sent to the printers, are not second drafts or fair copies, but the original manuscripts, uncannily clean for the most part of any but occasional small changes. Trollope claimed that keeping a journal for ten years had 'habituated me to the rapid use of pen and ink, and taught me how to express myself with facility'; another help was writing Post Office reports, of which he wrote 'thousands' and with which he took pains so as to compose them immediately into final form. He seemed to regard making a revised version of anything, novel, report, or letter, as somehow dishonest, or at least unhelpful. Rewriting, or 'polishing' as he called it, led to the smell of the polishing oil, or, in another favourite metaphor, made the rewritten work appear to be 'upon stilts'. He also thought rewriting a waste of time. But the facility and discipline that could readily produce the equivalent of two three-volume novels a year was still a long way off. *The Macdermots of Ballycloran* 'hung' with him, and by the time of his marriage, some nine months later, he had completed only one third of the book.[5] Still, for a first book, written in the midst of long hours of postal work and continual travelling, it was a good enough pace.

Anthony told his mother and brother of his engagement only in the spring of 1844. Mrs Trollope and Tom were visiting the Tilleys at Penrith that summer, but they did not go to Rotherham for the wedding; it was not very far for inveterate travellers like themselves—perhaps Anthony did not urge the matter; perhaps, though this is less likely, Mrs Trollope was slightly ruffled at not having been told of the engagement earlier.

Rose and Anthony were married on 11 June 1844, in the parish church at Rotherham. In *An Autobiography* Trollope wrote, 'perhaps I ought to name that happy day as the commencement of my better life, rather than the day on which I first landed in Ireland.' It was a needless gallantry. Ireland had wrought the change. Trollope is almost entirely silent about Rose in *An Autobiography*: 'My marriage was like the marriage of other people, and of no special interest to any one except my wife and me. . . . We were not very rich, having about £400 a year on which to live. Many people would say that we were two fools to encounter such poverty together. I can only reply that since that day I have never been without money in my pocket, and that I soon acquired the means of paying what I owed.'[6] Rose, in 1875, preparing a list of dates and events to help her husband write *An Autobiography*, has for her first entry, '1844. Married 11th June (hurrah).'[7] The honeymoon was in the Lake District, and part of it was spent with Mrs Trollope, Tom, and the Tilleys at Penrith. (Carlton Hill now belonged to the Tilleys, for Mrs Trollope, restless as ever, had lived in her new house only nine months before deciding to abandon it to live abroad with Tom; after considering Dresden, Rome, Paris, and Venice, they decided to settle permanently in Florence.[8]) Rose Trollope in old age said of her first meeting with Mrs Trollope, 'Nothing could have been kinder or more affectionate than the way she received me—kind, good, and loving, then and ever afterwards.' No surviving evidence contradicts these sentiments. Frances Trollope and Rose were together on some half a dozen occasions, and cordiality and friendliness seem to have prevailed. Rose remembered Mrs Trollope at Carlton Hill as full of cheer and wit, the life of every party, excursion, and picnic; she also recalled the famous energy: Mrs Trollope 'rose very early and made her own tea . . . then sat at her writing-table until the allotted task of so many pages was completed; and was usually on the lawn before the family breakfast-bell rang.'[9]

Anthony then took Rose to Kingstown, where they had met two years earlier; by 10 July he was back at work, Rose being quickly inaugurated into the routine of having her husband away more nights than he was home. This was to be the pattern of their married life for the next fifteen years, mitigated somewhat after the transfer to England in 1859. On 2 August the couple arrived at Banagher, the trip enlivened by a slight mishap, the jaunting car that carried them having driven into the Shannon Canal. [10] Trollope left no account of his early days of marriage, but a passage from *The Bertrams*, a novel containing a good share of personal reminiscences, reflects his feelings: 'To neither man nor woman does the world fairly begin till seated together in their first mutual home they bethink themselves that the excitement of their honeymoon is over. It would seem that the full meaning of the word marriage can never be known by those who, at their first outspring into life, are surrounded by all that money can give. It requires the single sitting-room, the single fire, the necessary little efforts of self-devotion, the inward declaration that some struggle shall be made for that other one, some world's struggle of which wealth can know nothing. One would almost wish to be poor, that one might work for one's wife; almost wish to be ill-used, that one might fight for her.'[11] At Banagher Rose had not long to endure the snubs that Anthony feared she might be subjected to since he had 'behaved badly' in marrying out of Ireland, nor the presumably cramped and inconvenient hotel rooms which local tradition says Trollope occupied in Banagher. He had already put in for a transfer; his first choice, the northern district, which might have permitted him to live at Dublin, was denied him, but hopes were held out for a move to the south. Old Mrs Trollope, answering on 7 August a letter from Rose, entered into the new wife's fears of living in backwater Banagher, saying she was glad that the circulating library subscription had been paid and trusting that Rose had taken to Banagher a 'good package, to comfort you in your retreat'.[12] She also commiserated with them about the vexatious delay in hearing about the transfer. But the wait was not long; on 27 August the change to the southern district was made official.[13]

Here his superior was James Kendrick, a more conscientious civil servant than Drought, and a man with whom Trollope got on very well. Trollope's headquarters were to be Clonmel, County Tipperary. But first he was given a few assignments that put him temporarily in charge of local post offices, and to these places Rose accompanied him, the two taking such lodgings as could be found quickly. First Trollope was sent to Cork, where the couple lived from early September 1844 to mid-February 1845. Trollope would use Cork's down-at-heel South Main Street for the grubby

Kanturk Hotel scenes in *Castle Richmond*. For the next
couple lived in Milltown Malbay, a small town in County
from the sea. From here he and Rose visited the nearby
which took hold of Trollope's imagination and later bec
of the short tragic novel *An Eye For An Eye*. In Octobe
lived in Kilkenny, and from 6 November 1845 to 20 Fe
Fermoy.

But aside from these interludes, their home for the next three years, and
where they settled in June 1845, was in Clonmel, an attractive and
prosperous town on the banks of the Suir in the South Riding of County
Tipperary. Clonmel is famous for the five-week defence of the city in 1650
by Hugh Dubh O'Neill against Oliver Cromwell and nine thousand
soldiers of his Model Army. (Carlyle called O'Neill's force 'the stoutest
Enemy this Army had ever met in Ireland'.) The Trollopes are said to have
taken spacious rooms in the very house (since destroyed) in which
Cromwell resided after finally capturing the town.[14] One notable citizen of
Clonmel and the town's mayor in 1845–6, Charles Bianconi, Trollope
already knew well. Bianconi was the inventor of the famous cars that bore
his name. His coach service was nation-wide, and in the years before the
railways Bianconi cars carried most of the mails in Ireland, his routes
encompassing close to 4,000 miles. In 1857, in a brief 'History of the Irish
Post Office', prepared by Trollope as part of the Postmaster-General's
report, he said of Bianconi that 'perhaps . . . no living man has worked
more than he has for the benefit of the sister kingdom.'[15] Still later,
Trollope's son Henry would ghost-write a life of Bianconi. Trollope made
many friends, especially among the Anglo-Irish of his district and among
the hunting set. Near Clonmel was a rock formation portentously named
'Palliser's Castle'.[16]

At Clonmel Trollope's two sons were born: Henry Merivale Trollope,
on 13 March 1846 and Frederic James Anthony Trollope on 27 September
1847. In *An Autobiography* Trollope mentions the births only while
describing events of 1852–3, admitting that his sons 'certainly were
important enough to have been mentioned sooner'.[17] His work, as always,
kept him much from home; when Henry was born he had been away for
the previous week, and it is not clear whether he was able to make a flying
visit to Clonmel on the day of the birth or whether he first saw his son three
days later, on the evening of the 17 March; thereafter he was again away
until the end of the month when he was a week at Clonmel. When
Frederic was born Trollope had been away the two previous weeks and
arrived home the day following the birth; then after a week in Clonmel he

s travelling again, able to touch back at Clonmel only about once a week for the next month. Rose occasionally complained of his being away so much. Revisiting Ireland in 1882, a few months before his death, Trollope wrote to her: 'I will give up being Surveyors clerk as you dont seem to like it, but in that case must take to being guide at Killarney.'[18] Henry— 'Harry' to the family—was named after Trollope's brother who had died at Bruges; Merivale derived from Anthony's great friend John Merivale, who was one of the child's godparents. The other godparents were his uncle Thomas Adolphus Trollope and his grandmother Frances Trollope. Frederic was probably named after a brother of Rose; his godparents were Trollope's brother-in-law, John Tilley, Trollope's boss, the surveyor James Kendrick, and Rose's sister Isabella. Both children were baptized in St Mary's Church, Clonmel.[19]

Marriage spurred Trollope on in the writing of his novel, for by July of 1845 he had the three-volume work completed. He took the manuscript with him to Penrith, where the family, including Uncle Henry Milton and his wife, were again assembled. In *An Autobiography* Trollope relates how on this visit to Penrith he gave the manuscript of *The Macdermots of Ballycloran* to his mother in order that she might secure a publisher for it. They agreed that she should not look at the novel before it was in print: 'I knew that she did not give me credit for the sort of cleverness necessary for such work. I could see in the faces and hear in the voices of those of my friends who were around me at the house in Cumberland . . . that they had not expected me to come out as one of the family authors.' (His mother continued to produce popular novels at great speed; Tom was doing well with his miscellaneous and travel writing; Cecilia had a novel, *Chollerton*, in manuscript at the time.) Trollope said the family silently viewed his book as 'an unfortunate aggravation of the disease'.[20] His account seems to conflate two visits, that of 1844 on his honeymoon and this one, for Tom was present on the first visit and not on the second. Trollope coloured the picture a little too darkly when describing the cool reception his family gave his admission of having written a novel. He had already told his mother and Tom about his partially completed novel during the honeymoon visit to Penrith. A few weeks after that, Mrs Trollope, writing to Rose, 'rejoiced' at the news that Anthony's manuscript, which had been lost, was found; she added, 'and I trust he will lose no *idle* time, but give all he can, without breaking in upon his professional labours, to finish it.'[21] This amounted to approval, even encouragement, of Anthony's novel writing, provided it did not jeopardize his Post Office career.

Mrs Trollope, with her host of literary connections, lost no time in securing a publisher. She did not, however, arrange for the book to be taken by one of her own publishers; evidently the best she could do was Thomas Cautley Newby, of Mortimer Street, Cavendish Square. Newby was a minor London publisher with no big-name author on his list, and little financial means. He eventually developed a reputation for dishonesty. (Publisher Richard Bentley on one occasion refused to talk with him without a witness in the room; Bentley's reader rejected a manuscript with the words 'good enough for Newby'.[22]) But Trollope was glad at the simple prospect of getting into print and trusted his mother's judgement that Newby was as high as he ought to aim with a first book.

Newby sent Trollope the agreement on 15 September 1845. The publisher would print 400 copies; Trollope was to receive half-profits after expenses, which meant that after the sale of 190 copies he would receive 10s. 1½d. for each additional copy sold.[23] Like most nineteenth-century novels, the book would be published in three volumes and sell for 31s. 6d. The formula of a small printing, a high price, and the often putative half-profits made it possible for publishers to bring out new or little-known novelists without much risk. The half-profits system was one Trollope came to detest because the author had no way of telling how fair the reckoning of expenses was. But a beginning author had no choice.

Newby explained that, much as he would like to publish the novel late in 1845, the best he could manage would be February 1846. But he procrastinated. Victorian publishers could put a novel through the press in six weeks or fewer if they chose, but Newby was in no hurry, and he had little capital. Mrs Trollope, in London in August 1846, saw Newby about Anthony's book, but, as she told Cecilia: 'He, like everybody else, gives a most wretched account of the novel-market. . . . He says that he thinks [*The Macdermots*] very cleverly written, but that Irish stories are very unpopular.'[24] (At about this time, Charlotte Brontë complained to her publisher about Newby's delays in bringing out her sisters' combined volume of *Wuthering Heights* and *Agnes Grey*: 'Mr. Newby shuffles, gives his word, and breaks it.'[25]) Finally, in March 1847, when Anthony was almost 32, *The Macdermots of Ballycloran* appeared.

Part of his apprenticeship for the book was his reading of Irish tales and novels. He had known since boyhood Maria Edgeworth's *Castle Rackrent* (1800) and *The Absentee* (in *Tales of Fashionable Life*, 1812); both were 'landlord novels', as were all but one of Trollope's Irish novels. According to Escott, Trollope's knowledge of Irish fiction was greatly extended through his frequent visits to his old Harrow contemporary, William

Gregory, at Coole Park, Co. Galway, where he had the run of the library. There he became acquainted with William Carleton's authentic stories of Irish peasant life, of which he most admired the powerful and tragic *Fardorougha the Miser* (1839) and *Tales of Ireland* (1834); he was greatly impressed by Gerald Griffin's popular and melodramatic *The Collegians* (1829)—Henry Taylor recounted how Trollope, on a visit to Killarney, the scene of the novel, had fallen into company with a priest, to whom he remarked that somewhere hereabouts the story's villain Hardress had drowned a woman: 'What a scene! what passion, what character, what skill I find in that novel! What a frightful history it tells!' The priest remained silent, and then said, 'Hardress was my first cousin, and I stood on the steps of the scaffold when he was hung.'[26] At Coole Park, too, Trollope met Charles Lever; his comic, picaresque novels of Irish army life did not influence Trollope, but the success of his *Confessions of Harry Lorrequer* (1839) and *Charles O'Malley, the Irish Dragoon* (1841) encouraged the younger man's aspirations.[27] But the influence of Trollope's reading of Irish novels should not be overstated. *The Macdermots*, like his later fiction, sprang chiefly from a close observation of daily life, a naturally good ear for dialogue, and the habit of day-dreaming, ruminating, 'living with' his characters in imagination before setting them to paper, coupled with a firm long-held determination—inspired by his early dislike of the fiction of Bulwer and G. P. R. James, and probably that of Dickens and his own mother—to avoid the 'unnatural' in character and the 'improbable' in plot.[28]

The Macdermots of Ballycloran is the story of a decaying Irish Catholic family: Larry Macdermot, the father, overwhelmed by the mortgage debt on his house and sinking into idiocy; Thady, his son, a decent but somewhat slow-witted man, trying futilely to run the estate and collect rents from peasants unable to pay; and Feemy, the daughter, headstrong and determined to love Myles Ussher, a Protestant captain of the hated Revenue Police. When Thady comes upon Ussher attempting to elope with Feemy, he kills him, thinking Ussher is taking her away by force. Thady is tried for murder; Feemy, who had been seduced by Ussher, dies of a miscarriage during the trial, and Thady is hanged for the crime. Trollope said, 'I do not know that I ever made [a plot] so good,—or, at any rate, one so susceptible of pathos. I am aware that I broke down in the telling, not having yet studied the art.'[29] That old Larry Macdermot was drawn in part—perhaps to some extent unconsciously—from Trollope's father is beyond doubt: Macdermot is old before his time, unable to manage money, beaten by the world; he suffers from an irrational temper,

THE MACDERMOTS

OF

BALLYCLORAN,

BY

Mr. A. TROLLOPE.

IN THREE VOLUMES.

VOL. I.

LONDON:

THOMAS CAUTLEY NEWBY, PUBLISHER
72, MORTIMER St., CAVENDISH Sq.

1847.

Title-page of *The Macdermots of Ballycloran*.

and is drifting into madness; his case is many times worse than Thomas Anthony's, but the parallels are unmistakable. And Thady Macdermot is something of a self-portrait of the earlier Anthony, generally ineffectual and unable to cope with his problems.

In this first novel Trollope shows that disapproval of heroes and villains that was to characterize all his fiction. No one is thoroughly virtuous or thoroughly evil, and Trollope engages a qualified sympathy for almost everyone: Larry Macdermot may be drifting toward alcoholic imbecility and an irrational hostility towards his dutiful son, but we feel pity for him. Thady, the central figure, is honest and hard-working, but hardly heroic; he is slow-thinking, plodding, sullen, and inarticulate. Feemy is no simpering, weeping victim, but the first of Trollope's headstrong young women. Even Ussher, the nominal villain, has an animal courage that is admirable. Father John McGrath (claimed to have been based on the priest Trollope once threw down the stairs, as told in 'Father Giles of Ballymoy'),[30] the moral centre of the book, friend of all his flock, jovial, hospitable, learned, tolerant of human weaknesses and even of Protestants, is none the less no paragon, being slightly cruel in his humour, erroneous in judgement, and not above demanding monetary recompense for his ministrations; he is even physically unattractive, 'very short, and very fat, and had little or no appearance of neck'.[31] Trollope would have called his fictional people 'realistic'. His early commonplace-book had attested to a vehement dislike of 'unnatural' or exaggerated fictional characters, and in his first novel he stayed well clear of that fault. He wanted his characters firmly planted in the actual world as he saw it, the products of long day-dreaming and imaginary dialogue, all of it tending to produce what he hoped would be believable stories with 'real people' in them. An enormous fictional parade—it was to stretch out into forty-seven novels and sixty short stories—had begun.

The Macdermots has its shortcomings: inflated style ('I began to perceive evident signs on the part of the road, of retrograding into laneism'[32]); sprawling dialogue; interpolated passages of explanation and commentary; and the melodramatic timing of Feemy's death, this last especially unlike Trollope's usual later work. But it surpassed most of the novels that were to follow in rendering private lives emblematic of a whole society; this it did as convincingly as the later *The Way We Live Now*; it dramatizes the complex tensions between Irish and English without taking sides, although compelling the reader's sympathies for the Irish poor.[33] What makes it unique among Trollope's writings, however, is its intensity of tragic feeling. Trollope wrote other tragic novels, or novels in part tragic, like *Castle Richmond*, *An Eye for an Eye* (both set in Ireland), *Orley Farm*, *He Knew He Was Right*, and *Sir Harry Hotspur of Humble-thwaite*; but never was another Trollope novel to be so unrelievedly sombre and serious—in spite of some humour—as *The Macdermots of Ballycloran*.

The book did not sell. Newby resorted in vain to advertisements attributing authorship to Mrs Trollope. (He also attempted to make it seem that the enormously popular *Jane Eyre* had been written by his author, 'Ellis' Bell—Emily Brontë—and, much later, that *Adam Bede Junior* was by George Eliot.[34]) Nor did it help for Newby in 1848 to rebind sheets of the original edition with a new title-page that added the misleading subtitle, 'A Historical Romance'. Trollope in *An Autobiography* commented that, as he had expected, he got neither money nor recognition; he said he never heard of anyone reading it, that he saw no review; that he asked no questions of the publisher, that he said no word about it, even to his wife.[35] In some of this Trollope may have either misremembered or exaggerated, for *The Macdermots* had not been stillborn: it received at least thirteen reviews, most of them favourable. The most damning came from the *Critic*, where the writer, while admitting that the plot was 'interesting and ingenious' complained of 'slovenly writing' and asserted that 'every page is crowded with tautologies'; he hoped Trollope were a youth, for if he had already reached maturity, 'his case is hopeless'. But *Douglas Jerrold's Shilling Magazine* called *The Macdermots* 'strictly natural, as life-like and vigorous as could be desired'; it said the 'Irish dialogue is smartly and judiciously written, and is the evident result of residence. . . . There are some stirring and life-like scenes in it, and we augur from it a successful career to the author. He evidently has inherited a keenness of observation and power of narrative.' Other critics, predictably, also linked Trollope with his mother: *Howitt's Journal* said that 'the son assuredly inherits a considerable portion of the mother's talent. It is a story of intense interest, and is written by a bold and skilful hand.' The *Spectator* went further, saying that although the subject was one Mrs Trollope might have chosen, *The Macdermots* had 'more of mellowness in the composition . . . and less of forced contrivance in the management of his story, than the fluent lady has ever displayed.' The *Athenaeum* declared: 'Twenty years ago "The Macdermots" would have made a reputation for its author'; the reviewer hoped Trollope would in the future deal less in misery and develop his humour. *John Bull*, however, found 'rare and singular merit' in the novel's realism, and compared his knowledge of Ireland with that of Maria Edgeworth.[36]

The poor sales, then, were not owing to the reviews. A major problem was the book's timing. Since the beginning of 1846 English newspapers had been full of the sufferings of Ireland under the potato famine and the dangers of Irish nationalism, and the public had little inclination to read fiction about Irish troubles. Before the publication of *The Macdermots*, Trollope had embarked on a second Irish novel, *The Kellys and the O'Kellys*, this time trying his hand at comic rather than tragic realism. He completed it in 1847, undeterred by the failure of *The Macdermots*. Determined to find a more reputable publisher, he offered it to Richard Bentley. The firm was in some financial trouble in the 1840s; but this was not generally known, and Trollope would have been impressed by Bentley's large general list, including the popular *Ingoldsby Legends* of R. H. Barham, memoirs and travels, and a series of 'Standard Authors', as well as three-volume novels by known and unknown authors. W. H. Ainsworth and G. P. R. James were among Bentley's authors; Frances Trollope had also been one until 1842, when she left him for Colburn. With Bentley, Trollope attempted to take a strong line, asserting that he would not part with the manuscript on *'any other terms than that of payment for it'*, would not accept half-profits or in any way have the payment conditional on sale. A publisher, Trollope asserted, will have it in his interest to 'push' a book that is his own property.[37] Bentley declined to take the book for cash, returned the manuscript, and four months later Trollope sent it to Henry Colburn, now the regular publisher of Mrs Trollope. Previously a partner with Bentley and now his arch-rival (Mrs Gore called them the Scylla and Charybdis of Victorian publishing), Colburn was nicknamed 'The Prince of Puffers', for his notorious advertising; he had been a pioneer in the publishing of the 'silver fork' (aristocratic) novel; he had published Disraeli, Bulwer Lytton, Captain Marryat, and G. P. R. James.[38] In the 1840s the mainstays of his fiction list were Mrs Gore, Mrs Marsh, and Mrs Trollope—whose influence with the publisher was considerable. Anthony, retreating from the position he had taken with Bentley, though still professing dislike for the half-profits system, accepted Colburn's offer to publish *The Kellys* on terms nearly identical to those Newby had given him for *The Macdermots*, except that even fewer copies, 375, were to be printed. Colburn returned a memorandum of agreement on 30 March 1848, saying also that as the book was 'illustrative of Irish Society, it should appear as soon as it could be printed'.[39] Colburn, very unlike Newby, was as good as his word, and *The Kellys and the O'Kellys* appeared on 27 June 1848.

The novel opens in early 1844 in Dublin during the famous seditious conspiracy trials of Daniel O'Connell, part of which Trollope, who was in the city briefly in January and February, seems to have witnessed. But the great bulk of the story takes place in the west, in Trollope's first postal district, specifically in the village of Dunmore near Tuam in Galway at the County Mayo border. This novel is much more typically 'Trollopian' than *The Macdermots*, exhibiting features he would return to again and again in later works: *The Kellys* is a comedy, its humour constant in spite of some terribly dark shadows; it is a love story, or rather two, with parallel plot lines; its first hero Lord Ballindine is weak and hesitant; its heroine, or one of them at least, Fanny Wyndham, though modest and in some ways timid, is stubborn and faithful to her unsure lover; another heroine, Anty Lynch, shows uncalled-for devotion to a worthless brother; small segments of confrontational dialogue exuberate into memorable stories in their own right; it has father and son enmity; and it features an older woman, the widow Kelly, as the best fun in the book; *The Kellys* also deftly incorporates written correspondence between characters. (Henry James was to remark that Trollope dealt more in letters than any other contemporary novelist and to suggest that this 'unfailing resource' may have derived from Trollope's many years' work in the management of the Post Office: James could imagine 'no experience more fitted to impress a man with the diversity of human relations'.[40]) On the other hand, Barry Lynch is more villainous than Trollope's usual dark characters, and many of his lines are stagey; Barry's abused and saintly sister is equally uncharacteristic and unconvincing, and their sessions together unworthy of the mature Trollope.

But perhaps especially in its satiric pictures of aristocrats, here the family of Lord Cashel, *The Kellys* is full-bloom Trollope. As in the later books, such characters are often introduced by trenchant thumb-nail sketches:* the empty, self-important Lord Cashel

had been an earl, with a large income, for thirty years; and in that time he had learned to look collected, even when his ideas were confused; to keep his eye

---

* Typical examples of Trollope's penchant for brief, apparently random descriptions of less important personages: Sir Alured Wharton 'was a melancholy, proud, ignorant man, who could not endure a personal liberty, and who thought the assertion of social equality on the part of men of lower rank to amount to taking personal liberty;—who read little or nothing, and thought that he knew the history of his country because he knew that Charles I had had his head cut off, and that the Georges had come from Hanover'. Sir Anthony Aylmer was a 'heavy man, over seventy years of age, much afflicted with gout, and given to no pursuit on earth which was now available for his comfort. . . . He was a big man, with a broad chest, and a red face, and a quantity of white hair,—and was much given to abusing his servants. . . . With his eldest son . . . he was not on very good terms.'[41]

steady, and to make a few words go a long way. He had never been intemperate, and was, therefore, strong and hale for his years,—he had not done many glaringly foolish things, and, therefore, had a character for wisdom and judgment. He had run away with no man's wife, and, since his marriage, had seduced no man's daughter; he was, therefore, considered a moral man.

The Earl's harmless wife, Lady Cashel, who does nothing in life but knit, knows young noblemen like her son were 'extravagant, and wicked, and lascivious, habitual breakers of the commandments, and self-idolators; it was their nature.' She ranks these evils with measles and whooping cough, which should be gone through early in life: 'She had a kind of hazy idea that an opera dancer [i.e. a mistress] and a gambling club were indispensable in fitting a young aristocrat for his future career' and would have agreed to 'innoculating a son of hers with these ailments in a mild degree,— vaccinating him as it were with dissipation, in order that he might not catch the disease late in life in a violent and fatal form'. [42] The Cashel family are worthy predecessors of the countless troubled and troubling aristocrats that would enrich the fictional world of Trollope's later creating.

The Kelly's and the O'Kellys also contained the first of Trollope's many hunting scenes, complete in this instance with that controversial figure, a hunting parson. Writing was a pleasant work for Trollope and hunting his most pleasurable activity in life, so why not combine them? He would later say, only partly tongue-in-cheek, that he 'dragged' too much hunting into his novels, his only excuse being that he felt 'deprived of a legitimate joy' if his story were such as not to allow him at least one hunting chapter. [43]

Trollope judged *The Kellys* inferior to *The Macdermots* in plot, but 'superior in the mode of telling'. The book was another failure, but the reviews were again generally favourable. The *Athenaeum* preferred *The O'Kellys* to *The Macdermots* as being 'less painful. . . . Humour pervades its scenes,' and said that some of the characters were worthy of Jane Austen; *Jerrold's Weekly Newspaper* approved the unsensational yet amusing presentation, free from 'that outrageous exaggeration which is so common in sketches of Irish life and character'. *Sharpe's London Magazine*, in a review that adumbrated much of the later contemporary criticism of Trollope's novels, complained at discovering no 'moral' in the book: it merely amused and did not instruct; it contained nothing 'elevated'; the characters were as commonplace 'as if you had sent for them *all haphazard* out of the street'; the reviewer followed the word 'heroes' with '(?)'; he approved of the hunting scenes, and labelled the novel '*remarkably easy to read*', its style—whatever it lacked in polish and eloquence— 'lively, clever, and uniformly amusing'. [44]

This time Trollope certainly read at least one review, for a friend of his had mentioned the book to a magnate of *The Times* who promised to have the book reviewed. Trollope watched carefully for this notice (all Englishmen read *The Times*, even in Ireland), and when it appeared in September 1848 learned it by heart, so much so that he could quote from it almost verbatim thirty years later. The purport of the review was that *The Kellys*, in its 'native humour and . . . bold reality in the delineation of the characters' was 'substantial fare', like the familiar mutton chop, but, like mutton, also somewhat 'coarse'.[45] The review was pleasant enough, but Trollope resolved henceforth to have no dealings on his own behalf with critics. The commencement of his writing career at a time when 'puffing' reviews were commonly obtained by publishers and by some authors must have influenced his lifelong determination to distance himself from reviewers.

Like *The Macdermots*, *The Kellys and the O'Kellys* did not sell. But Colburn, unlike Newby, sent Trollope an account of the sale. The publisher reported on 11 November that, in spite of the 'greatest efforts' to promote the book—some modest advertising—he had sold, out of 375 copies printed, only 140 (presumably, Trollope noted, to those who liked substantial though coarse fare), and the publisher was at this time £63. 10s. 1½d. out of pocket. Readers, Colburn went on, 'do not like novels on Irish subjects', and it was impossible for him to give Trollope any encouragement to go on writing novels. Then, perhaps because Mrs Trollope was one of his star novelists or because Trollope's latest work in progress, *La Vendée*, was not Irish, Colburn asked to see the manuscript when finished. Trollope says he took in good part Colburn's warning about continuing the career of novelist, though it did not influence him; the odds, he figured, were about twenty to one against him; yet he had only pen and paper to lose and so much, possibly, to win.[46]

For all the writing of books, Trollope's chief concern was the Post Office; this was true not only in the early years in Ireland when his books were bringing him neither recognition nor money, but even later when he was turning out two books a year and making six times as much money from writing as from postal work. And when in 1864, at the height of a popularity as novelist many times greater than any he would early on have dared to have hoped for, he put himself vigorously forward for the number two position in the service, he did so knowing he would have had to curtail his writing had he been given the promotion. Throughout the 1840s his work for the service was performed with increasing 'energy'. He developed an aggressive style, a self-confident, even bullying manner that included loud, peremptory, disputatious talk. He was not yet famous enough for many people to record his way; and thus it is not clear how early his bold, outspoken conduct developed. As this noisy manner later seemed entirely in character, it must have been there in seed from the start, but it first took hold when he found himself in authority in Ireland, among people whom the young deputy surveyor had to impress and to order about. As this new manner succeeded so well, Trollope cultivated it until his aggressive behaviour became his habitual way of meeting the world; this new 'persona' he extended beyond his professional work, and it eventually became the Anthony Trollope of record. As he grew older, the scorched-earth conversational style, with the loud, at times shouting intonation, became more pronounced. (Those who knew him well, who recognized the still-shy outsider behind the argumentative man seem almost universally to have forgiven him.) Not only his speech, but his physical activity had about it a whole-heartedness, an aggressiveness that seemed to possess him. He had the ability to give all his attention, all his physical and mental energy, to the matter at hand. His brother Tom recorded one instance of Anthony's 'promptness' in the line of duty: during the late 1840s, in the south-west of Ireland, Trollope visited a postmaster and observed him in the course of the interview carefully locking a desk in the office. Two days later postal headquarters urgently inquired about a lost letter with valuable contents. This report reached James Kendrick late at night, and he immediately put the matter into his assistant's hands. Unwilling to wait for a public conveyance the next morning, Trollope hired a horse, rode hard, and in the small hours of the morning knocked up the postmaster he had recently interviewed. When told that the key to the desk was lost, Trollope 'smashed the desk with one kick' and found the stolen letter.[47]

Trollope could control his tempestuous bearing when he chose. An instance of such restraint was fully documented in local papers. On the scent of a mail thief in Tralee, in September 1848, he enclosed a marked sovereign in a letter posted at Newcastle in Limerick to a fictitious Jemima Cotton at Ardfert. Trollope went there, and when the letter was not in the mailbag, which had to be opened at Tralee, he hurried to Tralee, obtained a search warrant and, with a policemen, accosted the postmaster and his assistant, one Mary O'Reilly. When her purse yielded the marked sovereign, she was committed to jail. The accused was young, pretty, and very popular locally, and a guilty verdict would not be easily had. Reporting her first trial, in the March 1849 assizes at Tralee, the *Tralee Chronicle* said that Trollope as a witness showed 'a great deal of cleverness', especially when the cross-examiner implied that Trollope, as one who 'dabbled in novels', dealt too much in fiction. But after one of the jurors was taken ill, a mistrial was declared, and the prisoner held over till the next assizes.[48] At her second trial, in July, the defence was in the hands of the formidable Isaac Butt, later the leading Irish barrister of his time and the founder of the Home Rule movement. Trollope, who had an obsessive interest in the law and particularly in the liberties—he considered them abuses—permitted to cross-examiners, seems to have enjoyed this test of his ability to keep calm and unflustered. He adopted a comic stance, and Butt played along with it. The Kerry *Evening Post* gave a verbatim account of much of the cross-examination. Trollope testified that he marked the coin 'under the neck on the head' (meaning the side of the coin bearing the Sovereign's head):

Mr. Butt—On the head under the neck!
Mr. Trollope—I did not say that. You are making more mistakes than I am.
Mr. Butt—I ask you was it on the head?
Mr. Trollope—I marked it under the neck on the head (great laughter).
Mr. Butt—You marked it under the neck on the head. You are acquainted with the English language, writing it occasionally?
Mr. Trollope—Occasionally.
Mr. Butt—And yet you cannot give an intelligible answer on this head.
Mr. Trollope—You had better give it up.
Mr. Butt—But—You—marked it on—what was it?
Mr. Trollope—I marked it under the neck on the head (renewed laughter).

Trollope also said that he had put a second scratch on the coin 'to enable him to know it if altered while in the hands of lawyers (laughter)'. Questioned about his eyesight, he said he used 'short sighted glasses', not magnifying glasses. The judge interposed, 'Then they magnify,' but Trollope insisted, 'No; their effect is to make my sight equal to that of other people.' Butt led his witness into a little by-play about the addressee, 'Miss Jemima Cotton', drawing from Trollope the admission that she was purely fictitious. Asked by Butt if he knew *The Macdermots of Ballycloran*, Trollope replied that he knew 'a book of that name'. Did he remember a barrister in that novel called 'Allwind'? Was it Trollope's intention to 'favour the world with the beau ideal of a good cross-examiner'? 'Yes. I dreamed of you (loud laughter).' Butt then read from the book the passage about the red moreen above the judge's head, how 'if it could only speak, if it had a tongue to tell, what an indifferent account it could give of the conscience of judges and the veracity of lawyers (loud laughter)':

Mr. Butt—I hope you do not think that now.

Mr. Trollope—I'm rather strengthened in my opinion (tremendous laughter).

Mr. Butt—[reading from *The Macdermots*]: 'He told them what he had to say would be very brief, and considering he was a lawyer and a barrister, he kept his word with tolerable fidelity' (loud laughter). You pictured to yourself a model cross-examiner?

Mr. Trollope: I dreamed of someone like you in cross-examination (laughter). 49

The newspaper account, with its parenthetical indications of laughter, clearly showed the surveyor's clerk victorious in his skirmish with the barrister—although the trial resulted in a hung jury. An eyewitness, Justin McCarthy, said that Butt himself felt 'that he had not quite the better of it'. 50 Escott, who got the information from Trollope himself, claimed that during the cross-examination, Trollope, intent on keeping his composure, soothed himself by recalling how Irish Members of Parliament had recently been referred to as 'talking potatoes'. 51 In *Castle Richmond*, Trollope referred obliquely to the trial when he has a character muse that in London courts 'there was no life and amusement such as he had seen at the Assize Court in county Cork . . . [where] the gentlemen in wigs . . . laughed and winked and talked together joyously' and where a delightful 'substratum below of Irish fun . . . showed to everybody that it was not all quite in earnest'. 52 Trollope's great barrister Chaffanbrass may have been drawn in part on Butt; certainly the scene in *Phineas Redux* where Chaffanbrass cross-examines the novelist Bouncer about novelists' not daring to violate probability in their plots recalls the Tralee court-room scene of two decades earlier.

But with postal underlings Trollope took few pains to keep unruffled. In December 1848 he got into a fairly violent quarrel with a mail guard named Conolly and wished to bar him from the Fermoy Post Office. Both men filed written accusations and the matter eventually was laid before the Postmaster-General. Maberly admonished the two of them, telling Conolly to treat superior officers with deference and respect, and Trollope to conduct himself in a manner so as 'not to give rise to these unpleasant charges against him'. Thereupon Trollope intemperately 'remonstrated' against the warning and was told by Maberly that he had been at fault. 53

Trollope had in these days not many contacts with London headquarters. But he naturally looked with interest at developments there, and was made privy to some of them through his brother-in-law, John Tilley, by now his most intimate friend. An anomalous situation obtained at the very top of the administration. Although Colonel Maberly continued as Secretary, Rowland Hill, who, from his position in the Treasury, had in

1840 introduced the penny post, was in 1846 named 'Secretary to the Postmaster General'.[54] The two carried on uneasily, Hill trying his best to dislodge Maberly. Whatever Trollope's misunderstandings with Maberly, he was ever to resent Hill, whom he considered an outsider who had usurped high rank in the service. One curious development that Trollope followed closely was an attempt by Thackeray in September 1848 to be named Assistant Secretary in the Post Office. Thackeray thought the position did not involve very much work: 'What a place for a man of letters!' he wrote to his friend Lady Blessington, who interceded on his behalf with the Postmaster-General, Lord Clanricarde.[55] Thackeray's celebrity and Lady Blessington's influence seemed for a while likely to succeed. But Maberly and the establishment closed ranks and dissuaded Clanricarde from giving the place to Thackeray. According to Trollope's later account, Clanricarde was told that the service wanted a man experienced in postal matters, that the 'feelings of other gentlemen' should be consulted, that those serving many years in an office did not like to see 'even a man of genius' put over their heads. Lord Clanricarde, who, Trollope said, was 'not scrupulous' in matters of patronage, gracefully followed this advice and appointed the 'Official nominee' from within the Department.[56] This was John Tilley, and Trollope had henceforth a close ally at court.

At about the same time, in the autumn of 1848, the Trollopes moved to Mallow, a market town on the River Blackwater in Co. Cork. Ireland had been given a fourth surveyor's district earlier in the year. Clonmel was in the new one, and Trollope, after some hesitation about moving, decided to remain with Kendrick and migrated some fifty miles westward.[57] At Mallow the Trollopes were able to rent an entire house, a three-storey Georgian building on the High Street. It was pleasant to be out of lodgings. Another attraction of Mallow was the hunt: at Clonmel, hunting with the Tipperary Foxhounds had been good, but at Mallow, with its Dunhallow Hunt at the very centre of the hunting country, Trollope found even better opportunities to indulge his passion for the sport. He would make the area around Mallow the setting for *Castle Richmond*, his farewell-to-Ireland novel, written 1859–60. The story has a secondary hero, a kind of hero *manqué*, Owen Fitzgerald, who in some ways resembles Trollope himself: 'reckless, passionate, prone to depreciate the opinion of others, extravagant in his thoughts and habits, ever ready to fight, both morally and physically, those who did not at a moment's notice agree with him' and 'in every way unreasonable,—as unreasonable in his generosity as he was in his claims . . . one whom one would fain conquer by arguments were it possible, [but] . . . the very man on whom arguments have no avail.'[58] One of Owen's endearing, and for Trollope redeeming, features is his inordinate love for the Dunhallow Hunt.

10

Conservative Liberal

AT Mallow, Trollope continued to work fitfully on *La Vendée*. For his third book he had looked about for a subject, scene, and time altogether different from that of his first two Irish novels with their contemporaneous settings. He decided upon an historical novel, a romanticized account of the unsuccessful royalist uprising in La Vendée against the French Republic in 1794–5. Although the writing of *La Vendée* may have been in part prompted by the European revolutions of 1848, Trollope himself had no fear of revolution in Ireland or England: as he told his mother in the spring of 1848, 'Everybody now magnifies the rows at a distance from him': he gets letters from England asking how he could allow his wife and children to remain in Ireland, but the only Irish rows he sees are in *The Times*.[1] Like everyone else in Ireland his attention was directed briefly to the Young Ireland 'insurrection' in July, which never got further than a few shots exchanged between Smith O'Brien and the police in the Widow McCormack's cabbage patch near Ballingarry, Co. Tipperary. Revolution remained a continental matter. In any event, Trollope's novel would have been too late to serve as a tract for revolutionary times, for he did not finish it till 1850, when the European convulsions of 1848 seemed entirely quieted.

On 15 February 1850, Colburn, in spite of his reservations about Trollope's career as novelist, gave him better terms than he had had for the first two novels: the publisher would print 500 copies, and pay £20 down, with the (unlikely) prospect of an additional £30 if sales reached 350 copies, or a further £50 if they reached 450 within six months. Trollope knew he had not really earned the £20: the money had been 'talked out of' Colburn by Tom Trollope, who was now acting with the publisher for his mother and himself.[2] Thus did Trollope, having written three three-decker novels, receive his first money from his writing, at Tom's importuning of Colburn. The book failed, even more thoroughly than had the first two.

But unlike the first two, *La Vendée* deserved its fate. Trollope himself rightly judged *La Vendée* 'certainly inferior' to the two earlier novels. The problem was that he had got it up out of books, chiefly out of one book, Madame de La Rochejaquelein's *Mémoires* (1815), which Trollope read in Walter Scott's 1826 translation (others were Carlyle's *French Revolution* and Archibald Alison's *History of Europe*). Scott's saying in his Preface that 'The Civil War of La Vendée forms one of the most interesting events of the Revolution in France'3 may have prompted Trollope to think it a good subject for a novel. Trollope saw his error too late: 'I knew accurately the life of people in Ireland, and knew, in truth, nothing of the La Vendée country.'4 *La Vendée* lacks the sense of immediate 'reality' that one invariably discovers in Trollope. (A Dublin lady friend of Trollope said that his 'close looking into the commonest objects of daily life always reminded her of a woman in a shop examining the materials for a new dress'.5) He could not observe his French subjects first hand, and the novel suffers accordingly. The story is also un-Trollopian in its one-sidedness, being almost a hagiography of the royalists, with its pictures of fearless leaders and saintly French Catholic peasantry. *La Vendée* was Trollope's weakest effort ever, his least convincing novel, weaker certainly than his other attempt at something outside his ken, the futuristic *Fixed Period*, written in 1880. With *La Vendée*, Trollope's writing career reached its nadir.

In the autumn of 1849, the same conservatism that informed *La Vendée* led to his first fling at journalism. In politics this conservatism kept clashing with his more theoretical liberalism (he later denominated himself 'an advanced, but still a conservative Liberal').6 He was a lifelong opponent of Tories and later a staunch Gladstonian Liberal. That he now held a not inconsiderable post in the Civil Service shored up the conservative side of his politics; all his life he opposed attacks on government officials, especially attacks from outsiders, philanthropists, reformers, and newspaper writers. In the late 1840s Trollope was much annoyed by criticism of the Whig government's handling of the Great Famine in Ireland. Especially offensive to him were the letters to *The Times* in June 1849 from Sidney Godolphin Osborn (described in the *Dictionary of National Biography* as 'a philanthropist of a militant and almost ferocious type'). Trollope was convinced he knew famine Ireland better than Osborn; indeed, because of his constant travelling throughout the southwest of Ireland, the areas hardest hit, he believed that he had observed more of the catastrophe than any other Englishman. Eager to have his say, he fired off a lengthy response to Osborn which the *Examiner* published on 25 August 1849. How, Trollope asks, can Osborn predict that the numbers of starving victims will increase? Are not the numbers decreasing? Osborn's brief visit took place precisely when poverty in Ireland is always most oppressive, just before the maturity of the potato crop, and when cholera, fever, and dysentery, 'the legacies of the famine', were at their worst; but the tide has been turned. As for the complaint about arable land being left untilled, this year's crop 'bids fair to equal that ever produced in the country'. Trollope could, he says, match Osborn's woeful pictures of miseries in the famine- and plague-stricken country, but what do such pictures prove except that there has been famine and plague? Trollope concedes that the government-instituted public works (at first, there was no outdoor relief, and a man had to work for his Indian corn) resulted in the spoiling of old roads, in new roads started and abandoned, in 'mountains' of wheelbarrows left unattended. But such phenomena betokened not incompetence on the part of the government but rather 'the severity of circumstances ordained by Providence'. The government had no time; the work was instituted to save the people; that task, in a crisis that was truly overwhelming, the government did as well as it could.[7]

Anxious to give a more detailed analysis of the situation, Trollope, in London the following February, sought out John Forster, editor of the *Examiner*, with a proposal that he write a series of some half-dozen letters on the 'The Real State of Ireland'. Trollope and Forster later became friends, although Trollope, like many others, considered him somewhat 'coarse' and over-opinionated. But now he approached 'the great man' at his Lincoln's Inn Fields home with some diffidence, feeling he belonged only 'in part' to the literary guild. Forster cautiously declared he would accept the letters if they were found suitable in 'style and matter'.[8] They passed muster, and appeared from April to June 1850, with Trollope vigorously defending the New Poor Law and the Encumbered Estates Bill (which took holdings from indebted and incompetent landlords). As for the Famine itself, the situation was not as lurid as reported; he himself, visiting the most afflicted areas of the country, did not see 'corpses lying exposed, unheeded and in heaps'. The Irish press, 'not proverbial for a strict adherence to unadorned truth', spread 'horrid novels' of this kind that were copied into English newspapers. Of course the governmental work programme involved some waste and left room for some fraud; it was no easy task suddenly to organize half a million men to a new kind of work ('there are not three men in England who could get 50,000 soldiers out of Hyde Park'). But the nation was 'saved'.[9]

In *An Autobiography* Trollope remarks wryly that after his letters appeared 'The world in Ireland did not declare that the Government had at last been adequately defended, nor did the treasurer of the *Examiner* send me a cheque in return.'[10] In *Castle Richmond* (1860) he refers obliquely to his *Examiner* letters: 'I was in the country, travelling always through it, during the whole period, and I have to say—as I did say at the time with a voice that was not very audible—that in my opinion the measures of the government were prompt, wise, and beneficent; and I have to say that the efforts of those who managed the poor were, as a rule, unremitting, honest, impartial, and successful. The feeding of four million starving people with food, to be brought from foreign lands, is not an easy job.' *Castle Richmond*, set against the obtrusive background of the first year of the Great Hunger, the winter of 1846–7, was another attempt to have his say about the Famine, sometimes through essays interpolated in the text of the novel. Trollope, never a particularly religious man, says time after time that the destruction of the potato was 'the work of God'; he announces that he does not believe in trying to 'deprecate' the Almighty; nor does he think that 'men's prayer [could] hinder that which [God's] wisdom had seen to be good and right.' It is absurd, Trollope insists, for Englishmen to blame the famine on Ireland's popery or its mild sedition— of the kind manifested in the débâcle at Ballingarry. The fault in Ireland lay with its idle middle classes, Protestant as well as Roman Catholic, especially young men brought up to do nothing, owning property but acknowledging no duty arising from property; tenants trying to be gentle- men; absentee landlords and, even worse, their surrogates, the greedy self-serving estate managers the absentees left behind them. Misuse of land by the idle gentry had been so rampant that 'a merciful God' had sent an avenging remedy in the form of famine and pestilence. Such means of cleansing the country were 'frightful' and 'violent', but they brought Ireland out of its misfortunes.[11]

Trollope as narrator/essayist in *Castle Richmond* can be stonily strong- minded: he says, for example, that the best workers among the poor had learned not to be struck to the heart by the look of death, 'the drag', in the face of the dying: 'In administering relief one may rob five unseen sufferers of what would keep them in life if one is moved to bestow all that is comfortable on one sufferer that is seen.' Those could best help the poor who were hardest of heart, most obdurate in their denials: 'It was strange to see devoted women neglecting the wants of the dying so that they might husband their strength and time and means for the wants of those who might still be kept among the living.' Trollope interjects an account of one woman in the far south-west telling him of a young boy who stood by listening, '"It's no use in life meddling with him; he's gone."' . . . And then she pointed out to me the signs on the lad's face, and I found her reading correct'; he concedes, 'Her delicacy did not equal her energy for doing good . . . but in truth it was difficult to be delicate when the hands were so full.' Only when dramatizing scenes of individual suffering does Trollope's narrator himself become delicate and show a side of himself more humane, more tender than that seen in his disquisitions on letting God's providence take its course. One such scene has Herbert Fitzgerald, heir to Castle Richmond, seek shelter from the rain in a dilapidated cabin, where he finds a dying woman, barely covered with rags, her eyes gleaming brightly, her face clouded in apathy, holding a dying baby, a few feet from the dead body of her other child. Fitzgerald attempts to arrange that she be taken to the poorhouse, but aid arrives too late and she and her two children have perished. Had there been outdoor relief—the outright dole that Trollope opposed—they would have survived. The rule against outdoor relief, the narrator comments, was 'salutary', but it 'pressed very cruelly. Exceptions were of course made in such cases, if they were known; but then it was so hard to know them!'[12]

Trollope was troubled by the famine scenes he continually witnessed in Cork and Kerry and Clare, but he came to terms with these tragedies by falling back on a kind of blind belief in what he calls 'God's work'. His analysis seems rather murderous—and Swiftian—in the abstract; but it apparently satisfied him at least, and as Ireland rose up again from her knees he became all the more convinced he was right. The long-standing problem of unemployment was largely solved by the death of about a million people and the emigration of another million. Ireland survived the Great Hunger, and by the end of the 1850s, when Trollope was leaving Ireland, he saw the country as better off than it had been in pre-Famine years. Irish ginger was, Trollope said, again hot in the mouth, Irish cakes were again baked, Irish ale brewed: 'And now again the fields in Ireland are green, and the markets are busy, and money is chucked to and fro. . . . Agricultural wages have been nearly doubled in Ireland during the last fifteen years. . . . Life and soul were kept together in those terrible days;—that is, the Irish life and soul generally. There were many slips, in which the union was violently dissolved. . . . But millions are still there, a thriving people; for His mercy endureth for ever.'[13] The piety doesn't go deep: God, or rather God's work, was for Trollope whatever could not be altered by human intervention or hand-wringing.

The old scourge of the Trollope family returned once more: Cecilia Trollope Tilley, now the mother of five children, showed signs of consumption, and in August 1847 she was ordered by doctors to pass two years in Italy. Tom hurried over to England to escort her, only to find a note at Ramsgate from John Tilley saying Cecilia had been found unequal to the land voyage and had been sent by steamer to Leghorn. Old Mrs Trollope met her pale daughter at Leghorn and took her home to Florence. There a homeopathic physician determined that the winter climate of Florence would be injurious to Cecilia, and so Mrs Trollope took her to Rome. (In Rome Tom became engaged to Theodosia Garrow, an 'exotic' young woman of English, Indian, and Jewish origins, a poet and staunch advocate of Italian independence; in April 1848 they were married, against the wishes of her father.) In May Cecilia returned to England, Italy not having been of any avail; at home she learned that the eldest of her five little children, Frances, was also 'in decline' from the same disease. Cecilia rallied for a while, but in early 1849 began to fail rapidly. Anthony took leave from his work and hurried to her bedside (the Tilleys, after John's promotion to Assistant Secretary in the Post Office, had moved to Allen Place, Kensington). Mrs Trollope arrived on 10 March, her seventieth birthday, to tend her fourth family death watch. Once again, though not in the financial straits of former times at Bruges and Hadley, she attempted to care for the dying and to write fiction. Her publisher, Henry Colburn, actually stopped by once to prod her on, as she was somewhat behind on her current book; the old lady complained that she had trouble finding a quiet half-hour a day, could manage no more than a page a sitting, and hardly knew what it was she was writing. [14] Cecilia died on 4 April 1849. Anthony answered John Tilley's letter with the news by saying that once it became certain she could never recover, he had 'almost wished that her sufferings should end'. He apologized for not coming over for the funeral but he could not do so 'without crippling myself with regard to money, in [a] way which not even that object would justify . . . it is a great comfort to me to have seen her so shortly before her death.' Trollope's letter closed, 'I sometimes feel that I led you into more sorrow than happiness in taking you to Hadley.' [15]

Trollope took into his home one of Cecilia's daughters, Edith Diana Mary Tilley. He seems to have brought her back to Mallow after last visiting Cecilia. Probably the arrangement was made more definite after the death of the child's mother a few days later; but it was understood from the first that were Tilley to remarry he might have her returned to him. Mrs Trollope, answering a letter from Rose, thanked her for taking the child: 'We shall none of us ever forget it. . . . John Tilley is not a demonstrative man—as Anthony knows—but his eyes filled with tears when he read your mention of his poor little Edith.'[16] Tilley had been an extraordinarily caring husband; the medical men who attended Cecilia said they 'had never seen as fond and devoted a husband', and he seems to have promised Cecilia on her deathbed to marry Mary Anne Partington, a cousin, the daughter of Penelope Trollope, Thomas Anthony's sister. Mary Anne Partington had been a great friend of Cecilia's, and, according to one witness, 'almost lived with' the Tilleys during their marriage.[17] Tilley would marry Mary Anne as soon as decency permitted, though the deaths of four of his young children within the year following his wife's death postponed the marriage a few months. With all but one of his children dead and a new wife about to be taken, Tilley wanted Edith back, and the little girl, who had been with the Trollopes less than a year, was returned to her father's house. Anthony wrote to his mother, 'We are very sorry. But we have no right to complain. Indeed, the incurring the chance of losing her at any moment after we had become fond of her, was the only drawback to the pleasure of taking her.'[18] About a year later Tilley's new wife died, three weeks after giving birth to a son, Arthur. Of Arthur Tilley, Anthony in later years was very fond; and, in due course, he would become the affectionate godfather of Arthur's half-brother John Anthony, son of John Tilley and his third wife.

Tilley, at Anthony's suggestion, brought Mrs Trollope to Mallow. Anthony and Rose pleased her with 'new-laid eggs, salmon curry, Irish potatoes (1849) and bread and butter, together with a little honey and a little coffee and a little porter from the same green land'.[19] When Anthony introduced 'old Spellen the piper' into the sitting-room she was at first dismayed but soon dissolved in tears at the pathos of his music. They took her to Killarney, which delighted her, as did Lord Kenmare's park. She walked through the Gap of Dunloe with the ease of a woman forty years her junior; they also went with her in a Bianconi car to Glengarriff, a seaside village on Bantry Bay and one of Trollope's favourite beauty spots in Ireland, although this junket did not please her as much: the journey was tiring, the tea was 'rubbish', the food detestable, the bedrooms 'pokey', the turf fires disagreeable. Back in Mallow she saw an old man breaking stones in the road, pattered downstairs and gave the astonished pauper sixpence. Barney, Trollope's groom since Banagher days, would tell the story to the family's honour until the sixpence grew into half-a-crown, bestowed daily for a month. Anthony, Rose, and Mrs Trollope planned 'mightily' for Mrs Trollope to return to Ireland with Tom, but she never did so, and Anthony next saw his mother when he and Rose managed their first trip abroad in April 1853.[20]

A few days after Cecilia's death, Mrs Trollope had written to Rose, 'I am *very* glad that my dear Anthony saw [Cecilia] on her death bed—The impression left on his mind, however painful at the moment of receiving it, will remain with him for ever more as consolation, than sorrow.'[21] These may not have been merely conventional pious sentiments on her part. Anthony, like his mother and everyone around Cecilia, had been struck by the strength of her religious faith. She had become a Puseyite; her novel, *Chollerton*, published anonymously—'By A Lady'—in 1846, was a high-church tale of a clerical hero fresh from Oxford. (It fared poorly with the critics: the *Spectator* said its philosophy was 'very poor' and its morality 'not much better'; the *Athenaeum* asked why such 'weak sectarian novels' seemed always to be the products of 'feminine enthusiasm' for teaching 'patent piety'.[22]) Cecilia's faith became, according to her brother Tom, 'nearly the whole of her life'.[23] She was the only one of the Trollope family who was ever more than routinely religious; Anthony, like the others, was a nominal, latitudinarian, tolerant, Church of England adherent, more worldly than otherwise. And Cecilia's faith, a consolation and strength to her throughout the unequal struggle with disease, may have strengthened Anthony's preference for high church to low church, even as he preferred, in his words, 'papistical to presbyterian tendencies'.[24] Trollope would sometimes gently satirize high churchmen, like the Reverend Caleb Oriel in *Doctor Thorne* who delights in Catholic-like services 'at dark hours of winter mornings when no one would attend', who eschews matrimony and fasts on Fridays;[25] or the Reverend Francis Arabin in *Barchester Towers* who almost followed Newman to Rome; but both of these clerics are worthy of conversion to sensible ways through worldly marriages. On the other hand, Trollope's treatment of low-church people, clerical and lay, 'ultra protestants' as he called them, is sometimes harsh. Their greatest absurdity is their intolerance of Roman Catholics and their extraordinary fear and hatred of Tractarians. The most celebrated examples were to be Obadiah Slope and Mrs Proudie, neither of whom can bear the mildest manifestation of Puseyism. Mrs Proudie once accused the wife of a clergyman of 'idolatry' because she dated a letter 'St. John's Eve';[26] for Slope, 'a full-breasted black silk waistcoat is with him a symbol of Satan'.[27] The most fanatical anti-Catholics were Church of Ireland adherents. In *The Kellys and the O'Kellys*, Mr O'Joscelyn, rector of Kilcullen, Co. Kildare, is 'a most ultra and even furious Protestant. . . . He pitied the ignorance of the heathen, the credulity of the Mahommedan, the desolateness of the Jew, even the infidelity of the atheist; but he execrated, abhorred, and abominated the church of Rome.'[28]

In *Castle Richmond*, old maid Aunt Letty Fitzgerald professes she would sooner be a Muhammadan than a papist (when her nephew tells her she would alter her opinion after one week in a harem, the old lady rejoins that she'd prefer that to going to confession). In the same novel, the staunch Protestantism of the Revd Aeneas Townsend and his wife consists largely in a hatred of popery. For them, 'the cross—which should, I presume, be the emblem of salvation to us all—creates a feeling of dismay and often of disgust instead of love and reverence.' Trollope ridicules the 'souping system' of Protestants that could not bestow charity without proselytizing: 'If [Townsend] could find hungry Papists and convert them into well-fed Protestants . . . he must be doing a double good.' Altogether, the Protestant clergymen come off second best to their Catholic opposite numbers; the novel's Catholic priest is much more humane and sensible, much more 'a man of the world' than his protestant colleague—the expression always a mark of approbation in Trollope. Trollope's hero, Herbert Fitzgerald, thinks Roman Catholic clergymen more 'liberal in their ideas and moral in their conduct'.[29]

Part of the difficulty, as Trollope saw it, was that Protestant ministers in Ireland did not have enough parishioners; everyone around them is Roman Catholic. In *The Kellys and the O'Kellys* the Revd Joseph Armstrong's congregation consists of one old lady, her daughters, and three Protestant policemen. Armstrong, when urged to praise Protestant Sunday schools against the 'abominations' of the national school system, can say nothing: he has no Sunday school in his own parish because he is 'the father of all the Protestant children to be found there—without the slightest slur on his reputation be it said'.[30] In *Castle Richmond* Trollope inserts, with due apology, an extraneous 'episode': an old Irish Catholic gentleman defended a local parson, one Mr Hobbs, who was accused of pocketing £12 charity money sent him from England by some pious ladies. Hobbs had undoubtedly done the deed, the Irishman said, but it was not robbery: 'the excellent Miss Walkers sent their money for the Protestant poor of the parish . . . and Mr Hobbs is the only Protestant within it.'[31]

When in 1850 Pope Pius IX re-created the Roman Catholic hierarchy in England, Trollope thought the anti-Catholic furore that followed silly. He disapproved of Prime Minister Lord John Russell's Ecclesiastical Titles Bill that forbade Catholic priests to accept English bishoprics from Rome (some Irish Catholic members put up a fight, and a watered-down version of the law was passed). Trollope's view was that nothing should have been done about 'Papal Aggression': 'I would have let the whole thing sink by its own weight.'[32] A few years later, in *The Warden*, Trollope had Sir

Abraham Haphazard, the Attorney-General, introduce into Parliament a 'Convent Custody Bill', the mainstay of which, its 107th clause, 'ordered the bodily searching of nuns for Jesuitical symbols by aged clergymen'.[33] The episode was not as absurd as it sounds: there was such a bill, introduced in the House of Commons by one Thomas Chambers (10 May 1853; dropped 10 August), to facilitate inspection of nunneries; in March 1854 James Whiteside brought in a bill to restrict the disposal of personal property by nuns (dropped 12 July).

After giving the manuscript of *La Vendée* to Colburn in February 1850, Trollope hit upon the idea of writing a tourists' guidebook of Ireland. While in London in February 1850 he saw, in Albemarle Street, John Murray, the son of the publisher who had brought out one of his mother's books and the first and only volume of his father's ill-fated *Ecclesiastical Encyclopedia*. The present Murray, whose *Handbooks for Travellers* were a great success, said he would look at a sample of the work, so Trollope went back and 'did' Dublin, Kerry, and the route from Dublin to Killarney, about a quarter of the proposed book, and sent it to the publisher. But a tourists' guide to that stricken country, which even in good times had little attraction for English travellers, must have been at the very bottom of Murray's list of interests, and the manuscript lay unopened in his office for nine months. It was returned, after 'a very angry letter' from Trollope. Had Murray, Trollope observed, 'been less dilatory, [he] would have got a very good Irish Guide at a cheap rate'.[34] Murray was to be one of the very few major publishers over whose imprint Trollope was never to come out.

When it quickly became apparent that *La Vendée*, published in June 1850, had failed even more resoundingly than had the previous two books, Trollope began to wonder whether novel writing was his 'proper line'. But although he did not write another word of prose fiction for three years, he did not lay down his pen. While waiting impatiently to hear from John Murray about the guidebook, he took to writing a play, a comedy, partly in blank verse and partly in prose. It was set in Flanders at the time of the Revolutionary wars, but was less 'historical' than *La Vendée*. Into this effort, *The Noble Jilt*, Trollope thought he put 'the best of my intellect'. He evidently worked slowly and painstakingly on the play, giving what was for him, even at this early stage of his career, an unusual amount of time to reworking, copying, and recopying it, 'touching' it—allowable since it was in verse—and was himself much pleased with the result. In June 1851, he sent the play to an old friend of his mother, George Bartley, a former comic actor and theatre manager. A frank opinion was asked and received: the serious parts, Bartley replied, were 'deficient in interest' and the comic ones were 'overlaid with repetitions'; there was not one character 'to challenge the sympathy of the audience'; it was 'a five act play without a hero'. Bartley reluctantly concluded that had he still been a theatre manager, he could not have recommended the play for production. Trollope says he accepted this 'altogether condemnatory' judgement but none the less felt its sting more than neglect or adverse criticism of his novels. Over the years he more than once took out both play and Bartley's letter; and, while admitting that Bartley was right, he persisted in thinking the dialogue good and some of the comic scenes perhaps 'the brightest and best work I ever did'—a most erratic pronouncement.[35] Trollope may have savoured lines such as those when the heroine's friend belittles romantic notions:

> Oh, love? Yes, love; love is a sauce to life,
> a very piquant, palatable sauce, not life itself.
> One cannot live on love—
> nor yet upon anchovies.

Or, with his mother's distressed revolutionaries in mind, he may have been proud of having a character observe, 'I never knew a patriot with a balance at his bankers.'[36] A dozen years later he would resurrect the plot and characters of *The Noble Jilt* and transform the play into a successful novel, *Can You Forgive Her?*, the first of what became the Palliser novels. And another ten years later, in *The Eustace Diamonds*, in a little private joke probably enjoyed only by himself and Rose, Trollope had a new play called 'The Noble Jilt'—'from the hand of a very eminent author'—appear on the stage of the Haymarket Theatre. The criticisms afforded it by the novel's characters were those given by Bartley, especially its having 'no scope for sympathy' from the audience. 'The Noble Jilt' in its fictional appearance has a run of 'four or five dozen' nights.[37] The actual play has never been produced.

Trollope also struck out in still another direction. This new literary interest had its roots in his reading of the first two volumes of Charles Merivale's *History of the Romans Under the Empire* (1850, 1851), and in engaging John Merivale in correspondence about his brother's views on Caesar. Trollope took it upon himself to investigate 'the character of probably the greatest man who ever lived', by which he meant the greatest of those 'who have moved the world'.[38] Determined to review Merivale's work creditably, Trollope immersed himself in a mass of supplementary reading that, as he told himself, a magazine article by itself hardly justified. Moreover, as he did with his fictional characters, he 'lived in Caesar, and debated with myself constantly whether he crossed the Rubicon as a tyrant or as a patriot'. Trollope was not sanguine that the article would be accepted, but the *Dublin University Magazine* published the review in May 1851. Trollope's heartiest praise throughout the lengthy 10,000-word article is for Merivale's unobtrusive style—one that 'never forces itself on the attention of the reader' (similar remarks were to be made countless times on Trollope's own style). The story of the Gallic campaigns, which Trollope thought the least interesting portion of Caesar's career, Merivale tells 'with infinite skill'; he 'has the rare gift of making a dry subject readable'. Trollope liked Merivale's ability to give absorbing accounts of well-known stories, that, for example, of Cato's divorcing his fruitful wife in order that his voluptuary friend Hortensius might marry her and have children, only to remarry her on the premature death of the second husband. But most of the review is given to attacking Merivale's uncritical praise of Caesar. Trollope will grant Caesar little beyond having effected 'perhaps the greatest series of military exploits ever performed by one man'.39 One wonders how, as Trollope asserted, Merivale himself could have sent him word that it was 'the best review of the work which had appeared'.40

Trollope was surprised that the magazine did not pay him for the review, but the editor told him that 'such articles were generally written to oblige friends', and as such carried no payment. Trollope was a friend of sorts of Charles Merivale, but indignantly resented the implication; he certainly had not written his review to oblige the author. In the long run, however, he was grateful that he had made the effort of tackling Merivale; his new-found interest in the ancient Romans would eventually lead to a little book on Caesar's *Commentaries*—in 1870—and a large one on Cicero—in 1880—and to 'a taste generally for Latin literature, which has been one of the chief delights of my later life'.41

Trollope was on holiday in June 1851, during which time he and Rose visited the Great Exhibition of Industry of All Nations in London. The Exhibition had dominated the news for at least the previous year. Dedicated to peace and prosperity among all nations, it pretty obviously underscored Britain's economic superiority. England's exhibits, together with those of her colonies, occupied the entire western nave, or one half of the Exhibition. The chief attraction was the enormous glass building itself, designed by Joseph Paxton, head gardener and designer of greenhouses for the Duke of Devonshire. Some people, like Colonel Charles de Laet Waldo Sibthorp, outspoken Member for Lincoln, repeatedly warned about the immoral foreigners the Exhibition would attract: Britons would find that 'Their property, their wives, and families would be at the mercy of pickpockets and whoremongers from every part of the earth.'[42] But most Englishmen would have agreed with the *Morning Advertiser* that there was little danger of infection, and that 'foreigners from all lands will morally, as well as politically and socially, profit from their intercourse with us, and return to their own countries better as well as wiser men.'[43] Trollope planned his visit a year in advance: in May 1850 he told his mother that he hoped she, with Tom and his wife, would meet Rose and him at the Exhibition 'under the shadow of some huge, newly invented machine. . . . I mean to exhibit four 3 vol. novels—all failures!—which I look on as a great proof of industry at any rate.' But Tom was still too busy fixing up his new home, the 'Villino Trollope' in the north-west corner of the Piazza Barbano,* and by March 1851 he sent his regrets. Anthony was disappointed: '*We* intend going to see the *furriners* in June. I think it will be great fun seeing such a crowd. As for the Exhibition itself, I would not give a straw for it,—except the building itself, and my wife's piece of work which is in it.' (Rose's embroidered screen, featuring a knight bearing the Trollope crest, would win a bronze medal.) On 7 May Anthony wrote to his mother, 'I regret more and more every day that Tom is not to see the Exhibition. I am sure it is a thing a man ought to see. John Tilley is enthusiastic, and knew all about it before it was opened. . . . I think he is right. It is a great thing to get a new pleasure. . . . We are all agog about going to London. Rose is looking up her silk dresses, and I am meditating a new hat!'[44]

* Later Piazza Indipendenza. The Villino, purchased in March 1850, became a luxurious setting for entertaining the Anglo-Florentine set and visitors; after his wife's death in 1865 Tom sold the house, feeling he could no longer live there because of the memories it held. Nearly a century later Anthony's granddaughter Muriel Trollope would recall spending school years in Florence with her parents during the 1890s and becoming dismayed at seeing 'my own name on the caps of the porter and page boy and on the omnibus at the door. . . . For the Villino Trollope had become a *pension* and bore its former owner's name!'[45]

11

The West Country and The Warden

TROLLOPE returned from London to Mallow, and spent July working his district. His task had lately consisted largely in extending the rural posts, and he performed this duty with such energy and efficiency that Rowland Hill now 'lent' him to the south-west district of England. Trollope arrived in Bristol, having sailed from Cork, on 1 August 1851. Since this was to be a lengthy assignment, Rose accompanied him, and they took rooms at Exeter, as his first work was to be in Devonshire, the county he came to consider the most beautiful in England.

Reorganization and extension of the rural posts was a large part of Rowland Hill's reform in the Post Office. Up to that time rural delivery had been erratic, and largely, as Trollope said, at the convenience of influential people who exerted pressure for delivery of their letters. Districts without such influence were not served at all, and their inhabitants had to fetch their letters from a post office, often at a considerable distance from their homes. Another problem was frequency of delivery—two or three times a week was, Trollope said, too 'halting' because Englishmen thought 'delivery much delayed . . . worse than none at all'. Trollope had to map out routes for letter-carriers, determine their length, and discover if the volume of letters, counted at a halfpenny a letter, would pay the wages of the carriers. But as the counting of letters was the responsibility of the postal authorities, Trollope could be 'sanguine' in his figures: 'I did not prepare false accounts; but I fear that the postmasters and clerks who absolutely had the counting to do became aware that I was anxious for good results.' A rural letter-carrier was not required to walk more than sixteen miles a day, and Trollope took special delight in finding short cuts, and sending his carriers on routes he laid out across fields. He himself travelled on horseback, averaging forty miles a day, and as he was reimbursed sixpence a mile, his exertions were doubly rewarding; the extra money made it possible for him to have his Irish groom Barney with him, to support two hunters of his own and sometimes a third horse, so that he managed to keep up his hunting while extending the post. Sometimes he was a peculiar sight, dressed in red coat, boots, and breeches, swooping down at nine in the morning on a country postmaster demanding to know the disposal of every letter that arrived in his office. And, often similarly attired, he would surprise farmers, parsons, lone country residents and their wives by suddenly appearing and asking questions about the delivery of their letters. Part of his mission was to stamp out the 'damnable habit' by which letter-carriers charged a penny a letter for delivery. This sin, for which Trollope saw no pardon, he did pretty much eliminate. He considered himself 'a beneficent angel to the public', even though the public did not always understand how this was so. His tactic was to come down on people 'as a summer storm': he had to startle them, for their own good, into revealing abuses: if given time to think they would not divulge the 'robbery', fearing to alienate their postmen. Trollope was 'altogether in earnest' and came to be much satisfied with the results of his labours: 'I believe that many a farmer now has his letters brought daily to his house free of charge, who but for me would still have had to send to the post-town for them twice a week, or to have paid a man for bringing them irregularly to his door.' To establish a regular and fair rural delivery system, 'to cover the country with rural letter-carriers' became 'the ambition of my life'. He could almost stand beside himself and see the process: 'It is amusing,' he wrote, 'to watch how a passion will grow upon a man.'[1]

Trollope visited all of Devon, and then went on to Cornwall, Somerset, and much of Dorset; the Channel Islands; parts of Oxfordshire, Wiltshire, Gloucestershire, Worcestershire, Herefordshire, Monmouthshire, and the six southern counties of Wales. Many of these locales would eventually turn up in his novels; most memorably, Somerset, Wiltshire, and Devon would be transformed into Barsetshire (the cathedral city of Barchester would draw chiefly on Winchester and Salisbury). He so thoroughly investigated all of the West Country, that, as he put it, 'I had an opportunity of seeing a considerable portion of Great Britain, with a minuteness which few have enjoyed.' He visited 'almost every house—I think I may say every house of importance—in this large district'. Busy as he was, he touched 'home' usually no more than a few days a month, and home kept changing, as the Trollopes, after Exeter, lived at Bristol, Carmarthen, Cheltenham, and Worcester.[2] The English assignment was to be stretched out to two years (interrupted for three months at the end of

December 1851 when at the urgent pleading of his superior he was returned to his Irish district). They were two of the happiest years of Trollope's life.

His 'energetic' style seems to have increased in fury when he came to the south-west of England, as his 'passion' to cover the land with rural letter-carriers grew on him. Some record survives of Trollope in action at this time. A postal worker, J. G. Uren, who encountered him at Falmouth, wrote: 'I remember his stalking into the office, booted and spurred, much to the consternation of the maiden lady in charge. He seemed to us then the very incarnation of a martinet, though I have since heard that he really was a kind-hearted man, and that this was the way he had of showing it. At any rate, he frightened the unfortunate rural messenger, whose walk he was about to test, almost out of his wits.' According to Uren, Trollope 'met his match' at Penzance in the person of the postmistress, Miss Ellen Catherine Swain, who told him he was 'no gentleman' and ordered him out of the house. (Later, the two became 'capital friends'.[3])

In South Wales a postal worker reported Trollope marching into the office 'at a 6-mile-an-hour stride', announcing he had just walked up from Cardiff (a distance of twenty-four miles), asking for the best hotel, and promising to come back as soon as he had had a raw beefsteak. On his return, a postman threatened he would give up his position if his request for increased pay were denied. 'Look here, my man,' Trollope exclaimed, 'don't think that we cannot manage without you. Throw it up; there will be twenty after your place to-morrow.' But he then entered into the facts of the case and gave the man the increase.[4]

At the seaside village of Mousehole, Cornwall, the sub-postmistress, Miss Betsy Trembath, was recorded as having this conversation:

Mr. Trollope: I am an Inspector from the General Post Office, and I wish to make some enquiries about the posts in this neighbourhood.

Miss Trembath: From the General Post Office, arta? I' bra glad to see he sure 'nuf. Wusta ha' a dish o' tay?

Mr. Trollope: I say I wish to make some enquiries. Can you tell me where—

Miss Trembath: Lor' bless the man. Doantee be in such a pore. I can't tellee noathin' if thee'st stand glazing at me like a chuked pig, as thee art now.

Mr. Trollope (losing his temper): Don't thee and thou me my good woman, but answer my questions. I will report you.

Miss Trembath: Good woman am I? Report me wusta? And I be'n so civil toee, too. Thees't better report my tuppence farden a day.[5]

In *The Small House at Allington*, the country postmistress, Mrs Crump, complains bitterly:

'Oh, letters! Drat them for letters. I wish there weren't no sich things. There was a man here yesterday with his imperence. I don't know where he come from,— down from Lun'on, I b'leeve: and this was wrong, and that was wrong, and everything wrong; and then he said he'd have me discharged the sarvice. . . . Discharged the sarvice! Tuppence farden a day. So I told 'un to discharge hisself, and take all the old bundles and things away upon his shoulders. Letters indeed! What business have they with post-missusses, if they cannot pay 'em better nor tuppence farden a day?'[6]

Yet only occasionally does Trollope introduce the post as such into his fiction—unlike hunting, for which he could always find room—and when he does so it is invariably with a sense of fun. In *He Knew He Was Right*, in the village of Nuncombe Putney, Devon, the post came in at eight in the morning, carried by a wooden-legged man on a donkey, who always arrived half an hour late and 'was very slow in stumping round the village': 'There is a general understanding that the wooden-legged men in country parishes should be employed as postmen, owing to the great steadiness of demeanour which a wooden leg is generally found to produce. It may be that such men are slower in their operation than would be biped postmen; but as all private employers of labour demand labourers with two legs, it is well that the lame and the halt should find a refuge in the less exacting service of the government.'[7] In *Framley Parsonage* Robin the postman explains to the parsonage cook that he had not been permitted to leave the letter for Mrs Robarts at Framley Court, where he knew her to be, because 'the law made it imperative on him to bring the letter to the very house that was indicated, let the owner of the letter be where she might.'[8] In *The American Senator*, a woman wants to retrieve a letter mistakenly placed in the wrong envelope and already deposited in the post; the postmaster nearly accommodated her but then this 'servant of the public,—who had been thoroughly grounded in his duties by one of these trusty guardians of our correspondence who inspect and survey our provincial post offices,—remembered himself at the last moment and expressing the violence of his regret, replaced the letter in the box'.[9]

Trollope had not been long in the south-west when his work took him, for twenty days in November 1851, to the Channel Islands; there he completely reorganized the postmen's routes, arranged for horse posts to distant areas, and increased the number of daily deliveries. And at St Helier, Jersey he put forth a carefully argued case for roadside letter-boxes ('pillar boxes'), such as were already in use in nearby France; he observed that although stamps were sold 'in every street', people in distant parts of town had to travel nearly a mile to the principal office to post letters; all that was needed was a 'safe receptacle' either free standing or fixed into permanent walls. The Postmaster-General, with urging from Tilley, accepted the suggestion. The first boxes, hexagonal and about four feet high, were cast at a cost of £7 each by John Vaudin of St Helier (they became known as 'Vaudins'); and one year later, on 23 November 1852, were put into use in St Helier at David Place, New Street, Cheapside, and St Clements Road. Trollope also urged boxes for St Peter Port, Guernsey, and on 8 February 1853 three were erected there. Public response was enthusiastic. The first pillar-box on the mainland was erected at Botchergate, Carlisle, in September 1853; and three months later, again at Trollope's bidding, they were installed at Gloucester; the first for Ireland were sent to Trollope in March 1855 for May, Ballymena, and Belfast. Within a few years pillar-boxes were installed throughout Great Britain.[10] The introduction of pillar-boxes was to be Trollope's most memorable innovation in the postal service. He himself was rather more proud of his work at extending the rural posts throughout much of Ireland and England. But the public, understandably, were most grateful for the pillar-box. It was only a radical conservative such as Miss Jemima Stanbury of Exeter in *He Knew He Was Right*, who could possibly object to the innovation:

Miss Stanbury carried her letter all the way to the chief post-office in the city, having no faith whatever in those little subsidiary receiving houses which are established in different parts of the city. As for the iron pillar boxes which had been erected of late years for the receipt of letters, one of which,—a most hateful thing to her,—stood almost close to her own hall door, she had not the faintest belief that any letter put into one of them would ever reach its destination. She could not understand why people should not walk with their letters to the respectable post-office instead of chucking them into an iron stump,—as she called it,—out in the middle of the street with nobody to look after it. Positive orders had been given that no letter from her house should ever be put into the iron post.[11]

Trollope for some time and with good reason had been hoping for promotion; his efficiency and energy were becoming proverbial. In John Tilley he had a strong ally at St Martin's-le-Grand. Rowland Hill and Colonel Maberly were both impressed by Trollope's services, but distrustful. Maberly probably still could not altogether believe that the ne'er-do-well of the 1830s was making his way up towards the top of the service; and Hill seems to have been suspicious of a cabal between Trollope and Tilley that would advocate Tilley's eventual accession to Maberly's Secretaryship, something Hill coveted for himself. When the post of Superintendent of Mail Coaches became vacant in the autumn of 1852, Trollope, living at the time in Gloucester, applied for the job, a position that would have situated him in London. Sir John Trollope, a distant relation and wealthy landowning MP from Lincoln, wrote to the Post Office on his behalf, although Trollope felt, as he told his mother, 'I ought not to want any private interest. The more I see the way in which the post-office work is done, the more aggrieved I feel at not receiving the promotion I have a right to expect.' Then he added (what was true but as he very well knew not directly pertinent to his desire for advancement): 'However, this does not really annoy me. I can't fancy any one being much happier than I am,—or having less in the world to complain of. It often strikes me how wonderfully well I have fallen on my feet.' His own letter to the Postmaster-General, the Earl of Hardwicke, cited his eighteen years of service and 'confidently' suggested that Colonel Maberly would testify to his fitness. But Maberly had recently urged that Trollope's special assign-ment with the rural posts be extended, telling Hardwicke how Trollope's 'very prompt & satisfactory manner' in revising the rural posts in Ireland had led to his being sent to assist surveyors in England and Wales. Actually the superintendency was in Maberly's gift, and he had Hardwicke appoint W. T. Wedderburn, chief clerk in the mail coach department itself, and whose own letter of application to Hardwicke cited twenty-six years of experience therein (this last something Trollope himself would have respected).[12]

Trollope and Rose had long been hoping to spend his annual leave in travel abroad and visiting Mrs Trollope and Tom. The summer of 1852 had seemed a likely time, but the pressure of work interfered. In March Anthony thanked Tom for not 'scolding' him, and set a new target of the following year: 'A twelvemonth does not seem so long to wait now as it did ten years ago. It ought to seem longer, for as one has fewer months to come one should make more of them. But somehow, the months and years so jostle one another, that I seem to be living away at a perpetual gallop. I wish I could make the pace a little slower.' At this time Trollope was working in South Wales (a place he decidedly did not like), while Rose and the two boys stayed at the seaside village of Llanstephan; the family was to live in Carmarthen in November and in Gloucester for the winter. His children, Trollope told his brother, 'are very nice boys:—very different in disposition but neither with anything that I could wish altered'. Informed that Tom was to become a father, Anthony told him he was glad: 'One wants some one to exercise unlimited authority over, as one gets old and cross.' Servants leave, and a wife can be 'too much for one', but 'children can be blown up to any amount without damage,—at any rate, for a considerable number of years.' A father may 'flog daily, and always quote Scripture to prove that it is a duty'. Trollope then cuts short his joking and assures his brother that 'nothing that could happen to you will be so likely to add to your happiness as this.—(You know all about the fox who lost his tail!).'[13]

Very little is known of Trollope as father.*

In the spring of 1853—a year for which not one personal letter survives—Anthony and Rose were able to go abroad for the first time. The only record is Rose's notes, compiled in 1876 to help Trollope write his autobiography. They left from Cheltenham, their abode at the time, travelled to London, where they picked up John Tilley, and continued to Paris, Châlon-sur-Saône, Lyons, Chambéry, the Mont Cenis Pass, Turin, and on to Genoa. There they met up with Tom, who, with his mania for punctuality, scolded them for being four hours late. Thence the party travelled, after two days in Genoa, to Florence via La Spezia. After three weeks in Florence, they journeyed home via Leghorn, Genoa, Novara, Bellinzona, the St Gotthard Pass, Lucerne, the Rigi, Basle, Mannheim, Cologne, Antwerp, and Ostend. Rose's notes hint at Anthony's combativeness as traveller: near La Spezia, Rose recalls 'row with the driver when we start' and, after the St Gotthard Pass, 'Places taken from us by two Germans.'[14] But on the whole the Trollopes found the trip delightful. Anthony would go abroad almost every year of his life henceforth. Sometimes a special Post Office assignment would prompt the trip, sometimes the desire to write a travel book, but most often it was a matter of a six-week holiday with Rose, taken usually in late summer/early autumn. He was a robust, indefatigable, unstoppable traveller. In due course foreign scenes would enter his fiction, his short stories at first: Egypt, the Holy Land, Malta, Spain, the West Indies, Bermuda, America, Belgium, southern France, Switzerland, Italy, Bavaria, Austria, and the Tyrol. Later, Prague, Nuremberg, Alsace Lorraine, and Australia would provide settings for entire novels. Even in old age, Trollope (in James Anthony Froude's words) went on 'banging about the world'.[15] The year of his death would find him twice travelling to Ireland.

---

* Harry Trollope, writing to Michael Sadleir in 1923 (and trying to discourage him from writing a biography of Trollope) said: 'Letter writing is a big subject, but my brother, now dead, and I, both thought that our father in his letters to us confined himself to the matter on hand and wrote shortly. He loved us both very dearly, but I think he had too much writing (P. O. work and books) to do to make him wish to dally pleasantly with his pen in writing to us. In talking he enjoyed heartily play of that kind, but writing savoured of business.'[16]

Trollope was so busy with his postal work that his literary career had to come to a halt. His writing had been floundering even before the move to England: *La Vendée* had failed more thoroughly than the previous two novels; the Irish guidebook had come to nothing; 'The Noble Jilt' had been condemned in manuscript; the review of Merivale had been a creditable performance, but Trollope clearly could not make his writing career in classical studies. Moreover, once he was in the West Country writing seemed impossible: the 'passion' with which he did his work, the incessant daily riding and the writing of lengthy reports, took up all his time. It made no difference that the pressure was self-imposed, never from head-quarters, which, as he said 'more than once expressed itself astonished at my celerity'. So enwrapped was he in postal duties that for a while he had to forgo even his programme, begun in December 1850, of systematically reading the plays of Beaumont and Fletcher (he eventually read through thirty-five of them by 1853).[17] Still, 'from day to day' he thought about writing. Then, having been working in England for just less than a year, in late May 1852, at Salisbury, 'whilst wandering there on a midsummer evening round the purlieus of the cathedral I conceived the story of *The Warden*,—from whence came that series of novels of which Barchester, with its bishops, deans, and archdeacon, was the central site.' Trollope did not write anything then, rather he simply 'thought about' the novel, 'lived with his characters'. Then, more than a year later, on 29 July 1853 at Tenbury in Herefordshire, he began to write the book, called tentatively 'The Precentor'. Determined to 'moderate' his postal work somewhat so as to resume his writing career, he wrote the first chapter.[18]

But just at this time he was recalled to Ireland, to be acting surveyor of the Northern District of Ireland. Acting surveyor was a good deal further up the ladder of promotion than surveyor's clerk, no matter how respected and valued the clerk. It was with mixed feelings, however, that Trollope returned to Ireland, and took lodgings in Belfast, which would be home for almost two years. For one thing, the Protestant North of Ireland did not appeal to him as much as the Catholic South; moreover—had other things been equal—he would have much preferred to stay in England. He felt 'warmly wedded' to the extension of the rural post there: 'Other parts of England were being done by other men, and I had nearly finished the area which had been entrusted to me. I should have liked to ride over the whole country, and to have sent a rural post letter-carrier to every parish, every village, every hamlet, and every grange in England.'[19]

The position of acting surveyor carried with it the implied promise of a surveyorship in the future. On 28 June of the following year, 1854, while at

Trollope's travel diary for May 1852 in the West Country. The columns after the place-names indicate miles travelled that day, and expenses for bed and board. The entry for Saturday the 22nd shows him in Salisbury, where 'wandering . . . round the purlieus of the cathedral I conceived the story of *The Warden*.'

Coleraine, Co. Londonderry, he wrote to his mother at three in the morning to tell her he had received 'what is tantamount to a direct promise' of a surveyorship; it was 'a certainty', though he feared it would not come as quickly as he liked; his salary, exclusive of reimbursements and perquisites would rise to about £650; he would have liked to return to England, though he seemed slated for the Northern Irish district. In the same letter he laid out plans for another visit to Florence and Venice, asking his brother to map out a route including a return via Innsbruck, Munich, Frankfurt, Cologne. But as Trollope had feared, some hitch in his promotion developed, and his intended holiday leave could not be managed that summer. By 24 July Trollope's mother wrote to condole with him on the postponement; she closed: 'God bless you and yours— Bear your plagues, as you have always done—*philosophically.*' Tom, in a postscript, said, 'The conduct, shabby, *unjust*, and insolently tyrannical of your superiors, makes me feel *very* radically inclined. . . . [It] would convert me into a Post-office Guy [Fawkes]. And I have no belief in your promotion, till you get it. Damn them all! Amen.'[20] Anthony and Rose managed only a week's holiday in Scotland, at Oban, Tarbert, and Stirling.

Then, on 9 October 1854 he was officially appointed surveyor for the Northern District of Ireland.[21] The pleasure may have been diminished in that it had been so long in coming; nevertheless, for the man who in 1834, precisely twenty years earlier, had begun so unpromisingly as a junior clerk in the Secretary's office in London, who for seven years had failed to catch on, who was often on the verge of dismissal, it was one of the major victories of his life. In rank, surveyors were equal to the heads of London postal departments and inferior only to the Secretary and the Assistant Secretary. And, though the North of Ireland was not Trollope's preferred locale, a surveyor's chance of transferring was very real. In the mean time, he set in motion a request that he be permitted to reside in Dublin rather than in the North.

Another important milestone had been reached the day before the promotion became official, though at the time Trollope could not have realized its full implications. On 8 October he posted the manuscript of his short novel, still called 'The Precentor', to William Longman. Longman's was the oldest London publishing house, having been established in Paternoster Row in 1724; they felt themselves somewhat above fiction,[22] and the strength of their list lay in poetry and history: they had published the poems of Scott and of the enormously popular Thomas Moore; in the 1840s and 1850s their leading author was Macaulay. They had published Charles Merivale's *History of the Romans*, and it was through John

Merivale that Trollope, the previous July, met Longman. The publisher had the manuscript read by Joseph Cauvin, a minor author and translator, who quickly sent a glowing report to the publisher: although Cauvin seems oddly to have placed the 'main interest' of the story in John Bold's internal conflict between love and duty, he liked the 'well drawn and happily distinguished' characters and the 'vein of quiet humour' throughout; he thought the send-up of *The Times* as good as 'anything of the kind that was ever written for geniality and truth'; he predicted a 'large sale' for the work. On 24 October Longman sent Trollope an agreement—again for the half-profits Trollope hated; there was not even the £20 advance *La Vendée* had brought him from Colburn. Still, Longman was Longman, and his mother had not had to lend support for the book's acceptance. It was published on 5 January 1855.[23]

In *The Warden* Trollope chose to deal with two evils—the misuse of charitable endowments by bishops and clergy of the Church of England, and the 'undeserved severity' with which the press treated those clergy-men paid large sums from such funds. The scandal of the misapplication of endowments was made a subject of popular concern by two long-running campaigns in *The Times* from 1849 onwards. The paper reported and commented on the case arising from the disclosure by the headmaster of Rochester Cathedral School that the vastly increased income arising from original endowments was going to the dean and chapter instead of providing free education for local boys. *The Times* also gleefully pursued the clerical Master of St Cross Hospital, Winchester, where fifteen old men were maintained and paid a small annual sum, while the handsome income now arising from the endowment was paid to the Master, who retained as much as £3,000 a year for himself. The situation at St Cross was in some respects close to that in *The Warden*; Trollope, however, made his case morally more interesting, because his central figure, Mr Harding, was not, like the Master at Winchester, a pluralist, who performed his functions at the hospital through an ill-paid deputy. Nevertheless, Mr Harding would have come under the lash of *The Times*, as a beneficiary of the system it was attacking. Even the more worldly clerics of the actual cases could be seen as treated by the leader-writers with 'undeserved severity', since, as Trollope said, 'When a man is appointed to a place . . . it is seldom that he will be the first to find out that his services are overpaid.' Trollope was not interested in propaganda for or against either side through what he considered Dickensian stereotypes: either a red-nosed bloated parson conspicuously neglecting all his duties, or a devoted, hard-working, underpaid clergyman subjected to the abuse of the daily press. Instead he put a good, almost saintly man, Harding, in the bad position of receiving high pay for little work. Trollope said his attempt to treat both evils was 'altogether wrong', a view eventually repudiated by later readers who would appreciate the novel's delicate balance.[24]

Trollope's judgement here must in part have resulted from the reviewers, many of whom disliked the ambiguity of the novel: the *Spectator* complained that 'the object of the writer is not clear'; John Forster in the *Examiner* professed himself in confusion 'as to Mr Trollope's real meaning'; the *Athenaeum* said the story suffered from the 'grave drawback' of 'too much indifference as to the rights of the case. The conclusion is inconclusive enough'; the *Leader* found the ending 'defective'—'careless and unsatisfactory—as if the author had got tired of his subject before he had done with it'. Another difficulty for some reviewers, and many readers since, was the satire and parodies of Carlyle and Dickens as Dr Pessimist Anticant and Mr Popular Sentiment. Forster, a close friend of Dickens and Carlyle, pronounced these satires 'in very bad taste'. The *Leader* concurred, calling the satire on living authors under 'farcically fictitious names' a mistake: 'Mr. Trollope is far too clever a man . . . to descend successfully to such low literary work.' On the other hand most reviewers, like Forster, praised the book as 'clever' and admired the characters, especially the Warden himself. The *Athenaeum*, for example, called the novel 'extremely clever and amusing. . . . all the characters are well and vigorously sketched.' The *Spectator* praised the 'keen observation of public affairs, a pungent closeness of style, and great cleverness'. The *Leader* innocently said that *The Warden* 'certainly promises well for the author's future, if he gives us more books'.[25]

The Warden was not a financial success: Trollope received payments of £9. 8s. 8d. for 1855, and £10. 15s. 1d. for 1856. Stonebreaking, he remarked, would have been more remunerative. None the less, the book had fair critical and, more important, fair popular success. As Trollope put it, 'The novel-reading world did not go mad about *The Warden*; but I soon felt that it had not failed as the others had failed. . . . and I could discover that people around me knew that I had written a book.'[26]

Only six weeks after the publication of *The Warden*, Trollope wrote to his publisher inquiring about its sale. He had, he told Longman, from the first intended a sequel to the story, and if *The Warden* were successful, he would have the manuscript of the new novel in the publisher's hands by May. Longman's reply was discouraging. Precisely what he said is unknown, but it was bad enough to make Trollope break off *Barchester*

Towers, of which he had written some eighty-five manuscript pages.[27]
Even though *The Warden* had not failed with the public as had the earlier
novels, and in spite of generally favourable reviews, Trollope turned his
hand to non-fiction, in the form of a broad survey of English institutions
called *The New Zealander.* It would be a year and a half before he would
return to novel writing.

The New Zealander derived its title from Macaulay's famous 'prophecy'
in 1840 that the day was coming when a visitor from New Zealand would
sketch the ruins of St Paul's Cathedral from a broken arch of London
Bridge.[28] Trollope's book was intended as a 'condition of England'
treatise, addressed specifically to the question of whether Great Britain
was beginning to show signs of that decay which is inevitable to all great
empires and nations. Trollope's answer was a very qualified yes. Convinced that England was no exception, he still felt the day of England's
decline was far off; he sees only some incipient indications of decadence,
all revolving around the question of honesty, particularly public acceptance of dishonesty. It was a Carlylean theme, but treated in a very
different manner from that of the Chelsea sage. In 1851, on first reading
the *Latter-Day Pamphlets,* wherein Carlyle's shrill denunciations of England reached their zenith, Trollope wrote to his mother:

To me it appears that the grain of sense is so smothered up in a sack of the sheerest
trash, that the former is valueless. . . . He has one idea,—a hatred of spoken and
acted falsehood; and on that he harps through the whole eight pamphlets. I look on
him as a man who was always in danger of going mad in literature, and who has now
done so.[29]

Four years later, in *The Warden,* Trollope gave public voice to this
judgement in his heavy-handed satire of Carlyle as Dr Pessimist Anticant,
who 'astonished the reading public by the vigour of his thoughts, put forth
in the quaintest language'; then popularity spoiled him, and he 'mistook
the signs of the times and the minds of men, and instituted himself censor
of things in general, and began the great task of reprobating everything
and everybody'.[30] In *The New Zealander* Trollope too is alarmed at the
dishonesty he sees in Great Britain, but his treatment is anything but
fanatic; it lacks the boldness that sweeps aside all counter-arguments;
Trollope frequently qualifies his argument, so as to make for very
lukewarm pamphleteering. Only when inveighing against the monopoly
exercised over public opinion by that tyrannical 'God', *The Times,* is
Trollope intemperate ('Men think, and speak, and act the Times news-

paper. . . . at every political conversation a man is tempted to remind the speaker that he has already seen the paper').³¹

In the most Carlylean chapter of the book, 'The People and Their Rulers', Trollope naïvely wants all men to learn 'to love their labour, to do loving work' (perhaps in the way he himself loved work). As it is, miners of Cornwall and Glamorganshire, for example, exist in 'strange and mon- strous villages', where gin and 'unrestrained immorality and uninspired labour' produce 'the look of hell'. British workers of all kinds—far worse off than their German, Italian, or Tyrolean counterparts—must have their work reordered, made interesting and inspiring, under the guidance of 'aristocrats', who, for Trollope, include anyone charged with overseeing the work of others, down to the small grocer with a single shopboy. With the behaviour of the hereditary aristocracy itself, Trollope is on the whole contented, debauchery among them being pretty much a thing of the past: a Prime Minister today will 'live with his wife' and pay his tradesmen; the heir to an earldom 'does not, as a matter of course, and merely because he is such, keep a harem of opera dancers [mistresses]'. Even Trollope's prose, usually simple and straightforward—and more so as he matured as a novelist—is in *The New Zealander* occasionally elaborate, unnatural, sometimes assuming a kind of pseudo-biblical/prophetic voice addressing the reader: 'Oh, man, if on no other terms than these ['money profits'] thou canst be gotten to love thy work, thou must go on, and suffer. Creep on, thou base one, and let thy soul rot, steeped in the stagnant pool of thy unmanly apathy.' Such strained efforts may reflect a grudging debt to or even clumsy imitation of Carlyle's style, something he at once admired and disliked.³²

With honesty as his touchstone, Trollope finds much else to criticize in mid-century England: religion is dishonest when it advocates sabbatarian beliefs that even its preachers must see as abhorrent to reason; both high and low church are dishonest in exhorting people to despise material prosperity; Members of Parliament are dishonest when they are willing to vote that black is white as their party bids them; both Members and their constituents are dishonest in their demand for political 'purism', angelic private lives in public figures, and in their feigned horror of election bribery; lawyers are dishonest who use legal ruses to defend prisoners they know are guilty. Tradesmen seem to think they can live by standards different from the rest of mankind, passing off chicory for coffee, cotton for linen. Imitations are substituted for the paintings of masters; mesmerism and quackery are invading medicine; advertisements are lies and puffery. Englishmen even pretend to be enjoying themselves at dinners and parties that bore them to death. These were themes Trollope returned to again and again in his novels. The attack on low-church doctrine and practice would be prominent in his next novel, *Barchester Towers* (1857), and would continue through others, most pointedly in *Rachel Ray* (1865) and *John Caldigate* (1878); that Christians should love 'the good things of the world' is an abiding Trollopian gospel. He would engage the question of party loyalty in far more sophisticated fashion by the time of the Palliser novels; his conviction that laws against election bribery were puritanical and hypocritical continued in *Doctor Thorne* (1858), would be drastically altered by the time of *Ralph the Heir* (1871), the defeat by bribery of his own attempt to sit in Parliament having taught him differently. Aristocrats, who come off fairly well in *The New Zealander*, are more often than not targets of satire; dishonesty in trade and advertisement would receive less than successful treatment in *The Struggles of Brown, Jones, and Robinson*; as for dinner parties, tedious or otherwise, few novelists depicted more of them than Trollope. In *The Way We Live Now* he would address almost every species of dishonesty discussed in *The New Zealander*.

The New Zealander also manifests the 'conservative liberalism' Trollope would ascribe to himself in *An Autobiography*: he supports the police against the charge of brutality in their handling of Hyde Park disturbances (the newspapers have given unfair accounts of the incident), but he criticizes churchmen for intolerance of Roman Catholics (a very liberal view in mid-Victorian England); he defends the Duke of Newcastle and Lord Raglan for their conduct of the Crimean War as victims of the country's unrealistic expectations (the war required more, not less 'red tape' in the sense of orderly routine), but he complains that young men who serve their country in the army and navy get a very poor bargain for themselves; he believes in 'beating Russia' in the Crimean War, but thinks victory ultimately of little importance compared with the problem of educating England's young; he contends that Britain is the greatest nation in the world, but feels this glory is of little use to governesses paid £10 a year or ploughmen who exist almost at the level of brutes; he is impatient with native criticism of things British, from foreign policy to the architecture of the new Parliament buildings, but will lament that Britons are too proud to take needful lessons from foreigners, to study, for example, the social graces of the French; he decries tender treatment of criminals, but can flail away at the law's delay as well as any reformer; he fears democracy as 'mob' rule, but is altogether intolerant of the thirteenth-century attitudes of the House of Lords.

Finally, in *The New Zealander* Trollope lists his eighteen 'giants' English literature:

Spenser	Swift	Burns
Shakespeare	Pope	Scott
Fletcher	Thomson	Byron
Milton*	Johnson	Southey
Dryden	Goldsmith	Taylor
Defoe	Cowper	Tennyson

His decision to begin the list with the Elizabethans accounts for the omission of Chaucer, whom he admired. It is, however, a noticeably conservative choice, explicitly intended to represent an 'uninterrupted succession', and omitting the innovators and radicals, Wordsworth, Coleridge, Shelley, who broke away from their eighteenth-century predecessors. In the last six years of his life the record of his reading aloud did include Shelley (*The Revolt of Islam*) and Wordsworth (*The Excursion*), while giving evidence that he retained his early love of Pope, Goldsmith, Cowper, Thomson's *Seasons*, and Byron. Only two living poets appeared in the *New Zealander* list, Henry Taylor and Tennyson. Trollope more than shared his contemporaries' admiration of Taylor's now forgotten *Philip van Artevelde*, 'that one, long, sustained and precious song'; in Tennyson he recognized a 'mysterious, heavenly melody [and] . . . that poetic electricity, felt but indefinable . . . which . . . touches, and but touches, the chords of the heart'. All on Trollope's list are famed as poets, except Defoe and Johnson, who are included because of their influence on English literary history. So superior to prose did Trollope think poetry, that not even Macaulay, for whose writings Trollope had immense regard, qualifies, much less any novelist. While he continued all his life to regard poetry as essentially superior to prose, he came gradually to have more respect for the novel. It is likely that had he revised the list twenty years later, he would have included Jane Austen and Thackeray. In 1856 there was more condescension than irony in the judgement, '. . . that [railway] travellers should read little else but novels was perhaps to be expected.'33

While Trollope was in London on postal business during the last week of January 1856, he saw William Longman, who expressed a willingness to look at *The New Zealander*. On 27 March Trollope sent him the

* Milton was, after Shakespeare, Trollope's favourite English poet; and, after *Macbeth* and *Hamlet*, 'Lycidas' the work most alluded to in his writings, especially the lines about sporting 'with Amaryllis in the shade', about the sun that 'tricks his beams', and about ambition as 'that last infirmity of noble mind'.

manuscript, saying that if Longman accepted the work he ought, because of its topical nature, to publish it as soon as possible.[34] Joseph Cauvin, Longman's reader, could not believe that this wrathful attack on 'all the leading influences and institutions of the State' was by the author of *The Warden*: 'All the good points in the work have already been treated of by Mr. Carlyle, of whose *Latter-Day Pamphlets* this work, *both in style and matter*, is a most feeble imitation.' Cauvin advised against publication on any terms.[35] His analysis was cruelly acerbic, but his caution to Longman was sound enough and, in the long run, fortunate for Trollope. *The New Zealander* would have brought ridicule on him just at a time when *The Warden* had given him popularity. Trollope in 1856 could not of course have understood what became clear only years later, that *The Warden*, launching him into novels with English, specifically Barchester, settings, was the crucial turning-point in his writing career. It is not known how much of Cauvin's harsh critique Longman transmitted to his author, but certainly the publisher gave him the burden of it. Trollope smarted for a while, tinkered a bit with the text, and then put it in his drawer.* It was not till later that he realized how correct Longman's reader had been, how inferior the tone—not to mention content—of the hortatory, preachy, stubbornly opinionated *New Zealander* was to the generous, fair-minded, tolerant, low-keyed voice of his fiction. In *An Autobiography*, for all its candid revelations of his miserable youth, of false starts in writing, of books he considered failures, he never mentions *The New Zealander*, the manuscript of which he still kept. He seems to have become almost ashamed of it.

In 1856 Trollope was especially preoccupied with his Post Office work. It was his first full year as surveyor, and his travel diary shows him continually on the move. Moreover, he was soon frequently travelling greater distances in Ireland because he had received permission to live out of his district, and in June, on return from the continent—for he and Rose had managed to make the postponed trip to Venice, where they met up with his mother and Tom—the Trollopes moved into a spacious three-storey

---

* Trollope did not submit the manuscript to another publisher, but he managed to salvage some of the text: an entire chapter, 'The Civil Service', missing from the manuscript, was apparently inserted pretty much as written as the chapter of the same name in *The Three Clerks*; the other missing chapter, 'Trade', may have been incorporated, with considerable changes, into *The Struggles of Brown, Jones, and Robinson*, a satire on trade and advertising; he inserted verbatim other passages from *The New Zealander* into *The Three Clerks* (in the chapter called 'The Parliamentary Committee') and also into *Doctor Thorne*, in the account of the election and unseating of Sir Roger Scatcherd. *The New Zealander* itself was not published until 1972.

red-brick house at 5 Seaview Terrace, Donnybrook, a Dublin suburb. It was a hundred miles to Belfast, the central city of his district.

Trollope was called to London by the Post Office during the summer to give evidence before the Select Committee on Postal Arrangements in Ireland, which was mainly concerned with investigating the benefits of making greater use of railways to carry mail. Trollope was the chief witness, testifying for almost four days between 16 and 27 July, whereas three, four, or five witnesses a day were heard at earlier sessions; he himself told the Committee: 'I do not think any other officer has local knowledge of the whole district except myself; I have local knowledge over the whole of Ireland.' With a detailed use of timetables he showed that railways were not always cheaper and more efficient than cars; between Waterford and Clonmel such replacement had caused a deterioration in service, a subject 'on which my own opinion as to what would improve the town is not a speculative opinion'; questioned about another witness's suggestion that the postal messenger might be an old woman, he replied, 'I think that was an allegorical statement.' He more than hinted that petitions for railways had been contrived by the railway companies, and when challenged, responded, 'I do not wish to withdraw the words I used.'[36]

The Civil Service was at this time undergoing great change; a huge blue book, the work of Sir Charles Trevelyan and Sir Stafford Northcote, with the assistance of the Oxford scholar Benjamin Jowett, paved the way for a complete reordering of the recruiting system for the Civil Service, incorporating competitive examinations aimed at getting the best candidate for each available position. Trollope, himself the product of a very different system of recruitment, fired back from Ireland in an article published (anonymously) in October 1855 in the *Dublin University Magazine*. Trollope saw the Report as unfair and wrong-headed, the whole based on the inaccurate assumption that the Civil Service recruited its members 'from the idle, the weak in mind, the infirm in body, the unambitious, the jolterheads, the ne'er do wells, the puny, and the diseased'. Using the Report's own figures, Trollope finds that in the Public Records Department—depicted as 'the very hospital of public offices'—twenty-one clerks over a five-year period had an average of seventeen days' absence per annum, and, as one man accounted for many absences, the average in this 'lazar house of invalids' was more like fourteen days per year, a figure medical men would find normal among the general population. It is true that men will take more frequent absences for sickness in jobs in which they can do so without losing pay; but this, Trollope insists, is 'human nature'.

The essence of the reform was to be an examination system intended to do away with patronage and attract the very best to the 'elysium of Somerset House'. So irresistible will be the glory of passing the examination that it will 'deprive the bar of its brightest aspirants, limit the hospitals to mediocrity, and carry off even a portion of the austere virtue that now ornaments the Church'; the mere honour of scoring high on Jowett's examination lists will bring the most ambitious, gifted, and educated young men in the kingdom into the Civil Service, for the Report says not a word, 'not a syllable', about the quid pro quo. (Trollope, complaining also about the thwarting of ambition within the Civil Service by the practice of giving high appointments to outsiders, mentions cases by name, including that of Rowland Hill, who 'invented penny-postage stamps, and so brought himself into place'.) Not only are the expectations about attracting the best of the nation to low-paying, unrewarding jobs 'Utopian', but the proposed examination itself is ludicrously unrealistic: a week-long series of written essays and a one-hour viva voce, beginning with a first-day 'preliminary' examination intended to test for 'a fast and neat handwriting, a thorough knowledge of book-keeping, and English composition'. The last especially strikes Trollope's fancy; he claims not to meet many of these 'juvenile Macaulays', and points out that Jowett himself 'has sinned against the rules of English composition in the very sentence in which he requires a knowledge of them as a first preliminary in his youthful candidates'. As for the other subjects, 'history, jurisprudence, political economy, modern languages, political and physical geography, and other matters, besides the staple of classics and mathematics', proficiency in which the examination will discover, these are 'rare attainments' in university graduates and all but impossible in boys of seventeen.[37] But Trollope's was a rearguard action, and the Civil Service Commission was established to oversee the examinations.

12

<hr />

Barchester Towers
and Success

It was not until 12 May 1856 that Trollope resumed *Barchester Towers*. He felt that he had pretty much wasted a year and a half on the ill-fated *New Zealander*; and so, returning to fiction, he determined to work more industriously and more systematically. He adopted two strategies for increased efficiency. First, be began his practice of writing while travelling. By now he moved about not so much on horseback or horse-drawn coach, but by railway: 'Like others,' Trollope recalled, 'I used to read,— though Carlyle has since told me that a man when travelling should not read, but "sit still and label his thoughts". But if I intended to make a profitable business out of my writing, and, at the same time, to do my best for the Post Office, I must turn these hours to more account than I could do even by reading.' Trollope made up a writing tablet and soon found that he could compose as quickly in a railway carriage as at his desk.[1] Years later he would have carpenters build writing desks in his cabins on ocean-crossing steamers.

The second system adopted at this time was a working diary of his writing. For years he had been making scrupulous records of his daily travels and expenditures for the Post Office, keeping track of every mile, every shilling and penny. In his commonplace-book of the 1830s he had said a young man ought to keep a careful account book of every monetary transaction, that his own failure to do so had brought him near to 'utter ruin'. Now, past 40, he adapted ledger-like columned record-keeping for his writing, marking off the days in weekly sections, entering daily the number of pages written each session, and then noting the week's total. His 'page' had approximately 250 words. He set a goal of 40 manuscript pages per week. He would have preferred to work seven days a week, but of course there were weeks when he could only manage a few days, and some weeks when illness or pressures of other work kept him from writing altogether. He usually managed the forty pages per week; on a few occasions he pushed himself to more than a hundred pages in a week. The working diaries were an extraordinary exercise in self-discipline. For whereas his postal work had its daily and weekly obligations—including frequent and lengthy written reports—his novel writing was under no compulsion, no deadline, other than his own will, and the result had been what Trollope termed 'spasmodic' efforts only. He wanted a self-induced system of 'task work'. Henceforth Trollope wrote under the watchfulness, as it were, of these diaries, with the result that 'if at any time I have slipped into idleness for a day or two, the record of that idleness has been there, staring me in the face, and demanding of me increased labour, so that the deficiency might be supplied.' A week without a sufficient number of pages was 'a blister to my eye', Trollope wrote, and a month would have been 'a sorrow to my heart'.[2] Lapses were indicated by entries such as 'Sore throat', 'Ill', 'Hunting', 'Alas', or 'Ah me!'. But such interruptions were to remain relatively few; by and large the working diaries recorded a steady outpouring of pages that must have provided a deep source of satisfaction. This diary-regulated writing would lead to startling results: with *Barchester Towers*, Trollope's famous, or infamous, productivity took hold, and for good.*

Just as Anthony was putting his novel production into high gear, his mother was ending her own literary career. She was a few years shy of 80, and her last book, *Fashionable Life, or Paris and London*, was about to be published. She had written 41 books—the individual volumes number 115—and her first had appeared when she was 53. Now, on 8 July 1856, she wrote to her younger son, who, with the publication of *The Warden*, was finally beginning to make a name for himself as novelist:

I am in truth grown woefully idle, and, worse still, woefully *lazy*, and this symptom is both new and disagreeable to *me*. But the degree of activity of which I have been wont to boast . . . might have been accounted in my very best days as positive *idleness* when compared to what you manifest. Tom and I agree in thinking that you exceed in this respect any individual that we have ever known or heard of—and I am proud of being your mother—as well for this reason as for sundry others. I rejoice to think that you have considerably more than the third of a century to gallop through yet before reaching the age at which I first felt inclined to cry halta la![3]

---

* Tom Trollope, when he cared to do so, could write prodigiously fast. He wrote the novel *Beppo the Conscript* (1864), 600 manuscript pages, in 23 days; on one single day he wrote 33 pages: 'My brother used to say that he could not do the like to save his life and that of all those dearest to him.'[4]

Anthony had not by any means reached his full stride as productive novelist, and Mrs Trollope's letter had a certain prescience that neither of them could have realized at the time. Still, here was praise from a very special quarter; and he, never given to keeping letters, kept this one.

Trollope finished *Barchester Towers* on 9 November 1856, the greater part of it having been written in railway carriages, with his working diary 'staring' him in the face when he slackened off. The book had been written at a pace more than five times faster than that which produced *The Warden*. He submitted the manuscript to Longman, and on 8 December Joseph Cauvin sent the publisher a mixed report. On the whole he considered the new novel inferior to *The Warden*; 'Plot there is none,' Cauvin said, but a greater defect was 'the low-mindedness and vulgarity of the chief actors. There is hardly a "lady" or "gentleman" among them. Such a bishop and his wife as Dr. and Mrs. Proudie have certainly not appeared in our time.' Worst of all was Signora Neroni, whom he deemed 'most repulsive, exaggerated and unnatural' and 'a great blot on the work'. Cauvin's strongest objection here was on the grounds of sexual explicitness—the examples he gives are the chapters 'Mrs. Proudie's Reception' and 'A Love Scene'. On the other hand, Cauvin found the book far from uninteresting, with part of it 'on a level with the best morsels by contemporary novelists'—though he thought the novel could be reduced to one volume. His only shrewd observation concerned Trollope's 'facility in the execution that makes you fancy that the author is playing with his reader, showing how easy it is for him to write a novel in three volumes'.[5]

Trollope, writing from Derry on 20 December 1856, answered Longman that he was willing to negotiate over the objectionable passages, though he doubted he could 'in utter ignorance have committed a volume of indecencies. . . . Of course [Signora Neroni] is intended to [appear] as indifferent to all moralities and decent behaviour—but such a character may I think be drawn without offence if her vice be made not attractive.' He flatly refused to reduce the novel to two volumes (Longman had wisely not endorsed his reader's suggestion of one volume). Postal work must have pressed especially hard at the time, for Trollope made the extraordinary suggestion that John Tilley call on Longman with 'carte blanche to act for me in any way' with regard to the indelicate passages.[6] As it turned out, Trollope himself made all the changes by mail.

But the question of objectionable passages almost became irrelevant, as Tilley reported back that Longman was unwilling to pay an advance of £100 for the novel. Trollope, encouraged by the attention *The Warden* had attracted, stood firm. (Had he known that Longman the previous year had paid Macaulay £20,000 for Volumes III and IV of his *History of England*, he would have been all the more determined to have his mite.) He wrote to the publisher on 10 January 1857: 'It appears that you think £100 too high a sum to pay in advance for the book. It seems to me that if a three vol. novel be worth anything it must be worth that.' He conceded, perhaps ironically, that it would be prejudicial to his own interests to change publishers and lose the value of Longman's prestige; but, he said, if his novel were not worth £100, he had in fact no interests to prejudice. He added that he also thought that the copyright should revert to the author after a stated number of years. Longman then agreed to the £100 advance against half-profits, and Trollope, on 18 January, accepted, saying that he would give way on the matter of the publisher's continued right of publication 'at present'. Actually, Longman did pretty well paying Trollope half-profits over the years, the total on *The Warden* and *Barchester Towers* coming to £727 11s 3d. by 1879.[7]

Retelling his negotiations with Longman twenty years later prompted Trollope to discourse on writing for money: 'I received my £100, in advance, with profound delight. . . . I am well aware that there are many who think that an author in his authorship should not regard money,—nor a painter, or sculptor, or composer in his art'; but for artists to claim to disregard money is as foolish and hypocritical as clergymen's preachments against worldly gain:

the love of money is so distinctive a characteristic of humanity that such sermons are mere platitudes called for by customary but unintelligent piety. All material progress has come from man's desire to do the best he can for himself and those about him, and civilisation and Christianity itself have been made possible by such progress. . . . it is a mistake to suppose that a man is a better man because he despises money. Few do so, and those few in so doing suffer a defect.[8]

(In *Can You forgive Her?* Plantagenet Palliser claims, 'There is no vulgar error so vulgar,—that is to say, common or erroneous,—as that by which men have been taught to say that mercenary tendencies are bad. A desire for wealth is the source of all progress. Civilization comes from what men call greed.'[9]) To expect writers to devote their 'unbought brains' to the public welfare is silly: 'Take away from English authors their copyrights, and you would very soon take away also from England her authors.' In 1883 this passage was to disturb publisher William Blackwood, who wanted at least the part about material progress making Christianity possible deleted from *An Autobiography* as it went through the press. Trollope's son Harry, in whose hands the matter lay, insisted on keeping it. Trollope would have applauded his doing so in the face of 'customary but unintelligent piety'.[10]

By 1 February 1857 Trollope sent Longman the revisions: 'I have de bon cœur changed all the passages marked as being too warm';* he cut out or rewrote passages Cauvin labelled 'ineffective', but let stand two whole chapters that had been been called 'tedious': 'I will not praise myself by saying they are not so, but I must profess that I cannot make them less so. I am sure you do not expect a perfect novel from me.' (Unfortunately the manuscript has not survived, and *Barchester Towers* in its original form is lost.) A month later, Trollope 'in a great hurry in boots and breeches, just as I am going to hunt' told Longman that by all means the words 'foul breathing' could come out and 'fat stomach' be changed to 'deep chest'. But Trollope vetoed Longman's suggestion for a different title, insisting that neither of the Proudies was to be considered the chief character in the book, and that the name *Barchester Towers* was 'at least inoffensive and easy of pronunciation'.[11] (Argument still obtains about the pronunciation of 'Proudie'.)

In *Barchester Towers*, Trollope took to heart some of the strictures voiced in the reviews of *The Warden*. The sequel contained nothing like the parodies of Dickens and Carlyle. The criticism of *The Times* was somewhat muted, although the paper's reviewer, otherwise most favourable to the novel, understandably objected to the further satire of the newspaper as 'The Jupiter', likening Trollope's treatment to the work of G. M. Reynolds in *Mysteries of the Court of London*—a way of saying it was vulgar and sensational.[12] Trollope very much resented the implication that Tom Towers was a caricature of a specific individual; he insisted he knew no one at *The Times* and could not have had an actual person in mind. On the other hand, Trollope paid no attention to the caution about facetious names. Until the very end he would use names like Blowhard and Flutey for musicians, Slow and Bideawhile for lawyers, Fillgrave and Rearchild for physicians, Midlothian and Auld Reekie for titled Scottish families, Neefit for a tailor, Sir Damask Monogram for a rich parvenu. His notion, a very old one, was that in comedy it did no harm to remind people that this was a make-believe world. The playful names were usually, but not always, reserved for minor characters. In *Barchester Towers* the fairly

---

* An example of bowdlerized wording can be seen in Chapter 48, where the Revd Francis Arabin, having successfully proposed to Eleanor Bold, 'bowing his face down over hers, pressed his lips upon her brow; his virgin lips, which since a beard first grew upon his chin, had never yet tasted the luxury of a woman's cheek.' About which passage Trollope told publisher George Smith in 1860, 'I shall never forget a terrible & killing correspondence which I had with W. Longman because I would make a clergyman kiss a lady whom he proposed to marry.'[13]

colourless name Slope for a central figure is turned into a joke by its derivation from Sterne's Dr Slop, and that of Mr Quiverful, for a man with fourteen children ('fourteen of them *living*', as Mrs Quiverful says) could not fail to remind readers familiar with the Bible and Prayer Book of the words of Psalm 128 about children being like arrows blessing 'the man that hath his quiver full of them'. (Henry James wrote of Quiverful: 'We can believe in the name and we can believe in the children; but we cannot manage the combination.'[14])*

Trollope heeded the most persistent criticism of *The Warden*, its ambiguity of purpose—reviewers had wanted to know where he stood on ecclesiastical reform. For Trollope the answer was to get away from the novel of 'purpose'. In *Barchester Towers* the wardenship is eventually given to Quiverful, but the old scandal and the rights and wrongs of the case no longer matter; the issue of reform has been lost to the personalities of the protagonists. And although *Barchester Towers*, like the *The Warden*, was again about clergymen, and, being a sequel, largely about the same clergymen, Trollope dealt with his clerics in their social and economic rather than in their religious lives. As the review in *The Times* put it, 'all the ideas are ecclesiastical, the dresses are canonical, and the conversations have a rubrical tinge. Yet the subject is so fresh and the representation so vivid, that the contracted limits of the story are forgotten.'[15] *Barchester Towers* does touch upon the controversy between high church and low church, with the latter not unexpectedly coming off much more poorly. Trollope's lifelong aversion to evangelicalism persists, but he does not try to interest his readers in doctrinal matters. Warden Harding, Archdeacon Grantly, the bishops, Mr Slope and Mr Arabin might almost have been barristers or military men. The Church itself he saw as a sort of privileged division of the Civil Service. Trollope had begun the series by taking as his subject the reform of ecclesiastical abuses in a cathedral town, and the characters followed as a matter of course. He had stumbled, as it were, upon clergymen, and discovered that he had a knack for delineating them. He said that no one could have had less reason for writing about clergymen; he claimed, either unthinkingly or disingenuously, never to have lived in a cathedral city except London, and to have no knowledge of any cathedral close (he had lived—as a schoolboy—in Winchester, and later for brief periods at Exeter, Bristol, and Worcester). Archdeacon Grantly, he said, was 'the simple result of an effort of my moral conscious-

---

* Perhaps the most important character in all Trollope to carry a facetious name is the Duke of Omnium, a quiet Latin joke in its deliberately clumsy double genitive, literally 'The Duke of of All' as the title for the richest of all dukes.

ness. It was such as that, in my opinion, that an archdeacon should be . . . and lo! an archdeacon was produced who has been declared by competent authorities to be a real archdeacon down to the very ground. And,yet as far as I can remember, I had not then ever spoken to an archdeacon. . . . The archdeacon came whole from my brain.'[16]

When *Barchester Towers* at last appeared in May 1857, it met almost unanimous praise from the critics, and again the label 'clever' appeared everywhere. The *Leader* called the novel 'uncommonly graphic and clever'; George Meredith in the *Westminster Review* wrote that *Barchester Towers* was 'decidedly the cleverest novel of the season' and recommended that any novel reader who had not read Trollope get the book and its 'dashing predecessor' immediately. The *Athenaeum* was glad to find characters from *The Warden* continuing their story; readers were already interested in them, but *Barchester Towers* was even more satisfactory, more dramatic in construction, the characters more vivid, and the romance infused with 'lightness and brightness'. The *Saturday Review* called the book 'very clever . . . if anything, too clever', being a 'series of brilliant but disjointed sketches. . . . Every chapter is full of fresh amusement'; the book succeeded 'wonderfully' in treating theological disputes 'without bitterness, injustice, or profanity'; the reviewer then set forth what became commonplaces of Trollope criticism: that he is not a 'party writer' who paints the wrong party 'all black and the right party all white'; that he avoids 'the excess of exaggeration'; and that he 'possesses an especial talent for drawing what may be called the second-class of good people—characters not noble, superior, or perfect, after the standard of human perfection, but still good and honest, with a fundamental basis of sincerity, kindliness, and religious principle, yet with a considerable proneness to temptation, and a strong consciousness that they live, and like to live, in a struggling, party-giving, comfort-seeking world'.[17] (With this generally positive notice, the *Saturday Review* began its close watch on Trollope. Started by university men in 1855, the *Saturday* was a conservative, high-toned, notoriously 'clever' publication, much given to attacking popular phenomena, including, most notably, Dickens; John Bright dubbed it the 'Saturday Reviler'; Thackeray called it the 'Superfine Review' and asked whether the world were 'one great school of little boys, and the *Saturday Review* its great usher'. The *Saturday* would eventually review more than fifty of Trollope's books, providing much censure together with a good share of praise.[18])

One reader capable of appreciating Trollope's literary artistry, and knowledgeable about Anglican clergy, began a lifelong enjoyment of his fiction with this novel: John Henry Newman, former leader of the Tractarian Movement and now living in hard-working obscurity as Superior of the Birmingham Oratory, woke himself up laughing one night in 1858 at the memory of the book he had been reading—*Barchester Towers*.[19]

If the reviews of *Barchester Towers* were excellent, Trollope himself could afford years later in *An Autobiography* to be more modest, saying only that *Barchester Towers*, like *The Warden*, 'achieved no great reputation, but it was one of the novels which novel readers were called upon to read'. It became, he went on, 'one of those novels which do not die quite at once, which live and are read for perhaps a quarter of a century'.[20] In fact, *Barchester Towers* has come down to posterity as the quintessential Trollope novel. To be sure, it is still 'early' Trollope—though written when he was 41—and it lacks some of the control that came with greater maturity. The writing is in places showy, with an uncomfortable share of admonitory 'thees' and 'thous' addressed to the reader and even to the characters, and is more laden with Latin tags, foreign phrases, and literary allusions than is customary in Trollope's prose. On the other hand, this style, together with the very loose plot, is not out of place in this the most avowedly 'comic' of his novels. The book has a generous share of the mock heroic, of farce and slapstick; and Mr Slope, as a comic figure, can be more two-dimensional, more cartoon-like, than most of Trollope's characters. And yet, *Barchester Towers* is also rich in what have come to be regarded as characteristically Trollopian strengths. There are Trollope's 'personages', some carried over from *The Warden*: Archdeacon Grantly, who becomes a more sympathetic, indeed lovable character, with a worldliness that itself makes him, though a churchman, more attractive; Septimus Harding, who, though less the focus of attention than in the earlier novel, is none the less still Trollope's unlikely hero, a timid old man with a conscience who wins his distinctions by declining advancement.[21] The newcomers include the hen-pecked Bishop Proudie, the formidable Mrs Proudie, their hypocritical chaplain Mr Slope, and the unsettling family of Dr Vesey Stanhope, the absentee vicar who has spent long years collecting butterflies on Lake Como. The most memorable has proved to be the combative Mrs Proudie, more than a match for her husband and Mr Slope combined and a worthy adversary for Dr Grantly; in her militant Sabbatarianism, she is the classic killjoy of comedy, yet capable of evoking the reader's sympathy when she uses her power to champion Mrs Quiverful and her fourteen children. Slope is banished from Barchester at the novel's close; nor will he be reintroduced in future novels of the series, and no one really misses him. But many regret that Trollope never brought the Stanhope children back to Barchester. Trollope's affection for the slightly effeminate Bertie Stanhope is obvious; the narrator interjects at one point, 'Is it not a pity that people who are bright and clever should so often be exceedingly improper? and that those who are never improper should so often be dull and heavy?'[22] Though some of Bertie's irreverence is Trollope's own, perhaps this dilettantish and free-spirited artist was too clever, too jesting a critic of Trollope's beloved shire. Signora Neroni, invalid siren, luring clerics of all ranks to her couchside, flaunting her sexuality in a fashion rare in Victorian fiction (and this even after all the purifying of the text at Cauvin's insistence), may have been barred from returning in future novels by Mrs Grundy. Whatever the reason, though Stanhope *père* is briefly mentioned in later novels, his iconoclastic children are never heard from again.

Barchester Towers also boasts some of the *loci classici* of comic Trollopian dialogue, as when Bertie Stanhope befuddles the uncomprehending, newly appointed Bishop Proudie, asking him if he likes Barchester, whether he were a bishop 'before', remarking that bishops' salaries have been cut down 'to pretty nearly the same figure', that he himself had once thought of becoming a bishop, though, 'on the whole, I like the Church of Rome the best', and capping everything by announcing, 'I was a Jew once myself.'[23] Almost any snippet of dialogue has the right ring to it. Dr Stanhope and his son have this passage of arms:

> 'Yes, sir, to-morrow,' said the doctor. 'You shall leave this house to-morrow.'
> 'Very well, sir. Will the 4.30 P.M. train be soon enough?' . . .
> 'You may go how and when and where you please, so that you leave my house to-morrow. You have disgraced me, sir; you have disgraced yourself, and me, and your sisters.'
> 'I am glad at least, sir, that I have not disgraced my mother,' said Bertie.[24]

(The *Saturday*, reviewing *Can You Forgive Her?* in 1865 would remark on 'those wonderful dialogues . . . which [Trollope] goes on writing out with such amazing patience, and which are so exactly like the dialogues we hear . . . in real life. The people do not let off epigrams at one another, nor make long speeches. . . . They do literally talk.'[25] Trollope himself said that dialogue in a novel should not replicate actual speech but only 'seem to be real'.[26])

Memorable characters and convincing dialogue are augmented in *Barchester Towers* to an extraordinary degree by the character of the narrator,

\se remarks are in effect his dialogue. If a reader is to like Trollope, he must like the narrator, always present, always commenting, ever at the reader's elbow, even confiding to him some of the problems and conventions of story-telling. This kind of narrator was present in earlier Trollope, but not to an equal degree. Some celebrated instances of the narrator's commentary in *Barchester Towers* have become part of English literary history, their effectiveness much argued about over the years. The most commented upon happens in Chapter 15, less than a third of the way through the book: the heroine is being courted by two unsatisfactory suitors when the narrator breaks in: 'But let the gentle-hearted reader be under no apprehension whatsoever. It is not destined that Eleanor shall marry Mr. Slope or Bertie Stanhope.' The narrator then says he will not conceal until the end of the third volume the fate of his heroine and goes so far as to invite the reader to look through the last pages of the book, suggesting that 'the story shall have lost none of its interest. . . . Our doctrine is, that the author and reader should move along together in full confidence with each other. Let the personages of the drama undergo ever so complete a comedy of errors among themselves, but let the spectator never mistake the Syracusan for the Ephesian.' The reader need not be troubled, the novel's outcome will not be in the least painful. To have said so much does not, for Trollope, mean that he has given anything away.*

Barchester Towers, lacking some of the novel-making skills of the later books as well as their seriousness, has nevertheless a sustained gaiety and quiet irreverence, an exuberant, sunny joyfulness that have made it Trollope's most enduring comedy. For many, *Barchester Towers* remains *the* Trollope novel, and as the title most available through the years, doubtless the most popular Trollope novel.[27]

With *Barchester Towers*, his career as novelist took off. For him, this meant not only public recognition but increased pay for his manuscripts,

---

* Other notable examples of authorial 'intrusion' in the novel: in Chapter 30 (about mid-way in the story) the narrator explains that if Eleanor had given way to tears, her lover Arabin would have realized how they stood: 'But then where would have been my novel?' In Chapter 43 the narrator says, 'But we must go back a little . . . for a difficulty begins to make itself manifest in the necessity of disposing of all our friends in the small remainder of this one volume. Oh, that Mr. Longman would allow me a fourth!' Chapter 51 begins, 'We must now take leave of Mr. Slope, and of the bishop also, and of Mrs. Proudie. These leave-takings in novels are as disagreeable as they are in real life.' The concluding chapter opens, 'The end of a novel, like the end of a children's dinner party, must be made up of sweetmeats and sugar plums [i.e. a wedding].' It was such passages as these that prompted Henry James to object to Trollope's 'suicidal satisfaction in reminding the reader that the story he was telling was only, after all, a make-believe. He habitually referred to the work in hand (in the course of that work) as a novel, and to himself as a novelist. . . . These little slaps at credulity . . . are deliberately inartistic.' For James, the only legitimate stance for the novelist was that of historian; for Trollope, as for Thackeray, it included—especially in comedy—that of the artist as creator or maker.[28]

and his rate of remuneration would henceforth increase continuously, sometimes in nearly quantum leaps, until levelling off a decade later. Trollope says bluntly in *An Autobiography* that he wrote his books for money. But he confessed privately in his letters that he most assuredly would have written novels even without pay, and that his 'only doubt as to finding a heaven for myself at last, arises from the fear that the disembodied and beatified spirits will not want novels'.[29] Moreover, in *An Autobiography*, in the midst of the remarks on writing for money that his account of receiving £100 for *Barchester Towers* inspired, Trollope inserted a paragraph on 'the charms of reputation' that somewhat undercuts all the talk of money: 'I wished from the beginning to be something more than a clerk in the Post Office. To be known as somebody,—to be Anthony Trollope if it be no more,—is to me much.'[30] With *Barchester Towers* he was well on his way.

Meanwhile, even as *Barchester Towers* was receiving such good notices, Trollope was half-way through another three-decker novel, *The Three Clerks*. (The legend that Trollope began a new novel the day after completing the previous one rests on two or three such instances; usually there was a decent, even substantial interval; here, for example, he gave himself three months' rest between finishing *Barchester Towers* and commencing the new novel. He had also to do his 'castle-building' or day-dreaming about his characters.) By writing steadily he was able on 15 July 1857 to tell Longman that the new three-volume novel was 'all but finished'; he also asked whether at Christmas Longman would be interested in a short, one-volume novel to be called *The Struggles of Brown, Jones, and Robinson*—'intended as a hit at the present system of advertising'. He added smilingly, 'Publishers' advertisements are not reflected on.' Longman stalled on the short novel as well as on the more serious issue of the success of the sales of *Barchester Towers*, which would have a definite bearing on the price to be paid for the next novel. Trollope wrote with only thinly disguised impatience on 21 August asking whether Longman was willing to deal with him 'on such terms as are usual for works of fiction of fair success'; he wanted a price he could consider 'in some way remunerative'.[31]

Longman's answer can be gleaned from Trollope's reply a week later: 'I certainly did mean you to understand by my last letter that I should want a better price for another novel;' he would accept nothing less than double that which he had received for *Barchester Towers*. If Longman were unwilling to give more than a £100 advance, it was hardly worth while for the publisher to have the manuscript read: 'I am sure you do not regard £100 as adequate payment for a 3 vol. novel. Of course an unsuccessful novel may be worth much less—worth indeed less than nothing. And it may very likely be that I cannot write a successful novel, but if I cannot obtain moderate success I will give over, and leave the business alone. I certainly will not willingly go on working at such a rate of pay.'[32] This was bargaining bluster, for Trollope was already addicted to novel writing and would by no means have left off; moreover, as both he and Longman knew, *Barchester Towers* had brought its author considerable popularity. Trollope believed his reputation was now such that the publisher was taking no great risk with another novel; furthermore, he wanted a lump sum down, rather than a 'deferred annuity'; he believed he had reached a point at which he deserved something more definite than 'half-profits'. Longman tried once more the argument about the prestige of his firm's name on the title-page as worth more than increased payment. To Trollope this smacked of that 'high-flown doctrine of the contempt of money which I have never admired. I did think much of Messrs. Longman's name, but I liked it best at the bottom of a cheque.' The publisher's refusal of increased payment for *The Three Clerks* threw cold water on the short novel about advertising, and Trollope broke off after having worked on it for only two weeks. The rupture with Longman's confirmed Trollope's suspicion that the publisher had little regard for fiction; earlier, on one of his infrequent visits to the firm's place of business he had already been somewhat put off, or, as he said, 'scared from the august columns of Paternoster Row' by a remark of one of Longman's firm to him censuring a fertile writer of novels (probably G. P. R. James) who 'had spawned upon them (the publishers) three novels a year'.[33] The words struck him as wrong-headed and funny; they stuck in his mind, and he alluded to them with suppressed glee four times in *An Autobiography.*

Trollope next offered *The Three Clerks* to Hurst & Blackett, successors since 1855 to Colburn. He had an appointment with the publisher on the one day available to him on his way through London en route to a holiday with Rose in Italy. He waited with growing impatience for an hour in the office in Great Marlborough Street for the 'peccant publisher' who did not keep his appointment. As Trollope was going the foreman begged him to leave the manuscript, but Trollope wanted immediate acceptance. The foreman, lacking authority to oblige, instead gave him some advice: 'I hope it's not historical, Mr. Trollope? . . . Whatever you do, don't be historical; your historical novel is not worth a damn.'[34] The man was unaware that Trollope's one historical novel, published in 1850 by Hurst &

Blackett's predecessor, pretty much fitted that description. Trollope liked the man's phrase, and later incorporated the incident in the opening pages of *Castle Richmond*; similarly in *The Way We Live Now*, a publisher tells Lady Carbury, who is about to take up novel writing, that her book must be a love story, that it must not end unhappily ('people like it in a play, they hate it in a book'), and that, above all, it must not be historical: 'Your historical novel, Lady Carbury, isn't worth a ——.'[35]

Trollope then took the manuscript unannounced to Richard Bentley, who ten years earlier had turned down *The Kellys and the O'Kellys*. In *An Autobiography* Trollope said that he succeeded in selling it on the spot, unread, for £250; in fact, he left the manuscript with Bentley, and acceptance was not made until he passed through London on his return from abroad, on 17 October. But the increase to £250 was real enough.[36]

The Three Clerks was a novel close to Trollope's heart, for the story's setting was the Civil Service, something he knew intimately and, by now, loved dearly. In such a novel he could display his insider's knowledge of the system, from Secretaries and Assistant Secretaries down through the various ranks to the lowliest of clerks; he could incorporate the recent experience of his long and creditable stint before a Parliamentary Committee. Having attacked the new system of competitive examinations in a magazine essay (and countless times in private discussion), he now did so with a lighter touch: Sir Charles Trevelyan, the 'great apostle' of Civil Service reform, would be good-naturedly caricatured as Sir Gregory Hardlines (Trollope and Trevelyan later became friends; Lady Trevelyan said that after the novel Trevelyan was always called Sir Gregory). Sir Stafford Northcote would appear under what Trollope deemed the 'feebly facetious name' of Sir Warwick West End.[37] Some of Benjamin Jowett's sanguine energies for examinations would be lampooned in the Revd Mr Jobbles; during a viva voce Jobbles puts questions to a candidate, Mr Alphabet Precis:

'Could you tell me now, how would you calculate the distance in inches, say from London Bridge to the nearest portion of Jupiter's disc, at twelve o'clock on the 1st of April?' Mr. Jobbles . . . spoke in a tone conciliating and gentle, as though he were asking Mr. Precis to dine with him. . . . But, nevertheless, Mr. Precis looked very blank. 'I am not asking the distance, you know,' said Mr. Jobbles, smiling sweeter than ever; 'I am only asking how you would compute it.' But still Mr. Precis looked exceedingly blank.[38]

The novel was a satiric but affectionate look at the Civil Service. But what most compelled Trollope's attachment to the book was its picture of one of the three government clerks of the title, Charley Tudor. Trollope places him in a very inefficient imaginary department, Internal (or 'Infernal') Navigation (the other two are clerks in the efficient and very real Weights and Measures Department). Tudor, unhappy in his work, in debt, getting in with fast friends, nearly marrying a barmaid, all the while aspiring to authorship, is a not too carefully disguised self-portrait, though nowhere near as doleful a figure as the young clerk Trollope described as himself in *An Autobiography*.

The Three Clerks also has a prominent court-room scene, something Trollope, like so many Victorian novelists, relished. (Trollope's novels feature eleven jury trials, well over a hundred lawyers, and innumerable points of law; lawyers and the law were a career-long obsession with him.) The trial opened the way for the barrister Chaffanbrass, a character in whom Trollope took great pride and satisfaction. Chaffanbrass grew out of 'Mr. Allwinde', the barrister of *The New Zealander* who is so roundly criticized by Trollope for using the technicalities of law to defend a murderer; Allwinde's greatest sin is his browbeating and 'bamboozling' of witnesses until the poor wretches don't know their left hand from their right. (In Trollope's view, everyone concerned in a trial, including defence counsel, ought to have as his object the 'truth'.) Chaffanbrass similarly makes it his speciality to confuse juries by abusing witnesses, but since he is attacking a witness who is himself the chief swindler in his client's case, the reader delights in seeing his victim sweat and contradict himself to the derision of the court. Chaffanbrass would reappear, in *Orley Farm*, again defending a guilty party, but because she is so decent a person, her one illegal act so understandable, and because her adversaries are so greedy, the reader cannot help but applaud Chaffanbrass's performance on her behalf. And in *Phineas Redux*, Chaffanbrass has the reader entirely on his side as he defends the innocent Finn by destroying the testimony of the befuddled Lord Fawn. Over the years the simplicities of *The New Zealander* were abandoned. Chaffanbrass has been called Victorian fiction's most memorable barrister, and Trollope had good reason to be proud of him. All in all Trollope thought *The Three Clerks* 'certainly the best novel I had as yet written', believing it had more 'continued interest' throughout, his first 'well-described love-scene', and a scene of pathos—Katie Woodward's near death-bed farewell to her lover—that years later could still bring tears to his eyes.[39]

Trollope's own fondness for *The Three Clerks* is more understandable than that of his contemporary critics and readers, who, differing radically with the verdict of posterity, generally agreed that *The Three Clerks* was an improvement on *Barchester Towers*. The *Leader* thought *The Three Clerks* the best of his novels: 'the scene of action is wider, the interest is more varied, characters are drawn from more general classes'; the reviewer also found more of the tragic than in the earlier books. The *Saturday Review* said *The Three Clerks*, in spite of some faults, was more rich in promise, particularly because of its heroines: 'These girls are like real girls. They have the strong and the weak points of young women in real life. . . . neither too good nor too bad, and with more freshness and life about them than is to be seen in the heroines of one novel out of a hundred.'[40] In Florence, Thomas Adolphus lent the book to the Brownings, and Elizabeth Barrett wrote back: 'We both quite agree with you in considering it the best of the three clever novels before the public. My husband, who can seldom get a novel to hold him, has been held by all three, and by this the strongest. Also, it has qualities which the others gave no sign of. For instance, I was wrung to tears by the third volume.' And Thackeray himself, Trollope's idol in the distance, would eventually tell Trollope that here was one novel that could hold him awake after dinner.[41]

There were objections too, of course. The *Athenaeum* complained of the book as 'rambling and straggling in its construction', and marred by digressions and irrelevancies. The *Saturday* hoped Trollope would tone down his 'smarter style', tidy up 'traces of rapid writing', and eliminate such glaring blunders as the pamphlet-like chapter on the Civil Service; the same reviewer found Trollope's law wrong, in having his villain tried under the Fraudulent Trustee Act before it received royal assent, and in allowing the defence counsel to threaten to put a witness into the dock and the prisoner into the witness-box; 'Why do not novelists consult some legal friend before they write about law? Is it impossible to find a barrister who has a hobby for criminal law and also a hobby for criticizing novels?' In *Doctor Thorne*, his next novel, Trollope has the narrator allude three times to the *Saturday*'s suggestion, saying he would be happy to pay his share, but insisting that until novelists have in fact clubbed together to keep a barrister, he shall have to arrange legal matters as 'the course of my narrative . . . demands'. A little later the narrator says, 'I know I am wrong, my much and truly-honoured critic, about these title-deeds and documents. But when we've got that barrister in hand, then if I go wrong after that, let the blame be on my own shoulders—or on his.'[42] The *Saturday*, in turn, reviewing *Doctor Thorne* alluded to Trollope's taking notice of their criticism: 'We are flattered by his readiness to take advice . . . but . . . Mr. Trollope does not meet our point. . . . he wantonly points out the difficulties of his task, and says that there is a way out of them, but that he does not choose to take the trouble to find it.'[43] This was far from the last of Trollope's difficulties with critics over his handling of the law, nor was it by any means his last contest with the *Saturday*.

13

<hr>

Egypt and the Holy Land

IN January 1858, when Trollope was half-way through writing *Doctor Thorne*, the 'great men at the General Post Office' asked him to go to Egypt to arrange a postal treaty and afterwards to inspect postal operations at Malta and Gibraltar. He arrived in London on 20 January and spent ten days being briefed on his assignment, during which time he was unable to write anything of the novel. He did, however, while in the capital, go to work among the publishers. Convinced that by now he could get a good price for a novel while it was being written, he saw Bentley and 'demanded' £400 for the entire copyright of *Doctor Thorne*. Bentley agreed, but the next day, according to Trollope, came around to the General Post Office, saying that he had miscalculated the sale of *The Three Clerks* and could offer but £300, a figure he put in writing on 25 January. On the 27th Bentley sweetened the offer somewhat: £300 for the first 1,250 copies, an additional £50 on the sale of these and a further £100 for a future printing. But Trollope wanted his price outright, independent of sales, and went 'in furious haste,—for I had but an hour then at my disposal'—to Chapman & Hall in Piccadilly. This was the firm that had, famously, launched the unknown Charles Dickens in 1836 with *Pickwick Papers*, introduced monthly shilling-part serialization of novels, and been one of the pioneers in publishing cheap reprints. In Edward Chapman's 'back-shop', Trollope in a 'quick torrent of words' stated his case and asked £400 for the novel in progress. The publisher, in Trollope's account, regarding his visitor as he might 'a highway robber who had stopped him on Hounslow Heath', and holding the fire poker in his hand all the time Trollope was speaking, said 'he supposed he might as well do as I desired'.[1] The agreement was signed on 29 January, and the next day Trollope left for the East. Trollope's publishing connection with Chapman & Hall was to continue, side by side with many others, until his death.

The Dover–Calais passage made him, though an experienced traveller, 'very sick', as he told Rose, and he was hardly himself even the next day in

Paris, in spite of a very good dinner at the Hôtel des Princes, with Tom Trollope (who was selling off some of his belongings to get over financial trouble). On 1 February, Trollope visited Chartres, and wrote home the following day promising to take Rose there, as the 'magnificent' stained glass struck him, like everyone else, as 'the finest in the world'. He had also got back to writing *Doctor Thorne* in spite of other provocations to sightseeing, especially tempting in Tom's company: 'I have not been inside the Louvre,' he told Rose. 'It is now one, and I have been writing all day—I must do 5 of my pages daily, or I cannot accomplish my task—Do not be dismal if you can help it—I feel a little that way inclined, but hard work will I know keep it off.'² He wrote steadily, missing only occasional days between then and the completion of the book at the end of March. From Paris Trollope travelled across France to Marseilles, whence he sailed, via Malta, for Alexandria. The voyage was made in miserable February weather, but Trollope, in spite of seasickness, still managed his daily stint of writing: 'more than once I left my paper on the cabin table, rushing away to be sick in the privacy of my state room. . . . real exertion will enable most men to work at almost any season.'³

He arrived at Alexandria on 10 February and quickly discharged his secondary assignment, that of rendering a judgement on the substitution of bags for boxes for mail sent through Egypt to India and Australia. Trollope was all in favour of the change, but only after the railway line from Alexandria to Suez was completed. With a caravan of eighty or ninety camels, 'where so many Arabs are employed—one namely to each camel—it is impossible to answer for the conduct of them all.'⁴ Trollope's advice was followed, and eventually the use of bags become universal.

The real business of the mission, negotiating a postal treaty with the Egyptians for the conveyance of mail overland from Alexandria to Suez via the soon-to-be-completed railway line, took more time and patience. Trollope's dealings were with Nubar Bey, of the Egyptian Transit Administration, an Armenian-born diplomat who later, as 'Nubar Pasha', became three times premier of Egypt. Nubar Bey came to Trollope's hotel every other day, bringing with him servants, pipes, and coffee. Trollope found him 'a most courteous gentleman' and his company enjoyable. Nubar Bey quickly acceded to most of the British terms, including money (much of the treaty having been worked out in advance by John Green, Acting British Consul General and postal agent at Alexandria), but he stubbornly held out for allowing forty-eight hours for the transport of mail from Alexandria to Suez, while Trollope insisted on twenty-four hours, 'sea to sea'. Nubar Bey claimed that if the Pasha signed the treaty he himself should resign, saying, according to Trollope, that the 'loss of life and bloodshed which would certainly follow so rash an attempt should not be on his head'. Trollope divined that the insistence on 'tranquillity' rather than 'celerity' in transit came from the (British) Peninsular and Oriental Steamship Company, to whom the Egyptians were beholden for a debt of some seventy or eighty thousand pounds. So Trollope adopted a stance he called 'oriental quiescence' combined with 'British firmness'.[5] (Nubar Bey, in the 1880s, said that Trollope's 'manner of negotiating had about it less of the diplomatist than of the author who might have meditated scolding his publisher if he did not come round to his terms, and of carrying his literary wares elsewhere'.[6]) Eventually the Egyptians relented, and most cordially. All the objections had been, Trollope later told headquarters, 'moonshine': 'I believe that one should never give way in any thing to an Oriental. Nubar Bey, who now that the treaty is signed declares that there will be no difficulty in carrying it out, assured me at least a dozen times, that if the viceroy insisted on signing such an agreement he would at once abandon his office, seeing that the work . . . would be absolutely impracticable!' The treaty was signed in London on 16 July, and Trollope was commended in the Postmaster-General's Annual Report to Parliament.[7]

Trollope enjoyed seeing the 'picturesque' East. In the midst of the negotiations with Nubar Bey at Alexandria, he went on business to Cairo for a week and Suez for five days, and took a holiday of ten days in the Holy Land. Looking about, even as he was working almost daily on *Doctor Thorne*, he was taking mental notes on his travels that he would incorporate into his next novel (*The Bertrams*), a work which in some ways anticipated his travel books. The narrator keeps apologizing for the travel commentary, but doing it all the same. (*Bentley's Quarterly Review* regarded Trollope's insertion of descriptions of his own travel as a 'detriment' to the novel; the *Athenaeum* complained, 'To be taken to the East twice in one novel, passes permission with the most patient reader.'[8]) The novel says that though Alexandria was the mother of science and once the favoured seat of the earth's learning, it is now the 'most detestable of cities. . . . it has all the filth of the East without any of that picturesque beauty with which the East abounds; and it has the eternal, grasping, solemn love of lucre that pervades our western marts, but wholly unredeemed by the society, the science, and civilization of the West.' Suez is a 'triste, unhappy, wretched place . . . a small Oriental town, now much be-Europeanized. . . . it has neither water, air, nor verdure. No trees grow there, no rivers flow there. Men drink brine and eat goats; and the thermometer stands at eighty in the shade in winter. The oranges are the only luxury.' Cairo, on the other hand, is much more alluring, 'a beautiful old city—so old in realities of age that it is crumbling into dust on every side. . . . It is full of romance, of picturesque Oriental wonders, of strange sights, strange noises, and strange smells.' He will not, the narrator says, write a description of the city, but he does spend ten pages telling about the whirling dervishes there. The nearby pyramids are spoiled by the guides who 'in their stench, their obscene indecency, their chattering noise, their rapacity, exercised without a moment's intercession . . . make a visit to the Pyramids no delightful recreation'; moreover, the interiors of the great monuments have nothing to offer the visitor but 'dirt, noise, stench, vermin, abuse, and want of air'. Another, very different attraction of Cairo (and one which he recommended to his Post Office colleague Edmund Yates) was Shepheard's Hotel, playfully described as 'the centre of Egypt' for Englishmen: 'our countrymen have made this spot more English than England itself. If ever John Bull reigned triumphant any where; if ever he shows his nature plainly marked by rough plenty, coarseness, and good intention, he does so at Shepheard's Hotel.'9

The novel's hero, George Bertram, who as traveller is for all practical purposes Trollope himself, is displeased with Jerusalem; he arrives sore of body from riding in a Turkish saddle, and has difficulty finding his 'd——d hotel' in a 'steep, narrow, ill-paved lane, with a half-formed gully in the middle, very slippery with orange-peel and old vegetables'; he visits the Church of the Holy Sepulchre, at Easter time, and views all the 'absurdity' within, including five different churches under one roof, from the 'gaudy and glittering' shrine of the Greeks to the 'dark, unfurnished, gloomy cave in which the Syrian Christians worship'; from a gallery above he glimpses the 'mumblement, jumblement' of a Greek mass. Struggling to get to the tomb believed to be the holy sepulchre, he is bothered by the 'unpleasant, unwashed, uncleanly Christians of so many nations' who hardly seem brothers of his own creed. He touches the slab of the tomb, as dangerous-looking, skin-clothed, dirty young Greeks reverently kiss the sepulchre: 'It was thus that Bertram . . . would have felt, thus that he would have acted had he been able.'10 Only the Mount of Olives, with its quiet view of the Holy City, impresses Bertram.

But the criticism falls quickly back on English travellers: a jolly, fat maiden lady of about 40, good-natured but indifferent to foreign sensitivities, holds a picnic outside Jerusalem for a party of eleven. Her food hampers are set up 'immediately opposite [the tomb] of St. James the Less . . . situated in the middle of the valley of Jehoshaphat, in the centre of myriads of Jewish tombs, directly opposite to the wall built with those huge temple stones, not many feet over the then dry watercourse of the brook Kedron. Such was the spot chosen by Miss Todd for her cold chickens and Champagne.' The narrator observes: 'Here, in England, one would hardly inaugurate a picnic to Kensal Green, or the Highgate Cemetery, nor select the tombs of our departed great ones as a shelter under which to draw one's corks'; but away from home English people, uniquely, do such things: 'To other people is wanting sufficient pluck for such enterprises; is wanting also a certain mixture of fun, honest independence, and bad taste.' The narrator is provoked to expand on the theme of the Englishman abroad:

Let us go into some church on the Continent—in Italy, we will say—where the walls of the churches still boast of the great works of the great masters. Look at that man standing on the very altar-step while the priest is saying his mass; look at his gray shooting-coat, his thick shoes, his wide-awake hat stuck under one arm, and his stick under the other, while he holds his opera-glass to his eyes. How he shuffles about to get the best point of sight, quite indifferent as to clergy or laity! All that bell-ringing, incense-flinging, and breast-striking is nothing to him: he has paid dearly to be brought thither; he has paid the guide who is kneeling a little behind him; he is going to pay the sacristan who attends him; he is quite ready to pay the priest himself . . . but he has come there to see that fresco, and see it he will. . . . Perhaps some servant of the Church . . . begs him to step back for just a moment. The lover of art glares at him with insulted look, and hardly deigns to notice him farther; he merely turns his eye to his Murray, puts his hat down on the altar-step, and goes on studying his subject. All the world—German, Frenchman, Italian, Spaniard—all men of all nations know that that ugly gray shooting-coat contains an Englishman.[11]

That which Dickens, half a dozen years later, would call podsnappery had an unfailing allure for Trollope.

Trollope returned to Alexandria on 24 March; on the 31st he completed *Doctor Thorne* and the next day began *The Bertrams*. On 4 April he sailed for Malta, a five-day voyage, where he stayed for a week, inspecting postal arrangements there. His report to Rowland Hill is typical of his efficient, no-nonsense, yet humane approach to such inspections. He has brought 'some points' to the postmaster's attention, but nothing requiring the notice of the Postmaster-General; he finds the personnel too numerous for the work, even in so hot a climate; of the eight employees, two, a clerk and a stamper, could be dispensed with; but no clerk should be dismissed as it would 'probably be considered a hardship to deprive the man of his situation', and Trollope suggests instead that the next vacancy should not be filled up, and the money of that salary used to increase the pay of the remaining five clerks; the stamper would become a letter-carrier. Trollope also thought the hours too long, and that at least three hours per week could be taken from each clerk's schedule. He believed the account forms used in Malta created unnecessary labour and should be simplified. All his recommendations were approved by the Postmaster-General.[12] Trollope liked Malta, and in *The Bertrams* had the narrator say, 'Of Malta I should like to write a book, and may perhaps do so some day; but I shall hardly have time to discuss its sunlight, and fortifications, and hospitality, and old magnificence in the fag-end of this volume.'[13]

Trollope then sailed for Gibraltar, where he made a similar postal inspection, and was able to take a six-day holiday about southern Spain. In a short story, 'John Bull on the Guadalquivir', Trollope would recount one of his own experiences when the narrator and a friend, travelling up the Guadalquivir (a 'brown and dirty' river in no way 'as lovely and poetical as its name') to Seville, mistake a Spanish duke—who understood English— for a bullfighter; the two Englishmen admire his 'outlandish' dress, finger the gold buttons and tags, even hold up the man's arm to 'see the cut of his coat', making all the while condescending remarks. The Spaniard takes the incident good-humouredly, but (as Trollope said in *An Autobiography*) when his identity is made known, 'how thoroughly he covered us with ridicule!'[14] At Seville, the narrator is 'inexpressibly charmed with the whole city' and especially with the cathedral: 'There hardly stands . . . on earth a building more remarkable than the cathedral of Seville, and hardly one more grand. Its enormous size; its gloom and darkness; the richness of ornamentation in the details, contrasted with the severe simplicity of the larger outlines; the variety of its architecture; the glory of its paintings; and the wondrous splendour of its metallic decoration, its altar-friezes, screens, rails, gates, and the like, render it, to my mind, the first in interest among churches.' In the cathedral he encounters a boisterous party of his countrymen, among them three young gentlemen, swinging big sticks, laughing and talking loudly as they hurry along, boorishly unheedful 'that the edifice they were treading was a church, and that the silence they were invading was the cherished property of a courteous people'.[15] 'John Bull on the Guadalquivir' was aptly named.

Trollope sailed from Gibraltar on 3 May, arriving at Southampton on 10 May, and the next day was in London, where he remained for ten days, making further reports to headquarters on his mission. *Doctor Thorne*, the second half of the manuscript having been mailed to the publisher from Egypt, was about to be published. This novel was the one instance in which Trollope admitted to having used someone's else's story: while in Florence the previous September he had been unsuccessfully cudgelling his brain for a new plot and had asked help from Tom, who then sketched for him the story that became *Doctor Thorne*.[16] The plot, as Trollope developed it, is more contrived, more sensational than usual (at least at this stage of his career): the family of the Squire of Greshamsbury oppose the marriage of the son and heir Frank Gresham to Mary Thorne, the niece of the village physician, Doctor Thorne; they insist that Frank 'marry money', because the estate is embarrassed, some of it sold to and the rest mortgaged to a self-made millionaire railway builder, Sir Roger Scatcherd. Unknown to all but her uncle, Mary is actually the illegitimate daughter of Scatcherd's sister, who twenty years earlier had been seduced by Dr Thorne's brother. The enraged Scatcherd, then a stonemason, murdered the seducer and was sent briefly to prison for manslaughter; the young mother emigrated to Australia, secretly leaving the child everyone believed to have died in the care of Doctor Thorne. Twenty years later the now wealthy Scatcherd, an incurable alcoholic, drinks himself to death, leaving a will stipulating that his fortune shall go to his son at the age of 25; should he die earlier, it is to go to his sister's 'eldest child'. The son dies; Mary, Scatcherd's sister's 'eldest child', inherits, and Frank Gresham 'marries money'. In some ways the plot stretches credulity: as one reviewer remarked, it seemed almost 'an abuse of the bottle in fiction' to have both Scatcherds, father and son, conveniently die of *delirium tremens* to arrange the denouement.[17]

But the public liked the story very much. It was a critical and commercial success on its first appearance and was reprinted during Trollope's lifetime more often than any other of his novels.* Trollope saw its popularity as amounting to evidence that 'plot' was very important to the public, whereas to him a novel was essentially a picture crowded with 'real portraits', a depiction of 'common life enlivened by humour and sweetened by pathos'.[18] Yet the ingenious plot of *Doctor Thorne*, whether or not it is 'better' than those of his own devising, does not set it much apart from Trollope's other novels: here as elsewhere in Trollope, it is the process that

* One survey shows *Doctor Thorne* reissued 34 times during Trollope's lifetime (20 English issues, 8 American, 6 continental); its nearest competitor was *Framley Parsonage* with 23 issues (10 English, 8 American, 5 continental); other frequently reissued titles included *The Warden*, *Barchester Towers*, *Orley Farm*, *Can You Forgive Her?*, and, surprisingly, *The Bertrams*, *Castle Richmond*, and *The Belton Estate*. The figures can be misleading, as the size of the issues is not known, nor, in some cases, the extent to which a 'new edition' was in fact no more than the binding up of old sheets with new title-pages; still, the figures for *Doctor Thorne* are impressive.[19]

interests. The reader knows, hundreds of pages ahead of time, that Scatcherd's son will die before his twenty-fifth birthday, that Mary will inherit the fortune and marry Frank, that the old Greshamsbury estates will be united. It is, after all, in spite of its somewhat serious and melodramatic outline, a satiric comedy, and marked, as reviewers said, by 'piquant' and 'broad' yet sympathetic and restrained humour.[20]

Trollope placed the story in Barsetshire (another reason for its success), and used it as a vehicle for looking closely at rural England. The opening speaks of the West Country county of Barsetshire as

not so full of life, indeed, nor so widely spoken of as some of its manufacturing leviathan brethren in the north, but which is, nevertheless, very dear to those who know it well. Its green pastures, its waving wheat, its deep and shady and— let us add—dirty lanes, its paths and stiles, its tawny-coloured, well-built rural churches, its avenues of beeches, and frequent Tudor mansions, its constant county hunt, its social graces, and the general air of clanship which pervades it, has made it to its own inhabitants a favoured land of Goschen. It is purely agricultural; agricultural in its produce, agricultural in its poor, and agricultural in its pleasures.

The narrator clearly loves rural England* and is more drawn to 'landed powers' than to the new captains of industry or commerce. And yet Barsetshire's own landed Whig aristocracy is satirized rather than the representatives of commerce or new money—the millionaire railway builder Scatcherd, or Miss Dunstable, the charmingly irreverent heiress of the 'Ointment of Lebanon' money. The Duke of Omnium, the richest duke in England, here makes his first, albeit brief entrance—literally, for he comes in by a side door to one of the occasional 'hospitable' dinners he gives for the important people of the county, talks to no one, eats his dinner, and departs. A tall, thin, plain man, undistinguished in appearance except for a gleam of pride in his eye always proclaiming, 'I am

---

* Trollope said in *Australia and New Zealand*: 'A writer attempting to describe England . . . would fill those chapters with strongest interest in which he painted various forms of English country life. He would know, and he would teach his readers, that the English character with its faults and virtues, its prejudices and steadfastness, can be better studied in the mansions of noblemen, in country-houses, in parsonages, in farms and small meaningless towns, than in the great cities, devoted as is London to politics and gaiety, or as are Glasgow, Manchester, Birmingham, and others like them, to manufactures and commerce. I doubt whether this be so in any other country. France has many aspects, but the Parisian aspect is more French than any other. Italy is seen only in her cities. In the United States the towns altogether overrule and subdue the country. . . . But the visitors to England who have not sojourned at a country-house, whether it be squire's, parson's, or farmer's, have not seen the most English phase of the country.'[21]

the Duke of Omnium,' he is unmarried, and said to be a 'great debauchee' and indifferent to everything but his own pleasure. He will remain a constant and important background presence in the remaining Barsetshire novels and gain still more prominence in the first three Palliser novels. Towards the Duke the author's attitude is one of disapproval mixed with grudging admiration; towards the other great Whig family, the De Courcys, it is altogether critical. Trollope's comic attack on aristocrats extends from the beginning to the end of his career; he is always after them, sometimes playfully, sometimes harshly (the great exception will be Plantagenet Palliser, the next Duke of Omnium). The De Courcys are self-satisfied, arrogant, venal, and money-grubbing. The Earl himself is withdrawn and disagreeable; his haughty, scheming wife is the great advocate of 'marrying money'. The Earl's sister, Lady Arabella, married to Squire Gresham, follows the same doctrine, and never lets anyone forget she is a De Courcy (after the birth of her son, she 'of course could not suckle the young heir herself. Ladies Arabella never can. They are gifted with the powers of being mothers, but not nursing-mothers. Nature gives them bosoms for show, but not for use'). The eldest De Courcy son, Lord Porlock, who has quarrelled with his family, is not much in evidence, but his brothers are: the second son cynically proposes marriage to Miss Dunstable, whom he barely knows, in a transparent bid for her fortune, telling her that his eldest brother is unmarried and not likely to perpetuate the family honours because of 'all manner of troublesome liaisons'. The third son laments bitterly that there is little chance for him, very small hope that 'all those who were nearest and dearest to him should die out of the way, and leave him to the sweet enjoyment of an earl's coronet and fortune'.[22] (In *The Small House at Allington*, where the entire De Courcy clan are leading figures, Porlock, late in life, will marry to spite his brothers.) A De Courcy daughter, Lady Amelia, talks her cousin Augusta Gresham out of marrying a mere lawyer, urging how in families like theirs blood is everything; four years later, the Lady Amelia marries him herself.

The strategy of making Doctor Thorne the central figure was doubtless Trollope's own, rather than Tom's. In *The Three Clerks* he had depicted in Charley Tudor a fictional version of himself as a young man; in Thomas Thorne he presented, perhaps largely unconsciously, a portrait, somewhat idealized, of himself in his forties. Thorne, like Trollope, came from an ancient but no longer thriving family; he is proud of his blood, but rebellious against rank; 'he did not absolutely tell the Earl De Courcy in words, that the privilege of dining at Courcy Castle was to him no greater than the privilege of dining at Courcy Parsonage; but there was that in his manner that told it.' He befriends the low-born, drunken, but talented Scatcherd; he believes his illegitimate niece worthy of the hand of any Gresham. But in spite of his 'democratic' views, 'at heart he was a thorough Conservative.' Without an income from old money, Doctor Thorne, like Trollope, must earn his way by a 'professional career', at which he works hard: 'It was something in his favour that he understood his business; something that he was willing to labour at it with energy; and resolved to labour at it conscientiously.' When excited, he can be very 'wrathful'; he is 'combative' and 'vehement' in opinions and action; when it appears possible, for example, that his adopted daughter will become an heiress, he is 'unable to prevent himself from building happy castles in the air'. Especially in his public career, his disposition, 'until it was understood, did not ingratiate him' with others: 'He was brusque, authoritative, given to contradiction, rough though never dirty in his personal belongings, and inclined to indulge in a sort of quiet raillery, which sometimes was not thoroughly understood. People did not always know whether he was laughing at them or with them.' But underneath Thorne's professional and 'manly' vigour he is mush—possessed of 'an almost womanly tenderness'. Thorne shares with Trollope 'an aptitude for the society of children. He delighted to talk to children, and to play with them. He would carry them on his back, three or four at a time, roll with them on the ground, race with them in the gardens, invent games for them, contrive amusements in circumstances which seemed quite adverse to all manner of delight.'[23] The book's descriptions of Doctor Thorne echo almost literally what contemporaries were to write about Trollope. Doctor Thorne was Trollope's kind of hero.

While in London in May, Trollope saw Edward Chapman and was paid the £400 for *Doctor Thorne*. The publisher, apparently at this time (the agreement is undated), contracted to pay £400 for *The Bertrams*; moreover, half of the copyright was to revert to Trollope after three years, in the kind of arrangement he had sought in vain from Longman. Trollope also raised the possibility of the short, one-volume novel, *Brown, Jones, and Robinson*, to be published at Christmas, priced £150 with his name, £120 if published anonymously, Trollope's preference being for the latter arrangement. After a month, Chapman declined the short novel: 'I should not like to do it without your name & at the same time I feel convinced that it is better that your name should be withheld, for there is a strong impression abroad that you are writing too rapidly for your permanent fame.'[24] Chapman had just read Sir Henry Maine's article in the *Saturday*

Review which said that though *Doctor Thorne*, the latest proof of Trollope's 'fecundity', was good news, it none the less caused uneasiness about the 'rapid multiplication of his progeny'. A few months later, the *National Review*, in a favourable overview of the four novels that began with *The Warden*, complained that the production of two three-volume novels within ten months did not allow an author time to 'to give due polish and completion' to his work, and regretted that Trollope 'should be guilty of the bad taste of counting quantity before quality'. Of Trollope's next novel, the *Spectator* said, 'The fact is he writes too fast. An average six or eight months is too short a time for the gestation and production of a first-class novel.'[25] Trollope, though he now gave close attention to reviews, dismissed these warnings. Writing later about his beginning *The Bertrams* the day after he finished *Doctor Thorne*, he said, with some irony, that he had determined 'to excel, if not in quality, at any rate in quantity'. He considered himself a workman, and was proud of never having 'scamped' his work. Then, without irony, he went on: 'My novels, whether good or bad, have been as good as I could make them. Had I taken three months of idleness between each they would have been no better.' This much he firmly believed. But he paid heed to complaints of overproduction to the extent of keeping alive in the back of his mind the plan for anonymous publication. In due course he would try it. In the mean time, he was happy with his pace, his reputation, and with his rate of remuneration. Reviews had been generally very favourable, and he had signed consecutive agreements for £400 per novel. He had, he later said, at this point, 'achieved my object': he stood well with publishers and could certainly sell any novel he wrote, and if he wrote three novels every two years, just half the fertility of the author who had so annoyed the publisher in Paternoster Row, he would, at this rate of payment, add £600 to his yearly income, raising it to a comfortable £1,400. Such success 'had been slow in coming, but was very pleasant when it came'.[26]

Rose joined him in London in mid-May and then accompanied him on postal duties to Mansfield in Nottinghamshire, to Ollerton near Sherwood Forest, and then to York and Edinburgh. After three days' work in Edinburgh Trollope took a ten-day leave while he and Rose toured Scotland, going as far north as Inverness, and then back down to Glasgow, where she left for Ireland, and Trollope remained, revising the Glasgow Post Office.

Trollope spent most of the summer there, returning to work at home for only three weeks in July and also putting in time briefly at Liverpool,

Manchester, Edinburgh, and Fort William (whence he took a five-day holiday by himself in the Isle of Skye). At Glasgow Trollope walked through the entire city with the letter-carriers, going up to the top-floor flats of the houses in the midsummer heat. He found it weary work, and so did the men—but they, he said, did not have to go home and write love scenes. And those that he wrote at Glasgow, for *The Bertrams*, he considered 'not good'.[27] In fact he was unable to write much at Glasgow or elsewhere this summer, and during one stretch, from 6 August to 19 September, he did no work at all on the novel, and entered a woeful 'Ah me!' four times in the working diary of *The Bertrams*. He did manage during this time to cut *The Three Clerks* for Bentley's five-shilling edition of the novel, 'working very painfully' to eliminate sixty-four pages, including the entire essay-like chapter on the Civil Service. A year later he told Bentley, who wanted a further reduction, 'It gives more trouble to strike out pages, than to write new ones, as the whole sequence of a story, hangs page on page.' During that time, when Trollope's earlier books, including the Irish ones, were being reissued in cheap editions, he reduced *The Macdermots*, cutting about a hundred pages, including three entire chapters, for Chapman & Hall's one-volume edition (effecting considerable improvement in the novel, especially in the ending). But he greatly disliked revising published work, and for all practical purposes never did so again.[28]

14

◆─▶◀◀◀─◆

The West Indies

TROLLOPE was in Ireland by 12 September and working his own district, with frequent trips to Belfast. But he was gaining a reputation as trouble-shooter for the Post Office, and his success in Egypt prompted officials to send him on a more difficult and complex mission, to the West Indies.

On 2 November he arrived in London for two weeks' briefing. While there he took part in the meeting that organized the Post Office Library and Literary Association, and was asked to second the resolution officially establishing it. In his speech he called on his listeners to take pride in the Civil Service ('I, myself, love the Post Office. I have belonged to it since I left school. I work with all my heart'). He expressed optimism about the Library, which had received many books: 'I thought the titles of all the books printed within the last three centuries were going to be read out' (the first donation was from Dickens, a seventeen-volume run of *House-hold Words*); he suggested the Library become a sort of club, and urged that the authorities make available a comfortable room, with armchairs, 'a good fire and a nice carpet', instead of the Returned Letter Room with its deal benches. The Library opened on 3 January, with some 2,000 books and 367 subscribers.[1]

On 17 November, Trollope sailed aboard the *Atrato*, from Southampton, for the West Indies. Preparations in London for the mission must have been fairly hectic, for Trollope had been unable to work on *The Bertrams* while in the capital. But on the second day at sea he settled into steady daily writing. Being able to do so made his first transatlantic crossing more satisfactory and gave a greater legitimacy to his leisure time. He entered whole-heartedly into the social life aboard ship, where people exist in a manner 'so unlike their customary conventional life': new friendships and new enmities are formed, and 'certain lines of temporary politics are originated'; by noon of the fourth day, after seasickness and gloom have been dispersed, 'the men begin to think that the women are not so ugly,

[171]

vulgar, and insipid; and the women drop their monosyllables, discontinue the close adherence to their own niches . . . and become affectionate, perhaps even beyond their wont ashore'; romantic friendships arise, which, however sweet, are 'generally short-lived and delusive'. Ocean crossings, of which Trollope was to make many, and their distinctive 'social politics', never lost their appeal for him. He used his experiences on the *Atrato* as the basis for 'The Journey to Panama', a short story with an unexpected and sad ending.[2]

Trollope first touched tropical soil at the Danish island of St Thomas on 2 December. As he was leaving the boat, a 'beautifully, nay, elegantly dressed' black woman handed him a rose saying, 'That's for love, dear.' Trollope liked this—'What was it to me that she was as black as my boot, or that she had come to look after the ship's washing?' But he did not like St Thomas, 'a Niggery-Hispano-Dano-Yankee-Doodle place; in which, per-haps, the Yankee-Doodle element, declaring itself in nasal twang and sherry cobblers, seems to be of the strongest flavor'. St Thomas was merely his port of changing ships, and he immediately sailed to Kingston, Jamaica.[3]

Trollope was on a many-sided mission for the Post Office. At Kingston—and similarly in British Guiana—he was to persuade the authorities that the local colonial government, rather than London headquarters, had to administer and take responsibility for the Post Office; this plan met with opposition, as it involved the end of the London subsidy, the fear of nepotism, and the loss of positions among London-appointed postal officials. In the end, Trollope simply insisted that London would effect the change. He was also to negotiate treaties with the Spanish government for a reduction in rates charged in Cuba and Puerto Rico for mail sent to Great Britain. He was to settle with New Granada (Colombia) for a drastic reduction of the tax levied on British mail passing through the country on the railway between Panama and Colon, and to arrange with the (Amer-ican owned) Panama Railway Company for a flat-rate contract for mail so carried.[4] His assignment also called for him, in his words, to 'cleanse the Augean stables' of the British Post Office throughout the colonies, includ-ing Jamaica, British Guiana, Barbados, Trinidad, and Granada. The colonial post offices had been managed from St Martin's-le-Grand, and the men sent out as officers had been 'sometimes more conspicuous for want of income than for official zeal and ability'.[5] This part of his assignment called for much travelling about, and on one occasion, intent on proving over the protests of local postal officials that their three-day allowance for a particular journey ought to be reduced to two, he rode the distance with the mail courier. His horse and saddle—the latter an 'instrument of torture' as he told Tom Trollope—were chosen by his hosts in order to defeat his purpose, and by the first night he was so saddle-sore that he nearly relented. But, as that would have been 'dreadful' to him, he ordered two bottles of brandy, 'poured them into a wash-hand basin, and *sat in it!*' The result was temporarily agonizing, but the next day he was able to ride, and of course made the journey in two days.[6]

The foreign travel connected with the Post Office assignment to Egypt had supplied some background for *The Bertrams* and would provide the setting for four short stories. The longer mission to the West Indies furnished material for five short stories and Trollope's first travel book.[7] In a letter to Chapman, written from Kingston on 11 January 1859, Trollope said that, having 'always a prudent eye to the future', he would like to know whether the publisher would be interested in a travel book on Jamaica, Cuba, British Guiana, Panama '& God knows what other latitudes or longitudes'; he asked £250 for 450 pages of the size printed in *Doctor Thorne*, the whole to be ready by 31 October (and 'most probably a good deal earlier'). Chapman replied that he wished Trollope's prudent eye for the future wasn't such a 'piercer' going 'quite through my heart and out at the bottom of my pocket' and asked for 550 to 600 pages—'a hundred pages more or less is nothing to you when you are writing.'[8] Trollope began the book on 25 January, a week after finishing *The Bertrams*, and before he had received Chapman's response. He took no notes, simply wrote down his observations, he said, 'hot on to the paper from their causes'[9]—actually he often wrote of events about a month old, but his memory was such as to keep them vividly present. *The West Indies and the Spanish Main* opens with Trollope recounting the present moment as he sits disconsolately becalmed in a sailing vessel between Jamaica and Cien Fuegos, Cuba ('in these days a man should never be tempted to leave the steam-boats,' Trollope wrote to his mother from shipboard).[10] He had been told this smaller ship might save him time, but in fact it would cost him precious days, as the ship made no headway, simply rolled about 'in a nauseous manner'; the food was meagre, eked out only by a ham and box of sardines picked up at Kingston and his own bottle of 'medicinal' brandy. His Post Office travel/account book shows the entry 'Alas!' on the third day at sea increasing impatiently to five such entries after as many days. This 'perfidious bark', the *Linwood*, took nine days rather than the purported three. But after a few pages of grousing, the narrative returns to the beginning of his voyage, and then devotes almost a third of the book to Jamaica.[11]

For Kingston itself, Trollope did not care: 'Of all the towns that I ever saw, Kingston is perhaps, on the whole, the least alluring.' Its unpaved, ragged, unlighted streets with their run-down unpainted wooden houses appear 'bankrupt'; everything, from the ugly public buildings to the dockyard at Port Royal, 'a naval hospital, a pile of invalided anchors', is 'a disgrace to the country that owns it'. Nearby Spanish Town, where he went to see the Governor, seemed if anything worse, a forbidding 'city of the dead'; his interview there quickly over, he had to kill some time and saw no living creatures in the streets except long, skinny pigs. But in the countryside he enjoyed the company of hospitable colonists; for a short time the social life, the dancing, and the 'long' drinks rendered the *dolce far niente* of rural Jamaica almost palatable to his 'Saxon energies'. Throughout the island he was amused by the Englishness of the place, especially in food: the white inhabitants eat beefsteaks and onions, bread and cheese, and beer; they affect to despise yams, avocado pears, cabbage, plantain, and 'twenty other delicious vegetables', and insist on eating bad English potatoes; the desire for English pickles is 'quite a passion'. [12]

Intent on seeing everything possible, he arranged with a companion and five black servants to climb and camp overnight on Blue Mountain Peak, in order to 'worship' a sunrise. At the top, enveloped in a cloudy, cold mist, wet through, they built a hut for sleeping and made a fire, but in trying to dry themselves managed only to scorch their clothes and burn their boots: 'Mournfully we turned ourselves before the fire—slowly, like badly roasted joints of meat; and the result was exactly that: we were badly roasted—roasted and raw at the same time'; it was so cold they were unable to sleep, and the morning brought only a dull 'muddy light' in the constant mist, but no sunrise. The impulse to explore did not desert him, however, and two months later, for example, he would insist on visiting Irazu, a volcanic mountain in central Costa Rica, in spite of the onset of the rainy season; shivering with cold, he and a friend inspected an extinct crater and even managed to approach a live volcano spewing dark yellow sulphur smoke that at one moment seemed about to suffocate them. [13]

Amidst the travel particulars and personal anecdotes in Trollope's book are disquisitions, most notable among which is an extended discussion of blacks. Trollope, like most of his contemporaries, believed the negro to be racially inferior. Well aware that he would offend 'philanthropists' at home, he set forth his views on the West Indian negro—only recently emancipated from slavery, 1833–9. Emancipation was 'clearly right', but one must not expect too quick a result from it. He did find the good humour and drollery of the negro prepossessing; he was struck by the way black women could wear finery without looking, as did so many English women, like 'hogs in armour'; a black woman seems at home in her clothes: 'she is never shame-faced. Then she has very frequently a good figure, and having it, knows how to make the best of it. She has a natural skill in dress, and will be seen with a boddice fitted to her as though it had been made and laced in Paris.' Nevertheless, 'These people are a servile race, gifted by nature for the hardest physical work, and apparently at present fitted for little else'; they are not yet truly civilized. The Christian religion, in spite of the hymn singing, has not entered their minds. The negro, Trollope says, must be given time to develop. At present he seems to have no desire for advancement, but is content to lie in the sun—and here Trollope echoes Carlyle—finding in fertile Jamaica 'unbounded facility for squatting and availing himself of the fruits of the land,' for lying 'at his ease under the cotton-tree and declining to work after ten o'clock in the morning'. The negro must be taught that work is the lot of Adam's children, and an influx of competitors, Indian and Chinese workers, may do the trick. Trollope did find some hard-working, industrious blacks: for example, at New Amsterdam in the province of Berbice, British Guiana, he stayed at a hotel, kept by a former slave, one Mr Paris Brittain, which Trollope pronounced 'without hesitation, the best inn, not only in that colony, but in any of these Western colonies belonging to Great Britain'. [14] But Trollope saw such a man, with his energy and ambition, as the exception that proved the rule. Little can be said to mitigate the insensitivity of Trollope's views on blacks, except that, in addition to the fact that the majority of Englishmen shared his view, he had the honesty to write out his thoughts (however benighted they were) for any reader who wished to challenge him.

But if his opinions of West Indian blacks would offend philanthropists and others at home, what he had to say of 'coloured' people—those of mixed blood—would offend, he feared, his new friends in the colonies. Trollope's 'theory' for the West Indies maintained that 'Providence has sent white men and black men to these regions in order that from them may spring a race fitted by intellect for civilization; and fitted also by physical organization for tropical labor.' Even as the Englishman would not be what he is now except for the 'wild and savage energy which has come to him from his Vandal forefathers', so a mixture of black with English or European blood will produce the man of coloured race, to whom the Anglo-Saxon must ultimately yield the West Indies. If such an idea is deemed unpatriotic and 'unworthy of an Englishman', so be it:

patriotism, Trollope writes, is a very 'finite' virtue; Britons should be satisfied with 'begetting' nations, and not intent on ruling them; they should not be so patriotic as to 'regret' the United States; they must look to the 'welfare of the coming world' and not their own national needs. [15]

In Cuba, Trollope managed without difficulty to visit and inspect a slave plantation, fifteen miles from Cien Fuegos, where some 150 blacks toiled in sugar fields. Trollope reported what he was shown or told, and seemed very little shocked: 'During the crop time . . . which generally lasts from November till May, the negroes sleep during six hours out of the twenty-four, have two for meals, and work for sixteen! No difference is made on Sunday. Their food is plentiful, and of a good and strong description. They are sleek and fat and large, like well-preserved brewers' horses. . . . During the remainder of the year the labour of the negroes averages twelve hours a day, and one day of rest is usually allowed to them.' Trollope was not permitted to witness any 'coercive measures' used on the slaves: 'No doubt the whip is in use, but I did not see it,' and he lacked the nerve to inquire of the owner about punishment. He learned that all plantation slaves were baptized at birth into the Roman Catholic Church: 'They have the advantage, whatever it may be, of that ceremony in infancy; and from that time forth they are treated as the beasts of the stall.' If the negro slaves had been beasts they could be said to be treated well: in spite of their incredibly long hours, 'the men do not apparently lose their health, though, no doubt, they become prematurely old, and as a rule die early. The property is too valuable to be neglected or ill-used.' The tour over, the owner gave Trollope a sumptuous late breakfast—'a delicious soup . . . a bottle of excellent claret, a paté de foie gras, some game deliciously dressed, and half a dozen kinds of vegetables'—and, without Trollope's knowing it, courteously paid his train ticket back to Cien Fuegos: 'If one was but convinced that those sleek, fat, smiling bipeds were but two legged beasts of burden, and nothing more, all would have been well at the estate which we visited.' [16]

From Havana Trollope sailed to St Thomas, the hub around which all British shipping in the area revolved. Thence he travelled via Barbados to Georgetown in the province of Demerara, British Guiana, where his work kept him for two weeks: he contradicted popular report that Demerara was a swampy, muddy place infested with yellow fever, a miserable backwater of unendurable heat and stagnant society; rather, he liked it best of all the places he visited, and said, facetiously, 'If there were but a snug little secretaryship vacant there . . . how I would invoke the goddess of patronage; how I would nibble round the officials of the Colonial Office;

1. Julians. Recent photograph of the house built in 1817–18 by Trollope's father.

2. Julian Hill. Nineteenth-century photograph of the Harrow farmhouse where Anthony grew up.

3. Frances Trollope. Portrait by Auguste Hervieu, *c*.1832.

4. Trollope's home at Mallow, Co. Cork, Ireland.

5. 5 Seaview Terrace, Donnybrook, near Dublin, Ireland.

6. Anthony Trollope, *c*.1855.

7. Thomas Adolphus Trollope and
Anthony Trollope, *c*.1860. Trollope
wrote: 'You will perceive that my
brother is pitching into me. He
always did.'

8. Trollope. Photograph by Herbert Watkins, *c*.1860.

9. Trollope. Photograph by Julia Cameron, October 1864.

10. Waltham House, Waltham Cross, where Trollope lived from December 1859 until March 1871.

11. William Makepeace Thackeray. Portrait by Samuel Laurence, 1864.

12. John Everett Millais. Photograph by Lewis Carroll, 1865.

13. George Eliot. Chalk drawing by Frederick Burton, 1865.

14. G. H. Lewes. Drawing by Rudolf Lehmann, 1867.

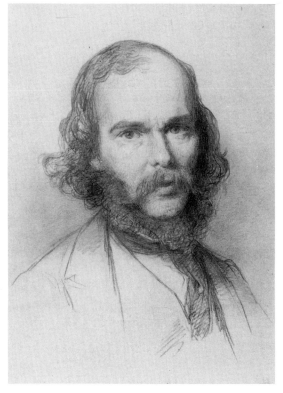

how I would stir up my friends' friends to write little notes to their friends!'[17]

Trollope next went to work at Barbados, then Trinidad, and returned, again via Barbados, to St Thomas; he sailed then for New Granada, coming ashore first at Santa Marta, a 'wretched village' of a city, where Great Britain, 'with intense cruelty', maintained a British Consul and a British Post Office. 'Every one of my predecessors here died of fever,' the Consul told Trollope. What, Trollope asked himself, could he say to the man? Cartagena, the next stop, though even hotter in climate than Santa Marta, was a 'much better town'. He sailed for Colon, or Aspinwall, as it was called by the Americans, who had built the railway here across the isthmus to Panama. He found the place 'a wretched, unhealthy, miserably situated but thriving little American town, created by and for the railway and the passenger traffic'. He granted that the railway was a 'great fact' and very expensive to build and maintain, but he considered the charge of $25 (five pounds) excessive, especially when seen in light of other connected fares: steerage passage from New York to San Francisco, a journey of about six thousand miles that included two sea voyages of about eleven days each, went for $50, half of which had to be paid to the railway for the fifty-mile train crossing at the isthmus.[18] He took the railroad to the west coast at Panama where he negotiated with the New Granada government about mail taxes and with the Railway Company about mail fees.[19]

At Panama, the heat—over 90 degrees—made him 'uncomfortable' but never ill; he did lose 'all pleasure in eating'. He was invited aboard the USS *Merrimac*, which was coaling at the port. The battleship impressed Trollope with its very large guns and its very good sherry. (Three years later, and while Trollope was visiting the United States, the ironclad *Merrimac*, fallen into Confederate hands, would nearly break the Union blockade at Hampton Roads Estuary, Virginia, only to be stopped in an indecisive encounter with another and smaller ironclad vessel, the *Monitor*.) Trollope embarked at Panama aboard the British man-of-war *Vixen* for Punta Arenas, Costa Rica, whence he planned to cross Central America overland to Greytown (San Juan del Norte). Fitted out in a short canvas smock-frock, coarse holland trousers and a Panama straw hat 'with an amazing brim' that made him look, he thought, like an American 'filibuster', or freebooter, he first made his way, with the captain and master of the *Vixen*, by mule to the inland capital of San José. It was a fairly arduous three-day journey, Trollope's huge portmanteau causing trouble by frequently slipping from its donkey; that portmanteau 'had been condemned in the Holy Land, in Jamaica, in Costa Rica, wherever it has had to be fixed on any animal's back. On this occasion it nearly broke both the heart of the muleteer and the back of the mule.'²⁰

At San José Trollope stayed at a pleasant little German inn, but spent all his free time in the British mission at the corner of the town plaza where Sir William Ouseley, Minister Extraordinary to the Central American governments, was staying. When Trollope first sent his card up to Sir William he could hear the legation Secretary say in a loud voice, 'Oh, tell Mr Trollope to go to the devil. It's much too hot to see anyone.'²¹ But Trollope and the Secretary, William Webb Follett Synge, 'a very prince of good fellows', soon became fast friends, and Trollope was much in Synge's company. The Secretary's quarters were in a commandeered haber-dashery beneath the rooms of Ouseley's temporary legation: 'I shall never forget the hours I spent in that linen-draper's shop,' Trollope wrote. It became for ten days a 'pleasant accustomed haunt', to which he could retire and 'pretend to read, while in truth the hours [were] passed in talking, with some few short intervals devoted to contemplation and tobacco'. Some of the talk between the two men must have been of Thackeray, with whom Synge was very friendly, and whom Trollope considered the greatest of English novelists. Not many months later Trollope would make the overture to Thackeray that resulted in the literary and personal connection that was to shape much of his subsequent career. In 1879 Trollope recalled an incident he said was illustrative of Thackeray's 'excessive' generosity:

I heard once a story of woe from a man who was the dear friend of both of us. The gentleman wanted a large sum of money instantly,—something under two thousand pounds,—had no natural friends who could provide it, but must go utterly to the wall without it. Pondering over this sad condition of things just revealed to me, I met Thackeray between the two mounted heroes at the Horse Guards, and told him the story. 'Do you mean to say that I am to find two thousand pounds?' he said, angrily, with some expletives. I explained that I had not even suggested the doing of anything,—only that we might discuss the matter. Then there came over his face a peculiar smile, and a wink in his eyes, and he whispered his suggestion, as though half ashamed of his meanness. 'I'll go half,' he said, 'if anybody will do the rest.' And he did go half, at a day or two's notice, though the gentleman was no more than simply a friend.²²

The unnamed friend was Synge, about to leave for Honolulu where he had been named consul in May 1862, and it was Trollope who supplied the other half of the loan. (Thackeray wrote to Synge, 'I have just met a Trojan of the name of Trollope in the street . . . and the upshot is that we will do what you want between us.'23) Perhaps Trollope's own openhandedness arose from a gratitude to Synge for having indirectly abetted his own association with Thackeray.

The scenery around San José Trollope thought 'striking' but not enough to make one 'rave' about it. The natives were more interesting. The women, for example, were addicted to crinoline: 'In the churches they squat down on the ground, in lieu of kneeling, with their dresses and petticoats arranged around them, looking like huge turnips with cropped heads—like turnips that, by their persevering growth, had got half their roots above the ground. Now women looking like turnips are not specially attractive.' Trollope was visiting the city during Passion Week and could observe Roman Catholic processions and services; the ceremonies included no bishop; Costa Rica no longer had a bishop of its own, the president having banished the one they had; and the people got their priests, when they needed them, from Guatemala, an arrangement that prompted Trollope to muse: 'If we could save all our bishoping, and get our priests as we want them from Guatemala, or any other factory, how excellent would be the economy!'24

After ten days at San José, Trollope set forth on the difficult trek down to the Atlantic coast. He had to go by mule through thick forests to the Serapiqui River, travel down to where it joined the San Juan River, and then down that river to Greytown. A few days before Trollope had reached San José, an Englishman and his wife had started for England via the same route. The wife had suffered greatly during the land crossing, and believed she would die en route; but reaching the Serapiqui River, the worst part behind them, she and her husband boarded the canoe only to have it overturn one hundred yards downstream on the snag of a tree. The woman drowned, and the grief-stricken husband, unwilling to meet his young wife's mother with such news in England, returned to San José. Trollope then took the same journey, in the company of the naval lieutenant who had accompanied the husband back. Trollope retold her story in 'Returning Home', keeping close to the facts of the incident as told to him and recorded in his travel book; the detailed account of the miserable three days on mule through the forest, the mules struggling in mud, the riders trying all the way to keep their knees and shins from being banged or crushed against trees, clearly draws on his own experience. Once aboard the canoe on the Serapiqui all was well: 'Here, for the first time in my life, I found my bulk and size to be of advantage to me. . . . I sat, having a seat to myself, being too weighty to share a bench with a neighbour. I therefore could lean back among the luggage; and with a cigar in my mouth, with a little wooden bicher of weak brandy and water beside me, I found that the position had its charms.'[25]

From Greytown he sailed again for Colon, aboard the British steam-packet *Trent* (the ship from which, during the American Civil War and while Trollope was in the States, two Confederate envoys would be removed by the US Navy, a move that nearly precipitated war between England and the North). From Colon Trollope immediately travelled by rail again to Panama. (He was convinced that a Panama Canal could never be built; and, if a waterway over the isthmus was insisted upon, he thought the best route would be via the San Juan River in Costa Rica and the Nicaraguan Lakes.) His business with New Granada officials and the railway company completed, he returned again to Colon and thence to St Thomas. From there he sailed to Bermuda, having arranged a little sightseeing for himself on the way home. In his book Trollope's focus at Bermuda was the prison colony, a facility for some 1,500 English 'hardened thieves' and other serious offenders. Trollope objects strongly to a system that gives the prisoners, on their two small islands, comparative freedom, a liberty that resulted in murder and in riots between Irish and English prisoners. He also questions why a Bermudan prisoner should have a daily diet better than that of soldiers, sailors, or mechanics, or why he should work fewer hours than English labourers. The Bermudan jail, Trollope insists, is failing in its chief object, that of visiting on inmates such 'condign punishment' as to deter others from a life of crime.[26] On the other hand, Trollope wrote a short story about Bermuda, 'Aaron Trow', a harrowing tale of an escaped convict that is quite unlike Trollope's usual manner, but a good example of how his conservative views—here a conviction that prisoners usually deserve miserable fates—are invariably qualified when treated fictionally. The escapee, in desperate search for food and money, violently assaults a young woman in an isolated seaside cottage, threatening to disfigure her face, to take her honour, even her life; she fights back like an enraged animal: 'foam came to her mouth, and fire sprang from her eyes, and the muscles of her body worked as though she had been trained to deeds of violence.' Frightened off, the convict is hunted down by the girl's fiancé, a meek Presbyterian minister, a devout 'man of peace', changed now into a bloodthirsty avenger. The convict is killed in a desperate struggle in the water, but the story's sympathies have tilted towards him (his original crime had been committed during a labour riot: 'Had the world used him well, giving him when he was young ample wages and separating him from turbulent spirits, he also might have used the world well'); and the minister is appalled at his own violence.[27]

On 2 June Trollope sailed aboard the *Henrietta* for New York (earlier plans that Rose would join him there had been abandoned), whence, after four days, he travelled up the Hudson River to Albany and then by rail to Niagara ('Nothing ever disappointed me less that the Falls of Niagara— but my raptures did not truly commence for the first half-day. Their charms grow upon one like the conversation of a brilliant man'). Announcing that he will not 'do the Falls' in his book, he recorded briefly how he went next via Lake Ontario and the St Lawrence to Montreal; then via Lake Champlain to Saratoga Springs, and finally back to New York, where he embarked, on 22 June, aboard the *Africa* for Liverpool.[28]

During the crossing he became a good friend of an American widow, Mrs Harriet Knower, and her 20-year-old daughter Mary. He met with them whenever possible over the next twenty years, either in London or in America, and even kept up a sporadic transatlantic correspondence with the two. He was especially drawn to Mary; in 1866 he wrote to her mother, 'We were so glad to have Mary's photograph! It is now hung in our bed room among others of people whom we love well.' It seems likely that Mary was the original for the heroine, the daughter of a widow in Albany, New York (the Knowers were an old Albany family), in the slight short story 'The Courtship of Susan Bell'.[29]

Aboard the *Africa* Trollope finished writing *The West Indies and the Spanish Main*. It was published by Chapman & Hall in October. Trollope later made the extraordinary claim that it was 'on the whole . . . the best book that has come from my pen. It is short . . . amusing, useful, and true.'[30] One likes to think he meant best among his various books of non-fiction, but that is not what he said. Perhaps his desire to be regarded as a 'serious' writer rather than a mere spinner of novels best explains the statement. Or, perhaps he was just provoking his readers, a tactic of which he was certainly capable.

Trollope arrived at Liverpool on 3 July, and was back home at Donnybrook the next day, stopping for a week before going to London to discuss his mission with headquarters. There he argued persuasively that Kingston rather than St Thomas should be the central base for the British mail packets; he believed the harbour at St Thomas to be pestilential with yellow fever, inconvenient, and expensive; he calculated that the change to Kingston could save yearly some £15,000 through re-routing mail packets. The Packet Company, which was paid by the mile, strongly objected. The Admiralty, to whom Trollope appealed, supported him, as did the Treasury; but the Packet Company managed to block the changes, although the threat of putting Trollope's plan into effect was held over the

Company's head in an effort to make services more efficient. The Post-master-General's Report generously acknowledged all of Trollope's accomplishments in the West Indies.[31]

While Trollope had been abroad, *The Bertrams* had been published in March. It had been written under 'very vagrant circumstances'—at Alexandria, Malta, Gibraltar, London, Glasgow, Dublin, Belfast, Coleraine, Derry, and Kingston, and aboard ship on four separate sea voyages. With interruptions, he had spent nearly ten months on the novel, about twice as long as he had on the previous one. *The Bertrams* has its gentle comic irony, but this does not modify its moody, serious, dark tone. Money is given Trollope's usual realistic concern. Much of the story is concerned with how young men, like George Bertram and Arthur Wilkinson, can earn their living, and how old men, like George's rich miserly uncle, use their money, and with how money problems delay or prevent young people from marrying. (The rich uncle is revealed to be the heroine's grandfather, but unlike in the fairy-tale, or, Trollope would have said, in Dickens, he stubbornly refuses to leave his fortune either to her or to Bertram.) But the book contains striking departures from Trollope's more usual paths: the heroine, Caroline Waddington, instead of remaining loyal to her first and affianced love, as is almost universal in Trollope, bluntly refuses to marry in poverty; she won't have love in a cottage; she and Bertram, both stiff-necked, torture each other for two years and then break off the engagement; she punishes herself by marrying a man she does not love (during their 'dreary' honeymoon he is almost tempted 'to tell her that he had paid too high for the privilege of pressing such an icicle to his bosom'). The marriage between cold wife and cruelly jealous husband, ending in his suicide, is unrelievedly dark; nor is the darkness much lightened by Caroline's eventual marriage with Bertram (in Hadley church, with its sad associations for Trollope). They are childless, their house is quiet, 'but they are not unhappy'.[32]

The melancholy tone suffuses the account, unique in Trollope, of a religious experience and its rejection for sensible, worldly values. Trollope, fresh from his own visit to the Holy Land, has George Bertram spend hours alone on the Mount of Olives, of which the narrator says: 'Let me take any ordinary believing Protestant Christian to that spot, and I will as broadly defy him to doubt there as I will defy him to believe in that filthy church of the holy places.' On the Mount of Olives the young man is inspired to a life of devotion to Christ as a priest of the Church of England. But his sense of vocation soon fades: 'It was so natural, that wish to do a great thing, so hard that daily task of bathing in Jordan.' The chief cause for his changing his mind is Caroline Waddington, who, with worldly contempt, tells him that clergymen tend to 'grovel' and asks whether the clerics he knows are 'generally men of wide views and enlightened principles' (some passages in *The Bertrams* amount almost to anticlericalism, very different from Trollope's usual gentle satire of moderate Church of England clergymen). Bertram's father, Sir Lionel, though hardly an admirable character or wise man, says that the Church as a profession, as a way of obtaining life's 'good things', is even more 'beggarly' than the army. The narrator comments that although Sir Lionel's attitude was 'commonplace', it was also 'common sense'. Trollope's own view of holy orders as merely one profession among others, and a 'beggarly' one at that, is borne out in the novel by the case of George's cousin Arthur Wilkinson, who realizes that he had become a clergyman 'because he had failed in obtaining the power of following any other profession'. Bertram himself comes to think that the best professions are those of author or politician.33 These, for all Trollope's growing reputation as a masterful delineator of clergymen, were his own thoughts on the subject. Discussing professions in 1860 with G. H. Lewes, he referred to the clerical life as a 'pill' to be swallowed, as something that 'incapacitates a man for most other work'. In 1881 Trollope told young Arthur Tilley, whom someone had suspected of intending to be ordained, 'Dont. Nothing cripples a man more certainly.'34

Bertram not only gives up all thought of the Church, he becomes a freethinker, and takes to writing controversial books. 'The Romance of Scripture' impugned the truth of the Bible; it reminded readers that the inspired writers were Orientals who wrote with 'the customary grandiloquence of Orientalism', with 'poetic exaggeration', and 'in ignorance of those natural truths which men had now acquired by experience and induction'. His next book, 'The Fallacies of Early History', more radical still, flatly calls the whole story of Creation a myth. Bertram tries to lure his clergyman cousin Arthur into argument on matters of belief:* did he really hold, for example, with the resurrection of the body? Wilkinson can only say that 'Nothing is impossible with God.' Bertram replies that it is impossible that God's 'great laws' should change: 'Your body . . . will turn itself, through the prolific chemistry of nature, into various productive gases, by which other bodies will be formed. With which body will you see

---

* Even in lighter contexts, Bertram keeps up the pressure: 'Come, Arthur, be honest, if a man with thirty-nine articles round his neck can be honest. . . . Do you love Adela, or do you not?'35

Christ?' Wilkinson cannot answer, and falls back on scripture. But clerics who argue in this manner, Bertram insists, only make faith more difficult. To tell one to rely on scripture is to 'argue in a circle. I am to have faith because of the Bible, but I am to take the Bible through faith.' To send one to prayer as the fountainhead of that faith is similarly circuitous: how can one pray without faith? While seeing Christ's words as 'irresistible evidence of his fitness to teach', he refuses to accept the whole package, one that requires belief in 'the sun standing still upon Gibeon no less than the divine wisdom which showed that Caesar's tribute should be paid to Caesar' (the latter a curiously Trollopian example of scriptural wisdom, and one easily enough believed). On the other hand, when people take Bertram for an infidel, he remonstrates. The narrator remarks, 'He had intended to be honest in his remonstrance, but it is not every man who exactly knows what he does believe. Every man! Is there, one may almost ask, any man who has such knowledge?' Bertram 'was angry with himself for not believing, and angry with others that they did believe'. If faith, Bertram argues, were something 'to come at, as a man wishes, who would doubt?'[36] Trollope, similarly, wanted to believe, and he did, after a fashion. Socially and publicly, he was, as George Eliot said, 'a Church of England man, clinging to whatever is, on the whole, and without fine distinctions, honest, lovely and of good report'. G. H. Lewes in 1866 recorded having Trollope, John Dennis, Alexander Bain, and Madame Bodichon to dinner: 'Bain startled us by his antichristian onslaught, and Trollope amused us by his defence.'[37] Trollope, like so many Victorians, wanted to believe, but belief itself was so much a mystery to him that, as Bertram says, he hardly knew, privately, what he believed. That segment of the Church of England informally denominated 'broad' suited Trollope nicely; he could pretty much dismiss the Old Testament, admire the moral teachings of Christ, and keep up an ill-defined belief in a supreme being and a vague hope of some kind of immortality.

WALTHAM CROSS

Few men I think ever lived a fuller life.

An Autobiography, ch. 15

15

Waltham House and the Cornhill

THE summer of 1859 brought a turning-point in Trollope's life as fortunate as his departure for Ireland in 1841. Summing up the personal and professional achievements of those eighteen Irish years in *An Autobiography* he wrote:

My life in England for twenty-six years from the time of my birth to the day on which I left it, had been wretched. I had been poor, friendless, and joyless. In Ireland it had constantly been happy. I had achieved the respect of all with whom I was concerned, I had made for myself a comfortable home, and I had enjoyed many pleasures.

Nevertheless he had for some time been hankering after a return to his own country, an emotional pull decisively reinforced by his consciousness that the Post Office was no longer his only career. *The Warden* and its successors had made of him a professional writer of reputation; and he thought that 'a man who could write books ought not to live in Ireland,— ought to live within the reach of the publishers, the clubs, and the dinner parties of the metropolis.' The opportunity for that move presented itself when he arrived in London to prepare his reports on the West Indies. The surveyorship of the Eastern District—which would enable him to live near London—had fallen vacant, and Trollope secured it. This he did 'with some little difficulty', because he 'did not stand very well with the dominant interest at the General Post Office', that is, with Rowland Hill, now Chief Secretary, and his brother, Frederick Hill, junior Assistant Secretary. He gleefully recalled the source of their animus as partly the publication of *The Three Clerks* and, more or less continuously, his outspoken criticisms of procedures and management: 'I have no doubt that I often made myself very disagreeable. I know that I sometimes tried to do so.' However, in view of his special services, the transfer could not be refused.[1]

The appointment to England would not be official until the following 10 January, but he was to take up his duties by late November. He quickly went house-hunting and discovered an old red-brick house, dating perhaps from as early as William III's time, with some large rooms and a good staircase, and standing in old-fashioned grounds.[2] On 2 August Trollope wrote to Rose in playful and jubilant 'olde English': 'Havinge withe infinite trouble & pain inspected & surveyed and pokèd manie and diverse holes in ye aforesaid mansion, I have at ye laste hiréd and taken it for yr. moste excellente ladieship.'[3] Waltham House, at Waltham Cross in Hertfordshire, on the boundaries of Essex and Middlesex, was well located in respect to his new district, which comprised Essex, Suffolk, Norfolk, Cambridgeshire, Huntingdonshire, and the eastern parts of Hertfordshire and Bedfordshire. More important, it was but twelve miles north of London and conveniently served by direct train from the Shoreditch Station.

On the very day on which Trollope was leasing Waltham House, Chapman & Hall agreed to pay £600 for the three-year copyright of his next novel, an increase of £200 over what they had paid for *The Bertrams*. In *An Autobiography* Trollope mistakenly says that he was prompted to 'demand' this higher price from Chapman directly as the result of positive reviews of the West Indies book in *The Times*, criticism that 'much raised' him in his 'position as an author'.[4] It is correct that the two-part review by E. S. Dallas was certainly laudatory: it stressed the serious aspects of Trollope's book, exactly the kind of praise he was looking for, and strongly endorsed all of Trollope's positions, from his views on the Jamaican black to the infeasibility of a canal across the isthmus (a 'glorious' French dream).[5] But *The West Indies* was not published until two months after he had signed the £600 agreement for the new novel, and *The Times* reviews appeared only in the following January. ('I am not good at dates,' Trollope baldly asserted in *The West Indies*.[6]) But Dallas, from his eminence as writer for the most influential publication of the day, had earlier written an article, confused by Trollope with the later ones, that did in fact give his reputation an enormous boost. This was a review, published in *The Times* on 23 May 1859—while Trollope was still abroad—which gave an overview of his fiction from *The Warden* to *The Bertrams*. Dallas said that if Charles Mudie, 'the Apollo of the circulating library', the 'great literary middleman', were asked who was the greatest of living men, he would unhesitatingly say Trollope. For Mudie, at the present moment one writer in England is paramount above all others, and his name is Trollope. He is at the top of the tree; he stands alone; there is nobody to be compared with him. He writes faster than we can read, and the more that the pensive public reads the more does it desire to read. Mr. Anthony Trollope is, in fact, the most fertile, the most popular, the most successful author—that is to say, of the circulating library sort.

The qualification only partly withdrew the compliment: books popular with lending libraries may not always be the product of 'genius', Dallas says, but 'genius is not everything. . . . There are people who find Mr. Thackeray too thoughtful and Mr. Dickens too minute.' The review goes on to observe that, oddly, Trollope's novels are 'free from those faults which we naturally associate with the circulating library—extravagance, trickery, false sentiment, morbid pictures. His style is the very opposite of melodramatic; it is plain and straightforward, utterly devoid of clap-trap. It is the style of a man who has a good deal to say, who can afford to say it simply.' Dallas suggests that even those who usually prefer reading blue books and statistics, who indulge only occasionally in 'the enormity of romance', will find Trollope rewarding.[7] Reviews in *The Times* were—like practically all reviews—unsigned, but Trollope learned that Dallas wrote this one: 'I told him that he had done me a greater service than can often be done by one man to another, but that I was under no obligation to him. I do not think that he saw the matter quite in the same light.'*[8]

To understand the force of Dallas's review one must keep in mind the major role played by the lending libraries in making books available to the public. Most readers did not purchase novels in their original three-volume form because of their prohibitively high expense, a guinea and a half, 31s. 6d.† Subscribers to Mudie's, whose library opened in 1842 and soon dominated the market, might borrow one volume at a time for an annual fee of one guinea (an arrangement neatly fitted to encourage publication in three volumes). Mudie, through his pointedly named 'Select Library', was also influential in determining which books should be made available to readers. He insisted on delicacy in sexual matters and propriety if not orthodoxy in religious matters. But then, so did most of his subscribers. After complaints from readers about Meredith's *The Ordeal*

---

* Years later, Trollope, in a review article of Dallas's abridgement of *Clarissa*, was not very kind; for Trollope *Clarissa* was unsalvageable, too long, too improbable, even in Dallas's abridgement, and he said so; moreover, it was Dallas of whom in *An Autobiography* Trollope said, while withholding his name, that the gift, from 'probably the most popular author of the day' (Dickens), of a manuscript (*Our Mutual Friend*) to Dallas 'as an acknowledgement for a laudatory review . . . should neither have been given nor have been taken'.[9]

† Readers did buy in large numbers the 'cheap' editions of successful novels, generally in one volume at five or six shillings, and usually published within a year or two of the first edition.

of Richard Feverel (1859), Mudie withdrew his order for 300 copies ('I am tabooed from all decent drawing-room tables,' Meredith complained).[10] Joseph Cauvin in censoring much in *Barchester Towers* had Mudie's in mind. It is known that Mudie's bought 200 of the 750 copies printed of that novel and fully half of the 1,000 copies printed of *The Three Clerks*. The figures for *Doctor Thorne* and *The Bertrams* are not available, but Mudie almost certainly took at least 500 copies of each.[11]

On 4 August, two days after signing the agreement with Chapman for *Castle Richmond*, Trollope began the book. A kind of farewell to his adopted country, it opens with the narrator wondering 'whether the novel-reading world . . . will be offended if I lay the plot of this story in Ireland! . . . I am now leaving the Green Isle and my old friends, and would fain say a word of them as I do so.' While busy writing the novel and winding up his affairs in Ireland, Trollope was also projecting a collection of short stories. He had already sent two stories, written in July, 'The Courtship of Susan Bell' and 'Relics of General Chassé', to Fletcher Harper, the New York publishing colossus, who paid him £20 each for publication in *Harper's New Monthly Magazine*. On 1 September Trollope wrote to Harper that he was thinking of writing a series of short stories to be collected in two volumes after their magazine appearance. Like the stories Harper already had, all were to have foreign settings, places Trollope had visited. When reissued, they would be called *Tales of All Countries*. If Harper agreed to take one story a month, he could have the next one by the end of October '& then the series regularly as fast as you would want them'.[12] That same day, without waiting for a reply, Trollope broke off *Castle Richmond* and devoted the next two months to writing short stories. During most of this time he was in the Pyrenees on holiday with Rose, Tom Trollope, and John Tilley, their many stops including Le Puy, the setting for 'The Château of Prince Polignac' and Vernet-les-Bains, a small bathing spa in the Eastern Pyrenees that formed the setting for 'La Mère Bauche'.[13] He returned home to Ireland, with five stories completed, to find that Harper did not want more than one story every other month. Trollope also saw the advertisements for a new shilling magazine, the *Cornhill*, to be launched in January 1860, published by Smith, Elder, with Thackeray as editor. Trollope now made the move that greatly accelerated his steady progress as a popular writer. Two days after arriving home he addressed a letter, on 23 October, to Thackeray, offering himself as one of the 'staff' of the new monthly. He proposed that Thackeray accept every other month for two years—alternating with Harper—the short stories that were to comprise the two *Tales of All*

Countries collections; alternatively he was prepared to sell the whole series to the *Cornhill*. It was a characteristically frank letter, stating what Harper was paying him, and asking for a quick reply as he had a letter from Harper to answer. Thackeray conferred with George Smith, and it was decided that Smith would make Trollope an offer for a full-length novel, and then Thackeray would write 'saying how much we want him'. (Thackeray was more or less a figurehead for the *Cornhill*: 'I am only a sham editor,' he told a friend, 'Mr. Smith, the publisher, does most of the work and likes it. He has no confidence in my judgment, and a great deal in his.') Smith's letter, written on 26 October, first expressed a willingness to take the series of short stories and to pay Trollope twice the fee paid by Harper, but then went on to say that he would much prefer 'a continuous story', the equivalent of a three-volume novel, for which he would pay £1,000.[14]

Two days later came an urbane and generous letter from Thackeray, welcoming Trollope, saying how glad he was to have him as 'a Cooperator in our New Magazine' and asking him for other contributions as well: 'Whatever a man knows about life and its doings that let us hear about. You must have tossed a deal about the world, and have countless sketches in your memory and your portfolio. Please to think if you can furbish up any of these besides the novel. When events occur on wh. you can have a good lively talk, bear us in mind.' The magazine, he said, would not rely solely on fiction—not that he meant to disparage novels, especially Trollope's; he hoped the *Cornhill* would have 'as pleasant a story' as *The Three Clerks*.[15]

Trollope was happily surprised. There was never a question of his saying no to the offer. One thousand pounds was more than twice his best payment for a novel so far and almost twice what he was to receive for his latest, *Castle Richmond*, on the stocks for Chapman. And it represented considerably more than a year's salary at the Post Office. But more surprising was the evident fact that so near the announced date for the start of the magazine, a lead novel was still not settled upon. Smith had intended that Thackeray himself should contribute the chief fiction, offering £350 for each of twelve monthly instalments, or £4,200 for a three-volume novel, but Thackeray, who had just finished *The Virginians* in September and who was not in good health, had to postpone writing a major novel. Instead he was preparing a six-part short fiction, *Lovel the Widower*, a reworking of an earlier comedy, *The Wolves and the Lamb*.[16] Trollope later wrote: '*Lovel the Widower* was not substantial enough to appear as the principal joint at the banquet. Though your guests will undoubtedly dine off the little delicacies you provide for them, there must be a heavy saddle of mutton among the viands prepared. I was the saddle of mutton, Thackeray having omitted to get his joint down to the fire in time enough. My fitness lay in my capacity for quick roasting.'[17]

Trollope hurried to London, where on Thursday 3 November he went first to 193 Piccadilly where Edward Chapman graciously said he might take *Castle Richmond* to the *Cornhill*, and that if it did not suit the magazine, Trollope was at liberty either to keep or delay his March deadline for delivery of the manuscript. Trollope then went to 65 Cornhill in the City, where he had his first interview with George Smith. The publisher made it clear that an Irish story would not be suitable for the commencement of the magazine, and that he would have no objection to the publication of *Castle Richmond* by Chapman while the new novel by Trollope was running in the *Cornhill*; he himself wanted 'an English tale, on English life, with a clerical flavour'. In a word, Smith wanted a Barsetshire novel. Trollope wrote that the money offered was so generous that 'had a couple of archbishops been demanded, I should have produced them'.[18]

Trollope said that 'on these orders' he went to work and 'framed what I suppose I must call the plot of *Framley Parsonage*', and wrote the first few pages of the story in the railway carriage during the journey back to Ireland. However, his memory is contradicted by the working diary for the novel, which shows that he wrote the first seven pages of the story on Wednesday, probably while travelling to London: even before his meeting with Smith he had suspected that the Irish novel would not be acceptable, and had thought about, and indeed begun, the 'morsel of the biography of an English clergyman' that was *Framley Parsonage*.[19]

The agreement with Smith, Elder, signed that 3 November, called for delivery of the first part of the manuscript on 1 December. Such a deadline was no problem for Trollope, even though he had not had time to work the story and characters through in his head as much as he liked to do. Actually, the first number (48 manuscript pages, 24 *Cornhill* pages) was completed by 8 November, five days after the meeting with Smith. Indeed, by 23 December Trollope had finished the eighth part, or exactly one half of the novel. But if the deadline was no problem, Trollope had been mildly disconcerted at having to break his 'principle' that no part of a story should be published until the entire work were completed. The artist, he insisted, 'should keep in his hand the power of fitting the beginning of his work to the end'.[20] Of course he had previously never published serially, so the temptation to do otherwise had not been there.

Trollope's working diary for *Framley Parsonage*, 1 November 1859 to 9 April 1860. It records date (with 'X' to indicate Sunday) and numbered pages written each day, and gives daily, weekly, and cumulative page totals. It also shows that he broke off between 1 January and 31 March 1860 to write the 'two last volumes of C Richmond', and resumed *Framley Parsonage* on 3 April.

In *An Autobiography* he claimed never to have broken the rule again, but in fact he did so in four of the five novels that immediately followed *Framley Parsonage*.

By late November Trollope had moved into Waltham House. His duties kept him on the move: during his first ten days he made two visits to Ipswich and one each to Maldon and Cambridge, as well as three to Post Office headquarters (in which he had an office near the gates at the end of Newgate Street). He had also to arrange for the transfer of Harry and Fred from St Columba's, Dublin, to an English school (the boys had previously attended school at Cork and at Chester). After some investigation he enrolled them at St Andrew's College, Bradfield, near Reading. It had been founded in 1850 by the Reverend Thomas Stevens, who had been at Oriel with Newman and was influenced to start Bradfield by the Tractarian Movement—the school's stated purpose being 'the careful education of boys into loving children of the Church of England'.[21] Trollope discovered that Bradfield had a far better ratio of masters to students, one to thirteen or fourteen, compared to Harrow's one to twenty-two or Eton's one to twenty-five; moreover, Eton had but one instructor in foreign languages for 906 boys; and, for that matter, Eton, he found, was not open to boys born in Ireland. But perhaps his own experience had been too bitter for him seriously to consider sending his sons to one of the famous old schools. In any event, the cost was considerably less at Bradfield, about £130 a year per pupil.[22] At first there was some difficulty about one of the boys, who, as Trollope had to tell Stevens, was in 'disgrace' at St Columba's for some breach of discipline and also for subsequently lying about the fault. But when Stevens wrote concerning the matter to the Warden of St Columba's, the reply he received served to convince him that the Warden was 'only fit to be employed in Ireland—an awful muff!! A sort of donkey that would be likely to make hypocrites of honest boys. He does not understand his work one bit. I hope the boys will do well here.' They did do fairly well (though for a while in late 1860 Trollope considered sending them to the continent for school).[23] Fred, who had not yet lost his Irish brogue and was known to the boys as 'Paddy Minor', developed a reputation in his dormitory as an excellent story-teller. But he distinguished himself more in an 'historic' fight long remembered at the school, much in the manner of Dobbin's great battle with Cuff in *Vanity Fair*. Fred took up the cause of a small boy, Richmond, against an older boy named Ward, and in a long fist-fight finally beat his bigger and stronger opponent, though he was himself so knocked about that he could not go home for the first few days of the next holidays.[24] Anthony must have been proud. He had never told his sons of his own big fight, that 'solitary glory' of his school days, his battle at Harrow with James Lewis. Fred would learn of it only twenty years later, in Australia, when he came upon Henry Stuart Russell, Trollope's unofficial fag at Harrow, who, as Fred told his father, 'said that you once had a great fight and at last beat your man'.[25]

Trollope brought with him to Waltham Cross his Irish groom, Barney, who had worked in Trollope's employ since Banagher. (He was said to have put little Harry and Fred on horseback before they could walk.[26]) Now Barney was entrusted with the duty of calling Trollope at 5 o'clock every morning so that he could be at his desk by 5.30. For this service, which included bringing a cup of coffee, Barney was paid an additional £5 yearly. Trollope wrote that during all the Waltham Cross years, Barney was never late: 'I do not know that I ought not to feel that I owe more to him than to any one else for the success I have had. By beginning at that hour I could complete my literary work before I dressed for breakfast.' The first half-hour would be spent in reading the previous day's work, and then, with watch open before him, he strove to write a page, or 250 words, every fifteen minutes, or some ten pages daily. If a writer of fiction, Trollope said, has done his thinking about his characters, his day-dreaming, he could work continuously for the three hours, there being no need to 'sit nibbling his pen, and gazing at the wall'. A pace of ten pages per day would have produced in ten months three three-volume novels, the very amount that had so angered the publisher in Paternoster Row.[27] Trollope often averaged about six volumes a year. His daily output over the years was under ten pages per sitting; nor was it anywhere near constant, often varying between as few as four and as many as sixteen pages. (The fastest burst of his writing career came in July 1864 when for fourteen days straight he composed daily fifteen pages of *Miss Mackenzie*; his most productive single day seems to have been 16 June 1867, when he wrote twenty pages of *Linda Tressel*—he regularly managed more pages per diem when writing short novels.) But what really kept the production down below the bothersome total of three long novels per year were interruptions: illness, holidays, extra postal work, unusually difficult travel, other writing such as articles for magazines. Only on extraordinary occasions did he manage to write a novel pretty much straight through without pause. (Naturally, a short novel, and one written during a holiday, had a better chance of being written uninterruptedly: *Lady Anna* had but one day of stoppage—for illness; *Dr Wortle's School* had none at all.)

On 23 December the first issue of the *Cornhill Magazine* appeared on the news-stands. A few days later Trollope wrote to Thackeray, whom he had still not met, 'Allow me to congratulate you on the first number of the magazine. Putting aside my own contribution . . . I certainly do conceive that nothing equal to it of its kind was ever hitherto put forth'; the magazine contained 'nothing that is not readable . . . and very little that is not thoroughly worth reading'.[28] The public certainly found the *Cornhill* worth reading. Smith had carefully orchestrated its appearance, spending £5,000 on pre-publication advertisements. That Thackeray was to be editor and chief contributor had made the magazine the subject of much talk. The first issue sold nearly 120,000 copies and was estimated to have had half a million readers. Smith could proudly call its reception the 'literary event of the year'.[29] The *Daily News* said, 'It is a long time since any event unconnected with politics or battles has been so eagerly looked for as the appearance of the first number of the *Cornhill*.' The *Illustrated Times* said that the first number had fulfilled the high anticipation which rumour had excited and was 'a marvel of elegance and cheapness'.[30] (Smith's aim was to give the public a bargain: for one shilling, the usual price for a monthly part of a novel, the *Cornhill* provided not only as much—and usually more— serial fiction, but also factual and critical articles, poetry, and illustrations.) Monckton Milnes told Thackeray that the *Cornhill* was 'almost too good for the public it is written for and the money it has to earn'.[31]

A great deal of the success, especially the continued success—for although circulation did not stay at 120,000, it hovered somewhere near 80,000—was due to *Framley Parsonage*. The novel had been given pride of place in the magazine. Smith wrote many years later that this was 'pure courtesy' on Thackeray's part, the host's inviting a guest to walk into a room before himself.[32] But Smith's recollections were frequently inaccurate, and it was natural that the major fiction should have been placed first. In any case, *Framley Parsonage* was far more popular than Thackeray's *Lovel the Widower*, which appeared through the first six months. Later, when Thackeray began a long novel, *Philip*, for the *Cornhill*, he told Charles Lever that he intended to make it 'as strong as I can to fetch up the ground wh. I have—not lost, I trust, but only barely kept. I sang purposely small [in *Lovel the Widower*]; wishing to keep my strongest for a later day, and give Trollope the honors of *Violono* [*sic*] *primo*.' But even Thackeray's more ambitious novel did not keep pace with Trollope's. After *Framley Parsonage* and *Philip* had run together in the pages of the *Cornhill* from January to April 1861, Thackeray told a friend, 'I think Trollope is much more popular with the *Cornhill Magazine* readers that I am.'[33] *Framley Parsonage* was unquestionably the chief attraction of the magazine during those first sixteen months. Elizabeth Barrett Browning thought the novel 'perfect'; Mrs Gaskell wrote to George Smith, 'I wish Mr. Trollope would go on writing Framley Parsonage for ever. I don't see any reason why it should come to an end, and every one I know is always dreading the *last* number.'[34]

The reviews of the book issue of *Framley Parsonage*, even those that were grudging in their praise, testified to the novel's extraordinary popularity. The *Saturday Review* styled Trollope little more than an amusing story-teller—'he is far less of a novelist than a good diner-out'— but had to admit that

At the beginning of every month the new number of his book has ranked almost as one of the delicacies of the season; and no London belle dared to pretend to consider herself literary, who did not know the very latest intelligence about the state of Lucy Robarts' heart, and of Griselda Grantly's flounces. It is a difficult thing to estimate the exact position and merit of a book with which we are all so familiar, and which has diverted us so long. It seems a kind of breach of hospitality to criticise *Framley Parsonage* at all. It has been an intimate of the drawing-room—it has travelled with us in the train—it has lain on the breakfast-table. We feel as if we had met Lady Lufton at a country house, admired Lord Dumbello at a ball, and seen Mrs. Proudie at an episcopal evening party.

Sharpe's London Magazine, in a harsh notice that said the novel represented solely the manners of the day and was a 'huge mass of conventionalism', admitted that in taking this position they had 'show[n] that we differ from all the world in our estimate of [Trollope's] novels. He is now, perhaps, the most popular of our modern novelists.'[35]

Trollope, who had been, at least according to *The Times*, the most popular author among lending library readers, now was accorded a similar status among the even more numerous readers of magazine fiction. A fortunate confluence of circumstances had benefited both Trollope and the *Cornhill*. Neither alone would have enjoyed such spectacular success. Writing in 1879, Trollope said that *Framley Parsonage* 'was received with greater favour than any [book] I had written before or have written since'.[36] In *An Autobiography* Trollope explained, with his usual self-depreciation, that to the story of the embarrassed young clergyman he added that of Lucy Robarts and Lord Lufton 'because there must be love in a novel'. The result was a 'hodge-podge', but the characters were 'so well handled, that the work from the first to the last was popular,—and was received . . . with still increasing favour by both Editor and proprietors of the magazine'. He thought his heroine 'perhaps the most natural English girl that I ever drew . . . of those who have been good girls'. In writing the book so quickly to order, Trollope had not had much time to think about his characters, and by placing the novel in Barsetshire he was able 'to fall back upon my old friends Mrs. Proudie and the Archdeacon':

As I wrote it I became more closely acquainted than ever with the new shire which I had added to the English counties. I had it all in my mind,—its roads and railroads, its towns and parishes, its members of Parliament, and the different hunts which rode over it. I knew all the great lords and their castles, the squires and their parks, the rectors and their churches. This was the fourth novel of which I had placed the scene in Barsetshire, and as I wrote it I made a map of the dear county. Throughout these stories there has been no name given to a fictitious site which does not represent to me a spot of which I know all the accessories, as though I had lived and wandered there.[37]

16

Literary London

Trollope's connection with the *Cornhill Magazine* served quickly to introduce him to the literary world that had been denied to him by his residence in Ireland. Of special service was the cordiality and hospitality of his publisher. George Smith, eldest son of the founder of Smith, Elder, had entered the family business before he was 20, and by the time of his father's death in 1846, when Smith was scarcely 22, he took charge of the entire enterprise—of which publishing was but a small part. The firm's extensive banking and commercial activities so prospered under Smith that he was able to take considerable risks as a publisher. He loved books and the company of authors, and he was the friend and publisher of Ruskin, Charlotte Brontë,* Mrs Gaskell, Matthew Arnold, Browning, and numerous others. Though Smith had earlier published three works of Thackeray, including *Henry Esmond*, he came to be his exclusive publisher only through the *Cornhill* arrangement. Smith had a reputation for generosity and even extravagance, especially in connection with his beloved *Cornhill Magazine*, for which his payments to authors were, in his words, 'lavish almost to the point of recklessness'. In 1862 he offered George Eliot £10,000 for *Romola* and succeeded briefly in luring her away from Blackwood (the figure was reduced to £7,000 because she would not permit sixteen rather than twelve instalments of the novel).[1] It was not only open-handedness, but shrewdness also that brought Smith success. Trollope said that Smith, like Blackwood, never 'let anything worth doing slip through his fingers, rated a manuscript's value too high or too low, or ever misjudged the humour of the hour and the taste of the public'.[2]

It was at the first of George Smith's celebrated *Cornhill* dinners, given in late January 1860 at his house in Gloucester Square, that Trollope met many of the men who were to be his associates and friends. He was 45, and

---

* The story of his publishing of *Jane Eyre* is one of the best known of Victorian literary history; he was said to have been the original for Dr John Bretton in Charlotte Brontë's *Villette*.

somewhat self-conscious in such company for the first time, and conducted himself with predictable compensating forcefulness. George Augustus Sala described him on this occasion:

Anthony Trollope was very much to the fore, contradicting everybody; afterwards saying kind things to everybody, and occasionally going to sleep on sofas or chairs; or leaning against sideboards, and even somnolent while standing erect on the hearthrug. I never knew a man who could take so many spells of 'forty winks' at unexpected moments, and then turn up quite wakeful, alert, and pugnacious, as the author of 'Barchester Towers,' who had nothing of the bear but his skin, but whose ursine envelope was assuredly of the most grisly texture.[3]

The night had not gone altogether smoothly. When Smith introduced Trollope to his editor, Thackeray curtly said, 'How do?' and turned on his heel to hide a sudden spasm of pain. Trollope, ignorant of the malady, was greatly offended. Smith patched things up, and Trollope and Thackeray became close friends.[4] Trollope came to have as high a regard for Thackeray the man as he did for Thackeray the author of *Esmond*. Most of of the newcomer's literary and artistic friends and acquaintances were to be from Thackeray's circle. That Trollope never became intimate with Dickens or with many of his satellites was at least in part because of his allegiance to Thackeray.

The morning after his début into the glittering London world of authors and artists, Trollope unwittingly provoked a prolongation of the celebrated 'Garrick Club affair'. That involved fracas had begun in 1858 and had pitted Thackeray and the 'gentlemanly' faction of the club against young Edmund Yates and the 'bohemian' faction. More important, it pitted Thackeray against Dickens, who supported Yates, and even collaborated in Yates's written responses. The dispute began when Yates, part-time journalist and, like Trollope, an employee of the Post Office, attacked Thackeray in a penny paper called *Town Talk*. Thackeray regarded the article as an invasion of the privacy and gentlemanly code of the Garrick Club, and eventually, in spite of Dickens's efforts, Yates was voted out of the club. Dickens's championship of Yates was partly motivated by the long-standing, smouldering rivalry between the two giants of the Victorian novel, a situation made worse because Thackeray had recently seemed to side with Catherine Dickens when Dickens separated from her after twenty years of marriage and ten children.

Then in late May 1860 Yates renewed his attack, publishing in the *New York Times* a piece called 'Echoes from London Clubs' in which he claimed, among other things, that Smith's *Cornhill* dinners were 'tremendously heavy': he described Thackeray as the 'big gun', designated G. H. Lewes 'Mr. Bede', and called George Smith a 'very good man of business, but totally unread' ('his business is to sell books, not to read them'); he told how Thackeray struggled to get Smith to acknowledge his joke about having Dr Johnson behind the screen, and how Smith, having 'probably never heard of Dr. Johnson and his screen dinner', drew laughter from the table. Smith said the joke lay in Thackeray's having mistakenly referred to the dinner, in which Johnson, ashamed of his poverty, took his dinner behind a screen, as taking place at Curle's rather than Tonson's, as in Boswell. In Trollope's version (cancelled by his own hand in the *Autobiography*) Smith was too deep in conversation with another guest, and the fun consisted in Thackeray's 'vain attempts to have his allusion recognized'. Whatever the facts, Yates's version made Thackeray look unkind and Smith ignorant. The publication of the article in the *New York Times* would have gone almost completely unnoticed in London, had not the *Saturday Review* reprinted Yates's comments with the ostensible object of censuring them. Thackeray, according to Trollope, was much 'afflicted' and Smith greatly 'annoyed', while he himself was deeply chagrined on realizing that he had unthinkingly discussed the dinner with a friend in the presence of Yates, a 'literary gutter-scraper'. Trollope confessed his fault to Smith and Thackeray and was 'pardoned'.[5] Smith was for ignoring the article, but his wife insisted that it be answered. Thackeray produced a 'Roundabout Paper' that reproved 'Mr. Saturday Reviewer' for picking 'this wretched garbage out of a New York street, and hold[ing] it up for your readers' amusement' and took Yates ('Mr. Name-less') to task, noting how different would have been the account if he had been one of the contributors to the magazine. Trollope wrote to Smith that the Roundabout Paper was 'not so severe as I thought it would be—but it is better so'. Trollope 'taxed the gutter-scraper with his offence, and he owned his sin, praying to be forgiven'.[6] Trollope and Yates were never again on good terms, though some semblance of outward cordiality was maintained, as when Trollope invited Yates to participate in a series of lectures by literary people for postal employees. But one can imagine Trollope's annoyance at being asked, in August 1861 by John Maxwell, to be nominal editor of the *Temple Bar*, all the 'real work' being done by its sub-editor, Yates. Trollope replied that he would not undertake a 'mock Editorship' and that his hands were too full to undertake a novel for the magazine.[7]

On that January night in Gloucester Square Trollope met for the first time and became friends with, among others, Field Marshal Burgoyne,

Frederick Leighton, Robert Browning, Edwin Landseer, Godfrey Sykes, designer of the cover for the magazine, Matthew Higgins ('Jacob Omnium'), Albert Smith, the elderly novelist and essayist, E. S. Dallas, G. A. Sala, and Fitzjames Stephen. Other more intimate friendships also started that evening. Besides Thackeray himself, these included Sir Charles Taylor ('than whom', Trollope wrote, 'in latter life I have loved no man better'), Robert Bell, G. H. Lewes, Richard Monckton Milnes, William Russell, and John Everett Millais. With all these Trollope lived afterwards on affectionate terms.[8]

Some of these friendships developed more quickly than others. That with George Lewes did so as a consequence of Trollope's assistance in getting Lewes's son Charles Lee placed in the Post Office. Young Lewes, Trollope explained to the boy's father, would have to take a competitive examination that Trollope believed the twelve most popular authors in England would fail: 'For myself I should not dream of passing. I sd. break down in figures & spelling too, not to talk of handwriting.' But should Charles make the grade, the Civil Service was just the thing for a young man because it did not 'create dishonesty' as did the law, nor 'incapacitate' a man for other work as did the Church; nor did it require all that one could give, as did medicine; rather it left 'ample time for other work'. On 9 August, when he learned that Charles Lee had come in at the head of the examination list, Trollope wrote to congratulate his father, again with a little homily on the Civil Service: 'Do not let him begin life with any idea that his profession is inferior to others'; the Civil Service might not offer great prizes, but it allowed men to earn them elsewhere: 'One such man [Henry Reeve] in our days edits the Edinbro . . . another [Henry Taylor] has written the best poem of these days [*Philip van Artevelde*]; a third [Tom Taylor] supplies all our theatres with their new plays; and a fourth [Trollope himself] plies a small literary trade as a poor novelist. We boast also of artists, philosophers, newspaper politicians, & what not.'[9] Trollope liked G. H. Lewes enormously (he also thought him the 'acutest' and 'severest' critic he knew).[10] Lewes's irregular union with George Eliot posed no problem for the worldly Trollope (nor for Tom Trollope and Theodosia, who met them both in Florence that spring) and, at a time when many still shunned her, Trollope went out of his way to become friends with the two together. By November George Eliot was entering in her journal, 'Pleasant evening. Anthony Trollope dined with us, and made us like him very much by his straightforward, wholesome *Wesen*.' Lewes in his journal for 15 April 1861 wrote, 'Went down to Waltham to dine and sleep at Trollope's. He has a charming house and grounds, and I like him very much, so wholesome and straightforward a man.' George Eliot within two years was referring to Trollope as 'our excellent friend . . . one of the heartiest, most genuine, moral and generous men we know'.[11]

Another of the people Trollope met at Smith's that night was to become not only an intimate but a collaborator. When Trollope met John Everett Millais, the painter had pretty much turned his back on his early and radical Pre-Raphaelite days. A child prodigy, Millais had at 9 won a silver medal from the Society of Arts; at 11 he entered the Royal Academy Schools, the youngest student ever admitted; at 14 he won the medal for drawing from the antique; at 18 he took the gold medal for oil painting; in 1848 he had been one of the founders of the Pre-Raphaelite Brotherhood. His paintings had sparked much controversy, and spice was added to his career when in 1855 he married Effie Gray, whose six-year marriage to Ruskin had been annulled for non-consummation. (She was to have eight children with Millais.) During the 1860s Millais emerged as a more conventional painter, chiefly of portraits. But he was also to become one of the foremost illustrators in black and white during the great years of English wood engraving; it can be convincingly argued that his dozen years of black and white work, beginning with Allingham's *Music Master* in 1855 and the Moxon *Tennyson* in 1857 up to the drawings for periodicals such as the *Cornhill* and *Good Words*, together with his illustrations for Trollope, represent an accomplishment comparable to anything he did other than the celebrated Pre-Raphaelite oils of the 1850s.[12]

In the hurry of getting out the first issue of the *Cornhill*, no illustration attended *Framley Parsonage*, although the magazine prided itself on its artwork (Thackeray's *Lovel the Widower* had one full-page illustration and a vignette, both his own drawing). Smith set about securing an artist for Trollope's novel and asked him to select a subject for illustration. After further delays Smith hinted to Trollope that he was negotiating with Millais, to which news Trollope responded, 'Should I live to see my story illustrated by Millais no body would be able to hold me.' One wonders if Trollope had forgotten his sly joke in *The Warden* about the villainous Tom Towers adorning his quarters with a painting by Millais of a 'devotional lady looking intently at a lily as no lady ever looked before',[13] a comment all the more embarrassing in that it apparently attributed Charles Collins's *Convent Thoughts* to Millais. No record survives of Trollope's reaction to Millais's first illustration to *Framley Parsonage*, that for the fourth instalment, depicting Lord Lufton and Lucy Robarts. But when he saw in proof the second illustration, that of Lucy in a crinoline dress weeping on her bed, Trollope wrote angrily to Smith that it would be better to omit the drawing altogether: it was 'simply ludicrous', and some people would think it intentionally so; it was a 'burlesque', but so poorly executed as not to pass muster even for *Punch*; presumably, 'Mr. Millais has not time to devote to these illustrations, & if so, will it not be better to give them up?' As reviewers of the book noted, Lucy's dress, rather than Lucy, seems to be the subject of the drawing. Smith calmed his author's temper; and the next illustration, two months later, pleased Trollope: 'The Crawley family is very good,' he wrote, '& I will now consent to forget the flounced dress'; furthermore, life seemed to be imitating art, 'I saw the *very pattern of that dress* some time after the picture came out.' Things went smoothly for the remaining illustrations. In all Millais supplied six drawings for *Framley Parsonage*, an unusually meagre number for a long novel. But the collaboration had begun, which would lead to Millais's drawing eighty-seven full-page plates and nineteen elaborate vignettes for Trollope, who later wrote: 'I do not think that more conscientious work was ever done by man. . . . In every figure he drew it was his object to promote the views of the writer whose work he had undertaken to illustrate, and he never spared himself any pains in studying that work, so as to enable himself to do so. I have carried on some of those characters from book to book, and have had my own early ideas impressed indelibly on my memory by the excellence of his delineations.'14

Trollope had his commitment to keep with Chapman & Hall, and on 2 January 1860, putting *Framley Parsonage* on hold, he resumed *Castle Richmond* and worked steadily until completing it by the end of March. Such an interruption, he said, presented no difficulty: 'In our lives, we are always weaving novels, and we manage to keep the different tales distinct. . . . Had I left either *Framley Parsonage* or *Castle Richmond* half-finished fifteen years ago, I think I could complete the tales now [in 1876] with very little trouble.'15 He considered *Castle Richmond* one of his failures, and so has posterity; on the other hand, the reviews were fairly good. The *Spectator* called it 'a clever and amusing novel'; the *Athenaeum* said it was 'a spirited novel; the characters are life-like, and the incidents real.' The *Saturday Review* introduced the analogy that Trollope himself loved to propagate, that of the writer who 'makes a novel just as he might make a pair of shoes, with a certain workmanlike satisfaction in turning out a good article'; the reviewer thought *Castle Richmond* lacked the 'freshness and zest' of his earlier novels and regretted that, though Trollope has something to say about the Irish Famine, he did not mix this material well with his story.[16] But on the whole, *Castle Richmond*, though less widely noticed than *Framley Parsonage*, received at least as favourable a reception from the critics. But not from the public, to whom Irish novels were still distasteful. The hoped-for victory over this English prejudice expressed in the opening of the novel was not to be had. Trollope would not return to an Irish setting for a novel until 1870 when he wrote a short, tragic story called *An Eye for an Eye*, a work he did not publish until eight years later.

Upon finishing *Castle Richmond*, Trollope immediately resumed *Framley Parsonage*, which he completed on 27 June. During June he was also negotiating the sale of his next novel (*Orley Farm*). Trollope had determined that his new work, which was to be his longest to date, would appear in instalments. In fact, in the very first paragraph and throughout the novel he would refer to it as a 'serial work'. *Framley Parsonage* had turned him for good into a serial novelist. Of the thirty-nine novels published after *Framley Parsonage*, only four were released originally in book form, and of these two had been intended for serial publication that had gone awry; and the one that was published posthumously would have been placed with a magazine had Trollope lived. Thus *Miss Mackenzie* (1865) was the only novel he wrote after *Framley Parsonage* that was not intended for serial publication. His 'mechanical genius', as he laughingly called it, enabled him to write his novels to exactly prescribed limits—instalments per novel, chapters per instalment, pages per chapter, words per page.

The 'mechanically' apportioned instalments of a novel were meant to encase sections of the story that would hang together and at the same time 'entice the reader' to come back to the next number. A serial should have 'at least an attempt at murder in every number', Trollope once told a publisher, though he himself could 'never get beyond giving my people an attack of fever or a broken leg'.[17] Moreover, serial publication, he said, 'forces upon the author the conviction that he should not allow himself to be tedious in any single part'. Trollope admitted he himself was often tedious, but insisted that the serial writer must feel that he 'cannot afford to have many pages skipped out of the few which are to meet the reader's eye at the same time. Who can imagine the first half of the first volume of *Waverley* coming out in shilling numbers?' These ideas came to him while writing *Framley Parsonage*, which novel, in spite of its failings, had, he thought, at least 'no long succession of dull pages'. It can be argued that *Framley Parsonage* did more than give his popularity a tremendous boost and turn him for good into a serial novelist; it would in the long run make him more careful in the balancing of plots and counter-plots, and to this extent, serial publication made him a better novelist. [18]

The great popularity of *Framley Parsonage* boosted the interest of both Edward Chapman and George Smith in Trollope's next novel. Smith certainly meant to keep his star novelist, and sometime in June he made Trollope a threefold proposal: £3,000 for a non-fiction book in two volumes on India, £1,800 for a novel (*Orley Farm*) to appear in twelve issues of the *Cornhill*, and £600 for a short novel to appear in the magazine in 1862. In respect to the book on India, Smith knew of the success of Trollope's work on the West Indies; and his own extensive shipping/importing business with India provided an added incentive for the project. The £3,000 for that book would not be all profit for Trollope because he would have to take leave without pay from the Post Office for at least nine months and would have to pay his own expenses. Still, the total, £5,400, was impressive. On the other hand, Trollope felt some loyalty to Chapman, who had published three of his last four books, and who, in his dealings, 'always acceded to every suggestion made to him . . . never refused a book, and never haggled at a price'. [19] Trollope probably realized that he could one way or another continue to publish with Smith while keeping his connection with Chapman & Hall. Moreover, he was evidently anxious to try serialization in shilling monthly parts, a form of publication for popular novels pioneered by Chapman & Hall some quarter of a century earlier when they issued Dickens's *Pickwick Papers* in parts with enormous success. The form was specially associated with Dickens, but had been used by other novelists, including Ainsworth, Lever, Mrs Trollope, and Thackeray. Part publication usually called for twenty instalments in nineteen numbers, the last a double issue. Such novels were invariably longer than the standard Victorian three-volume novel (being roughly the equivalent of five such volumes); they were illustrated (usually two plates per part). At a shilling a number the total cost was one pound, plus a nominal fee for binding, considerably less money than the usual 31s. 6d. price for the conventional three-volume novel. Moreover, payment for a novel in parts was spread over nearly two years. From every viewpoint (except the size of the print), the novel in shilling parts was a bargain. It was the popularity of this form that Smith and Thackeray were challenging with a magazine that cost the same shilling but included not only illustrated fiction but much else besides. By the end of the decade the magazine would dominate the field.

Whatever Trollope's motives, he gave *Orley Farm* to Chapman & Hall. Chapman's £2,500 and half-profits after 10,000 copies—which latter eventually netted him more than £600 in addition—must have appeared about equal to Smith's straight £1,800. The difference was attributable to length, which was crucial to both writers and publishers. Trollope calculated his novels according to their number of 'volumes'—which for him meant the equivalent of one volume of the traditional nineteenth-century three-decker novel (approximately 60,000 to 80,000 words). *Orley Farm*, written to Chapman's purposes, was a five-volume novel; Smith's would have been three volumes. But the increase over what he had been paid by these publishers for his two recent books was considerable: Chapman was tripling his payment for *Castle Richmond*, which had been in effect £200 per volume unit; and Smith's offer would have almost doubled the figure paid for *Framley Parsonage* nine months earlier.

On the very day Trollope signed for *Orley Farm* with Chapman, 3 July, he offered to accept Smith's terms for the Indian book and for the short novel for the *Cornhill*. Smith dropped the Indian project, but agreed to pay £600 for the short novel for the *Cornhill*. Smith and Trollope had been in consultation about this story even before negotiations for the longer works had come to the boil. All the talk about Trollope writing too much raised again the idea of publishing a novel anonymously. (Novels published in the *Cornhill* were unsigned, but their authorship was generally known.) One possibility was a tale laid in Italy: he had, he told Smith, the plot in mind, and he thought an Italian story would be less easily identified as his than one about London advertising (*Brown, Jones, and Robinson*), although he feared that 'these things always get wind'. Smith chose *Brown, Jones, and Robinson*. The book Trollope had tried to sell to Longman back in 1857 and to Chapman the next year, of which he had written thirty-two manuscript pages in 1857, finally had a buyer. It is unlikely that George Smith would have rejected any novel from Trollope's pen at this point. *Brown, Jones, and Robinson* was to turn out to be, as Trollope said almost penitently, 'the hardest bargain I ever sold to a publisher'.[20]

However, Smith was prepared to reject two of Trollope's short stories as unsuitable for the *Cornhill*. The first, submitted on 29 July 1860, was 'The Banks of the Jordan'. This tale of a young woman masquerading as a man so that she might accompany the unsuspecting narrator on a tour of the Holy Land was filled with sexual resonances that Smith and Thackeray felt too explicit for the magazine. The narrator, for example, takes hold of his companion's leg by the calf to show where a Turkish saddle would chafe; he innocently offers to massage the saddle-sore young woman with brandy; he falls asleep with his head in her lap. Smith did not reject the story outright, but wanted the offending material removed and the whole thing shortened. 'You city publishers', Trollope wrote back, 'are so uncommonly delicate, whereas anything passes at the West End!' (Smith, Elder's premises were in Cornhill, the City; Chapman & Hall were in Piccadilly, the West End.) But although he could 'arrange' such details as that of the saddle, he could not cut the story from thirty to twenty pages: 'One cannot shorten a story. Little passages are sure to hang on to what is taken out.'[21]

Then, on 6 November, Trollope tried to place 'Mrs General Talboys' with the *Cornhill*, promising George Smith '18 pages exact'. The difficulty this time could not be length. Rose had thought the story 'ill-natured', but Smith and Thackeray found it dangerous. (Trollope was convinced Thackeray himself had not read it, but left the task to some 'moral deputy'—Smith.) The rejection drew from Trollope a good-natured but carefully argued letter to Thackeray: Trollope was unwilling to allow that he was 'indecent', while insisting that 'squeamishness'—though not delicacy—ought to be disregarded by a writer. In justifying allusions to illegitimate children and such like sources of 'impurities' in fiction, he gave instances from Scott, Charlotte Brontë, George Eliot, Dickens, and from Thackeray himself, calling him 'our second modern great gun', second only to Scott ('Observe how civil I am to you after the injury you have done me'); he saw Thackeray as disregarding squeamishness in his own writing for the *Cornhill* itself, in *The Four Georges*, and in innuendoes about ballet girls in *Lovel the Widower*. 'I of course look forward', Trollope went on, 'to bringing out my own story in a magazine of my own—It will be called "The Marble Arch," and I trust to confound you by the popularity of Mrs. Talboys.' Thackeray, who had been ill and dreaded facing Trollope's letter, had one of his girls read it first. Relieved, he wrote back: 'I am another, am I? I always said so. "The Marble Arch" is such a good name that I have a months mind to take it for my own story.'[22]

The two stories were eventually sold, along with six others, to the *London Review*, whose business manager, William Little, gave Trollope £50 apiece for them. 'The Banks of the Jordan' and 'Mrs General Talboys' appeared in January and February 1861, and their fate proved that Smith and Thackeray knew their business. Laurence Oliphant, a miscellaneous writer and one of the proprietors of the *London Review*, wrote to Trollope about the 'disapprobation' with which their readers had received the stories; Oliphant quoted one of the 'mildest' of the many letters to their editor, this reader speaking of destroying the supplements in which the stories were printed and giving up the paper, while inquiring whether the proprietors meant to appeal to men of 'intelligence & high moral feeling' or those of a 'morbid imagination & *a low tone of morals*'.[23] The *London*

Review published only one more story by Trollope and then sold the remaining five to the newly established weekly, *Public Opinion*.

The rejection of his stories had no effect on the growing cordiality between Trollope and George Smith. By September Trollope had dropped the 'Mr' from his salutation in letters to Smith, had entertained Smith and Thackeray at Waltham, and found himself thanking Smith for the gift of an elaborate travelling bag:

No one is more accessible to a present than I am. I gloat over it like a child, and comfort myself in school hours by thinking how nice it will be to go back to it in play time. In that respect I have by no means outgrown my round jacket, & boy's appurtenances. . . . I argue from your good nature that you are satisfied with the work I have done for you, & that after all is better than any present. I also feel that I owe you some cadeau of worth, seeing that you have brought me in contact with readers to [be] counted by hundreds of thousands, instead of by hundreds.[24]

Smith had sent the travelling bag in time for Trollope's holiday. On 24 September he and Rose left for the continent to visit the T. A. Trollopes in Florence. There he met Kate Field.

Mary Katherine Keemle 'Kate' Field was born in St Louis, Missouri, on 1 October 1838, the daughter of Joseph M. Field and Eliza Riddle; both her parents were on the stage; her father was also a theatre owner/manager, playwright, and a friend of various literary people, including Edgar Allan Poe. Kate was a clever child, extremely sensitive and strong-willed; she had a good voice and considerable musical talent; she had the family flair for the stage. After the unexpectedly sudden death of her father early in 1856, she was looked after for a time by her mother's sister, Cordelia Riddle Sanford, the wife of a Newport millionaire, Milton Sanford. Mrs Sanford was a generous patron of the arts, and at Newport entertained many distinguished people, including actress Charlotte Cushman, actor Edwin Booth, writer Edwin Whipple, sculptor Thomas Ball, abolitionist Charles Coleman, feminist Julia Ward Howe, and singer Adelaide Phillipps—stimulating company for young Kate, and the kind of company she was to shine in all her life. Indeed her later society would be more brilliant than her aunt's. But lacking independent means, she struggled, successfully but arduously, to maintain her place and her independence in that society. An entry in her journal from her seventeenth year expresses the wish that she were a man; as a woman she must 'crush' her ambitions and impulses, because a woman must 'content herself with indoor life, with sewing and babies'; those who say this is God's intention '*lie*'. (The same entry includes a passionate desire for 'a room religiously your own . . . a sanctuary to which you retire to ponder, think, weep, write, read, *pray*, knowing that there you may indulge your feelings as the emotions and passions dictate, and no one will dare intrude—no one will scrutinize you'.) She wrestled with the alternatives: to live quietly upon the bounty of her uncle and aunt or try her fortune upon the stage or perhaps at writing. She was realistic: 'I've just talent enough to make me despise humble occupations and long for that which it seems to me I can never attain.' Uncle Milton, against whom she privately complained at times that he would not let her love him 'in a fatherly way', helped resolve the uncertainty by deciding that she should study music in Italy. Before sailing for Europe with her uncle and aunt in January 1859, Kate, who was 21, arranged with George Lunt, editor of the Boston *Courier*, to write letters from abroad for the paper. Lunt provided her with introductions to the Brownings, the T. A. Trollopes, and Hawthorne. Kate fell in love with Italy; took voice lessons from Sebastiani and Romani; became a friend of Charlotte Cushman and intimate with both Brownings (Robert told her she was 'the most ambitious person of my acquaintance') and with the Tom Trollopes ('Mr. Trollope is such a fine man. His wife is promiscuously talented . . . but does not go very far in any one thing'). In Florence too she formed a close friendship with Isa Blagden, Mrs Browning's great friend (who called Kate's mother a 'dove who had hatched an eagle'). She met the feminist Frances Power Cobbe, the painter Elihu Vedder, Boston publisher James T. Fields, sculptor Harriet Hosmer. She became a friend of (and later an authority on) the Italian tragedienne Adelaide Ristori. She also met George Eliot ('a woman whose whole face is of the horse make') and G. H. Lewes ('a very ugly man, but very charming in conversation'). Old Walter Savage Landor, smitten, said she was the most charming young lady he had ever seen ('and you know, he has seen a great many,' Elizabeth Barrett Browning told Kate). He wrote her poems and gave her gifts, flowers, grapes, and, as Kate wrote, 'all the manuscript scraps in his possession, which I am to edit and publish after his death'. She had to attend him every morning, while he taught her Latin, which time she sometimes begrudged him. [25]

Kate had auburn hair and blue eyes; she was shortish, girlish but with a full figure, and all her life would look much younger than her years. Trollope met her at his brother's and was immediately drawn to her combination of charming femininity, independence of mind, and frank, easy companionableness. He knew and appreciated, as his novels testify, pretty, intelligent girls of the English middle class; but their upbringing and education precluded the making of choices about their way of life:

they were being prepared for early marriage and were not permitted the aspirations and wide interests of this 'exotic' American. With Kate friendship was possible, and Trollope soon formed for her a romantic attachment that lasted until his death. Her first impression of him is recorded in a letter to her aunt: 'Anthony Trollope is a very delightful companion. I see a great deal of him. He has promised to send me a copy of the "Arabian Nights" (which I have never read) in which he intends to write "Kate Field, from the Author", and to write me a four-page letter on condition that I answer it.'[26] Trollope was to say of her in his *Autobiography*:

There is an American woman, of whom not to speak in a work purporting to [be] a memoir of my own life would be to omit all allusion to one of the chief pleasures which has graced my later years. In the last fifteen years she has been, out of my own family, my most chosen friend. She is a ray of light to me, from which I can always strike a spark by thinking of her. . . . But not to allude to her in these pages would amount almost to a falsehood. I could not write truly of myself without saying that such a friend had been vouchsafed to me.[27]

Especially noteworthy is the reference to 'thinking of her' because they were not often in each other's company. Nor, apparently, did he write to her except when he was near her and about to meet up or when there was some business immediately at hand. Only twenty letters from Trollope to her survive, though there is evidence that he sent her more than that number. Unfortunately all of hers to Trollope he destroyed; but from his side of the correspondence (and from her letters to others), one can gather that hers were frank and, like his, sometimes tactless. But that very frankness bespeaks a familiarity so well-founded as to support such outspoken contrariety. As a married man twenty-three years her senior, Trollope's tactic was constantly to emphasize this age difference, and act the avuncular, even fatherly, adviser, one who with her own good in mind found fault and gave difficult advice. This was evidently the way he delivered himself of shyness and fought off some feelings of guilt. He frequently sermonizes, scolds, bullies her, then admits that he does so. His letters, with their teasing and occasional tenderness, all express friendship and concern, with a confident spontaneity that must have come from his assurance that she accepted and returned his affection. How much their relationship lighted up life for him, he expressed in *An Autobiography*; there can be no doubt that she valued the man whom her biographer called her 'ardent friend'. There were other men in her life— admirers and eligible suitors, of whom she had many—for she was the

centre of attraction wherever she went and by her own admission preferred the company of men to that of women; with none, however, did she
maintain such an easy friendship, over time and distance, as that with the
much older, happily married (and therefore unthreatening) English
novelist, whom she had laid under her spell in Florence.

Upon his return to London, Trollope sent the promised copy of the
Arabian Nights, playfully telling her the tales would do her good 'mentally
& morally': 'Don't attempt to read them . . . through at a burst, but take
them slowly & with deliberation & you will find them salutary.' The letter
takes on an obliquely personal tone in its second paragraph:

I am beginning to feel towards you & your whereabouts as did your high-flown
American correspondent. Undying art, Italian skies, the warmth of southern,
sunny love, the poetry of the Arno and the cloud clapt Apennines, are beginning
again to have all the charms which distance gives. I enjoy these delicacies in
England—when I am in Italy in the flesh, my mind runs chiefly on grapes, roast
chestnuts, cigars, and lemonade. [28]

At home Trollope apparently made no secret of his attraction to Kate
('friendship' would have been the word he used), and Rose evidently made
no or little fuss. In a late novel, the narrator says it is conducive to
'matrimonial comfort' that a husband be caught in some 'family
peccadillo'—such as when 'a letter from a lady falls into wrong hands'. The
wife can then, in the face of her husband's 'assumed divine superiority',
pardon 'such evidence of human imperfection', and achieve equality. [29]

The year 1861 began with George Smith assuring a sensitive Trollope that
Thackeray had agreed there should be no 'editorial revision' of *Brown,
Jones, and Robinson* to fit it for appearance in the *Cornhill*. At this time
Trollope had not yet written more than the thirty-two manuscript pages
produced in 1857. The concern of Smith and Thackeray was probably
based not on a sight of this fragment but on the indelicacies they detected
in his short stories. Trollope's answer shows how important Smith's
assurance was: 'I should have been unhappy to feel myself severed from
the most popular periodical publication of the day, & assure you that I will
do the best I can for you with B. J. & R.'[30] Being asked to tone down stories
was one thing; novels were a very different matter. Memories of
Longman's changes in *Barchester Towers* still rankled.

Trollope attempted to write *Brown, Jones, and Robinson* in 'a style for
which I certainly was not qualified', as he admitted. [31] In fact he attempted
to write in the humorous vein of Thackeray, and also, to a lesser extent, in

that of Dickens. The novel also differed from his others in that it is supposedly told, not by the usual Trollopian narrator, who is so often a rather undisguised Anthony Trollope, but by one of the protagonists, George Robinson, one of three proprietors of a luckless haberdashery store. Moreover, the first chapter, called a 'Preface', explains that Robinson's text has been put into publishable form by 'one of Smith and Elder's young men'. The editor of the magazine tells Robinson that 'in fiction . . . your own unaided talents would doubtless make you great . . . but . . . I do think that in the delicate task of composing memoirs a little assistance may perhaps be not inexpedient.' This was one of Trollope's little private jokes, a nice irony that the story should be described as having been put together in the very fashion which if insisted upon would have driven him from the *Cornhill*, in spite of all the magazine had meant to him.

Although looking ahead to the continuation of *Brown, Jones, and Robinson* (not begun until June 1861) and writing short stories, his chief task at hand every morning was the enormously long *Orley Farm* for Chapman. He would work on it steadily with but slight interruptions for other writing for almost a year, from 4 July 1860 until 22 June 1861. One very heartening aspect of *Orley Farm* emerged when, before 1860 was out, Chapman engaged Millais to do the illustrations, two per number, forty in all. Millais had trouble visualizing, from Trollope's description, the very first illustration, that of Orley Farm itself, and Trollope suggested Millais might go down to see the house or that a photographer might be sent. But for all he knew the house might have been altered: 'There are two houses which did belong to my father, & were then called "Julians". . . . In one, the larger, Mr Cunningham the rector of Harrow still I believe lives. The other which is a little lower down the hill, and a little further from the high road, is the house in question. I will however write to Harrow & learn the name of the occupier.'[32] Cunningham, who did not die until 1861, was indeed still living in the grander of the two houses, the one Trollope's father had built and then ignominiously vacated after living there little more than a year. Julian Hill, the farmhouse, was owned at this time by Edward Ridley Hastings, who used it for a preparatory school. After *Orley Farm* was published Hastings got Trollope's permission to name his school Orley Farm School (under which name it still exists today, though it was moved to new quarters in 1901).

Not only was 'Orley Farm' based on Julian Hill, but 'Hamworth' and 'Hamworth Hill', the setting of the novel, plainly echo Harrow and Harrow-on-the-Hill. (Harrow with its painful memories was but a few miles from where Trollope now lived at Waltham Cross, and although he went continually about England and visited just about everywhere—either officially or socially—there is no record of his ever returning to Harrow.) *Orley Farm* is the sad, tragic story of a middle-aged widow, Lady Mason. The other prominent elements, a secondary plot about young lovers, comic sections centring around commercial salesmen, and hunting scenes, tend to make *Orley Farm* a somewhat sprawling novel, the result probably of Trollope's first working in so lengthy and constrained a format, twenty instalments of thirty-two densely printed pages each. Lady Mason is a good woman, a caring mother who forges a codicil to a will in order that her son Lucius, an honest but priggish young man, may inherit Orley Farm instead of his obnoxious half-brother to whom it legally belongs. Her deed brings her twice into court, and *Orley Farm* is Trollope's most extended treatment of the law, with a long list of solicitors and barristers of every variety, including the redoubtable Chaffanbrass. Trollope's old notion that no honest lawyer should defend one whom he thinks guilty is ostensibly a major theme, one propounded by the narrator and by Felix Graham, a naïve fledgling barrister. On the other hand, the story itself undercuts such a simplistic view: Lady Mason is so decent a person, her cause so reasonable—though dishonest—and her antagonists are so despicable and so mean, that the reader welcomes the apparent miscarriage of justice when she is wrongly declared innocent. By having her, after the trial, voluntarily surrender the property Trollope can come down on the side of justice, in spite of the law's failings. In Lady Mason herself Trollope explores, in a way he had not attempted since *The Macdermots*, tragic emotions, pathos, guilt, and mental anguish, something he would do with even more success in Josiah Crawley and Louis Trevelyan.

Millais's illustrations for *Orley Farm* seemed perfectly to fit the text; Trollope went so far as to have the narrator say in a late chapter that the reader's idea of Lady Mason's sorrow 'will have come to him from the skill of the artist, and not from the words of the writer', and he even suggests that the reader turn back hundreds of pages and look again at the illustration.[33] So pleased with the illustrations was Trollope that he had a set of artist's proofs of the drawings bound in a half-morocco volume, in which he wrote: 'I have never known a set of illustrations so carefully true, as are these, to the conception of the writer of the book illustrated. I say that as a writer. As a lover of Art I will add that I know no book graced with more exquisite pictures.'[34] In *An Autobiography* Trollope called Millais's illustrations for *Orley Farm* 'the best I have seen in any novel in any language'.[35]

Continued collaboration with Millais served to enhance the intimacy between the two men. That Millais was a professional artist must have made his friendship all the more welcome to Trollope, an inveterate museum-goer. Trollope had the educated Victorian's trust in his own judgement in art, and was not averse to expressing it in print. In 1856 he had written a chapter on art for the ill-fated *New Zealander*; now in May 1861 he interrupted work on *Orley Farm* to write a lecture on the National Gallery. He sent Millais tickets, but for reasons unknown the lecture was never given, and Trollope published it in Mrs S. C. Hall's *Saint James's Magazine*. In the article he defends the controversial National Gallery, of which Englishmen, with their natural bent for national self-criticism, generally feel they have made a 'mess'. Although the new building by William Wilkins had been subjected to unmitigated abuse, the problems he faced were considerable: he was crippled as regards space, money, and materials ('he was called on to use columns from other places'). Of course the Louvre is a grander building, but England cannot expect anything like that 'until, as a first step, we bless ourselves with a French Government'. But as a place for *seeing* pictures the National Gallery is superior. In the Louvre there is but one enormous—and 'very dirty'—velvet settee, from which one cannot see half the pictures. At Munich, there is no seat at all, 'and the work of seeing the pictures is terrible. I used to lie along on the dirty floor; but there are many picture-seekers who would not like that.' The Pitti has 'luxurious' chairs, but the pictures cannot be seen from them. At Trafalgar Square one can sit anywhere in the room and make the best of the pictures.

Along with a discussion of the prices of the Gallery's major purchases, Trollope cannot resist some art criticism, which for him involves no 'arcana'. How does a man learn to love a great picture? By standing in front of it 'till he does love it, or till he drops'. The old Tuscan masters are especially dear to him, for among them can be traced 'that painful thinking, those ungrudged efforts after excellence, which by degrees brought up the art of painting to the highest excellence it has ever reached'. Later came the want of effort that led to decay. Raphael, though a 'wonderful' artist, 'prepared absolute ruin for all who were to come after him. . . . Raphael's grace had been the grace of fiction, and not the grace of nature. The artists of Italy were stricken with wonder, and followed the falsehood faithfully, without attaining the grace. It was he and Michael Angelo, between them, who did the mischief.' One wonders how much of this sprang from talk with Millais. Trollope closes on a prosaic, and characteristic, note, a suggestion that the building ought to open at eight, not ten, in the morning.[36]

Trollope's move to England had brought him success as a writer, a place in the literary, artistic, and political circles of the capital, and new friends. It also brought the blessing of being thoroughly settled, for the first time, in his own home, Waltham House. It was a four-storey house of the early eighteenth century, with two wings, one of them used as an office for his clerks, the other as stables for his horses. Trollope at first had a lease, but decided to purchase after spending £1,000 on improvements during 1861–2, including the addition of a drawing-room on the ground floor, its outer walls carefully matched to the mellow brick of the house. The old walled garden, with its sundial, stone-edged pool, and summerhouse, was a great delight to the Trollopes, who brought it to such perfection that two landscape gardeners told a later purchaser: 'Leave it alone; as an old garden it is inimitable.' Gardeners must have been employed, though no references to them survive; however the 1861 Census does enumerate the staff living in the house: groom, dairymaid, cook, under-cook, and house-maid. Looking back to 1861 in *An Autobiography*, Trollope wrote, 'I was now settled at Waltham Cross, in a house in which I could entertain a few friends modestly, where we grew our own cabbages and strawberries, made our own butter, and killed our own pigs. I occupied it for twelve years, and they were years to me of great prosperity.' The approaching end of those twelve years he made the occasion for a valedictory description, characteristically mingling deprecation with affection:

I had, some time since, bought the house . . . and had added rooms to it, and made it, for our purposes, very comfortable. It was, however, a ricketty old place, requiring much repair, and occasionally not as weather-tight as it should be. We had a domain there sufficient for three cows, and for the making of our own butter and hay. For strawberries, asparagus, green peas, out-of-door peaches, for roses especially, and such every-day luxuries, no place was ever more excellent.[37]

The entertainment of friends in his country house was one of Trollope's great pleasures. The earliest known invitation is to Mrs Knower, suggesting that she and her daughter should spend some days with the Trollopes in June 1860. In April 1861 he assured G. H. Lewes: 'Of course a man who comes here sleeps here.' Many invitations mention the 5.10 p.m. train from Shoreditch Station, which brought visitors down in time for six o'clock dinner. Often a little party was assembled, as in June 1863 when William Russell of *The Times* was invited along with Robert Bell, Jacques Blumenthal the composer, and 'that female Caxton of the Age', Emily Faithfull, founder of the Victoria Press; or when Millais was asked to settle a day—with promised 'consumption of all our cream and strawberries'—

with the Thackerays, Charles Collins and his wife Kate (Dickens's daughter), and Admiral Robert Fitzroy. Another friend recalled how 'in the warm summer evenings the party would adjourn after dinner to the lawn, where wines and fruit were laid out under the fine old cedar tree, and good stories were told, while the tobacco smoke went curling up into the twilight.' George Smith recorded that once while he was staying overnight at Waltham, he rose early, looked out his window, and 'saw Trollope dragging a garden roller at what might be called a canter round the garden', something he did for exercise when not hunting. (Trollope also proposed 'out of the mere kindness of his heart' that Smith's wife might amuse herself by jumping over a bar on his favourite hunter. Trollope, Smith said, 'had scarcely imagination enough to comprehend the limitation of those who did not share his own round and over-running vigour'.) The Trollopes entertained in the winter also: Annie Thackeray saw it at that season, 'a sweet old prim chill house wrapped in snow'; and one of Trollope's nephews recalled that the children's parties at Christmas were in every detail like the ones at Noningsby described by Trollope in *Orley Farm*, with Trollope joining in games of 'Commerce' and contriving that the children hold the winning cards. (John Morley and Mrs Humphry Ward closed a review of *An Autobiography* with the remark that 'children delighted in him'.)[38]

In the winter he was also able to offer visitors a day out with the hounds. His greatest regret on leaving Ireland had been that hunting would prove too expensive for him in England; however, as the income from his books increased he could soon afford to keep at least four hunters in his stables and to pay the annual subscriptions to the Essex Foxhounds, on the edge of whose country he lived; he sometimes hunted with the East Essex, near his friend Lady Wood and her daughter Anna Steele* at Witham; he was also within easy distance of the Roothing country, and made occasional forays into Oxfordshire and other hunting counties. In the hunting scenes of *Can You Forgive Her?* Trollope inserted a satiric picture of himself as the fifteen-stone 'heavy-weight sporting literary gentleman', the novelist Pollock, even the name echoing his own. Like Trollope, Pollock is the subject of good-natured joking about his extraordinary efforts to get to the hunt. A fellow hunting man exclaims:

'By George, there's Pollock! . . . I'll bet half a crown that he's come down from London this morning, that he was up all night last night, and that he tells us so three times before the hounds go out of the paddock.'

* Lady Wood and her daughter were both novelists; among Lady Wood's other 12 children was a young daughter Katherine, later Mrs Kitty O'Shea, so fatally involved with Parnell.

And sure enough Pollock announces:

'By George . . . just down from London by the 8.30 from Euston Square, and got over here from Winslow in a trap. . . . I had to leave Onslow Crescent at a quarter before eight, and I did three hours' work before I started.'

'Then you did it by candle-light.' . . .

'Of course I did; and why shouldn't I? Do you suppose no one can work by candle-light except a lawyer?'[39]

Like Pollock, Trollope rode hard in spite of his weight, and had countless tumbles and disasters with horses that could carry him no farther. (The granddaughter of Lady Wood remembered his hunters as 'more like coach horses than anything else, but his huge squat bulk required weight carriers, and they were safe conveyances and clever fencers over the trappy Essex ditches'.) As Trollope's near-sightedness grew progressively more severe,* his mishaps became more frequent: 'Few have investigated', Trollope wrote, 'more closely than I have done the depth, and breadth, and water-holding capacities of an Essex ditch.' Not being able to see the nature of a fence, his practice was either to follow someone closely or simply ride straight for the fence 'with the full conviction that I may be going into a horse-pond or a gravel-pit'. Trollope took his share of mockery about his calamities in the field: George Smith records Trollope, his head heavily bandaged from a hunting accident, telling him that his hunting pals, 'those brutes in Essex, insisted on inquiring after the *horse's hoofs*, pretending to believe that *they* must have sustained more damage than my head!' The only concession Trollope made to his more than busy schedule was to hunt two rather than the ideal three days a week: 'Mortal man', he told Smith, 'cannot write novels, do the Post Office, and go out three days.'[40] But, as in the old days in Ireland, nothing was allowed to interfere with hunting, neither writing nor Post Office work. No one at the Post Office complained, at least not publicly. His hunting meant that from November to April he had to be 'especially alert', as he said, and to work in the evenings and on Sundays. But these exertions daunted him not at all. Being able to resume hunting capped the pleasure that his return to England and the success of *Framley Parsonage* had brought him. At Waltham Cross Trollope gradually acquired the character of an Essex squire. At the same time, from Waltham he kept up an increasingly busy literary and social life in the capital. The years of great prosperity had begun.

* By the 1870s a visitor to Trollope's study would speak of his fumbling about 'amongst a whole army of spectacles for the exact pair which would enable him to read the face of his guest'.[41]

Trollope's progress into the fashionable literary and artistic world moved forward when on 24 April 1861 (his forty-sixth birthday) he heard from Richard Monckton Milnes that he was elected to the Cosmopolitan Club. He had written to Milnes the previous July, asking that Milnes put his name down. Tom Taylor would second him. It was another instance of Thackeray's circle advancing Trollope. The Cosmopolitan Club met on Wednesdays and Sundays in the studio of the painter Henry Wyndham Phillips, in Charles Street, Berkeley Square. J. L. Motley said its purpose was 'to collect noted people and smoke very bad cigars', and quoted Thackeray as saying, 'Everybody is or is supposed to be a celebrity; nobody ever says anything worth hearing; and every one goes there with his white choker at midnight, to appear as if he had just been dining with the aristocracy.'⁴² The club supplied its members and their friends with free tea and brandy and water. Trollope found the gatherings 'delightful'; there he would meet Milnes and Thackeray, Tom Taylor, Millais, Browning, Tennyson, Austin Layard, Tom Hughes, Arthur Russell, George Barrington, Laurence Oliphant, Matthew Higgins, William Stirling, Henry Reeve, Frederick Locker-Lampson. A special attraction of the Cosmopolitan for Trollope was the presence of notable Liberal politicians: Lord Ripon, Lord Stanley, William Forster, Lord Enfield, Lord Kimberley, George Bentinck, Vernon Harcourt, Davenport Bromley, E. H. Knatchbull-Hugessen. These, and many others, Trollope relates, 'used to whisper the secrets of Parliament with free tongues'.⁴³ Cosmopolitan Club intimacy with politicians must have been heady stuff to an amateur politician like Trollope. As a civil servant he had been on the edge of the political world, and had used his glimpses of it in *The Three Clerks*, especially in the career of the venal politician, Undy Scott, and in the party intrigues of the Parliamentary Committee on the proposed Limehouse Bridge. The world of party politics loomed large—and was confidently handled—in *Framley Parsonage*, with its 'gods' (Whig-Liberals) and 'Giants' (Tories), the plot turning on Harold Smith's exercise of patronage during his brief spell in the cabinet, just before the fall of Brock's government (clearly echoing that of Palmerston's Whig-Liberal administration in 1858). But the friendships Trollope made at the Cosmopolitan added greatly to his knowledge, and prepared the way for the later political novels. Trollope would model the 'Universe Club' of *Phineas Redux* on the Cosmopolitan.

Another indication of Trollope's rise in the literary world was the start of his lifelong and devoted involvement with the Royal Literary Fund. He was recruited in May 1861 for the Fund by Robert Bell, Thackeray's close friend, who became one of Trollope's intimates. Bell had always lived by his pen; he was a journalist, biographer, an editor of poets, and author of some unsuccessful plays and novels. Trollope wrote that Bell 'never made that mark which his industry and talents would have seemed to ensure. He was a man well known to literary men, but not known to readers.' Trollope asserted that he knew no one better read in English literature; Bell's conversation charmed far more than his pen; moreover, he liked to hear the chimes at midnight, at which times, Trollope said, none surpassed him in wit and 'gentle revelry'.[44] Bell was an indefatigable worker for the General Committee of the Royal Literary Fund, the group of twenty-four that managed the Fund and allocated grants to needy writers. The fund was founded in 1790 to help—as it still does today—impoverished authors or their widows and dependents. Trollope had little use for most public charities, and even had his doubts about private giving. He once told a friend that 'all charity is wrong,—and only to be excused by the comfort it gives to the giver.'[45] But he viewed the Royal Literary Fund differently and came to have a positive attachment to this remarkable institution, of which he became a life member by a donation of £10. The Fund's annual anniversary dinner was a main source of income, and Trollope expended much energy seeking out stewards and arranging for speakers. On seven occasions he himself spoke, usually in answer to the toast to literature. The first such occasion was on 15 May 1861 when the dinner was held at Freemasons' Hall, Great Queen Street, Lincoln's Inn Fields. Trollope's brief speech hit a characteristic note, 'the prosaic side' of his subject:

I think the time is coming when literature will be regarded as a profession in this country, as the law, the church, and physic, are now regarded. But the mainstay of all professions is the *honorarium*. Men must live; and, as I take it, literary men must live as well as others; and I am inclined to think that in no respect has literature, during the last ten years, made greater progress than in this;—that those who set themselves to work at it with honest industry and with fair intellectual powers, can live by their work in comfort.

A familiar theme, and most appropriate for a fund-raising dinner for indigent authors; but it was also something close to the speaker's heart. Trollope was seated at dinner with Bell, Thackeray, E. S. Dallas, Frederic Chapman (cousin and partner of Edward Chapman, and who by this time was conducting the firm's negotiations with Trollope), and Sir William Frederick Pollock. Trollope was gratified to be associated with literary figures, 'men of his own kind', and answering the toast to 'The Literature of England coupled with the name of Mr. Anthony Trollope'.[46]

Trollope had long had it in mind to write a book about America; he had said so in the closing pages of his book on the West Indies, suggesting that 'the government and social life of the people there—of that people who are our children—afford the most interesting phenomena which we find as to the new world;—the best means of prophesying . . . what the world will next be, and what men will next do.'[47] And so, on 20 March 1861, he signed an agreement with Chapman & Hall for £1,250 for the first 2,500 copies to be published of a two-volume travel book on America. Earlier he had told George Smith that a leave for the purpose of writing a book on India would not present any difficulty. But difficulty did arise, the source of the trouble having been brewing for some time. The old feud of Tilley and Trollope against Sir Rowland Hill had been warming up ever since Trollope had come to England. Hill must have sensed trouble at having the loud and gruff Trollope near headquarters and in frequent communication with his brother-in-law, the Assistant Secretary who so often balked him. Trouble was not long in coming. Trollope was just settled into his new duties when a long article appeared in *The Times* of 29 and 30 March 1860, urging an inquiry into how the Post Office operated, especially in the London area. It particularly criticized the poor pay of the lower staff. The Postmaster-General, Lord Elgin, established a Committee of Inquiry, of which Trollope was named a member. Hill, who was absent on sick leave at the time, saw the committee as an intrigue against him and tried to slow its work through his brother, an Assistant Secretary like Tilley, but junior to him in length of service. The committee resigned, although Tilley protested vigorously that it should continue without interference from Frederick Hill. Then Rowland Hill suspended the committee, pending the appointment of a new Postmaster-General. After considerable infighting, and out of fear of the workers' displeasure, the committee was reformed, with Trollope again a member. It began hearing complaints from workers' groups on 16 May, and on 21 July its report called for considerable pay increases and the improvement of working conditions for the lower employees. It also recommended promotion by seniority for these workers. Rowland Hill fumed and called upon the new Postmaster-General, Lord Stanley of Alderley, to wait upon his return before acting. But Tilley and Trollope won their point, as seniority became again the basis for promotion among lower workers. (Hill later entered in his diary, 'Don't believe in T's sincerity—no man both clever and honest could be a party to the elaborate misrepresentations in the two Reports of the Committee on the Circulation office, and as T. is undoubtedly clever, it follows in my opinion that he is dishonest.'[48]) In April Tilley and Trollope had also testified before a Parliamentary Committee against the suitability of Civil Service examinations for entrants to the minor establishment, once more flying in the face of Hill's policies.

The Trollope–Hill feud flared up again in early 1861 when Trollope organized a series of lectures by literary men for postal employees— G. H. Lewes, Edmund Yates, Thomas Hughes, and Trollope himself. (Thackeray declined, saying he had only 'that stale old Humour & Charity' talk and that he was too busy 'preparing my friend Philip' to write a new lecture.⁴⁹) Trollope gave the first lecture, on 4 January at St Martin's-le-Grand. He vigorously defended the Civil Service as a profession: some pundits claimed that appointments in the service 'were looked for by the indolent and incapable, by those afflicted with physical infirmity, and by young men unfit for active exertions'; but Trollope held that no other profession admitted 'of a brighter honesty, of a nobler purpose, or of a more manly action'. Can soldiers, lawyers, Members of Parliament, he asked, be sure they are 'doing good'? He vigorously attacked promotion by merit, the system beloved of Hill, as invidious in that it enabled a senior officer to 'put unfairly forward his special friends'. Trollope also energetically advocated more independence for civil servants, especially the right to vote. He said that every time a new Reform Bill on the franchise came up he had applied to 'some big wig'—to Lord John Russell, for example, or Lord Elgin. But a lone voice was helpless, and civil servants must come forward and be heard. His listeners cheered, and the papers were generally enthusiastic in reporting the speech, though as Trollope wryly remarked to George Smith, 'The Civil Service Gazette I think I may say did not report the lecture.'⁵⁰ Trollope proceeded to publish it in the *Cornhill* in defiance of Hill, who represented the Postmaster-General, Lord Stanley, as disapproving of the lecture. This was a far greater provocation to Hill than the criticism of the Civil Service in *The Three Clerks*; he promptly requested the Postmaster-General to censure the offender, only to find that Trollope had forestalled him by showing the article in proof to Stanley, with whom he was on good terms. Trollope recalled that Stanley told him that Hill had asked for his dismissal. 'When I asked his lordship whether he was prepared to dismiss me, he only laughed. The threat was no threat to me, as I knew myself to be too good to be treated in that fashion.'⁵¹

Rowland Hill seemed to be losing round after round. One can imagine, then, his indignation at Trollope's requesting, a few months later, a seven-month leave of absence. Trollope says he went direct to Stanley, who asked the robust Trollope if it were on the plea of ill health. No, he wanted to write a book, and based his plea on having 'done my duty well by the service'. The application had to go through the ordinary channels, and Hill opposed the leave as without precedent and 'in many respects objectionable'; he then conceded that the leave might be granted 'with the distinct understanding that the indulgence be considered a full compensation for the special services [in Egypt and the West Indies] on which he rests his claim.' Stanley in turn thought Trollope might be asked to help negotiate postal arrangements with the US, but Hill vetoed that idea. Stanley granted the leave. Trollope took issue with the 'special services' clause, which Stanley had probably not meant to endorse in any case, and Stanley then sternly rebuked Hill, writing that he did not intend the leave to be considered compensation, that Trollope had never asked for any, and that the leave should in no way diminish any claims Trollope might have in view of his past 'Zeal Diligence & Ability'. It was a rebuff that long rankled with Hill.[52]

When Trollope sailed with Rose for America on 24 August, he could well afford to take a break from fiction, for he did appear to be 'crowding the market': *Framley Parsonage* had finished in the *Cornhill* in April, at which time the three-volume book edition appeared. *Orley Farm* had made its first shilling-part appearance the previous month and would run until October 1862; the first number of *Brown, Jones, and Robinson* had just been published in the August number of the *Cornhill*; his first collected volume of short stories was scheduled to come out in November, and a Christmas story, 'The Mistletoe Bough', had been bought by the *Illustrated London News*. In his desk at home he had a generous contract from George Smith (£2,500 and reversion of copyright after eighteen months), signed the previous month, for a long, twenty-part novel for the *Cornhill*, scheduled to commence in the magazine in September 1862. He could readily put aside the 'spinning of tales' for a while and devote his energies to the travel book.

It was his purpose, as he said in the opening pages of the work, to write a book very different from his mother's *Domestic Manners of the Americans*: hers he deemed 'essentially a woman's book', which rather unjustly described with a 'light but graphic pen, the social defects and absurdities' of 'our near relatives'. His would examine the 'political arrangements' of the new country; he wished also to 'add something to the familiarity of Englishmen with Americans'. Whereas her book had created laughter in England and 'soreness' in America, his would, he hoped, mitigate the latter and 'add to the good feeling which should exist between two nations which ought to love each other so well'.[53] He had planned the book before the outbreak of the Civil War, and would not purposely have chosen this time for his visit, as it surely interfered with his work—he never got to any of the seceding states. On the other hand, the book was written chiefly for an English audience, and the war quickened the English interest in America.

17

North America

AFTER touching first at Halifax, Trollope and Rose arrived at Boston on 5 September 1861, where he found himself welcomed by new friends. His chief contact was James T. Fields, the Boston publisher and editor of the *Atlantic Monthly*, whom Trollope had met in London at a *Cornhill* dinner. Henry James described Fields and his wife as 'addicted to the cultivation of talk and wit and to the ingenious multiplication of such ties as could link the upper half of the title-page with the lower'; he said their house overlooking the River Charles had such a collection of rare books and literary curiosities that it amounted to a 'waterside museum'.[1] Into their literary and artistic set of friends, which included all the Boston Brahmins, the Fields welcomed writers from abroad. Dickens and Thackeray had become their friends, and their hospitality helped Trollope to fall in love with Boston. Of the city and her people Trollope wrote that he knew 'no place at which an Englishman may drop suddenly among a pleasanter circle of acquaintance, or find himself among a more clever circle of men, than he can do at Boston'. Yet England's neutral stance in the American Civil War made his position an uneasy one. He found that most Bostonians thought the English had let their love of the cotton trade overcome their better instincts, an attitude Trollope believed understandable but uninformed. Another barrier was the ordinary American's contempt for what he had learned of England's government and its class system. Trollope was asked such questions as whether lords in England ever spoke to men who were not lords. When Rose, asked if she admired American institutions, agreed with only moderate enthusiasm, an American remarked that he had 'never yet met the down-trodden subject of a despot who did not hug his chains'. Rose was also asked by a woman if she had changed her opinion about America; Rose tried to explain that she was not the author of the *Domestic Manners of the Americans*, but the questioner quietly persisted, 'I guess you wrote that book.'[2]

After a week in Boston the mosquitoes drove him to Newport, Rhode

Island—'the Brighton, and Tenby, and Scarborough of New England'. On arrival at the Ocean Hotel, Trollope asked the clerk whether there were any rooms: 'Rooms enough' he was told, for Newport was deserted, and the hotel, with accommodation for 600 people had as few as twenty-five guests during the melancholy week the Trollopes stayed there. The ladies' drawing-room of the hotel, large enough for 'a very good House of Commons for the British nation', depressed him; American women, who were usually talkative, were unapproachable in hotel drawing-rooms, places so comfortless that even lovers were unable 'to remain five minutes in the same room', and he was driven on a few occasions to desert his wife for the 'nasty bar'. In the hotel dining-room—and elsewhere in America—the behaviour of children annoyed him. The 'adult infant lisps to the waiter for everything at table, handles his fish with epicurean delicacy, is choice in his selection of pickles, very particular that his beefsteak at breakfast shall be hot, and is instant in his demand for fresh ice in his water.' If the child be a girl, she caps everything by her exit: whereas an English child would scramble down, the American youngster 'glides' to the floor and then 'swims' out of the room with a 'dorsal wriggle', employing a kind of gait often seen in 'second rate French towns, and among fourth rate French women'.3

He found the coast at Newport not as fine as those in Wales or Cornwall, not to mention Clare or Kerry. Newport itself he thought would be pleasant if full of visitors. The most enjoyable part of his stay at Newport was seeing young Mary Knower.

The Trollopes returned to Boston for two days, where he dined at the Fields' with James Russell Lowell, Hawthorne, Emerson, and Holmes: Lowell recorded that he found Trollope 'a big red-faced rather underbred Englishman of the bald-with-spectacles type. A good roaring positive fellow who deafened me.' Trollope regaled the company with accounts of his going to work on a novel 'just like a shoemaker on a shoe', rising at five, writing so many pages each day. Holmes and Trollope were 'very entertaining': the American tried his paradoxes on Trollope, but it was 'pelting a rhinoceros with seed-pearl'; when Holmes attempted to draw him out on Englishmen and wine, Trollope pretended no knowledge, roaring, 'I *won't* be asshored' at Holmes: 'Trollope', Lowell wrote, 'wouldn't give him any chance. Meanwhile, Emerson and I, who sat between them, crouched down out of range . . . with the shot hurtling overhead. . . . I rather liked Trollope.'4 Fields told Hawthorne: 'Trollope fell in love with you at first sight and went off moaning that he could not see you again. He swears you are the handsomest Yankee that ever walked this planet.'5 Hawthorne, before Trollope knew either him or Fields, had written to Fields the now-famous letter—which Trollope partly reproduced in *An Autobiography*—saying that Trollope's novels 'precisely suit my taste,—solid and substantial, written on the strength of beef and through the inspiration of ale, and just as real as if some giant had hewn a great lump out of the earth and put it under a glass case, with all its inhabitants going about their daily business, and not suspecting that they were being made a show of.'[6] In *North America* Trollope called Hawthorne 'the first of American novelists'.[7]

While at Boston Trollope began his book. It was his practice to write of places and people usually a few weeks after seeing them. As with his work on the West Indies, *North America* was written 'almost without a note'; his memory was such that he could record detailed accounts of places visited earlier. The time-lag also provided context. He could write of Detroit, for example, that it was 'a large well-built half-finished city . . . not so pleasant as Milwaukee, nor so picturesque as St. Paul, nor so grand as Chicago, nor so civilized as Cleveland, nor as busy as Buffalo'. From Boston the Trollopes went north to Portland, Maine, a city that struck him as idyllic: 'It has an air of supreme plenty. . . . The faces of the people tell of three regular meals of meat a day, and of digestive powers in proportion. They get up early, and go to bed early. The women are comely and sturdy . . . the men are sedate, obliging, and industrious.' All life in Portland seemed 'orderly, sleek, and unobtrusive. Probably of all modes of life . . . this is the most happy.' The only fault was prohibition. 'But they advertise beer in the shop-windows,' Trollope said to his driver. Could not a man get drunk on Scotch ale and bitter beer? 'Wa'al, yes. If he goes to work hard, and drinks a bucketful . . . perhaps he may,' was the reply. The White Mountains of Vermont had scenery Trollope called superior to much of that in the famed mountains of Europe. America's autumn colours were unmatched anywhere.[8]

The most exciting part of his brief visit to Canada seems to have occurred when he and Rose climbed—against advice—a mountain called Owl's Head, near Magog, a few miles north of the Vermont border, got lost in the rain, and had to be rescued by men hallooing in the dark for them. Niagara Falls, as on his earlier visit, absolutely entranced Trollope: of all sights including 'all buildings, pictures, statues, and wonders of art . . . and also all beauties of nature . . . I know no other one thing so beautiful, so glorious, and so powerful'. From Niagara he went west to the Mississippi and as far north as St Paul and the Falls of St Anthony, and then down river to Dubuque, Iowa. Milwaukee impressed him: although the highest level of education and refinement in any large English town would be superior, 'the general level of these things, of material and intellectual well being—of beef, that is, and book learning—is no doubt infinitely higher in a new American than in an old European town. Such an animal as a beggar is as much unknown as a mastodon. Men out of work and in want are almost unknown.' About the frontiersman, Trollope sounds almost Emersonian: 'this man has his romance, his high poetic feeling, and above all his manly dignity. Visit him, and you will find him without coat or waistcoat, unshorn, in ragged blue trousers and old flannel shirt, too often bearing on his lantern jaws the signs of ague and sickness; but he will stand upright before you and speak to you with all the ease of a lettered gentleman in his own library. . . . When he questions you about the old country he astonishes you by the extent of his knowledge. I defy you not to feel that he is superior to the race from whence he has sprung in England or in Ireland.' Visiting one such frontiersman's cabin north of Dubuque, Trollope found it 'neat and well furnished'. He also noted that he saw there 'Harper's everlasting magazine' in which, although he does not say so, *Orley Farm* was appearing at the time.⁹

Trollope sorrowed to see able-bodied men siphoned off from the newly settled West for the war. In England, when poor yokels are enlisted 'with a shilling and promise of unlimited beer and glory', they go to a mode of life not much inferior from that which they leave; but 'of those men whom I saw entering on their [military] career upon the banks of the Mississippi, many were fathers of families, many were workers of lands, many were educated men capable of high aspiration—all were serviceable members of their State.' The Irish seemed to make especially good conscripts into the army, though not all of them. When he asked a burly Irish driver in a western city why he didn't join, the man replied: 'I'm not a sound man yer honour. I'm deficient in me liver.'¹⁰

At Dubuque, Iowa, he ate the 'best apple' he ever encountered. But he was amused at assertions such as 'Your [English] peaches are fine to look at, but they have no flavour.' Another told him, 'My great objection to your country, sir, is that you have got no vegetables.' Trollope admitted only that Englishmen raised no squash—which he thought was 'the pulp of the pumpkin'; but he himself in his 'little patches' at home grew more than twenty kinds of vegetable. But the western land did burst with its own produce. At Chicago and Buffalo he went down granaries, and climbed up elevators; he saw wheat 'running in rivers from one vessel into another, and from railroad vans up into the huge bins on the top stores of the warehouses'; he saw corn 'measured by the forty bushel measure with as much ease as we measure an ounce of cheese'. He began to know, he said, 'what it was for a country to overflow with milk and honey, to burst with its own fruits, and be smothered by its own riches'.[11]

At Albany, New York, the State legislature was not sitting, and he passed through quickly, making little more observation than that 'the manner in which the railway cars are made to run backward and forward through the crowded streets of the town must cause a frequent loss of human life. One is led to suppose that children in Albany can hardly have a chance of coming to maturity.' West Point he found of great interest: here a lad 'is called upon for an amount of labour, and a degree of conduct, which would be considered quite transcendental and out of the question in England', though on visiting 'an embryo warrior' in his private quarters during study time he found him asleep. Trollope disapproved of the 'Draconian code of morals'—the complete prohibition of strong drink and of any contact with 'feminine allurements' under pain of expulsion. But on the whole he pronounced the Academy excellent. He did doubt that the government should have placed it at West Point, the 'prettiest spot' in the country.[12]

Trollope arrived at New York on 31 October. There he had fewer social contacts than in Boston, though he did visit the historian George Bancroft and probably saw Mrs Knower and Mary. His strongest impression of the city was its inhabitants' devotion to making money: 'Every man worships the dollar, and is down before his shrine from morning to night.' Trollope said he believed in money as much as the next man; he wished only that New Yorkers would use more of the art of concealing art and banish something of the 'savour of dollars which pervades the atmosphere of New York'. 'I have never walked down Fifth Avenue alone without thinking of money,' he wrote. In social intercourse, the stranger who is not interested in stock percentages 'perceives that he is out of his element, and had better go away'.[13]

'Have you seen any of our great institootions, sir?' was a question that Trollope as a visiting Englishman continually encountered in New York. He saw most of them, including institutes for the deaf and dumb, water works, historical societies, telegraph offices, and large commercial establishments. In such institutions New York was 'pre-eminently great': 'The hospitals are almost alluring. The lunatic asylum which I saw was perfect, —though I did not feel obliged to the resident physician for introducing me to all the worst patients as countrymen of my own. "An English lady, Mr. Trollope. I'll introduce you. Quite a hopeless case. Two old women. They've been here fifty years. They're English. Another gentleman from England, Mr. Trollope. A very interesting case! Confirmed inebriety."'[14]

Trollope found it almost impossible to give too much praise to New York schools. Nothing, he wrote, would surprise an Englishman more than the contrast between a London free school and a New York one. The New York pupil is neither ragged nor dirty nor stigmatized socially. One knows not if the youngster's father makes a dollar a day or $3,000 a year. The amount of learning is 'terrific': in one classroom of girls that he visited, the discussion about the properties of the hypotenuse quite overwhelmed him. In another class, on ancient Roman history, he felt more at ease. The mistress asked the girls why the Romans ran away with the Sabine women. 'Because they were pretty,' answered one little girl. There followed a 'somewhat abstruse' explanation about populating colonies. The girls, he said, knew who the Romans and Sabines were as well as he did. The students were 'leagues beyond that terrible repetition of A B C' to which most English metropolitan school pupils were limited. Trollope was suddenly called on to say a few words to five or six hundred girls gathered in one room to sing. 'What could I say but that they were all very pretty. . . . Very pretty they were. . . . but among them all there was not a pair of rosy cheeks.' Like most visiting Englishmen he found central heating—'those damnable hot-air pipes'—the curse of America: 'Men at thirty and women at twenty-five have had all semblance of youth baked out of them.'[15]

He did not like huge stores like Stewart's, which occupied an entire city block between Broadway and Fourth Avenue at Ninth Street. 'You have nothing like that in England,' said a friend. 'I wish we had nothing approaching to it,' Trollope told him; he preferred old-fashioned— English-style—small speciality shops. Harpers publishing establishment he found full of wonders: 'Everything is done on the premises, down to the very colouring of the paper which lines the covers, and places the gilding on their backs. The firm prints, engraves, electroplates, sews, binds, publishes, and sells wholesale and retail. I had no doubt that the authors have rooms in the attics where the other slight initiatory step is taken towards the production of literature.'[16]

His business talk with Fletcher Harper, though not a matter for discussion in *North America*, did not get very far. Harper had been reprinting his books, sometimes paying some little sum to the English publisher. In 1859 he had declined to buy early sheets for *The West Indies*, but then published the book anyway. Trollope later wrote that he 'explained to him, with what courtesy I could use, that I did not quite like his mode of republishing my books. He was civil enough to assure me that the transactions had been gratifying to him.'[17] Trollope probably stormed and fumed. Harper did promise that if Trollope came to an agreement with another American publisher for *North America*, he would not reprint it—but he broke his word the moment the book appeared in England.

In discussing New York, Trollope indulged in a diatribe against vulgar American women, first apologizing for doing so, saying that all were industrious, respectable, and intelligent, though their manners were 'to me more odious than those of any other human beings that I ever met anywhere'. He elaborately excluded from his censure 'some American women' whom he knew and meant to continue to know, who were as bright, beautiful, graceful, and sweet as was imaginable, and 'charming beyond expression'. Kate Field, and Mary Knower also, must have felt the allusion to themselves. But for many American women, especially those of New York, he entertained the kind of feeling brought on by the presence of an 'unclean animal'. He describes one such woman entering a street car:

[She] drags after her a misshapen, dirty mass of battered wirework, which she calls her crinoline, and which adds as much to her grace and comfort as a log of wood does to a donkey when tied to the animal's leg in a paddock. Of this she takes much heed, not managing it so that it may be conveyed up the carriage with some decency, but striking it about against men's legs, and heaving it with violence over people's knees. The touch of a real woman's dress is in itself delicate; but these blows from a harpy's fins are loathsome. . . . though not modest, the woman I describe is ferocious in her propriety. She ignores the whole world around her. . . . She speaks as though to her, in her womanhood, the neighbourhood of men was the same as that of dogs or cats. . . . She looks square at you in the face, and you rise to give her your seat. . . . She takes the place from which you have moved without a word or a bow. . . . In England women become ladylike or vulgar. In the States they are either charming or odious.

Harper's New Monthly Magazine, in a review of *North America*, agreed with Trollope on such women, calling his picture a 'true one' that 'faithfully daguerreotypes the species'; *Harper's* also said everyone knew the 'fantastic wriggle' of the little girl in the hotel. [18]

Trollope's fault-finding with New York may have owed something to his disappointment at not meeting Kate Field there. She had returned from Florence in October. Espousing the abolitionist view of the war in her journalism had cost her dearly: Kate's conservative millionaire uncle, who was childless, had intended to make her his heir. When at his ultimatum she refused to desist from her radical writings, he altered those intentions, and Kate was left to support herself and her invalid mother. [19] It was a development worthy of a Trollope novel, though he apparently knew nothing about it; he seems never to have quite understood her precarious situation, having always to work hard to keep her head above water while moving among well-to-do society. From New York he wrote to her on 5 November, saying he was 'amused by the audacity' of her letter: she had said she would be in New York; but he was willing to 'forgive' her on condition that she remain in Boston where he and Rose would arrive the next week; he counted 'not . . . a little' on her presence there.[20] Arriving in Boston on 12 November, he finally caught up with her. He had not seen her for a year, since Florence. During his three-week stay in Boston he must have seen her as often as possible; he certainly attended at least one lecture with her and probably more, as she was part of the Fields' set of friends with whom Trollope was most closely connected.

His first night back in Boston, Trollope attended a lecture at Tremont Temple by Emerson, whom he had feared might be too 'transcendental' for him. But there was nothing 'mystic' about his talk, and Trollope especially relished Emerson's caveat about the American eagle becoming the American peacock. With a party that included Kate Field, he went to hear Edward Everett on 22 November at Roxborough, where he was seated on the platform 'among the bald-headed ones and the superlatively wise'. He disliked Everett's lecture, which he considered 'neither bold nor honest' for its newly-born anti-southern fervour and for snide remarks on England. Trollope disliked even more a lecture by Wendell Phillips, 'an abolitionist by profession', delivered at Boston on 27 November. To Trollope, though his sympathies were always with the North, Phillips's call for the immediate enfranchisement of the slaves to confound the South was a doctrine of 'rapine, bloodshed, and social destruction'.[21]

Trollope was much impressed on visiting the Boston Public Library, which he described as a 'gratuitous circulating library open to all Boston, rich or poor, young or old'. The reading-room was full, and the call for books at the counter brisk. 'My own productions were in enormous demand,' he observed wryly. Why should not 'the great Mr. Mudie' introduce a library of this kind in London? Trollope visited Harvard College, which, he said, provided a higher level of education than did the English universities: 'study is more absolutely the business of the place than it is at our Universities.' He journeyed to Lowell and was favourably taken with its female 'philanthropic manufacturing college'; a 'discreet matron' even showed him through the upper floor of a residence, where he found everything 'cleanly, well-ordered, and feminine'. Returning from Lowell to Boston by train, Trollope was delighted by an old man who identified him as an Englishman without his having spoken a word: 'There is no mistaking you with your round face and your red cheeks. They don't look like that here.' Trollope offered him a cigar. [22]

But the great furore over the *Trent* affair, at its height while Trollope was in Boston, disturbed his otherwise happy visit. James Mason and John Slidell, Confederate commissioners to London and Paris, respectively, had been taken by force from a British ship on the high seas by Captain Charles Wilkes—either the nephew or grand-nephew of the Charles Wilkes who had befriended Mrs Trollope in 1827[23]—and the two men were detained at Fort Warren in Boston Harbor. Most Northerners contended that the envoys were 'contraband' and had been lawfully removed from the ship. Everyone was quoting legal authorities. 'Wheaton is quite clear about it,' one young girl told Trollope. He had never heard of Wheaton, but insisted that common sense was on the English side, v.natever the ladies and the lawyers thought: 'This stopping of an English mail steamer was too much for me.' Both sides feared that England would go to war with the North. [24]

Rose left Boston for England on 27 November. As Trollope told Kate Field, his wife had 'a house, and children & cows & horses and dogs & pigs—and all the stern necessities of an English home'. [25] Six days later he began his journey southward to Washington. At Philadelphia he met for the first time 'live secessionists', people who admitted themselves to be such. At Baltimore, a Southern city north of Washington, General John Adams Dix showed Trollope the cannon by which he held the city in his grip. But in spite of martial law, cakes and ale seemed to prevail. Baltimore reminded him of England: foxhounds were kept there, and the country around the city, so unlike anything he had seen in New England or New York, looked good for fox-hunting. An old inn with an old sign, with soiled and battered wagons in front of it, at the corner of Eutaw and Franklin Streets, was just such as could be found in Somerset or other agricultural counties of England. Trollope declined to go duck shooting; he did not shoot, for one thing, and he would not wait alone for hours in a 'wet wooden box' on the edge of Chesapeake Bay. [26]

Washington, where he arrived on 14 December, he thought a 'failure' as a city. Commerce had made New York and Philadelphia great cities, second only to London and Paris. But Washington had only politics. It was 'ungainly' and 'pretentious' and existed chiefly in theory: Massachusetts Avenue on the maps was four miles long, but on visiting it one soon found oneself outside the town, in an 'uncultivated, undrained wilderness', wading through bogs among 'rude hillocks'. The Capitol Building itself faced the wrong way, and everybody went in the back door. The heavy wings added to the building seemed larger than the original structure and 'destroyed the symmetry of the whole'. The Washington Monument, about one third complete, and not promising to come to anything, was 'a fair type of the city'.[27]

The presence of some 200,000 soldiers in Washington distressed him. Mounted sentries, shivering in the cold and besmeared with mud, stood on every corner; army wagons thronged the streets night and day; military tents were pitched throughout the city. All this filled Trollope, who hated 'military belongings', with sorrow. Rough-shod generals were in the ascendancy. Legislators were 'at a discount': 'Pack them up in boxes, and send them home,' one officer told Trollope.[28]

Trollope did not try to see Lincoln; he had no business to discuss with the President and did not like to press for an introduction. He watched with eager interest the Congress in session, remarking the sad absence of so many places because of secession. In the Senate he heard but was not much impressed by Massachusetts Senator Charles Sumner's speech on the *Trent* affair. Trollope felt sure war with England over the imprisoning of Slidell and Mason was imminent, and, like other Englishmen visiting the States, he was prepared for a quick return to his own country. Everyone was very polite, and no one abused England in his presence, except Commodore Wilkes himself. Sharp debate within the Lincoln administration was led by Secretary of State William Henry Seward, who favoured release of the prisoners, and Senator Sumner, who opposed it. Seward (whom Trollope criticized harshly on other points) reportedly prevailed with President Lincoln, and relations with England remained intact. Trollope dined at Seward's house, along with Sumner, on 27 December, the day the decision was made.[29]

Trollope spent the first three days of 1862 among the officers of the Army of the Potomac, sleeping in a tent four miles from the Confederate lines. He watched General McClellan reviewing his troops and felt sure the exercise showed nothing except that the general rode very well. Military 'pomps and circumstances' affected him with melancholy: 'Soldiers gathered together at camp are uncouth and ugly when they are idle; and when they are at work their work is worse than idleness.' The drills seemed so silly, men prodding at the air with bayonets and trotting back and forth, 'miserably conscious of the absurdity of their own performances'. Such drills, he wrote, always made him think how little had been the world's advance in civilization: 'There must be soldiers, and soldiers must be taught. But not the less pitiful is it to see men

of thirty undergoing the goose-step and tortured by
proper mode of handling a long instrument which is h
spear.'³⁰

As was only natural, Trollope, in most places he visited
eye at the Post Office. At Washington there was only one
letter-boxes throughout the city, no subsidiary offices at
might be bought or letters posted, and no general system of l
Most letters had to be picked up at the window, and the ᴜᴇʀᴋ had no
system for finding letters by initial, but 'turned letter by letter through his
hand'. The queue was sometimes out on to the street. Stamps could be
purchased at only one window in a corner, to which there was no regular
ingress or egress. The Post Office building itself was very graceful, and the
supervisors gentlemen of great courtesy, but the service Trollope judged
'absolutely barbarous'.³¹

While in Washington Trollope kept up correspondence with Kate
Field. He expected to see the manuscript of a story she was to write, but
feared she was idle and going after 'false gods', like abolitionist Wendell
Phillips and spiritualist Elizabeth Doten; he told her she was ambitious
but would not make enough effort: 'You would whistle for a storm like a
witch. . . . You must sit down with a trumpet and blow at it till your
cheeks would split. . . . something of a puff of wind will come at last. Now
I hope you will find yourself well rated, & will send me your story off
hand.' Two days later, addressing her as 'Dearest Kate', Trollope sent her
an elaborate and altogether negative critique of a poem she had sent him,
finding fault with everything from the rhyme 'Smile on' with 'union' to the
thought, imagery, and jokes—'Jokes in poetry should be clear as crystal.'
Poetry would only come after hard, slow work. Besides, 'Philanthropical
ratiocination is your line, not philandering amatory poetising.' He told her
it pained him to say such things, but insisted she would do better as a
writer of prose. He added, 'I know from *much* experience how bitter are
the sapient criticisms of one's elders on the effusions of one's youth! I too
have written verses, & have been told that they were nought.' His
previous 'jobation' letter was written before he got the poetry, but he
urged her to stick to the story: 'It is a great profession that of writing; but
you must spoil much paper, & undergo many doubting, weary, wretched,
hours. But I do think you can write good nervous readable prose.' A few
days later he wrote again, wondering whether ill health, hinted at in her
latest letter, had held up the story. She may have 'troubles and sorrows by
the score' of which he knows nothing.³²

Trollope stayed exactly one month in Washington, having lived mfortably in the hotel of 'one Wormley, a coloured man, in I Street, to whose attention I can recommend any Englishman who may chance to want quarters in Washington'. He left the capital for the West on 14 January 1862, with a vague hope of getting into the South. Pittsburgh he found the 'blackest' place he ever saw, sootier and dingier than Swansea, Merthyr Tydfil, and South Shields combined. With curious feelings he visited Cincinnati and the building his mother had erected there when he was a boy at Winchester, more than thirty years past. The structure, however odd, had been in her time the most imposing in town, but was now sadly eclipsed. It had become a 'Physico-medical Institute', housing both 'a quack doctor' and 'a college of rights-of-women female medical professors'. The present proprietor told Trollope that it was his belief that 'no man or woman ever yet made a dollar in that building.' Cincinnati was the hog-slaughtering centre of the West, which it had been in the process of becoming during his mother's sojourn there, when she complained of the difficulty of crossing Main Street without brushing up against a hog's dripping snout. Englishmen, Trollope mused, feel that pigs are somehow 'not as honourable in their bearings as sheep and oxen', a prejudice that had no place in Cincinnati. He went to see a hog killing, but declined to describe it; at first he rather despised the man whose job was 'specially disagreeable', until learning that he made five dollars a day.[33]

Trollope next entered Kentucky, a border state, where slavery was still legal. In the Blue Grass country, between Lexington and Stockfort, he visited the Woodford Stud Farm, kept by a slave-owner who bred horses, cattle, and sheep. Trollope inspected some of the slave cottages and found them superior in size, furniture, and comfort to those of agricultural workers back home: 'Any comparison between the material comfort of a Kentucky slave and an English ditcher and delver would be preposterous. The Kentucky slave never wants for clothing fitted to the weather. He eats meat twice a day, and has three good meals; he knows no limit but his own appetite; his work is light; he has many varieties of amusement; he receives instant medical assistance at all periods of necessity for himself, his wife, and his children. Of course he pays no rent, fears no baker, knows no hunger.' Trollope explained that he did not mean to equate such comforts with freedom, but he did think that any discussion of the condition of the negro ought to consider the advantages of which abolition would deprive him.[34]

At St Louis, where General Henry Halleck had imposed martial law, Trollope found the war had disturbed everything. The most memorable feature of his four-day stay, a visit to the army barracks, was frightening:

1861–1862

'The stench of those places was foul beyond description. Never in my life had I been in a place so horrible to the eyes and nose as Benton Barracks. . . . It may be that dirt, and wretchedness, disease and listless idleness, a descent from manhood to habits lower that those of the beasts, are necessary in warfare. . . . [But] the degradation of men to the state in which I saw the American soldiers in Benton Barracks, is disgraceful to humanity.' At Rolla, Missouri, falling in the snow as he struggled towards his hotel he had a moment of doubt: 'Why is it that a stout Englishman bordering on fifty years finds himself in such a predicament as that? No Frenchman, no Italian, no German, would so place himself, unless under that stress of unsurmountable circumstances. No American would do so. . . . As I slipped about on the ice and groaned with that terrible fardle on my back, burdened with a dozen shirts, and a suit of dress clothes, and three pair of boots, and four or five thick volumes, and a set of maps, and a box of cigars, and a washing-tub, I confessed to myself that I was a fool.'35

But of course he pushed on. His picture of Cairo, Illinois, is as dismal as that by Dickens in *Martin Chuzzlewit*. Inhabitants seemed to revel in dirt. In the forlorn hotel he had to use the public washroom: 'I did not dare to brush my teeth lest I should give offence; and I saw at once that I was regarded with suspicion when I used my own comb instead of that provided for the public.'36 While at Cairo he wrote to Kate Field, thanking her for pardoning his criticism of her writing. He had heard she was not well. 'I know that you are not a female Hercules. None but Englishwomen are.' He told her he didn't like the West and that until he came to Cairo he thought St Louis (her birthplace) 'the dirtiest place in the world'. He also told her that at St Louis he had had a talk with an old friend of the Field family, William Greenleaf Eliot, Unitarian minister, founder of Washington University (and grandfather of T. S. Eliot), who said that Kate ought to marry a husband, the 'best career' for a woman, with which sentiment Trollope said he agreed.37 He did not know that at the time Kate was suffering a rather violent passion for an apparently fickle American artist whom she had met at Florence and Paris, and whom she would have married had he asked her.38

After an inspection of yet another major military establishment, Camp Wood near Louisville, Kentucky, Trollope started back eastward. He was detained for a few hours in Seymour, Indiana, and again in Crossline, Ohio, and used the time to discover what sort of life people led in towns that were entirely the products of the locomotive. Rails ran through the centre of the town; any street not touching the railway was in disfavour with the inhabitants; 'The panting and groaning, and whistling of engines

[237]

is continual. . . . This is the life of the town.' No such places exist in Europe, where towns preceded the railways and where the locomotive is a 'beast of prey' against which one should be on guard and warn one's children. But in the western states the locomotive is a domestic animal; nobody fears it, and little children 'run about almost among its wheels'. In Seymour and Crossline the railway is 'the first necessity of life, and gives the only hope of wealth'. The European visitor may find these towns disagreeable and ugly, but they thrive and prosper, and should be judged not against old towns with congregated wealth, but against other new settlements that lack railways.[39]

Trollope passed again through Cincinnati, Pittsburgh, Baltimore, Washington—'still under the empire of King Mud'—and New York on his way to Boston. He had promised himself a final week there, in spite of the fact that his sailing was to be from New York. He was happy to be again in the East. He did not like the West or Westerners; he had found the men gloomy and silent, almost sullen: 'A dozen of them will sit for hours round a stove, speechless. They chew tobacco and ruminate. They are not offended if you speak to them, but they are not pleased. . . . They are essentially a dirty people. Dirt, untidiness, and noise, seem in nowise to afflict them. Things are constantly done before your eyes which should be done and might be done behind your back.'[40] By contrast he remained 'enamoured' of Boston and his friends in that city. He saw Kate Field and put a sketch of her in a short story, 'Miss Ophelia Gledd': the heroine is 'the belle of Boston', very fond of men's society, very relaxed with them; she never flirts, but has interesting conversations; she goes everywhere on her own—balls, lectures, 'meetings of wise men', and political debates. The narrator, an Englishman of about Trollope's age, becomes her staunch friend and adviser about her various suitors. He takes her sleighing: 'As I started with her out of the city warmly enveloped in buffalo furs, I could not but think how nice it would be to drive on and on, so that nobody should ever catch us. There was a sense of companionship about her in which no woman that I have ever known excelled her. She had a way of adapting herself to the friend of the moment which was beyond anything winning. . . . I wasn't in love with her myself, and didn't want to fall in love with her. But I felt that I should have liked to cross the Rocky Mountains with her, over to the Pacific, and to have come round home by California, Peru and the Pampas.' At the close of the story, she chooses to become engaged to another Englishman, a literary man fourteen years her senior.[41] (In *North America* Trollope recounted how when he tried to drive a sleigh, his inexpertise caused the horses to run away, bringing him to 'grief and shame', and how he had momentarily felt 'doomed to consign to a snowy grave' the lady who accompanied him. [42])

Trollope left Boston on Sunday, 9 March, went to New York, visited the Knowers the following day, then the Bancrofts, and sailed on Wednesday the 12th for Liverpool. His ship stopped briefly at Queenstown, and he was delighted to find himself again in Ireland. But as he was mobbed by a crowd of beggars, mostly 'sturdy and fat' women in rags protesting they were starving, he could not help but contrast these Irish with those in America: 'The Irishman when he expatriates himself to one of these American States loses much of that affectionate, confiding, master-worshipping nature which makes him so good a fellow when at home. . . . To me personally he has perhaps become less pleasant than he was. But to himself—! It seems to me that such a man must feel himself half a god, if he has the power of comparing what he is with what he was.' [43] He arrived in Liverpool on 25 March and was home on the following day.

Within a month he completed *North America*. He reworked his chapter on the constitution, corresponding with R. H. Dana on the subject, and contending that Lincoln had acted unconstitutionally in suspending habeas corpus. He could not resist inserting an entire chapter on the US Postal Service, which was in fact considerably inferior to England's. In a penultimate chapter he wrote that while Americans have done remarkably well as 'producers' of literature, they are 'the most conspicuous people on the earth' as consumers of books. English publishers think in terms of thousands of copies, American publishers in tens of thousands. Everyone in America reads; cabmen, ticket-porters, warehousemen, and agricultural labourers have 'libraries'; American readers prefer English books to their own, and some English authors may be unaware that their influence is undoubtedly greater in the States than at home. The English authors most popular in America seem to be Dickens, Tennyson, Buckle, Tom Hughes, Martin Tupper, and Thackeray. [44]

He closed the book with a nostalgic goodbye to Boston and the haunts he had come to know so well and the people he had come to admire and love, including such lights of this 'western Athens' as William Prescott, George Bancroft, J. L. Motley, Professor Louis Agassiz, Longfellow, Lowell, Emerson, Dana, Holmes, and Hawthorne. Trollope wrote that he would never again visit Boston because he had written that which would make him unwelcome in America. Such was hardly the case, in spite of his criticisms of New York ladies, Washington, the West, and corruption in government war contracts. Many of his Boston friends would, it is true, disagree with his stand against immediate abolition, and they would not accept his belief that although the North would win the war and dictate the terms of the peace, there could never again be 'amicable union' between North and South, and that the Gulf states would be allowed to form into some kind of second-rate confederation. On the other hand, he thought the war would be worth the result it would bring: the border states would be saved for the union, and four million white people would be rescued from 'the stain and evil of slavery'. Though opposed to slavery, and though he maintained that slavery was the 'single and necessary' cause of the war, Trollope seemed to oppose it chiefly for the dehumanizing effect it had on slave holders, for whom it was a 'deadly curse'. Abolition by ordinance would not really 'emancipate' the four million slaves, but would bring chaos upon the land. Emancipation would have to come gradually; Trollope has no patience with the Boston abolitionist who says, 'I could arrange it all to-morrow morning.' Trollope believed the southern slave to be 'as a rule well treated', while the free negro was generally ill-treated in the North, in New York for example, where he was subject to special voting qualifications that in effect disfranchised him, and where he had to use separate street cars. Trollope does not think the black man the white man's equal, and insists that Northerners, including abolitionists, do not really think so either. [45] However benighted Trollope's ideas on abolition may appear today, it is worth remembering that his view was shared by most Europeans, and indeed by most Americans in the North itself, including most of her soldiers. Abolitionists—like Kate Field—were a decided minority.

North America did not offend as Trollope thought it would. The book was largely a comparison of American and English societies, and Trollope's conclusion was encapsulated in the judgement that 'nine tenths [of the English population] would have had a better life as Americans than they can have in their spheres as Englishmen.'[46] The book had a remarkably warm reception in England, in spite of its strong pro-Northern stance. The *Saturday Review*, it is true, called *North America* 'most terribly wind-baggy', and insisted that no matter how pleasant Trollope's style, the book was 'about as thin-spun, tedious, mooning a journal of travel and discussion as has been offered to the public in a long time', and could have said its say in about fifty pages. But the *British Quarterly* admired how little seemed to have escaped Trollope's attention, how well he had used his six months' time in America, and how well he blended 'seriousness and lightness' in the book. The *Athenaeum*, in a long and favourable review, remarked that Trollope went to America 'with a full sense of his mother's sins weighing upon him', intent on writing a fair book. The *Spectator* said the book was pleasurable reading, and would 'probably far exceed the best novel of the season in temporary circulation'. G. H. Lewes in the *Cornhill* called *North America* fresh and honest, a work that 'never flatters nor libels'.[47] Englishmen bought the book, Chapman & Hall providing three editions in the original format, and cheaper fourth and fifth editions through 1866. Trollope thought the book full of information but 'tedious and confused'. But he remained proud of its 'assured confidence' that the North would win, in spite of the fact that it was written before the war was a year old, during the time when the Southern forces were more success-ful.[48]

Trollope sent copies of the book to some of his Boston friends: Fields, Longfellow, Dana, Dr Lothrop and Mrs Charles Homans. He did not, however, present one to Kate Field. He playfully parried her reproaches ('You are a young lady.—A ring, a lock of my hair, or a rosebud would be the proper present for you; not two huge volumes weighing no end of pounds') before responding to her comments:

Your criticisms are in part just—in part unjust,—in great part biassed by your personal (—may I say love?) for the author. The book is vague. But remember, I had to write a book of travels, not a book of political essays—and yet I was anxious so to write my travels, as to introduce, on the sly, my political opinions. The attempt has not been altogether successful. The book is regarded as readable,— and that is saying as much for it, as I can say honestly. Your injustice regards chiefly abolition ideas, [General John] Freemont & such like; on which matters we are poles asunder.

In condemning the recent introduction of conscription in the North, he gave her his notion of the limits of patriotism:

My feeling is that a man should die rather than be made a soldier against his will. One's country has no right to demand everything. There is much that is higher & better & greater than one's country. One is patriotic only because one is too small & too weak to be cosmopolitan.

Nevertheless he remained sanguine about the outcome of the war, and to this dear American friend made a remarkable declaration of the effect on him of visiting her country:

I was thinking today that nature intended me for an American rather than an Englishman. I think I should have made a better American. Yet I hold it higher to be a bad Englishman, as I am, than a good American,—as I am not. If that makes you angry, see if you would not say the reverse of yourself.

He sends personal news: as Waltham House is being enlarged, they are not going to Italy in the autumn ('The bricklayers would run away with the forks'). He would like to know more of her work and social life and whereabouts. In his roundabout way he protests his love: 'How little we often know in such respects of those we love dearest. Of what I am at home, you can have no idea;—not that I mean to imply that I am of those you love dearest. And yet I hope I am.'49

Trollope also mentioned to Kate the letter he was shortly to publish about 'that beast Harper' ('Why don't they draught him?'). It was a lengthy discussion of the international copyright question, and particularly the unscrupulous conduct of Harper, set forth in the form of a letter to James Russell Lowell and published in the *Athenaeum* of 2 September. Harper was free, Trollope admits, like any American publisher, to publish English works without compensating the author. This was bad enough. But Harper had agreed not to publish any book for which Trollope made special arrangements with another American publisher. This Trollope had done with Lippincott of Philadelphia for a two-volume edition of *North America* from which Trollope was to receive a royalty (12½ per cent after 2,000 copies); but Harper had rushed into print before Lippincott with a cheap sixty-cent one-volume edition. Was this not 'literary piracy'? Harper replied in the *Athenaeum*, his strongest point being that Trollope's letter had been addressed to 'W. Russell Lowell', an error Trollope had too late tried to correct before the *Athenaeum* went to press.50

Rowland Hill read the *Athenaeum* the day it carried Trollope's letter, and noted in his journal: '*Trollope* is suspected of neglecting his official duties to attend to his literary labours. Engagement in connection with the Cornhill Magazine and another periodical whose name I do not recollect—numerous novels—Trip to the United States . . . and work thereon—In confirmation see in Athenaeum of this day letter from Trollope in which he speaks of earning "his bread by writing"—as though literature were his "profession" &c.'51 Nothing came of Hill's private grumblings.

18

Almost a National Institution

TROLLOPE had been out of England for all but the first of the eight monthly appearances in the *Cornhill Magazine* of *The Struggles of Brown, Jones, and Robinson*. This was perhaps just as well. When the first instalment appeared, the *Illustrated London News* remarked that Trollope's 'newly devised comic epic gives . . . but modified satisfaction to the readers of the Cornhill. The complaint is that nobody can understand what Mr. Trollope means.' The complaints got worse as the story progressed. The *Saturday Review* later said of it that 'the chief characters, motives, and incidents were so odiously vulgar and stupid that the staunchest champions of realism were forced to give up in disgust. It may be questioned whether any living being ever got to the end of *Brown, Jones, and Robinson*.' George Smith did not bring out *Brown, Jones, and Robinson* in book form until eight years later (there was an unauthorized American edition in 1862). At that time, 1870, dressed up with four undistinguished plates, the novel fell flat. The *Westminster Review*, in one of the few notices to appear, said they regretted the book had been published: 'It was universally felt, when the story first appeared in the "Cornhill Magazine," that the whole affair was a blunder. Most people were unwilling to believe that the author of "Framley Parsonage" could have written such unmitigated rubbish.'[1] Trollope admitted the novel's faults, and he never attempted anything in that line again; but he felt none the less that there was 'some good fun in it'. George Robinson, the narrator/advertiser does have a lively imagination. For him, capital in a business venture is a 'bugbear', and 'unreserved credit' is everything: 'When a man advertises that he has 40,000 new paletots, he does not mean that he has got that number packed up in a box. . . . A long row of figures in trade is but an elegant use of the superlative.' Advertisements need not be 'true': 'No man,—no woman believes them. They are not lies; for it is not intended that they should obtain credit. . . . The groundwork of advertisement is romance. It is poetry in its very essence. Is Hamlet true?' ('I really do not know,' answers his partner. [2]) Trollope acknowledged that he never heard anyone say a good word about the book. In fact no one, he recorded, ever said anything about it to him except George Smith, 'who kindly remarked that he did not think it was equal to my usual work'. [3]

Another book that had made its appearance during Trollope's absence was *Tales of All Countries*—the first of five volumes of collected short stories he eventually published. The *Saturday Review* said that Trollope was 'alone in his power of telling a story about absolutely nothing'; the reviewer especially marvelled at stories such as 'The O'Conors of Castle Conor' and 'The Relics of General Chassé': 'All is narrative—easy, continuous, and flowing. Every page is in its way entertaining, and is written with a certain force and grace, and yet it is all about nothing whatever.' The *Spectator* mentioned these two stories as best, saying they bore comparison with 'some of the most laughable scenes in "Pickwick" itself'. [4]

On 5 April 1862, after he had been home two weeks, Trollope was elected a member of the Garrick Club (in the *Autobiography* Trollope mistakenly gives 1861). He had been nominated on the previous 5 May, proposed by Robert Bell, seconded by Thackeray; other signatures supporting his nomination included J. E. Millais, Shirley Brooks, Frederic Chapman, Tom Taylor, Henry O'Neil, Wilkie Collins, Charles Reade, and fourteen others; his profession was given as 'author'. [5] Trollope later explained what election to the Garrick Club meant to him:

Having up to that time lived but very little among men, having known hitherto nothing of clubs, having even as a boy been banished from social gatherings, I enjoyed infinitely at first the gaiety of the Garrick. It was a festival to me to dine there . . . and a great delight to play a rubber in the little room upstairs of an afternoon. . . . I think that I became popular among those with whom I associated. I have long been aware of a certain weakness in my own character, which I may call a craving for love. I have ever had a wish to be liked by those around me,—a wish that during the first half of my life was never gratified. In my schooldays no small part of my misery came from the envy with which I regarded the popularity of popular boys. . . . And afterwards, when I was in London as a young man, I had but few friends. Among the clerks in the Post Office I held my own fairly after the first two or three years; but even then I regarded myself as something of a Pariah. My Irish life had been much better. I had had my wife and children, and had been sustained by a feeling of general respect. But even in Ireland I had in truth lived but little in society. . . . The Garrick Club was the first assemblage of men at which I felt myself to be popular. [6]

Trollope became, as he put it, 'much identified' with the Garrick. He was a regular at whist there, entertained and was entertained there, had much to do with the election of members, including his brother Tom in 1864, George Smith in 1865, and his son Harry in 1867.

In September Trollope took a ten-day flying visit with John Tilley to Holland, which provided him with an occasion to write an article for the November number of the *Cornhill*. 'My Tour in Holland' is really another excursion on one of Trollope's favourite hobby horses, art criticism, and, one might add, museum criticism: at The Hague in the Steengratz Collection the pictures 'may be seen without trouble'; the Public Museum at Amsterdam is 'badly lighted, and the keepers seem to be averse to fresh air'; the Vander Hoop gallery charges a small fee and consequently the tourist 'has the rooms all to himself'. Trollope's comments on pictures are impressionistic: 'Rembrandt's portrait of the old Burgomaster . . . has perhaps in it more of dignity than any face that he ever painted.' The finest Dow in the world is 'the young woman handing a basket out of a window. You should certainly go to Holland, if only to see that young woman'; the remarkable thing about Rembrandt's 'Doctors round a Dead Body on a Dissecting-Table' is 'that such a picture should have in it so little that is painful'. Vander Helst's 'Banquet of the Civil Guard' is a 'wonderful performance if looked upon as a gallery of portraits, but I cannot call it a good picture'. A few travel anecdotes frame the discussion: Trollope nearly caused a scene because his Dutch bathing suit could have clothed 'no moderate-sized Englishman' and, as he was already in the machine he had no alternative but to go in naked and seek deep water to cover himself. It was fair time when he visited Amsterdam, and Trollope and Tilley stood out as strangers: 'The girls laughed at us . . . and the elder women stared and whispered. . . . through Mexico or Moscow I might walk at any time without observation. It is not distance that makes things strange.' The merry-go-round, the like of which did not exist in England, attracted not only children, but 'staid young women of five-and-twenty sat on them as gracefully as beauties ride in Hyde Park.' He longed to try the merry-go-round, 'to mount one of those timber griffins, and go round in company with a demure Dutch damsel that was there, but my courage failed me'.[7]

Trollope came home from Holland to the reviews of *Orley Farm*. There were some of the by-now-usual complaints: The *Dublin University Magazine* said that Trollope did not go 'below the surface'; the *National Review* insisted he was a 'mere photographer', that he was armed only with 'a number of commonplaces on religion, morals, politics, social and domestic philosophy'; the *London Review* declared that Trollope enjoyed, like W. P. Frith, 'the very best of second-rate reputations'—everybody has read *Framley Parsonage* and everybody has seen *Derby Day*; both show great ease. Trollope's handling of the law again came in for special censure: E. S. Dallas in *The Times* said the author believed 'that lawyers are all liars, and that the procedure of our courts is less adapted to elicit than to conceal the truth. He thinks that barristers should be judges rather than advocates, should say no more than they think, [and] should refuse to accept a brief where they believe that their proposed client is guilty.' The *London Review*, in a second article, claimed that Trollope 'cannot bear a lawyer. They are all rogues, not by nature, but by profession.' On the other hand, the *Examiner* said *Orley Farm* was not only Trollope's 'best novel [but] one of the best novels of the day, and of its kind,—an excellent kind, honest and natural,—one of the best that has been written in any day'. The *Saturday* said that *Orley Farm* was 'one of the best of his many novels', and that 'no one has ever drawn English families better'. In the *Spectator* Richard Holt Hutton wrote that *Orley Farm*, in some respects Trollope's greatest work, displayed 'the nearest approach that he has made to the depth and force of tragedy'. Hutton thought the lawyers here as good as the clergymen in the Barchester series: 'No English novelist has ever yet delineated the finer professional lines of English character with anything like his subtlety and power.' Hutton hoped Trollope would reintroduce in future novels some of the *Orley Farm* characters (only Chaffanbrass would reappear). Dallas conceded that *Orley Farm* had 'a tragic force, or something like it'. The *Cornhill Magazine*, in a notice perhaps written by G. H. Lewes, and voicing a sentiment George Eliot later expressed on Trollope's fiction, claimed that *Orley Farm* was a book likely 'to make [readers] better for the rest of their days—a book not only stirring their interest, but enlarging their sympathies by its pictures of life'.* And the *National Review*, in spite of its reservations, claimed that Trollope's popularity served as the perfect refutation of E. D. Forgues' recent article about the 'degenerence' of the English novel:

[*Orley Farm*] is the precise standard of English taste, sentiment, and conviction. Mr. Trollope has become almost a national institution. The *Cornhill* counts its readers by millions, and it is to his contributions, in ninety-nine cases out of a hundred, that the reader first betakes himself. So great is his popularity, so

* George Eliot wrote to Sara Hennell, 'I have read most of. . . Orley Farm, and admire it very much. . . . Anthony Trollope is admirable in the presentation of even, average life and character, and he is so thoroughly wholesome-minded that one delights in seeing his books lie about to be read.'[8]

familiar are his chief characters to his countrymen, so wide-spread is the interest felt about his tales, that they necessarily form part of the common stock-in-trade with which the social commerce of the day is carried on. . . . The characters are public property. . . . More than a million people habitually read Mr. Trollope.[9]

Many of Trollope's friends thought *Orley Farm* his best book. He demurred: the plot—which he thought of as secondary—although 'probably the best I ever made', was weakened by the fault of 'declaring itself' in Lady Mason's confession about half-way through the book. He could not seriously have believed her revelation much of a mistake, given his avowed purpose of keeping no mysteries from his readers; in the book itself, just after she admits her guilt—a scene Trollope proudly bracketed with passages from Scott, Charlotte Brontë, and Thackeray as properly 'sensational'—the narrator says he hopes that her doing so will not have surprised anybody: 'If such surprise be felt I must have told my tale badly. I do not like such revulsions of feeling with regard to my characters as surprises of this nature must generate.'[10] While realizing that in Lady Mason he had fallen well short of that 'perfect delineation of character' which to him was the highest merit in any novel, Trollope was none the less proud of *Orley Farm*.[11]

Writing in retrospect, Trollope said that in 1862 he felt he had 'gained [his] object'. He had timidly hoped for success through writing when he first came to London in 1834, had made his first effort towards that success in 1843 when he began writing *The Macdermots*. Although 'no man in his youth had less prospect' of the comforts of moderate wealth, success was now here, a position among literary men and a 'comfortable' income of about £4,500 a year. He generally spent about two-thirds of this, for the comfort extended itself to include 'many luxuries' (of which hunting was the most expensive). This 'easy income' meant a relaxing of care: 'Not to have to think of sixpences, or very much of shillings; not to be unhappy because the coals have been burned too quickly, and the house linen wants renewing; not to be debarred by the rigour of necessity from opening one's hands, perhaps foolishly, to one's friends.' But for all the characteristic emphasis on money, he felt constrained to add that none the less, 'the respect, the friendships, and the mode of life' were sweeter than the money.[12]

It was with that consciousness of having 'gained his object' that Trollope began a long novel on his return from America. It was to appear in twenty instalments in the *Cornhill*, beginning in September 1862 (by which time

Trollope had completed scarcely half the novel). Smith at first offered £3,500 for the entire copyright; Trollope balked, mistakenly thinking he would do better by retaining some portion of the copyright, and agreed instead to £2,500 for serial rights and eighteen months' license for two book editions. (Trollope did not exercise his option to buy the remaining stock and resume copyright of the novel; instead he allowed Smith to purchase the copyright for £500. The resulting net loss of £500 to Trollope gave him pause about retaining ownership of his copyrights; by the late 1860s he was selling the complete rights to his books to his publishers. He told Thomas Hardy, in 1877, 'I sell everything out and out to my publishers, so that I may have no further bargainings. When I used to hold the cheap edition in my own hand it was my practice to sell the half-profits for such or such a time;—but it never came to much with me. There can be no doubt that the royalty system is the best [i.e., better also than the vague half-profits] if you can get a publisher to give you a royalty, & if you are not in want of immediate money.'13)

Before he started the novel, in May 1862, Trollope had intended that it should be called 'The Two Pearls of Allington', a title to which Smith objected because Harriet Beecher Stowe's *The Pearl of Orr's Island* was currently being serialized in England. Although no admirer of Mrs Beecher Stowe—he thought her novels 'falsely sensational and therefore abominable'—Trollope grumbled only a little and allowed Smith to steer him towards the superior name, *The Small House at Allington*.14 Its 'two pearls' were the heroine Lily Dale and her sister Bell; and the central male character was the young London Civil Service clerk Johnny Eames, a partial self-portrait of the youthful Anthony Trollope. Eames is a hobble-dehoy, awkward, ungainly, shy in the presence of women, much given to solitary walks and castle-building, a late bloomer; though tempted, he won't marry someone socially beneath him, but sticks to his unhappy passion for Lily Dale, who cannot return his love. Throughout this novel and *The Last Chronicle* she remains faithful to her faithless first love. (In spite of public clamour for Lily's marriage to Eames, Trollope kept his 'female prig'15 a self-imposed old maid.)

The Small House at Allington introduces Plantagenet Palliser and forms a bridge between the Barsetshire and the Palliser novels. Palliser's first appearance is inauspicious: the nephew and heir of the Duke of Omnium, he is about twenty-five, unmarried, rich, and with prospects of enormous wealth; a rising politician, serious and hard-working, Palliser is indifferent to hunting or shooting or yachting, or any amusement; he is a great reader of serious books, a 'thin-minded, plodding, respectable man, willing to devote all his youth to work, in order that in old age he might be allowed to sit among the Councillors of the Land'. In *The Small House* Palliser becomes involved in what seems—from what we later learn of him—an unlikely flirtation with a married woman, Lady Dumbello, daughter of Archdeacon Grantly. But one word from Mrs Grantly sends Lady Dumbello back into her husband's good graces, and Palliser ends up in the unwilling arms of Lady Glencora MacCluskie. This wealthy young woman is in love with a scapegrace, Burgo Fitzgerald, but pressures from her family and Palliser's prevail. Palliser 'had danced with her twice, and had spoken his mind', had done his duty, and the two marry. [16] This frequently unhappy couple form the basis and centre for the series of six Palliser novels, which Trollope would begin half a year later with *Can You Forgive Her?* Palliser and Lady Glencora are very minor figures in *The Small House*, Glencora figuring in scarcely two pages. One wonders whether Trollope at this time had any idea that he would in subsequent novels lavish more attention on these two than on any of the hundreds of characters he created.

The new novel was a great success: it 'redeemed' his reputation with George Smith, after the damage done by *Brown, Jones, and Robinson*. Millais again did the illustrations, one full-page and one chapter-heading vignette for each instalment. The critics liked the novel, although they almost unanimously thought Eames the weakest character, and the unfaithful lover Crosbie the best. The *London Review* said that Trollope knew more about womankind than most novelists of either sex, the *Saturday Review* that he handled love affairs as did Jane Austen; Hutton in the *Spectator* made perceptive comments about Trollope's grasp of the 'social strategies', the 'moral "hooks and eyes" of life', by which people get holds over others; the *Athenaeum* said that, during serialization, the question of whether Johnny Eames would marry Lily Dale was as much speculated upon as any '"marriage on the tapis" . . . in any town or village in Great Britain', and demanded emphatically that Trollope reopen the story of the leading characters; similarly the *Illustrated London News* insisted that the 'unsatisfactory conclusion' of the novel be righted in another tale: 'Flesh and blood cannot endure that [Lily Dale] should be sentenced to lead the life of a "widowed maid".' Only the *Saturday* persisted in the view that characters should not be carried over from one novel to another, protesting against the reappearance of Mr Harding, Archdeacon Grantly, and Lady Dumbello: 'This is all very good fun for [Trollope], but it is very poor fun for his readers.' [17]

While *The Small House* was running in the *Cornhill*, Chapman & Hall published, in February 1863, Trollope's second series of *Tales of All Countries*. It contained 'The Banks of the Jordan', here renamed 'A Ride Across Palestine', and 'Mrs General Talboys', the stories that had proved too indelicate for the *Cornhill*, and too indelicate even for the *London Review*. The volume also reprinted 'Aaron Trow', which, with its violent scene of an attempted disfigurement and threatened rape of a woman, would doubtless also have been accounted too strong for those publications; in his short stories Trollope sometimes experimented with subjects he was chary of in his longer fiction. But the reviewers weren't troubled; in fact the *Spectator* singled out 'Mrs General Talboys' for praise, calling it 'certainly clever', if rather coarse, adding that it read more like the production of Trollope's mother. On the other hand, the same reviewer noted what was to become a commonplace of Trollope criticism: 'No writer requires more the freedom and continuity of an extended narrative in order to produce his best effects.' The *Saturday Review* compared the short stories to the 'first faint sketches' which great painters make as studies for larger works, and dilated on the excellences of 'The Parson's Daughter of Oxney Colne'. (The heroine of that tale, a young woman who had given her whole heart to the wrong man and embraced a permanent, disappointed, single existence because the 'the romance of her life was played out', may well have been a kind of preliminary Lily Dale. [18]) The reviewer also claimed that Trollope stood 'without a rival' in describing young ladies and was above all successful at proposal scenes: 'It is almost as hard to write a good proposal about imaginary people as to make one in the flesh to a real girl. Mr. Trollope, however, almost always succeeds . . . because he takes great pains and does not shrink from going at consider-able detail into all that is said, or should be said, or might be said on such occasions.' The writer thought Trollope could do 'naughty' girls too, as in 'A Ride Across Palestine', which he considered the best story in the collection. [19] Certainly the second series of *Tales of All Countries* was an improvement over the first. Once again, as in the earlier series, some of the stories are based upon incidents that happened to Trollope while abroad and are quite plainly autobiographical. The narrator/traveller of these stories seems very like Trollope the traveller: frequently a solo sojourner, he is fond of the company of pretty women; he never bothers to lock his things up; he laments that he had never been taught French and is amazed at the facility of other peoples like Arabs who learn 'all languages under the sun'; he is content to meet all reasonable costs ('There is nothing in the world like paying for what you use'); he has frequent trouble maintaining his 'personal dignity', as when doggedly sitting on a mule in Costa Rica or being dragged in a 'wooden box' of an omnibus across Egypt to Suez; he revives himself with brandy and water and cigars; he is happy to see the world, but convinced that 'for a life of daily excitement, there is no life like life in England'.[20]

Trollope had expected another novel to start serialization in the summer of 1863, in the popular evangelical monthly *Good Words*, and had already secured George Smith's consent to its overlapping with the long novel in the *Cornhill*. The editor of *Good Words* was the well-known liberal Scottish preacher Norman Macleod, minister of the Barony Church, Glasgow. Macleod was a man of great charm, physical size, and zeal, beloved of the poor (he conducted Sunday evening services to which only people wearing working clothes were admitted);[21] he was one of the Scottish chaplains to the Queen, and in fact her friend and adviser (his enemies accused him of drinking whisky and smoking with Prince Albert at 'ungodly hours').[22] The proprietor of *Good Words* was the irrepressible Alexander Strahan, another Scotsman, who conducted a publishing business, largely in religious books, at Edinburgh. His magazine attempted to attract varying sectors of evangelical Christianity, including that within the Established Scottish Church, the more strictly Calvinistic Scottish Free Church,* and even the Anglican Church. Since its first issue in January 1860 (at the same time as the *Cornhill*), *Good Words* had increased its circulation and widened its appeal far beyond evangelicals, with fiction (by authors including Dinah Mulock and 'Sarah Tytler', a *Cornhill* writer) and articles on subjects of general interest, including science; illustrations were a special feature, and one of its artists was Millais. As with the *Cornhill*, the publisher/proprietor did more of the editorial work than did the editor. Trollope was already a friend of Macleod (who had enlisted him as a member of the 'Gaiters Club', a little group who made walking tours in Scotland), and in April 1862 Macleod decided to sign him up for *Good Words*. Macleod began in a jocular vein: 'You never perhaps heard of Good Words? . . . Enough that our circulation is now 70,000—& that *I* am Editor!' Strahan, he said, would meet Trollope's requirements as to money. 'You & Kingsley', Macleod added,

* Established in 1843 when 473 ministers seceded from what they considered to be the too lax Church of Scotland. Anglican divine Sydney Smith (whose writings Trollope admired) said that though John Murray had explained the Scottish Church to him ten times, and Francis Jeffrey twenty times, it was all still a mystery to him: 'I know it has something to do with oatmeal, but beyond that I am in utter darkness.'[23]

'are the only two men whom I should like to have a story from . . . I think you could let out the *best* side of your soul in Good Words—better far than even in Cornhill.'[24] Trollope said he tried to dissuade Macleod, told him that 'a novel from me would hardly be what he wanted, and that I could not undertake to write either with any specially religious tendency, or in any fashion different from that which was usual to me.'[25] But Macleod persisted, and Trollope accordingly saw Strahan, who agreed on 7 April to pay £600 for the serial rights of a short novel, to run from July to December 1863. The young publisher, who had moved his business to Ludgate Hill, London, was well aware of the value of a serial by Trollope in his campaign for a wider readership. In November he offered Trollope £100 for a short Christmas tale, and soon proceeded to make a new agreement for the novel, by which he would pay £1,000 for a doubling in length. The January issue of *Good Words* contained Trollope's 'Widow's Mite', and Strahan's advertisements announced proudly the coming serialization in the magazine of a new novel by the 'author of "Framley Parsonage"', to be illustrated, like that one, by Millais.[26]

Then in April the *Record*, an Anglican evangelical weekly, subject to strong Scottish Calvinist influences, began a six-article campaign against *Good Words*, deploring the high proportion of purely secular material in the magazine and its dilution of the pure milk of Calvinism; it lamented the fact that 'our own beloved [Anglican] Church' should be represented by such broad churchmen as Charles Kingsley and A. P. Stanley; it did not fail to draw attention to the advertisements of Anthony Trollope, whom it labelled 'this year's chief sensation-writer for *Good Words*'. The *Record* shuddered at the 'conjunction of names—Anthony Trollope and Dr. Guthrie' (the Scottish apostle of the 'ragged schools').[27] When it came out that the writer of the articles was not, as he said, an Anglican, but Thomas Alexander, a Free Church Presbyterian Scot, Macleod scored some points; and when it was reported that the Free Church Presbytery at Strathbogie in the Highlands had gathered up all the local copies of *Good Words* and publicly burned them, the secular press gleefully entered the controversy, even to the extent of sniffing out an especially high rate of illegitimate births in book-burning Strathbogie.[28] The fuss was all good publicity for Strahan,* but Macleod was uneasy, and insisted that Strahan henceforth send him all proofs for vetting. When at the end of May he received proofs for the greater part of *Rachel Ray*, he was dismayed to find

---

* *Good Words* continued to increase steadily in circulation, and, according to Strahan, by the late 1860s, it had reached a readership of 160,000, outselling by a margin of at least two to one all other monthlies, including the *Cornhill Magazine*.[29]

it totally unsuitable for *Good Words*. Negotiations to end the agreement he left to Strahan, whom he told: 'I don't blame [Trollope] a bit . . . I might have assumed that he could not and . . . would not change his way of treating at human life to please the readers of Good Words . . . [But *Rachel Ray*] would land me in a series of fights with Parsons, Parties, Churches, and Reviewers. . . . I have twice sat down to write to him but to tell the truth I feel so utterly spoony about it as if I were doing something wicked that I cannot at present.'[30] When he did write to Trollope, on 11 June 1863, it was a terribly long letter, explaining how he attempted to run the magazine on a middle ground, avoiding the narrowness and strictness of most religious periodicals while striving none the less not to offend the 'sincere convictions and feelings of fair & reasonable Evangelical men'. Macleod insisted he had not 'sacrificed' Trollope to the 'vile Record'; he had hoped that Trollope would write a novel which, instead of demonstrating what was 'weak, false, disgusting in professing Christians', would show Christianity as an unmatched power for good. But in *Rachel Ray* Macleod sees nothing but an attack on the Low Church: 'a gloom over Dorcas Societies, & a glory over balls till 4 in the morning,—in short, it is the old story—the shadow over the Church is broad & deep, & over every other quarter sunshine reigns—that is the *general impression* which the story gives.'[31]

Trollope's later comment was that the story must be allowed to speak for itself: 'It is not brilliant, nor in any way very excellent; but it certainly is not very wicked. There is some dancing in one of the early chapters, described, no doubt, with that approval of the amusement which I have always entertained.'[32] This is really a less than accurate assessment of the novel: *Rachel Ray* is a rough attack on evangelical prejudices, an onslaught worthy of Frances Trollope. It is hardly the dancing that Macleod found objectionable, but rather, as his letter shows, the continual presentation of unhealthy religious influences.

Set in rural Devon and more 'provincial' than any of the Barsetshire novels—it is reminiscent of George Eliot's *Scenes from Clerical Life*— *Rachel Ray* offers a tale of evangelical prudery, fanaticism, puritanism, sexual repressiveness, and intolerance. Trollope, all his protestations notwithstanding, seems to have been unable to resist the temptation to attack the evangelicals in one of their own journals. The heroine's evangelical sister, the widow Dorothea Prime, a character almost as prominent as Rachel herself, considers Rachel a 'castaway' because she is discovered to have spent a few moments alone with a man, and, rather than stay under the same roof with her sister, leaves home. This 'lady preacher' is courted by Samuel Prong, a hard-working but ungentlemanly and sanctimonious evangelical clergyman, who wants to marry Dorothea for her small income—telling her all the while that 'Money is but dross'. But Dorothea, in spite of her unworldliness, puts the control of her own money before marriage. ('Defend me from a lone widow,' says the agent who arranges her quarterly payments, 'especially if she's Evangelical.') Rachel's timorous mother, a woman of good impulses weakened by religion, is so gullible that 'she believed too much. She could never divide the minister from the Bible;—nay, the very clerk in the church was sacred to her while exercising his function therein. . . . So also when the clergyman in his sermon told her that she should live simply and altogether for heaven, that all thoughts as to this world were wicked thoughts, and that nothing belonging to this world could be other than painful, full of sorrow and vexations, she would go home believing him absolutely.'[33] And Dr Comfort, a parson Calvinistic in his preaching though not in his way of life, gives Mrs Ray utterly unsound counsel in regard to Rachel's involvement with her suitor. Macleod was right, the shadow over the Church is broad and deep.

When the *Good Words* publication fell through, Trollope arranged for Chapman & Hall to give him £1,000 for the right to print 3,000 copies (instead of £500 for 1,500 copies) since there was to be no serial edition. Then he demanded £500 from Strahan, although legally he could have held the publisher responsible for the £1,000. 'I have written for you', Trollope told him, 'such a story as you had a right to expect from me,— judging as you of course did judge from my former works.' Trollope said he desired only to make what he would have by the original agreement, and Strahan readily agreed to the 'reasonableness' of this proposition and paid the £500.[34] The friendship between Macleod and Trollope was unaffected by the *Rachel Ray* incident. Moreover, Trollope continued to write for *Good Words*: in December 1863 the magazine published 'The Two Generals', and a year later 'Malachi's Cove', one of Trollope's most unusual fictions (it reads like something from D. H. Lawrence); one wonders Macleod did not find it too earthy. In 1872 *The Golden Lion of Granpere*, a rather innocuous short novel, ran in the magazine for eight months under Macleod's editorship.

The real disappointment of the *Rachel Ray* débâcle in *Good Words* was that Millais, whose much-praised *Parables of Our Lord* were appearing in the magazine, would not now illustrate the novel. '[*Good Words*] has thrown me over,' Trollope wrote to Millais, in what seems a triumphant tone, 'They write me word that I am too wicked . . . I won't try to set you against them, because you can do Parables and other fish fit for their net; but I am altogether unsuited to the regenerated . . . and trust I may remain so, wishing to preserve a character for honest intentions.'[35] The only vestige of the originally projected illustrations was a frontispiece for Chapman & Hall's one-volume 'Seventh edition' of 1864.[36]

Trollope's greatest satisfaction with the novel came from George Eliot's appraisal. In July she had sent him a copy of *Romola*, a book Trollope told her would 'assuredly' live after her; he then sent her a copy of *Rachel Ray*, 'You know that my novels are not sensational. In Rachel Ray I have attempted to confine myself absolutely to the commonest details of commonplace life among the most ordinary people, allowing myself no incident that would be even remarkable in every day life. I have shorn my fiction of all romance.'[37] She wrote back:

Rachel has a formidable rival in The Small House, which seems peculiarly felicitous in its conception & good for all souls to read. But I am much struck in Rachel with the skill with which you have organized thoroughly natural everyday incidents into a strictly related well proportioned whole, natty & complete as a nut on its stem. Such construction is among those subtleties of art which can hardly be appreciated except by those who have striven after the same result with conscious failure. Rachel herself is a sweet maidenly figure & her poor mother's spiritual confusions are excellently observed. But there is something else I care yet more about, which has impressed me very happily in all those writings of yours that I know—it is that people are breathing good bracing air in reading them—it is that they, the books are filled with belief in goodness without the slightest tinge of maudlin. They are like pleasant public gardens, where people go for amusement, & whether they think of it or not, get health as well. It seems rather preachy and assuming in one way that, out of all the other things I might say. But it is what I feel strongly & I can't help thinking that it is what you care about also, though such things are rather a result of what an author is than of what he intends.[38]

The *Athenaeum* seemed almost to paraphrase the exchange between Trollope and George Eliot, inquiring how, at a time when the public appetite had been whetted for mystery, crime, and surprise in fiction, this 'simple story of doings in a picturesque nook of Devonshire is as delightful as it is healthy'. The writer added that 'no artist but Mr Trollope could produce' such intimate portraits of women. Reviewers of *Rachel Ray* repeated themselves on this latter point: *The Times* said '[he] is, of all our novelists, the ladies' man of our time'; his portraiture of women 'has made him the pet of our drawing-rooms. The women adore him. Nobody understands the gentle dames and damsels of modern life half so well as this modern Anthony. . . . he is the great lady-killer of the age.' The

Saturday Review called Trollope 'quite a young lady's man. . . . His young women are capital—very like real young women. . . . There is a brisk market for descriptions of the inner life of young women, and Mr. Trollope is the chief agent in supplying the market.'[39] Trollope's special talent for depicting women had been noticed since *Barchester Towers*; in 1858 T. C. Haliburton, author of *Sam Slick* and an old friend of Mrs Trollope's, had written him congratulations 'upon attaining the enviable distinction of being by far the best delineator of female character of the present day'. Emily Hall recorded in December 1860: 'I think Trollope is closer to describing women, in drawing their minds and the wanderings of their feelings, than any writer of modern days.' A woman once said to him, 'I understand, Mr. Trollope, your knowing what a young gentleman and a young lady say to each other when they are alone together; but how can you possibly know the way that two young ladies talk to each other while brushing their hair?' Naturally, he offered no explanation—beyond saying he never listened at keyholes.[40] (In its obituary of Trollope the *Saturday Review* retold this anecdote, adding that Trollope 'was in the best sense of the word a masculine man and writer, and yet he knew more of the feminine mind and nature than any author of his generation.'[41]) Trollope, like Paul Montague in *The Way We Live Now*, was one of those men who 'have their strongest affinities and sympathies with women, and are rarely altogether happy when removed from their influence'.[42]

Eighteen-sixty-three brought two important changes in Trollope's personal life. The first came in March, when his household was increased by one. An eight-year-old niece, Florence Nightingale Bland, came permanently to live at Waltham House. She was the recently orphaned daughter of Rose's sister Isabella and Joseph Bland, a clerk in the Rotherham bank once managed by his father-in-law. The little girl became in effect Trollope's daughter, and henceforth the narrator's comments about what 'we' want for 'our daughters' had some personal experience behind them. But almost nothing is known about Florence Bland. Trollope speaks affectionately of her as the 'tyrant' he must take riding in the park; she went with the family on their continental holidays, and when older she was included in their dinner parties and visitings. She attended school at Aachen.* When Florence was about 20 Trollope described her in a letter

* A schoolmate there, Ada Strickland, whom Florence often brought home on holidays, eventually married Harry Trollope, in 1884; Ada said that as a young girl she was 'head over ears in love with [Anthony] and used to have a furiously gay time at their house. . . . I was kind to [Harry] and liked him because he was Anthony's son.'[43]

to a friend as 'clever but not demonstrative';[44] she became, late in Trollope's career, his part-time amanuensis, taking down from his dictation some of his letters and parts of novels. In the last year of his life she twice accompanied him to Ireland where he gathered materials for *The Landleaguers*.

The second was the death of Frances Trollope soon after Anthony's last meeting with her in Florence. He had taken his family, including Florence Bland, for a holiday in Switzerland from 20 July to 15 August; then on 10 September he had accompanied his elder boy, Harry—now 17 and having left Bradfield—to Florence, where he was to remain for tutoring. Trollope had only just returned to England when his mother died in Florence on 6 October. She was 84. Trollope, who did not go to Florence for the funeral, asked Hepworth Dixon, editor of the *Athenaeum*, to put a short notice in the paper; he supplied a few facts that might be incorporated into the piece: that she began writing at 50 and did so simply to provide an income because of his father's very bad circumstances, that she continued to write for a quarter of a century, until she was 77, her last work having been published in 1856. John Doran wrote the notice, and Trollope thanked him for the 'kindliness, heartiness, as well as excellent taste' of the article. Doran said, among other things, that Mrs Trollope's literary career 'made her one of the most remarkable women of her period. . . . The venerable lady has passed tranquilly out of life, leaving a name in English Literature, and a memory to be honoured by her two surviving sons.' Trollope wrote to his old family friend of their Harrow days, Mary Grant Christie: 'My dear mother died full of years and without anything of the suffering of old age. For two years her memory had gone. But she ate & slept & drank, till the lamp went altogether out; but there was nothing of the usual struggle of death. I think that no one ever suffered less in dying.' T. A. Trollope, who took care of her those last years, said privately that 'her mind was in fact *gone*'. But before she died she had been able to get about, and was bedridden only a day or two before the end came. Tom kept a promise to her that he would open a vein in her arm lest she be buried alive, and then had her buried in the Protestant Cemetery in Florence; he himself composed a Latin inscription which said in marble that her 'special divine spirit needs no marble monument'.[45]

The death of his mother in old age had been accepted by Trollope as the passing of an inevitable milestone. He experienced a much sharper grief at the untimely death of Thackeray some three months later, on 24 December 1863, a death for which none of Thackeray's friends was prepared, in spite of his deteriorating health. Trollope heard the news on Christmas Day. In a note to Chapman he said, 'I have been greatly cut up by Thackerays death, which I only learned in the Times. It has not been a merry Christmas with us. I loved him dearly.' To George Smith he wrote: 'I have been stopped . . . in every thing. . . . I felt it as a very heavy blow.' He offered to write something about Thackeray in the next *Cornhill*: 'If you have no one better, I will do it gladly. Lewes, or Bell, or Russell would do it better. . . . I have not the heart to wish any one a merry Christmas.'[46] He attended the funeral, one of a crowd of some 1,500, in All Souls Cemetery, Kensal Green, the place where he himself would be buried twenty years later. In his *Cornhill* tribute, which appeared together with one from Dickens and a poem by Lord Houghton, Trollope rated *Henry Esmond* 'the first and finest novel in the English language' and Colonel Newcome 'the finest single character in English fiction'. Of Thackeray himself, Trollope wrote, 'One loved him almost as one loves a woman, tenderly and with thoughtfulness,—thinking of him when away from him as a source of joy which cannot be analysed, but is full of comfort.'[47]

However grievous the death of Thackeray, the departure of this giant among contemporary novelists tended to increase Trollope's own prominence in the London literary world. He succeeded Thackeray as the leading author on Smith, Elder's list. Within a short time he too would become involved in the editorship and management of periodicals. At the Garrick Club he was invited to take his dead friend's place on the Committee. Soon afterwards the club moved from its tiny premises in King Street, Covent Garden, to the fine new building, designed by Frederick Marrable, in New King Street (later renamed, at the members' request, Garrick Street); there Trollope presided at the inaugural dinner on 6 July 1863, proposing the toast to Thackeray's memory. He was instrumental in the Club's commissioning of a bust of Thackeray by Joseph Durham (and later in J. E. Boehm's putting it into marble); he played the leading part in his commemoration in Poets' Corner, with a bust by Marochetti.[48] Thackeray was gone. Dickens and George Eliot remained pre-eminent, but Trollope was admitted to be the prolific, well-loved king of serial novelists.

Trollope continued at the height of his powers as a novelist in 1864. The year opened with the publication by Chapman & Hall of the first of twenty monthly parts of *Can You Forgive Her?*. Trollope had started writing the story in August 1863 and finished it at the end of April 1864 (another instance of a novel beginning to appear before being completed), taking only eight months for what he called a 'five volume' novel, a speed comparable to that which completed the 'four volume' *Small House* in five months. He proceeded, after less than a month's break, to write a short novel, *Miss Mackenzie*, for publication in two volumes by Chapman & Hall. (In choosing volume publication without prior serialization he was encouraged by the success of *Rachel Ray*: 'After all,' he told Chapman, 'the old fashioned mode of publishing does very well now and then as a change.'⁴⁹) No sooner had he finished *Miss Mackenzie* than he embarked on *The Claverings* (to be serialized in the *Cornhill*, 1867–8), which occupied him until the end of the year. During 1864 he produced the equivalent of nearly eight 'volumes', the closest he ever came to the dreaded figure of three three-decker novels that so distressed the publisher in Paternoster Row. His earnings were high: £3,000 for *Can You Forgive Her?* (half-profits eventually raised the figure to £3,525, the most he received for any of his works), £1,500 for *Rachel Ray*, and £2,800 for the serial and book rights of *The Claverings*, which—as it was the equivalent of a three-volume novel—Trollope declared 'the highest rate of pay that was ever accorded to me'.⁵⁰ It was probably of *The Claverings* that George Smith, whose recollections are very unreliable, told a partially invented story: Trollope came to Smith's office to arrange for a serial, was offered £2,000, demurred at this, saying he was hoping for £3,000. Smith shook his head no, whereupon Trollope suggested they toss a coin for the extra £1,000.* Smith professed hesitancy: what would his banker say? What would his clerks think if they saw him tossing with an author for his manuscript? The two men came to agreement, Smith wrote, on 'my terms, which were sufficiently liberal', and he then invited Trollope to the privacy of his club where he would willingly toss for the extra £1,000. 'Mr. Trollope did not accept the offer.'⁵¹ The difference in Smith's account between his offer and Trollope's expectations is altogether unlikely, but the anecdote is emblematic of the two men's easy and cordial relationship.

The productivity recorded above, extraordinary even for Trollope, would not have been possible had he obtained the advancement in his Post Office career that seemed briefly within his grasp in 1864. In March of that year his old adversary Rowland Hill retired, a retirement Trollope marked with a conciliatory letter, saluting Hill's reforms: 'I have regarded you for many years as one of the essential benefactors, not only of your own

---

* 'There are Englishmen who think that every man differing with them is bound to bet with them on any point in dispute' ('The Widow's Mite', *Lotta Schmidt: And Other Stories*). When Mr Dockwrath refuses to bet with Mr Moulder on the outcome of the great Orley Farm case, Moulder laughs, 'What criterion is there by which a man can test the validity of his own opinion if he be not willing to support it by a bet? A man is bound to do so, else to give way and apologize.'⁵²

country, but of all the civilized world. I think that the thing you have done has had in it more of general utility than any other measure which has been achieved in my time.' Hill recorded the receipt of 'an excellent letter' from Trollope among the congratulatory letters from men he had long regarded as hostile.[53] (When Trollope's *Autobiography* was published in October 1883 with its unflattering comments about Hill, the *Postal, Telegraphic, and Telephonic Gazette* published this letter—and *The Times* followed suit—as evidence of Trollope's differing private and official opinions. Trollope would have insisted on his admiration for Hill's extension of the rural post and other reforms; but in fact the letter is fulsome in its praise.) Hill's place as Secretary was promptly filled by John Tilley, whereupon Trollope applied for Tilley's vacant Assistant Secretaryship, to which he felt entitled on grounds of seniority and distinguished service. The application demonstrated his commitment to the Post Office. As he said in *An Autobiography*:

Had I obtained this [promotion] I should have given up my hunting, have given up much of my literary work,—at any rate would have edited no magazine,—and would have returned to the habit of my youth in going daily to the General Post Office. There was very much against such a change in life. The increase in salary would not have amounted to above £400 a year, and I should have lost much more than that in literary remuneration. I should have felt bitterly the slavery of attendance at an office, from which I had been exempt for five-and-twenty years. I should, too, have greatly missed the sport which I loved. But I was attached to the department, had imbued myself with a thorough love of letters,—I mean the letters which are carried by the post,—and was anxious for their welfare as though they were all my own. In short, I wished to continue the connexion. I did not wish, moreover, that any younger officer should again pass over my head.

That, however, was what happened. Tilley, tied to Trollope though he was by friendship and by marriage, recommended a man six years his junior in the service, Frank Ives Scudamore. In recounting the episode Trollope conceded Scudamore's superiority in the understanding of accounts (he was Receiver and Accountant General of the Post Office), while contending that he himself 'might have been more useful in regard to the labours and wages of the immense body of men [some 20,000] employed by the Post Office'.[54]

The disappointment of his hopes and a natural resentment that Tilley had not recognized his claim may have contributed to the obstinacy and ill temper with which he pursued the new Secretary on the surveyors' long-standing grievance about the widening gap between their salary scale and that of the Assistant Secretaries and the London heads of departments. He first wrote as a representative of the surveyors; but when Tilley refused to admit that a case had been made, justifying the differential by a reference to 'special services', Trollope continued the battle on his own. In July, in an official letter of remonstrance, he dismissed the 'special service' argument, and described Tilley's reply as 'studiously offensive'; his parting shot was to say that he would be justified in asking the Postmaster-General 'to recommend the newly appointed Secretary to be more considerate of the feelings of those officers among whom he passed his official life, till he received his promotion'. This 'most intemperate letter' brought a further rebuke from Tilley, but Trollope refused to consider the subject closed and addressed a final letter to the Postmaster-General, knowing that it would go to the Secretary. He commented on Tilley's refusal to reconsider the salary scales: 'It was exactly the way in which Oliver was treated when he came forward on behalf of the Charity boys to ask for more;—and I own that I thought Mr Tilley was very like Bumble in the style of the answer he gave us.' Tilley, however, stood firm. Rowland Hill took a sour pleasure in hearing what he regarded as 'the conspirators against me . . . quarrelling as to the division of the spoil', with 'a fearful passage of arms between Trollope and Tilley—Trollope, of course, being the aggressor'.[55] But 'the aggressor' was soon reconciled with Tilley—who well knew how short-lived were Trollope's outbursts of temper when criticizing a colleague.

The Post Office establishment, perhaps to mollify Trollope, offered him a postal mission to the East the following year, but he declined. In 1866 he was given the arduous task of reorganizing the sorting and delivery of letters in London. For some years the metropolitan area had been divided into postal districts (the familiar W, WC, etc.), all under the supervision of one controller in the Circulation Department. Since the time of the Inquiry Committee it had been under consideration that the job was too much for one individual, and in March Tilley proposed to the Postmaster-General that someone be selected to report on the feasibility of converting eight of the ten London postal districts into individual 'post towns', each with its own postmaster. Trollope was asked to do the report, quickly submitted one, and by 15 June the new arrangement was being put in place, with Trollope acting as temporary surveyor of the new 'district'. His headquarters were set up at the Vere Street post office, by Cavendish Square.[56] A postal employee recalled him at work:

I have seen him slogging away at papers at a stand-up desk, with his handkerchief stuffed into his mouth, and his hair on end, as though he could barely contain himself. He struck me as being rather a fierce-looking man, and a remark which he made to a postmaster on one occasion did not appear to me to savour either of courtesy or kindness. This poor fellow, who had probably seen 30 years' service, and who was wedded to the old system of working the districts, was fretting terribly at the prospect of becoming a postmaster and of being left to his own resources, so to speak, when Trollope turned round on him with the remark: 'Why don't you pay an old woman six pence a week to fret for you?'

(The worrier may have been one Mr Smith, who, Trollope told Tilley, was too old to take up new work; Mr Salisbury would fill the position better, and besides, he 'has 8 children'.57) The new arrangement completed, Trollope was then offered the permanent surveyor's position for the Metropolitan District, but he immediately refused. It would have raised his salary by £100, but it would have meant spending too many days in town; moreover, he had determined to retire early from the service. He recalled in *An Autobiography* that Scudamore's appointment had reinforced an earlier decision, taken with Rose's concurrence, 'to abandon the Post Office when I had put by enough to give me an income equal to the pension to which I should be entitled if I remained in the department till I was sixty'. Explaining that decision, he sketches his way of life from 1860 until his retirement:

I got up always very early; but even this did not suffice. I worked always on Sundays,—as to which no scruple of religion made me unhappy,—and not unfrequently I was driven to work at night. In winter when the hunting was going on, I had to keep myself very much on the alert. And during the London season, when I was generally two or three days of the week in town, I found the official work to be a burden.58

Trollope had failed to obtain higher advancement in the Post Office in 1864, but his stature as a man of letters was steadily rising. On 9 March he joined the Committee of the Royal Literary Fund, becoming the colleague of such men as Lord Stanhope, Lord John Manners, J. A. Froude, Dean Stanley, and Bishop Wilberforce. These dignitaries were responsible, with the help of a paid Secretary, for the administration of the funds of the charity and the allocation of grants to impoverished writers or to the dependants of deceased writers. The Committee met at least once a month during nine months of the year. In 1864 the Fund was fulfilling the functions for which it had been set up in 1790 by essentially the same means. Ten years earlier, however, there had been a campaign for radical reform led by Dickens and John Forster in alliance with C. W. Dilke, T. K. Hervey, and Hepworth Dixon. Their targets were costly, ineffective administration and the low level of grants; but their object, as became increasingly clear, was also to transform the Fund into an association of professional literary men and to remove the influence of wealthy and aristocratic patrons. Although they came close to success in 1855 when a committee (on which the reformers were well represented) was set up to consider framing a new charter, their attack on the administration was pushed to such unfair lengths that by 1859 they had alienated most of the subscribers. Dickens's chief adversaries were Octavian Blewitt, Secretary of the Fund since 1839, and Robert Bell, later Trollope's good friend. Most of the subscribers rallied to Blewitt's defence, regarding him as a hard-working and competent administrator, devoted to the Fund, which he continued to serve as Secretary until his death in 1884. Trollope himself, while a supporter of the organization's objectives and administration, did make modestly successful efforts to increase the size of the grants; his correspondence shows the time and energy he devoted to the sad cases brought to his notice; he argued, for example, in favour of a grant for 'a dear old lady', Miss Helen Crickmaur, who wrote children's stories and was now 'almost starving'. From 1864 until his death, he seldom missed a meeting of the Committee except when out of the country. In 1869 he became one of the three treasurers of the Fund, which position he also held until his death.[59]

Another sign of his high place in the literary world of London came on 12 April 1864, when Lord Stanhope secured for him election to the Athenaeum Club under Rule II, the rule which admits members by special invitation without the normal delay. As Trollope told Squire Bancroft in 1878, under Rule II the 'selected heroes' are usually

learned pundits, philosophers, doctors who have invented new diseases, and scientific fogies with bleared eyes. Become such a one and you will be brought in at once—or be made a bishop, or a Cabinet Minister, and the thing is done. By the other mode candidates await their turns. Yours will come in 15 years,—unless the process becomes slower. . . . This will be quite soon enough for you as it is essentially an old man's club—I, if I am allowed by post-mortem arrangements, will then come down,—or up—and give such ghostly assistance as may be possible.

(Bancroft was elected a member in 1909.[60]) Though the Garrick remained Trollope's favourite club, he would, in spite of his occasional grumbling about the Athenaeum's 'ponderosities', use the club frequently and play countless games of whist there, right up to the time of his death.

Membership in the Cosmopolitan and the Garrick had already made Trollope a dedicated clubman; membership in the Athenaeum increased still further his immersion in the London club world. Club life fed his desire for standing with his peers, for camaraderie, for 'manly' company, card-playing, smoking, elaborate meals for small informal groups. Living as he did outside London proper, he could use clubs to offer hospitality and dinners to friends in the city. He also joined the Arts Club in Hanover Square in 1864, but resigned because he never used it; at the instigation of friends in the Post Office, he was one of the originators of the Civil Service Club, but never went there and withdrew; for a brief time he was a member of the Turf Club, serviceable to him 'only for the playing of whist at high points'; in 1874 he declined to join the Reform Club—'I belong to 3 clubs, which are two more than a man needs.' Late in life, in August 1881, he was elected to the United Service Club in Pall Mall: 'I find all the old generals very good fellows, and one of them yesterday called me Sir Anthony, which I thought very civil. Perhaps he took me to be a General myself.'⁶¹ Trollope's novels teem with clubmen.

Largely through his clubs, then, Trollope became a great diner-out in London. (When he stayed overnight in town it was at Garlant's Hotel, Suffolk Street, near Haymarket.) He also loved to extend hospitality at his own comfortable house, and was a guest at the country houses of his London friends and that of his cousin Sir John Trollope. He met leading politicians at Lady Amberley's dinner parties; and he and Rose stayed often at such houses as Sir Arthur Annesley's Bletchington Park, the poet Sir Henry Taylor's at Brighton, and with Lord Houghton at Fryston in Yorkshire. One of his most hospitable friends remained George Smith. The Trollopes stayed with him at Brighton, his winter residence, whence he travelled up to London daily. Trollope also became one of the *habitués* at the Friday night dinners given by the Smiths at Oak Hill Lodge, Hampstead, the house they had taken in 1863; their friends had an open invitation to these dinners, with no notice required—an idea said to have been partly inspired by Thackeray. Smith's two young daughters used to watch from the balcony as the guests arrived, counting them so that the butler would know how many places to lay for dinner; they waited expectantly for Trollope, for he had the habit of looking in the mirror and ruffling his hair before entering the drawing-room with a great roar of greeting.⁶²

George Smith's warm relationship with Trollope was also marked by his gift, in 1864, of one of Samuel Laurence's chalk portraits of Thackeray; at the same time Smith commissioned from Laurence a portrait of Trollope himself, for presentation to its subject. More than a week of sitting was necessary, Laurence telling his sitter that he was 'very difficult to draw'; it was an ordeal for the impatient Trollope, although he found the painter's voluble conversation pleasant. He admitted to Smith that the finished portrait was done 'to the life, in a wonderfully vigorous manner', showing him a 'wonderfully solid old fellow', and reported that Rose declared it 'very like,—& not a bit more solid than the original'. Laurence's was the first portrait of Trollope, though he had already been photographed, a process he always found disagreeable ('I *hate* sitting for a photograph'), entailing as it did holding a pose for an uncomfortably long time. He sat to the well-known London photographer Herbert Watkins in April 1860, and commented on the result: 'It looks uncommon feirce [*sic*], as that of a dog about to bite; but that I fear is the nature of the animal portrayed.' Photographs captured Trollope's bluff, aggressive mask, but nothing of his other side, something Charles Kent remarked in writing of a later photograph that the 'bearded leonine face of the man, with its bold front-look, is but a mask before a nature intensely sympathetic.' In 1875 Trollope himself said of photographs, 'Some people wont come out well. Mine are always wretched.'[63]

Two of the three novels on which he was engaged in 1864 drew on his increasingly intimate knowledge of London society and country-house life. *Can You Forgive Her?* also extended his range as an observer of the contemporary political scene, while *The Claverings* involved its vacillating hero Harry Clavering and the passionate Lady Ongar in the raffish fringe of metropolitan life. This novel, which Trollope thought 'good'— except for the weak character of its hero—but which he thought would find no readers in posterity, has a general unpleasantness that has made some people uncomfortable. Many also find the ending unsatisfactory, as Harry Clavering, in ill health, is gently brow-beaten into marrying the meek, faithful heroine, rather than his first love, the now-widowed Lady Ongar; and the convenient death at sea of two unworthy cousins, which brings him a titled estate and wealth, seems contrived. One noteworthy distinction of *The Claverings* is its sympathetic portrayal of an evangelical clergyman, the Revd Samuel Saul.[64] A short book, also written that year, *Miss Mackenzie*, was a bold and successful experiment in making the central character a spinster of 35, neither witty nor very attractive, and keeping the reader always in company with her: there are no sub-plots, and no other characters that the reader is likely to find engaging. Trollope claimed that it 'was written with a desire to prove that a novel may be produced without any love';[65] however, he rewarded the unworldly spinster for her integrity and courage with a happy marriage and release from money troubles. He must have been gratified, when the two volumes appeared in 1865, by the reviewers' recognition of its distinctive achievement: the *London Review* thought it a 'bold undertaking . . . to ask his readers to take an interest in the fortunes of such a heroine . . . but Mr. Trollope revels in risk'; the *Reader* saluted it as a novel that 'no one but Mr. Trollope would have had either the hardihood to undertake, or the ability to write so as to be readable'; the *Westminster Review*, calling Trollope 'Our most popular novelist', said that 'among his many female characters he has never drawn a better than this of Miss Mackenzie'. *The Times* wrote, 'We know not any other living writer of fiction who would have been so bold as to undertake the dealing with such a subject. . . . Mr. Trollope touches it with his wonted ease. . . . He gives us pictures which are not dull of dull lives, dull households, dull dinner parties, dull teas, and dull prayer meetings. The amount of amusement . . . is certainly remarkable.' The *Saturday Review* found that, whereas much of Trollope's popularity arose from the 'nice people' in his fiction, in *Miss Mackenzie* he had deliberately carried his readers into the midst of 'poverty-stricken gentry, dull old maids, unthrifty shopkeepers, and rapacious parsons' and apparently got away with it: 'Nobody but Mr. Trollope would have dared to marry a heroine of some forty years to a widower of fifty with nine children.'[66] Sir Edward Bulwer Lytton, not yet acquainted with Trollope personally, wrote to tell him how much he admired 'the conception and execution' of the central character, so 'full of most delicate beauty'.[67] The one discordant voice came from the other side of the Atlantic. Henry James, then 22, in the first of four reviews of Trollope in the New York *Nation*, objected to his 'devotion to little things', complaining that Trollope's work was too detailed, too laden with 'the virtues of the photograph'.[68]

19

Pallisers and Periodicals

IN *An Autobiography* Trollope expressed his special satisfaction for *Can You Forgive Her?* In his defence of the great speed at which this novel and *The Small House at Allington* had been written, he said of the two, 'taking these books all through, I do not think that I have ever done better work.'[1] The story of Alice Vavasor and her two suitors was based on his old unpublished play 'The Noble Jilt'; the dilemma, as the authorial commentator presents it, owes something to Trollope's argument with Kate Field: Alice's mind 'had become filled with some un-defined idea of the importance to her of her own life. What should a woman do with her life? There had arisen round her a flock of learned ladies asking that question.' The narrator's bluff, and only mildly ironic answer is, 'Fall in love, marry the man, have two children, and live happy ever afterwards.'[2] But what endeared the novel to him was not the somewhat 'wearying' character of the heroine, but the presentation of Plantagenet Palliser and his wife, Lady Glencora. These two very slight figures from *The Small House at Allington* had exuberated into fully realized individuals. Palliser and Glencora became his favourite fictional creations, and he used them time after time to express his political, social, and moral convictions: these two, together with their 'belongings', he wrote, 'have been as real to me as free trade was to Mr. Cobden, or the dominion of a party to Mr. Disraeli; and as I have not been able to speak from the benches of the House of Commons, or to thunder from platforms, or to be efficacious as a lecturer, they have served me as safety-valves by which to deliver my soul.'[3]

Trollope was proud of having created in Palliser 'a very noble gentleman,—such a one as justifies to the nation the seeming anomaly of an hereditary peerage and of primogeniture', and insisted that Glencora was 'in all respects inferior' to her husband.[4] Nevertheless, from her first appearance in *Can You Forgive Her?* he engaged the reader's sympathy in her behalf, gifting her with a quick wit and strong rebellious spirit. He treats with sensitivity her continuing love for the handsome impoverished rogue, Burgo Fitzgerald, after her relatives have forced her into marriage with Palliser, and the way she is brought to the brink of leaving her husband for Fitzgerald. After she has been reconciled to marriage and to Palliser, she retains the mischievousness that is her most charming quality: pregnant at last with the heir apparent to the greatest dukedom in the land, she tells the old Duke of Omnium that she hopes the baby is a girl. Although the Pallisers find a *modus vivendi*, in this and in subsequent novels Trollope never blinks the harsh facts of her story. 'The romance of her life is gone' with Burgo, and the tale of her difficult marriage to Palliser will form a large part of the six-novel series that begins with this one. Here is a colossal exception to the time-honoured comic tradition Trollope so often followed of ending his stories with wedding bells and happy prospects. The story of Glencora and Palliser begins with their marriage, one of the least 'romantic' marriages in English fiction. It is also one of the most closely chronicled marriages in Victorian fiction. Not all his readers appreciated his treatment of the strain on the Palliser marriage. He might have complained with Glencora, 'one does get so hampered, right and left, for fear of Mrs. Grundy,'[5] when he received a letter from a 'a distinguished dignitary of our Church', lamenting that one of the great innocent joys of his life had to be discontinued because he could no longer have his daughters read Trollope's novels to him. Trollope answered respectfully, and rather formally:

The subject of adultery is one very difficult of discussion. You have probably found it so in preaching. . . . But the bible does not scruple to speak to us of adultery as openly as of other sins. You do not leave out the seventh Commandment. The young girl for whom . . . you are so tender is not ignorant of the sin;—and, as I think, it would not be well that she should be ignorant of it. . . . Thinking as I do that ignorance is not innocence I do not avoid, as you would wish me to do, the mention of things which are to me more shocking in their facts than in their names. I do not think that any girl can be injured by reading the character whose thoughts I have endeavoured to describe. . . . It is not probable that I shall carry you with me, but I may perhaps succeed in inducing you to believe that I do not write in the manner of which you complain without thought or without a principle.[6]

The illustrations for *Can You Forgive Her?* were by Hablot Knight Browne, who, as 'Phiz', had begun his famous collaboration with Dickens in 1836. When Dickens decided to have *Our Mutual Friend* illustrated by Marcus Stone, Browne was furious: 'Dickens probably thinks', he wrote to a friend, 'a new hand would give his old puppets a fresh look, or perhaps he does not like my illustrating Trollope neck-and-neck with him—though, by Jingo, he need fear no rivalry *there*! Confound all authors and publishers, say I. There is no pleasing one or t'other.'[7] He certainly did not please Trollope, who undoubtedly realized that he was getting Browne's services at the fag-end of his career and after his talent was largely exhausted (he was also in failing health). But Trollope's principal objections rested on the incompatibility of his own style with Browne's; Trollope and Browne were as ill-attuned to each other as Dickens and Browne had been suited to each other. To say this is to underscore the very different approach that Dickens and Trollope brought to fiction. Trollope, in *An Autobiography*, placed Dickens third among the novelists of his time, behind Thackeray and George Eliot; he acknowledged that certain Dickens characters—Mrs Gamp, Micawber, Pecksniff—had become 'household words'; but they were not 'human': 'It has been the peculiarity and the marvel of [Dickens's] power, that he has invested his puppets with a charm that has enabled him to dispense with human nature. . . . Nor is the pathos of Dickens human. It is stagey and melodramatic.'[8] It annoyed Trollope to see in the characters that Browne drew for *Can You Forgive Her?* such clear family resemblances to Dickens's. 'Inhuman' and unnatural 'puppets' out of Dickens seemed to have wandered on to his pages. He begged Millais to take over, and even offered to make up himself the difference in price (Browne was getting about five pounds a drawing, Millais five times as much). But Millais, under press of other work, declined, and the unhappy Trollope–Browne collaboration struggled on; Trollope became infuriated at the illustrator's inattention to detail, as when he caught in a preliminary drawing Browne giving Burgo Fitzgerald a beard—in plain contradiction to the text. Half-way through the novel, Trollope had Browne dismissed, and replaced him with a Miss Taylor of St Leonards, an amateur of very little talent. But she was a Millais-style 'sixties' illustrator, and this was what Trollope wanted.[9]

Towards the end of 1864 Trollope and Frederic Chapman were shaping plans for a new periodical. A year earlier author and publisher had come close to starting a weekly magazine, with a serial novel as its main attraction. They thought it would be possible to rival the *Cornhill's* unprecedented initial success as a monthly, due largely to Thackeray's name as editor, by having their weekly edited by Trollope, now an equally well-known name to readers and contributors, with a novel by him appearing throughout the first year. During September the projected 'New Weekly—Conducted by Anthony Trollope', which was to commence publication in January 1864, engaged Trollope's attention. He and Chapman discussed page size, whether or not to use bi-columned pages,

whether the sheets for the book edition of the novel Trollope was to write
for the new venture could not be pulled from the magazine's type, the
desirability of a cover in colour, and other such details. Robert Bell was to
have been assistant editor. Trollope somewhat testily told Chapman that
although he could not 'sacrifice' *Can You Forgive Her?* by making it
shorter to suit the periodical, he could fit the whole novel into one year's
weekly parts. No record survives of why this short-lived scheme was given
up; there is no reference to it in letters later than 19 September 1863.[10]

Now, a year later, Trollope and Chapman were again planning to launch
a new periodical, although of a different kind from the 'New Weekly'. They
believed that there were many people who would welcome a magazine
more fresh and lively in its thinking and style than the existing quarterlies,
but intellectually more demanding than the weeklies or monthlies. Trollope's inspiration was the *Revue des deux mondes*, so strongly recommended by Matthew Arnold in 'The Future of Criticism at the Present
Time'. Arnold's article had appeared in the November 1864 issue of the
ten-year-old *National Review*, the first—and as it proved the last—of a
new series of the magazine that changed it from a quarterly to a monthly
and adopted a policy of signed articles. Chapman & Hall, its publishers,
had invested in the *National* in 1861, by which time under its original
editors, Walter Bagehot (also editor of the *Economist*) and R. H. Hutton
(also joint editor of the *Spectator*), it had achieved a high reputation and a
respectable sale. That sale, however, had never recovered from the loss of
its large American circulation during the Civil War, leading to dependence on its Unitarian backers, who were unwilling to sustain it. With its
demise, Chapman & Hall were prepared to launch a new periodical, freed
from the *National*'s tie to Unitarianism but with an equal commitment to
free and intelligent discussion of politics, philosophy, and science. They
also planned to hedge their bets by having serial fiction to attract a wider
readership than the *National* attained or than any English version of the
Revue des deux mondes could expect. Bagehot was among those consulted
about the new venture in December 1864, and would have been in
sympathy with aims so close in many respects to those set out in the
original prospectus of the *National*.[11]

Chapman & Hall were to be 'publishers' only, that is, distributors of the
magazine, which would be the property of independent projectors, each of
whom subscribed £1,250, bonded together as a limited company (Trollope
told Herman Merivale in March 1865 that the paid capital was £8,000).
Known Members were Trollope, Frederick Chapman, Henry Danby
Seymour (Liberal Member for Poole), Charles Waring (later Seymour's

successor at Poole), James Cotter Morison, a writer and biographer, and Charles Rea, a Post Office colleague of Trollope's; James Sprent Virtue, Morison's brother-in-law, who was to be the printer for the new magazine, may have been a projector, and also Lord Houghton, said by Escott to have forwarded it 'not only with his blessing but his purse'. Trollope was elected chairman of the board by which the finances were run. Meetings of the proprietors were held in the Albany chambers of Charles Waring, probably their richest member, enlisted at Trollope's instance by E. F. S. Pigott; at a later stage when the periodical was purchased by its publishers, Waring is said to have thought of buying it back, a move opposed by Trollope.[12]

The character of the periodical and the method of finance having been settled, the first priority was to find an editor. In November Danby Seymour had been in favour of George Meredith; but Trollope chose the older and more distinguished G. H. Lewes, who had been editor of E. F. S. Pigott's *Leader* and mainstay of the *Westminster*, and who had himself published much in philosophy, science, and the arts, English and European. By early December Trollope and Chapman had dined with Lewes and George Eliot and secured his tentative agreement. Lewes at first found the prospect of 'pleasant work' and a steady income of £600 attractive; but shortly before Christmas he changed his mind, fearing the work would be too heavy for his health and would also 'disturb our domestic habits'. Trollope responded with what Lewes called a 'charming' letter: he sympathized with Lewes's misgivings, while stressing that he sought not simply a competent editor, but one 'with whom I could hold close friendly intercourse. I do not care to put myself at the beck of any one whom I do not know, or whom, when known, I may not like.'[13] Trollope prevailed, and Lewes accepted. Trollope also chose the name, the *Fortnightly Review*, a good straightforward choice since it was to follow the *Revue des deux mondes* in appearing once every two weeks.

One distinctive feature of the periodical, specially favoured by Trollope and on which there was complete agreement, was that all articles should be signed. The practice of giving authors' names was, for England, highly innovative; it was also successful, and the *Fortnightly* was to set an example for other magazines, including the *Contemporary Review* and the *Nineteenth Century*. Trollope said, 'I think that the name of the author does tend to honesty, and that the knowledge that it will be inserted adds much to the author's industry and care.'[14] Trollope contributed an article to the *Fortnightly* on anonymous literature, in which he contended that all periodical literature (except, oddly, on 'current politics') ought to carry the author's name. Signed book reviews, for example, would result in more 'real criticism'; he dismissed the fear that only praise would be forthcoming, maintaining that 'almost all the best criticism . . . has been eulogistic'; as to warning readers about bad books, especially by 'the early snuffing out of young literary or young artistic imbeciles', that might be left to the indifference of the reading public.[15]

Fortnightly publication, title, and the signing of articles were not contentious issues; and they were decisions for which Trollope was largely responsible. From his account in *An Autobiography* it is clear, however, that in the discussions about drafting the prospectus and preparing the first issues, his was sometimes a dissenting voice. Announcements in the weeklies of 25 March 1865 acknowledged the *Revue des deux mondes* as their model, and promised to 'remove all those restrictions of party and of editorial "consistency" which in other journals hamper the full expression of opinion': no writer would be 'required to express the view of an Editor or a Party'. A statement that 'the Review will be liberal' disappeared in later and shorter announcements, which said merely that 'The object of the *Fortnightly Review* is to become an organ for the unbiased expression of many and various minds on topics of general interest in Politics, Literature, Philosophy, Science and Art.'[16] Trollope commented, 'The matter on which we were all agreed was freedom of speech, combined with personal responsibility. We would be neither conservative nor liberal, neither religious nor free-thinking, neither popular nor exclusive;—but we would let any man who had a thing to say, and knew how to say it, speak freely.' Such intellectual independence was all well and good in theory, but Trollope himself immediately violated the principle 'most irrationally' by declaring that 'nothing should appear denying or questioning the divinity of Christ'. Trollope confessed that his proviso was 'most preposterous' in view of the stated principle, and agreed that it drove one or two writers from the magazine, but he persisted none the less. Trollope was in fact considerably less enthusiastic about liberal principles than most of the others, including Lewes. Tension was present from the first. Subsequently the magazine moved more and more decidedly to the left, and Trollope, in retrospect, saw that his idea of a truly 'eclectic' or independent journal with a genuine mix of liberal and conservative thinking was 'altogether impracticable': 'Liberalism, free-thinking, and open inquiry will never object to appear in company with their opposites, because they have the conceit to think that they can quell those opposites; but the opposites will not appear in conjunction with liberalism, free-thinking, and open inquiry. As a natural consequence, our new publication became an organ of liberalism, free-thinking, and open inquiry.'[17]

The first number of the *Fortnightly Review* appeared on 15 May 1865. The opening paper was the first of the nine instalments of Bagehot's *English Constitution*, a brilliant fulfilment of the *Review*'s ideals in its original and independent treatment of the subject and its immense readability. Among the other contributors were Lewes, George Eliot, Frederic Harrison, and J. W. F. Herschel. It also carried the first instalment of Trollope's *The Belton Estate*, his opposition to the inclusion of fiction having been overcome by the rest of the board. His close involvement in the review appears in two letters to Lewes, written during his absence from London on Post Office business between 23 May and 15 June. One knowledgeably praised E. S. Beesly's article on Catiline; the other was on the practicalities of editing, not only content and order but appearance (the pages might be 'less pressed'). He insisted that although *The Belton Estate* might occasionally be placed first, this must not become regular practice as it would indicate that fiction was 'our staple'. He also commented on Lewes's 'Principles of Success in Literature' in the second number, calling it 'beautiful, but, oh, so cruel', almost as much so as Carlyle but 'without the salve which one has for Carlyle's blows, in the feeling that they are all struck in the dark, & may probably, after all, not be deserved'. As for his own 'travels': 'Enjoying myself! revising a post office with 300 men, the work and wages of all of whom are to be fixed on one's own responsibility! Come & try it, & then go back to the delicious ease & perfect freedom of your Editors chair!'[18] He had written eight pages of *The Belton Estate* that morning, and would write twelve the next morning.

Trollope wrote much non-fiction for the *Fortnightly*, the earliest a review of the three-volume collected poems of Henry Taylor. Long an enthusiastic admirer of *Philip Van Artevelde*, and his ranking of Taylor among the eighteen 'giants' of English literature having gone unpublished in *The New Zealander*, Trollope now did his best to boost Taylor's reputation: *Van Artevelde*, he wrote, is notable for its 'plain narrative' which, among the 'plain English' people, is everything in verse or prose; and in lucid narrative Taylor surpasses even Tennyson, Mrs Browning, and Robert Browning. The review was so lengthy that Trollope apologized, 'I have loved [Taylor's works] so long and well, that I cannot allow this opportunity of speaking of them in good company to pass by me. They are well known,—but not yet well known up to the measure of their deserts.'[19]

Trollope liked Henry Taylor all the more for his being a civil servant, having served in the Colonial Office since 1824; all his writing, like Trollope's, had been done as a second vocation.

The 1 July issue of the *Fortnightly* contained Trollope's defence of the magazine's policy of signed articles and reviews, and in the following issue Trollope made no bones about going into print under his own name with a scathing review of Ruskin's *Sesame and Lilies*: Ruskin has discussed art 'in language so beautiful, and with words so powerful, that he has carried men and women away with him in crowds'. But the shoemaker should stick to his last, and Ruskin as political economist will not get a hearing; he has taken his preachings from Carlyle, who has been recognized as a preacher and 'almost as a prophet', one whom Englishmen 'are ready to pardon the abuse he showers upon us, on account of the good that we know that he has done to us'. But they do not want to be told by Ruskin that their judgement is 'mere sham prejudice, and drifted, helpless, entangled weed of cast-away thought'. To tell people they must read 'attentively' is well enough, but Ruskin 'mounts so high into the clouds, that what he says,—if it were not altogether so cloudy as to be meaningless and inoperative—would quench all reading rather than encourage it. Young or old, boys or girls, should have our Greek alphabets, and get good dictionaries in Saxon, German, French, Latin, and Greek, in order that we may trace out the real meaning of the words which we read!' Ruskin complains that Englishmen 'despise' literature, proving the assertion by saying that 'men will give more for a large turbot than for a book'; and he tells them they are '"filthy" because [they] all thumb the same books from circulating libraries'.[20] One can understand the pique of one who was hailed as the king of circulating-library novelists. Carlyle saw Trollope's review and wrote to his wife that Ruskin's book 'must be a pretty little thing. Trollope, in reviewing it with considerable insolence stupidity and vulgarity, produces little specimens far beyond any Trollope sphere of speculation. A distylish little pug, that Trollope; irredeemably imbedded in commonplace, and grown fat upon it, and prosperous to an unwholesome degree. Don't *you* return his love; nasty gritty creature, with no eye for "the Beautiful the" etc.—and awfully "interesting to himself" he be.' Trollope had met Carlyle a number of times, first in 1861 through G. H. Lewes, who related that 'as [Trollope] had never seen Carlyle, he was glad to go down with us to tea at Chelsea. Carlyle had read and *agreed* with the West Indian book, and the two got on very well together.' Trollope again visited Carlyle in 1864, and wrote to Lewes, 'Oh, heavens;—what a mixture of wisdom & folly flows from him!'[21]

Trollope's other *Fortnightly* articles focus on his pet themes: of the Established Irish Church, for example, he wrote that the British people endure such an anomaly because it is an old, venerable, and 'picturesque' institution. Nothing characterizes an Englishman more in regard to political and social institutions than 'the loving tenderness with which admitted abuses are endured and palliated'. But the Irish Church, in spite of its age, its quaintness, its picturesqueness, must be disestablished. Trollope won't be impressed by arguments such as the Reverend Alfred Lee's, the gist of which is that St Patrick was a Protestant because he landed in 432 and papal supremacy, according to Lee, was not acknowledged until 1152. Nor will Trollope listen to talk about Irish Church temporalities being switched to the Church of England by Henry VIII. The fact is that the Church temporalities were set apart for teaching the people, and the people are nine-tenths Roman Catholic.[22]

Another article, 'The Civil Service', is a tireless discussion of his old bugbear, the Civil Service examinations as discussed in that 'dread document', the annual *Report of the Civil Service Commissioners*. This was the Tenth Report, the first having come out in 1856 after the Northcote–Trevelyan paper of 1853. Trollope, who had been opposing Civil Service examinations from the beginning, at last concedes that the 'primary idea' of looking into the physical and intellectual fitness of candidates will now be denied by few. But as for the practice, he is as quarrelsome as ever: the examination for the Indian Civil Service, for example, is so demanding that Trollope thinks those sent to India 'must have been educated to a pitch of which we have, I fear, but few examples among those who remain at home'. The candidate is tested in English, Latin, Greek, French, German, Italian, Sanskrit, and Aramaic; pure mathematics, mixed mathematics, natural and moral science. In English the candidate is asked, for example, to discuss the statement of Dr Johnson that 'translation is the pest of language' and to name 'the earlier English dramatists from whom Shakespeare borrowed', illustrating his answer by reference to various plays. 'That any young man of twenty-one should answer such questions as these from real knowledge of his own' is, if not 'incredible' at least 'miraculous'. Trollope wishes the Report gave the answers as well as the questions.[23]

The shorter book reviews Trollope wrote for the *Fortnightly* also reflected his interests. He admired Charles Buxton's *Ideas of the Day on Policy*, a book written by a politician for politicians: 'If read by a political tyro . . . it will leave behind more of political knowledge than can be gained by twelve months' study of leading articles, and of speeches either in the House or in the provinces.' One can't help thinking that Trollope, who was bringing more and more politics into his novels, learned from Buxton's book. Trollope is struck, for example, by the argument that the young Member who 'in his early career endeavours to take his own special course' is imprudently making himself into a black sheep. This sounds remarkably like Phineas Finn. Buxton, a Liberal Member for Surrey, became a dear friend of Trollope's; he was also a great hunting enthusiast, and he was the man who later persuaded Trollope to run for Parliament. [24]

R. H. Hutton's *Studies in Parliament* had the same appeal to Trollope's political sense; that Hutton regularly reviewed Trollope added to his interest. Trollope generously lauds Hutton's sketches of the 'political characters' of leading statesmen; a political education, Trollope asserts, is incomplete without a knowledge of the personal yet still public character of politicians: Hutton 'must have passed many a long hour, many a long night, in the galleries of the Houses of Parliament, almost unconsciously laying bare and separating the nerves and veins of the characters before him with the dissecting knife of his observant intellect, till he has obtained an insight into the minds of the men, and a grasp of their capacities and energies'; [25] Trollope later took a leaf from Hutton's book and sat nightly in the visitors' gallery of the House for a few months, doing just what he congratulates Hutton for having done.

Trollope's interest in America led him to Sir M. Peto's *Resources and Prosperity of America* (basically a study of facts and statistics, the kind of book Trollope could enjoy more than most people) and Goldwin Smith's *Civil War in America*. He again took aim at Ruskin as prophet, saying of *The Crown of Wild Olive* that one could learn nothing of value about political economy from the art critic. But one wonders why Trollope should have bothered to review Captain W. A. Baker's *The Day and the Hour*, 'the work of a man apparently driven mad by the intricacies of Prophecy', who thought that Napoleon III was the Antichrist, that Victoria was the new Queen of Sheba, and that the world would end in 1878. [26] Perhaps Trollope saw the book as good fun.

The enormous popularity of pietistic literature explains why Trollope troubled to break on the wheel of the *Fortnightly* such a butterfly as Mrs Sewell's *The Rose of Cheriton*, a worthless little book of essays in verse. Trollope speaks of 'the millions' of such works that are published, all urging, innocently enough, that the godly life is the proper life, but foolishly advocating that it consists in 'a renunciation of worldly things'. Mrs Sewell would shut up beer shops and gin palaces, thinking that such measures would alleviate evils that in his view only education could address. As for the £70 million she says are spent annually on drink, Trollope, with his incurable love for statistics, calculates that this comes to about three halfpence a day all around: 'The allowance seems to be moderate.'²⁷

The *Fortnightly Review*, though it enjoyed great respect among certain liberal circles, was not a commercial success. Trollope attributed this largely to the magazine's 'colourlessness', in that it was not for or against some set of positions. But in fact, quite to the contrary, the review was identified from the start with Lewes's well-known liberalism—moral as well as political. As Henry Rogers remarked, 'Nobody could be more impartial than Mr. Lewes . . . but this did not prevent [the *Fortnightly*'s] being extensively stigmatized as "an infidel publication," "a positivist magazine, you know," and the like.'²⁸

One of the journal's problems was easily overcome; distributors had difficulty handling a bi-monthly magazine, and at a meeting in August 1866 the board decided to make the *Fortnightly* a monthly. After some discussion they decided to keep the name. Trollope found it ironic and amusing that the *Fortnightly*, which he deemed the 'most serious, the most earnest, the least devoted to amusement, the least flippant, the least jocose' journal of his day, had now 'the face to show itself month after month to the world, with so absurd a misnomer', a name for which he had been responsible.²⁹

Trollope's hopes for the *Fortnightly* took a further plunge in November when Lewes resigned as editor; Trollope wrote to him saying how deeply he regretted the loss to the magazine, but agreeing that Lewes's time was 'too valuable to be frittered away in reading Mss'. He suggested that either John Morley should be asked or Trollope himself would undertake the editorship for six months; but he had doubts about Morley: 'If I found that the Review had drifted into the hands of a literary hack . . . I should wash my hands of it. . . . You will understand what I mean when I say that should I find I dont like the nose on our new Editors face, I must simply drop the Review; and that therefore I cannot but be very anxious. Let me know what you think about Morley.'³⁰ Morley passed muster with Lewes, and, with strong support on the board from James Cotter Morison, was named editor. Many years later Morley told how Trollope 'once had an interview with a writer whom he wished to make the editor of a Review. "Now, do you," he asked, glaring as if in fury through his spectacles, and roaring like a bull of Bashan, "do you believe in the divinity of our blessed Lord and Saviour Jesus Christ?"' The interviewee was of course Morley himself. Trollope might badger Morley, though he would hardly have put the question to the free-thinking Lewes. In fact Trollope was in deep with a group far more liberal than himself, disciples of J. S. Mill and other radical thinkers. Morley related how Mill expressed a desire to meet Trollope, 'and it was arranged that Trollope should go down to dine at Blackheath one Sunday afternoon. He came up from Essex [i.e. Waltham] for the express purpose, and said to a younger friend who was convoying him down, "Stuart Mill is the only man in the whole world for the sake of seeing whom I would leave my own house on a Sunday." The party was only a moderate success. The contrast was too violent between the modesty and courtesy of the host and the blustering fashions of Trollope. . . . It was a relief to get the bull safely away from the china-shop.' Another witness recorded hearing Trollope deliver, at St James's Hall, 'a short and forcible' speech on behalf of Mill's candidacy for Westminster ('the physical contrast between [Mill] and his distinguished supporter was almost ludicrously strong. Mr. Trollope's clear ringing accents could be heard all over the large hall. Mr. Mill was almost inaudible, even to persons sitting within three or four yards of him').[31] Trollope had, none the less, mixed feelings about Mill—'whose name', he once wrote, 'is supposed to be a guarantee for wisdom', and yet who could propose for Ireland that the land be given to the tenants while the government compensated the dispossessed owners, a scheme Trollope deemed 'doubly dangerous in that it came from a man with a world-wide reputation for wisdom, and was yet visionary, impracticable, and revolutionary'.[32] He also judged Mill quixotic on women's rights. It is not known for sure what he thought of Mill's famous motion during the Reform Bill debate of 1867 to replace the word 'man' with 'person', thereby extending the vote to women. But in *He Knew He Was Right*, begun late that year, Trollope has Jonas Spalding, the fatuous American minister to Florence, say to Charles Glascock:

'Your John S. Mill is a great man.'
'They tell me so. I don't read him myself.'
'He is a far-seeing man,' continued the minister. 'He is one of the few Europeans who can look forward, and see how the rivers of civilization are running on. He has understood that women must at last be put upon an equality with men.'
'Can he arrange that the men shall have half the babies?' said Mr. Glascock.[33]

Such probably would have been Trollope's reaction. Nor is it known what he thought of Mill's 'persecution' of Edward John Eyre, for his atrocities as Governor of Jamaica, where he put down a rebellion by indiscriminate murdering of hundreds of natives; here one suspects Trollope sided with

Mill—at least in the early stages of the affair, his close friend and political sponsor Charles Buxton having been one of the original founders of the Jamaica Committee. That the opposition Eyre Defence Committee was championed by Carlyle and supported by Ruskin and Dickens would have helped tilt Trollope towards Mill. In any case, the *Fortnightly* was now in the hands of Morley, an avowed disciple of Mill. The 'Saint of Rationalism' contributed articles to the magazine, and during Morley's illness in 1870 even volunteered to take over the editorship temporarily.[34]

The *Fortnightly* became a monthly in November 1866, but the change was hardly enough to save the magazine for its proprietors. They had spent their money liberally on securing contributions, and near the end of the same year, their resources exhausted, they made over to Chapman & Hall, 'for a trifle', as Trollope put it, the almost valueless copyright. One of Trollope's last acts as chairman of the finance board was to allow Morley to give Swinburne 20 guineas (considerably more than the usual fee) for 'Child's Song in Winter', an 'exquisite' work, Morley told Trollope, 'without any of those unfortunate characteristics with wh. Mr. Swinburne's name is at the present moment connected'. Reporting the payment to Chapman—who was about to become sole proprietor—Trollope said he hoped he was right to have done so.[35]

Trollope was out of his element amid Morley, Mill, Huxley, Harrison—and the literary likes of Swinburne, Rossetti, Meredith. Trollope's liberalism was an old-fashioned desire for gradual social amelioration, the liberalism of Palmerston, Gladstone, and the Liberal party, hardly that of Joseph Chamberlain and Charles Dilke. Only rarely would he again write articles for the *Fortnightly*; he did publish two novels in the magazine, *The Eustace Diamonds*, 1871–3, and *Lady Anna*, 1873–4, the arrangements for which were in the hands of Chapman the publisher. Fiction in the magazine had no particular bias, and it was by accident that *Lady Anna*, in which the titled heroine marries a tailor, may have seemed peculiarly appropriate for the liberal *Fortnightly*.

Trollope's dream of 'eclecticism'—publishing opinions on both sides of issues—had proved impractical, and he wistfully admitted that it had to be so; he also somewhat grudgingly admitted the magazine's success under Morley, keeping his reservations about its more radical principles. In fact, the *Fortnightly Review*, during Morley's tenure as editor, went on to become the great liberal English journal of its time. The magazine Trollope had founded was published until 1954, when it was absorbed by the *Contemporary Review*, the journal started as its rival and still published today.[36]

While Trollope and others were busy projecting the *Fortnightly Review*, George Smith was planning a daily afternoon newspaper, *The Pall Mall Gazette*, named after the fictional journal in Thackeray's novel *Pendennis*. The *Pall Mall* offered the news in summarized form and stressed extensive literary and political commentary, together with original articles. Smith, as he had done with the *Cornhill*, shouldered much of the work, although Frederick Greenwood was the editor.* From the first Trollope considered himself 'one of the staff', and though he had none of the 'parent's solicitude' for the *Pall Mall Gazette* that he felt for the *Fortnightly*, he was keenly interested in the paper and wrote more non-fiction for it than for any other publication.[37] Trollope had a piece on the American Question in the very first issue, that of 7 February 1865. Naturally, the Civil Service continued a concern for Trollope; in one piece, clearly drawing on his own experiences as a young man and repeating his familiar theme of the difficulties of living in London on a clerk's £100 a year, he argued that Civil Service clerks ought not to be liable for dismissal for dealing with money-lenders, but should have the ordinary citizen's right of resort to the bankruptcy court without risking their jobs.[38]

A noteworthy effort for the *Pall Mall* was 'A Zulu in London', Trollope's report on one of the May Meetings of evangelicals at Exeter Hall, a session devoted to promoting Christianity among the Jews. Trollope gives his account as coming from a visiting Zulu from Natal, a friend of a 'well-known bishop' who was anathema to the evangelicals. (The bishop was of course John Colenso, Bishop of Natal, who loved the Zulus and respected their polygamous marriages and their questionings of the Old Testament; he himself came to believe the Pentateuch a late forgery, and his published commentary to that effect caused great outcry and controversy; it also provoked jokes about the bishop who went out to convert the savages and was converted by them.[39]) The audience comprised some 150 gentlemen, mostly clergymen, on the platform; and thousands of ladies with needle and thread below ('Whether they were pretty I could not see, but they were very industrious'). A stout gentleman gave a paper on conversions of Jews; the statistics were pretty poor, but then 'the Jews are a stubborn people'. Another speaker, a canon, attacked non-literalist readings of the Old Testament such as the African visitor himself espoused. But the audience 'would listen to no arguments opposed to their

* When *An Autobiography* was published in 1883, Greenwood was angered by Trollope's failure to credit him as the originator of the *Pall Mall Gazette* and furious that he should have written of George Smith as 'chief editor' in the paper's early days.[40]

own', a stark contrast to conferences in Zululand where the bishop 'had learned, perhaps, more than he had taught'. The Zulu also remarks that the treatment of women in the hall reminded him of a 'Mahomedan congregation in which the weakness of the woman is held in contempt by the strength and wisdom of man', especially when the canon turned his back upon the ladies and spoke to the men, imploring them to keep any religious doubts to themselves, begging them not to 'vex with such reasonings the minds of these poor ignorant ones whom it is your duty to guide in the right way'. Zulu women, the visitor insists, would stand for no such treatment. Zulus, men or women, would accept nothing 'too gross for the belief of their teachers'. When the speaker finished, the 'ignorant' ladies cheered him, and the Zulu determined to avoid Exeter Hall in the future.[41] So did Trollope, who reported back to Smith that he could positively not do another such article: 'Suicide would intervene after the third or fourth, or I should give myself up to the police as [a] murderer.' He had brought his son Harry along, but the young man could be of no use in reporting the meetings, as he had gone to sleep throughout.[42]

Trollope's most sustained and best efforts for the *Pall Mall* were three series of connected essays on topics dear to his heart: hunting, travel, and clergymen. Each was subsequently brought out by Chapman & Hall as a small book. The first series, *Hunting Sketches*, had begun on the third day of the newspaper's publication and consisted in pictures of hunting types. There is the man who hunts but doesn't like it, for whom the season itself is a penance, whose chief pleasure is talking about hunting during the off season and taking pride in his wardrobe. The hunting parson, Trollope reluctantly concludes, had better give up the sport because he is flying in the face of public opinion; but as far as Trollope can see, the argument about hunting wasting a clergyman's time is silly: the country parson 'may hunt twice a week with less objection in regard to [loss of] time than any other man who has to earn his bread by his profession'. The happiest person in the sport is the Master of Fox Hounds (Sir John Trollope, Anthony's cousin, was MFH of the Cottesmore); the Master of an old-fashioned hunt, like the country gentleman with £10,000 a year, or the Member of Parliament from the county, is the envy of the whole world. 'For myself,' Trollope says, 'I would sooner be a master of hounds than a Lord Mayor.' Except for this last, *Hunting Sketches* is hardly the enthusings of a fanatical hunter, but a rather sobering look at the sport: even the sketch of 'The Man who Hunts and does Like it'—very much Trollope himself—tells of his moments of doubt: the sport costs him about £500 a season, and the season usually has one good day, three days that were not bad, and 'all the rest have been vanity and vexation of spirit'. Hunting requires everything from a man, 'his time, his money, his social hours, his rest, his sweet morning sleep; nay his very dinners'.⁴³ *Hunting Sketches* has little about the unfathomable, irrational hold the sport had on such men as himself.

In the midst of all his writing for the *Pall Mall* Trollope had been able to do something towards repaying George Smith for his many social courtesies, the latest of which were the *Pall Mall* dinners which he gave his contributors. In January Trollope proposed Smith for the Garrick Club, and he was quickly elected, on 1 April. Within a few days Trollope was inviting Smith to a dinner at the Garrick along with Billy Russell, Charles Taylor, Frank Fladgate—all special friends of Thackeray, and now of Trollope: 'Taylor has bespoken up from his country quarters a young suckling pig. At any rate, whether sucking pig be or be not to your taste come & join us, & we will be very jolly.' But shortly after the Garrick Club pleasantries and still in the midst of Trollope's steady writing for the *Pall Mall*, there nearly occurred a falling out. On 9 May Trollope sent back a cheque to Smith saying he could not be paid at 'the rate of two guineas and a half for articles about the length of a leader in the Times'; he begged Smith to understand that he would be glad to send him things from time to time gratis—'all for love'—but could not 'afford to work as a professional man at wages which I should be ashamed to acknowledge'. He would be happy to do a series of sketches on tourists at the rate of four guineas a column. Smith sent Trollope what must have been a calming, soothing note, for Trollope answered that he was obliged for Smith's kindness, was glad that they understood each other, and agreed that Smith should send back the cheque.⁴⁴ Trollope's account book shows he earned £234. 14*s*. 6*d*. for his *Pall Mall* writings in 1865 and £97. 2*s*. 6*d*. in 1866.

The sketches of travellers—written at a rate of four guineas a column—appearing in the paper from 3 August to 6 September, are, like so much of his non-fiction, valuable chiefly for their satiric self-portraits: the travelling paterfamilias—'paying the bills, strapping up the coats, scolding the waiters, obeying, but not placidly obeying the female behests to which he is subject, and too frequently fretting uncomfortably beneath the burden of the day, the heat and the dust, the absence of his slippers, and the gross weight of his too-matured proportions.' On the solitary traveller, Trollope is almost Hobbesian: 'we avoid him sedulously because we have it in our power to give him that one thing that he wants,—company'; other travellers shun the lone traveller they encounter, 'indulging that joy of ascendancy which naturally belongs to us when we have discovered any one low enough to require our assistance'. If the solitary traveller had some work to do—if only to carry a teapot to the Foreign Office at Vienna, this would have been enough to support him, but then 'work is always so much easier than play.' Trollope says the tourist in search of knowledge is a pretentious bore, but this particular bore sounds rather like Trollope when gathering materials for travel writing:

He will listen with wondrous patience to the details of guides, jotting down figures in a little book, and asking wonder-working questions which no guide can answer. And he looks into municipal matters wherever he goes, learning all details as to mayors, aldermen, and councillors, as to custom duties on provisions, as to import duties on manufactures, as to schools, convents, and gaols, to scholars, mendicants, and criminals. He does not often care much for scenery, but he will be careful to inquire how many passengers the steamboats carry on the lakes, and what average of souls is boarded and lodged at each large hotel that he passes. He would like to know how many eggs are consumed annually, and probably does ask some question as to the amount of soap used in the laundries.

The English ignorance of foreign languages is admitted with amusement and made to serve Trollope's hearty endorsement of amateurism; he always held that things need not be done terribly well to be enjoyed: 'To wander along the shores of lakes, to climb up mountains, to visit cities, to see pictures, and stand amidst the architecture of the old or of the new world, is very good, even though the man who does these things can speak no word out of his own language.' The traveller must cut his coat according to his cloth: if he can't argue about his bed and supper in good Tuscan, why trouble? 'Be content to speak your two words ungrammatically, or, if that be beyond you, be content not to speak them at all. The mountains and valleys will render themselves to you without French. Pictures on the walls will not twit you with your ignorance. . . . To be able to be happy and at rest among the mountains is better than talking French in saloons.'[45]

During the winter and spring of 1864–5 Trollope was preparing for the launch of the *Fortnightly*, writing for the *Pall Mall Gazette*, and performing his Post Office duties. He also found time for a flying visit to Florence, following the death on 13 April of his brother's wife Theodosia. Trollope took their daughter Bice home with him; he was exceedingly fond of his niece, who at this time was 12. That feeling comes through in a letter written to her from Belfast shortly after she had come to Waltham Cross: 'Your great aunt Mrs. Clyde,—my mothers sister,—who is a very old

ıan living in Exeter has sent you a present of ten guineas. We must
e a great consultation between you, and aunt Rose, and papa, and
rney [the groom], and all the other wise people, as to what you had
better buy. What do you say to a new cow? Or perhaps ten guineas worth
of chocolate bonbons? . . . Your own affectionate uncle | T | (for Toney).'46
Trollope himself seems to have supplied her with a pony. Over the years
Bice was frequently to spend long spells in England, sometimes staying
with the Trollopes; she later went to school in Brighton. On their first
return to Waltham, Trollope had arranged that the young girl, who was
reputed to have a marvellous singing voice, be instructed in music by
Frances Eleanor Ternan. Fanny Ternan was a member of an Irish theatrical family, whom Anthony and Rose had known for some years; she and
her two sisters had been professional actresses. (One of her sisters was
Ellen, said to have been Dickens's mistress.47) Fanny spent alternate
weekends at Waltham, giving Bice music lessons. Trollope's care for Bice
indirectly brought about his brother's second marriage. In the autumn
Fanny travelled to the continent with Anthony, Rose, Fred, and Bice,
together with Tom, who had come to England to fetch his daughter. It was
arranged, again with Trollope's assistance, that Fanny should reside at
Florence as Bice's governess, and soon Tom and she were engaged.
Trollope seems to have been scheming for just such an event, and when
Tom wrote to tell him he was going to marry Fanny, Anthony replied,
'Yes, of course! I knew you would.'48 In October 1866 Trollope, on holiday
leave from the Post Office, went to collect Tom at Florence and accompany
him to Paris, where Rose and Harry joined the party to celebrate the
wedding, which took place on 29 October at the British Embassy. Trollope
acted as one of the witnesses. Frances's mother was present, as was Ellen.
Dickens sent his congratulations to the couple. Tom and Frances seem to
have made a happy marriage.

Meanwhile a great change took place in Trollope's own household. In
September 1865 his second son Fred, who was on the eve of turning 18,
was about to leave for Australia. The boy had determined to try a colonial
career as sheep farmer after, as Trollope put it, Fred 'found that boys who
did not grow so fast as he did got above him at school'. He was a big lad and
good at sports, having taken various athletic prizes at Bradfield. His
masters are said to have encouraged him to matriculate at Cambridge, but
the young man, who shared his father's obstinacy, wanted to go to
Australia. In *An Autobiography* Trollope wrote that Fred's 'departure was
a great pang to his mother and me'. In *North America*, Trollope had
written that however emigration might benefit so many Englishmen,

especially of the poorer classes, he would 'not willingly select a frontier life' for his own children.[49] He could understand the lure of owning one's own land, being one's own master. But the new land was so unlike the old one. Trollope dearly wished he had the knowledge of Australia that he had of America. He himself later wrote the kind of book on the Australian colonies he should have liked to have been able to consult in 1865. Trollope permitted Fred to leave on condition that he return when he was 21 and decide only at that time whether or not to settle permanently in the colonies. On 16 September Trollope, Rose, and Fred together with Bice and Fanny Ternan left for the continent. At Koblenz they met up with Harry; at Linz Trollope left Harry and Rose, and together with E. F. S. Pigott, whom he had met at Salzburg, took Fred to Vienna, whence the young man left for Australia.[50] Trollope would not see him for three years.

In 1865 Trollope determined once again to try an experiment in anonymity. He feared he was overcrowding the fictional market; he also felt, he said, the injustice of praise heaped indiscriminately on well-known writers. Though not in such exalted company—he may have had Dickens especially in mind—still his work was now received with too much uncritical regard. Thus he began a course of novels to see if he might establish 'a second identity', the secret of authorship to be more closely guarded than in the case of *Brown, Jones, and Robinson*. In order the better to conceal his authorship, he decided to place these stories in foreign settings—the first two in Prague and Nuremberg, which he had just visited: 'Of course I had endeavoured to change not only my manner of language, but my manner of story-telling also; and in this . . . I think that I was successful. English life in them there was none. There was more of romance proper than had been usual with me. And I made an attempt at local colouring, at description of scenes and places, which has not been usual with me. In all this I am confident that I was in a measure successful. . . . Prague is Prague, and Nuremberg is Nuremberg.'[51] It is curious that this determination to publish books without his name came a few months after he had written in the *Fortnightly* his article which claimed that anonymous literature was a thing of the past, that there would never be another concealed name such as Scott created, that if *Pickwick* were making its first appearance today it would not have 'Boz' on its title-page but Charles Dickens.[52]

Trollope began writing *Nina Balatka* on 3 November 1865 and finished it on 31 December. On 9 March he offered George Smith this short novel, set in Prague, for anonymous publication; he asked £300 for the *Cornhill* serialization and £300 for book publication (1,500 copies), or £500 for the entire copyright. The novel, like *Brown, Jones, and Robinson*, was of single-volume length, and Trollope probably would have asked £600 for it with his name. When Smith declined, Trollope took the refusal in good grace: 'All right about N.B. Would you kindly send her back—to Waltham? She won't mind travelling alone. Whether I shall put her by, or try another venture with her I don't quite know. At any rate you are too much the gent to claim acquaintance if you meet her in the street'—i.e., to give away Trollope's authorship.[53] Trollope quickly tried another publisher, Blackwood of Edinburgh. Under John Blackwood, whose father had begun business as a second-hand bookseller in 1804, the firm had become an important publishing house; George Eliot was its current star novelist; and *Blackwood's Magazine* was an old and respected monthly. Trollope approached Blackwood through Joseph Munt Langford, London manager for Blackwood and a Garrick Club friend (and probably with encouragement from George Lewes). Blackwood wrote to Langford that he was much puzzled by the story: it 'shows the hand of the accomplished artist throughout. . . . Nina's warm frank outpouring of her love is a most beautiful piece of painting but as the story goes on one cannot sympathise with her in her love for her cold suspicious Jew.' Trollope, Blackwood comments, had 'thrown a perfectly foreign Prague atmosphere about all his characters so perfectly unEnglish that there is the sort of air of hardness about the story that one feels in reading a translation'. He thought— perhaps with some regret—that Trollope's authorship would remain undetected 'as there is nothing in the Tale to recall the popular painter of Englishwomen in the drawing room & on the Lawn'. Expecting little popularity for the anonymous story, Blackwood came to terms with Trollope for £200 for serial and £250 for the remaining copyright, only £50 less than the terms Smith refused.[54] Blackwood wanted to publish Trollope, and he would for the time being humour him in his quixotic chase of a second reputation. Over the years Blackwood became Trollope's closest friend among his many publishers, in spite of the fact that he often offered him somewhat lesser prices for his books. Blackwood was his own reader, and Trollope, especially as their publishing connection developed, listened to suggestions and criticisms from Blackwood that he would not have suffered from others. And because the Blackwood firm kept scrupulous letter books, practically the entire Blackwood–Trollope correspondence survives. The letters reveal a give-and-take exercised over Trollope's text which, while it in no way approached the mutilation Longman's reader had inflicted on *Barchester Towers*, still makes one wonder at Trollope's readiness to entertain, at this stage of his career, such criticism.

Blackwood, for example, repeated to Trollope his concern about the coldness of Anton Trendellsohn, the heroine's Jewish lover, and while correcting proofs Trollope admitted to Blackwood, 'the man comes out too black. I think I'll make him give her a diamond necklace in the last chapter.'[55] He did not.

Nina Balatka, which appeared in *Blackwood's Magazine* over seven months, from July 1866 to January 1867, was certainly a change in Trollope's fictional method. Blackwood was correct about the hardness and the translation-like feel of the writing. As for the more-than-usual 'romance proper' Trollope said he put into the story, he explained that this meant attempting to tell 'some pathetic incident' rather than to portray 'a number of living human beings'. Here it consists of making the heroine pass almost mindlessly through a series of tests until at the end the lovers are united; many of the traditional conventions of this kind of romance appear: persecution by relatives, scheming, betraying servants, missing documents; poverty, near starvation; pawning of one's last possessions, near suicide.[56] The plot is much more manipulated than is usual with Trollope; moreover, the story contains practically no authorial comment, and no humour (unless one were to count the observation made by a maid that Nina could not be spirited off to Italy out of the way as in the old days because 'the English people would hear of it, and there would be the very mischief').[57]

Nina Balatka has particular interest for its treatment of anti-Semitism; Trollope himself had many of the prejudices of most of his upper-middle-class contemporaries in England—though he certainly did not share their anti-Catholic and anti-Irish bias. But Jews in his stories are often unattractive, especially in the minor roles of usurious money-lenders—Jabesh M'Ruen in *The Three Clerks*, Tom and John Tozer in *Framley Parsonage*, Mr Clarkson in *Phineas Finn*, Abraham Hart in *Sir Harry Hotspur*, Samuel Hart in *Mr Scarborough's Family*. More prominent is Joseph Emilius, in *The Eustace Diamonds* and *Phineas Redux*, a converted Bohemian Jew who becomes a popular London preacher, a dishonest, money-hungry hypocrite eventually turned murderer. Two figures even more central, Ferdinand Lopez, the dishonest adventurer in *The Prime Minister*, and Augustus Melmotte, the great swindler in *The Way We Live Now*, are of doubtfully Jewish origins. On the other hand Madame Max Goesler, one of Trollope's most attractive creations, is of vaguely Austrian background and rumoured to be at least partly Jewish. Anti-Semitism is satirized in *Rachel Ray* where the hypocritical Mrs Prime violently opposes the candidacy of a rich Jewish tailor for Parliament; no Christian, she insists, should ever vote for a Jew: 'a curse has gone out from the Lord against that people; and gentlemen had no more right than ladies to go against the will of the Lord,' and she rejoices when the Jew loses (by one vote). The narrator comments, 'To [Jews] she would have denied all civil rights, and almost all social rights. . . . They in England who are now keenest against the Jews, who would again take away from them rights that they have lately won, are certainly those who think most of the faith of a Christian.'[58] In *The Way We Live Now* the anti-Semitism of the Longe-staffe family against the Jewish banker Brehgert is depicted as positively disgusting. In *South Africa*, Trollope says he has 'invariably found Jews to be more liberal than other men'.[59] But in *Nina Balatka* Trollope presented an unequivocal indictment of anti-Semitism, or at least of the old world anti-Semitism of Eastern Europe. The first, spare sentence of the novel sets the stage: 'Nina Balatka was a maiden of Prague, born of Christian parents, and herself a Christian—but she loved a Jew; and this is her story.' Everyone, Christian and Jew, opposes the marriage of Nina to Anton Trendellsohn, but the Christians are far more deeply prejudiced, more venal, dishonest, unscrupulous, inhuman. The Jewish hero, while no paragon—he is cold, suspicious, and stern—remains constant of purpose towards Nina. Honest and forbearing, he explains to Nina that Christians who display insolence toward Jews 'are poor in heart and ignorant'. The reader's sympathies are with the Jews, who are courteous, honest, decent people. The Christians, on the contrary, aside from Nina herself, present a sorry lot indeed. Nina's horrible aunt Sophie Zamenoy seems to be the Christian spokesman, and she continually talks of Nina as 'degrading' herself by a connection with Anton: 'Your troth to a Jew is nothing. Father Jerome will tell you so'; Nina's engagement she terms 'terrible, abomin-able, and damnable'; Trendellsohn is an 'accursed Jew'; she and other Christians will stoop to any means to prevent the marriage: 'I do hate them! Anything is fair against a Jew.'[60] It is a dark, sombre, depressing story, and its happy ending, though certainly muted, seems out of place. Indeed Trollope himself later forgot that *Nina Balatka* ended happily.[61]

Nina Balatka, which came out as a 'first novel', enjoyed almost uni-formly good reviews. Trollope's anonymity seems to have been pretty well kept, except for Hutton in the *Spectator* who sniffed out the author: 'If criticism be not a delusion from the very bottom,' he began, 'this pleasant little story is written by Mr. Anthony Trollope.' Hutton had spotted a usage he thought almost exclusively Trollope's, the phrase 'made his way' applied to walking but implying 'a certain moral hesitation as to the end and aim of the walking'. Hutton thought the tale very 'pleasant', the main idea one of force, and the description of Prague scenery and customs done with grace. The *Examiner* judged the novel 'very simple and very charming' and, for readers who want a novel with a purpose, 'a very trenchant argument against the hundred-headed prejudice' that erects barriers between people of different religions, nationalities, and social classes. The *Athenaeum* said the story was told 'so clearly and tersely, and with so much real feeling, as to retain the reader to the last' and, in a comment Trollope welcomed heartily, commended the book to thoughtful people to whom 'the study of character is more interesting than the entanglements and extrications of a complicated and unnatural plot'. The *London Review* called *Nina Balatka* 'one of the most charming stories we have read for a long time'.[62] But the notices, however favourable, were not sufficient to create much sale, and Blackwood took a considerable loss on the venture, as he bluntly told Trollope. The secrecy of Trollope's authorship seems to have been well enough kept; people on the whole did not believe Hutton correct. According to W. H. Pollock, a good many thought Tom Trollope was the author.[63]

These positive reviews of the anonymous *Nina Balatka* may have compensated for the critical depreciation of *The Belton Estate*, which completed serialization in the *Fortnightly Review* of 1 January 1866. The novel did not achieve great popularity as a serial; it could not have been expected to do for the *Fortnightly* what *Framley Parsonage* had done for the *Cornhill*—the new magazine was too serious, too intellectual for that. Trollope himself said of *The Belton Estate* that it was 'readable, and contains scenes which are true to life; but it has no peculiar merits, and will add nothing to my reputation as a novelist. . . . I seem to remember almost less of it than of any book that I have written.'[64] Nevertheless, later readers have found much to praise and to interest them in the story. The hero is in many ways rather like Trollope: Will Belton is blunt, florid of face, an early riser ('What's the use of laying in bed, when one had had enough of sleep?' he asks); stalwart, self-confident, with 'a grain or two of tyranny in his composition', a man of enormous energies for whatever work came to hand, whether farming or eating breakfast, a sportsman enamoured of hunting and shooting; 'furious' when his back is up; a man in whom the 'habitual impatience of his nature predominated'; restless, unable to stand idleness ('I wish it wasn't Sunday because then I could go and do something. . . . I'd fill a dung-cart or two'); he is impatient, not good at waiting; his loss of temper sometimes makes a fool of him; he is down to earth, with little delight in ceremony: Belton's view on weddings, for example, is that 'it would be best just to walk to church and to walk home again without saying anything to any body. I hate fuss and non-sense.'[65] He is given to long walks to 'cool' his mind, and does a great deal of imaginative and highly detailed day-dreaming.

A prominent feature of *The Belton Estate* is the situation of Mr and Mrs Askerton: she had been married to a 'drunken brute', had left him 'under the protection' of Mr Askerton, with whom she had lived for three years before her dissolute husband died and she was able to marry Askerton. Much of the story revolves upon the question of whether the heroine and others ought to accept the Askertons. Heroine Clara Amedroz does, but only gradually is full sympathy given to the Askertons by Clara, by Belton himself, by the narrator. One wonders what George Lewes and George Eliot, conscious of their slow yet always incomplete climb back into respectability, thought about this aspect of the story, appearing in the magazine edited by Lewes.

The reviewers found it disappointing: they said it dragged, that its 'realism' of the sordid and mean in life was unbecoming. In the New York *Nation*, Henry James wrote another of his scathing early reviews of Trollope. He had been warming to his subject. *Miss Mackenzie* had irritated him by its 'vulgarity', and *Can You Forgive Her?* by not being 'serious'. Now, though James found *The Belton Estate* 'more readable than many of its predecessors', it was none the less 'as flat as a Dutch landscape', inducing in the reader a 'gentle slumber'. Will Belton was excellently drawn and Captain Aylmer not badly. The real objection is that *The Belton Estate* seems to be written for children: it is 'a *stupid* book . . . essentially, organically, consistently stupid; stupid in direct proportion to its strength. It is without a single idea.' It cannot suggest thought: 'Mr. Trollope is a good observer; but he is literally nothing else.'[66] On the other hand, many readers liked the book; Jane Carlyle, for one, told a friend: 'I hope you read that tale going on in the "Fortnightly"—"The Belton Estate" (by Anthony Trollope). It is charming, like all he writes;— I quite weary for the next number.'[67]

20

Farewells and Saint Pauls Magazine

ALL in all, *The Belton Estate* had the poorest reviews of any Trollope novel since he started publishing. But of greater concern to him were the inroads periodical writing had made in his production of fiction: in 1865 he had produced for the *Pall Mall Gazette* nearly fifty pieces of journalism (some quite short) and for the *Fortnightly Review* six long articles and thirteen book reviews. The two novels written in 1865 were relatively short ones, *The Belton Estate* and *Nina Balatka* together coming to three 'volumes' by Trollope's reckoning, in contrast to the previous year when he had completed more than twice as much fiction. He determined now to make a major effort. Accordingly on 2 January 1866 he wrote to George Smith, proposing a long novel, to be published in twenty shilling parts rather than in the *Cornhill Magazine* because the much-delayed *Claverings* had yet to begin in its pages.[1]

On 3 February Smith answered that he was not sure about shilling-part serialization; he would prefer to pay £3,000 for the right to print any kind of part issue and a first book edition, with profits of future editions to be shared equally between Trollope and Smith, Elder. Trollope agreed, stipulating only that the novel appear in the course of 1867 and 1868. Smith then wrote back that he might like to run the story to thirty instead of the usual twenty numbers. Trollope responded with a letter that candidly and modestly revealed his virtuosity in treating the problem of length in serial fiction. If the story must be written for possible twenty- or thirty-instalment publication, preparation must be made to accommodate the larger number of parts:

It would not be practicable to divide 20 numbers into 30 equal parts, unless the work be specially done with this intent. I commonly divide a number of 32 pages (such as the numbers of 'Orley Farm') into 4 chapters each. If you wish the work to be so arranged as to run either to 20 or to 30 numbers, I must work each of the 20 numbers by 6 chapters, taking care that the chapters run so equally, two and two, as to make each four into one equal part or each 6 into one equal part. There will be some trouble in this, but having a mechanical mind I think I can do it. . . . you will also understand that if your mind be made up either to 30 or to 20, you need not put my mechanical genius to work.

On 24 February Smith decided on 20 monthly parts; two days later he changed his mind and was leaning towards weekly publication in 32 parts, this last being that which he eventually settled upon.[2]

Trollope, who had begun writing the novel on 19 January, made no mention of the subject to Smith, but had decided to write another Barchester novel, to have one final go with his archdeacon, with the Proudies, and indeed with almost all the inhabitants of his 'beloved county'. That return to Barsetshire, eventually entitled *The Last Chronicle of Barset*, worthily crowns the series in adding to it a new dimension. Its distinctive quality lies in the dominating presence of Mr Crawley, a character from *Framley Parsonage*. Here, although his story is allowed to end happily, Crawley is essentially a tragic figure. In him Trollope combined what he had learned from his father's unhappy years of poverty and near madness with his now expert knowledge of the straits to which many poor clergy were reduced.

The best background to his depiction of Crawley's plight and to other clergymen as they appear in the *Last Chronicle* and the earlier books in the series (*The Warden* and *Barchester Towers* in particular) is Trollope's *Clergymen of the Church of England*. This volume, published by Chapman & Hall in March 1866, was the collection of his clerical sketches written for the *Pall Mall Gazette* during the previous autumn.

Present-day bishops, Trollope says, are by and large hard-working, a development he attributes to the Oxford Movement. No longer are bishops the wealthy barons of the days of George IV, who got their sees by editing Greek plays, tutoring noble pupils, or charming the royal ear. Trollope makes the sensible but irreverent suggestion that the Crown choose bishops 'by rotation', high-, broad-, and low-church in turn. One bit of the old corruption remains, the right of patronage, and bishops still present their best livings to their friends; indeed they are expected, even 'supposed', to do so.[3]

As for deans, with the changes over the centuries, their 'real work' has gone. A dean need do no more now than reside in the cathedral city and occasionally 'show himself'. He has a quaint old house, garden, and close, and no expensive duties in London, though he will for a month or so each year 'revisit the glimpses of the metropolitan moon'. Trollope's typical dean is a man who has no real vocation to the clerical life; holy orders were somehow placed in his path early in life; he is fond of literature, has done well at university, been a fellow, was perhaps tutor of his college, written a book or two, and probably shown himself too liberal for the Bishops' Bench. Trollope mischievously inquires why the authorities did not get over the trouble with Bishop Colenso by making him a dean in England.[4]

An archdeacon, Trollope writes, has more work to do than a dean; he has a good living, is 'seldom allowed to starve', and is perhaps the son or nephew of a bishop; above all the archdeacon is a man of the world, 'a bishop in little', concerned with the physical aspect of his churches: 'It is . . . easier to see whether the windows of a church are in repair . . . than it is to be intelligibly and effectively explicit on [the behaviour] of canons.' The archdeacon is strongly conservative, but tolerant with clerical sinners: 'No one knows so well as an archdeacon . . . that it is needless and absurd to look for a St. Paul in every parsonage. He would, indeed, be very little at his ease with a local St. Paul, much preferring a comfortable rector, who can take his glass of wine after dinner and talk pleasantly of old college days.'[5]

For the country parson, of whom Trollope knew so many, he has genuine affection, at least for the old-fashioned kind: Oxford or Cambridge educated, urbane, genial, probably the son of a squire or clergyman, the country parson 'does not expect much of poor human nature, and is thankful for moderate results' (a judgement reminiscent of Sydney Smith's). His home is among the most pleasant in the land, 'just reaching in well-being and abundance that point at which perfect comfort exists and magnificence has not yet begun to display itself'. He is a superb host: 'the eye of no man beams so kindly on me as I fill my glass for the third time after dinner as does the eye of the parson of the parish.'[6]

On the subject of curates Trollope becomes more the reformer than the amused observer: 'It is notorious that a rector in the Church of England, in possession of, let us say, a living of a thousand a year, shall employ a curate at seventy pounds a year, that the curate shall do three-fourths or more of the work of the parish, that he shall remain in that position for twenty years, taking one-fourteenth of the wages and doing three-fourths of the work, and that nobody shall think the rector is wrong or the curate ill-used!'[7]

Trollope is also the reformer, predictably, on the Irish Protestant clergyman, 'a severe, sombre man', who cannot as much as 'shake hands with you without leaving a text or two in your palm'; bigoted, illiberal, hating the Roman Catholics who surround him, he knows that 'sermons preached to his own family, to three policemen and his clerk, cannot be said to have been preached to much effect'. Only disestablishment of the Irish Church (something Trollope campaigned for until its enactment in 1869), makes sense.[8]

In 'The Clergyman who Subscribes for Colenso', Trollope quietly takes his stand against biblical literalism. Colenso's attack on the historical truth of the Pentateuch had brought him excommunication from the Bishop of Cape Town and great legal expenses in his (eventually successful) struggle to regain his episcopal income; his supporters, including Darwin and Lyell, sought contributions on his behalf, and England's clergymen had to take a stand. Trollope's broad churchman bravely puts down his name on the subscription list for Colenso, facing the scorn of the majority of his colleagues. But, Trollope says, 'the incompatibility of the teaching of Old Testament records with the new teaching of the rocks and stones'—along with Bishop Colenso—has made it impossible for many to stay with the old teachings, much as they might like to do so. In 'The Clergyman who Subscribes for Colenso' Trollope shows himself mildly forward-thinking in the doctrinal crisis affecting practically all Christians of his day.[9]

Most of the types in *Clergymen of the Church of England* seem right out of Barsetshire. Bishop Proudie, whatever his weaknesses or faults, is hardly an old-time wealthy bishop baron who got his see by editing Greek plays or tutoring nobility; he is low church, appointed by a Whig government, and assuredly does not keep race horses. Grantly is the worldly archdeacon, the country gentleman, defender of the Church's temporalities. Arabin is the rich dean, formerly fellow of an Oxford college, with little to do, whose absence on the continent seems natural enough as it assumes so important a place in *The Last Chronicle*. And Josiah Crawley (a lowly incumbent, not an assistant, though technically called a 'Perpetual Curate') is quintessentially the underpaid cleric, the embodiment of a plight that seemed always on Trollope's mind when he turned to the Church.

Clergymen of the Church of England, with its worldly and knowing tone, made smarter by its lightness of touch, annoyed some clerical sensibilities. Here was a layman, an outsider, claiming an insider's savvy. The book was important enough, Trollope says in *An Autobiography*, to bring down on his head 'the most ill-natured review' any work of his ever received, written by a 'great dean of that period': 'The critic told me that I did not understand Greek. . . . [He] had been driven to wrath by my saying that Deans of the Church of England loved to revisit the glimpses of the metropolitan moon.'[10] The critic was Henry Alford, Dean of Canterbury, a voluminous writer and scholar; he had been one of the Tennysonian set at Cambridge, had published his own poetry and edited an edition of Donne (with the 'licentious' poems omitted), translated the *Odyssey* and edited a Greek New Testament. Though evangelically trained, he was liberal and tolerant, knowledgeable about German biblical criticism, and editor of Alexander Strahan's *Contemporary Review*.[11] It would perhaps have been hard for any dean, but especially for Alford, to have stomached Trollope's notion that the 'chief qualification' for a modern dean was a taste for literature. Alford, in twenty-two closely printed pages, attacked Trollope on all fronts, castigating him for flippancy, want of earnestness, and amateurism; he faulted his grammar, his ignorance of Greek etymologies, caught him in error about college fellows having originally been monks, and denounced his treatment of curates' incomes and the Irish Church. In sum Alford saw the book as 'deplorably frivolous' and 'a serious public evil'. Nevertheless, at the close he said he could 'almost unreservedly praise' Trollope's essay on Colenso, although even in this single commendation he could not resist another criticism: '[Trollope] is evidently more at home among the phenomena of unbelief than among those of undoubting faith and obedience.'[12]

Then the Anglican *Guardian* also attacked Trollope on curates' incomes, though it subsequently was fair enough to print a letter in Trollope's defence from an impoverished curate who cited his own case: he had laboured as a curate for forty years, earning stipends ranging from £70 to £100; he was never offered anything better, nor was his case considered a hard one.[13] The *Pall Mall* welcomed this real-life confirmation of Trollope's figures, and Trollope himself wrote a letter printed in the *Pall Mall* saying how he was 'roughly handled' by some cleric—'probably not a curate'—for naming £70 per annum as the normal income for curates whereas a law existed that put the minimum at £80 and the maximum at 'the liberal remuneration of £150'. Trollope pointed out that the law referred only to curates in parishes without resident clergymen; but even granting—in the face of contrary evidence—the £80 to £150 scale, what was one to think of a profession that could not reward efficient men working for ten or twenty years in the prime of their life with better wages than that?[14]

Trollope took this kind of skirmishing seriously; for though he claimed to write only about the social lives of his clergymen, that spectrum assuredly included the economic lives of clergymen; indeed, pounds-per-year seem to be the central fact around which so many of his 'clerical' stories revolve, and in *The Last Chronicle* it is Mr Crawley's poverty-inducing stipend of

£130 that drives him to near insanity. Only at the end of the novel, with the presentation to him of the living worth £350, does his near-tragic tale revert to the traditional comic ending. Trollope, when treating of the clergy, liked to feel he was on sure ground; furthermore, a careful reading of the novels shows that, in spite of his protestations to the contrary, he did not hesitate to touch upon the spiritual lives of his clerical characters, too. He manages to do so amid so many worldly matters as to have them almost escape notice. But from the beginning, from *The Warden* with Mr Harding's doubts about the morality of keeping a stipend of £800 for little work, through the account in *Barchester Towers* of Arabin's drift towards asceticism and Rome, to *Framley Parsonage* with Mark Robarts's temptations to unseemly involvements with fast-moving men like Sowerby, to *The Last Chronicle* with Mr Crawley's questionings about the divine justice of his lot, something more than the 'social lives' of these men concerns Trollope. And when the series comes to an end, with the death of Mr Harding, it is surely more than social and money matters that count— even in the midst of comedy. Trollope's touch is a sure one: 'And so they buried Mr. Septimus Harding, formerly Warden of Hiram's Hospital in the city of Barchester, of whom the chronicler may say that the city never knew a sweeter gentleman or a better Christian.'[15]

The mild clerical uproar about *Clergymen of the Church of England* followed close upon another tiff in the public press: when his old friend Norman Macleod was attacked by Scottish Calvinists and Free Churchmen in 1865 for his unorthodox views on Sunday observance, Trollope wrote a spirited defence of those views in the *Fortnightly Review*. Trollope's article commends Macleod for speaking out, in the very midst of the Glasgow presbytery, about sabbath observance (the occasion being the recent introduction of a Sunday train service between Edinburgh and Glasgow). Calling sabbatarian rigour in Glasgow 'more rigid, more pharisaical' than anywhere else in Scotland,* he endorsed Macleod's view that the Old Testament proscription of sabbath-day work was 'ceremonial' and intended only for the Jews of that time. But Trollope's argument is clearly his own, set forth in terms a later generation would have called Shavian: we are to pray and not to work on the sabbath, but 'Is there any work harder than prayer to the man who really prays? Is there any task more tedious than that of listening to sermons to the man who really listens? Is

---

* Macleod was hissed at in the streets of Glasgow, and, like the title character in Trollope's *Vicar of Bullhampton*, who has an ugly Methodist chapel erected in front of his church, Macleod saw his enemies open a Free Church mission next door to his Barony Church.[16]

the reading of religious literature a pleasant, light occupation, or is it not work of the hardest kind? Would not any man undergoing his education rather get up a chorus of Sophocles than go through a hundred pages of the ordinary Sunday reading? . . . The Sunday prescribed for us has, in fact, been a day of work so hard as to make it a day of torment.'[17] The *Saturday Review* attacked Trollope's article in a piece called 'An Amateur Theologian'. It asked why Trollope was not satisfied with the 'place in English literature from which there is little danger that he will be dislodged. . . . Are not his novels . . . enough to fill his time,' especially since he 'can write novels as easily as hens lay eggs'? How can he possibly think he has anything new to say on the subject of Sabbatarianism? He writes with a 'most frank, but certainly not engaging, ignorance' of the subject; he 'slays the slain with almost ludicrous energy'. Trollope's expressed views— except on prayer—are 'the opinions of almost all educated men'. The article likens Trollope, in his delight in commonplace knowledge, to La Fontaine, who in old age happened upon a New Testament, was charmed, and went off to tell a friendly priest of the treasure he had found. Trollope prevailed on George Smith to print in the *Pall Mall* his signed reply, in which he charged that the *Saturday* had 'no special fault to find with my remarks,—always excepting the great vice of a novelist choosing to make remarks'. This had not been Trollope's first crossing of swords on topical matters with the *Saturday*; some few months earlier, Trollope's letter to the *Pall Mall* on the death of Abraham Lincoln had drawn fire. Trollope had written that he could not allow the event to pass without 'mingling my voice of lamentation with those of others'; whereupon the *Saturday*, in an article called 'Mistaken Estimates of Self', complained that 'Instead of mingling his voice with the lamentations of others, [Trollope] goes out of his way to set up a little solitary howl of his own. He confesses that "any prolonged utterance of individual grief would in him be an impertinence", and then prolongs his utterance over a large column'; Trollope's 'whole letter is an extraordinary illustration of the way in which a charming novelist may flounder about in platitudes and almost penny-a-lining commonplaces when he turns political philosopher.' The *Pall Mall* came to Trollope's defence, adding that it was no wonder the *Saturday* preferred unsigned articles since their writers had been 'discoursing for months past' on how the American South would never surrender, whereas Trollope, consistently supporting the Northern cause, had long predicted Northern victory.[18]

As these contributions to the *Pall Mall* demonstrate, Trollope was a doughty controversialist; but such battles did little to distract the novelist. During the first half of 1866, although engaged sharply with the *Saturday* and with the clerical critics of *Clergymen of the Church of England*, his creative energies were devoted to the fictional world of Barsetshire. In that world his controversial concern over curates' incomes was absorbed in and transmuted by the triumphant depiction of Mr Crawley. In early August he delivered the first part of *The Last Chronicle of Barset* to George Smith, whose immediate pleased response delighted him: 'When I have worked to order,' Trollope wrote back, 'the only criticism for which I care much is the criticism of the buyer who has trusted me so far as to purchase what he has not seen.'[19] One development neither Smith nor anyone else could have foreseen from the early portions of the novel was the death of Mrs Proudie. *An Autobiography* records the now famous incident: Trollope, who during the season often spent two nights a week in London, was at work on the novel in the drawing-room of the Athenaeum Club, when he heard two clergymen discussing his work. Seated either side of the fireplace, each with a magazine in his hand in which was appearing a Trollope novel, they were abusing his practice of using reappearing characters: the archdeacon 'whom we have had in every novel he has ever written' and that old duke 'whom he has talked about till everybody is tired of him'. At this point 'one of them fell foul of Mrs. Proudie. It was impossible for me not to hear their words, and almost impossible to hear them and be quiet. I got up, and standing between them, I acknowledged myself to be the culprit. "As to Mrs. Proudie," I said, "I will go home and kill her before the week is over." And so I did. The two gentlemen were utterly confounded, and one of them begged me to forget his frivolous observations.' Different versions of the incident survive: In Walter Herries Pollock's account, Trollope referred to 'a group of young clergymen' as triggering his decision; as Cecilia Meetkerke told the story, one of the two men in the Athenaeum was reading a part of *The Last Chronicle*; in another variation, recorded by Augustus Hare as given to him by Mrs Duncan Stewart to whom Trollope is supposed to have told the story, he overheard some critic complain and promised that 'Mrs. Proudie shall die in the very next book I write.' (All three accounts predate the publication of *An Autobiography*.[20]) It is impossible to sort out the exact facts, except that the persons who annoyed Trollope by their remarks could not have been reading *The Last Chronicle* because the novel was finished before the first part was published; moreover, his only magazine serial going at the time of writing the novel was *The Claverings*, not one of the Barsetshire novels, and one containing but the briefest mention of Proudie and his wife, the bishop having put an end to the Revd Mr Clavering's hunting. But the quickness and surprising manner of Mrs Proudie's death suggests that the novel was indeed in progress when he determined to kill her off. (She has a heart attack in Chapter 66; a possible hint, or what can in retrospect be seen as a hint of this development occurs in Chapter 47; in any case, he did not go back and insert the earlier material, as the manuscript indicates.) Trollope may have exaggerated the speed with which he disposed of his character. More interesting is whether or not he intended the novel from the start to be the last of the Barchester series: probably he did—though for that matter it might have continued without her. (The title *Last Chronicle* was not decided upon until the novel was almost finished: on 24 June it was still 'The Story of a Cheque for £20, and of the Mischief Which It Did'; in late September Trollope wanted 'The Last of the Chronicles of Barset'; Smith, who had apparently dislodged the inane 'Cheque' version, eventually brought him round to the deft and crisp title, *The Last Chronicle of Barset*.[21])

For many years Trollope, for all the serious consideration he gave reviews, had disregarded critical strictures against the reintroduction of characters and situations into later novels: the *Saturday Review* had objected that *Framley Parsonage* was mere '*réchauffé*' of *Barchester Towers*, and that by 'borrowing from himself' the novelist lost much in freshness and vigour; introducing episodes connected to previous novels was 'a lazy and seductive artifice'. Similarly, the *Dublin University Magazine* had complained of *Framley Parsonage*: 'When are we to see the last of Bishop and Mrs. Proudie, of the Grantlys, of Tom Towers, of Dr. Thorne? This merciless reintroduction of old friends saves a novelist so much of the time and trouble needed for coining new ones.'[22] On the other hand, other and more numerous reviewers approved of the connected stories. But perhaps he felt he had done all he could profitably do with his clerical provincial world; perhaps the restlessness that made him attempt a second literary career with anonymous novels prompted him now to leave off the older series and give himself to a new one. In any case, having completed *The Last Chronicle*, he would travel and rest his pen for two months, though doubtless continuing his day-dreaming, and then begin the second novel in the Palliser series. None the less, Trollope occasionally regretted having burned his bridges to Barsetshire, and said he sometimes regretted having killed Mrs Proudie—'so great was my delight in writing about Mrs. Proudie, so thorough was my knowledge of all the little shades of her character. . . . Since her time others have grown up equally dear to me,—Lady Glencora and her husband, for instance; but I have never dissevered myself from Mrs. Proudie, and still live much in company with her ghost.'23

In August, Trollope asked Millais to illustrate *The Last Chronicle*: 'Many of the characters (indeed most of them) are people you already know well—Mr. Crawley, Mr. Harding, Lily Dale, Crosbie, John Eam[e]s, and Lady Lufton. George Smith is very anxious that you should consent, and you may imagine that I am equally so.' Millais, who had pretty much given up illustration altogether in favour of his more lucrative painting, had informally promised Trollope he would illustrate one more of his novels. Now he told Trollope he would think it over: 'If it had been 2 drawings a month I would have said yes at once, but this weekly business is a problem in the middle of painting.' Trollope waited two weeks and then wrote again: 'But how about the illustrations. You promised me a further answer. Do *do* them! They wont take you above half an hour each.' Millais, who, though ordinarily a quick worker, sometimes spent days on a single illustration, at last refused. Smith's unlucky decision to publish in weekly parts weighed too heavily. No other illustrator had drawn for the Barchester series, but now George Housman Thomas was commissioned to illustrate the final novel, and Trollope had Smith send him copies of *Framley Parsonage* and *The Small House* so that Thomas 'should see the personages as Millais has made them'. The drawings drew mixed appraisals from Trollope: Thomas's Grace Crawley 'has fat cheeks, & is not Grace Crawley'; Mr Crawley before the magistrates 'is very good. So is the bishop. Mrs. Proudie is not quite my Mrs. Proudie.'24

Smith, Elder published *The Last Chronicle* in two volumes in July 1867. Hutton, like other reviewers of the book, greeted the announcement, as conveyed in the title and in the concluding pages, that the Barchester series was hereby brought to a close, with only partially mock despair. 'What am I to do without ever meeting Archdeacon Grantly?' Hutton quotes a friend as saying, 'He was one of my best and most intimate friends. . . . It was bad enough to lose the Old Warden, Mr. Septimus Harding, but that was a natural death. . . . Mr. Trollope has no right to break old ties in this cruel and reckless way.' Hutton professed 'loneliness very oppressive' at the prospect of never again meeting 'the best known and most typical of his fellow-countrymen' and was indulging thoughts of leaving England for ever. The *London Review* expressed 'gentle melancholy' at the leave-taking from Barsetshire, and, paraphrasing Trollope's words, said: 'To us, as well as to him, Barset has long been a real county, and its city a real city; and the spires and towers have been before our eyes, and the voices of the people are known to our ears, and the pavements of the city ways are familiar to our footsteps.' Geraldine Jewsbury in the *Athenaeum* remarked on Trollope's closing paragraphs, 'We only hope he will *not* keep his word.' Mrs Oliphant, in *Blackwood's*, wrote, 'We did not ask that this chronicle should be the last. We were in no hurry to be done with our old friends. And there are certain things which he has done without consulting us against which we greatly demur. To kill Mrs. Proudie was murder, or manslaughter at the least. We do not believe she had any disease of the heart; she died not by natural causes, but by [Trollope's] hand in a fit of weariness or passion.' The reviews also singled out the novel as Trollope's best so far, and Mr Crawley as Trollope's highest achievement. Hutton, for example, thought *The Last Chronicle* 'the richest and completest of Mr. Trollope's works', and Mr Crawley his 'noblest and most unique acquaintance', and the last days of Mr Harding 'the most *delicate* piece of moral portraiture ever completed by Mr. Trollope'; Harding's death, Hutton said, had drawn tears from people who are strangers to crying. Hutton even liked the 'vulgar people' of the London scenes. 'Of its own light kind,' he concluded, 'there has been no better novel ever written than the *Last Chronicle of Barset*.' For Mrs Oliphant, the book 'struck a higher note than [Trollope] has yet attempted'; she knew no character of his 'so profound and so tragic' as Mr Crawley: 'there is a grandeur about the half-crazed, wildered man—a mingled simplicity and subtlety in the conception—to which we cannot easily find a parallel in fiction.' Geraldine Jewsbury and some others thought the London characters a 'mistake', a view shared by many readers since.[25] But even granting the objections to the London scenes, the reviews of *The Last Chronicle* were the best Trollope ever received. His reputation had never been higher. He too thought *The Last Chronicle* his highest achievement: 'Taking it as a whole,' he said in *An Autobiography*, 'I regard this as the best novel I have written.' As always, he would add a qualification: 'I was never quite satisfied with the development of the plot. . . . I cannot quite make myself believe that even such a man as Mr. Crawley could have forgotten how he got [the cheque]. . . . But . . . I claim to have portrayed the mind of the unfortunate man with great accuracy and great delicacy. The pride, the humility, the manliness, the weakness, the conscientious rectitude and bitter prejudices of Mr. Crawley were, I feel, true to nature and were well described.'[26]

Josiah Crawley remains Trollope's most admired single creation. Much of Crawley came from Trollope's father. Crawley and his wife 'had had many children, and three were still alive'; inordinately anxious about educating his children, Crawley is incapable of inspiring affection in them; he is distressed by the success of men who cannot match him intellectually; he is moody, depressed, difficult, angry; his mind is clear, logical to a fault, except on everyday matters; he is a great trial to his wife, who at times fears that his mind is 'astray'. Lawyer Thomas Toogood says, with insight upon which Trollope's own irony plays, that Crawley is unlike 'anybody else that ever was born. . . . I never heard of such a man. . . . Somebody ought to write a book about it.'[27]

Another presence in *The Last Chronicle* from Trollope's early years is the partly autobiographical Johnny Eames, continuing the good progress towards respectable manhood he manifested in *The Small House at Allington*. The hobbledehoy has almost completely disappeared: Eames is now a respected civil servant, performing many works far better than his superiors—Sir Raffle Buffle, for example, cannot write letters, an art at which Eames is adept. Eames takes delight in occasionally antagonizing his superiors, although even old Buffle admits Johnny is 'clever'. Eames talks about marked sovereigns in tracing money, bringing to mind one of Trollope's more spectacular manœuvres in his Irish Post Office days. He displays Trollope's energies in travelling on his 'heroic' trip to Paris and Florence to search out Mrs Arabin, refusing to sleep en route, and drawing from the narrator the remark, 'I think he would have been pleased had he heard that Mrs. Arabin had retreated from Florence to Rome. . . . he would have folded his cloak around him and have gone on.' (And after accompanying her back to England, he escorts her to 'a certain quiet clerical hotel at the top of Suffolk Street, much patronized by bishops and deans of the better sort'—Garlant's Hotel.)[28] Eames is treated throughout with good-natured irony, the kind Trollope used continually on himself. As for his hopeless passion for Lily Dale, Eames resolves that the only cure was hard work; he might go deep into Greek or 'exact science'; he might resign his Civil Service post and take up the literary life, this last the very thing Trollope himself was about to do.

The pleasure taken by Trollope's readers in his practice of reintroducing characters in subsequent novels was expressed at the annual Literary Fund dinner on 15 May 1867 by Earl Stanhope, President of the Fund, who called it an 'invention, attended with most successful results, of which, as far as I know, the original merit belongs to M. de Balzac'. Trollope, in answering the toast to literature, said that he would be happy to drink long life to Balzac: 'I am told that he was the man who invented that style of fiction in which I have attempted to work'; he assured aspiring writers that they could find no 'easier' format, but said that while carrying over characters from one novel to another was 'very pleasant to the author', he doubted readers would always participate in the same pleasure.*[29] Trollope was much given to this kind of half-ironic apology for his use of recurring characters, although he knew that most of his reading public favoured his practice. His hearers at the dinner realized of course that the novel currently drawing near its completion in weekly part publication, emphatically called *The Last Chronicle of Barset*, would bring that series to a close. But they had no way of knowing that Trollope had determined to continue on with the Pallisers, begun in *Can You Forgive Her?*, and had in fact that very morning finished *Phineas Finn*, the second book in the new series.

One man of letters and friend of Trollope sadly absent from the dinner was Robert Bell; long in ill health, he had died on 12 April. Trollope inserted an obituary in the *Pall Mall*, praising him as a professional literary man who had worked hard at letters for more than forty years. Trollope attended the burial service, at Kensal Green, near Thackeray's grave. He helped instigate an effort to obtain a Civil List pension for the widow, writing to various people, including Dickens, who answered that on hearing from Trollope he had immediately gone and signed the petition. 'I had heard with much satisfaction', Dickens added, 'that poor Mrs. Bell had found a friend in you, for I knew she could have no stauncher or truer friend.' Two months later Trollope heard that Mrs Bell had put up her husband's library for auction; he went to the executors, had the auction arrangements cancelled, and bought the whole library above market price. 'We all know', he is reported to have said, 'the difference in value between buying and selling books.'[30]

The year 1867 saw not only the publication of the *Last Chronicle*, but the appearance of another collection of Trollope's short stories and his second experiment in anonymous writing. In March Strahan put into type for book publication ten short stories, all but two of which had appeared in Strahan's publications, *Good Words* and the *Argosy*. Trollope intended to call the volume 'Tales of All Countries, Third Series', but Strahan hoped a different 'happy *saleable* title' would suggest itself to Trollope. Sending Trollope the first budget of proofs, Strahan said he found the stories would make two volumes, and 'if I make a little more profit to myself I am

---

* Trollope's own mother had featured the widow Martha Barnaby in three novels, 1839–43.

sure you will not object'.[31] Strahan did not know his man. Two years earlier Trollope had been infuriated when Frederic Chapman had 'surreptitiously' printed the short two-volume-length *Belton Estate* in three volumes—the only occasion on which 'a publisher got the better of me in a matter of volumes'.[32] Now Trollope fired back immediately, 'altogether' refusing his sanction. The stories had been sold to Strahan as one volume: 'I have always endeavored to give good measure to the public'; these printed pages looked 'so thin and desolated, and contain such a poor rill of type meandering thro' a desert of margin, as to make me ashamed of the idea of putting my name to the book'. Trollope said he was grieved that the costs of a second printing should fall on Strahan, and offered to share the expense.[33] Strahan did not want to quarrel with Trollope, who could have made his objection public and hurt sales. The book was published in one volume. On the other hand, Trollope's offer to share the costs of reprinting was almost unexampled. The title became *Lotta Schmidt: And Other Stories*, whether more saleable than the older title it is impossible to say.

That April, John Blackwood in Edinburgh was pleased to learn through Joseph Langford that Trollope was willing to offer him another novel. The publisher hoped that the 'Author of "Nina Balatka"' just might catch on. Although the book was not selling, the authorship was still talked about. Early in July Blackwood came to London and stayed with the Trollopes at Waltham, and by 10 July Trollope posted to him the manuscript of *Linda Tressel*, a short novel he had just completed. The story was a companion to *Nina Balatka*, again with a foreign setting and more of 'romance proper' than usual for Trollope. Blackwood agreed to pay £450, the same price he paid for *Nina Balatka*; he added that he had not sold 500 copies of the first novel, incurring thereby a 'heavy loss', but hoping that the 'well earned reputation [that] could not help Nina herself will help Linda'.[34] Blackwood probably hoped enough people knew of Trollope's authorship to make the secret an open one.

By 13 September the publisher had read the entire novel, and while mailing Trollope the proofs of the first instalment, announced, 'I fear you have made a blunder and so have I. There is no adequate motive for Madame Staubachs conduct & her persistence becomes irritatingly wearisome. You really have no right to say that it was the Calvinistic old jades *virtues* that caused poor Linda's sufferings. I hope devoutly that I may turn out wrong in my opinion but the provoking sameness of each step of the story weighed very heavily upon me as I read.' (He took comfort in the fact that Rose liked the story.) Trollope answered immediately that Blackwood was 'quite at liberty to give up the story if you do not mind the expense of having put it into type. Do not consider yourself to be in the least bound by your offer . . . and feel quite sure that your returning it to me will moult no feather between you & me.' Blackwood determined to go ahead, and only then did Trollope offer some reply to the publisher's objections: 'It is hardly possible for a novelist who depends more on character than on incident for his interest always to make the chief personages of his stories pleasant acquaintances'; he could not arrange things so that 'a nice young man should always be there to be married to the nice young woman'; a writer like Scott, who deals chiefly in incidents, always has 'a Rowena ready for [his] Ivanhoe'. Trollope was not, he said, turning up his nose at stories of action, only explaining that his were different. In *Linda Tressel* he 'wanted to shew how religion, if misunderstood, may play the very Devil in a house'.[35]

Linda's tragedy does indeed grow out of her aunt's 'too rigid' religion. Aunt Staubach is a staunch Protestant, living in Nuremberg, that Protestant stronghold in the midst of Catholic Bavaria. Her 'manners and gait were the manners and gait of a Calvinist'. Her religiously motivated persecution of her niece and charge Linda takes the form, as often in Trollope, of sexual suppression; she thinks Linda a 'castaway' because she has spoken with a young man whom the aunt considers a wastrel; she mounts an unrelenting campaign to make the girl marry a repulsive old suitor named Steinmarc. There is a perfectly frightful scene in which after three hours of the aunt's prayers and shriekings the young woman succumbs and agrees to marry Steinmarc. Linda's inability to resist her aunt arises from her own Calvinistic training; submissive and meek, she comes to believe that her aunt is correct, that she herself 'was a thing set apart as vile and bad. There grew upon her a conviction that she was one of the non-elect.' As forced religious observances become odious to her, she takes this as 'certain sign that the devil had fought for her soul and had conquered'; she could not 'disbelieve her aunt's religious menaces'.[36] In *Linda Tressel* Trollope attempted a novel completely serious and tragic, for the story has no forced happy ending as had *Nina Balatka*. *Linda Tressel* is an unrelentingly depressing tale, one that many readers found unpleasant. Decency and virtue appear helpless before misguided religion. The novel seemed almost calculated to offend the religious tenets of the Scottish city in which it was published. No wonder Blackwood had his reservations.

While Trollope was composing his farewell to Barsetshire, *The Last Chronicle of Barset*, he was approaching a farewell to his official career in the Post Office and the beginning of a deeper involvement in the world of periodical publishing. Early retirement was made more attractive by a new venture offered to him just as the future of the *Fortnightly Review* looked bleakest. In the autumn of 1866 he was approached by James Virtue about editing a magazine, of which Virtue was to be owner and publisher. James Virtue headed a prosperous printing business and published art and devotional books; he printed for many publishers, among them Chapman & Hall, and had from the start been printer of the *Fortnightly*. He also printed for the erratic Alexander Strahan, and in order to recoup a part of his printing bills was now considering taking over one of Strahan's magazines, the *Argosy*, and giving the editorship to Trollope, who had already published three short stories in the magazine. According to *An Autobiography*, Trollope tried to discourage Virtue from undertaking the scheme on the grounds of its slim chances of making money. But Virtue came to Waltham and 'listened to my arguments with great patience, and then told me that if I would not do the work he would find some other editor'.[37] He then decided not to take over the *Argosy*, but to launch a new magazine; Trollope would be editor with a salary of £1,000 per annum and complete control over arrangements with contributors, both writers and illustrators. Virtue added, optimistically, 'it will be hard if we cannot hold our own against such as "Belgravia" and "Temple Bar".' But of course the model and the competition he and Trollope had in mind was the *Cornhill*. Trollope agreed, but wanted a two-year contract. Virtue consented, and then outlined his ideas: he thought to pay the contributors well to get good talent, 'an average of 20*l*. a page ought to do'; he calculated that a circulation of 25,000—a rather sanguine figure—would pay, and asked meekly if there were any possibility of Trollope himself supplying the first novel, even a short one.[38] The next day, Trollope began *Phineas Finn: The Irish Member*, a novel more overtly political than any he had written. From the first Trollope wished his magazine to have a decidedly political, and by his lights, decidedly 'liberal' (which is to say Liberal party) bias. The *Fortnightly* had demonstrated for him that there had to be a bias; his own magazine would have a distinctly Gladstonian-liberal direction.

On 14 December Trollope in business-like fashion outlined to Virtue his proposals for the magazine: a feasible starting date would be 1 October 1867, in which case he would 'give all the intervening time to preparing a story for the magazine, and doing other work for it'. There should be a monthly political article, alternating home and foreign politics ('I think that during the Session I would endeavour to explain in a few pages what Parliament is doing'), but little or no reviewing. He would open the magazine with a novel of his own and carry it through twenty numbers, a work the length of *The Small House*; his price would be £3,200 for a novel this size, the equivalent of four 'ordinary volumes'. He reiterated the stipulation for a two-year contract at £1,000 per annum. He was secretly calculating the monetary effects of resigning from the Post Office. No matter how secure his income from writing appeared, surrendering an annual salary and an eventual pension gave him pause. For at least two years he would have this additional income. By 24 January there was a signing of letters of agreement. 'I do not think we shall want any lawyers work between us,' Trollope wrote to Virtue. 'I have never found the need of any yet with a publisher.'39

The Trollopes took their continental holiday early so that Anthony might be in London during the time immediately preceding the appearance of the new magazine. They were gone from 18 July to 20 August, during which time he visited the Vosges mountains in Lorraine, which provided the setting for *The Golden Lion of Granpere*, the third novel in the 'romantic' vein of his new anonymous persona. On returning home he wrote the story in twenty-seven days. *The Golden Lion*, a light comedy, very different from *Nina Balatka* and *Linda Tressel*, was in Trollope's view—and everyone else's—'very inferior to either of them'.40 But the new novel was not destined to be part of the experiment in anonymity: *Linda Tressel* had sales as meagre as had *Nina Balatka*; moreover, it had received less notice and less favour with the reviewers. One notable exception was Henry James, writing again in the New York *Nation*: clearly, he says, *Linda Tressel* and its predecessor, *Nina Balatka*, are by Trollope, whose style 'is as little to be mistaken as it is to be imitated'; both are 'rich with their own intrinsic merits, and . . . contain more of the real substance of common life and more natural energy of conception than any of the clever novels now begotten by our much-tried English speech'; both works require that the reader have patience with a kind of simple, uninspired dullness of narrative manner; but the stories themselves are 'full of truthfulness and pathos'; in *Linda Tressel*, especially, the story 'forces its way up into truly tragic interest and dignity'; the narrative is not seasoned with wit or poetry, only 'common sense and common sensibility. The whole force of the story lies just where, after all, it should—*in the story*, in its movement, its action, and the fidelity with which it reflects the little patch of human life which the author unrolls, heaven-wise, above it.'[41] James's volte-face on Trollope was continued, most memorably, in a long essay occasioned by Trollope's death, in which, while claiming that Trollope 'abused his gift' by writing too much, and quarrelling with his narrative strategies, James insisted on calling Trollope 'a man of genius', 'a knowing psychologist', in virtue of his 'happy instinctive perception of human varieties'; he marvelled at what he called Trollope's 'complete appreciation of the real' and admired his depictions of English women and of Americans; Trollope often, James said, 'achieved a conspicuous intensity of the tragical'; James was among the first to emphasize Trollope's extraordinary facility in using letters as an 'unfailing resource' in his fiction. Trollope would endure, James claimed, as 'one of the most trustworthy, though not one of the most eloquent, of the writers who have helped the heart of man to know itself'.[42]

Blackwood, Trollope wrote, would have undoubtedly continued the experiment in anonymity had Trollope contributed the novels free: 'Another ten years of unpaid unflagging labour might have built up a second reputation.'[43] W. H. Pollock wrote that Trollope explained that he had not continued in the vein of *Nina Balatka* and *Linda Tressel* because 'the public—the big public—did not care for them, and it was to the big public that he had to appeal'.[44] Trollope had not the heart to offer *The Golden Lion* to Blackwood at this time; instead he kept the manuscript in his desk and two years later tried to sell it to Chapman & Hall with magazine rights to go to the American publisher Appleton. Nothing came of these negotiations, and in February 1871 he offered it to Blackwood, to be published with his name along with permission to use his name on any subsequent republication of *Nina Balatka* and *Linda Tressel*; he told Blackwood to name his own price, and added that *The Golden Lion* had a happy ending. Blackwood answered that sales of the earlier books had been so disappointing that he could offer no more than £300 for the entire copyright. Trollope considered this too little, and he sold the story—which contained nothing to offend religious sensibilities—to *Good Words*, still edited by his old friend Norman Macleod, and owned by Strahan, for the good sum of £550.[45]

Plans for his new magazine had occupied Trollope much of the year; he had been writing a long novel, *Phineas Finn*, with which to open the publication. Pleading the special circumstances of inaugurating his own magazine, he had persuaded Millais to illustrate the novel. Millais had promised to 'do one more', and *Phineas* required only twenty plates in all, and at monthly intervals. The cover of the new magazine was to carry the prominent legend 'With Illustrations by J. E. Millais, R.A.', though he illustrated nothing except Trollope's novel. Robert Bell having died, Trollope gave the job of sub-editor to Edward Dicey (a writer who later became editor of the *Observer*), at a salary of £250, to be paid out of Trollope's yearly £1,000. Trollope lined up various writers he wanted to get into his stable, including A. H. Layard and George Goschen for politics, Francis Lawley and Leslie Stephen for sports, Henry Nelson O'Neil and Percy Fitzgerald for arts and theatre. He could count on his brother and sister-in-law for Italian politics and fiction. Somewhat surprisingly, he abandoned the policy he had so strongly urged on the *Fortnightly* of putting authors' names to their articles; for his own magazine he felt safer with the practice of the successful *Cornhill*.

Finding a name for the magazine took a long time. Trollope's early suggestions, 'The Monthly Westminster' and 'The Monthly Liberal', had been discarded; Virtue most likely saw them as too overtly political. A proprietary name, such as *Blackwood's* or *Fraser's*, would not do, because, as Trollope said, 'Virtue's Magazine' sounded 'too attractive'; Trollope had vetoed Virtue's suggestion of 'Trollope's Monthly' or 'Anthony Trollope's Magazine', as meaning nothing after he would have left the journal; doubtless also he thought it a bit too self-aggrandizing; even Dickens had not gone that far. By April Trollope favoured 'The Whitehall Magazine', but this was again probably too political for Virtue. Only by late August was the name *Saint Pauls Magazine* decided upon, and Trollope wrote to Millais asking if he would do a sketch of the cathedral for the cover of the magazine. (The drawing eventually used seems too mechanically architectural to be by Millais.[46]) Virtue had long had his bookselling/publishing business at Amen Corner, close by St Paul's Cathedral, and in taking the name from a geographical location, Trollope and Virtue were following, as in so many other details—one shilling price, 128 pages, incorporation of illustrated fiction with general interest subjects—the pattern set by the *Cornhill*. (Other magazines such as *Saint James's, Belgravia, Temple Bar* had already imitated the *Cornhill* closely.) But whatever the magazine was to be called, Virtue saw Trollope's name as his drawing card, and as late as a month before the launch of the magazine advertised it simply as a 'NEW MONTHLY MAGAZINE BY ANTHONY TROLLOPE'; indeed, he was still doing pretty much the same thing half a year later.[47]

October saw the first issue of *Saint Pauls Magazine* on the news-vendors' stalls. Trollope opened the magazine with a disarmingly frank editorial, assuring the public that *Saint Pauls* 'is not established . . . on any rooted and matured conviction that such a periodical is the great and pressing want of the age'. Rather, the proprietors believed they could make the venture 'commercially profitable'. Although there were other worthwhile magazines, the more such magazines the better. People who disparaged magazines claimed that they offered nothing more than novels, the non-fiction being mere 'padding'. But this so-called padding, Trollope insisted, had come from great writers: Sydney Smith, Macaulay, Thomas Hood, Whewell, Carlyle, Thackeray, Tennyson, Mrs Browning, Bulwer, Dickens, Froude, Stanley, Lewes, Tyndal, Huxley, Ruskin, Arnold, and others. *Saint Pauls* would be distinctive in following a middle course between those magazines whose purpose was declaredly that of 'tripping along ever upon the light fantastic toe'—an obvious reference to the *Cornhill*—and that one magazine that had marched forward 'with the steady gait of self-conscious information, professing to be instructive and daring to be grave'—an equally clear reference to the *Fortnightly*. The new magazine's gravity would arise from its political emphasis; the editor and his contributors believed that politics was 'the first and the finest' of all studies; their support would be for the Liberal party, 'that side in the House of Commons which in truth represents the majority of the constituencies.' As for novels, the editor himself, who had for so long sung 'love ditties', would here 'warble' another from month to month. Trollope's editorial, for all its Thackerayan ring, was an odd performance.[48] One wonders what Virtue thought of it.

Trollope's novel was, naturally enough, the chief attraction of the magazine; the public seemed to like *Phineas Finn*, and Trollope, balancing as he said the political interest along with 'love and intrigue, social incidents, with perhaps a dash of sport', considered it 'successful from first to last'.[49] *Phineas Finn* was accompanied in *Saint Pauls* by a short novel (eight instalments), *All for Greed*, by Madame Blaze de Bury, a development that might have told Trollope that *Saint Pauls* was no *Cornhill*: in the previous January Trollope had been asked by Sir Charles Taylor about Madame de Bury's prospects for publishing the novel, and Trollope replied that, as she for so long a time had published nothing, she would be treated 'almost as a new novelist', and that George Smith, for example, would certainly not take the manuscript for the *Cornhill*. Trollope would 'have it read,—or read it; and no doubt could get it sold if it was liked. She must not however expect a long price.' In the event Trollope himself paid her about a pound a page, or just under £150 for the story.[50] The non-fiction for the first issue included 'The Leap in the Dark' by George Goschen; 'The Ethics of Trades' Unions' by Edward Dicey; articles on the turf by Francis Lawley, on taste, by Henry O'Neil, and one by Trollope himself on sovereignty, a dull if workmanlike defence of constitutional monarchy. The mix of fiction and articles on politics, topical subjects, sport, and art was typical of what the magazine was to contain henceforth.

Having waited until *Saint Pauls Magazine* had made its début, Trollope sent to John Tilley on 2 October, for forwarding to the Duke of Montrose, Postmaster-General at the time, his letter of resignation from the Post Office. Tilley wrote a letter accepting the resignation on the Duke's behalf, saying that Trollope was 'among the most conspicuous servants' of the Post Office, that he had never permitted his 'other avocations to interfere with . . . Post Office work, which has always been faithfully, and, indeed energetically, performed.'51 The word 'energetically', Trollope said, with its 'touch of irony' did not displease him; he reprinted the entire letter in *An Autobiography*, because, he said, in spite of its 'official flummery' it was evidence that he did not allow his literary labours to interfere with his postal work. Trollope was violently indignant at the suggestion, doubtless made often enough out of his presence, that he had resigned under pressure because of his literary work and hunting. In 1876, writing *An Autobiography*, he admitted to being 'still a little sore on the subject'. Nothing would enrage him more than as much as a hint that he was among those who took public money without earning it. He got up early every day, he worked on Sundays, he frequently worked in the evening. He had 'applied' the thirty-three best years of his life to the Post Office—he had not 'devoted' them, he explained, because he did not entirely surrender himself to his work in the sense that he did nothing else; still, 'during all those years I had thought very much more about the Post Office than I had of my literary work, and had given to it a more unflagging attention'. He claimed not to have been angry when his novels were slighted, but to have suffered bitterly when his plans for the Post Office were not adopted; he had been passionately anxious that the public in small villages should be able to buy postage stamps with ease; that mails should be delivered free, and early, to the people in rural areas; that pay to sorters and carriers should be adequate, and 'above all' that such pay should be truly earned.52 But literary work of late had made encroachments on his time that may have troubled him. Just ten days before leaving the service, he wrote privately to a fellow surveyor, Christopher Hodgson, 'It is not so much that the office is no long[er] worth my while, as you say, as that other things have grown upon [me] so fast that I feel myself beginning to neglect the office and I am sure you will acknowledge that

.t is the case it had better be given up.'[53] It had been the ป of *Saint Pauls* that had been encroaching on his time and s. His new salary from the magazine would amount to £750 or much what he was earning from the Post Office, and thus for two , at least he would suffer no loss of income because of leaving the service. He did, however, forfeit a pension of about £500 per annum which would have been his had he remained another eight years in the Post Office, that is, until he was 60. Had he been named Assistant Secretary in 1864 he would doubtless not have resigned, though this is not the same as saying that he resigned because the position went to another. That disappointment had been three years before, and it cannot have been the immediate cause of his resignation. But having been denied the Under-Secretaryship made him more open to deeper literary involvement, and more likely to retire early. George Eliot had misgivings about the move: 'I cannot help being rather sorry,' she wrote to John Blackwood, 'it seems to me a thing greatly to be dreaded for a man that he should be in any way led to excessive writing.'[54] As it turned out, Trollope would write somewhat less after leaving the service than while engaged in two professions (he maintained that three hours a day of writing was about all that one could do anyway).[55] During the eight years previous to retirement he wrote fifteen novels (in forty-two of his 'volumes'), one travel book, three collections of short stories, and enough journalism to fill a large-size volume. During the following eight years he wrote thirteen novels (in forty 'volumes'), one travel book, one collection of short stories and less journalism; thus the latter pace was only slightly slower than that of the period prior to retirement; and that of the last eight years of his life was in turn again only slightly slower than that preceding it.

On his last day as a civil servant, 31 October 1867, 'the chaps in the GPO' gave him a farewell dinner at the Albion Tavern, an affair attended by some hundred people. Trollope was reported in the press as expressing 'melancholy' at leaving the service.[56] None the less, he must have found the celebration cheering, especially since he was not retiring into leisure, but into increased literary work. *Saint Pauls* had apparently got off to a reasonably good start; and during recent months *The Last Chronicle* had received the most adulatory reviews of any of his novels. Whatever his misgivings about leaving the service, he could not help seeing favourable signs for the future. (The timing was also good for hunting: 1 November meant the beginning of the season, and he was able to return to going out three days a week.) He was heartened too by the first agreement he signed with a publisher after leaving the Post Office: two weeks after the celebratory goodbyes, and after two issues of *Saint Pauls Magazine* had appeared, Virtue agreed to pay £3,200 for the complete copyright of a new novel (*He Knew He Was Right*). Like *The Last Chronicle*, the new work was to appear in thirty-two weekly parts and be the equivalent of a five-volume novel. The rate of pay was roughly the same for the two, for Smith, while paying £3,000 for *The Last Chronicle*, had purchased only half-copyright of subsequent editions. From Virtue's standpoint, £3,200 represented a better value than *Phineas Finn*, for that novel, bought at the same price, was but four volumes. Whether the plan for the weekly part publication was Virtue's idea or Trollope's is not known; the arrangement had not been particularly remunerative for Smith; but Virtue would not have known this, and he may have been emulating the successful publisher in choosing this form of publication.

The agreement with Virtue for *He Knew He Was Right* linked Trollope more closely with his new publisher. Trollope, by setting up his own magazine, a rival to the *Cornhill*, had pretty much cut himself off professionally from George Smith. He contributed practically nothing further to the *Pall Mall*, although Frederick Greenwood, the paper's editor, claimed later that this silencing was his doing: an intense anti-Gladstonian Conservative, Greenwood said Trollope's political contributions to the paper had been 'so intolerably empty and wordy that the editor was compelled to put a stop to them, even at the risk of mortal offence—which ensued'.[57] In any case, Trollope remained on good personal terms with George Smith, and in December approached him with a scheme for bringing out a uniform collected edition of the Barsetshire novels (he said *Doctor Thorne* was not absolutely essential to the series). He had had such a project in mind for some time, and the reviews of *The Last Chronicle* encouraged him, especially that of the *Examiner*, which, after calling the Barsetshire stories 'the best set of "sequels" in our literature', said that 'in justice to Mr. Trollope and to itself, the public should have these Barsetshire novels . . . duly bound, lettered, and bought as a connected series'.[58] Smith held three of the copyrights, and the others could have been purchased, but he declined to act. It may have been a purely business consideration, as had his earlier refusal to buy up Trollope's other copyrights (they had eventually gone to W. H. Smith, who published the books over the Chapman & Hall imprint), or Smith may have cooled somewhat towards publishing Trollope after 'his' *Cornhill* novelist had come out with a magazine of his own. On the other hand, Smith was a sound businessman, and given the modest sales of *The Last Chronicle* in weekly issue, and the fact that the book edition was still in its first half-year, it was understandable that he should hesitate. Trollope was to wait ten years before seeing a uniform edition of the Barsetshire Chronicles published.

Trollope kept the editorial chair of *Saint Pauls Magazine* for almost three years. He was a conscientious but not overbearing editor. Only a fraction of the correspondence survives, but enough to indicate something of his working style. He had necessarily to read 'basketfulls of manuscripts', and to reject countless submissions. He sometimes turned away articles as being out of his ken: he declined, for example, an article on ozone, as probably 'correct' in its account but 'altogether beyond my own powers of criticism'; he returned a paper to J. E. Taylor, explaining, 'I am afraid of the subject of Darwin. I am myself so ignorant on it, that I should fear to be in the position of editing a paper on the subject.' He wanted articles of general interest to his readers, and he declined what he considered a sound paper on the War Department as being too much an 'official Report', and lacking 'that sharpness (often prejudicial to justice) which would charm the readers of a magazine'; he refused a paper on Dürer's life, telling the author that readers would not care much whether or not the artist's wife was a shrew: 'I am sure you will understand me when I say that I am bound to get matter such as will find readers, not among the highest class of men & women,—but with that class by which a magazine is mainly supported.' He turned down an essay by Millicent Fawcett on the radical MP William Johnson Fox: 'I am afraid that the memory of Mr. Fox has so far died out that we should hardly succeed in resuscitating it by the article.' Often, of course, he simply disagreed with the article: he refused an essay by Octavia Hill, submitted with the blessing of no less a friend than G. H. Lewes, whose son had married into the Hill family: her paper on housing for the poor Trollope judged 'Utopian': 'You cannot', he wrote to Lewes, 'inspect people into Godliness, cleanliness, and good grub. I do think you may educate them to it.'59

He could be persuasive in commissioning material, as when he talked George Macdonald into writing a Christmas story (a genre Trollope himself detested): 'Let it not be sensible;—but weird rather, and of a Christmas-ghostly flavour. . . . I don't know whether Pudding and Hades can be brought together;—but if any man can do it, you can.' With lesser talents he could be insistent; he printed up proofs of Mrs Annie Cudlip's short story, but told her it would not be used unles she changed the ending: hers destroyed 'all our sympathy for a very prettily drawn girl' and 'wounds all our ideas of probability'; he outlined a totally different ending, but consoled her that she need only change the last two pages. Mrs Cudlip followed his instructions exactly. But usually, once a piece was accepted, he did little tinkering with it. He asked A. H. Layard to soften words about the 'limited capacity' of the Tory party and class; he altered the (now lost) title of one of Charles Lever's articles because 'to town-living people here in England, who have dirty minds, [it] would have given rise to nasty suggestions touching dissenteric troubles.' With poetry, on the other hand, especially that of his chief contributor of verse, Austin Dobson, he made countless suggestions. Dobson, who in effect was a 'discovery' of Trollope's, accepted most of his advice: the editor objected, for example, to the 'pseudo word' *abeat*; a passage about blessings given by the blind drew the comment: 'I may be stupid, but I see no idea in this. The blind, if they bless, bless without seeing. But the blind are not specially given to conferring of blessings'; the phrase 'Knew in her cheek a little colour burn' he found 'certainly involved' and 'generally unintelligible'. Trollope contended that poetry for a magazine should be readily comprehensible to 'uneducated, but perhaps intelligent, minds'.[60]

21

Washington and Beverley

TROLLOPE had not been two months out of the Post Office when John Tilley talked him into undertaking to make a new postal treaty, or convention as it was called, with the United States. Tilley told the Postmaster-General that it was necessary to send 'a strong man'—because the British, who were terminating the existing treaty, were not in a good bargaining position. Trollope's 'personal popularity with the Americans' would be important; Tilley believed 'no one else would do the work so well'. The hope was that Trollope could get the Americans to agree to join the British in sending mail exclusively through the ports of Queenstown, County Cork, and Liverpool, using only Cunard mail packets, with three regular sailings per week. Trollope, a private citizen now, thought the honour of presentation at court might enhance his status as emissary, and he asked Lord Houghton to have him presented at court before his departure for America. He was presented to the Prince of Wales, by Lord Stanhope, at a levee on 17 March.[1]

A. H. Layard joked with Trollope about making money in America by public readings—something that Dickens had been doing for the past six months. Trollope said he feared he would bring back 'a very small bag'.[2] He had spoken at the great farewell dinner for Dickens on the eve of his departure for his lecture tour—given two days after Trollope's own dinner on leaving the Post Office. Asked to answer the toast to Literature, he did not like to refuse, even though, as he told a friend, he was 'not specially in that set'. According to the 'Authentic Record' of the dinner Trollope rose to 'general and prolonged cheering'. He made little reference to Dickens beyond calling him 'a great chieftain in literature' and instead devoted his talk to attacking Carlyle's hobby-horse that fiction came perilously close to lying.[3] On 11 April Trollope sailed from Liverpool and arrived at New York Harbor on 22 April, just in time to go out in a mail tender and board Dickens's departing ship to shake hands with him. 'It was most heartily done,' Dickens reported to James Fields.[4]

Two days later Trollope reached Washington, to learn to his displeasure that the American Postmaster-General, Alexander Randall, could not much attend to the matter of a postal treaty because of the impeachment trial of President Andrew Johnson. Randall would have to resign if Johnson were convicted and had to await the outcome of the trial. Trollope, though he understood Randall's position, fumed at the delay. Mrs James Fields wrote to Kate Field, 'Mr. Trollope is here expressing in no mild or measured terms his disgust for Washington and Impeachment.' Ten days later she was reporting another 'very pleasant visit from good whole-souled Mr. Trollope. A few such men redeemed Nineveh. He always seems the soul of honesty.' But not of patience. He had hated Washington in 1861–2, and this time he found the heat of summer in the capital worse than the snow and mud of that winter. But two days after Johnson's acquittal, on 16 May (by a margin of one vote), Randall and his senior clerk, Joseph Fanwood ('the only man here who really understands' the treaty, Trollope said) gave him an entire day, but the outlook was gloomy for British prospects. The American public, Trollope reported to Tilley, 'is more patient than ours . . . less driven than are we in the matters of [postal] quickness and punctuality'. Six weeks later the American position had become even less tractable because of pressure from Congressmen who supported American shipping lines. Trollope sent Tilley a copy of the *Washington Morning Chronicle* in which an article described 'the wise-acre who controls the British Postal Department'—Tilley—as having cancelled the old convention in the interest of its own subsidized line of steamers, Cunard. Then Randall went away to attend the Democratic Convention in New York, and negotiations dragged on. Trollope had come to take a strong dislike for Randall, who, he declared, not only did not understand the postal matters but 'would make appointments with me and then not keep them'. At one point Trollope threatened to report that he could do nothing and go home, until he reminded himself that this would be playing into the hands of the Americans. The British were disturbing the existing treaty and therefore, as he told Tilley, the Americans 'had the whip hand of us altogether'. The treaty Trollope eventually arranged was substantially the same as the one it replaced. No one in London blamed him.[5]

Trollope had also been commissioned by the Foreign Office to make some attempts towards forwarding the establishment of international copyright. It was Trollope's conviction till the end that American op-position to international copyright came not from American readers, lawmakers, or booksellers, but from a handful of big publishing houses, especially Harpers. Nothing came of his efforts in Washington for international copyright.[6]

His only consolation amidst the delays and frustrations, heat, mosquitoes, and a stone-deaf American Senator who insisted on dining with him every day (at Wormley's Hotel on I Street, where he again lodged) was his contact with Kate Field. He began again writing to her, after a long interval (long at least on the evidence of surviving letters). He was not the kind of person who attempted to keep a friendship, however warm, alive by the post. In *Phineas Redux* he wrote:

for the maintenance of love and friendship, continued correspondence between distant friends is naught. Distance in time and place, but especially in time, will diminish friendship. It is a rule of nature that it should be so, and thus the friendships which a man most fosters are those which he can best enjoy. If your friend leave you, and seek a residence in Patagonia, make a niche for him in your memory, and keep him there as warm as you may. Perchance he may return from Patagonia and the old joys may be repeated. But never think that those joys can be maintained by ocean postage.[7]

In their resumed correspondence he gave Kate the benefit of detailed and shrewd comments on her writings, published and in manuscript. He sent stringent criticisms of her plotting, construction, and tendency to turn a story into an essay; moreover, he dismissed spiritualism, and the planchette, a subject on which she was about to publish a little book. (In 1855 Trollope had attended a seance conducted at Ealing by the young American medium Daniel Hume—later 'Home', and the original for Browning's 'Mr Sludge, the Medium'; old Mrs Trollope had been trying to get in touch with her departed loved ones, especially her children, but Anthony detested the whole proceeding, and, as he now told Kate, found spiritualism 'unworthy of the previous grand ceremony of death'.[8]) The trouble he took in advising her to 'exercise [her] mind' when telling a story demonstrates his belief in her promise; he went so far as to invite her to write a story for *Saint Pauls*; Kate confided to her journal, 'If I can, it will be a feather in my cap.' He reminded her of the plan, after his return to England: 'I would willingly see myself in some little way helping you in a profession which I regard as being the finest in the world.'[9] But Kate did not write the story. He also thought well enough of her *Pen Photographs of Charles Dickens' Readings*, based on his public reading in New York that January, to attempt to gain for it English publication, an attempt frustrated by Dickens's opposition.

Kate and Trollope enjoyed meetings as well as correspondence. Of the earliest, at Washington on 25 May, her journal says tersely: 'Met Anthony

Trollope. Same as ever.'¹⁰ In June he made a ten-day journey away from the capital, spending most of the time in New York City, where he and Kate had their photographs taken by Napoleon Sarony, of 630 Broadway. The photographer was evidently tipsy, and Trollope in writing to Kate of the photographs said he hoped 'that horrid little Silenus' would be 'drowned in Burgundy and that his deputy with the dirty sleeves will photograph him in his last gasp'. Trollope would like one of the photographs of her, 'standing up, facing full front, with your hat. I think it would have your natural look, & you cant conceive how little I shall think of the detrimental skirt of which our Silenus complained.' On 8 July he wrote to her from Washington saying he had framed a section of her photograph 'down to the mere hat and eyes and nose. It is all I have of you except a smudged (but originally very pretty) portrait taken from a picture.' He thanked her for a newspaper account describing him as a 'strange looking person. His head is shaped like a minnie ball, with the point rounded down a little, like the half of a lemon cut transversely in two. It is small, almost sharp at the top, and bald, increasing in size until it reaches his neck. His complexion and general bearing are much like Dickens's. His body is large and well preserved. He dresses like a gentleman and not like a fop, but he squeezes his small, well-shaped hand into a very small pair of colored kids. He "wears a cane," as all Englishmen do.' 'I never wear gloves,' he told Kate. Trollope suggested she adopt a middle initial like other 'strong-minded' American women—'Kate X. Field' would serve. He told her how he was still 'killed' by the heat and the mosquitoes; he had set fire to the netting trying to burn the mosquitoes and didn't sleep a wink. He did not know for sure that she and Mrs Homans would be in Boston and so he might not go there; if Kate could get down 'close to the sea, & near enough for me to get at you, I would then go to you'. This letter he closed, 'Give my kindest love to your mother. The same to yourself dear Kate—if I do not see you again,—with a kiss that shall be semi-paternal—one third brotherly, and as regards the small remainder, as loving as you please,'—a fairly accurate statement of how he felt towards her.¹¹

From New York, he wrote to Kate that he was in fact going to Boston for one day. He would be within twelve miles of her but would not be able to see her: 'I wish I could have seen your dear old face once more, (before the gray hairs come, or the wings which you will wear in heaven)—but I do not see how it is to be.' He made a mysterious reference to 'the black phantom'. Perhaps someone had linked their names indelicately: 'I hope he has winged his way to distant worlds. He did not hurt me,—but a man is tough in these matters. It vexed you and teased my wife.' He closed, 'I wish I thought I might see your clever laughing eyes again before the days of the spectacles.' At Boston, visiting Mrs Homans, he was told Kate was expected there that day; but she did not arrive, and Trollope had, as he later wrote to her, 'a melancholy day'. If he was to see Kate again, it must depend on her coming to England: 'I am becoming an infirm old man, too fat to travel so far.'[12]

Trollope arrived home on 26 July and was duly thanked by the Postmaster-General for his services in securing the new treaty. He was also paid five guineas a day plus expenses. Trollope wrote to his brother that after this 'most disagreeable' trip to America he did not intend 'to go on any more ambassadorial business'.[13] *Saint Pauls*, which had been left in Edward Dicey's hands, required his attention; as for his own writing, that had gone on apace during his absence, for he had completed *He Knew He was Right* in Washington, and three days later had begun *The Vicar of Bullhampton*. He and Rose took a four weeks' holiday in Scotland, returning 13 September, when he resumed writing *The Vicar of Bullhampton*.

In October the editing of *Saint Pauls* brought him the special pleasure of G. H. Lewes's paper on 'The Dangers and Delights of Tobacco'. 'No doubt,' he wrote to Lewes, 'all good smokers will express their lasting gratitude in some substantial form;—a pyramid of cigar ashes—or a mausoleum for, long-delayed, future use, constructed of old pipe stems and tobacco stoppers.'[14] Trollope himself was a cigar smoker almost all his adult life; he customarily smoked three or four large cigars daily, and during his more affluent years would order as many as 12,000 cigars at a time from Havana, sometimes supplying friends like George Smith and Lewes with a share. Henry Brackenbury reported that 'One wall of [Trollope's] library where he worked was entirely hidden by small cupboards or bins, each with a separate glass door, and filled with cigars, stacked across each other "headers and stretchers" like timber, so as to allow free circulation of air. . . . There was a pointed stud stuck into the wood above the door of the bin in use, and as soon as this bin was empty the stud was moved to the next bin, and the empty one filled from the chest.'[15] In the late 1870s he gave up smoking because he thought it was making his hand shake and causing 'somnolency', but after two years he resumed, a doctor telling him that smaller cigars would not be injurious. Thereafter, apparently till the end, he smoked '3 small cigars (very small)' daily without evident ill effect.[16] Cigar smoking was always one of the great satisfactions of his life.

In the midst of the work of editing and writing that occupied him in the autumn of 1868, Trollope took time to compose for his friend Lady Wood a formal defence of her novel *Sorrow on the Sea*. The book had been labelled immoral by the *Athenaeum* in a review that caused the publisher, Tinsley, to withdraw it from circulation and refuse payment to the author. The reviewer began by saying that *Sorrow on the Sea* 'is a very bad novel' and ended by saying that 'the details of these volumes are literally unfit for presentation in any language'. Trollope found nothing objectionable in the novel, and further insisted that that which 'is unfit for publication in one language, must be unfit for publication in any other'; the reviewer intended to make readers believe that an English lady had 'written in English that which would be held to be disgraceful even in the literature of countries which are less severe on such matters', and Trollope called this 'manifestly unjust', even maliciously so; and he was willing to testify in court to this effect. (One of the objections was the novel's treatment of baby farming. Lady Wood's brother-in-law, Lord Hatherley, is said to have bought up all available copies and had them burned. [17]) A few months earlier, from Washington, Trollope had written an encouraging letter to Rhoda Broughton, who had had similar troubles with Mrs Grundy: Trollope told her that some lady friend of his, 'a good critic', had recommended her work to him and he had accordingly read *Not Wisely But Too Well*. He had been told that her works were written in a strain 'not . . . becoming any woman', but he found 'not a word that I would not have had written by my sister, or my daughter—if I had one'. He could not understand critics who came down with 'claws and beaks' on a story that taught 'a wholesome lesson without an impure picture or a faulty expression'. He added that in his view she was making the prosaic in life too prosaic, the poetic too poetic. Still, he read the book with 'intense interest. I wept over it . . . and came to the conclusion that there had come up another sister among us, of whose name we should be proud.' [18] To Miss Broughton, a novelist who outlived her reputation for audacity ('I began life as Zola, I finish it as Miss Yonge'), [19] Trollope's unsolicited letter is said to have brought a renewal of confidence. But in 1876 she complained that Frederick Locker had told her that 'Anthony Trollope says I might have done something if I had taken pains. But then he never praises any writer except Thackeray, at least I never heard him.' [20]

As soon as he had left the Civil Service, Trollope tells us, he had been stirred to look for the opportunity to run for Parliament. In *Can You Forgive Her?* he had written a deeply personal passage:

There is on the left-hand side of our great national hall . . . a pair of gilded lamps, with a door between them, near to which a privileged old dame sells her apples and her oranges. . . . Between those lamps is the entrance to the House of Commons, and none but Members may go that way! It is the only gate before which I have ever stood filled with envy,—sorrowing to think that my steps might never pass under it. . . . I have told myself, in anger and in grief, that to die and not to have won that right of way, though but for a session . . . is to die and not to have done that which it most becomes an Englishman to have achieved. . . . It is the highest and most legitimate pride of an Englishman to have the letters M.P. written after his name.[21]

The sentiments were old ones for Trollope: he still remembered his Uncle Milton's taunt back in the 1830s that few Post Office clerks became Members of Parliament. And so, in the very first month of his freedom from the Civil Service, driven by 'an almost insane desire' to sit in Parliament, he volunteered to stand for one of the two divisions of Essex. His adviser was his hunting friend Charles Buxton, himself Liberal Member for Surrey. Essex was a Tory stronghold, and Trollope was to lay out some £2,000 in expenses, with practically no chance of winning. He must have secretly thought that his popular name would have given him some chance, although he said later in *An Autobiography* that the attempt would have been 'absolutely in vain', his candidacy being chiefly a matter of not allowing the Tories to retain the seat without a contest. But there was no dissolution, and no election took place in 1867, as Disraeli passed his Reform Bill. However, by the new Redistribution Bill, Essex was extended to three divisions, and that adjacent to London was expected to be Liberal. In early 1868 there was again rumour of a dissolution, and Trollope understandably thought that after he had promised to make the hopeless run earlier, he would have been selected as one of the candidates for a now safe South Essex seat. Buxton proposed him. But Andrew Johnson, Chairman of the Essex County Council, who had strongly urged Trollope to announce his candidacy in 1867, and who himself declined to do so at that time, was put forward by 'the dissenting interest', and Johnson and another Liberal were eventually elected for South Essex unopposed. Trollope was sorely aggrieved.[22]

Upon his return from America in the summer of 1868, again at the urging of Buxton and other friends, he agreed to stand for another 'impossible borough' that the Liberals did not want to allow the Conservatives to win uncontested. After turning down one or two places, Trollope settled for Beverley, capital of the West Riding of Yorkshire. Beverley was a borough of 12,000 people and, under the newly enacted Reform Bill of

1867, had about 2,100 electors.[23] Trollope was well aware of Beverley's reputation for unsavoury elections: on the evening of departing for Yorkshire he wrote to Mrs Pollock that he believed Beverley to be 'one of the most degraded boroughs in England'.[24] But it was a heady time for Liberals—about half the voters were new—and Trollope doubtless thought he had some real hope of being returned. In 1867, Disraeli, Chancellor of the Exchequer for Lord Derby but Prime Minister in all but name, had passed his great Reform Bill, with its famous Hodgkinson amendment that in effect granted household suffrage to the boroughs, where it was expected to strengthen the Liberals. By his Redistribution Bill Disraeli had attempted to keep the counties rural and Conservative, by granting them additional seats and giving seats to hitherto unrepresented towns and transferring many suburban voters into the boroughs—where the vote was more likely to be Liberal anyway.[25] Thus both measures should have made contesting Beverley less quixotic. Moreover, Disraeli, who had become Prime Minister in February upon Derby's resignation for reasons of ill health, seemed to be heading for sure defeat. In April Gladstone had beaten the government on a resolution respecting the disestablishment of the Irish Church. Disraeli, presiding over a government that did not command a majority in the House, hung on, and only in November did he finally go to the country with a general election. The Liberals and Gladstone looked to triumph soundly. Trollope was caught up in the optimism; perhaps the newly-enfranchised electors of Beverley would turn matters round in spite of their long history of corruption and of sending Conservatives to Parliament; perhaps they would be pleased to be represented by a famous author.

Trollope's agent in Beverley was a local solicitor, W. S. Hind, himself a former Member of Parliament. He told Trollope he hadn't a chance of getting elected, that he would spend £1,000, that the elected Members would be thrown out on petitions, and that a commission would then disfranchise the borough: 'For a beginner such as you are, that will be a great success.'[26] But Trollope persisted. Dickens told Thomas Adolphus Trollope that 'Anthony's ambition [to stand for Parliament] is inscrutable to me. Still, it is the ambition of many men; and the honester the man who entertains it, the better for the rest of us, I suppose.'[27]

Beverley returned two Members. One incumbent, Sir Henry Edwards, chairman of the Beverley Iron and Waggon Company, which manufactured railway cars and farm machinery, had held his Conservative seat for ten years; he contributed much to local charities and paid handsomely for the favour of sitting in Parliament. Trollope said of him that 'he had contracted a close intimacy with [Beverley] for the sake of the seat. There had been many contests, many petitions, many void elections, many members, but, through it all, Sir Henry had kept his seat, if not permanently, still with a fixity of tenure next door to permanence.'[28] The other Conservative incumbent, Christopher Sykes, perhaps fearing the newly-enfranchised electors or perhaps the challenge from the broadly rising Liberal tide, took himself instead to contest the East Riding; and Captain Edmund Kennard, a wealthy young man willing to spend freely to gain a seat in Parliament, became the other Conservative candidate. Trollope's Liberal colleague was Marmaduke Maxwell, eldest son and heir of Lord Herries, a Scottish Roman Catholic peer who lived in the neighbourhood. Maxwell had read Trollope's novels and was pleased to be joined with him.

From Waltham, Trollope wrote on 28 October his election address, in which he affirmed that his purpose if elected would be to give 'active, constant, and unwearied support to Mr. Gladstone' and the Liberal party. The Reform Bill, Trollope said, should not have been passed under the auspices of Disraeli 'in whom, certainly, the nation has no confidence'. As for the leading issue of the campaign, Trollope said that for years he had denounced 'the gross injustice and absurd uselessness of the Irish Church Establishment . . . the ascendency of the rich over the poor, of the great over the little, of the high over the low'. The Irish Protestant Church 'assumes the virtues of the Pharisee' and is 'hated instead of loved by the people'. On another prominent issue, education, he said that 'every poor man should have brought within his reach the means of educating his children, and that those means should be provided by the State.'[29]

Trollope arrived in Beverley on Friday evening, 30 October, and addressed a crowd from the balcony of a tailor's establishment in the Market Square. The avowedly Liberal *Beverley Recorder* gushingly called his speech 'one of the ablest and most fluent addresses ever heard in Beverley'. Trollope, although an adequate speaker, was, according to his own testimony, not a particularly good one; his delivery was monotone, and somewhat hurried; he could not, he said, combine memorized text with impromptu remarks. In this first speech at Beverley he told his hearers it was 'not natural' for electors of a place like Beverley to be Tories: a Conservative farmer or landlord was understandable, but not a Conservative town-dweller. If the Borough returned him to Parliament, he would function as a faithful Liberal party member; he said that no man had a right to go into the House and call himself an 'Independent' member: 'You must work in bodies, in drilled regiments, to do any political good.'[30] Trollope paid his agent £300 (an additional £100 was later required) and left town. Three days later, on 2 November, Trollope being absent, the municipal elections were held, and it was at this time that the actual bribery took place. Sir Henry's agent withdrew £800 from the bank and, stationing himself at a tavern called, appropriately enough, 'The Golden Ball', paid off the voters and entered their names and the amount in his book. The bribes ranged from 15 to 20 shillings, considerably up from that offered at past elections, because the money was for a 'double event'—the municipal election and the parliamentary one two weeks hence. Between 800 and 1,000 bribes were taken. The *Hull and Eastern Counties Herald* noted that the Tories had openly boasted that any amount of money would be used to ensure their victory. The election was as good as over by noon, and the buying off of electors had resulted in much drinking and later street fighting. The Tories took all six council seats, and a brass band paraded the streets that evening celebrating their victory.[31]

Trollope returned to Beverley on Tuesday, 3 November, the day after the municipal election, for what he told Lord Houghton would be 'that desperate work of canvassing,—than which no Life upon earth can be more absolute hell'.[32] In *An Autobiography* he wrote that 'From morning to evening every day I was taken round the lanes and byeways of that uninteresting town, canvassing every voter, exposed to the rain, up to my knees in slush, and utterly unable to assume that air of triumphant joy with which a jolly, successful candidate should be invested.'[33] In *The Duke's Children*, the narrator says of canvassing for parliamentary election: 'Perhaps nothing more disagreeable, more squalid, more revolting to the senses, more opposed to personal dignity, can be conceived. The same words have to be repeated over and over again in the cottages, hovels, and lodgings of poor men and women who only understand that the time has come round in which they are to be flattered instead of being the flatterers.' The candidate eventually comes to 'hate the poor creatures to whom he is forced to address himself, with a most cordial hatred'.[34] One wonders how many of the electors recognized the famous novelist. When Thackeray stood for Oxford he wrote to Dickens urging him to 'come down and make a speech, and tell them who he was, for he doubted whether more than two of the electors had ever heard of him, and he thought there might be as many as six or eight who had heard of [Dickens]'.[35]

Trollope had to speak almost every night; this was bad enough, but, impatient as he was, listening to others' speeches was far worse. Moreover, he did not get along well with his supporters, most of whom he found to be 'grinding vulgar tyrants'. They were trying to get him elected, and he would not follow the rules. When he wanted to take a day off for hunting, he was assured by an influential supporter, a publican, that all Beverley would desert him. For Trollope, the biggest disillusionment came in the knowledge, quickly acquired, that no one, not the most ardent of his supporters, cared in the least about his political opinions. They could not even understand why he should have any particular political beliefs; he was there to cause trouble and inconvenience and expense to Sir Henry. All in all, among the assorted miseries of canvassing, speech-making, and the 'tyranny' and indifference of his supporters, he labelled his Beverley electioneering 'the most wretched fortnight of my manhood'.[36] But Trollope seems to have been reasonably effective, for in spite of the previously paid bribes, there was some worry in the Tory camp, and the Conservatives, according to Escott's account, proposed withdrawing Kennard if the Liberals would withdraw Trollope—leaving Sir Henry and Maxwell uncontested winners. The offer was refused.[37]

In his speeches Trollope hammered away at Disraeli, a 'maid-of-all-work' as he called him, and at the Established Church of Ireland. At the mayor's dinner, where the speeches were supposed to be non-political, one of the canons of Beverley Minster, J. B. Birtwhistle, offended Trollope by speaking of Liberals as 'foes of the Protestant Church'. In a later speech Trollope found himself saying, 'I am a member, and a very sincere member—I wish I might say a devout member—but certainly a believing and an admiring member—of a Protestant Church.'[38] When Trollope proposed he attend the Minster on Sunday, he was told by his supporters that Sir Henry 'goes there in a kind of official procession' and that Trollope had better stay away.[39]

In spite of his continued talk about party loyalty, Trollope differed from most Liberals about the ballot, and on this subject he probably would have hurt his cause, if his opinions had gone for anything. He told the voters, with an irony that must have mystified some of them, that he was 'too great a Radical to love the ballot': an elector should not hide behind a secret ballot, but should discharge 'his noblest duty openly and independently'. It was the kind of thinking that in other contexts Trollope criticized as 'Utopian'. In fact a secret ballot might have won him the election; the two Liberals appear to have been far the more popular candidates, and had there been a secret ballot enough of the already-bribed voters might have gone back on their pledges to vote Conservative in the parliamentary election. Trollope also came out against the Liberal party on the Permissive Drink Bill, which would have regulated public consumption of alcohol. State regulation of liquor sale, like the ballot, was in Trollope's view an 'unmanly restraint', unworthy of a great people.[40]

The nomination of candidates took place, in the rain, at the hustings in the Market Square on Monday, 16 November. Trollope in his final campaign speech focused on the contrasting prospects of being ruled either by Gladstone 'with the assistance of such men as Mr. Bright' or by Disraeli and such 'deep-dyed' Tories as Gathorne Hardy and Sir John Pakington. Trollope referred repeatedly to Gladstone and Bright—'They are dear to your hearts, they are dear to mine.' The professed allegiance to Bright was disingenuous, for he detested Bright, thinking him an irresponsible demagogue. But Bright, with his 'monster rallies' across the North, had been the real moving force behind the passage of the Reform Bill, and doubtless Trollope knew his hearers wanted him acknowledged. In an oblique reference to bribery, he told the electors that they had 'no business to send [Edwards and Kennard into Parliament] if you differ from them'. The mayor called for a show of hands and announced that the Liberals had the majority. Of course the Tories demanded a poll, and the election took place the next day, Tuesday, 17 November. The Liberals got off to a fast start: after the polls had been open one hour Maxwell had 208 votes, Trollope 202, Edwards 168, and Kennard 159. But three hours later, the two Conservatives had edged ahead. The crowd became rowdy at what they saw happening; a group of Liberals, headed by one of Trollope's close supporters, broke into a Tory committee room and took possession of incriminating evidence of bribery. Fights occurred in the streets. When the polls closed at 4 p.m., the mayor announced his count:

> Edwards 1,132
> Kennard 986
> Maxwell 895
> Trollope 740

According to newspaper accounts, Sir Henry and Captain Kennard did not show up at the hustings for the actual announcement of the results, and when they did arrive were greeted by shouts of 'Bribery!' and 'We'll soon have you unseated'. The barricades were torn down; 'large beams of wood' and rocks were thrown; Sir Henry and Captain Kennard retreated 'only just in time to escape by a back street when the crowd rushed to meet them'. Maxwell and Trollope received an 'ovation' from a crowd estimated at 5,000: 'No one could have believed that they were the defeated candidates,' reported the *Beverley Recorder*. The beaten Liberals made a few remarks, Trollope being reported as saying that he went from the contest with a 'clear conscience and with a grateful heart. It may be that I shall appear before you again'—sentiments he reiterated the following day in a farewell address, written from Waltham.[41]

A leading article of the *Beverley Recorder* said that the election result was 'a matter for congratulation to the Liberal Party. They fought heroically and nobly, and although well aware that the expenditure of a few pounds would have secured for them a successful issue, they rigidly abstained from giving even a glass of beer to any voter.' The paper predicted the unseating of the Tories and insisted that 'the great majority of [the electors] are at heart Liberals'.[42] Even after discounting the sanctimonious party talk, the substance seems true enough. Had no money passed hands and no 'undue' influence been exerted, Trollope and Maxwell would apparently have won easily. Trollope could not but have been chagrined by the fact that the Liberals elsewhere had done so well: 222 new members got their seats for the first time, and the Liberals brought in a majority of 112. Gladstone, whom Trollope so admired, became Prime Minister, and the Liberals remained in power until 1874.

Waltham must never have seemed more pleasant than after his two weeks in Beverley. By Friday he was riding to the hounds again, and telling his hunting friend Anna Steele that 'as for the election, I let that run like water off a ducks back'. He admitted a grievance about South Essex, but a 'walkover for the county was too good a thing for me to expect. I shall have another fly at it somewhere some day, unless I feel myself to be growing too old.'[43] Thackeray had said that he took his election defeat at Oxford as the English schoolboy does his floggings, 'sullenly and in silence'.[44] Similarly, Trollope had no hand in bringing the petition against the election results. That was the work of Liberal Beverley townsmen. The trial was held in March 1869 before Baron Samuel Martin. The judge found 104 persons guilty of corrupt election practices (the worst offender being a local draper) and declared the election void.[45] Trollope was not called to testify. Nor was he anxious to appear before the Parliamentary Commission inquiring into bribery at Beverley. He told an official of the commission beforehand, 'I cannot imagine that I have anything to tell the commissioners, which will be worth their hearing.'[46] The commission, sitting at Beverley from 24 August to 17 November 1869, heard from 700 witnesses and uncovered a long, dreary history of corruption; it was revealed, for example, that in the prior six elections, all had been corrupt except that of 1854, when, as *The Times* put it, an honest election had taken place quite by 'accident'.[47] Trollope was called to give evidence on 3 September. He testified that he had paid £400 in all. Yes, he had been told that the parliamentary election results 'might rely a good deal on the issue of the municipal election'; it had been 'hinted' to him that money had been spent on the municipal, but he had been assured that 'every shilling' of his own money had been used in legal ways: 'To my knowledge,' Trollope said, 'none of the money was used to corrupt the electors, either by money or beer, or any other way.' As if in proof, he added, 'I stood at the bottom of the poll.' The commission declared itself satisfied that neither Trollope nor Maxwell had been parties 'directly or indirectly to bribery'. The Borough of Beverley, which first returned Members to Parliament in 1295, was disfranchised. Sir Henry Edwards was later tried for illegal election practices but acquitted.[48]

Trollope said he did 'not altogether regret' his attempt to sit in Parliament for Beverley. Perhaps Sir Henry could have been relegated to private life without such trouble and £400 on Trollope's part, and without the 'fortnight of misery', but he flattered himself that he had done some good: 'nothing could be worse, nothing more unpatriotic, nothing more absolutely opposed to the system of representative government' than the ingrained election practices of Beverley. There had been 'something grand in the scorn with which a leading Liberal there turned up his nose at me when I told him that there should be no bribery, no treating, not even a pot of beer on our side!' To have had a part in putting an end to crooked electioneering was a satisfaction.[49]

What he had seen first hand of elections was too good not to use in his fiction. But not immediately. First he wrote a short novel, *Sir Harry Hotspur of Humblethwaite*, which he had probably been building in his mind at the time, and then, in April 1869, began *Ralph the Heir* in which he took his revenge on Beverley. There had been other elections in Trollope: in *The Three Clerks, Doctor Thorne, Can You Forgive her?, Rachel Ray*, and *Phineas Finn*. But the election scenes in *Ralph the Heir*, presented with a Dickensian comic liveliness unlike Trollope's usual wont, are far richer in detail; they have also a new seriousness. The corruption is real, and genuinely harmful.

In the character of Sir Thomas Underwood, the best thing in the book, Trollope presented a disguised self-portrait of himself as aspiring politician, a picture blurred by deliberate and ironic dissimilarities that make Sir Thomas ostensibly a man radically different from his creator. Sir Thomas Underwood is played out, debilitated by life: 'there are men who love work, who revel in that, who attack it daily with renewed energy, almost wallowing in it, greedy of work, who go to it almost as the drunkard goes to his bottle, or the gambler to his gaming-table. . . . But such a one was not Sir Thomas.' Underwood, moreover, is a blocked writer, forever contemplating a life of Bacon, going 'as it were, round and round the thing, never touching it', never writing a word.*[50] In politics, Sir Thomas is a staunch Conservative. But like Trollope, when invited to stand for Parliament, he is unable to resist the temptation despite disturbing worries and doubts; and he takes himself to the borough of Percycross, which, as Trollope admitted in *An Autobiography*, is 'one and the same place' with Beverley.[51] Like Trollope, Sir Thomas is warned by a 'learned pundit', in the precise words given in *An Autobiography*, that he will waste his money and lose the election, that the victors will be unseated by petition and the borough ultimately disfranchised. Like Trollope, he comes to despise his vulgar and venal supporters; utterly out of his element in the borough, he is tempted to withdraw. His Conservative colleague, the incumbent, Mr Griffenbottom, a thoroughly corrupt old Tory who has spent 'a treasure' on the borough, and for whom Sir Thomas develops an intense dislike, is a scarcely disguised Sir Henry Edwards. The Conservatives' chief agent, Mr Trigger, is Sir Henry's unscrupulous and dishonest agent, but Trollope's own supporters provided models for the committee that backs Griffenbottom and Underwood. When Underwood insists that no money be spent improperly, he is greeted with knowing smiles. Trigger is tempted to tell him he is meddling with matters that do not concern him. One of his committee, Mr Pile, becomes 'sick' at the very mention of 'purity' in elections: 'There was to him something absolutely mean and ignoble in the idea of a man coming forward to represent a borough in Parliament without paying the regular fees,' that is, bribes. 'Why', he asks Underwood, 'should a poor man lose a day's wages for the sake of making you a Parliament man?' The Wesleyan minister with a 'soft, greasy voice', Mr Pabsby, foremost among the 'horseleaches' who want money favours from incumbents, is Trollope's jab at Canon Birtwhistle, who had called him an enemy of the Protestant Church. One of Underwood's opponents on the Liberal side, Moggs the radical, experiences some of Trollope's difficulties. He finds people at Percycross 'more anxious to teach him than to receive his political lessons'; he feels he is 'a cat's-paw, brought there for certain objects which were not his objects—because they wanted money, and some one who would be fool enough to fight a losing battle'.[52] And Moggs, like Trollope, would not give as much as a glass of beer. The Conservatives do a great deal of bribing, behind Sir

---

* James Spedding—of whose industrious but drawn-out work on Bacon Trollope must have known—published Bacon's *Works* (7 vols., 1857–9) and *Life and Letters of Francis Bacon* (7 vols., 1861–74) and wrote *Life and Times of Bacon* (1878).[53]

Thomas's back. As at Beverley, the polls show the two Liberals ahead in the first hour of voting but in the end the Conservatives have won, the ineffable Griffenbottom/Edwards at the top of the poll, with Sir Thomas coming in second.

Sir Thomas has a worse time of it than had Trollope: he has his arm broken in the mêlée at the hustings and, though no one considered him guilty of bribery, he has to undergo the 'purgatory' of the petition trial, and the humiliation of being unseated. Underwood is extremely shy, thin-skinned and sensitive; Trollope had much the same disposition, but he dealt with it through his bluff, loud, barking, aggressive manner. But Underwood's thoughts at times closely parallel Trollope's: 'What excuse had he for placing himself in contact with such filth? Of what childishness had he not been the victim when he allowed himself to dream that he . . . could go among such impurity as he had found at Percycross, and come out, still clean and yet triumphant?' The narrator, remarking on Sir Thomas's discouragement, says, 'There come upon us all as we grow up in years, hours in which it is impossible to keep down the conviction that everything is vanity, that the life past is vain from folly, and that the life to come must be vain from impotence.'54 Such a passage points up a side of Trollope that it is easy to ignore in the midst of his whirlwind life and his blustery social behaviour, but he was also much given to dark thoughts. He is said to have told Millais: 'It is, I suppose, some weakness of temperament that makes me, without intelligible cause, such a pessimist at heart.' Escott said that Trollope had fits of despondency and melancholy, that his abrupt and at times imperious manner 'concealed an almost feminine sensibility to the opinions of others, a self-consciousness altogether abnormal in a seasoned and practical man of the world'; that he harboured so strong a desire for approbation from strangers and friends alike that the inevitable disappointment of this desire 'pained and ruffled him beyond his power to conceal'. The experience of Beverley did not embitter Trollope, though it must have brought out his pessimism and that 'genial air of grievance against the world in general, and those who personally valued him in particular' that his physician and friend Sir Richard Quain attributed to him.55

Ralph the Heir got generally favourable reviews, Hutton remarking that 'no episode of Mr. Trollope's ever surpassed in ability the episode of the Percycross election and the election petition'. *The Times* said that with Dickens departed, no one could have written of the electioneering experiences 'so humorously and so truthfully as Mr. Trollope'.56 Trollope himself thought the book 'one of the worst' he had written except for the election scenes.⁵⁷ But it was clearly a book he had wanted to write. He would later have another go at Sir Henry Edwards, a more sober account of election bribery, in *Phineas Redux*, where he caricatures him as Mr Browborough, a corrupt MP who, like Edwards, is put on trial for bribery but not convicted.

22

Other Politics

TROLLOPE'S sons were still unsettled in their lives. Fred had worked on sheep stations in Australia for three years, first at Barratta station near Deniliquin and later in Victoria. As agreed, he returned home to England in December 1868, had a full season's hunting with his father, and then, as 'his purpose was fixed', in the spring emigrated for good to Australia. With money from his father—something around £7,000—Fred bought and developed a sheep station, some 27,000 acres near Grenfell in New South Wales.[1]

As far back as 1864, shortly after Harry had left school at Bradfield, Trollope had unsuccessfully tried to get him—through Lord Houghton—a position in the Foreign Office or another branch of the government service (after first having had him study for eight months in Italy, supplemented by private tutoring in England and in Paris). Then Harry had read law with Montague Hughes Cookson at Lincoln's Inn and in June 1869 had been called to the Bar. He was 23. But Anthony, son of a failed barrister and unrelenting satirist of lawyers in his fiction, was not, as it turned out, to have a son a practising barrister. Just at this time another possible opening for Harry appeared. Frederic Chapman needed a partner who would bring some capital into Chapman & Hall. A Trollope family 'council' weighed a career for Harry in publishing against the 'terrible uncertainty of the Bar'. Trollope probably had as much to do with the decision as Harry himself; in any case, in August 1869 Trollope paid £10,000 for Harry's partnership, one that gave him in effect a one-third interest in Chapman & Hall. Trollope had, he told Lewes, 'an immense deal of trouble in arranging it.' Chapman & Hall, he added, 'is a fine business which has been awfully ill used by want of sufficient work and sufficient capital'. Trollope told Blackwood, who probably offered advice in the matter, that 'Harry is hard at work and comes home freighted with Mss. What he does with them I dont know; but I feel glad that I am not an author publishing with Chapman & Hall as I fancy he goes to sleep over them with a pipe in his mouth.'²

Eighteen sixty-nine, an anxious year for Trollope the parent, demonstrated the great range of Trollope the novelist: in March appeared the book edition of *Phineas Finn* and in May that of *He Knew He Was Right*. There was also a feeble reminder of the last and finest of the Barsetshire novels in the form of a three-act comedy *Did He Steal It?*, which John Hollingshead of the Gaiety Theatre persuaded Trollope to devise from the Crawley plot of *The Last Chronicle*. Fortunately Hollingshead recognized that it would fail, and Trollope accepted the verdict. Although the play was not performed or published, Trollope had it privately printed by Virtue, probably so as to make it easily readable by Hollingshead. With the narrator's disappearance all flavour of Trollope vanished; the dialogue was clumsy; Crawley was changed into a schoolmaster, and his words 'Peace, woman', from the most famous scene in the novel, are said not to Mrs Proudie but to a local magistrate's wife. People who admired the novel would have been dismayed.³

The Barsetshire novels had been concluded, but that county (already strongly connected to the world of contemporary politics in *Framley Parsonage*) was to reappear occasionally in the series of political novels upon which he had embarked. In *Phineas Finn* Trollope had for the first time set out to write 'a parliamentary story'. Of course *Phineas Finn* was only a 'semi-political' novel; for his readers' sake he put in love, intrigue, and sport, and peopled the novel with witty, bright, complex women, Lady Laura Standish, Violet Effingham, Lady Glencora, and Madame Max Goesler. But his intention was to be political, and he strove for more verisimilitude. He wanted to become 'conversant with the ways and doings of the House', and, having failed to gain a seat in Parliament, he went now to the Speaker of the House and begged a pass to the gallery. He took his seat there faithfully for a couple of months, long enough, he said, 'to enable me often to be very tired,—and, as I have been assured by members, to talk of the proceedings almost as well as though Fortune had enabled me to fall asleep within the House itself'.⁴

Phineas Finn is played out against the background of agitation for and passage of the Second Reform Bill. Gladstone's moderate Reform Bill had been defeated in June 1866, largely through the opposition of Robert Lowe and his Whig and Liberal followers. When Trollope began writing the novel in November 1866, Russell and Gladstone were out of office,

Derby was Prime Minister and Disraeli Chancellor of the Exchequer. The following February, Disraeli introduced a Tory-sponsored bill more radical than the earlier Liberal one, doing so with help of certain Members of the Opposition, in a move considered by Trollope and others as the height of opportunism. (Lord Carnarvon and two other members of the cabinet resigned when household suffrage was made part of the bill on 2 March.) In the novel Trollope does not follow these events literally; instead, he has the Liberals in office and the chief stumbling block to the Reform Bill come not from the Conservatives, nor the Cagliostro-like Daubeny (Disraeli), nor the defecting Liberals, but from the radicals, led by Turnbull (Bright). Described in the novel as the 'great radical', and the 'most popular politician in the country' among workers, Turnbull uncompromisingly ties reform to other demands, most notably the ballot and suppression of certain rotten boroughs. (Turnbull also espouses manhood suffrage, the 'reduction of the standing army till there should be no standing army', the political movements in America—for which he has 'an almost idolatrous admiration'—free trade 'in everything except malt', and the 'absolute extinction of a State Church'.5) With his 'mob', his enormous petition for the ballot, and his collusion with Daubeny (Disraeli) on the boroughs issue, Turnbull keeps handing the government defeats, enough to make old Mr Mildmay (Russell) retire and hand the reins of the Liberal party over to Gresham (Gladstone); but the Reform Bill passes, and by the hand of the Liberal party. Perhaps the actual facts were almost too strange for Trollope's kind of fiction, or, more likely, he had his story-line pretty much in mind before the strange events of February 1867 occurred—the novel was exactly half-finished at that time. In any case, Trollope would hold off incorporating Daubeny/Disraeli's audacious behaviour of keeping power by passing the Opposition's agenda into law until *Phineas Redux*, written some four years later.

The novel is largely about party loyalty, and Finn, a fledgling but fast-rising politician, eventually resigns his seat in Parliament because he votes according to his conscience on Irish tenant rights, in opposition to his party. Trollope's political sympathies with his hero come through here, as he himself supported moderate tenant rights (those advocated in the novel are sufficiently vague). Finn, like Trollope, opposes the ballot, on which subject Mr Monk, another sometime-spokesman for Trollope's views, says, 'Every man possessed of the franchise should dare to have and to express a political opinion of his own. . . . otherwise the franchise is not worth having.' And Finn continually argues within himself, 'Could a man be honest in Parliament, and yet abandon all idea of independence?'6 a question that Trollope says would have worried him had he himself got into Parliament: he feared that he was too 'visionary' to have become a practical political man, too impatient, too unwilling to conform. Should he have had a grievance—say with reference to 'over-taxed catchup'—he 'would always be flinging' that grievance in the face of the Chancellor of the Exchequer.⁷ One can believe it.

The book did not meet with the good press that his Barsetshire novels enjoyed. His great supporter, Hutton, in the *Spectator*, said that although it was superior to the 'lower level' of his work—novels such as *Miss Mackenzie* and *Rachel Ray*—it did not come up to *The Small House* or *Framley Parsonage* and was far below *The Last Chronicle*. He found the whole book 'tame', including the parliamentary life (ironically enough, in view of Trollope's own probable indebtedness to Hutton's *Studies in Parliament*—especially its characterization of Bright). The *Saturday* felt Trollope had strayed away from his real *métier*: 'Nobody can draw a clergyman better, and he is perhaps the most trustworthy male lecturer living on the mental anatomy of young ladies'; but the kind of 'light castigation' visited upon clerics and young women would not do for contemporary statesmen: 'If you throw mud at them at all, you had better throw it vigorously, or nobody will notice you.' Trollope's treatment of politicians is 'inoffensive and colourless' except for Turnbull/Bright: 'It is only the contemplation of Mr. Bright that acts upon Mr. Trollope as a red rag upon a bull.' Turnbull is invariably 'arrogant and devilishly cunning'; but he makes dull speeches—'surely an unpardonable solecism'. Trollope 'is cruelly careful that the veriest child shall not fail to recognize his pet aversion under the *alias* he has given him. With historical and needlessly elaborate minuteness [Trollope] describes his robustness, age, hair, height, gait, complexion, eyes, nose, lips, coat, trowsers, and waistcoat'; Turnbull is slow to perceive a joke, dictatorial, quarrelsome, sermonizing; indeed 'the future historian may refer to [this novel] to discover what was the material of which Mr. Bright's waistcoats were made'.⁸

Shortly after these reviews, the *Daily Telegraph*, in a leading article, attacked Trollope for drawing portraits of politicians, especially of Bright in Turnbull. Was it right for Trollope to put into a novel 'malignant little touches professing to lift the veil of private life' of the politician? Trollope fired back a somewhat disingenuous letter to the *Telegraph* the same day, in which he vigorously denied the accusation: in Turnbull, he wrote, 'I depicted Mr. Bright neither in his private or public character; and I cannot imagine how any likeness justifying such a charge against me can be found. The character that I have drawn has no resemblance to [Bright]. . . . It was my object to depict a turbulent demagogue.' Trollope went so far as to say that he deliberately tried to avoid any likeness to an actual politician of the day but had been 'unlucky,—as the charge brought by you against me shows'.⁹ In *An Autobiography* Trollope claimed that his statesmen—he mentions Brock, de Terrier, Monk, Gresham, Daubeny—'had been more or less portraits, not of living men, but of living political characters'. In a private letter to Mary Holmes, written a few months after completing the *Autobiography*, Trollope admitted that well-known political men such as Disraeli and Gladstone had been used as 'models' for the fictitious Daubeny and Gresham, but only as to their 'political tenets. There is nothing of personal characteristic here.'¹⁰ Trollope may have half-believed this to be the case, but he must have known as well as the next man that political behaviour is often the result of 'personal characteristics'; certainly Daubeny has all the daring and what Trollope considered the un-scrupulousness of the hated 'conjuror' and 'Cagliostro' Disraeli. Trollope's readers believed the Phineas Finn story was a *roman-à-clef*.* The very names Daubeny and Gresham are undisguisedly close to Disraeli and Gladstone; 'Daubeny' is even shortened to 'Dubby' occasionally. Trollope's denial in the *Daily Telegraph* is less than candid. He must have argued the matter vociferously many times, publicly insisting—although he privately admitted to drawing upon the 'political character' of real men—that there was nothing of their personal characteristics in the portraits. No one believed him.

He Knew He Was Right was published in May, Virtue having transferred the book rights to Strahan. Its claustrophobic atmosphere makes an extraordinary contrast to the public life of the 'parliamentary story' published two months earlier. The novel's main story, among the many sub-stories, told of the deterioration of Louis Trevelyan into madness from his combined unwillingness to allow his judgement to be questioned and his possessive sexual jealousy towards his wife. Henry James said that 'the long, slow progress of the conjugal wreck of Louis Trevelyan and his wife . . . arrives at last at an impressive completeness of misery. It is the history of an accidental rupture between two stiff-necked and ungracious people—"the little rift within the lute"—which widens at last into a gulf of

* Phineas himself was thought by some of Trollope's contemporaries to be taken from two originals, John Pope Hennessy, an Irishman from Cork who had a meteoric career in Parliament, and Joe Parkinson, an English journalist of impressive physical presence and captivating social manners, who married a millionaire's daughter. Another possibility is Chester Parkinson Fortescue, later Lord Carlingford, a young handsome Irish MP, who actually held offices attained by Finn, Under-Secretary for the Colonies and Chief Secretary for Ireland.¹¹

anguish.'[12] Trollope may have been prompted to write this tale of a 'modern Othello' by a review article entitled 'Madness in Literature' that appeared in the *Spectator* of 3 February 1866. The writer deplored the attributing in fiction of strong passions to madness, the currency of which practice he blamed on M. E. Braddon; he twice suggested that Trollope might be able to 'paint the morbid passion [of Othello] in its naturalistic nineteenth-century dress'.[13] Trollope thought—erratically—that in no other work had he fallen 'more completely short of my own intention than in this story'. He had failed, he said, to create sympathy for the unfortunate Trevelyan. The Exeter episodes involving old Miss Stanbury he considered good, but a novel weak in its main story could not be 'redeemed by the vitality of subordinate characters'.[14] Miss Stanbury—based on his aunt Fanny Bent—is indeed the best of his benign tyrants: a Tory of the old school, to whom 'all change was hateful and unnecessary', she disowns her nephew Hugh Stanbury because he writes for a penny newspaper, a journal she considered 'radical incendiary stuff, printed with ink that stinks, on paper made of straw'. Hugh Stanbury, it is worth noting, is another partial self-portrait: a product of Harrow, 30, 'five feet ten, with shoulders more than broad in proportion, stout limbed, rather awkward of his gait, with large feet and hands . . . [and] a broad, but by no means ugly, nose. . . . Hugh Stanbury was reputed to be somewhat hot in spirit and manner. He would be very sage in manner, pounding down his ideas on politics, religion, or social life with his fist as well as his voice. He was quick, perhaps, at making antipathies, and quick, too, in making friendships; impressionable, demonstrative, eager, rapid in his movements,— sometimes to the great detriment of his shins and knuckles; and he possessed the sweetest temper that was ever given to a man for the blessing of a woman.' Among his newspaper efforts were 'two or three rather stinging articles . . . as "to the assumed merits and actual demerits of the clergy of the Church of England"'.[15] Like Trollope, Stanbury is continually defending literature as a 'profession'.

The reviews of *He Knew He Was Right* were not particularly good, though they are not as harsh as Trollope's own verdict. Hutton was unusually severe. He thought the second volume especially wearisome, and that Trollope had wandered from his course which had at first been to make Trevelyan's wife Emily in her steely haughtiness more to blame for the tragedy; on the other hand, Miss Stanbury at Exeter Hutton deemed 'absolutely perfect', and Dorothy Stanbury the 'most delicate and fascinating of all Mr. Trollope's women'. *The Times* said the story was 'generally very interesting', but that Trollope's novels, including this one, 'have no aesthetic purpose; they mean nothing more than they say' and require little mental activity on the part of the reader; the simple fare that Trollope provides 'needs no educated taste, but only a healthy appetite'; this novel disappointed after the Barsetshire series; only the character of Bozzle the vulgar detective was truly remarkable, a welcome antidote to the romanticizing of the detective by other writers. The *British Quarterly Review* complained of Trollope's writing as 'uncompromisingly realistic' and contended that it was 'no justification of this Pre-Raphaelitism that it is true to life'; Art ought to elevate life, idealize it. And why this 'morbid infatuation' with conjugal infidelity? There was the usual marvelling at Trollope's fecundity, *The Times* remarking that his novels 'almost tread each other down'; like Nelson longing for a whole *Gazette*, Trollope had longed for a whole library of his own, and seemed to be getting his wish. Trollope reminded one of 'the conjuror who draws tape out of his mouth, snipping it at intervals, as long as anyone chooses to look at him. It is all the same, and cut in any lengths you please . . . you pay your money and take your choice.' The *Saturday Review*, which thought *He Knew He Was Right* 'on the whole rather superior' to Trollope's usual work, suggested that the library shelf in the British Museum containing his works should be revered as 'one of the most singular monuments we know of human industry'.[16]

The reviewers were silent, oddly, on one of the book's prominent emphases, that of 'the woman question'. Women's rights, or the want of them, in regard to marriage, property, work, and the franchise were much in the air at the time. Trollope's views on women's rights can be represented as the ordinary conservatism common in his day, especially if quoted selectively; and, at bottom, at least in theory, he believed that a woman's first purpose in life was to 'fall in love, marry the man, have two children, and live happy ever afterwards'.[17]

This conservative view Trollope propounded chiefly in his non-fiction. In *North America*, for example, he quipped of women's rights that 'the best right a woman has is the right to a husband'; he was willing to admit the 'conclusive' logic of arguments for granting women the vote, but, believing that female suffrage would disturb the 'mutual good relations between men and women', zanily advocated that women exercise the vote in alternate years with men.[18] Trollope's most detailed treatment of women's rights came in a lecture, 'Higher Education of Women', which he gave in various provincial towns in the late 1860s and early 1870s (he once claimed that he deserved credit for 'infinite pluck' for giving it to audiences of young women).[19] 'We cannot', he asserted, 'alter our natures'; 'we do not . . . want to assimilate men and women'; and if society attempts to do so, a 'higher law' would prevent it; Trollope opposed, even as he admired, the woman who proposed to do 'the work of the world', that is, man's work.* She was 'kicking against the pricks'. It was the duty of men to earn bread, and of women to 'guard and distribute it'. That was the lesson of nature, and was 'seen everywhere,—in all the attributes, organs, capabilities, and gifts of the two sexes'. Englishmen ought not to consider giving girls and boys the same education; they should not even be instructed under the same roof; what was good for the one was not good for the other. Men who advocated granting women equality with men in regard to political privileges, social standing, or education—a clear reference to Mill and his followers—were in the position of the good-natured bear who tried to drive the fly from his sleeping friend's face and knocked out his brains. Women's education had made great strides, Trollope insisted, since the time of Charles II; he himself had 'generally found the conversation of an Englishwoman of four-and-twenty to be superior to that of a man of the same age'; he was in favour of 'higher education' for women, but it was to be self-administered, at home, through reading and study. The great fault was that young 'emancipated' ladies spent all their free time reading novels; young women between the ages of 18 and 25, wanting to be 'settled'—married—must practise self-discipline, must turn to their Hallam and their German dictionaries, even their Shakespeare and Longfellow. Granting he was cutting his own throat here, he urged that novels be reserved for recreational reading; otherwise they became an opiate. Finally, young ladies ought to emulate their grandmothers who were 'very famous at the making of puddings and baking of pies'.[20]

On the other hand, when creating fictional characters, Trollope shows himself highly sensitive to wrongs done to women by society's rules and conventions. When writing fiction he seems able to detach himself from his opinions. In *He Knew He Was Right*, a novel of the struggle for 'mastery' in a marriage, Trollope puts acute observations into the mouths of the various women characters. Emily Trevelyan, the wife from whom Trevelyan separates himself, fears her husband will take their child from her. Everyone believes he is legally justified, that Trevelyan, as the man, has 'the power of doing as he pleased' in regard to their child. 'It is a very

---

* Trollope had contributed gratis two stories, 'Miss Ophelia Gledd'—the tale with a Kate Field-like heroine—and 'The Journey to Panama', for collections published by Emily Faithfull, a feminist who had established the Victoria Press, a publishing house staffed entirely by women; but he seems to have regarded doing so as a kind of friendly lark, done chiefly for the sake of Emily Faithfull herself.[21]

poor thing to be a woman,' she says to her sister Nora. 'It is perhaps better than being a dog,' Nora answers, 'but, of course, we can't compare ourselves to men.' Emily replies, 'It would be better to be a dog. One wouldn't have to suffer so much.' And Nora herself continually chafes under the restraints of her lot as a woman; she had been brought from the Mandarin Islands to live with Emily and her husband so that she might place herself in the marriage market: 'For a woman such as herself there was no path open to her energy, other than that of getting a husband. Nora Rowley thought of all this till she was almost sick of the prospect of her life.'[22] Tough-minded, she determines to fight her own battles, make her own decisions, choose her own man, reject whom she will, go into lodgings alone if necessary. Even the shy, usually retreating Dorothy Stanbury speaks up. She says that certain women do not seem to serve any purpose; they don't belong to anybody, and they don't seem to do any good:

'They're just nobodies. They are not anything particular to anybody, and so they go on living till they die. . . . A man who is a nobody can perhaps make himself somebody,—or, at any rate, he can try; but a woman has no means of trying. She is a nobody, and a nobody she must remain. She has her clothes and her food, but she isn't wanted anywhere. People put up with her, and that is about the best of her luck. If she were to die somebody perhaps would be sorry for her, but nobody would be worse off. She doesn't earn anything or do any good. She is just there and that is all.'

Dorothy's speech surprises her suitor, Brook Burgess, who admits that one does see such women 'now and then'. 'There are hundreds of them,' Dorothy fires back. As it happens, her own sister, Priscilla, is a 'nobody', a 'superfluous' woman for whom Trollope manages to create sympathy in spite of her acerbic personality. She is stubbornly brave and independent in her loneliness. Asked by Emily Trevelyan if she is 'contented', she answers:

'Well, no; I can't say that I am contented. . . . Should my mother die . . . I should be utterly alone in the world. Providence, or whatever you call it, has made me a lady after a fashion, so that I can't live with the ploughmen's wives, and at the same time has so used me in other respects that I can't live with anybody else.'
    'Why should you not get married?'
    'Who would have me? And if I had a husband I should want a good one,—a man with a head on his shoulders, and a heart. Even if I were young and good-looking, or rich, I doubt whether I could please myself. As it is I am as likely to be taken bodily into heaven, as to become any man's wife.'

When her sister asserts that women are altogether dependent on men, Priscilla says, 'I manage to get on somehow.' When told that 'the men-cooks are the best, and the men-tailors, and the men who wait at tables, and the men-poets, and the men-painters, and the men-nurses. All the things that women do, men do better,' Priscilla retorts, 'There are two things they can't do. . . . They can't suckle babies, and they can't forget themselves.'[23]

Instances from other novels abound in sympathetic presentation of the dependent position of women. In *The Belton Estate*, for example, Clara Amedroz says to Captain Aylmer that she should like to be able to do as she pleases, but of course 'women—women, that is of my age—are such slaves! We are forced to give an obedience for which we can see no cause, and for which we can understand no necessity.' Women, she insists, are unjustifiably dependent. 'Dependence is a disagreeable word,' Aylmer answers, 'and one never quite knows what it means.' 'If you were a woman you'd know,' she tells him. Why must she stay at home and listen to her aunt read sermons on Sunday? Why should not she do as she pleases? Go out to the club? She tells her aunt, 'I think it would be well if all single women were strangled by the time they are thirty.'[24] Especially in the later novels of the Palliser series did Trollope treat of intelligent women whose lot in life is frustrated by their position in society: Lady Glencora, Madame Max Goesler, both successful after a fashion, and Lady Laura Kennedy and Lady Mabel Grex, both tragic figures.

None the less, Trollope had no patience with political campaigns for women's rights, and in *He Knew He Was Right* where he introduced an American feminist, Wallachia Petrie, he descended to caricature and retreated into his conventional stance: Wallachia is a 'republican virago, with a red nose'; she had had success in 'that fatal triumph of a lecture on the joint rights of men and women, and it had rendered poor Wallachia Petrie unfit for ordinary society.' She is a fatuous, absurd bore, a 'poetess' (called 'the Republican Browning' for no reason other than her admiration for the Brownings), whom everyone avoids as much as possible. She couples her feminism with a strongly republican anti-British strain, and she fiercely opposes her friend Caroline Spalding's marriage to an English lord, named Glascock. English aristocrats, Petrie says, are 'dishonest, and rotten at the core'; 'Their country . . . is a game played out, while we [Americans] are still breasting the hill with our young lungs full of air'; she tells Caroline that once married to an Englishman, 'If you have a baby, they'll let you go and see it two or three times a day. I don't suppose you will be allowed to nurse it, because they never do in England. You have read what the Saturday Review says' (a reference to anti-feminist articles on women's rights by Mrs Eliza Lynn Linton appearing while Trollope was writing the novel; she strongly advocated mothers' breast-feeding their children).[25] For Wallachia Petrie, 'it was a thing very terrible that [Caroline] the chosen one of her heart should prefer the career of an English lord's wife to that of an American citizenness, with all manner of capability for female voting, female speech-making, female poetising, and, perhaps, female political action before her.' Wallachia leaves Florence before the wedding, 'and returned alone to the land of liberty'. 'Sour grapes,' says Glascock. The narrator remarks, 'There are certain forms of the American female so dreadful that no wise man would wilfully come in contact with them.'[26]

Wallachia Petrie had some successors in Trollope's fiction, most notably in characters associated with the 'Female Disabilities Institute' in *Is He Popenjoy?*, written 1874–5, at a time when women's rights might have been seen as making quicker advances than Trollope liked. When Trollope reached for caricature he tended to be heavy-handed. The German women's rights lecturer Baroness Banmann (based perhaps on Lydia Becker, born in Manchester of German parents, an outspoken orator against women's disabilities in the 1870s)[27] is 'a very stout woman, about fifty, with a double chin, a considerable moustache, a low broad forehead, and bright, round, black eyes, very far apart. . . . [She] was dressed in a black stuff gown, with a cloth jacket buttoned up to the neck, which hardly gave to her copious bust that appearance of manly firmness which the occasion almost required.' Addressing mixed audiences, the Baroness 'seemed to have no hesitation in speaking of man generally as a foul worm who ought to be put down and kept under, and merely allowed to be the father of children'. Her rival lecturer is the very thin, bespectacled American, 'Miss Doctor' Olivia Q. Fleabody (the name a play on Elizabeth Peabody, an American reformer), in whose case 'the jacket and collars were quite successful'. Her audience at the Institute is made up of 'strongly-visaged spinsters and mutinous wives, who twice a week were worked up by Dr. Fleabody to a full belief that a glorious era was at hand in which women would be chosen by constituencies, would wag their heads in courts of law, would buy and sell in Capel Court, and have balances at their bankers'.[28] Fleabody opportunistically makes a fortune at lecturing; the baroness turns out to be a complete fraud, eventually absconding with £1,000 given her by a weak-minded old man to pursue her court battle against the Institute.

Trollope found himself arguing about Wallachia Petrie with Kate Field.

vould be wrong to assert that he patterned Wallachia on Kate, though
there were some correspondences. Trollope wrote to her on 15 April 1870,
'I never said you were like W. Petrie. I said that that young woman did not
entertain a single opinion on public matters which you could repudiate,—
and that she was only absurd in her mode of expressing them.' This
explanation must have done little towards mollifying Kate, who would
have thought some of Wallachia Petrie's public opinions ridiculous,
irrespective of her manner. Since Trollope had last seen Kate in 1868, she
had entered upon a very successful career as a lecturer. She made a
brilliant début, with a talk called 'Women in the Lyceum', at Chickering
Hall, Boston, in March 1869; the press was very good (James T. Fields said
it was 'the most successful début that he ever saw'); her voice was deemed
'exceptionally musical, sweet, and agreeable', her manner 'refined'. Her
personal beauty and exquisite dress were often remarked upon. William
Lloyd Garrison said it was worth the price of admission merely to see Kate
Field on the platform. Various people, including Henry James, Senior
(who addressed her as 'Blessed child') and Oliver Wendell Holmes, urged
her on. With endorsement from such Boston Brahmins, whose 'acknowledged favorite' she had been for years, Kate took to speaking around the
country. She lectured in major cities like New York, Washington, and
Chicago, and in hundreds of small towns. A good business woman, she was
soon able to pay off her debts and to support her mother more comfortably.
When she wrote and told Trollope something of her successes, including
her having made $8,000, his return letter, now lost, must have, as usual,
said the wrong things, for it provoked another from her, which made him
try to explain what he had meant: he denied that he found fault with her for
lecturing; he congratulated her on making so much money, adding the
characteristic but useless rider that he was sure that however she earned
money 'it will be both honest and honourable'; he did not mean to deride
lecturing, it was just that he thought writing 'nicer for either man or
woman;—but that perhaps comes from the fact that I am better paid for
writing than for lecturing'. He told her he would love to hear her lecture,
but would like the privilege of going home to supper with her afterwards
and being 'allowed to express my opinion freely'. He had evidently also
been again at her to marry, and she 'flies' out at him in return. He did not,
he claimed, advise her to marry someone whom she did not care for: 'You
tell me I don't know you. I think I do,—as to character & mind.' What he
meant to say was that she should not bind herself 'to an idea of personal
independence' in such a way as to rule out marriage. He believed that 'at
any rate in middle life, married people have a better time than old

bachelors and spinsters.' (Kate apparently did distrust the possibilities of married happiness. She told Lilian Whiting that twice in her life she had been in love, and twice, without really knowing why, she shrank from marriage: 'I need a clear head to accomplish the work I must do in this world, and nothing so unfits a sensitive nature for mental exertion as emotional intensities'; she told her aunt that the marriages she knew of seemed 'terrible grinds', that she had had 'several escapes from matrimony, for which I thank God. . . . I believe in love. I don't believe in being tied to a man whom I cease to love. . . . My observation makes me afraid of lifelong experiments.') Finally, Kate had offered to write an article for *Saint Pauls* on her great favourite, the actor Charles Albert Fechter. Trollope explained how his control over the Magazine was ending, but that in any case, 'I myself hate Fechter as an actor, and I think the people here are sick of him.'[29] She took her material to the *Atlantic Monthly*, and there published two articles later in the year. Between Trollope and Kate there continued the pattern of frankness carried to the point of opposition; it almost seems as if there were some sharp hostility beneath the affection.

Trollope had irritated Kate the liberated woman by his depiction of Wallachia Petrie. He was himself upset—as a devout rider to hounds—by the admission into the *Fortnightly Review* for October 1869 of the historian Edward Freeman's article attacking the morality of fox-hunting. (The sport was at the height of popularity and Freeman's view was shared by only a small minority.) Trollope considered the article 'almost as the rising of a child against the father'. He had written nothing for the magazine for two and a half years, except for one very short review of George Rooper's *Flood, Field, and Forest*, a book he saw as a light-hearted reply to the French joke that Englishmen in want of recreation say, 'Ah, let us amuse ourselves; let us go and kill something.'[30] But Freeman's charge of immorality he felt obliged to answer. In conversation about such an indictment of hunting he would have blustered and roared, but when he put pen to paper he could remain calm and be reasonably fair to opponents, and his reply to Freeman is an instance of the kind of controlled response one would have expected from Trollope the novelist. One of Freeman's leading arguments was that all fox-hunters shrink from consideration of the moral implication of their sport, their great object being 'to avoid thought upon the subject'. Trollope contended that we are all apt to say such things of our opponents, like the 'eager Protestant [who] believes the Roman Catholic to be what he is because he will not try to open his eyes'.

Freeman twice quoted Cicero's question, 'What delight can the educated man take in such amusement?' (Cicero was referring to the slaughter
of animals on stage), and Trollope, who didn't know Freeman personally,
said he wished he did in order that he might 'hit' him in the same way: did
he play cards, did he read novels, climb Alps, or trundle the 'harmless and
academic bowl'? Was he good at croquet? To almost any recreation one
could put Cicero's question. Non-sporting men were like 'some old ladies
. . . who, living down in the country, think that a London club means
drunkenness, gambling, and wickedness'. The uninitiated reader of Freeman's attack would think that the ordinary English fox-hunter 'is always
riding about the country up to his elbows in fox's blood'. But the *delectatio*,
or pleasure from hunting, while it was various, did not consist in 'a
promiscuous intercourse with the mangled limbs of the quarry'. Rather,
'Men are thrown together who would not otherwise meet. . . . Perhaps of
all the delights of the hunting field conversation is the most general. . . .
A community is formed in which equality prevails, and the man with small
means and no rank holds his own with the lord or the millionaire as he can
nowhere else. . . . City-men learn country lore, and country-men are told
the ways of cities.' Trollope thought he saw a weakness in Freeman's
argument when he denied any difference between bull-baiting and fox-
hunting. 'No man', Trollope avers, 'goes out fox-hunting in order that he
may receive pleasure from pain inflicted . . . and therefore fox-hunting
stands on ground altogether different from that of bull-baiting, in which
the pleasure did consist in looking at the bull's suffering.' Freeman
maintained that he had 'no scruple as to taking life either of man or beast
when real need calls for it'. But what, Trollope asks, was real need? 'Ten or
twenty little animals are killed, away in a wild country in which they can do
no harm, that one lady may have a tippet.' Did she really need it? Not as
much, in Trollope's view, as the country needed the hunt. Moreover, the
fox, as even Freeman admitted, would be extinct but for the sport. The life
of a fox was pleasant as the lives of animals go—until the last ten minutes.
'Is his life as bad as that of a cab-horse, or of a half-starved dog, or of a caged
bird, or of an imprisoned fish?' Freeman, Trollope asserted, had
altogether failed to prove his sweeping assertion that cruelty is 'the
essence of the whole thing'.[31]

Freeman printed a rejoinder, to which Trollope was prepared to reply,
but *Fortnightly* editor John Morley, himself very much against hunting,
called a halt. Other publications took up the controversy; the *Saturday*
came down, though rather gently, against Trollope; Freeman took his case
through two lengthy letters to the *Daily Telegraph* (which supported his

views in a leader). A vigorous correspondence ensued in that paper, including a lofty letter from Ruskin, who reprobated fox-hunting not on the grounds of cruelty—'More pain is caused to the draught-horses of London in an hour by avariciously overloading them, than to all the foxes in England by the hunts of the year'—but rather because fox-hunting 'wastes the time, misapplies the energy, exhausts the wealth, narrows the capacity, debases the taste, and abates the honour of the upper classes of this country'.[32] One can imagine Trollope's disgust at this last from the author of *The Crown of Wild Olive* and *Sesame and Lilies*.

Publishers also proved a source of irritation to Trollope during 1869. In March trouble arose about *The Vicar of Bullhampton*, the novel Trollope had begun in America the previous June and finished by November. His friend E. S. Dallas had solicited the story for *Once A Week*, a flourishing magazine published by Bradbury & Evans, who generously offered to match his highest rate of pay, £2,800, for a novel the length of *The Claverings* (for reasons unknown, the price was eventually reduced to £2,500, apparently by mutual consent and in spite of the fact that it was only a few pages shorter than *The Claverings*). Acknowledging the agreement, Trollope added, almost prophetically, 'Of course it is understood that it is intended for your periodical, Once a Week.' Dallas wrote back, 'Mind I expect a stunner.' The novel was to begin serialization in May, in which month both *Phineas Finn* and *He Knew He Was Right* were to complete their serializations. When in January Dallas asked for a delay in commencing the novel in *Once A Week*, Trollope refused, and Dallas wrote to Trollope that to him it seemed 'a novelty' in the publishing business that an author consider it a grievance when a novel for which he would be paid all the same should be delayed a month or six weeks; Bradbury & Evans, he said, were paying Trollope a 'very large sum' on his recommendation, and he felt it hard on Trollope's part to charge him with breach of faith for asking for a little time to play with. Trollope relented and agreed to a two months' delay, with the novel rescheduled to begin in the first week of July. But worse was to come. In March Dallas wrote that he and the publisher were in 'great perplexity' (and, one suspects, some trepidation): they had bought Victor Hugo's new novel, *L'homme qui rit*, which would have begun in the magazine in January but for the 'incessant corrections of the author'; publication had to be delayed until April, and if Trollope's novel began in July as planned, the two would run side by side for three or four months, which situation, because they would have to increase the number of pages, would be 'death' for the magazine. Would

Trollope, 'like a good fellow', permit publication of *The Vicar of Bull-hampton* in the *Gentleman's Magazine*?33 (Founded in 1731 as a social 'intelligencer' with obituaries, antiquarian notes, and poetry, the *Gentle-man's Magazine* had recently begun publishing undistinguished fiction.34) It was, Dallas told Trollope, 'raised in character' and 'will do you no discredit'. Trollope's answer may have been delivered in person; in any case it has not survived, but in his account in *An Autobiography* he makes clear his 'disgust at this proposition', a disgust arising from a dislike for Hugo's 'pretentious' and unnatural later novels, and from indignation at being asked to make way for 'this sententious French Radical', whose delays had caused the problem.35 *The Vicar of Bullhampton* came out in separate numbers. In July Trollope published in *Saint Pauls* a very negative critique of *L'homme qui rit*, by his friend Juliet Pollock, who called the novel, which Hugo set in the England of Queen Anne, 'a stupendous anachronism', 'a ludicrous and exasperating jumble', written from a '"sell-your-wife-at-Smithfield" point of view'.36

The end of the year also brought a slight disappointment, when Trollope came to sell *The Eustace Diamonds*, the novel he had begun in early December. It was offered to Blackwood on 18 December, to begin appearing in the spring of 1871; Blackwood declined, saying he did not like to make arrangements that far in advance. He might have feared that his friend's price for a long novel would be too high; Trollope mentioned no asking figure in his inquiry to Blackwood, but he had earlier told him that he had no trouble in selling a long novel for £3,000. Trollope then took the 'four-volume' work to Chapman, who gave him £2,500, only a small decline from the £3,200 paid by Virtue for the five-volume *He Knew He Was Right*.37 (In 1873 he would enter agreements of £2,500 for the four-volume *Phineas Redux* and £3,000 for the five-volume *Way We Live Now*.) It is not known whether Trollope suspected that the prices he could command would decrease in the future. But the 1860s had been his period of greatest earning power, his greatest popularity.

Trollope had, during the 1860s, done a modest share of lecturing in London and about the country, talking on the Civil Service, on the American Civil War, on higher education for women, and on 'Politics as a Study for the Common People'. Now, in late January 1870, he planned a swing northward to speak on 'English Prose Fiction as a Rational Amuse-ment'. The lecture, a defence of the morality and usefulness of fiction, with emphasis on his favourites, Scott, Austen, and Thackeray, was a kind of outline of a book he had for years wanted to write but never did. Some of the impetus for this study had been received as far back as 1864 when William Thomson, Archbishop of York, had inveighed against the immorality of fiction. In the lecture Trollope remarked, 'A bishop gets up now and then to lecture against novels;—as I am now getting up to lecture in their defence.' There was present too Trollope's by now customary slap at Carlyle, qualified by fulsome praise (Trollope protesting that 'of all living men I feel perhaps the highest veneration' for Carlyle) but maintaining that Carlyle's assessment of novel writers as among 'the foolishest of existing mortals' had been of all such dispraise 'the most unjust and the most thoughtless'.[38]

Trollope gave the lecture at Hull on 24 January 1870, at Glasgow on the 27th, and at Edinburgh on the 28th, where he arranged to stay with John Blackwood. A 'learned pundit' of Edinburgh had offered him the hospitality of the city, but 'as it [meant] a half-formed introduction to the pickled snakes and a visit to the public library & the like I viewed [it] with horror and did not accept'.[39] This was not his first stay with the Blackwoods. He had visited them at Strathtyrum, Blackwood's home near St Andrews Golf Course, in August 1868 and, at a large dinner given in his honour, had deliberately scandalized the table. A. K. H. Boyd, one of the guests anxious to meet Trollope, found him 'singularly unkempt', his clothes wrinkled and ill-made. Moreover,

he was the only man I had heard swear in decent society for uncounted years. The swearing, which was repeated, was the most disagreeable of all: the actual asseverating, by the Holiest Name, of some trumpery statement.* How could that man have written the well-remembered sentences which had charmed one through these years? Then, by way of making himself pleasant to a gathering of Scotsmen, he proceeded . . . to villipend our beloved Sir Walter. . . . Mr. Trollope said that if any of Sir Walter's novels were offered to any London publisher of the present day, it would be at once rejected. We listened, humbly. Then it was asked whether this was because time had gone on and Sir Walter grown old-fashioned. 'Not a bit: it is just because [his novels] are so dull.'[40]

Trollope, who at times bemoaned dull stretches in Scott, was none the less a staunch admirer; he was putting his audience on; the swearing may also have been calculated to disturb his Scottish hearers. People frequently missed his conversational ironies.

---

* Evidence is contradictory on Trollope's swearing: Edmund Yates, no friend, responding to Boyd's article, declared, 'I do not remember ever having heard Trollope swear. He may have [used the word *damn*], but he certainly was not an habitual swearer.'[41]

Saint Pauls Magazine had never prospered. From the start it had reached at best a circulation of about 10,000, far below the 25,000 Virtue estimated necessary to make it remunerative. But the proprietor was patient, and continued on, hoping for an increase of readership. Virtue's patient but worried conduct is reflected in his response to a letter Trollope wrote to him in December 1868 with regard to future novels for the magazine: *Phineas Finn* was to finish in May of the following year; Trollope would supply another to begin in January 1870 or, if Virtue preferred, he would apply to George Eliot, whose work Trollope estimated would cost about double his own: 'No doubt it would be worth much more than mine. . . . Do not for a moment suppose that there will be any feeling of rivalry between her & me. I should like to do exactly what you think best.' Virtue did not bother to see if George Eliot were interested, and in April 1869 agreed to pay the £2,520 Trollope had named for *Ralph the Heir*. At about that time, Virtue tried to sell the magazine to Chapman & Hall, an arrangement that Trollope would have found agreeable. After this attempt failed, Virtue transferred the magazine in May 1869 to Alexander Strahan, whose business, because of long-standing debts for printing, Virtue largely owned.* Trollope stayed on as editor, but as the magazine continued to lose money, steps had to be taken to economize, and it came as no surprise to Trollope when Virtue told him in January 1870 that Strahan had determined to edit the magazine himself. Virtue said he very much regretted that Trollope and *Saint Pauls* should part company, their relationship had been 'so genial & pleasant', and although he could still exercise 'control' over Strahan, he always declined to do so, as there were many other considerations involved in the curious relationship between the two publishers. Strahan wrote to Trollope, saying that as the magazine was not remunerative and as Trollope had expressed a willingness 'to do whatever might be thought best in its interest', *Saint Pauls* was going to 'edit itself' after the fashion of *Blackwood's*: 'I would never think of making this proposal', Strahan added, 'were the Magazine in a flourishing state.' He trusted Trollope would 'approve of our motives' even if he could not commend the decision.[42] Trollope, though disappointed, did not quarrel with the decision.

In *An Autobiography* Trollope explained that the failure of the magazine had in no way been Virtue's fault. The publisher followed 'every

---

* The free-spending Strahan, ever in money difficulties, had worsened his situation in late 1868 when he added Tennyson to his list by contracting to pay the exorbitant sum of £4,000 per annum for the right to publish his *old* works, and agreeing to take but 5 per cent of the proceeds of new works.[43]

suggestion respecting the magazine that I made to him. If the use of large capital, combined with wide liberality and absolute confidence and perpetual good humour on the part of the proprietor, would have produced success, our magazine certainly would have succeeded.' Trollope says he read all the manuscripts submitted to him, got the services of able people (he also had his share of mediocre talents and unknowns). *Saint Pauls* did not, he believed, fail from bad editing; perhaps it failed because of 'too much editing'—by which he meant that he accepted articles of too rarefied a quality, not catering enough to the interests of his readers. Trollope came to believe that publishers like Smith and Blackwood were in fact the best editors of magazines, largely because they were less tempted to fall into 'that worst of literary quicksands, the publishing of matter not for the sake of the readers, but for that of the writer. I did not so sin very often, but often enough to feel that I was a coward. . . . Occasionally I know that I did give way on behalf of some literary aspirant whose work did not represent itself to me as being good; and as often as I did so, I broke my trust to those who employed me.'44 Like Thackeray, he was keenly sensitive to the thorns in the editor's cushion.

But his editorial trials bore fruit: towards the end of his tenure Trollope published, from November 1869 to May 1870, a series of short stories (later collected as *An Editor's Tales*) which offer a portrait of himself as editor of the magazine. Two themes dominate: his susceptibility to women contributors and the burden of reading worthless manuscripts. Though details are altered, the stories arose out of factual incidents. 'The Turkish Bath' tells of a Mr Molloy, an ingenious would-be contributor who creeps into the editor's confidence in a bath-house, and then 'plunged a dagger' into him by asking for an interview about a 'little manuscript'; Molloy's article turns out to be utterly useless; he is in fact mad.

In 'Josephine de Montmorenci', a young woman of that name writes and all but demands that he publish her story; the editor, who 'loved the rustle of feminine apparel, who delighted in the brightness of a woman's eye . . . and was not indifferent to the touch of a woman's hand', finds her story not altogether worthless, and goes to her house, hoping for an 'adventure'; there he discovers a little, wizened woman, young but haggard, a cripple with a twisted spine, whose real name is the unromantic Maryanne Puffle. (Her story is eventually accepted, not by the magazine but by a book publisher.)

In 'Mary Gresley' (Gresley being Trollope's maternal grandmother's name), the heroine is a young woman, in this case beautiful, with sparkling eyes and a fine sense of humour: 'Where is the man of fifty,' the narrator asks, 'who in the course of his life has not learned to love some woman simply because it has come in his way to help her, and to be good to her in her struggles? . . . We [the stories jokingly use the editorial plural throughout] were married and old; she was young, and engaged to be married. . . . She looked upon us no doubt . . . as a subsidiary old uncle whom Providence had supplied to her. . . . She charmed us. . . . We loved her, in short, as we should not have loved her, but that she was young and gentle, and could smile,—and, above all, but that she looked at us with those bright, beseeching, tear-laden eyes.' The hero of her novel is 'utterly untrue to nature', and the heroine is commonplace. But Mary Gresley, instancing the success of Charlotte Brontë, presses forward— drawing the comment from the editor that 'the injury which [Brontë] did after this fashion was almost equal to that perpetrated by Jack Sheppard' (the latter being the villain of Harrison Ainsworth's 1840 novel of that name; the murderer Courvoisier asserted that the character inspired him to his crime). Still, thinking it not beyond her powers to learn to write a novel, the editor undertakes to tutor her in the writing of fiction; he is relieved when she does not bring her mother up to the office: 'Even when you are past fifty, and intend only to preach a sermon, you do not wish to have a mother present.' He 'had made a clean breast of it at home in regard to our heart-flutterings, and had been met with the suggestion that some kindness might with propriety be shown to the old lady as well as to the young one.'

In 'The Spotted Dog' the editor makes great but vain efforts to reclaim a drunken scholar by inducing him to make one last effort at literary work. In 'Mrs Brumby' a hateful woman keeps forcing herself into his office, bullying him and threatening him with the law. One can easily imagine Virtue paying off such a trouble-maker with £10, as happens in the story. The curiously sad and even tragic little stories that make up *An Editor's Tales* were the best thing to come out of *Saint Pauls Magazine* and the best of his five volumes of collected short fiction.[45] James Payn, himself an editor, said that he considered *An Editor's Tales* 'as convincing a proof of the genius of the author as anything he ever wrote. I once expressed this opinion to Trollope, who assented to my view of the matter, but added, with a grim smile, that he doubted whether anybody had ever read the book except myself.'[46]

Trollope's non-fiction for *Saint Pauls* had followed pretty much along predictable lines: he wrote articles on hunting, on Gladstone, on the new cabinet, on the Irish Church; he attacked Carlylism; he wrote on American politics, he defended President Andrew Johnson. One article that did not fall within his usual range of comment was called 'The Uncontrolled Ruffianism of London', a lively little piece saying crime was not so bad in the great metropolis as word would have it, and that recent suggestions that Londoners not go out at night, or that they carry heavy sticks and walk in the middle of the street, were misguided inferences from statistics. What, for example, do 4,738 reported pickpocketed handkerchiefs mean among a population of 3,000,000? And do not New Yorkers and Parisians, for example, have worse problems than Londoners? 'Of the rowdyism of New York we have always entertained so strong a conviction, that we feared no comparison there.' He quotes the *Pall Mall* as showing that yearly summary convictions for crimes numbered 58,000 in London vs. 85,000 for Paris, a city one third less in population. In London, convictions for drunkenness and disorderly conduct outnumbered those in Paris by five to one, but Trollope is inclined to think that drunken people 'do more harm to themselves than to their neighbours'. He doubts people would know how to use nightsticks anyway, and those resorting to carrying loaded pistols would be in greater danger from themselves than from garrotters. He himself has been unable to meet anyone who has been garrotted. (Trollope had the fictional Mr Kennedy attacked by garrotters in *Phineas Finn*.[47])

All in all Trollope wrote twenty-one non-fiction articles for the magazine, of which two-thirds were political, the remainder literary and topical. Twice he attacked his *bête noire*, Disraeli. He first accused the Prime Minister of abusing political patronage: Disraeli gave a post in the Mint to a Treasury employee who had been his private secretary, and who, Trollope says, had never even seen the Mint; furthermore, Disraeli promoted this friend over a man who had been thirty-six years in the Mint and whose chiefs had recommended him for the post—Trollope was still fighting the battle against 'outsiders' given positions in disregard of seniority.[48] His other assault on Disraeli came just after Trollope had surrendered his editorial duties. The former Prime Minister, out of office since the November 1868 election, had written a novel, *Lothair*, his first since *Tancred* in 1847. Even before its publication on 2 May 1870, there had been speculation about how much Thomas Longman had paid him for the book. That Disraeli should have again taken to novel writing pained Trollope, and that he should be rumoured to be receiving a huge sum for the book made matters worse. Trollope bet £10 with Lord Houghton— who knew as much literary gossip as anyone in England—that no publisher had offered Disraeli £10,000. Houghton 'called' Trollope, saying quite rightly that E. S. Dallas had proposed to pay Disraeli £10,000, on behalf of Bradbury & Evans, for the book's serialization in *Once A Week*. Trollope, although paying up, insisted that the offer was not a genuine one, that it was as if he himself had offered half a million for Fryston, Houghton's Yorkshire estate, both of them knowing that Trollope would not have the money. Dallas, Trollope told Houghton, had been 'running a muck among novelists, offering to buy this and that'. Trollope insisted that no novel could be worth £10,000 to a publisher. 'I know pretty well the value of these articles,' he told Houghton; he said Dickens's last novel, *The Mystery of Edwin Drood*, which from a pecuniary point of view would have 'three times' the value of *Lothair*, had sold for 'considerably less'. Trollope was on surer ground here: Chapman & Hall—of which Trollope's son was a partner—had paid Dickens £7,500 plus half-profits after 25,000 copies. But Trollope did not know the upper end of the scale as well as he thought he did. He had no idea that Dickens had made some £11,000 on earlier novels such as *Bleak House* and *Little Dorrit*; nor did he know that George Smith had offered George Eliot £10,000 for *Romola*. Longman had in fact paid Disraeli only £1,000 outright for *Lothair*, with royalties after 2,000 copies (by 1876 he had cleared £7,500 on the novel and was so much in vogue that by 1880 Longman would offer him £10,000 for *Endymion*.)[49] *Lothair* enjoyed great popularity, though little critical acceptance. Trollope's disgust is unconcealed in the review he wrote for the August 1870 issue of *Saint Pauls*: he said that the ex-Prime Minister, determined to strike at the aristocracy, and believing they would accept anything from his hand, produced a story that was 'vulgar, ill-written, passing all previous measures in the absurdity of its adulation of rank, false as it can be made in its descriptions of life, stuffed with folly'. Whatever the book's popularity, Disraeli must be lonely in his success, 'as were Paracelsus, Cagliostro, Barry Lyndon, and other quacks and conjurers'. Trollope hopes England's aristocrats have learned a lesson and will not again install in the high place of Prime Minister one who will 'rub their noses in the dust, covering them with grotesque ridicule'. Disraeli had a right to be proud of the political position he had won, but he has now 'dragged his honours through the mud . . . by descending to personalities which would have disgraced the slightest novelist of the day, and has put his name on the title-page of a book as to which . . . it is impossible to invent any rational theory for its absurd puerilities.'[50] (That some people defended *Lothair* on the plea that it was written when Disraeli was too old, drew from Trollope the remark, 'though not too old to be Prime Minister'.[51]) Trollope's review of *Lothair* was the harshest thing he ever published.

Trollope's last issue of *Saint Pauls* was that of July 1870; he had been editor just short of three years. One can believe that he wished the magazine luck, though with little hope that it would succeed. Strahan lowered the price paid to contributors, decreased the proportion of political and serious matter, and enlisted less expensive fiction writers—Katherine Macquoid, Mrs Craik (Dinah Mulock), Jean Ingelow. A few of the old guard stayed on, including T. A. Trollope. Anthony's *Ralph the Heir* continued as a supplement to the magazine until July 1871. *Septimus*, a short novel by Nathaniel Hawthorne, appeared in its pages. But Strahan's publishing business continued to falter, and in 1871 Virtue persuaded Strahan to leave the firm, fellow creditors having prevailed upon Virtue to take over. Strahan was allowed to take *Saint Pauls* with him, but the following year ownership passed to Henry S. King, a brother-in-law and one-time partner to George Smith. Strahan hung on as King's editor of *Saint Pauls*; the fiction level sank lower still—Mortimer Collins ('the very dregs' Trollope once said of his work)[52] and others unknown to posterity: Edward Lovel, John Saunders, John Adam. Perhaps the piece in *Saint Pauls* most remembered after Trollope's departure is Robert Buchanan's 'The Monkey and the Microscope' (August 1872) a reply to Swinburne's *Under the Microscope*, itself a reply to Buchanan's infamous 'Fleshly School of Poetry' attack on Rossetti and Swinburne. *Saint Pauls Magazine* ceased publication in March 1874.[53]

Eighteen-seventy brought with it the disappointment of the failure of *Saint Pauls*; it also brought Trollope a commission which was a source of gratification and delight. While visiting Blackwood in Edinburgh that January, Trollope expressed admiration for the first two volumes of the publisher's 'Ancient Classics for English Readers'—the *Iliad* and the *Odyssey*—prepared by the editor of the series, W. Lucas Collins, a clergyman scholar, vicar of Kilsby and later rector of Lowick. Trollope volunteered to review these for *Saint Pauls*, a development that much pleased Blackwood, who wrote to Collins, 'As he is about the most shrewd & practical man of letters going it was very cheering to hear him.'[54] (In his review, Trollope praised the series as a means of removing the 'very dense ignorance' about classical authors, and especially recommended it to the 'educated lady'.[55]) When Blackwood suggested that Trollope himself write one of the volumes for the series, he decided upon the *Commentaries of Caesar*. It was a natural choice, given the great interest Merivale's *History of the Romans*—so largely about Caesar—had aroused in him in 1851.

On his return to Waltham, on 29 January, Trollope immediately began the *Caesar*, interrupting the writing of *The Eustace Diamonds*. For three months he worked harder on a book than he had ever done. Had it been a work of fiction of that size, three weeks would have been ample time. But this 'soaring out of my own peculiar line' put him on his guard. Ignoring translations, he read the *Commentaries* twice and went through works of critics George Long and Charles Merivale, and even 'that most futile book' of Napoleon III. By 10 March he sent Blackwood the first seven chapters, asking what Blackwood and Collins thought of it before he went on. Both men encouraged him, Collins pointing out a few 'mere trifles', taking issue, for example, with Trollope's light colloquial translations—'thick as blackberries' and 'as fast as he could lay leg to ground'. When Trollope finished the book, he told Blackwood he had enjoyed this tough bit of work 'amazingly': the change from novel writing had 'enabled me to surround myself for three months with books & almost to think myself a scholar'. *The Commentaries of Caesar* was a 'dear little book' to Trollope, yet another belated triumph for the poor, unpromising Harrow schoolboy. He made Blackwood a present of the copyright. The work had been its own reward. It returned him to Latin literature systematically, and henceforth he 'almost daily spent an hour with some Latin author'.[56] The project also brought him the friendship of Lucas Collins. On first meeting the Trollopes, in May 1870, Collins wrote to Blackwood 'The Trollopes came on Thursday and left on Saturday. We like them very much,—him especially, he was so very pleasant to talk to, and at the same time so perfectly unassuming.'[57]

In his *Commentaries of Caesar* Trollope seems still to think Caesar the greatest 'name' in history; Napoleon came next; Washington was perhaps the greatest of such men in 'moral attributes' because his work 'came altogether from patriotism—with no alloy of personal ambition'. Trollope saw Caesar's moral character as unspeakably cruel; the only excuse to be made for him was that he was Roman, and 'Romans were indifferent to blood'. Christ's coming, Trollope says, 'has changed all things', and though atrocities are still committed, men are not now as they were. Trollope's story-telling powers do not desert him as he condenses Caesar's *Commentaries*, nor does his eye for detail or light touch: 'Caesar estimates that thirty thousand arrows were thrown upon the men defending this tower [in the war with Pompey], and tells us of one Scaeva, an officer, who had two hundred and thirty holes made by these arrows in his own shield. We can only surmise that it must have been a very big shield, and that there must have been much trouble in counting the holes.'[58]

But the book brought him very little of the gratification he secretly craved from the critical and scholarly world: 'Nobody praised it,' and

Charles Merivale, sent a copy, thanked him for his 'comic Caesar'. This remark caused him great pain—never shown, he said, till the incident was recounted in the posthumously published *Autobiography*, though there Merivale's name is withheld.[59] But Merivale's comment was not as harsh as the review in the *Athenaeum*—a publication Trollope much respected—which said that Trollope lacked the required knowledge of or fondness for the theory of war to tackle such a subject, that he 'treats geography with a contempt that apparently springs from ignorance', that his 'jerky false style' sins against good taste and reveals 'an utter in-capability of appreciating historical causes and effects', and that while readers were looking forward to more 'Trollopean' parsons and doctors, 'we trust that we shall never meet again with the Trollopean Caesar.'[60] The review he must have been in most apprehension about never appeared, for the *Saturday* was silent. The book became a popular school reader for many years.[61]

In April *The Vicar of Bullhampton* was published by Bradbury & Evans. The novel was in part the story of a 'fallen woman'. The previous October Trollope had written an article for *Saint Pauls* about the furore caused by Dion Boucicault's play *Formosa*, which presented a prostitute on stage. Trollope belittled the notion that any mother could believe her twenty-one-year-old daughter ignorant of the existence of prostitutes. Keeping girls pure by trying to keep them in ignorance is a 'system of perpetuating childhood'. Moroever, 'to presume that to either boy or girl the repres-entation of a prostitute on stage teaches that which is already unknown is . . . as absurd as it would be to suppose that the representation of theft would teach the existence of thieves.' If one really wishes to teach in this regard, 'the character of some poor female from the street might be brought upon our stage in a manner to do infinite good,—so that women should be taught what misery there is around them'. The fault with *Formosa* is that the character—a prosperous prostitute—is 'utterly false, false to human nature and false to London life'. Trollope declares that the career of an English prostitute was the 'most miserable' in the world, that 'in no other career is misery produced by so slight an amount of ill-doing'. Moreover, their situation is made worse by the feeling that 'our wives and sisters would be degraded if they spoke to them, polluted if they touched them,—almost tainted if they even looked at them.'[62] Privately he told Anna Steele, 'The whole Formosa business was to my thinking detestably false. But a poor creature may fall,—as we call it—and yet be worth redeeming. Fathers & mothers will forgive anything in a son, debauchery, gambling, lying—even the worst dishonesty & fraud—but the "fallen" daughter is too often regarded as an outcast for whom no hope can be entertained. Excuse all this enthusiasm.'[63]

For the book edition of *The Vicar of Bullhampton* Trollope felt compelled to supply a preface (he customarily regarded dedications and the like as 'trash'), in which he argued the propriety and morality of presenting in fiction a 'castaway' in a sympathetic manner. Could not women learn to 'pity the sufferings of the vicious'? No moral lapse was punished as heavily as fornication or prostitution, and yet that fault was 'often so light in itself, but so terrible in its consequences to the less faulty of the two offenders'. If the subject be treated delicately and without glorifying the life of a fallen woman, perhaps some thoughtless girl 'may be made thoughtful, or some parent's heart may be softened'. It was a question to which Trollope returned often. In *John Caldigate*, the adventuress Mrs Smith makes good sense when she argues that 'women can't recuperate', though men can: 'If you had made a false step,' she tells Caldigate, 'got into debt and ran away, or [had] mistaken another man's wife for your own . . . you could retrieve your honour, and, sinking at twenty-five or thirty, could come up from out of the waters at thirty-five as capable of enjoyment and almost as fresh as ever'; in fact, a man 'is rather the better liked because he has sown his wild oats broadly'. A woman, on the other hand, 'does not bear submersion. She is draggled ever afterwards. She must hide everything by a life of lies, or she will get no admittance anywhere.'[64] In *An Eye for an Eye*, there is pointed criticism of women who are terribly strict in regard to sexual proprieties for girls but who actually like 'a little wickedness in a young man,—if only he does not carry it to the extent of marrying the wrong sort of young woman'; these women think that the pregnant girl 'should be punished as the sinner and that the man should be assisted to escape'.[65] If Trollope were worried about puritanical objections to *The Vicar of Bullhampton*, he need not have been. Carry Brattle is seen only after her 'fall', and the details of her behaviour are left altogether obscure. As the *Athenaeum* said, Trollope had 'not unnaturally' avoided a history of her sins. The *Saturday*, calling *The Vicar of Bullhampton* a 'not very satisfactory book' (while granting that 'Trollope's third rate is more readable than most novelists' best') had no complaint about his avowed aim to reclaim Carry Brattle from degradation: 'Mr. Trollope cannot be reproached with making vice attractive. He tells us that Carry is pretty—an impression of which the illustrator [Henry Woods] has done his best to disabuse us.' *The Times*, while saying that the novel would add little to

Trollope's reputation, pronounced it 'a nice, easy, safe reading book for old ladies and young ladies . . . welcome in all well-regulated families'.[66]

In November the book edition of *Sir Harry Hotspur of Humblethwaite* appeared. Trollope had sold the entire copyright to Alexander Macmillan for £750, a good price for so short a novel. The story was serialized in *Macmillan's Magazine*, where 'it did not make either [the proprietor's] fortune or that of his magazine'; thereupon Macmillan sold the book rights, for a nine-month period, to Hurst & Blackett. But when the latter firm set the book in two volumes, Trollope objected. 'The fact is', he told Macmillan, 'that as one pound of tea wont make two by any variance in packing the article,—so neither will a one-volume tale make two volumes. . . . to make two pounds out of one is more than can be done even in Marlboro Street [Hurst & Blackett's address].' Trollope was adamant, as he had been earlier with Strahan and the volume of short stories, and when Hurst & Blackett nearly called off the deal, Macmillan apparently moved in and paid part of the reprinting costs. The book duly appeared in one volume.[67] Trollope had made no complaint, however, when Blackwood published *Nina Balatka* and *Linda Tressel*, shorter even than *Sir Harry Hotspur*, each in two volumes (of course his name was not attached to the Blackwood books).

Sir Harry Hotspur of Humblethwaite, the tale of a conscientious father who, in refusing to allow his daughter to marry a scheming wastrel, destroys her, is Trollope's saddest story.* It was hailed by *The Times* as 'a return to what we must call Mr. Trollope's old form', a book filled with the 'vigour and boldness which have been wanting from [his] recent works'. The *Athenaeum* called it a 'brilliant novelette' and 'decidedly more successful than any other of Mr. Trollope's shorter stories'. Hutton, in the *Spectator*, while maintaining that 'Mr. Trollope's genius demands space', called the novel one of his 'very best short tales', saying that no subject ever suited Trollope better than the irresolution of old Sir Harry. Only the *Saturday* found fault, in this case with unsympathetic treatment of the aristocracy, though it admitted the book 'shows signs of greater care than Mr. Trollope always finds it worth while to take'.[68] In *An Autobiography* Trollope described the book as 'written on the same plan as *Nina Balatka* and *Linda Tressel* . . . [having] for its object the telling of some pathetic incident in life rather than the portraiture of a number of living human

---

* There is no external evidence of Henry James having borrowed from *Sir Harry Hotspur*, but *Washington Square* bears remarkable resemblances to Trollope's novel.[69]

beings'. It was therefore more properly a 'romance', while it differed from the anonymous books in that it was an English story.[70] Trollope treated the issue of a dissolute life in the weak villain George Hotspur deftly, stressing his dishonesty, gambling, and card sharping, but delicately presenting a sexual liaison with an actress. *The Times*, reiterating that *The Vicar of Bullhampton*, a book that it called 'dulness itself', was 'very safe reading for ladies' schools', said *Sir Harry Hotspur* had revelations 'anything but fitted for the perusal of the young'; on the other hand, the book 'may do good to many of both sexes more advanced in life'. Charles Kent, writing in the *Sun*, called the story 'a brilliant example of Anthony Trollope's power as novelist' and 'a radiant specimen of English imaginative literature'; Kent also admired Trollope's 'consummate delicacy' in handling his material in such a way that even 'the redoubtable Mr. Podsnap' would find nothing 'to bring a blush to the cheek of a young person'. Kent sent the review to Trollope, who answered, 'Such praise as yours is always most pleasant to an author. . . . I am always most doubtful about my work;— and in some moods am altogether beyond doubt.'[71]

On 9 June Charles Dickens died suddenly at Gad's Hill. Trollope, who had recently had a number of personal contacts with him on the subject of international copyright, wrote a signed obituary in *Saint Pauls*: 'No other writer of English language except Shakespeare has left so many types of characters as Dickens has done'; and whereas Shakespeare has comparatively few readers, Dickens's characters—Pickwick, Sam Weller, Mrs Nickleby, Wackford Squeers, Fagin, Bill Sikes, Micawber, Mrs Gamp, Pecksniff, and Bucket the detective—'are persons so well known to us that we think that they, who are in any way of the professions of these worthies, are untrue to themselves if they depart in aught from their recognised and understood portraits'. ('A boots at an hotel is more of a boots the closer he resembles Sam Weller. . . . Every detective is to us a Bucket.') On the other hand, it was a questionable compliment to say that Dickens knew especially how to 'tap the ever newly-growing mass of readers as it sprang up among the lower classes'; and there was more than a hint of further reservations about Dickens's 'want of art in the choice of words and want of nature in the creation of character'. Still, 'his words have been so potent . . . that they have justified themselves . . . and his characters, if unnatural, have made a second nature by their own force.' Trollope closed with praise customary for an obituary, even indulging in the inevitable 'we shall not look upon his like again'.[72]

Dickens's death was no personal loss for Trollope as had been

Thackeray's seven years earlier. But even as Thackeray's death at the close of 1863 had left the field more open to Trollope, so now Dickens's departure in 1870 did the same. At the Royal Academy of Arts dinner the following April Sir Francis Grant toasted Trollope, saying that while Dickens, who had been toasted the previous year, had left a celebrated name, he was glad 'to think we have still among us some others most distinguished in the literature of fiction,—if, indeed, the wonderful fidelity and truthfulness to nature which pervade the works of Anthony Trollope can be called fiction'.73 Among many readers, the field had really been narrowed to two, George Eliot and Trollope. Wilkie Collins was popular, but, in spite of the enormous success of *The Woman in White* and *The Moonstone*, was not thought of as in Trollope's class. Disraeli had popularity but not critical acclaim. The *Dublin Review* would call Trollope 'the first master of his craft now in existence'; he has 'the keenest powers of surface observation of any living novelist, and the finest humour'; some will award George Eliot 'higher intellectual status' but will refuse her precedence over him as novelist; Wilkie Collins is fatally uneven, while Trollope is 'a thoroughly consistent workman'; Trollope falls short in that his 'landscapes of life are deficient in perspective; and his men and women are deficient in soul'. None the less, 'Trollope has given life, and speech, and motion to scores of portraits, has sent them to walk abroad . . . and to have their names on men's lips when the actual every-day affairs and incidents of life are talked of.'74 Trollope would have considered that a fair assessment.

23

——— ◆∙▶◀∙◆ ———

Australia and New Zealand

LONG determined to visit Fred in Australia, Trollope finally made definite arrangements to do so. Being free of *Saint Pauls* helped. 'Of course', as he said in *An Autobiography*, he first made a contract for a travel book on the colony. On 12 January 1871 Chapman & Hall agreed to pay £1,250 for the work, about half the amount, Trollope figured, that fiction of comparable length would have brought him.[1] He also proposed a series of travel letters for the papers, which he offered to *The Times*. Mowbray Morris, declining, wrote that though flattered by the offer, he felt *The Times* could not give him ample room 'to do justice to your own style and mode of treatment'. Trollope then took his proposal to the *Daily Telegraph* (a penny daily with a circulation of some 200,000, by this time far outstripping even *The Times*), which accepted, and printed eleven lengthy letters over a period of one year, beginning in December 1871.[2]

The decision to visit Fred at this time included a resolve, accompanied by considerable regret, to give up Waltham House. Trollope would look back fondly on the 1860s as his best years. Certainly by 1876, when he wrote *An Autobiography*, he was convinced that 'few men . . . ever lived a fuller life' than he had during the Waltham years, with his almost unprecedented amount of writing, coupled with Post Office work, social life, hunting, and travelling. For all his love of London and of clubs, English country life was sweeter to him, and Waltham had been a compromise, close to London and yet rural. He hoped now that it would be less expensive to live in London; some economies were in order; he had given up his Post Office salary, and had then seen his editor's salary—which had matched his Post Office income—taken from him. Henceforth he was thrown solely on his writing. Hunting, he told himself, might have to be abandoned. He put the house up for lease or sale, but it was two years before it was sold, and at a loss of £800 ('I continually hear that other men make money by buying and selling houses. . . . I have never made money by selling anything except a manuscript').[3] Having disposed of the house and nearly all the furniture, he and Rose were distressed when a ship accident caused an eighteen-day delay in their departure, which was to have been on 6 May. This postponement necessitated their being involved 'in all the misery of living about among friends and pot-houses,—going through that very worst phase of life which consists in a continuous and ever failing attempt to be jolly, with nothing to do'.4

In the midst of leaving Waltham and the delay in sailing for Australia Trollope had written nothing since completing *Phineas Redux* on 1 April. On the other hand, he was, as usual, ahead of his market, and he would not be out of the public eye during his extended trip abroad: *Ralph the Heir* was to continue appearing in *Saint Pauls* until July, at which time *The Eustace Diamonds* would commence in the *Fortnightly*; he had just sold *The Golden Lion of Granpere* to *Good Words*, publication to begin in January. The manuscript for *Phineas Redux* he put into a strong-box for future arrangements, along with that of a short tragic Irish novel, *An Eye for an Eye*, written in four weeks the previous summer.

On 23 April he had attended one of the celebrated lunches given by George Eliot and Lewes at the Priory, other visitors including Lady Castledown, Turgenev, Viardot, Browning, and Burne-Jones (the next day Trollope arranged that the Athenaeum Club extend further courtesies to Turgenev, who had been an honorary member in 1857).5 It was at one such gathering that, according to Frederic Harrison, George Eliot 'positively quivered' with dismay as Trollope described writing every morning at 5.30 for three hours, with his watch on his desk, pushing on with his 250 words every quarter of an hour. She told him there were days on end when she could not write a line. 'Yes,' Trollope gallantly offered, 'with imaginative work like yours that is quite natural; but with my mechanical stuff it's a sheer matter of industry. It's not the head that does it—it's the cobbler's wax on the seat and the sticking to my chair!' And, according to another account, he drove home his point about the seat of inspiration with 'an inelegant vigour of gesture that sent a thrill of horror through the polite circle there assembled'. On the other hand, George Eliot is on record as saying, 'I am not at all sure that, but for Anthony Trollope, I should ever have planned my studies on so extensive a scale for *Middlemarch*, or that I should, through all of its episodes, have persevered with it to the close.'6

Trollope and Rose sailed on 24 May from Liverpool for Australia—via Suez and the Indian Ocean—and on the next day he began a novel, *Lady Anna*, the story of a granddaughter of an earl marrying a tailor. He worked steadily, averaging nine pages a day, missing only one day's work through illness, and finished the two-volume novel exactly eight weeks later, on 19 July. The entire book had been written at sea. The Trollopes arrived in Melbourne on 27 July 1871. Anthony did not immediately make for Fred's sheep station in New South Wales but travelled by sea to Brisbane, breaking his journey briefly at Sydney. From Brisbane he visited Queensland coastal towns as far north as Rockhampton and went inland to the rich pastures of the Darling Downs. The *Brisbane Courier* wrote that his tour 'is as carefully watched and recorded by the Press as a royal progress'; it reported, for example, how he had visited 'the Valley' near Gladstone and 'actually sat on the Bench at the Court-house, while one Boney, an aborigine, was being tried by Mr. Rich for being illegally on the premises of Mr. Breslin. We are happy to record that the great author gave evidence of his sanity by retiring before the case was finished.' At the end of September, after a month in Queensland, he returned to Sydney. The *Sydney Punch* addressed Trollope with lyrical fulsomeness: 'As noiselessly as the creatures of your own delightful fancy that have stolen into our hearts for years and made their home there, you have come amongst us, the brave master, the kindly magician, the eloquent teacher. The very city seems nobler when we think that you are walking its streets, and that its citizens may look upon one who has given so much happiness to millions.'[7]

Fred had come and met them at some point, and Rose had gone on ahead to Fred's station, Mortray, 250 miles west of Sydney. Trollope arrived in Grenfell ('a fearfully abominable place' he wrote in his travel notes), some ten miles south of Mortray, on 20 October, and there met Fred's fiancée, Susannah Farrand, the daughter of the police magistrate of Forbes (a town some thirty miles distant from Mortray). Trollope said in his notes that 'Susie' was 'very much prettier than her photograph, a good humoured pleasant little girl who I think will make Fred a good wife'.[8] He drove her to Mortray, getting lost in the forest along the way. He made Fred's sheep station the subject of a chapter in his book, 'Country Life in the Bush'. The brief stay with Fred also gave him the germ of a short novel, *Harry Heathcote of Gangoil* which Trollope would dash off in four weeks in June 1873:* As he told Mary Holmes, 'Harry Heathcote is my boy Frederic,—or very much the same.'[9] In this tale of the troubles of a squatter, the fictional picture of Fred is not altogether flattering: educated at an English public school, Heathcote, though now only 24, sees himself

---

* *Harry Heathcote of Gangoil* was to be the last of Trollope's novels with an entirely non-English setting (except for the futuristic *Fixed Period*, set in an imaginary country near New Zealand). In these books, along with *Nina Balatka, Linda Tressel, The Golden Lion of Granpere,* Trollope, hedging his bet, kept the story short.[10]

as a 'young patriarch' in the wilderness; he is imperious and obstinate, and his relationship with his workers has 'too much of master and man about it',[11] and he makes enemies among his equals. He has his good qualities, many of them Trollope's own: he is hard-working, truthful, forthright to a fault. The end of the story reflects Trollope's hopes for his son: Heathcote's sheep station survives economic problems (and arson), and he has a loving, supportive wife—she reads Shakespeare to him at night.

Trollope's visit to the station coincided with washing and shearing days, the busiest time of the year for Fred, who had to be out at five a.m. and was rarely back in time for dinner at eight p.m. It struck Trollope that the care of a small station, such as Fred's, some 27,500 acres, with 40 miles of fencing and 10,000 sheep, with very limited help, was a nearly impossible task; Fred seemed 'to have more [work] on hand than a British prime minister in June'. Trollope rode about on horseback, 'giving now and then a fantastic opinion as to the doing of the work, criticising the roughness of the mode in which the poor brutes were hauled into the water, or the cruelty with which they were wounded by the shearers'.[12] He also took enjoyable rides through the forest, did some kangaroo hunting, and enjoyed the strange remoteness of the countryside.

At Mortray, as in most of the other more than thirty bush homes he visited, Trollope was pleased at finding a plentiful provision of books, noting that the folly of owning but never looking at books was greater in English cities than in the Australian bush: 'the young squatter, when the evening comes upon him, has no other recreation to entice him. He has no club, no billiard table, no public-house which he can frequent.' The authors most likely to be owned were Shakespeare (often unread), Dickens, and Macaulay ('I would back the chance of finding Macaulay's *Essays* at a station against that of any book in the language except Shakespeare'). Trollope tells how young squatters marry early: 'The man is alone, and can have at any rate no female companionship unless he marry.' And it's easily done: the squatter 'simply goes out in his buggy and brings home the daughter of some other squatter,—after a little ceremony performed in the nearest church'.[13] This was pretty much what Fred did. He married Susannah at Forbes on 14 December 1871 (Fred was 24). By then Trollope and Rose were on their way via ship to Melbourne. The most likely explanation for their absence from the wedding—aside from Trollope's dislike for wedding ceremonies—is that for him his book was all important. For visiting his son, Trollope allowed—in addition to the times during which Fred was able to join him in his travels—about four weeks in October/November 1871 and another week the following June. The visit to Fred had occasioned the trip to Australia, but once there, the writing of the travel book took hold. This involved much greater effort than did the writing of a novel, an enormous amount of travel, much physical labour, the consulting of experts, and the use of histories and statistical studies. Rose, who frequently did not accompany Trollope to out-of-the-way destinations, stayed longer with Fred while Anthony roamed the colonies for information. (Australian Trollope family lore, as recorded by her grandson Gordon Trollope in 1930, had it that Rose 'hated the country, and said many unkind things about it'.[14])

From Mortray Trollope returned to Sydney, and after a further month in New South Wales visited all the remaining colonies—Victoria, Tasmania, Western Australia, and South Australia—before leaving Australia for New Zealand. He went at his travels combatively, as his sometimes circuitous routes took him thousands of miles by ship, rail, and coach; he went great distances in buggies, over the bush roads, and trails which in England would have not been considered roads; he also travelled much on horseback, sometimes managing 'forty, fifty, and even as much as sixty-four miles a day'; he covered hundreds of miles through forests and mountains 'so steep it was often impossible to sit on horseback'. In Western Australia, he arranged for the private use of a mail coach to travel from Albany to Perth, a four days' journey, camping out at night in the bush with a new-found young Scottish friend. They undertook the camping out partly to show the Australians that they could do so: 'We lit fires for ourselves, and boiled our tea in billies; and then regaled ourselves with bad brandy and water out of pannikins, cooked bacon and potatoes in a frying-pan and pretended to think that it was very jolly'; but at five in the morning, rising in damp clothes and boots he would have to wear through the day, packing up wet blankets, and trying to wake the snoring driver, he did not feel 'any ardent desire to throw off for ever the soft luxuries of an effeminate civilisation, in order that I might permanently enjoy the freedom of the bush'. At Gulgong, he had himself lowered 150 feet down the mine shaft of a gold mine with his foot in the noose of a rope. At Ballarat, he went down 'Winter's Freehold' mine, descending in an iron cage 450 feet, travelling 4,000 feet in a horse-drawn underground tramway and then climbing up a ladder to another tramway to where miners were at work. At Deloraine in Tasmania, in order to see the famous Chudleigh stalactite caves, he made his way for a mile underground—together with Governor Charles Du Cane and a guide—crawling, creeping, wading in waist-deep water, 'knocking one's head at every turn'; having seen 'not . . . half the wonders of the place,—which by-the-bye were invisible by reason of the outer darkness', the party waded back.[15] His more routine activities had him attending banquets in his honour, lecturing, calling on governors, colonial ministers, public officials, and great landowners. At Sydney he appeared before the New South Wales Select Parliamentary Committee on the Civil Service, predictably inveighing against competitive examinations.

There were also pleasant meetings with English residents, connected to his early life: Hugh Miles Milman, whose great-grandmother Trollope as a boy had known well at Harrow, was working as a meat-processor at Rockhampton; Colonel George Hamilton, who had been at school with him at Harrow, was Commissioner of Police at Adelaide; Gustavus Edward Cockburn Hare, a school-fellow at Winchester, was resident magistrate at Albany, Western Australia. At Melbourne Trollope called on one Miss Scott, whom he had known at Banagher. In Perth he stayed with Walter Savage Landor's young cousin Edward Wilson Landor, the police magistrate; the Landor family took him to an evening party, where he shocked Australian sensibilities by failing to wear evening clothes (perhaps he had none with him) and spilling coffee on the new white frock of the host's débutante daughter; the eccentric blue-shirted English novelist was long remembered.[16]

In his travel book, Trollope did his best to write about each colony from a slightly different aspect, although never failing to offer a summary of the history and social institutions of each. His interest, characteristically, was not scenery: of Mount Kosciusko, in the south of New South Wales, 7,300 feet high, the 'Mount Blanc' of Australia, he said that 'as the life of the men and women around me was more essential to my object than scenery, I was obliged to leave Kosciusko unseen'. On the other hand, he found almost any statistics touching human existence irresistible. He noted, for example, that greater Ballarat, Victoria, had in 1871 a population of 48,156, and 56 churches, 3 town halls, 477 hotels, 10,000 dwellings, 11 banks, 8 iron foundries, 13 breweries, 84 miles of streets, 164 miles of foot pavement—'there ought to be 168, if every mile of street were fairly dealt by'—and a municipal revenue of £50,000.[17] As not all readers find statistics as fascinating as did Trollope, the book's thoroughness and repetitiveness can in places make for heavy going. On the other hand, Trollope's eye for detail and his novelist's penchant for little vignettes and dramas, along with his generous use of personal anecdote, make for readability. His own interest can even make quite arresting things of very little promise, as the accounts of sheep-shearing and sheep-washing in Queensland.

The average English reader was probably chiefly interested in the much-publicized gold-mining (since the great discoveries at Ballarat in 1851). Trollope discussed gold-mining at length but predictably came down against it as a lure to would-be emigrants: it smacked too much of gambling. He admitted that the typical miner from Cornwall or Northumberland might in coming to the gold-mines get a lift in the world in regard to manners and habits as well as income. But the gentleman, even if he strikes gold, gets a fall, 'He loses his gentility, his love of cleanliness, his ease of words, his grace of bearing, his preference for good company, and his social exigencies.' At a gold-field in Currajong, New South Wales, Trollope met a young man he had known at home, someone who had gone to school with his sons and visited at Waltham:

I saw him in front of his little tent, which he occupied in partnership with an experienced working miner, eating a beefsteak out of his frying-pan with his claspknife. . . . He had no friend near him but his mining friend,—or mate, as he called him. . . . He had been softly nurtured, well educated, and was a handsome fellow to boot; and there he was eating a nauseous lump of beef out of a greasy frying-pan with his pocket-knife, just in front of the contiguous blankets stretched on the ground, which constituted the beds of himself and his companion. It may be that he will strike gold, and make a fortune.

This encounter supplied Trollope with the idea for a later novel, *John Caldigate*, four crucial chapters of which are set in Australia.[18]

Trollope visited not only most of the colonial Parliaments (where he found the members too long-winded and hardly up to English standards of oratory), but many schools, prisons, lunatic asylums, and, of course, post offices. Of the new Post Office at Adelaide, the grandest building in the town, he remarks that 'knowing something of post-offices, I regret to say that the arrangements might have been improved by consultation with English officials'. He was most impressed with the schools, and said that, aside from the great old English universities, Australia was far ahead of the mother country in educating its people. England left so many of its poor 'in almost brute-like ignorance', but the Australian colonies seemed to educate everyone. He says that at a large common school at Sydney the teacher would ask his pupils some such question as, 'If a man invest £197. 7s. 6d. at 4½ per cent., and get a rise in the rate of interest of ⅛ per cent. at the end of 23 days, what will his income amount to at the end of 42 days?' Whereupon a 'little boy does it out of head, looking innocently up to the ceiling for his answer'. Trollope presumed the boy was supplied with the answer; still, it was an impressive show. 'When a little boy gets up on

15. Trollope. Portrait by Samuel Laurence, 1864.

16. Frederic Chapman.

17. John Blackwood. Portrait by John Watson Gordon.

18. Trollope. Photograph by Elliot & Fry, *c.*1868.

19. Rose Trollope.

20 and 21. Trollope. Photographs by Sarony, New York, 1868.

22 and 23. Kate Field.

24. 39 Montagu Square, London, where Trollope lived from April 1873 until July 1880.

25. Trollope's home at South Harting, near Petersfield, where he lived from July 1880 until his death.

26. Trollope, 1877.

27. Trollope. A late photograph. His son Harry wrote:
'That is excellent: I have seen him so often in that mood.
I know exactly what he's going to say, & the tone of voice
in which he will say it.'

his legs, and without any aid of pen or pencil, does a sum in half a minute which I know that I could not do myself if I were locked up half a day with all necessaries, I hate that little boy.'[19]

In Tasmania he visited the prison at Port Arthur, and his account begins with the conservative line on law and order:

Of course there were horrors. The men who did escape . . . committed fresh crimes and underwent fresh trials,—with very small chance of verdicts in their favour. . . . Horrors are always so popular that of course such tales are told the loudest. . . . The system was one to which flogging was necessary. Tenderness had no part in the thing as it was established. . . . Either the government was to keep down the convicts, or the convicts would put down the government.

There was much 'comfort' in the system of convict labour: 'Good roads, handsome buildings, clean streets, and public gardens' are produced 'almost without apparent expense'. As always in Trollope, practical application brings a softening, as feelings take over:

There were some dozen or fifteen men imprisoned. These were the heroes of the place. There was an Irishman with one eye, named Doherty, who told us that for forty-two years he had never been a free man for an hour. He had been transported for mutiny when hardly more than a boy,—for he had enlisted as a boy,—and had since that time received nearly 3,000 lashes. In appearance he was a large man and still powerful,—well to look at in spite of his eye, lost as he told us through the misery of prison life. But he said that he was broken at last. If they would only treat him kindly, he would be as a lamb. But within the last few weeks he had escaped with three others, and had been brought back almost starved to death. . . . He had been always escaping, always rebelling, always fighting against authority,—and always being flogged. There had been a whole life of torment such as this;—forty-two years of it; and there he stood, speaking softly, arguing his case well, and pleading while the tears ran down his face for some kindness, for some mercy in his old age. 'I have tried to escape;—always to escape,' he said,— 'as a bird does out of a cage. Is that unnatural?' . . . I did feel for him. . . . I should have liked to take him out into the world, and have given him a month's comfort.

Then an underlying conservatism returns, as Trollope adds, 'He would probably, however, have knocked my brains out on the first opportunity.'[20]

In discussing Western Australia, Trollope emphasized the preponderance of transported convicts there and the stigma thus left on the colony. The home government made up for the dearth of female convicts by sending women emigrants, about whom the colonists made great complaint: 'It is said that the women were Irish, and were low, and were not calculated to make good mothers for future heroic settlers. . . . The women in question were sent that they might become the wives of convicts, and could not therefore have been expeditiously selected from the highest orders of the English aristocracy.' Trollope found all aspects of the convict legacy fascinating: 'If you dine out, the probability is that the man who waits upon you was a convict. The rural labourers are ticket-holders. . . . Many of the most thriving shopkeepers came out as convicts. There are convict editors of newspapers.' He thought the prisoners at Fremantle less interesting than those at Port Arthur and could recall specifically only one, a gentleman who had been tried in England for scuttling a ship: 'I saw him walking about with a very placid demeanour, and . . . I do not doubt but that he will be editor of a newspaper before long.' Because of its convict population, travellers from Western Australia could not be received into the other colonies without a certificate; and Trollope printed in full the brief document given him as he left, stating that 'A. Trollope . . . is not and never has been a prisoner of the Crown in Western Australia.'[21]

Trollope returned eastward through Adelaide and Mt. Gambier in South Australia, and on arriving at Melbourne found a letter written on 7 March from Charles Reade saying that he had dramatized *Ralph the Heir*. Reade pointed out that in law he was not bound to consult the author, but that in any case he had not had the time to consult Trollope (this was disingenuous, as Reade had finished writing this 'trifle', as he called it, after ten days' work, on 17 October 1871);[22] he planned to give Trollope credit in the billings and thus 'open the theatre' for him (in fact Trollope's name came first in some of the printed announcements). Reade was unable to say when the drama would be produced, but promised to send Trollope a prompt copy so that he might 'make a good deal of money by it if produced in Australia under your own eye'. Reade, who fancied himself a champion of authors' rights and who was much at law with publishers, actually thought he was acting magnanimously. But Trollope, who got Reade's letter on 20 May 1872, immediately fired off angry letters, the first to George Smith, telling him what Reade, 'an intimate friend of mine' had done: 'It is monstrous that I should be made to appear as a writer of plays without my own permission,—or that I should be coerced into a literary partnership with any man.' He begged Smith to print in the *Pall Mall* a (somewhat softer) letter, disclaiming any responsibility for the play, and saying, in part, 'I would as lief enter into such a partnership with Mr. Charles Reade as with any man I know,' but that the procedure was unfair: 'If the play should succeed, he will get all the money. Should it be damned—as, in spite of Mr. Reade's dramatic genius, is likely if he adhere with any fidelity to the very bad plot of the novel—I must share the penalty with him.' To Reade himself Trollope sent a copy of the *Pall Mall* letter, together with one saying, 'I am very far from a desire to quarrel with you. According to my ideas of right and wrong in such matters, you are wrong. And, according to my ideas also, I am bound to let it be known publicly that I have no hand in producing the play.'²³

The play, *Shilly-Shally*, produced by John Hollingshead (another friend of Trollope's) at the Gaiety Theatre, opened on 1 April 1872 (long before Trollope, in Australia, got Reade's letter). A farcical comedy that featured John Toole, the most popular comic actor of the day, in the leading role of Neefit the tailor, *Shilly-Shally* had a successful one-month run; Toole's performance 'literally brought down the house and made the audience rock with delight'.²⁴ But the play was attacked for 'indelicacy', notably by Clement Scott in the *Daily Telegraph*. Trollope became all the angrier when he learned this by reading Reade's rejoinder in the same paper, and he sent off another disclaimer to the *Telegraph*.* Reade had in the mean time sent Trollope a copy of the play. Trollope responded that he could not alter his opinion and would be 'pusillanimous' if he did not say so.²⁵ According to Joseph Langford, after Trollope returned home, Reade quarrelled but Trollope would not. That seems hard to believe, since Trollope felt sorely aggrieved. But Reade was more reckless in his anger: he 'denounced Trollope as a literary knob-stick and a publisher's rat, alluding to Trollope's methodical way of composing his novels'. The artist Henry O'Neil, a mutual friend, tried vainly to reconcile them. The two men would cross the street rather than meet; they would glare at each other in silent fury, and Reade himself told how they 'were actually wont to participate in a game of whist at the Garrick without deigning to speak to each other'. The ill will lingered on for five years, till 1877.²⁶

Trollope spent one year seeing the Australian colonies, and on 29 July 1872 he and Rose left Melbourne aboard the steamer *Albion* for New Zealand. He had expected a British Empire flavour in Australia, and had never felt very far from home, especially in New South Wales. New Zealand would be, he hoped, mysterious: 'If I could find myself in a Maori pah,—then indeed the flavour of the dust of Pall Mall would for the time depart from me altogether.' The steamer took him to The Bluffs, the sea port of the

---

* It was not till much later that Trollope heard of an even stronger charge, that of 'indecency', levelled in the *Morning Advertiser* by its drama critic, Richard Lee (the most offensive line seems to have been 'He must marry her in her smock'). Reade sued Lee for libel and was eventually awarded £200 in damages.²⁷

South Island, and thence he travelled by train to nearby Invercargill, capital of Southland. The place was in no way exotic: 'I felt exactly as I might have felt on getting out of a railway in some small English town, and by the time I had reached the inn, and gone through the customary battle as to bedrooms, a tub of cold water, and supper, all the feeling of mystery was gone.' He thought the average New Zealander 'more English than any Englishman at home'.[28]

Although New Zealand struck him as irremediably English, Trollope made the Maoris and the Maori wars central to his discussion of New Zealand. He found these natives, unlike the Australian aborigines, attractive people: 'Those of their deeds which were most horrible in our eyes were done in the performance of duties absolutely exacted by their laws.' He had a scarcely hidden admiration for the outlaw Maori chieftain Te Kooti: 'for four years . . . the New Zealand government and the New Zealand troops were employed in hunting him. . . . As many as 2,000 men have been in the field after him, and he has cost New Zealand the incredible sum of nearly half a million.' Trollope tells of Rauparaha, a certain 'representative man', a great Maori chieftain with a reputation for wisdom, who in 1843 had helped instigate the Maori wars of resistance against settlers; he was also reputed to have been 'a great cannibal' and a terrible scourge of other tribes, 'of whom he had devoured many'. Trollope met Rauparaha's son at the Governor's table and played battledore and shuttle-cock with him: 'It is said of him,—the present man,—that he has killed men, but never eaten them;—of his father . . . that he had killed and eaten men . . . but of his grandfather, that he had killed men and eaten them, and had then himself been killed and eaten, like a true old Maori warrior.' Trollope, who shared the widespread English curiosity about cannibalism, seems never able to omit a reference to the subject; he mentions Sydney Smith's grim joke in the 1840s about telling George Selwyn, the first bishop of New Zealand, to have a cold clergyman on the sideboard for his Maori guests; Trollope himself remarks that Selwyn 'has returned to us [in England] uneaten, and now . . . presides safely over a comfortable English diocese'.[29]

Trollope considered the Maoris a brave people whose early feelings towards the British were kindly and hospitable. But the Maoris were not improved by contact with Europeans: 'As they touch the higher race they are poisoned and melt away.' Trollope viewed missionary efforts among the Maoris as fruitless and misdirected: '[The Maori] have many virtues. They are too proud for petty dishonesty; they are good-natured, and have a manly respect for themselves and for others; they are, in the main, truthful and brave; and their hospitality is proverbial. But these were their virtues of old,—before we came to them; and many who know them will say that these virtues are fading under their assumed Christianity.' Trollope writes 'with pain' that this 'gallant people', who 'nearly have the gifts' to live with the white race on equal terms, are destined to perish.[30]

In New Zealand, Trollope saw the principal towns and sights, Christchurch, Wellington, Port Lyttelton, Dunedin; the Auckland gold-fields, Kauri gum trees, lakes and springs and forests. His visit was in the midst of a particularly severe winter, but he none the less determined to travel overland many difficult miles via Lake Wakatip from Invercargill to Dunedin. In his bed one night he heard his host at a 'metal inn' of corrugated iron—in which every word could be heard throughout the rooms—tell his wife that the celebrated Mr Trollope 'must be a [damned] fool to come travelling in this country in such weather as this'. Trollope was half-inclined to agree. At one point he had to get out of a coach and slog twelve miles through the snow and mud. Later, in the province of Auckland, along the Lower Waikato River, he did have the very un-English experience of spending a night in a Maori *pah*, and sleeping alone in a small Maori hut. At Ohinemutu, 'a poor little Maori village', he went one dark evening, together with Captain Gilbert Mair, to bathe in a hot spring, only to find the small pool already occupied by 'three Maori damsels'. He hesitated, but then crept down into the water, the young women offering encouraging pats on his back. Mair recorded that after some time in the water, Trollope told him he wished he had something to lean against; whereupon Mair whispered this 'to a fine young woman of splendid proportions . . . who immediately set her capacious back against him, whereat he exclaimed, "Well, Mair, this is very delightful, don't you know, but I think I did wise in leaving Mrs. Trollope in Auckland."' After a 'comfortable' half-hour, he plunged into a cold river and then came back to the hot water 'amidst the renewed welcomings of the Maori damsels', having passed the evening 'very pleasantly'.[31]

On 3 October Trollope started for home. He had been gathering information, seeing the sights, meeting people for fourteen months. His book was about three-quarters complete, and would engage him on the homeward journey and for another month after arriving in London. Like the earlier *West Indies*, *Australia and New Zealand* makes disturbing reading today when Trollope touches on native peoples. At times he can be sympathetic to the plight of the aborigines. White men came, many natives were starved, their accustomed food having been taken from them: 'The white man, of course, felt that he was introducing civilisation; but the black man did not want civilisation. He wanted fish, kangaroos, and liberty.' Again, 'It was impossible to explain to the natives that a bene-volent race of men had come to live among them, who were anxious to teach them all good things. Their kangaroos and fish were driven away, their land was taken from them, the strangers assumed to be masters, and the black men did not see the benevolence.' Trollope insists the aborigines were 'savage warriors, and not murderers' when they fought for their lands and livelihood. His tenacious honesty makes him at times veer against the white man: 'We have taken away [the blacks'] land, have destroyed their food, have made them subject to our laws which are antagonistic to their habits and traditions, have endeavoured to make them subject to our tastes, which they hate, have massacred them when they defended themselves. . . . Within the haunts of white men . . . they have learned to wear clothes, and to drink, and to be covetous of tobacco and money,— and sometimes to do a little work. But with their rags, and their pipes, and their broken English, they are less noble, less sensitive of duty . . . than they were in their savage but unsubdued condition.' He saw as vain, indeed as ridiculous, the notion of converting the natives into Christians 'so that they should go to heaven after the sorrows of this life are over'; no one any longer believes untaught savages will suffer eternal punishment; in fact, if their new Christianity be but 'pseudo faith', perhaps missionary efforts were if anything endangering their souls.[32]

On the other hand, Trollope viewed the displacement of blacks by whites as inevitable; he believed the Australian aborigines were 'savages of the lowest kind', and 'infinitely lower' in gifts than the African negro. Echoing Carlyle two decades earlier, Trollope says that the black dignity one reads of 'is simply the dignity of idleness'. Of the Rama Yuck settlement at Gippsland, Victoria, established for Christianizing and educating aborigines, Trollope wrote, 'We can teach them to sing psalms . . . with less labour than is generally necessary for white pupils. . . . To me it seems that the game is not worth the candle. . . . Their writing was peculiarly good, as was also their memory. They are mimetic people, very quick of copying, and gifted with strong memories. But they do not, I think, understand.' He asks whether any 'philanthro-pist' would maintain that England should not have struggled to possess Australia. Could anyone believe that the aborigines would have fared better under the Dutch or French? Sadly, Trollope concludes that it is the fate of the aborigines 'to be abolished'. 'Of the Australian black man we may certainly say that he has to go. That he should perish without unnecessary suffering should be the aim of all who are concerned in the matter.' Trollope's moral sense, like that of most of his contemporaries, simply did not register the horrors of this analysis.[33]

In *Australia and New Zealand* Trollope's verdict on the colonists is a laudatory one. He finds faults, of course, chiefly the relatively minor one of people doing too much bragging or 'blowing', a practice he ascribes to a pervading and unnecessary 'sense of inferiority': 'I must say . . . that the wonders performed in the way of riding, driving, fighting, walking, working, love-making, and speech-making . . . would have been worth recording in a separate volume had they been related by any but the heroes and heroines themselves.' He dissects the drunkenness of the labouring classes, especially in the bush; he says colonial statesmen have not had time to develop true patriotism. But on balance he is altogether positive about the colonies; he suggests that they must work together to effect a customs union, and is optimistic about self-determination and eventual separation from the mother country. Although Australians do not like to be told about future independence, the day must come; Trollope doesn't want colonies kept as 'gems' in England's diadem. When the time for separation comes, England must let the colonies have their independence; and the time must be determined by the colonists themselves. The present loyalty of colonists to the mother country is too strong: the colonist 'always speaks of England as home. He remembers the Queen's birthday, and knows the names of the Queen's grandchildren. He is jealous of the fame of Nelson and Wellington.'[34]

But clinging to the idea of England's glory, either by Englishmen at home or by colonists, will not help many people, will not 'remove those terrible burdens of poverty which every Englishman, proud as he may be of his country, should feel as an incubus to his soul. As we are the richest of people, so we are also among the poorest.' Only the upper middle class— among whom most of Trollope's readers were numbered—the people with shoes for their children, and plenty of food and fuel, can indulge in the thought of England's glory: 'But for that poor man . . . would not 5s. a day, with no song, be better than 2s. a day, and Rule Britannia? And for that young woman, would not £30 for a year's service, and at the end of it a husband able to keep her, be better than £16 a year and no husband, even though no regimental band should go by the windows once a fortnight, playing up "Steady, boys, steady" for the gratification of her patriotism?' Rose had brought along a cook from England, 'a good-looking strong woman, of excellent temper' who was capable of everything from hairdressing to brewing beer. After a month in the bush, she found a husband; Trollope was delighted to see her half a year later, '"quite the lady," but ready for any kind of work that might come in her way.' No woman of her class, he decided, ought to remain in England if she could take herself to the colonies.[35]

During his trip Trollope met hundreds of colonists and came to know scores of them, but he did not make many friends; for one thing he strongly felt that friends at a distance were almost as good as lost; moreover, as he wrote to George Smith from Melbourne, 'I have interested myself much with these colonial people,—as to habits, wages, ways of life & the like; but in regard to social delights I cannot cotton to them thoroughly.'[36] The one exception was George William Rusden, of Melbourne, Clerk of the Executive Council of Victoria and author of works on Australian education and history. Rusden, before meeting Trollope, had dedicated his pamphlet on the history of Port Philip to him. Though Trollope differed sharply with the old-fashioned Tory on the eventual separation of the colonies from England, he says in *Australia and New Zealand* that he 'found no one better informed on the affairs of Australia generally' than Rusden.[37] This new friend facilitated introductions to important people and had Trollope made an honorary member of the Melbourne Club. Trollope later got Rusden elected to the Garrick without a single black ball: 'Omne ignotum pro magnifico,' he joked—Every unknown is taken for a marvel.[38] Trollope also encouraged Rusden to write a 'magnum opus', a history of Australia and New Zealand, and arranged that Rusden come to England and have Chapman & Hall publish the volumes. And although Trollope denied the efficacy of ocean post to maintain friendships, his letters to Rusden are among the few truly personal ones he wrote.

The Trollopes' homeward journey carried them first to Honolulu aboard the SS *Nebraska*, and thence aboard the SS *Idaho* to San Francisco. From there they travelled overland by rail across the United States. One stop on the way was Salt Lake City, Utah, where Trollope called unannounced on Brigham Young and sent up his card:

He received me in his doorway, not asking me to enter, and inquired whether I were not a miner. When I told him that I was not a miner, he asked me whether I earned my bread. I told him I did. 'I guess you're a miner,' said he. I again assured him that I was not. 'Then how do you earn your bread?' I told him that I did so by writing books. 'I'm sure you're a miner,' said he. Then he turned upon his heel, went back into the house, and closed the door.[39]

This was proper punishment, Trollope conceded, for he had been vain enough to believe the Mormon leader would have heard of him. The Trollopes arrived in New York, on 25 November, stopping at the Brevort

Hotel in lower Fifth Avenue. They embarked for England two days later, and arrived in London in early December.

In all they had been away nineteen months. Waltham House was gone, and the Trollopes took temporary rooms at 3 Holles Street, Cavendish Square. Rather than give up hunting, as had been half in his mind when he divested himself of Waltham House, Trollope returned to the sport as energetically as ever. It had been hunting that he had most missed while out of England. Now he purchased another horse, so as to bring his stud back up to four, and took his horses to his old favourite, the Essex, and occasionally, to Leighton Buzzard under Baron Meyer de Rothschild and Selby Lowndes. [40]

He was happy to be back, but unpleasant news soon greeted him about Harry. The young man, as G. H. Lewes recorded, wanted 'to marry a woman of the town' (one version had her a French actress), and Trollope sent him to visit his brother in Australia. Trollope also confided the story to Charles Taylor and Henry O'Neil, and to Joseph Langford, who explained to John Blackwood that Harry had 'shown himself amenable to reason and obedient to parental authority. Trollope has behaved with his usual promptness.' [41] At about this time Harry also got out of publishing. He had been with Chapman & Hall about three and a half years: 'He did not like it,' Trollope wrote in *An Autobiography*, 'nor do I think he made a very good publisher.' Harry left the business with more monetary gain than might have been expected from his short stay, 'and has since taken himself to literature as a profession. Whether he will work at it so hard as his father, and write as many books, may be doubted.' [42] It was not easy being this famous father's son.

During most of the time while Trollope had been away, *The Eustace Diamonds* had been appearing monthly in the pages of the *Fortnightly*, and in Trollope's view it 'did much to repair the injury which I felt had come to my reputation in the novel-market by the works of the last few years'. [43] Trollope judged this novel his most successful since *The Small House*, which had appeared almost a decade earlier.

The Eustace Diamonds is the story of an adventuress, Lizzie Eustace, a widow in search of a second husband while attempting to keep as her own an enormously valuable necklace, which she claimed had been given to her by her deceased husband, but which his family said was an heirloom that had to be returned to them. The novel's popularity owed most to Lizzie herself, 'a cunning little woman of pseudo-fashion', whom readers and critics quickly compared to Becky Sharp. Trollope rather fuzzily explained: 'As I wrote the book, the idea constantly presented itself to me that Lizzie Eustace was but a second Beckey Sharpe [*sic*]; but in planning the character I had not thought of this, and I believe that Lizzie would have been just as she is though Beckie Sharpe [*sic*] had never been described.'[44] Trollope himself pointed to the connection early in the book by calling Lizzie an 'opulent and aristocratic Becky Sharp'.[45] The *Spectator* found her disappointing: 'We had supposed that in Lady Eustace we were to have Mr. Trollope's equivalent for Thackeray's "Becky Sharp," but we hardly think that we have got it; or if we have, Mr. Trollope's equivalent for Thackeray's "Becky Sharp" is but a poor one.' But the *Saturday Review* said that Trollope, 'having apparently set himself to draw a rival to Becky Sharp . . . has spared no pains. . . . His Lizzie stands out a distinct, strongly marked image and type, and will live among his characters.' Though 'a dishonest, lying, evil-minded harpy', she has a 'companionableness, a life and spirit, about her which keeps her within the bounds of humanity'.[46] Lizzie is in fact quite different from Becky, not least in that she has not Becky's 'sharpness'; while utterly given over to and fascinated with lying, she tends to be taken in by her own lies, something that could never be said of Becky Sharp. Moreover, Trollope in writing *The Eustace Diamonds* seems to have had Wilkie Collins in mind at least as much as Thackeray, for he adopts some of the strategies of the detective novel, epitomized by Collins's *The Moonstone* (1868), and those of the sensational novel, epitomized by *The Woman in White* (1860). In *An Autobiography* Trollope dismisses as a mistake the distinction made by the reading public between so-called sensational novels such as Collins's and 'realistic' novels such as his own; he says that a good novel should be both sensational and realistic, and he points to 'sensational' passages in novels admired by those who claim to detest sensationalism—in *Ivanhoe*, *Old Mortality*, *Jane Eyre*, *Henry Esmond*, and, excusing the liberty, in *Orley Farm*. No matter how sensational (or tragic), a story will charm if its characters are made of 'flesh and blood' and are such that the reader can sympathize with them. If the characters have this kind of human 'truth' about them, no novel can be too sensational. Trollope probably meant this, or believed he did, but in fact he thought the sensational and the realistic were seldom united successfully by popular novelists, certainly not by Collins or Dickens. Elsewhere in *An Autobiography* he makes it clear that in his view Collins is pretty inferior: he is 'all plot'; he carefully works out minute details, backwards and forwards, so as to effect perfect 'dove-tailing'. But such kind of excellence gives Trollope little pleasure because he can 'never lose the taste of the construction'. For himself,

'When I sit down to write a novel I do not at all know, and I do not very much care, how it is to end.' He admits that in *The Eustace Diamonds* he got his plot better arranged than was usual with him, but feels constrained to insist again that plot is not his line. This one 'produced itself without any forethought'.47

The *Saturday Review* was happy to pronounce that in *The Eustace Diamonds* 'Mr. Trollope is himself again'. *The Times* said, 'The Eustace Diamonds may fearlessly invite comparison with any of Mr. Trollope's earliest and best known novels,' and welcomed the reintroduction of 'some friends of bygone days', Lady Glencora, Plantagenet Palliser, and the old Duke of Omnium, but singled out Lord Fawn for special comment: '[Trollope] has done one of the most difficult things in the world—he has made a respectable man interesting.'48 One private reaction to the book Trollope would have valued was that of Edward FitzGerald, the translator of *The Rubáiyát*, who said *The Eustace Diamonds* interested him almost as much as the Tichborne case (high praise, since that sensational trial of a false claim to a title and its estates had all England by the ears, Trollope included).49 One private opinion he did learn of, perhaps to his wonderment. Shortly after *The Eustace Diamonds* appeared, Trollope, dining at Lord Stanhope's met, of all people, Disraeli. The former Prime Minister, who claimed that he did not read much contemporary fiction, that when he wanted to read a novel he wrote one, is quoted as saying to Trollope, 'I have long known, Mr. Trollope, your churchmen and churchwomen; may I congratulate you on the same happy lightness of touch in the portrait of your new adventuress?' He almost certainly had not read *Phineas Finn* with its unflattering portrait of 'Dubby' Daubeny.50

MONTAGU SQUARE

As to that leisure evening of life, I must say that I do not
want it. I can conceive of no contentment of which toil is
not to be the immediate parent.

Letter of 8 June 1876

24

The Way We Live Now

TROLLOPE's search for a new home in London took two months. Eventually he found an early nineteenth-century red-brick four-storey house (a fifth storey was added after Trollope's time) at 39 Montagu Square, Marylebone, just a few blocks north of Marble Arch. That Trollope's good friends Frederick and Juliet Pollock lived at number 59 Montagu Square was encouraging. Montagu Square was, Trollope told a friend, 'not a gorgeous neighbourhood, but one which will suit my declining years and modest resources'. For all its quiet gentility, the square was also but a few blocks from Northumberland Street by the Marylebone Workhouse, where he had lived so unhappily in gloomy lodgings nearly forty years earlier.* Trollope wrote to Rusden: 'We are taking . . . a house in London, and are going to enter into the ruinous pleasures and necessary agonies of furnishing it. I remember I used to hear . . . that a modest man might supply himself with beds, tables and a chair to sit on for £200. Now I am told that £1500 for the rough big things is absolutely indispensable, and that prettinesses may be supplied afterwards for a further £500.' Trollope got Chapman to expedite payment due him for *The Eustace Diamonds*, some £1,250, to help with the premium on the house.[1] He hoped this would be his last home; he thought he would die there.

When the Trollopes took possession of 39 Montagu Square in early April—hunting having conveniently just ended—his chief order of business was arranging his books, which he claimed were dearer to him than even his horses or the wine in his cellar.[2] Though not a bibliophile in the sense of taking an interest in books as objects or rarities, he was proud of his personal library and had catalogues printed in 1867 and 1874, for

---

* In *The Way We Live Now* Trollope makes a private joke about Marylebone: after Melmotte, the great financier/swindler and MP, disgraced and poisoned himself, Westminster 'never forgave him', but Marylebone, 'which is always merciful, took him up quite with affection', and even considered erecting a monument to him.[3]

Waltham House and Montagu Square. His catalogued collections numbered about 5,000 volumes; although he had acquired about 4,000 from
Robert Bell's library in 1867, he discarded many of them; the second
catalogue showed that during the intervening seven years he had discarded more than 1,000 volumes and acquired more than 800 new ones.
His collection was strong on drama and poetry; it contained more biography than history, and very little philosophy, theology, or natural
science; it was also relatively thin on fiction. Of course he did not keep and
catalogue all the books he read, nor did he own all the books he read.[4] At
Montagu Square, his book room, or study, was on the ground floor in the
back, behind the dining-room; extra books were placed in the recess at the
end of the double drawing-room one flight up.[5] When the library had been
put in place, Trollope began, on 1 May, a new novel: he had not written
anything since finishing *Australia and New Zealand* in mid-January; the
pressures of fox-hunting, house-hunting, and moving had resulted in a
three-and-a-half-month fallow period. Now he determined to make a
serious return to fiction; the result was *The Way We Live Now*, another
'five-volume' novel, his longest; it was also his most sustained satire, and
the one that many twentieth-century readers consider the most attuned to
their own concerns.

Of all his novels, *The Way We Live Now* is probably the most topical, the
most rooted in contemporary events, the most inspired, so to speak, by
newspaper accounts. The title was meant to be taken literally, in that the
story is set firmly in the year of its creation, 1873. Trollope's preliminary
notes indicate that Lady Carbury, 43 years old, a handsome, energetic,
flirtatious, and unscrupulous 'authoress', was to be 'the chief character',
and Roger Carbury, would-be suitor of Lady Carbury's daughter,
Henrietta, was to be the 'hero'. Melmotte the 'French swindler' is barely
mentioned, included only towards the end of the list of characters as the
father of Marie Melmotte, 'the heiress'.[6] But as Trollope wrote, Augustus
Melmotte took over, and the novel became an investigation into the
'commercial profligacy of the age'.[7] Melmotte takes London by storm: he
floats a phoney American–Mexican railway company and forges documents; he entertains royalty and the visiting Emperor of China; he is
elected to Parliament for Westminster—John Stuart Mill's old seat—and
by the ballot, which, to Trollope's annoyance, had been made into law in
1872; he is introduced to the House by the head of his party, unnamed in
the novel but unmistakably Disraeli. Melmotte's origins are murky; his
'fat' wife is a Bohemian Jewess, and he is perhaps Jewish himself, though
more likely the son of one Melmody, an Irish-American forger.

Melmotte's real-life originals appear to have been many: George Hudson, the 'railway King', who had died as recently as 1871; Napoleon III, who had indulged in and supported extravagant commercial speculation, and who died in exile in 1873; the chief original was John Sadleir, a banker and a Member of Parliament, who was revealed to be a swindler and forger on a grand scale, dealing fraudulently in railways and estates. When his attempt to brazen things out failed, he committed suicide by prussic acid in February 1856. His career and death had been put to powerful use by Dickens at the time in the history of Mr Merdle, the swindling financier and Member of Parliament in Dickens's *Little Dorrit*. In 1856 Trollope had incorporated a reference to him in the closing page of *The New Zealander*, as the incarnation of the swindling and lying that Britons were no longer recognizing for what they were. Melmotte's foreignness, and the theme of outsiders making dishonest fortunes in London, drew upon the recent celebrated 'Bank of England Forgery' case (in which four young Americans had bilked the Bank of England for £102,000 by forging signatures on bills of exchange) and upon questionable South American loans, especially that connected with the Honduras railway scandal of 1872 (the work of Charles 'Joachim' Lefevre, whose phoney railway laid no more than fifty miles of track before failing).[8]

Then the most colourful event of the year's London season lent itself to incorporation into Trollope's already-begun novel: on 18 June there arrived, on a three-week state visit, Nase-ed-din, the Shah of Persia. He was fêted in the City at an enormous entertainment at the Guildhall, with 3,000 guests, followed by a state dinner for ninety, with tickets at a premium. This became the dinner Melmotte is favoured to give for the visiting Emperor of China, at Grosvenor Square, in the presence of English royalty. In making the exotic foreign dignitary the Emperor of China, Trollope was having fun with another hit news item from earlier in the year, the marriage of the actual Emperor of China, a boy of 15.[9]

In *The Way We Live Now*, Trollope did not limit himself to commercial profligacy, but 'made an onslaught also on other vices,—on the intrigues of girls who want to get married, on the luxury of young men who prefer to remain single, and on the puffing propensities of authors who desire to cheat the public into buying their volumes'.[10] Dishonesty permeates every rank of society: Lady Carbury knows very well that her book, *Criminal Queens*, is worthless, but she has a 'conviction that her end was to be obtained not by producing good books, but by inducing certain people to say that her books were good'. She gains generous reviews by returning the favour. She later takes to novel writing at her publisher's urging: she had not 'any special tale to tell' and 'would have written a volume of sermons on the same encouragement'.[11]

Aristocrats and people of position are lazy do-nothings, and in their greed are easily cozened by Melmotte. And they are frequently the buyers in the marriage market, a sordid correlative to the financial market. Young Lord Nidderdale, a member of Melmotte's dummy railway board, has no purpose in life except to marry an heiress. Nidderdale offers to take Marie Melmotte 'for half a million down'. Discussing the marriage market with his nasty old father, the Marquis of Auld Reekie (who, as Lady Glencora MacCluskie's guardian, had many years and novels earlier arranged her loveless marriage to Plantagenet Palliser), Nidderdale says that there should be a 'regular statement' published stating the amount of money connected with each young unmarried woman: 'It'd save a deal of trouble.'[12]

The Longestaffes, the family of a Sussex Squire, are a sorry lot. The least unattractive is the son, Dolly, a foolish young man who is involved, like his father, with Melmotte. Dolly also is urged by his family to tackle Marie, but is too indolent. His sister Georgina has been many weary years struggling on the marriage market; now, almost thirty, embittered and desperate, she nearly marries the elderly Jewish banker Brehgert; whereupon her family flies into anti-Semitic rage. Her father, who had long fought to keep Jews out of Parliament ('When that had been done he was certain that the glory of England was sunk for ever'), swears he will turn her out of his house; the prospect of marriage to a Jew is 'disgusting,— degrading,—disgraceful'; her mother tells her the Jews are 'an accursed race . . . expelled from Paradise'. Even her maid leaves her. Brehgert is a decent man, but Georgina fails to see this; she especially misses what the narrator calls 'the single-minded genuine honesty' of his dealings with her.[13] A cynical mercenary herself, she balks at the likelihood of not having a London house. Brehgert claims, rightly, that he acted like a gentleman throughout, and old Longestaffe cannot gainsay him. Whatever Trollope's own mild and conventional prejudices about Jews, the Christians are clearly worse in the world of 'the way we live now'.

Worst of all is young Sir Felix Carbury, another nominal director of Melmotte's railway company, and the complete cad: he gambles; he never for a moment thinks of paying his bills; he wastes his own inheritance, then eats up that of his mother and sister; he tries to elope with Melmotte's daughter, but is too inept and drunken to pull it off; he plays shamelessly with the affections of a country girl, having no thought of marrying her—

he knows 'a trick worth two of that'. [14] Felix is one of Trollope's few young wasters to show no redeeming qualities at all.

Trollope, always wary of full-blown satire and mindful of some past failures when he had tried it, thought that in *The Way We Live Now* he had been too harsh and exaggerated in his satire. On the other hand, there is much of the usual Trollopian balance in the novel: Melmotte himself takes on a kind of Roman grandeur towards the end; Felix Carbury may be no good at all, but other young men like Nidderdale and Dolly Longestaffe have their compensating decencies; and they are funny, always a mark of grace in Trollope. Furthermore, the whole story is too entertaining to be as bleak as some would have it. The visit of and dinner for the Emperor of China are great fun. The second half of the book is lighter, particularly in the many pages that remain after Melmotte's suicide; and at the close there are no fewer than four weddings. [15] The foreign trouble-makers die or leave for America, and England is, apparently, more or less in place again. Many readers have mistakenly taken the cranky, puritanical Roger Carbury as Trollope's spokesman. When Carbury complains bitterly that the country is 'going to the dogs' (Trollope's precise description of Carlylism in *An Autobiography*), Bishop Yeld—based upon kindly Charles Longley, Trollope's old tutor at Harrow, the recently-deceased Archbishop of Canterbury—argues Trollope's own view: 'men on the whole do live better lives than they did a hundred years ago'; there is today more justice, more mercy, more charity, less of religious enthusiasm and of superstition. The 'grumblers' are not looking at the world at large. [16] In *An Autobiography* Trollope discusses the question in nearly identical words, dismissing such pessimists as Carlyle and Ruskin, whose extravagant and loud lamentations 'are so contrary to the convictions of men who cannot but see how comfort has been increased, how health has been improved, and education extended'. [17] Moreover Trollope, in spite of what he considered the novel's faults of exaggeration, certainly did not regard the book as a failure, and seems mistakenly to have thought that the reviewers gave it good notices.

In fact, the press was bad. The *Athenaeum* liked only the Longestaffes, calling the book 'carelessly constructed and carelessly written'. Meredith Townsend, in the *Spectator*, complained of the 'oppressive vulgarity of the characters', and asserted that there 'is not a decently honest man in the book who is not a fool, except the squire, Roger Carbury, and he is an overbearing prig'. The *Saturday Review* quarrelled with the 'incivility' of the title—'The way *we* live!'—and argued that until Trollope paused to relax and gather himself he would produce no more Archdeacon Grantlys,

Mrs Proudies, or Dr Thornes. The *Examiner* compared the book un-
favourably to *Vanity Fair* and regretted Trollope's 'haste both in conception and in execution'. The New York *Nation* crowed that the novel
justified Americans' love for their country: no English writer ever produced a description of America 'blacker than this picture of English
civilization by Mr. Trollope'. The *Westminster Review* went so far as
nastily to remark 'how closely Mr. Trollope himself resembles Lady
Carbury—how he too has written all sorts of books, a hack translation of
Caesar, a scratch volume of hunting sketches, a boys' Christmas book
of Australian adventure, all of them with no higher aim than Lady
Carbury's.'[18]

The important exception was *The Times*, which, in a review by Lady
Barker of 24 August 1875, whole-heartedly approved of the book, calling it
'only too faithful a portraiture' of present-day manners. The review
especially complimented Trollope on his fairness to his characters, even to
Melmotte, who for all his odiousness is credited with boldness and
'pluck'.[19] A fortnight earlier *The Times* had published an editorial by John
Delane and Tom Mozley, which, without mentioning Trollope's novel by
name, endorsed its view:

The country in general is now regarded as a prey upon which any number of
vultures, scenting it from afar, may safely light and securely gorge themselves.
The foul tribe is amply replenished by its congeners at home, and foreign invaders
find any number of men bearing good names ready to assist them in robberies far
more cruel and sweeping than those of the foot pad or the burglar. Gentlemen of
family and station are competing for the honour of helping Canadian, American,
French and German adventurers to fleece English society, and English society
has allowed its greediness for exorbitant gains to hurry it blindfolded into the
trap.[20]

Being out of the country at the time of the reviews, Trollope probably
missed most of them, but he doubtless saw these two *Times* items, and
they may have led him to believe the novel had been well received.

Shortly after establishing himself in Montagu Square Trollope had the
pleasure of welcoming Kate Field. In 1871 she and her mother, who was in
bad health, had sailed for England. Mrs Field died on arrival at Queenstown, Ireland, on 26 May. Trollope had left for Australia three days
earlier, or he surely would have been of help at this time. But Kate, as
popular as ever, began life anew in London. She had many old and new
friends to come to her side, including various friends of Trollope, Frances
Power Cobbe, Mr and Mrs Moncure Conway, George Smalley, Robert

Browning, G. H. Lewes and George Eliot, Lord Houghton, J. A. Froude, Alexander Kinglake, Alfred Austin. She wrote for newspapers and magazines, and composed 'comediettas' or curtain-raisers. Her political views took a more radically republican turn as she became sympathetic with and a close friend of Sir Charles Dilke. She even took up the militantly free-thinking Charles Bradlaugh, went to hear him address working men in the East End (she said that as an orator Bradlaugh 'would not have had his equal in England had he not occasionally dropped his *h's*'), and at Mayfair parties she defended him to the frank horror of other guests. She gave her first public lecture—on Dickens—in April 1872 (Sidney Colvin said that there had been no such voice as hers on the English stage in many years).[21] In September 1872 she returned to New York, but by June 1873 was back in London, and dined at the Trollopes' on her second evening in town. Trollope invited Wilkie Collins, who replied, 'Yes I have heard of the American lady—she is adored by everybody, and I am all ready to follow the general example.'[22] Kate, a veritable lioness, enjoyed a brilliant season, and everyone, especially men, called on her. Mark Twain went out of his way to meet her, at about the very time that Trollope introduced himself to Mark Twain. He wrote to Kate on 5 July that he was giving a dinner at the Garrick for 'two of the wildest of your countrymen', Mark Twain and Joachim Miller (a poet called 'the Oregon Byron'); Trollope joked: 'Pity you have not yet established the rights of your sex or you could come and meet them, and be *as jolly as men.*'*[23] According to Kate Field's biographer, Trollope called 'often' on Kate at this time, but we know nothing of the details.[24] She appeared as youthful as ever, while Trollope looked all the more avuncular and old beyond his years. They doubtless hit it off better in person than in letters, where Trollope's critical turn seems ever to have exercised itself towards her. Three years later, in *An Autobiography*, written in early 1876, she was still his 'most chosen friend', a 'ray of light' from which he could 'always strike a spark by thinking of her'.[25]

Instead of going to the continent as usual, the Trollopes took their September holiday in Killarney. On his return he answered a letter of his neighbour Lady Pollock, who was away for a time:

* Also present at this dinner were Leveson-Gower and Tom Hughes; Twain later wrote: 'Trollope was voluble and animated, and was but vaguely aware that any other person was present excepting him of the noble blood, Levison-Gower [*sic*]. . . . Joaquin Miller did his full share of the talking, but he was a discordant note. . . . He and Trollope talked all the time and both at the same time, Trollope pouring forth a smooth and limpid and sparkling stream of faultless English, and Joaquin discharging into it his muddy and tumultuous mountain torrent'[26]

The Way We Live Now

I have been troubled and in some sort unhappy. I fear I have lost the hearing of one
ear for always. For such troubles a man ought to be prepared as he grows old; and
this is comparatively so small a trouble, that I ought not to feel it a grievance. But
for a time it frets me, and confuses me. I fancy that I am always going to be run
over, and everybody seems to talk to me on the wrong side. I am told that a bone
has grown up inside the orifice. Oh dear! One does not understand it all. Why
should any bones grow, except useful, working, bones? Why should anything go
wrong in our bodies? Why should we not be all beautiful? Why should there be
decay?—why death?—and, oh why, damnation? The last we get out of by not
believing it, but when a man has a bone in his ear, so that everything makes a
rumbling noise and nothing is heard distinctly, he does believe it. But why;—why
is it there? I suppose I have done something or left undone something, which if left
undone or if done, would have saved me from the bone. But for the moment I
cannot get it out of my head.[27]

Poor hearing (which may have been a family failing; Tom Trollope became
quite deaf) brought with it increased feelings of age. Trollope was at this
time 58 and had long been in the habit of calling himself an old man (in his
novels people are 'old' at 50). But if dreary thoughts entered his mind
temporarily, he determined not to let them do so for long. He kept to his
writing, and threw himself with his usual zest into London life and, in
November, into hunting. Awareness that his hunting could not go on too
much longer made him 'more than ever' go to great lengths: he arranged
that three days a week a cab would be at his door by 7 a.m. (where the
driver would be accommodated with breakfast); after being driven to
Liverpool Street Station, he took the train into the hunting country,
travelled again by horse-drawn vehicle, usually some dozen miles, to the
Essex Hunt (sometimes to find that frost had cancelled the day's sport),
then returned again each evening by the same conveyances, proud that as
an 'old man' and 'comparatively a poor man' he managed this regimen,
strenuous enough for a young rich man.[28] Sometimes his schedule called
for a stop at Chapman & Hall in Piccadilly, and an old member of the staff
said that Trollope would 'tramp into the office, as soon as the doors were
open, clad in his pink coat, with a sheaf of proofs in his great side
pocket . . . he would bang on the table with his hunting crop, and swear
like a sergeant-major because there was no one in authority yet arrived to
receive his hectic instructions.'[29]

People with hearing problems are sometimes unwittingly loud; Trollope had ever been loud, but one suspects his partial deafness exacerbated
his penchant for shouting. All his friends testify to this defect: Lady
Amberley, as his hostess, complained that his voice was 'too loud', that it

drowned Thomas Huxley's pleasant, quiet voice.[30] Shirley Brooks
recorded in January 1873 that Trollope 'roars more than ever since
Australia'.[31] Frederick Locker-Lampson testified that Trollope's 'ordinary
tones had the penetrative capacity of two people quarrelling, and his voice
would ring through and through you, and shake the windows in their
frames, while all the time he was most amiably disposed towards you
under his waistcoat. To me his *viso sciolto* and bluff geniality were very
attractive, and so were his gusty denunciations.'[32] Wilkie Collins, calling
Trollope 'as good and staunch a friend as ever lived', admitted nevertheless that 'his immeasurable energies had a bewildering effect on my invalid
constitution. To me, he was an incarnate gale of wind. He blew off my hat;
he turned my umbrella inside out.'[33] Another friend said Trollope 'came in
at the door like a frantic windmill'. Another, writing in 1873, described a
visit by Trollope:

The bell would peal, the knocker begin thundering, the door be burst open, and
the next minute the house be filled with the big resonant voice inquiring who was
at home. I should say he had naturally a sweet voice, which through eagerness he
had spoilt by halloing. He was a big man, and the most noticeable thing about his
dress was a black handkerchief which he wore tied *twice* round his neck. A trick of
his was to put the end of a silk pocket-handkerchief in his mouth and to keep
gnawing at it—often biting it into holes in the excess of his energy. . . . His
manner was bluff, hearty, and genial, and he possessed to the full the great charm
of giving his undivided attention to the matter in hand. He was always enthusiastic
and energetic in whatever he did. He was of an eager disposition, and doing
nothing was a pain to him. . . . Either [hunting or books], however, and for the
matter of that I might add *any* subject, was attacked by him with equal energy. . . . While he talked to me, I and my interests might have been the only
things for which he cared; and any passing topic of conversation was, for the
moment, the one and absorbing topic in the world.[34]

An enemy like Edmund Yates, still nursing old animosities a decade after
Trollope's death, would read his behaviour very differently:

A man with worse or more offensive manners than Trollope I have rarely met. He
was coarse, boorish, rough, noisy, overbearing, insolent; he adopted the John-
sonian tactics of trying to outroar his adversary in argument; he spluttered and
shouted, and glared through his spectacles, and waved his arms about, a sight for
gods and men. . . . By persons in general society he was regarded with perturbed
wonder, as a specimen never before met with. By a few old whist-playing cronies
at the Garrick, whose acquaintance he only made late in life, he was greatly liked. I
have heard of several instances, and I know of one, to prove that he had a kind
heart, and that his roaring bluster and offensive contradiction was 'only his

manner'; but, as Mr. Mantalini says of Ralph Nickleby, it was 'a demd uncomfortable private-madhouse kind of manner' all the same.[35]

Tom Trollope, on reading Yates's article in 1892, told Harry Trollope that it was 'less venomous than those (now very few) who knew anything of the relations between your father and Mr. Yates, might have expected'.[36]

25

Pallisers Again

WHILE Trollope was writing *The Way We Live Now*, steadily from May to December, with a four-week interruption in June to write *Harry Heathcote*, he was of course appearing before the public in serial form: *Lady Anna*, the story written entirely on shipboard en route to Australia, about an Earl's granddaughter remaining faithful to her troth to a tailor, opened in the pages of the *Fortnightly* just as he was moving into Montagu Square. It did not fare well with the press; as Trollope said, 'every body found fault with me for marrying her to the tailor.'[1] The *Saturday Review* complained that the reading public would not stand this sort of thing 'except in a period of political storm and ferment,' that the book's similarity to George Eliot's *Felix Holt* could not be 'entirely accidental', although her tailor and Trollope's were Hyperion to a satyr. The reviewer went on to say that it had been heard that Trollope wrote the story on a bet.[2] (He was certainly capable of making such a wager, but would not have liked it known publicly.)

And in July there appeared, in the *Graphic*, the first instalments of *Phineas Redux*. Had things gone otherwise with *Saint Pauls Magazine*, he would have preferred to have published this sequel to *Phineas Finn* in its pages. As it turned out, he was already disassociated from the magazine by the time he began writing *Phineas Redux* and, even had he taken the book to *Saint Pauls*, the new proprietor would have been unable to meet his price. Arthur Locker, editor of the *Graphic*, a weekly that was successfully challenging the *Illustrated London News*, had written to Trollope in Australia to request a novel, claiming for the *Graphic* a circulation 'far exceeding that of any magazine'. Knowing of Trollope's 'unflagging industry', Locker said he expected Trollope would turn out a story on his homeward journey. Trollope answered that he had a novel already written, *Phineas Redux*, 'a sequel to one written by me called P. Finn; & of the same length'.[3] He asked £2,500 for the entire copyright, which terms Locker accepted; but on returning to London Trollope divided serial and book rights between the *Graphic* and Chapman & Hall, receiving £1,250 for each. This £2,500 represented a decline of £700 over what Virtue paid for *Phineas Finn*, exactly six years earlier. Locker was unhappy about the title, worrying that the public would think 'Redux' the hero's surname, but Trollope said he had 'no objection to them doing so'.4 (When Trollope gave Locker *Harry Heathcote of Gangoil* as a Christmas story for 1873, Locker also objected to that title, but Trollope insisted that he thought much about the names of his stories, a matter 'which must be left to the author'.5)

Trollope said with mock modesty that he had no right to expect that readers of *Phineas Redux* would remember characters who appeared six years previously, though he coyly admitted the sequel to have been equally successful with the public—especially, he noted, with men and women who lived in the sets depicted in the story. *Phineas Finn* and *Phineas Redux* were to him 'one novel', marred by the mistake of having the hero return to Ireland at the close of the first part to marry a simple Irish girl, whom he had to kill off to expedite Phineas's return, in the sequel, to London and politics, and, it should be said, to romance.6 *Phineas Redux* is a work distinctly more political, more sensational, and more sombre than the earlier story. That the comparative pessimism of *Phineas Redux* was in part owing to Trollope's election defeat at Beverley and the demise of *Saint Pauls Magazine*, both of which took place between the writing of the two stories, is likely but impossible to demonstrate.

In *Phineas Redux* Trollope drew on events of 1868–9 with regard to Irish Church disestablishment and again patterned his Conservative protagonist (Daubeny) on Disraeli. In February 1868 Disraeli, who had been Tory leader in the Commons, took over leadership of the party from the ailing Lord Derby. On 4 April Gladstone and the Liberals beat Disraeli by sixty votes in the Commons on Irish Church disestablishment; Disraeli refused to resign and hung on; finally, in November, Disraeli dissolved the House and lost heavily in the general election, one fought largely on the issue of Irish disestablishment. Disraeli still refused to resign; then in December Gladstone carried another resolution on disestablishment and Disraeli capitulated. In 1869 Gladstone disestablished the Irish Protestant Episcopal Church in Ireland. In *Phineas Redux* old Lord de Terrier retires and hands over leadership to Daubeny. Daubeny, we read, 'had achieved his place by skill rather than principle'; 'his utterances had been confusing, mysterious, and perhaps purposely unintelligible'; Daubeny's own party, like Disraeli's, distrusts him. For Daubeny, 'audacity in reform was the very backbone of conservatism'. Standing for East Barsetshire, Daubeny in an election speech cleverly mentions a plan to disestablish the Church of England, to an audience whose 'bucolic mind' cannot comprehend what he is saying.[7] Such a move represented what to Trollope was customary Conservative party opportunism, as in Catholic Emancipation and Corn Law repeal. But it especially echoed Disraeli's recent and audacious usurpation of the Liberal agenda for franchise reform. In some respects Trollope switches things around, in that Irish Church disestablishment had been carried through by Gladstone and the Liberals; and Daubeny/ Disraeli proposes disestablishing the Church of England, a much more radical move. The notion that Disraeli might attempt something very like this was already in Trollope's mind during 1868: in his Beverley election speech he said that if Disraeli and the Tories came to power, Disraeli would probably 'go over the most beautiful conjuring trick. It will be hocus pocus, square round, fly away, come again, up and down, turn a somer-sault, come down on his feet, and present you with a most beautiful bill to disendow the Irish church, and very likely to abolish Protestantism generally.'[8] *Phineas Redux* is the story of such an attempt.

The novel is not only more political but also more sensational than the earlier half of the story. Lady Laura, who 'worshipped' Phineas but had turned him down to marry the rich Robert Kennedy, withers away for love of him. Her husband in jealous rage fires a pistol at Phineas, and eventually lapses into madness, largely the result of the same jealousy. Finn 'doesn't seek out intrigues, they find him'. He becomes 'something of a hero': 'A man who is supposed to have caused a disturbance between two married people, in a certain rank of life, does generally receive a certain meed of admiration.'[9] Phineas's adventures take a truly sensational turn with his mistaken arrest and trial for the murder of his enemy Bonteen.

But more important to Trollope than the politics or the sensationalism of the book was the gradual growth of his characters with the passage of time. Palliser, Glencora, and the Duke, from earlier novels, along with some-what newer ones from the first Phineas novel, Finn himself, Lady Laura ('the best character in the two books' in Trollope's view), Violet Effingham, and Madame Max Goesler, kept 'luring' him back: 'So much of my inner life was passed in their company, that I was continually asking myself how this woman would act when this or that event had passed over her head, or how that man would carry himself when his youth had become manhood, or his manhood declined to old age.' Of the 'incidents' in the stories he claimed he knew practically nothing beforehand but devised them as he wrote. But by day-dreaming, by 'living with' his characters, he knew, he said, their personalities so thoroughly that the evil or good within them was as 'clear to me as are the stars on a summer night'.[10]

Phineas himself is not the optimistic young man of the first novel, though only two fictional years are meant to intervene. He is still likeable, though more subdued; his confidence is weakened; his cheerfulness diminished. His murder trial so unnerves him that he is changed for good; the ordeal almost 'unmans' him. Even eventual proof of his innocence cannot restore him: 'He had been so hacked and hewed about, so exposed to the gaze of the vulgar, so mauled by the public, that he could never more be anything but the wretched being who had been tried for the murder of his enemy. The pith had been taken out of him.'[11]

'The women' remain loyal to Phineas (though three-quarters of the House believe him guilty; to have known a murderer enlivened their day; and the police, zealous to do their duty, are willing to believe that Phineas and another suspect had committed the murder, both of them, independently). Madame Max busies herself uncovering helpful evidence against another possible suspect, Lizzie Eustace's husband Emilius; later she will save Phineas by marrying him. Glencora remains her marvellous irreverent self: 'I can hardly believe that Mr. Bonteen has been murdered, though I don't know why he should n't as well as anybody else. . . . Only think of Lady Laura,—with one mad and the other in Newgate.' Glencora will not believe Phineas had killed Bonteen, 'not though Lord Fawn swore that he had seen it. I never will believe what I don't like to believe, and nothing shall ever make me.' Any means of defending Phineas are fair: 'Could n't we get Sir Gregory Grogram [the prosecuting Attorney General] . . . I dare say it's very shocking, but I do think that twenty thousand pounds spent among the lawyers would get him off.' Were he to be convicted she would 'buy up the Home Secretary. . . . I know what Cabinet Ministers are.' The barrister Chaffanbrass (thought to have been based partly on William Ballantine, famous for his skill in cross examination) returns in full force. Older now, tempered somewhat, considerably more human, and, placed as he is this time, defending the innocent Phineas, he has the reader's complete sympathy. Actually, Chaffanbrass is mistakenly convinced of Phineas's guilt, but this makes no difference. His 'destruction' during cross examination of the inept Lord Fawn, a decent but foolish man, on whose confused testimony the case against Finn rests, is surely one of the high points of Victorian courtroom fiction. Chaffanbrass, 'in asking a man his name, and age, and calling . . . could produce an impression that the man was unwilling to tell anything, and that, therefore, the jury were entitled to regard his evidence with suspicion.' The befuddled Lord Fawn takes back most of the evidence he had given before the magistrates, and after his testimony, feels that he has been 'disgraced forever'.[12] The *Spectator* said that in the reappearance of 'our old friend, the Old-Bailey barrister, Mr. Chaffanbrass' were contained one or two of the 'finest touches' in all Trollope's fiction.[13]

The oldest old friend in *Phineas Redux* is the Duke of Omnium. He had first appeared in the Barsetshire series, in *Doctor Thorne*, where it was said that his revenues were about the same as the Queen's, except that 'the Duke's were his own'. He was a proud, self-indulgent man, determined to remain unwed, and rumoured to be a great womanizer. Now, many years and many books later, this profligate yet dignified presence is removed from the scene at last. As he lay dying, he was the talk of all the London drawing-rooms and clubs: 'It was acknowledged everywhere that he had played his part in a noble and even a princely manner. . . . And yet, perhaps, no man who had lived during the same period . . . had done less, or had devoted himself more entirely to the consumption of good things without the slightest idea of producing anything in return!' At his death, 'A clergyman attended him and gave him the sacrament. He took it,—as the champagne prescribed by Sir Omicron, or the few mouthfuls of chicken broth which were administered to him by the old lady with the smart cap; but it may be doubted whether he thought much more of the one remedy than of the other. He knew that he had lived, and that the thing was done. His courage never failed him.' A marvellous old pagan, quintessentially English, 'he knew who he was, and who other people were.'[14]

Given Trollope's aim of continued change and growth in these characters, he was especially heartened by Hutton's review in the *Spectator* which said that a rumour of Phineas's return had long been current: 'Indeed, we all of us know those of Mr. Trollope's characters who appear and reappear in the main line of his social tradition, so much better than we know ninety-nine hundredths of our own friends, that if by any chance we can gather news of their future fortunes, however indirectly, from the one depository of the secret of their existence, there is none of us who would not avail himself of that opportunity far more eagerly than of any of the ordinary sources of social gossip.'[15] To his readers, Trollope's creations seemed more real than their actual-life counterparts; they were becoming nearly as real to some readers as they were to Trollope. (Virginia Woolf was to say that we believe in Trollope's characters 'as we believe in the reality of our own weekly bills', that we get from his novels 'the same sort of refreshment and delight that we get from seeing something actually happen in the street below'.[16])

Having completed *The Way We Live Now* in late December 1873, Trollope wrote nothing for three months—it was the hunting season—and then on 2 April returned 'with a full heart' to the Pallisers. The good reviews of *Phineas Redux* may have influenced him. In any case, the passing of the old Duke's coronet to his conscientious, hardworking nephew Plantagenet Palliser paved the way for a novel more securely centred on him. He wanted to draw Palliser as a statesman; his Brocks, De Terriers, Monks, Greshams, Daubenys, 'more or less portraits, not of living men, but of living political characters', had been easy enough to create and 'required no imagination' on his part. In Palliser, however, he had intended to depict a statesman 'superior' to the usual hardened professional politician, and yet in some ways inferior: 'He should have rank, and intellect, and parliamentary habits . . . and . . . unblemished, unextinguishable, inexhaustible love of country. . . . But he should be scrupulous, and, as being scrupulous, weak.' The new Duke of Omnium, when called upon to be Prime Minister of a coalition government, should 'feel with true modesty his own insufficiency; but not the less should the greed of power grow upon him when he had once allowed himself to taste and to enjoy it'.[17] For all his timidity, he becomes autocratic and peevishly imperious; his colleagues are all more or less afraid of him, and they question whether his manner is the result of pride or of shyness; he grows ill-at-ease, moody, irritable, unhappy; he is so thin-skinned that 'any counsel offered to him took the form of criticism'. His closest friend, the Duke of St Bungay, gives him Trollopian advice: 'Think about your business as a shoemaker thinks of his. Do your best, and then let your customers judge for themselves.' But Palliser cannot adopt such a course; at times he seems so weak as to be 'positively unmanly'. 'Men shouldn't be men of Sèvres china,' says Lady Glencora. He seems at times almost mentally ill; he grows increasingly more 'quixotic' and stubbornly bestows a garter in a fashion that will bring cabinet resignations and the fall of his government. *The Prime Minister* becomes a chronicle of his weaknesses, many of them the result of his scrupulous honesty and idealism. 'He is a god,' says Lady Glencora, 'but I am not a goddess. . . . They should have made me Prime Minister. . . . I could have given away garters and ribbons, and made my bargains while giving them.'[18]

Trollope was pleased with *The Prime Minister*. In *An Autobiography* he said in his usual self-deprecatory manner that he had no right to hope that readers would understand Palliser and Glencora as he did; readers could not be expected to have remembered or even to have read all the previous novels, whereas Trollope's memory seems always to have had the whole story before him. He offered one example: the Duke as Prime Minister will not allow his wife to attach herself to any position in the Queen's court, saying, 'I should not choose that my wife should have any duties unconnected with our joint family and home.' Who, Trollope asks, while reading these words will remember that in a previous novel Palliser, on being twitted by his wife for his willingness to clean the Premier's shoes, had told her that he 'would even allow her to clean them if it were for the good of the country'? It was with connected details such as these that Trollope had been for many years 'manufacturing within my own mind the characters of the man and his wife'. At this point he adds the much-quoted lines summing up what he saw as his best work:

I think that Plantagenet Palliser, Duke of Omnium, is a perfect gentleman. If he be not, then am I unable to describe a gentleman. [Lady Glencora] is by no means a perfect lady;—but if she be not all over a woman, then am I not able to describe a woman. I do not think it probable that my name will remain among those who in the next century will be known as the writers of English prose fiction;—but if it does, that permanence of success will probably rest on the characters of Plantagenent Palliser, Lady Glencora, and the Rev. Mr. Crawley. [19]

Trollope gave Palliser many of his own political tenets; in a chapter called 'The Prime Minister's Political Creed' the Duke explains them to Phineas:

The conservative . . . wishes . . . to maintain the differences and distances which separate the highly placed from their lower brethren. He thinks that God has divided the world as he finds it divided, and that he may best do his duty by making the inferior man happy and contented in his position. . . . That lesson seems to me to be hardly compatible with continual improvement in the condition of the lower man. But with the conservative all such improvement is to be based on the idea of the maintenance of those distances. . . . The liberal, if he have any fixed idea at all, must I think have conceived the idea of lessening distances,—of bringing the coachman and the duke nearer together. [20]

Chapter XVI of *An Autobiography* expounds Trollope's own 'advanced conservative liberal' creed in practically identical words.

Personally, too, part of Palliser is Trollope himself. Like the Duke, he was preternaturally sensitive, 'thin-skinned'—a favourite word—though of course Trollope had an entirely different way of dealing with his own sensitivity. Trollope shouted and roared; kept up a whirlwind life of work, hunting, travelling, dining out, holidaying, writing, throwing himself entirely into whatever he was doing with an energy and enthusiasm that positively dismayed many of his contemporaries. Yet beneath it all was a sensitivity very similar to the Duke's, a sensitivity only a few people divined. The most astute observation of this came from Julian Hawthorne (son of the novelist), who met Trollope at a gathering of writers in 1879. Hawthorne found him speaking 'volubly and almost boisterously', his words 'bursting forth from beneath his white moustache with such an impetus of hearty breath that it seemed as if all opposing arguments must be blown quite away'. He turned briskly from one listener to another, all the while flourishing his walking stick and sometimes narrowly missing the heads of his listeners. He seemed a 'civilized and modernized Squire Western':

Looking at him more narrowly, however, you would have reconsidered this judgment. . . . His organization, though thoroughly healthy, was both complex and high-wrought; his character was simple and straightforward to a fault, but he was abnormally conscientious, and keenly alive to others' opinion concerning him. It might be thought that he was overburdened with self-esteem, and unduly opinionated; but, in fact, he was but over-anxious to secure the goodwill and agreement of all with whom he came in contact. There was some peculiarity in him—some element or bias in his composition that made him different from other men; but, on the other hand, there was an ardent solicitude to annul or reconcile this difference, and to prove himself to be, in fact, of absolutely the same cut and quality as all the rest of the world. Hence when he was in a demonstrative, expository or argumentative mood, he could not sit quiet in the face of a divergence between himself and his associates; he was incorrigibly strenuous to obliterate or harmonize the irreconcilable points between him and others; and since these points remained irreconcilable, he remained in a constant state of storm and stress on the subject.[21]

Trollope thought that in *The Prime Minister* he had another success, but the novel was not well received, and in 1878 he added a footnote to his already completed *Autobiography* saying that the book had been a 'failure' and 'was worse spoken of by the Press than any novel I had written. I was specially hurt by a criticism on it in the *Spectator*.'[22] Trollope mistakenly thought Hutton had written the review, which in fact was by Meredith White Townsend, who complained of nearly everything in the book, but especially that Trollope had 'smirched' his old characters, had inconsistently changed them: Palliser 'was always over-sensitive and over-fidgetty, but he never before was over-bearing, unjust, and . . . vulgar'; Lady Glencora in this book 'pushes like any parvenue who wants to become a personage, courts objectionable people, flatters politicians she hates, and turns her house into a menagerie of members. . . . Many a woman has played that part, but not Lady Glencora.' The *Saturday Review* said: 'When . . . we find that an author's work leaves the final impression of vulgarity, we may assume that the fault lies with him, and not with his subject, and it is on this ground we are forced to the conclusion that *The Prime Minister* represents a decadence in Mr. Trollope's powers. . . . The want of imagination, always sufficiently manifest in his treatment of the deeper problems of fiction, is now beginning to tell upon the execution of details.'[23] Even staunch admirer Edward FitzGerald* called *The Prime Minister* 'the only dull Novel I have read of Trollope's'.[24] Curiously, Tolstoy, another admirer of Trollope, thought *The Prime Minister* 'Excellent'.†

* FitzGerald's correspondence is sprinkled with generous comments on Trollope: he thought the account of Mr Harding with his violoncello in the *Last Chronicle of Barset* 'better than Sterne—in as much as it is more unaffected and true'; even with occasional 'longueurs' as in *He Knew He Was Right*, Trollope 'has a world of his own'; *The Eustace Diamonds* was his 'Evening Service'; when bored with George Eliot, 'the Greatest Novelist of the Day', he pined for 'more brave Trollope; who I am sure conceals a much profounder observation'; he found *Phineas Redux* 'infinitely better than Dizzy in the record of London Society, Clubs, Political Parties, etc., never a caricature'; he wished *Is He Popenjoy?*, 'or its like, would continue as long as I live'.[25]

† Tolstoy's favourite English novelists were Dickens, Eliot, Thackeray, and Trollope, in that order. Parts of *The Bertrams*, which Tolstoy read in 1865, provoked the comment, 'Trollope kills me with his virtuosity. I console myself that he has his skill and I have mine.'[26]

26

———⋄•❋•⋄———

An Autobiography

ON 1 March 1875 Trollope set out on his second trip to Australia, prompted by concern about his son's difficulties at Mortray. There had been a prolonged drought, and Fred had not the capital or the acreage to survive unaided. At the beginning of 1875 Trollope told John Blackwood: 'My boy in Australia is all in the right way. If he dont succeed in the long run I can no longer believe in honesty, industry, and conduct. But I believe I can give him a helping hand by going out. I can see what money I can advance to him out of my small means, and settle certain things with him.'[1] The expense of the journey was covered by an arrangement with Nicholas Trübner, made in December 1874, to write a series of twenty travel letters, at £15 apiece, for publication in various provincial papers, including the *Liverpool Mercury*, *Aberdeen Free Press*, and *North British Daily Mail*. His route took him via Paris and Bologna to Rome; from there he wrote to Rose, complaining that he did not care twopence for the Charles Kingsley Memorial, though he did in fact subscribe. With Tom he went to Naples, which he called 'by no means peculiarly interesting. The bay is not equal either to Dublin or New York'; he saw the art galleries and Pompeii. On ship from Brindisi to Alexandria he wrote his first travel letter, about Italy and Garibaldi, 'having pumped Tom for the contents'. Sailing from Suez, he again got his cabin fitted up with a writing desk, and resumed work on *Is He Popenjoy?*, a novel he had begun in October, and on which he had not made customary progress. He told Rose, 'Our passengers are not very bright but by no means unpleasant'; the food was abominable; he read James Emerson Tennent's *Ceylon* ('nothing longer or duller ever was written').[2]

At Columbo, Ceylon, he was entertained by a merchant he had met aboard ship, who owned a famous tortoise, the 'oldest inhabitant' of the island. This particular tortoise, 'very venerable, very lethargic, and very much respected', on whom two or three men could stand without inflicting injury, was 'almost the chief celebrity of Columbo', for otherwise Trollope found the place uninteresting. He travelled all about the island; at Kandy he visited the Buddhist temple famous for housing the tooth of Buddha: the keeper of the temple could not show him the tooth, that privilege being reserved for royalty: he was just as glad, as the place was as hot as an oven, and the tooth 'if real, if the undoubted tooth of Buddha, would not have given out its essence of reverence to eyes so irreverential as mine'. His visit to the mountain holiday resort of Nuwara Elliya was enlivened by his having to walk, alone, the last six miles: 'I lost my guide . . . it rained hard, and . . . on an unknown and unseen road amidst the mountains, on a road winding round a precipice half the way, I almost gave myself up for lost, and thought that my bones would be pecked by unclean insects in a Ceylon jungle.' Nuwara Elliya proved to be 'a regular little England' with cricket matches and football; he even joined in a hunt, for elk. He went into Dimbula, the great coffee plantation district; he nearly fulfilled his 'grand desire' of seeing a 'real wild elephant', but the beast crashed through the jungle, unseen, within thirty yards of him.[3] He stopped some time with William Gregory, the Governor, an old Harrow school fellow and friend from Galway: 'He is a very good fellow,' Trollope wrote to Millais, 'but his house was dull and there was nothing to do or be done. . . . A Governor has a great deal of luxury but very little comfort. He can admit no equals, and lives in a sort of petty bastard vice royalty which would kill me.'[4]

Trollope reached Melbourne on 4 May, having completed *Is He Popenjoy?* the previous day. Again on Australian soil, he used his travel letters as a platform for playful rejoinders to those local critics who had disliked his book on the colonies. (The Melbourne *Argus*, for example, had attacked Trollope for speaking with 'such an air of omniscience about men and manners, institutions and industries, society and politics, religion and education, legislation and commerce, scenery and statistics', and for doing so in such a way as to suggest that 'he is conferring a favour upon the colonies' by writing about them; the *Brisbane Courier* spoke of *Australia and New Zealand* as 'Mr. Trollope's latest work of fiction'.[5]) Trollope thought his book had praised the colonies exceedingly, had admired so much and disapproved of so little, that he was almost ashamed:

But, on reaching the colony again, I found myself to be regarded as rather a bad man, in having come a second time among people whom I had so grossly maligned. No good word that I had said was held in any remembrance; but any hint conveying censure was treasured up and quoted against me with indignation. I was shown an article in a newspaper in which my mendacity, malignity, and general fiendishness were dilated on with all an editor's eloquence. The custom-house officer who passed my luggage heaped coals of fire on my head by allowing my things to pass through without examination, although I had accused the colonies of 'blowing' . . . In writing of races as in speaking of individuals, nothing short of absolute unalloyed eulogy will suffice to give satisfaction.

Western Australia was 'still contaminated . . . by a convict element' and, though the colony had great promise, it continued to be looked down upon and despised by the other colonies. Trollope remained amused at com-plaints that the women whom the home government sent over at its own expense were not of the 'best class'. More seriously, he reiterated his stand on the value of emigration for the working man, and the fall it would occasion the 'gentleman'; he debunked gold-mining, quoting with approval those colonists who maintained that 'all the gold in Australia has been raised at a cost greater than its value'. He decried the annexation of the Fiji Islands,* took his stand against the proposed annexation of New Guinea, and criticized the current expedition there of William Mackay:

He and his party will, of course, have fire-arms, and fire-arms are at present unknown there. . . . A white man or two will be 'murdered' in their determina-tion to make themselves masters of the new land; but the savage will succumb, and be driven back—will be coaxed with red cloth and beads—will be perplexed beyond the extent of his poor intellect; and may think himself very lucky if he be not at last brought into the pale of civilisation and quickly polished off the face of the earth as beatified subjects of the British Crown.

In occupying the lands of native peoples Britons are committing 'a terrible injustice'; England could not go on indefinitely 'annexing one country after another'; a line must be drawn somewhere: 'It surely cannot be worth our while to annex New Guinea, in order that a few merchants may be enabled to live—or die—upon its shores.'6

Trollope reached Fred's sheep station at Mortray in late May and remained there about seven weeks. Shortly after he had settled in, he began writing *The American Senator* (a novel already promised to George Bentley, son and successor of Richard Bentley, for the firm's magazine, *Temple Bar*). After he had been one month with Fred, Trollope wrote to Millais: 'The one thing I regret most at being absent from England is not seeing the pictures. I like a man to be honest enough to say that he is proud

---

* Thakombau, King of Fiji, ceded the country to British rule in the person of Trollope's friend Sir Hercules Robinson, then Governor of New South Wales. Thakombau went home from Sydney a British pensioner, 'a singular termination to the career of one who has eaten his enemies, and who lived for sixty years as a heathen and cannibal'.7

of his own work and contented with what he has been able to do for himself. I hate the namby pamby humility of a man who thinks it necessary to belittle himself and his efforts. I know no one who has more right to be proud than you have.' The immediate reference was to Millais's paintings in that year's Royal Academy Summer Exhibition, but Trollope's words clearly are also about himself. And yet he frequently did precisely what he here deplored, namely belittle himself and his own works. He went on to describe his routine in the bush:

I write for four hours a day, then ride after sheep or chop wood or roam about in the endless forest up to my knees in mud. I eat a great deal of mutton, smoke a great deal of tobacco, and drink a moderate amount of brandy and water. At night I read, and before work in the morning I play with my grandchildren,—of whom I have two and a third coming.* Fred, my son here, is always on horseback and seems to me to have more troubles on his back than any human being I ever came across. I shall be miserable when I leave him because I do not know how I can look forward to seeing him again without again making this long journey. I do not dislike the journey, or the sea, or the hardship. But I was 60 the other day, and at that age a man has no right to look forward to making many more voyages round the world.[8]

Fred's sheep station was not turning a profit, in spite of his unending labours, and it was decided that he should examine the feasibility of selling the station. Trollope arranged that Sir Hercules Robinson should act on his behalf with power of attorney, stipulating that if Fred sold the station he would send his father details on any new speculation and that Trollope would write to Robinson as to the amount he would stand liable (an amount later set at £7,000). Before long the situation proved more disastrous than had been thought, and Fred sold the station, the account he sent his father in January 1876 showing that of the £6,000 Trollope had originally advanced toward the venture only £1,400 remained.[9] In *An Autobiography* Trollope says that 'several thousands of pounds which I had squeezed out of the pockets of perhaps too liberal publishers have been lost on the venture. But I rejoice to say that this has been in no way due to any fault of [Fred's]. I never knew a man work with more persistent honesty at his trade than he has done.'[10] Trollope wrote the same thing privately to Harry: 'The loss of money has been lamentable—over £4,600!!

---

* Another grandchild, Gordon Trollope, born ten years later, recorded the family tradition that Trollope showed Fred's wife Susannah 'invariable respect and affection. He used to love to sit and hear her sing, and there are still in existence some of the lovely ballads of the day which he gave to her. He so much regretted not having a daughter of his own that he went the length of adopting a girl [Florence Bland] into his family.'[11]

An Autobiography

But it is a kind of misfortune which I can bear. . . . Poor dear Fred. Do not suppose . . . that I blame him.'[12] Fred purchased another property, Booroondara East, near Cobar, but for reasons of health he was unable even to attempt working the station, and some time in 1876 became, like his father before him, a civil servant. He joined the Lands Department and remained in various capacities a member of that department until the year of his death, 1910.

On 28 August Trollope left for home, via New Zealand, and thence to Hawaii, a journey of some two weeks; to escape the heat of the cabins, Trollope slept on deck the whole trip, the only passenger to do so. Hawaii, or the Sandwich Islands as Captain Cook had named them, provoked in Trollope the observation that when the white man annexes a land, 'at the cost of a certain amount of blood', we are 'sorry' that he has had to kill natives; but when the native manages to kill a Briton, that invader has always been 'murdered'. As for Captain Cook, Trollope saw no need 'to execrate the homicidal tendency of the Hawaiian who killed him with a dagger in a free fight'.[13]

Trollope sailed then from Hawaii to San Francisco, observing that it was a voyage of 800 miles (it is in fact some 2,600). Aboard ship he completed *The American Senator*, two days before arriving in California on 26 September. Trollope wrote of San Francisco: 'I do not know that in all my travels I ever visited a city less interesting to the normal tourist, who, as a rule, does not care to investigate the ways of trade, or to employ himself in ascertaining how the people around him earn their bread. There is almost nothing to see in San Francisco that is worth seeing.' Such a place would in fact interest Trollope—by implication, no 'normal tourist' himself because of his relatively slight interest in scenery and 'sights'; he was most curious about trade and 'how people earn their bread'. Moreover, 'the trade of the place, and the way in which money is won and lost, are alike marvellous.' The most worthwhile sight was the Stock Exchange, where the 'fury . . . is even more demoniac than in Paris'. If San Francisco otherwise rather disappointed him, Yosemite did not: 'I know of no rocks in Europe or elsewhere which are to be compared to them. . . . the colours are beautiful, and the effects magnificent.' Trollope then began the transcontinental rail journey, to Boston, seven days and seven nights, made with little fatigue or discomfort.[14] From Boston he travelled to New York, where on 20 October he boarded the *Bothnia* for home.

In spite of some poor weather, he found the crossing enjoyable. He made friends with many people, including Colonel Henry Hozier (whose daughter was to marry Winston Churchill), General Richard Chambers

Taylor, and Mrs Katharine Bronson, an American woman who was shortly to become a fashionable hostess in Venice and friend to many writers and artists (most especially Browning). He also met younger women, including Mrs Bronson's daughter, three Miss Whitings, and a Miss Jane Dulany. This last was another of those who touched his susceptibility to female charms. A few months later he wrote to her in Paris—where she was pursuing a musical career—saying of a photograph of himself that he sent her, 'Some people wont come out well. Mine are always wretched'; he also gave her a copy of his privately printed play 'Did He Steal It?', doubting it would 'answer your purpose'. He lamented that, aside from the Bronsons, he had not seen any of his fellow *Bothnia* travellers: on ship, 'People are thrown together in absolute intimacy for a few days, till they have time for loves and quarrels, for sympathies & heart burnings, sometimes for tears & embracings, and then they part,—never to see each other again! You I hope I may see again, as I think I may probably be in Paris for a day or two in the spring. If so I shall certainly call on you. In the mean time I shall expect to hear from you, as you will certainly send me your photograph.'[15] In *John Caldigate* (written about a year later), the narrator observes that on trans-oceanic voyages 'there are many sources of joy of which the land knows nothing. You may flirt and dance at sixty; and if you are awkward in the turn of a valse, you may put it down to the motion of the ship. You need wear no gloves, and may drink your soda-and-brandy without being ashamed of it.'[16]

Another *Bothnia* passenger was Henry James, who wrote to his family on 1 November: 'We had also Anthony Trollope, who wrote novels in his state room all the morning (he does it literally every morning of his life, no matter where he may be,) and played cards with Mrs. Bronson all the evening. He has a gross and repulsive face and manner, but appears *bon enfant* when you talk with him. But he is the dullest Briton of them all.' After reaching London, James dined at Edward Dicey's with Trollope and 'found him a very good, genial, ordinary fellow—much better than he seemed on the steamer when I crossed with him'. In the essay written on the occasion of Trollope's death James spoke much more glowingly of those shipboard morning writing stints: '[I have] never forgotten the magnificent example of plain persistence that it was in the power of the eminent novelist to give. . . . The season was unpropitious, the vessel overcrowded, the voyage detestable; but Trollope shut himself up in his cabin every morning for a purpose which . . . could only be communion with the muse. He drove his pen as steadily on the tumbling ocean as in Montague Square.'[17]

Trollope was not, as James had surmised, writing a novel during the crossing; instead, he was beginning a 'Memoir' or autobiography. Aboard the *Bothnia* he wrote the first thirty-three manuscript pages—an unusually slow pace—the first two of the three restrained but powerful chapters about his unhappy childhood and youth, knowledge of which there would be almost literally none, were it not for his own account. The idea of writing his autobiography—and especially the need to describe and account for his wretched boyhood—must have been growing in Trollope's mind since his reading in 1872 of the first volume of John Forster's *Life of Charles Dickens*. In that volume Forster printed long extracts from the novelist's 'autobiographical fragment', telling how his happy childhood in Chatham had been succeeded by a period of poverty in London; his parents sent the boy to work in a blacking-warehouse and, when his father was confined in a debtors' prison, he had to fend for himself in lodgings. Forster also revealed how much of the early part of *David Copperfield* was autobiographical, and that Micawber was a portrait of Dickens's father. Posthumous publication of the fragment had been left to Forster's discretion, and Trollope found it 'distasteful'. To George Eliot and G. H. Lewes he commented: 'Dickens was no hero; he was a powerful, clever, humorous, and, in many respects, wise man;—very ignorant, and thick-skinned, who had taught himself to be his own God, and to believe himself to be a sufficient God for all who came near him;—not a hero at all. Forster tells of him things which should disgrace him,—as the picture he drew of his own father, & the hard words he intended to have published of his own mother.' Trollope's own memories of hardship and isolation made him incapable of doing justice to Dickens's treatment of such experiences; instead it inspired him to write of his own boyhood miseries with characteristic understatement and stoicism—although his method was equally calculated to evoke sympathy. Trollope found Dickens guilty of self-pity and egotism, and he had the same reaction to the lengthy extracts from W. C. Macready's diaries, published in 1875 by Sir Frederick Pollock in Macready's *Reminiscences*. He linked the two when he wrote to Rusden on 29 November that books like Macready's 'do not make one pleased with humanity. It is disgusting to see the self-consciousness and irritated craving for applause which such men as Macready & Dickens have exhibited;— & which dear old Thackeray did exhibit also. It astonishes me not that men should feel it, but that they shew it. I am sure of myself that whenever such a disease has been oppressing me I have been able to tread it out.' Half a year later, he returned to the subject in another letter to Rusden, revealing his aversion to Macready's evangelical religiosity. In response to Rusden's defence of Macready as showing humility before God, he made what for him was an unusually personal avowal:

I do not prize humility before God. I can understand that a man should be humble before his brother men the smallness of whose vision requires self-abasement in others;—but not that any one should be humble before God. To my God I can be but true, and if I think myself to have done well I cannot but say so. To you, if I speak of my own work, I must belittle myself. I must say that it is naught. But if I speak of it to my God, I say, 'Thou knowest that it is honest;—that I strove to do good;—that if ever there came to me the choice between success and truth, I stuck to truth.' And I own that I feel that it is impossible that the Lord should damn me, and how can I be humble before God when I tell him that I expect from him eternal bliss as the reward of my life here on earth. . . . I do not think myself to be a worm, and a grub, grass of the field fit only to be burned, a clod, a morsel of putrid atoms that should be thrown to the dungheap, ready for the nethermost pit. Nor if I did should I therefore expect to sit with Angels and Archangels. I must say that I judge a man by his actions with men, much more than by his declarations Godwards—When I find him to be envious, carping, spiteful, hating the successes of others, and complaining that the world has never done enough for him, I am apt to doubt whether his humility before God will atone for his want of manliness.[18]

He trusted his own autobiography had no such humility.

Trollope arrived at Montagu Square on 31 October, just in time for hunting. Another pleasure was finding a copy of G. H. Lewes's *On Actors and Acting* waiting for him, a book with a preface entitled 'Epistle to Anthony Trollope' in which Lewes explained that years ago Trollope had expressed a wish to see some of Lewes's dramatic criticism 'republished in a more accessible form than the pages of a periodical'. Yet another pleasure was the acceptance of the honorary freedom of the Grocers' Company, one of the wealthiest of the ancient London livery companies; the honour was also offered at this time to Disraeli, Lord Derby, Lord Stanhope, Lord Cockburn, and Sir James Paget; only Disraeli declined, for reasons of pressure of government business. Trollope's citation spoke of the 'great pleasure afforded to many thousands in their hours of relaxation by his admirable works of fiction; and of the valuable information imparted in the accounts of his travels'.[19]

Trollope delivered the manuscript of *The American Senator*—written entirely during the journey abroad—to the printers in December 1875, and engaged yet again in mild altercation over a title: 'I find that I cannot change the name,' he told George Bentley, 'which indeed . . . I feel to be in itself a good name. I am sure that nobody can give a name to a novel but the author.' Nevertheless he began the concluding chapter of the book by remarking, apparently with little irony, that the novel 'might perhaps have better been called "The Chronicle of a Winter at Dillsborough".' (Bentley was to go out of his way in the advertisements to indicate that the story 'is laid in England'.) At about the same time Trollope tried to persuade Bentley to accept for May publication in *Temple Bar* an entirely different novel, as yet unwritten (even though he had *Is He Popenjoy?* in his desk drawer). He may have wished to get another Palliser novel into print quickly; in any case, Bentley did not want a different novel, probably because Trollope told him he would not have the entire manuscript ready by the time the first instalment was scheduled to appear. Bentley then changed his mind, only to have Trollope tell him, on 17 January from Lowick in Northamptonshire, where he was visiting Lucas Collins and hunting, that it was now too late to change.[20] Trollope, who had not written anything since his return from Australia, had resumed, on 2 January, his autobiography.

The book was completed on 11 April. In its first sentence Trollope announced that he would call these pages an autobiography only for want of a better name, and that 'it will not be so much my intention to speak of the little details of my private life' but rather about what he and others have done in literature. He then admitted that the 'garrulity of old age'— he was 60—together with 'the aptitude of a man's mind to recur to the passages of his own life' may tempt him to 'say something' of himself. Thereafter follow three chapters of the most personal, moving, and convincing prose he ever wrote, the account of his miserable early life. The personal note becomes less intense once *An Autobiography* gets to Trollope's career as writer, but it is always there. The book details, for example, his obsessive writing habits, his irrational passion for hunting; it even speaks pointedly if guardedly (and without giving her name) of his love for Kate Field. Throughout, *An Autobiography* is a record of his desire, as he says, 'to be something more than a clerk in the Post Office'. Then, in a closing paragraph, he writes, tantalizingly:

It will not, I trust, be supposed by any reader that I have intended in this so-called autobiography to give a record of my inner life. No man ever did so truly,—and no man ever will. Rousseau probably attempted it, but who doubts but that Rousseau has confessed in much the thoughts and convictions rather than the facts of his life? If the rustle of a woman's petticoat has ever stirred my blood; if a cup of wine has been a joy to me; if I have thought tobacco at midnight in pleasant company to be one of the elements of an earthly Paradise; if now and again I have somewhat recklessly fluttered a £5 note over a card-table;—of what matter is that to any reader?[21]

His strategy in the book was to say deeply personal things while denying saying them (Trollope would have given the rhetorical device its Latin name, *praeteritio*, derived from his beloved Cicero). The very denials are revealing, and Trollope knew they were. Some have missed his ironies, but it was always part of Trollope's style to allow them to do so undisturbed.

Trollope locked the manuscript of *An Autobiography* in his desk, together with a letter to Harry, written 30 April 1876, by which he bequeathed the manuscript to him as a gift. Harry was to 'edit' the manuscript, and have discretionary powers of suppressing any passage, or indeed of not publishing the work at all, but he was not to add to the text, except in the form of a preface or introductory chapter. The letter expressed a wish that the book be published by Frederic Chapman, but gave Harry permission to do 'the best you can as to terms' with some other publisher if he chose. Publication, if made at all, was to be effected as soon as possible after his death. Trollope closed, 'Now I say how dearly I have loved you.'[22] Harry recorded how in 1878 Trollope, with the manuscript in his hand, told him about it and said, 'Now we'll lock it up [again] and say no more about it.' Then, while closing the drawer, ever the businessman with publishers, he was unable to resist telling Harry that he ought to ask £1,800 for the book.*[23]

Trollope's talk in *An Autobiography* of the mechanical aspects of writing, the downplaying of 'inspiration', the emphasis on monetary rewards for writers, the insistence on comparing the writing of novels to the making of shoes, led a few contemporaries and many subsequent critics to think mistakenly that the *Autobiography*, published in October 1883, ten months after his death, somehow demolished Trollope's already sinking reputation. For one thing, Trollope's working habits were scarcely a secret, as he continually went out of his way to talk about the very things thought to be the shocking 'revelations' in the *Autobiography*. For that matter, reviewers had discussed them. The *Westminster Review*, for example, said in passing, 'It is told of Mr. Trollope that he considers his

---

* After Trollope's death, Harry sold the rights not to Chapman, but to Blackwood; he asked £1,800 but received £1,000. He exercised very little editorial prerogative, suppressing only short passages on 'Billy' Russell (about his having 'fallen away latterly among Princes' and deserting his old friends) and Charles Reade (concerning his unauthorized adaptation of *Ralph the Heir*). Harry also omitted the word 'American' from the description of the unnamed woman (Kate Field) to whom his father was so attached.[24]

own method of art to be purely mechanical, and that he has declared that he could teach easily any one to write as good books as his own in a short space of time.' The *Saturday Review*, immediately after Trollope's death, but before the existence of *An Autobiography* was even heard of, said that only the 'stupid critic' would think 'that the steady regularity of Mr. Trollope's method of work is incompatible with genius'. Furthermore, *An Autobiography* was universally acclaimed on its publication in 1883. In *The Times*, Alexander Innes Shand (thought to be the original for Ferdinand Alf, a newspaper editor in *The Way We Live Now*), in a laudatory two-part article combined enthusiasm for 'this extremely frank autobiography' in which was found 'more of the sensational than in any of his novels', with an appreciative survey of his writings. The disclosures of Trollope's early miseries reminded the reviewer of those Dickens endured, a comparison made also by the *Daily Telegraph* and by many other reviews. The *Spectator* ran three reviews of *An Autobiography*, one by Meredith Townsend and two by R. H. Hutton. Townsend's notice was chiefly concerned with the extraordinary transformation of the unpopular 'heavy lad' into an efficient public servant, sociable man, and fine novelist. Hutton, while saying that *An Autobiography* demonstrated the axiom that a creative writer was rarely a fine critic, still found much to praise and judged the statement of the liberal creed in politics 'one of the wisest and tersest summaries of political principle, which we have ever come across'. The *Saturday Review* admitted to the suspicion that 'had Trollope been content to write a little less, he might have written a little better', but drew back, saying, 'it is possible that Trollope's system suited him best.' The *Fortnightly Review*, Trollope's 'own child', did not rise up against its parent, but called *An Autobiography* a 'most entertaining book', demonstrating the necessity of 'ceaseless devotion of mind and unintermitting labour of body'. The *Morning Post* commended its 'entire unreserve' and thought it would encourage 'despondent toilers' to persevere. The *Daily Telegraph* said the book was a 'flood of light' thrown on the 'inner life of Anthony Trollope . . . [which] will but serve to make his countrymen regard him with increased admiration and respect'. Other favourable reviews appeared in the *Athenaeum*, the *Academy*, the *Christian World*, the *Edinburgh Review*, and, of course, *Blackwood's Magazine*.[25] To say that *An Autobiography* killed or even lessened Trollope's reputation is to disregard the record.*

* Among the few people to raise the issue of Trollope's talk about his writing habits as harmful to his reputation was George Gissing, who gave the question his own twist, saying that he *hoped* it were true that 'the great big stupid public', was 'really, somewhere in its secret economy, offended by that revelation of mechanical methods'.[26]

Completing *An Autobiography* gave Trollope a feeling of fulfilment; he was sure he had not fallen into any self-serving stance such as Macready's or made any untoward family revelations as Dickens and Forster did (although the book certainly allowed for the inference that his busy, industrious and joyous mother had neglected him). Trollope now felt in a way complete, in spite of, or perhaps even because of, his naturally pessimistic streak. He wrote to Rusden:

As to that leisure evening of life, I must say that I do not want it. I can conceive of no contentment of which toil is not to be the immediate parent. As the time for passing away comes near me I have no fear as to the future—I am ready to go. I dread nothing but physical inability and that mental lethargy which is apt to accompany it. Since I saw you I have written a memoir of my own life;—not as regards its activity but solely in reference to its literary bearing, as to what I have done in literature and what I have thought about it,—and now I feel as though every thing were finished and I was ready to go. No man enjoys life more than I do, but no man dreads more than I do the time when life may not be enjoyable.[27]

As Trollope was finishing *An Autobiography*, he came, perhaps not altogether by coincidence, to the end of hunting. For thirty-five years he had ridden to hounds as often as humanly possible, every November to April. His attachment to the sport had been, as he said, such as he could neither fathom nor understand. His decision to give up hunting was not dictated by any accident in the field; the previous year he had indeed had an 'episode': 'I got into a muddy ditch,' he wrote to Alfred Austin, '& my horse had to blunder over me, through the mud. He trod 3 times on my head. When I saw the iron of his foot coming down on my head, I heard a man on the bank say—"He's dead." I am strapped up with plasters as to my forehead, but otherwise quite uninjured. You may imagine that in the scrimmage I had a queer moment.' But he had suffered as much at various times over the years. During his last season he had been especially assiduous to go out; he had, for example, excused himself to his good friend J. E. Sewell, Warden of New College, Oxford, for not dining there in December: 'Nothing breaks a man's heart so thoroughly as having a lot of horses and giving them nothing to do. . . . A hunting man is bound to hunt if he can hunt'; in January he spent time at Lucas Collins's Lowick Rectory in Thrapstone, Northamptonshire, whence he could ride with the Pytchley and Fitzwilliam hunts. He chose to give up hunting while still reasonably good at it, accepting, as he told John Blackwood, this abnegation 'gracefully' and not waiting 'to drain the cup to the last drop'.[28]

Now he closed the penultimate chapter of the account of his life saying, 'at last, in April 1876, I do think that my resolution has been taken. I am giving away my old horses, and any body is welcome to my saddles and horse-furniture.' For all the bravado, he was deeply moved, and offered his own somewhat lugubrious verse translations of two passages from Horace,* adding, 'I think that I may say with truth that I rode hard to the very end.' Although he would continue to bring hunting into novels, he never again spoke willingly of the sport.[29]

Like other people in their sixties he found friends dying. Shirley Brooks, *Punch* writer and editor, and for Trollope a link with Thackeray, died in February 1874; and Trollope, along with Tom Taylor, Millais, and W. P. Frith, worked hard to raise money for his widow. They collected £2,000, Trollope acting as treasurer, sending many begging letters—'and I hate begging,' as he told G. H. Lewes. He also assisted in getting the Royal Literary Fund to give her £100, and even mediated between her and George Godwin, London architect and editor of *The Builder*, who wanted to buy the chair that Brooks worked in.[30] A more personal loss came in August 1876 with the death of Sir Charles Taylor, one of his closest and dearest friends, the man who had driven him home in his brougham from George Smith's after the first *Cornhill* dinner in January 1860. Another member of the Thackeray set, Taylor was a wealthy bachelor, sportsman, and friend of literary men; he was known for the bitter aphorisms and cynicism that led him to be called 'Old Pleasant'.[31] Trollope told Rusden he hardly knew why he loved Taylor so: 'He was not very clever, nor specially well read,—was self-willed, cantankerous, and unpopular. But he was thoroughly manly, and among the friends of my latter life there was no one whom I more thoroughly loved. What the Garrick will do, which he managed as though it were his own house, we do not yet know.' In *An Autobiography* Trollope said of Taylor: 'He was our king at the Garrick Club. . . . He gave the best dinners of my time. . . . A man rough of tongue, brusque in manners, odious to those who dislike him, somewhat inclined to tyranny, he is the prince of friends, honest as the sun, and as open-handed as Charity itself.' The last sentence, as even Edmund Yates said, was an apt description of Trollope himself.[32]

For Trollope the answer to ageing, to the end of hunting, to the loss of friends, and to the vagaries of health, was hard work and, what was

---

* One of them reads:

> Years, as they roll, cut all our pleasures short;
> Our pleasant mirth, our loves, our wine, our sport.
> And then they stretch their power, and crush at last
> Even the power of singing of the past.
>
> *Epistles*, II. iii. 55

sometimes a subspecies of the same thing, reading. Trollope had always been an ambitious reader, even from his early London days, when he had read enough to envision writing a vast 'History of World Literature'. Throughout his career, he had, in addition to much desultory reading, made some sustained efforts at concentrated study: in the early 1850s he had read at least thirty-five Beaumont and Fletcher plays; in the 1860s he had gone through many novels, taking notes, in preparation for a 'History of English Prose Fiction'. After preliminary considerations of early works from the *Arcadia* onwards, including, for example, the 'detestable trash' of Mrs Aphra Behn, he planned to begin with *Robinson Crusoe*—which he considered the first 'really popular' novel—and treat all deceased English novelists; his purpose was to vindicate the profession of novelist against the prejudice that gave novel writing a relatively low character. Pressure from other work was bad enough, and when Dickens and Bulwer Lytton died, he abandoned the project.[33] After his work on Caesar in 1870, he read some classical Latin author almost daily. He studied Horace, Ovid, Quintilian, Sallust, Suetonius, Tacitus, Lucan, Livy, Virgil, Catullus, Pliny. From 1875 to 1880 his Latin reading would concentrate around Cicero, when writing his *Life of Cicero* took up much of Trollope's energies, though not interfering with his production of novels.

In the late 1860s Trollope had resumed reading old English dramatists, a project that gained momentum in the 1870s and carried through till his death. As he read, he made marginal notes and then wrote down his summary criticism of each play on the endpapers. He may even have considered writing a book about early drama, although the subject seemed endless. His busiest years for reading in old drama were 1871, 34 plays (including 28 of Shakespeare's aboard ship en route to Australia), 54 in 1874, and 35 in 1876, the year of *An Autobiography*, which closed with the statement that aside from the Latin classics, he found his greatest reading pleasure in old English dramatists—'not from any excessive love of their work, which often irritates me by its want of truth to nature, even while it charms me by its language,—but from curiosity in searching their plots and examining their characters'. He hoped to read, if he lived long enough, 'every play' written up to the end of the reign of James I. He read widely in the prolific authors, Beaumont and Fletcher, Jonson, Thomas Heywood, Massinger, Middleton, Marston, Ford.* He read at least a

---

* Other dramatists he read were Peele, Marlowe, Cooke, Chapman, Shirley, Greene, Glapthorne, Nash, Still, Lyly, Otway, Wilmot, Kyd, Dekker, Brewer, Cook, Tuke, Marmion, Bale, Edwards, Webster, Tourneur, Machin, Barry, Tailor, Tomkis, Fisher, May, Davenant, Rowley, Lodge, Habington, John Heywood, Suckling, Brome, Cartwright, Mayne, Randolph, Digby, Davenport, Killegrew, Wilkins, Nabbes.

dozen plays during the last year of his life. From 1866 to 1882 he read more than 270 plays, and many of them more than once. 'No one', he wrote, 'who has not looked closely into it knows how many there are.'[34]

Shakespeare, whom he read and reread throughout his lifetime, he placed in a class by himself. None the less Trollope finds faults: *The Tempest*, for example, he judges a 'very pretty play; but hardly in my mind equal to the praise bestowed upon it'; *Measure for Measure* is 'uneven' in language, plot, and taste; *Much Ado About Nothing*, while admirable for the stage, 'is but a poor play to read', and the same holds for *Love's Labour's Lost*. *A Midsummer Night's Dream*, after two acts of pretty poetry, 'falls off'; *Romeo and Juliet*, in spite of its 'rapturous' poetry, doesn't merit its great reputation; the plots of *All's Well that Ends Well*, *Measure for Measure*, *Much Ado About Nothing*, and *Twelfth Night* 'are [more] fitted for tales such as those of Boccaccio than for plays'; the *Henry IV* plays—though he has read them 'a score of times' and 'relished their fun'—offer overdone comedy and a 'vocabulary of abuse . . . almost nasty'; *Richard III* lacks a 'single character with whom to sympathise'.[35]

But in other works his enthusiasm carries him into superlatives: *The Merchant of Venice* 'has as much of the beauty of poetry as any written by Shakespeare. There is no better reading.' Trollope calls *As You Like It* 'perhaps . . . the prettiest comedy that ever was written in any language'. Of *King Lear* he says, 'There is nothing, perhaps, in the whole range of poetry to exceed the finest passages of Lear, and I know no character in which so grand a passion is displayed.' Brutus of *Julius Caesar* is 'perhaps the finest character ever drawn by Shakespeare'. *Macbeth* is 'on the whole the finest play of Shakespeare. The plot is better than that of any of the other tragedies, and the pathos better sustained to the end.' *Hamlet* is 'the greatest work of man. . . . [But] it is remarkable that in a play where all else is perfect, the last scene should be so incongruous and so little affecting.'[36]

Predictably, Trollope wants plots that do not pass belief and characters that are 'natural'. The notes contain endless railings against 'absurd' and 'purposeless' and 'confused' plots and 'unnatural' characters and passions: Trollope writes, for example, that Beaumont and Fletcher's *The Island Princess* manifests an 'infinite absurdity in the manipulation, certain persons being infamous murderers in one scene, and magnanimous & noble in the next'. Massinger's *The Fatal Dowry* suffers from 'a certain extravagance both of character and plot. Women are whores in one act and are ready to sacrifice their lives to ideas of chastity in the next. . . . Men are subjected to the same unnatural repentance.' Trollope was especially annoyed at inadequate characterization of women: Jonson, for one, 'never achieves a woman's part. He hardly even tries to make a woman charming. They are all whores or fools—generally both.'[37]

What is surprising is the vehemence of Trollope's denunciations of 'beastly' lewdness and indecency. He does admit that one must not judge another age by the present one, but cannot control his anger: *The Alchemist*—though 'a very great work'—he finds 'dirty, vulgar, and disgusting without ceasing for one act, one scene, one passage, or one line'. In Ford's *'Tis Pity She's A Whore*, 'the most striking fault . . . is that the plot does not at all require that the "whore's" lover should be her brother. The incest is added on as a makeweight to atrocities which certainly required no such addition. Nothing in fiction, prose or poetry, disgusts so much as unnecessary crime.' Beaumont and Fletcher's *The Coxcomb* is 'a most revolting play' and in parts 'so offensive as to make the reader wonder that it should not have offended even the taste of the age of James I. It is not only that the fool should by stratagem have got his friend to lie with his wife, but that the wife, with whom the reader is intended to sympathise, should have debased herself by yielding.'[38]

Few non-Shakespearean plays get all positive marks: standing almost alone is Habington's *The Queen of Arragon*, 'I am disposed to say that there is finer poetry in this play than in any other drama in the English language beyond Shakespeare. . . . And yet no one has read it.' Almost all Trollope's verdicts are mixed, and most are far more negative than positive; often praise is reserved for the language: Webster and Rowley's *The Thracian Wonder* 'is wonderfully confused and unmeaning in its plot; but it has some pretty poetry'; Marston's *History of Antonio and Mellida* is almost altogether bad except that 'Now and again a line occurs which is worth preserving'. Sometimes Trollope is altogether condemnatory: Middleton's *Your Five Gallants* is 'so tedious, so perplexed so uninterest-ing and so bad. . . . [that] to have read it is a sin, in the wasting of time'. And, once or twice, in spite of his indefatigable energy, Trollope simply could not finish a play: Middleton's *A Game at Chess* he found 'so unreal . . . and . . . so dull as to be unreadable'. Trollope registers so many objections and complaints, that one wonders how he kept going through this huge mass of reading. It was chiefly the poetry that sustained him; he simply loved to read long dramatic poetry. And of course there was his innate doggedness, the need to feel equal to any task he had set himself: he had determined to read through old English drama, and so he would. On Christmas Day, 1875, calling *Cynthia's Revels* by Jonson 'altogether inept', he concluded with typical self-irony, 'The work will have no future readers, unless it be some additional Editors or determined idler like myself.'[39]

As if his strenuous regimen of reading in the Latin classics and old English drama were not enough, Trollope engaged in the Victorian habit of family reading aloud (his listeners would have been Rose, Florence Bland, Harry when at home, and any guests). He kept a list of these readings from 1876 on, mostly narrative poetry of enormous length: Tennyson's *Idylls*, Spenser's *Faerie Queene*, various tales from Chaucer, Byron's *Childe Harold*, the *Odyssey* and *Iliad* in Pope's translation; *The Ring and the Book* (this entry followed by '!!'), *Paradise Lost*.*[40]

Trollope's reading notwithstanding, his real satisfaction came from writing: 'For what remains to me of life,' he says at the close of *An Autobiography*, 'I trust for my happiness still chiefly to my work—hoping that when the power of work be over with me, God may be pleased to take me from a world in which, according to my view, there can then be no joy.'[41] Shortly after writing those words, he took up, on 2 May 1876, another novel about the Pallisers, a mellow book about ageing and accommodating life as it is. The unkind reviews of *The Prime Minister* had not yet appeared; but he may have had his ear to the ground about how the public were receiving the story as it came out in large five-shilling parts. In any case, he planned *The Duke's Children* from the start as the last of the Palliser novels, and he worked away with scarcely any interruptions except for the five or six days' travelling to and from his continental holiday with Rose at Hollenthal, a valley in the Black Forest near Freiburg, and at Felsenegg, near Zug in Switzerland during August and September (places the Trollopes first visited in 1874); in fact at the latter place he often wrote twelve manuscript pages a day, well above his usual average. Though he finished the book by the end of October, he was apparently in no hurry to see it in print; it was not until the summer of 1878 that he sold the serial rights to *All the Year Round* for £400 and the book rights to Chapman & Hall for £1,000, the same arrangement as he had made for *Popenjoy*, except that Chapman & Hall had paid £200 more for the earlier book.

---

* Other works read included Denham's *Cynthia's Quest*, Byron's *Siege of Corinth*, Thomson's *Seasons*, Shelley's *Revolt of Islam*, Mrs Browning's *Aurora Leigh*, Wordsworth's *Excursion*, Longfellow's *Evangeline*, *Skeleton in Armour*, *Hiawatha*, and *Courtship of Miles Standish*, 'various' Tennyson, Goldsmith's *Deserted Village*, *Traveller*, and *Retaliation*, Cowper's *Task*, Thackeray's *Ballads*, Aytoun's *Bothwell*, John Sterling's *The Sexton's Daughter*, W. W. Story's 'A Jewish Rabbi in Rome', Bulwer Lytton's *New Timon* and Edward ('Owen Meredith') Lytton's *Lucile*.

Because Charles Dickens, jun., editor of the magazine, was unwilling to allow more space to the serialization than he had to that of *Popenjoy*, Trollope gave time in April and May 1878 to the skilful cutting of the manuscript of *The Duke's Children*; it had been intended as a 'four-volume' novel, eighty chapters in twenty monthly parts; it emerged a three-volume novel, its eighty chapters intact, but able to accommodate a nine-month run of short weekly instalments in the magazine. The reduction was a remarkable—and most unusual—feat for one who so disliked revising, polishing, or cutting novels in manuscript.[42]

In the autumn of 1876 Trollope got involved with yet another publisher, William Isbister. On 24 October Donald Macleod, brother of Norman Macleod and his successor as editor of *Good Words*, wrote to Trollope asking if he would write, 'for the sake of "Auld lang syne"' a 'storiette' for the magazine.[43] *Good Words* was no longer the property of the mercurial Alexander Strahan, but of Isbister, a long-time partner of Strahan's who eventually took over the firm (although James Virtue still owned much of the company). Trollope sent Isbister a long story, 'Why Frau Frohmann Raised Her Prices', which Isbister published in the magazine over four months, from February to May 1877. By January 1877 he had written two other pieces for Isbister, an article and a short story on the telegraph girls of the Post Office (who had greatly impressed Trollope on a visit to St Martin's-le-Grand). Trollope was to have considerable dealings with Isbister over the years until his death: *Good Words* would carry four stories, three articles, and serialize one novel; and Isbister would publish one collected book of short stories, *Why Frau Frohmann Raised Her Prices*, and Trollope's study of Palmerston. Trollope came to consider Isbister, as he told Harry—who also published with Isbister—'a fairly honest fellow but dilatory and vague', a publisher who knew little beyond 'the paper and printing part' of his trade and was 'altogether astray as to whether a book will or will not pay'. Trollope seemed to have become partly disillusioned with Fred Chapman; he explained to Harry that Isbister 'is very much like Chapman, only as I think truer and honester'. When Isbister had Trollope renew a bill for £150, Trollope considered it 'exactly the same as borrowing the money. . . . This is like Chapman.'[44]

Like other Britons in the latter half of 1876, Trollope was much exercised over the 'Eastern Question': 'Here we are all agog about the Turks and the Russians,' he wrote to Mrs Bronson, 'and are so hot that every body is ready to cut everybody's throat. I and my brother quarrel most ferociously per post. . . . To my thinking Disraeli is the meanest cuss we have ever had in this country;—but he, (my brother) makes a God of him and says his prayers to him.'[45] The great public debate grew out of the massacre in 1875 of thousands of Christians at the hands of the Turks in the Bulgarian provinces of Turkey, news of which had leaked out slowly. The Prime Minister, Disraeli, the Queen, the Conservatives, and the military saw Russia—which wanted to interfere, ostensibly on behalf of the Bulgarians, but largely in an effort to expand southwards into the Mediterranean—as a serious threat to Britain, and tried to downplay the Turkish atrocities. Gladstone, the Liberals, the working class, and churchmen of all sorts opposed the Turks, even at the expense of siding with Russia. Gladstone helped his cause with his spectacularly successful pamphlet, *The Bulgarian Horrors and the Question of the East*. Taking a high moral line, he described five million Bulgarians as oppressed and beaten down, unable 'to look upwards, even to their Father in heaven', but extending their hands to the British; Gladstone wanted the Turks, 'one and all, *bag and baggage* . . . out from the Province they have desolated and plundered', lest they renew 'these foul Satanic orgies' there.[46] Staunch Gladstonian Trollope read the pamphlet aloud to his family in October (the only non-literary reading, and the only one not in verse); he told Rusden, 'Gladstone has raised among the people such a flame of indignation against the Turks, that it would be impossible for any English Minister to go to war in their defence.'[47] Trollope was one of the speakers who denounced Disraeli's pro-Turkish policies at a public meeting held at St James's Hall on 8 December (other speakers included Gladstone, Lord Shaftesbury, Evelyn Ashley, and the Duke of Westminster). The *Pall Mall Gazette* reported that Trollope 'spoke of the splendid chance we gave Turkey by the Crimean War, but England would not, he said, repeat the experiment. (Cheers.) The Turk was incurable, because he did not see the difference between good and evil as we saw it; to him tyranny, cruelty and oppression were absolutely good. He was the worst citizen in the world, because arms were his glory, and he had no glory except in arms. He must be made to live in Europe under other laws, and to conform to other customs than his own. (Hear, hear.)' Thomas Hardy, who attended the meeting, recorded: 'Trollope outran the five or seven minutes allowed for each speech, and the Duke [of Westminster], who was chairman, after various soundings of the bell, and other hints that he must stop, tugged at Trollope's coat-tails in desperation. Trollope turned round, exclaimed parenthetically, "Please leave my coat alone", and went on speaking.'[48]

27

South Africa

In the spring of 1877 Trollope made firm plans to 'do' another British colony, South Africa. But first he wanted to complete his work on the new Copyright Commission, to which he had been appointed the previous year, and which took evidence over a twelve-month period, the last of its many meetings being held on 8 May. Trollope wrote to Sir Henry Holland, asking if the Copyright Commission might move more quickly in preparing its report, as he was going to be absent from England for six months.* He was also anxious to come to an agreement with John Blackwood for a three-volume novel, *John Caldigate*, two-thirds of which he had completed by late May. He arranged passage aboard one of Donald Currie's Castle steamships to the Cape Colony, and on 7 June attended a meeting of the Royal Colonial Institute at which Currie spoke on the issues then most current concerning South Africa—the annexation of the Transvaal and federation. Called upon to speak, Trollope sensibly replied that he should have more to say in nine months' time; he did, however, support J. A. Froude's plea that the future of the Zulus living in the Transvaal be safeguarded. He obtained letters of introduction, the most important being from Sir Henry Barkly, who had recently completed seven years as Governor of the Cape Colony.

Just as Trollope was preparing to leave for South Africa, *The American Senator* was published by Chapman & Hall. It is remarkable among Trollope's works for its sympathetic full-length portrait of the quintessential Trollopian husband-hunting female.[1] Arabella Trefoil 'had long known that it was her duty to marry, and especially her duty to marry well'. Beautiful, hard-hearted, and calculating, she had for many years been at

---

* In fact, the Commission was unable to make its report until 24 May 1878. In February of that year John Blackwood, relating how Trollope had come back from South Africa 'in great force', quoted Lord John Manners as saying he was likely 'to drive them all mad at the weary Copyright Commission, going over all the ground that has been discussed in his absence'.[2] The copyright laws themselves, especially the vexed problem of international copyright with America, were not changed during Trollope's lifetime.

the 'weary work' of marrying rank and riches; she had been engaged a few times, and once she had nearly married a young aristocrat of immense wealth, 'but just as she was landing her prey, the prey had been rescued from her by powerful friends'. Engaged now to John Morton, a decent man of moderate means in the diplomatic service, she tries none the less to snare the wealthy Lord Rufford. She loves neither man; indeed she 'hates' Rufford. Still, whatever her faults, Arabella, like all Trollope's protagon- ists, has sympathy-engaging qualities. She is brave and indefatigable and can behave admirably at times. When John Morton lies dying, she tells him how unworthy she has been of him and what 'an escape he had had not to marry me', confessing how she had attempted to ensnare Rufford while engaged to Morton. And when she faces down Rufford, accusing him of throwing her over at his sister's bidding, calling him unmanly and dastardly, in one of those little dramas of verbal confrontation that so enliven all of Trollope's narratives, the reader applauds. One's sympathies sway with events and seem to follow those of people in the book: after Rufford disentangles himself from her, 'There were many who thought that she had been ill-used. Had she succeeded, all the world would have pitied Lord Rufford.' One is grateful that John Morton left her a legacy in his will, and that she is finally wedded to Mounser Green, a clerk in the Foreign Office—no great catch but serviceable enough (described as 'a distinguished clerk . . . and distinguished also in various ways, being one of the fashionable men about town, a great adept at private theatricals, remarkable as a billiard player at his club, and a contributor to various magazines').[3] Trollope told Mary Holmes that in Arabella Trefoil he 'wished to express the depth of my scorn for women who run down husbands'; while the book was still in serial, he wrote to Anna Steele: 'I have been, and still am very much afraid of Arabella Trefoil. The critics have to come, and they will tell me that she is unwomanly, unnatural, turgid,—the creation of a morbid imagination. . . . But I swear I have known the woman,—not one special woman . . . but all the traits, all the cleverness, all the patience, all the courage, all the self-abnegation,—and all the failure.'[4] Trollope had good reason to be wary: the *Examiner*, for example, said Trollope apparently still suffered from the 'attack of mis- anthropy' that had produced *The Way We Live Now*: 'He seems still to keep a special inkstand supplied with gall, for use when describing fashionable society, against which his rancour appears to be unbounded. When he penned the character of the heroine of his present story, for instance, the very paper must have blanched under the withering impress of his quill.' *The Times* admitted that Arabella's chase after Lord Rufford was 'exciting' but complained that 'that mature young beauty and her scheming mother strike us as playing a more unblushing game than is even compatible with "the way we live now".'5

Elias Gotobed, the American Senator bent on investigating British customs and institutions, is interesting as embodying, for all his foolishness and gaucheries, the questioning, quarrelsome, occasionally foot-in-mouth side of Trollope himself. The Senator takes up, for example, Trollope's old *bête noire* of curates' incomes, offering the instance of one Mr Puttock, a rector who receives £800 a year and a house 'for doing nothing', and pays his curate £100 a year for doing all the work. The Senator also asks why the 'big plums find their way so often to the sons and sons-in-law and nephews of bishops'. The Senator has learned that a rich man may buy a living 'just as he might have bought a farm', and then in effect say to his parishioners, 'Come . . . hear me expound the Word of God because I have paid a heavy sum of money for the privilege of teaching you.' All this the Senator proclaims at the table of the Revd Mr Mainwaring, whose own living had been purchased with his wife's money. How was he to know, he later asks, that when 'in private society I inveigh against pickpockets . . . there should be a pickpocket in the company'. Gotobed admits he enjoys associating with English aristocrats who exhibit such 'easy grace'; yet he is troubled by their apparent conviction that they are 'God's viceregents here on earth', intended by the Almighty to keep things in just the state they are. He is not surprised that one man is rich and one man is poor, but he sees it as a 'miracle' that in England the poor, 'they who have been born to suffer . . . should also think it to be all right'.6

The climax of the Senator's investigation into British institutions comes in a lecture he delivers at St James's Hall, London, on 'English Irrationality'. The narrator explains that the Senator, though hurried, had done his work energetically; had visited Birmingham, Manchester, Liverpool, Glasgow, and other places:

He had poked his nose everywhere, and had scrupled to ask no question. He had seen the miseries of a casual ward, the despair of an expiring strike, the amenities of a city slum, and the stolid apathy of a rural labourer's home. He had measured the animal food consumed by the working classes, and knew the exact amount of alcohol swallowed by the average Briton. He had seen also the luxury of baronial halls, the pearl-drinking extravagances of commercial palaces, the unending labours of our pleasure-seekers.

(It is an only partly ironical picture of Trollope as traveller and travel writer.) The Senator tells his audience that Englishmen usually do not admit 'the light of reason' into private or public life but generally allow themselves to be guided by 'traditions, prejudices, and customs which should be obsolete.' He won't comment on the Monarchy except to say that 'its recondite forms are very hard to be understood by foreigners, and that they seem to me to be for the most part equally dark to natives.' He argues that the distribution of votes and representation in Parliament is all helter-skelter, a maze of old and new ways, hardly penetrable by analysis; what is more, the largest class of British labour, the agricultural, 'is excluded from the franchise in a country which boasts of equal representation'. As for the House of Lords, 'Is it possible that the theory of an hereditary legislature can be defended with reason? For a legislature you want the best and wisest of your people.' (A heckling voice cries out, 'You don't get them in America.' 'We try at any rate,' the Senator retorts.) Waxing more and more energetic, he attacks hereditary property, primogeniture, the 'feudalism' created by aristocracy. He inveighs against abuses in the Church, in words Trollope himself had used dozens of times, saying that 'even here in England', most businesses attempt to get the man most suited for the work at hand, except the Church, which still follows the old ways of patronage and nepotism. He similarly accuses the army of allowing its heroes to go without advancement if they cannot afford to buy promotion, 'whereas the young dandy who has done nothing more than glitter along the pavements with his sword and spurs shall have the command of men'. The crowd was becoming restive, a riot was feared, and though the Senator had not yet got to lawyers, the Civil Service, railways, commerce, and the labouring classes, Lord Drummond, his host for the occasion, ends the proceedings. Drummond deposits Gotobed at his hotel, telling him that he admired his purpose and courage but doubted it were wise for a man 'to tell any other man, much less a nation, of all his faults'. To which observation, Trollope—probably with his mother, Dickens, and himself in mind—has the Senator reply, 'You English tell us of ours pretty often.'[7]

Trollope, who privately told Mary Holmes that the Senator 'is not himself half so absurd as the things which he criticises',[8] must have been not altogether surprised at the press's reaction: the *Athenaeum* said, 'The Senator might be cut out of the book almost without affecting the story; and his lecture on British institutions . . . is as near to being a bore as anything Mr. Trollope could write.' The *Saturday*, while liking the novel, said the part of the Senator might have been omitted. *The Times* thought the Senator 'an excrescence on the work to which he gives his name'. T. W. Crawley in the *Academy* thought the Senator's denunciations too sweeping 'even for an American'. Moreover, apart from the role of the Senator, the book took a beating in the press, continuing the gradual slide that had begun with *Lady Anna* and *The Way We Live Now*. The *Spectator*, for example, said that although Trollope rarely writes a bad book he 'almost as rarely now writes one which may be distinctively called good. We take his more recent novels very much as we take English weather.' The New York *Nation*, perhaps predictably, found the Senator's part 'pleasantest'; but the book's other interests were 'in parts disagreeable, not to say repulsive'; the writer even claimed that certain chapters confirmed 'the hint which has reached us from England, that Mr. Trollope is beginning to "let out" portions of his novels to less renowned assistants.' The *Examiner* hoped the tropical sun of South Africa would 'reopen the petals of Mr. Trollope's imagination and elicit something more worthy than the "American Senator."'[9]

Trollope embarked for Cape Town on 29 June. He wrote to Harry: 'I dont like any one on board, but I hate two persons. There is an old man who plays the flute all the afternoon and evening. I think he and I will have to fight. And there is a beastly impudent young man with a voice like a cracked horn, who will talk to me. He is almost unsnubbable, but I think I will silence him at last, as far as conversation with me goes.' He feared he would find the Cape uninteresting: 'The people who are going there on board this ship are just the people who would go to an uninteresting Colony.'[10] Whatever the company, he did his writing as usual, and completed *John Caldigate* the day before reaching Cape Town. The ship entered the harbour early on Sunday morning 22 July. A mist hid the beauties of the setting, and Trollope had to stand 'at the gate of the dockyard for an hour and a quarter waiting for a Custom House officer to tell me that my things did not need examination'.[11] He had scarcely landed when he wrote to Chapman, 'I shall begin my book about South Africa tomorrow!!!' Writing by the same post to Blackwood, he said: 'As I have as yet only been on shore 12 hours I am not prepared to give a full & comprehensive description of the country. But it seems like a poor, niggery, yellowfaced, half-bred sort of a place, with an ugly Dutch flavour about it.'[12] But he soon found the people pleasant, and agreed with a colonist whom he quoted as saying, 'We have plenty to eat and plenty to drink, and manage to make out life very well. The girls are as pretty as they are any where else, and as kind;—and the brandy and water as plentiful.' With customary energy Trollope set about meeting important people and seeing institutions; he was entertained by the Governor, Sir Bartle Frere;

he met John Charles Molteno, the Prime Minister, and various members of Parliament, and, quite extraordinarily, he interviewed ex-President Thomas Burgers of the recently-annexed Transvaal Republic; he observed a session of Parliament, and visited the museum, the library, the botanic gardens, and the Castle. He inspected the Post Office, and as always, gave advice, which he knew would be courteously listened to and then ignored; he suggested that the public be not driven to buy stamps at a store across the street and that postal officials cease regarding the public as 'enemies' from whom they needed to be protected by 'fortifications in the shape of barred windows and closed walls'. Even bankers, he said, work over open counters. [13]

'Do you care for the stars?' Trollope was asked by the Astronomer Royal, E. J. Stone. 'In truth I do not care for the stars. I care, I think, only for men and women, and so I told him.' He later relented and visited the Observatory, was shown 'all the wonders of the Southern Heavens', but admitted that he did not understand much about them. [14]

After two weeks in Cape Town and environs Trollope sailed eastward to Mossel Bay and Port Elizabeth. At the latter place he was invited to hold a conference with some twenty Gaika Kaffir chiefs, whom some feared would join the Galeka Kaffirs in rebellion against the government. The account given in the book is told more bluntly in a letter to Harry:

Only one Chief talked, and he declared that everything was as bad as it could be; That the Kaffirs were horribly ill treated by the English;—That they were made to wear breeches instead [of] red paint, which was very cruel; and that upon the whole the English had done a great deal more harm than good. He was a dirty half-drunken savage, who wore a sixpenny watch key by way of earring in his ear. He ended by begging tobacco, and God-blessing me for giving him half a crown. [15]

(The chief whom Trollope met, Siwani, remained faithful to the government, and in fact led an army of loyal natives against the rebellion. [16])

Continuing eastward along the coast, Trollope visited Grahamstown, Fort Beaufort, King Williams Town, and East London; thence he sailed for Durban, in the colony of Natal, which he found very British. At the capital, Pietermaritzburg, the Governor, Sir Henry Bulwer, graciously insisted that Trollope leave his hotel and stay at Government House. A large public dinner was given in his honour, where Trollope pleased the audience by insisting that immigrants should not think of returning to the mother country. One of the dinner guests was Bishop Colenso, who in turn arranged that Trollope spend a day and a night at his home. Trollope had never met Colenso, Natal's most famous and controversial personage. In his book Trollope refused to take sides on the theological storm caused by Colenso's *Pentateuch Critically Examined*, and was silent on the fact that he himself had in 1865 been one of the subscribers to a fund that helped Colenso refer his case successfully to the Crown, or that in 1866 he had published 'The Clergyman Who Subscribes for Colenso'—Trollope's own condemnation of literalist interpretation of the scriptures. In his travel book, Trollope says only that he was much impressed by the bishop's preaching (high praise, as Trollope almost invariably detested sermons), and that on this occasion 'the most innocent and the most trusting young believer in every letter of the Old Testament would have heard nothing . . . to disturb a cherished conviction.'[17] But Colenso had become controversial also for his liberal political positions, most recently for his support of the Zulu chieftain Langalibalele. Colenso hoped to win Trollope to his opinion; as his son wrote at the time: 'We are almost afraid lest [Trollope] should fall completely into the hands of the officials and be hoodwinked. . . . It will be a great triumph if we can supply him with really trustworthy facts about Zululand. . . . Father is a great admirer of Trollope. The *Barchester Towers* series gave him immense enjoyment.'[18]

The Zulu whom Colenso championed, Langalibalele, had refused to appear before British authorities in Natal, who then pursued him with much bloodshed on both sides. Now under house arrest near Cape Town, Langalibalele wanted many of his wives and children to be allowed to join him (he had seventy wives and innumerable offspring). Colenso, various philanthropists, and other friends of the prisoner, outraged at the whole affair, were for accommodating him with regard to his wives and children, although, as Trollope—always happy to criticize what he regarded as misguided fanaticism—noted, 'it could hardly be that Exeter Hall and the philanthropists should desire to encourage polygamy by sending such a flock of wives after the favoured prisoner.' Only two wives and one son had been allowed to join this 'troublesome old pagan', and his supporters insisted that he was 'languishing for his wives'. Trollope saw half a dozen of the wives, reported to be ill or dying 'because of this cruel separation', and suggested that the government send him three or four more wives, 'seeing that to a man who has had seventy less than half a dozen must be almost worse than none'. On returning to Cape Town Trollope met the captured chieftain at his house of arrest: Langalibalele 'was very silent, hardly saying a word in answer to the questions put to him,—except that he should like to see his children in Natal'.[19] Trollope felt the government did right, and that natives needed to be shown a hard line on obeying British law; he opposed letting Langalibalele return free to Zululand. Bishop

Colenso and his family were disappointed at Trollope's somewhat flippant discussion of Langalibalele's case; on the other hand, they were pleased at having helped win him to the cause of the Zulus generally and their chief Cetywayo in particular.

For the Zulus Trollope developed a positive liking. 'They are good-humoured, anxious to oblige, offended at nothing, and extremely honest.' Physically, the Zulus were 'never awkward'; they had a charming way of wearing their European clothes, often rags: 'Whatever it be that the Zulu wears he always looks as though he had chosen that peculiar costume. . . . When you see him you are inclined to think, not that the clothes are tattered, but "curiously cut,"—like Catherine's gown.' Trollope believed the Kaffirs and the Zulus would become a labouring, educated, civilized people. He also (and here the influence of Colenso and his daughter was probably strong) defended Cetywayo, the powerful monarch of neighbouring Zululand; he thought the charges against Cetywayo of 'murdering his people right and left' were without foundation. Cetywayo kept on good terms with the British in Natal, while despising the Dutch in the Transvaal; British commissioner Theophilus Shepstone and Cetywayo respected each other, and Trollope viewed Cetywayo, by his opposition to the oppressive Dutch rule there, as 'probably . . . the indirect cause of the annexation' of the Transvaal. Trollope urged that Britain not extend its rule to Zululand, but quite accurately predicted that troubles were to come: 'if I know anything of British manners and British ways, there will be British interference in Zulu-land before long.'[20]

Trollope believed that the South African black had been given a bad press at home, and hoped, at least to some extent, to set the record straight: he had heard it said in the House of Commons that Kaffir wives were bought and sold; while it was true that wives were bought, they were never sold: 'But . . . the old and rich buy up the wives, leaving no wives for the young men. . . . The practice is abominable,—but we shall not alter it by conceiving or spreading false accounts of it.' He asserts that in general cannibalism has not been a vice of the South African natives, Kaffirs, Zulus, Hottentots, or Bushmen, while admitting that some cannibalism had been practised by the Basutos. Still fascinated with the subject, he quoted at length from an article about a cave discovered in 1868 and strewn with the gnawed bones of women and children (he even cites such grisly detail as the lack of charring on the bones as showing 'that the prevailing taste had been for boiled rather than for roast meat').[21]

From Pietermaritzburg the hardest travel lay ahead, about which friends had let Trollope understand that he was 'well—much too old for the journey'; he admitted that the trek to Pretoria in the Transvaal, thence to Kimberley and the Diamond Fields, thence to Bloemfontein in the Orange Free State, and back across the Cape Colony to Cape Town, some 1,500 miles overland 'under very rough circumstances', was an 'awful' prospect. He left Pietermaritzburg for the Transvaal on 13 September, travelling by post cart as far as the frontier town of Newcastle. On the way he had an altercation with a man who attempted to bring a large metal box containing bonnets into the coach at the book-parcel rate, something that 'struck my official mind with horror'. 'It is illegal,' cried Trollope, who blocked the way, refusing to leave his place for breakfast. The offending package was eventually secured outside the coach. At Newcastle, he dined in a tent with British officers; the dinner, together with everything else, was 'excellent', but the mess prided itself most on serving Bass's bitter beer: 'An Englishman in outlandish places . . . sticks to his Bass more constantly than to any other home comfort.'*[22] Also at Newcastle he met by prearrangement George Farrar, a young man with whom he purchased a cart and four horses. Thereafter Trollope's narrative is held together for many pages by the account of this cart, its expenses, and its problems.

Their first goal was Pretoria, capital of the newly annexed Transvaal, a place he had scarcely heard of six months before leaving home. Once there, he was disappointed to find that Sir Theophilus Shepstone, the man who had effected the annexation, was away visiting the provinces of the new colony. Taken in hand by Shepstone's cabinet and officers, Trollope was given the hospitality of Government House, whence he wrote to Shepstone thanking him for the courtesies, and adding: 'You were the one person whom I was most anxious to see in South Africa.' While 'most heartily' congratulating Shepstone on performing 'one of the most difficult services that have fallen to the lot of a British subject in latter days', it is clear that Trollope, while favouring the annexation, would have put some searching questions to Shepstone.[23] Most importantly, he wanted to know where annexation would stop.

The annexation of the Transvaal, although a *fait accompli*, looms large in Trollope's book. After considerable soul-searching he saw the action as warranted: former President Burgers, in Trollope's view a decent but inept man, had not known how to govern a new country; Burgers saw himself as 'competing with [George] Washington for public admiration'; he had failed to provide for the collection of tax revenues and the security

* 'When the student at Oxford was asked what man had most benefited humanity, and when he answered "Bass", I think that he should not have been plucked. It was a fair average answer' (*Rachel Ray*, ch. 3).

of property; instead he concentrated on producing a national flag and gold coinage with his own portrait thereon;* he established a code of law, something that could be done 'almost as easily as the flag', but he effected no means of enforcing the laws. Accordingly, 'The condition of the Transvaal was very bad. Slavery was rampant. The Natives were being encouraged to rebellion. The President was impotent. The Volksraad was stiff-necked and ignorant. . . . That we must interfere for our own protection in regard to the Natives seemed to be necessary.' Thereupon, Shepstone, 'a sturdy Englishmen had walked into the Republic with five and twenty policemen and a Union Jack and had taken possession of it. "Would the inhabitants of the Republic like to ask me to take it?" No, the people declined. "Then I shall take it without being asked." And he took it.' Trollope doubts 'whether there is a precedent for so high-handed a deed in British history' and admits that Shepstone seemed to have 'exceeded his orders' and effected the annexation 'without complete authority'. Nevertheless, 'A case of such a kind must in truth be governed by its own merits, and cannot be subjected to a fixed rule.' Trollope says that had he been in Shepstone's place he would have done the same thing and 'been proud of the way I had served my country'.[24] It is not known what Trollope thought of Britain's giving back the Republic in 1881.

One member of Shepstone's staff, Rider Haggard, then twenty-three and legal guardian of all the orphans in the Transvaal, returned to Government House late one evening to find someone sleeping in his bed asking 'who the deuce I was. I gave my name and asked who the deuce the speaker might be. "Anthony Trollope," replied the gruff voice, "Anthony Trollope".' Haggard found Trollope 'obstinate as a pig' and a man of 'the most peculiar ideas'. Doubtless Trollope had tried his combative conversational approach with the young man, probably challenging the annexation and other policies he himself embraced in an effort to provoke a spirited defence. Haggard later softened his assessment, saying, as did nearly everyone else, that Trollope was 'a man who concealed a kind heart under a somewhat rough manner'.[25]

En route to Kimberley, Trollope wrote to Harry from Potchefstroom in the Transvaal: 'I do so long to get home. South Africa is so dirty. But I shall

---

* In *The Fixed Period* (1882) President Neverbend of Britannula, lately a British colony, says, 'We have been a little slack perhaps in instituting a national mint,' and he has not 'put the portrait of the Britannulan President of the day,—mine for instance,—in the place where the British Monarch has hitherto held its own. I have never pushed the question much, lest I should seem, as have done some presidents, over anxious to exhibit myself.'[26]

not do so before the first week in January. Not all the books in Xendom shall make me later than that.'²⁷ The going was exhausting; one horse died and had to be replaced; the last miles into Kimberley were particularly trying, as he and Farrar had to walk the horses in 90° heat. On arriving at the town at 5 p.m., they discovered that one of their portmanteaus had fallen from the cart, and they had to walk back 'six weary miles' searching for it. The next morning it was discovered in the middle of the road, guarded by two Kaffirs who were waiting for the owner to turn up. Trollope does not mention that the trunk contained his manuscript.²⁸

At Kimberley he and Farrar sold at auction their cart, harnesses, and horses, the outlay for which had been £243: 'The auctioneer endeavoured to raise the speculative energy of his bidders by telling them that the horses had all been bred at "Orley Farm" for my own express use . . . but I do not know that this romance much affected the bidding.' The lot went for £100. To Harry Trollope confided, 'I shall not put in the book that I had to get the Governor to send the Inspector of Police to the auctioneer before I could get my money.'²⁹

Kimberley, capital of the Diamond Fields in Quirquiland West, a territory the British had annexed in 1871, Trollope found detestable for the heat, dust, flies, and lack of trees and grass. Moreover, 'the meat was bad, the butter uneatable, vegetables a rarity. . . . Milk and potatoes were luxuries so costly that one sinned almost in using them.' Diamonds and prospective wealth were the compensation: a man walking around with a pocketful of diamonds doesn't worry about such amenities. Trollope gaped at the diamonds: 'I was soon sick of looking at diamonds though the idea of holding ten or twenty thousand pounds lightly between my fingers did not quite lose its charm.' And in spite of his bias against what he considered gambling, Trollope could not help but be impressed. The Kimberley mine was 'one of the most remarkable spots on the face of the earth', 'the largest and most complete hole ever made by human agency', where thousands of men worked at one time. He saw Kimberley as a place in which blacks would find their way; it would become a large town with a settled native population gradually being 'civilized': 'Who can doubt but that work is the great civilizer of the world,—work and growing desire for those good things which work only will bring?'³⁰

On 22 October Trollope left Kimberley for the Orange Free State. He met many Dutch Boers, and took strong exception to the British stereotype of the Boer as 'a European who had retrograded from civilization, and had become savage, barbarous, and unkindly'. With a novelist's talent he moves his account from generalities to particularities:

The Dutch Boer does not love to pay wages,—does not love to spend money in any way. . . . [But he] is courteous and kind. . . . If you are hungry or thirsty you say so, and hurry on the dinner or the cup of tea. You require to be called at four in the morning and suggest that there be hot coffee at that hour. And he is equally familiar. He asks your age, and is very anxious to know how many children you have and what is their condition in the world. He generally boasts that he has more than you have,—and, if you yourself be so far advanced in age, that he has had grandchildren at a younger age than you. 'You won't have a baby born to you when you are 67 years old,' an old Boer said to me exulting. When I expressed a hope that I might be saved from such a fate, he chuckled and shook his head, clearly expressing an opinion that I would fain have a dozen children if Juno and the other celestials concerned would only be so good to me. His young wife sat by and laughed as it was all explained to her by the daughter of a former marriage who understood English.[31]

At Bloemfontein, Trollope met John Henry Brand, President of the Orange Free State. That Bloemfontein, small, quaint, and decent in the parched and barren land, was unimpressive mattered nothing ('It is needful that a country should have a Capital, and therefore the Orange Free State has Bloemfontein').[32] Trollope reiterates endlessly that there could be no possible excuse for Britain annexing the Orange Free State and no reason to confederate it with the British colonies.

Trollope headed back to Cape Town via Port Elizabeth and Mossel Bay. From the latter he wrote to Harry: 'I am at this moment in an awful scramble, going off in 20 minutes on an expedition with a man I never saw till an hour and a half ago [George Hudson, Resident Magistrate at Mossel Bay], in quest of grand scenery—The grandest scenery in the world to me would be Montagu Square.'[33] One of the features of this week-long excursion to George and Knysna, and more interesting to Trollope than the scenery, was the local phenomenon of ostrich farming, which seemed to be replacing sheep farming. Keen as ever about how men made their livelihoods, Trollope was fascinated but sceptical; he distrusted anything that smacked of gambling, and ostrich farming obviously depended too much on a 'freak of fashion'. At one ostrich farm he remarked, 'I could not but hope as I saw the huge birds stalking about with pompous air,—which as you approached them they would now and again change for a flirting gait, looking back over their shoulders as they skipped along with ruffled tails;—I have seen a woman do very much the same;—that they might soon be made to give place again to the modest sheep.'[34]

On Tuesday 11 December he sailed from Cape Town for England, the last entry in his notebook from the trip reading, 'Started for home!!! Never so home-sick in my life.'35 He wrote the last chapter of *South Africa* as he was crossing the Bay of Biscay, finishing the book the day before arriving on 3 January in London.

South Africa was his most discerning travel work; his thinking is more subtle, more progressive, more amenable to change, and certainly less prejudiced in regard to the native races. Trollope here was far less John Bullish than most of his countrymen. If he went to South Africa to learn, he did so. For he did not come back advocating federation, or the glories of the British life abroad, or colonial expansion, or South Africa as a place to which Britons might emigrate. On the contrary, he came back saying South Africa was not truly a British colony, that is, a place to which British working people could go to improve their lot. There is no talk in *South Africa* of the black natives having to 'go' to make way for the white man. Rather South Africa was and should continue to be a land of black men, and the British Parliament ought to attend to the needs of the native population. England had become the master of the destinies of millions of black people: 'We have imposed upon us the duty of civilizing, of training to the yoke of labour and releasing from the yoke of slavery a strong, vital, increasing and intelligent population.' South Africa, as 'a country of black men' ought to be a source of 'purer gratification' than the Canadas, Australia, New Zealand. In those 'successful' colonies, 'we have gone with our ploughs and with our brandy, with all the good and with all the evil which our civilization has produced, and throughout the lands the native races have perished by their contact with us.' But, Trollope avers, it must not be so in South Africa. British obligation to the blacks is not to teach them to sing hymns, but to 'civilize' them through labour. So far British intervention has, in Trollope's view, been salutary to the native populations.36

The reviews of *South Africa* were enthusiastic: the *Examiner* was startled by Trollope's ability to work so quickly: 'We may well doubt whether any country but our own could furnish such a marvel of productive energy'; the *Saturday*, while rather simplifying Trollope's argument that South Africa did not constitute a proper British colony ('A handful of struggling English people making bad brandy, collecting feathers, and cropping bad wool hardly answers our ordinary notions of a colony at all'), congratulated Trollope that 'on so very dull a subject as South Africa there is scarcely a dull page'. George Smalley, in a review in the New York *Tribune* so generous that Trollope wrote to Smalley to say how pleasant he found it, called *South Africa* 'the best existing book on its subject for the general reader'.37

South Africa sold well, running through four two-volume editions, followed by a one-volume abridged edition in 1879 that included a new chapter prompted by the Zulu War, which had broken out in January of that year. In Trollope's view, Sir Bartle Frere, British High Commissioner in South Africa, had provoked the war by making altogether unreasonable demands on the Zulu King Cetywayo. Expansion of British rule cannot continue unabated: 'Have we not stretched our arms far enough? . . . If it be our duty to civilize the world at large, should we not pause a little as we do it? . . . I have no fears myself that Natal will be overrun by hostile Zulus;—but much fear that Zululand should be overrun by hostile Britons.' Privately, Trollope wrote to Rusden, 'I can not tell you how much to blame I think we have been in attacking Cetywayo. Frere, for whom personally I have both respect and regard, is a man who thinks that it is England's duty to carry English civilization and English christianity among all Savages. Consequently, having the chance, he has waged war against these unfortunates,—who have lived along side of us in Natal for 25 years without ever having raised a hand against us! the consequence is that we have already slaughtered 10,000 of them, and rejoice in having done so. To me it seems like civilization gone mad!'[38] (Frere was censured by the government in 1879 and recalled after Gladstone took office in 1880.) On 19 January 1880 Frere sent Trollope a 105-page criticism of this chapter, adding in a covering letter, 'As I consider you entitled to an obelisk or pyramid or whatever may be the appropriate expression of African gratitude for the good work you have done in seeing for yourself and placing South Africa so graphically before English readers, I feel bound to let you know where I think you are wrong.'[39] Trollope was unmoved. He lectured on 'The Native Races of South Africa' at Manchester in 1878, and in 1879 he lectured on the Zulus at Nottingham and at Birmingham, taking the same line as in the Zululand chapter of his book. Bishop Colenso, who had been dissatisfied with some aspects of Trollope's *South Africa*, must have been agreeably pleased with his opposition to the Zulu War.

28

Popenjoy *and* Ayala

IN March 1878, so that Chapman & Hall might issue a collected edition of *The Chronicles of Barsetshire,* Trollope got permissions from Longman, W. H. Smith, and George Smith (the last involving complicated buying back of copyrights and paying of profits to Smith, Elder). The same project had come to grief in 1867, when Smith had declined to buy the Longman copyrights. Now at last the books were to appear, a uniform set that eventually comprised six titles in eight volumes (Trollope had not intended to include *The Small House at Allington* in the series, but did so at Chapman's urging; in 1867 he had told George Smith that *Doctor Thorne* was 'not essential' to the series but ought to be included).[1] F. A. Fraser, who had illustrated *Ralph the Heir* in serial appearance, was enlisted to supply frontispieces. Trollope wrote a brief Introduction, explaining how the books, except for *The Warden* and *Barchester Towers,* were not intended to form a sequence, though one did exist 'in the Author's mind': 'I . . . had formed for myself so complete a picture of the cathedral town and the county in which I had placed the scene, and had become by a long-continued mental dwelling in it, so intimate with sundry of its inhabitants, that to go back to it and write about it again and again have been one of the delights of my life.' On the other hand, he feared that few novels written 'in continuation' had been successful, that 'even Scott, even Thackeray had failed to renew great interest', and Fielding and Dickens 'never ventured the attempt'. Still, as the stories were now old, and 'not perhaps quite forgotten by the readers of the present day, and to my memory fresh as when they were written' they were being republished 'so that my records of a little bit of England which I have myself created may be brought into one set'. If Plantagenet Palliser and Lady Glencora were his favourite characters, the earlier Barsetshire novels were his—and the public's—favourites among his books. The collected set did not sell well. All the volumes had long been available individually in cheap editions; moreover, the uniform edition dribbled out a few volumes at a time between autumn 1878 and spring 1879. But Trollope did not bring out the set for profit. Their publication was a mildly self-indulgent monument to his achievement. He sent copies, with some satisfaction, to that scene of earlier disgrace, Winchester College.[2]

Kate Field was spending much time in England. She had steadily established a fair reputation as an actress and singer. Especially successful was her leading role, in London and throughout the country, in a comedietta, *Extremes Meet*, her own adaptation of a French play. Trollope saw her perform in it, at the Princess Theatre, in March 1877 and 'liked it very much', as he told playwright Tom Taylor, to whom he sent a letter introducing 'my old and very dear friend Kate Field'. At about the same time she asked his opinion and help in placing a paper on the lecturing woman, probably a reworking of her popular lecture, 'Women in the Lyceum'. Trollope, tactlessly frank as ever, told her that the article 'slaughters giants that have no existence' and fails to face the real objection to lecturing by women, namely, that 'oratory is connected chiefly with forensic, parliamentary, and pulpit pursuits for which women are unfitted because they are wanted elsewhere . . . at home.' Her paper is 'gay and lively'; 'Your fun is I think better than your facts,' but, as it stands, he thinks no editor, himself included, would take it. If she would make some changes, he will ask Bentley of the *Temple Bar* to consider the paper.[3] She seems not to have pursued the matter further. Trollope apparently had little active interest in Kate's campaign for acceptance of the telephone in England, though he did have Tom inquire about the expense of an Italian translation of her pamphlet on the subject. When Alexander Graham Bell was invited to exhibit the new device to the Queen at Osborne, Kate was chosen to talk to her over the wire. In fact she sang 'Kathleen Mavourneen' with much éclat ('I'm considered a great creature,' she wrote in her diary, 'because I've sung to the Queen'). The Prime Minister, Disraeli, wrote to say that the Queen was so interested in the telephone that a trial experiment was being arranged for the Home Office, and invited Kate to sing again, from the library to the rooms of the Minister. The Bell Company, out of gratitude for Kate's support, gave her shares that eventually netted her some $200,000, an entirely unexpected fortune that made her life less precarious, though no less active.[4] One trusts Trollope thought the money 'honestly earned'. But to another of her enthusiasms he was all but hostile. Kate had become deeply involved in the Shakespeare Memorial Association, which, with money from Charles Edward Flower, the Stratford brewer, sought to build an imposing theatre at

Stratford-on-Avon. She raised subscriptions, performed during the inaugural week's festival by reading the opening address—in verse—and by singing; she later arranged a successful benefit dramatic performance at London's Gaiety Theatre, for which she enlisted the services of various notables such as the Kendals, Hermann Vezin, and Ellen Terry. She got up a subscription from American friends for finishing the interior of the theatre, the contributors including Longfellow, James Fields, Edmund Stedman, and Henry James. Trollope, when she asked him for a contribution, answered: 'No;—I don't care two pence for the Shakespeare Memorial or Mr Flower. If there be any one who does not want more memorials than have been already given, it is Shakespeare! Mr Flower is a worthy old gent,—who wants to go down to posterity hanging on to some distant rag of the hindermost garment of the bard of Avon. . . . Surely he can hang on to a rag without costing me five guineas!' He had evidently earlier given her some money for herself, and added in a postscript: 'Now dont you turn around and be cross with me, and pitch my little mite of assistance to yourself at my teeth, as if I were bad at the core! For yourself there would be other mites if they were wanted.'5

Trollope's standing with the critics continued to fall with *Is He Popenjoy?*, published by Chapman & Hall in April 1878. The very title drew the comment from the *The Dublin University Magazine* that only a writer 'devoid of all sense' would call a book by such a name (Trollope may have been playing with the 'Is he Tichborne?' question).6 The *Academy* said *Popenjoy* represented Trollope's 'least pleasant' manner; The *Saturday* compared the book to 'a copper-plate by a good artist at its last stage. All the finer touches, the tender, subtle gradations are worn out, and strength is supplied by a hardening of the strongest lines. . . . all the delicacy and nicety of touch is gone'; *The Times* remarked that the novel 'would more than pass muster had it appeared anonymously, but it is by no means worthy of its author'; and the *Spectator* accused Trollope of trading on his reputation, writing inferior tales, this one 'poor as a work of art and to some extent unwholesome'.7 Such judgements seem hard to justify. It was as though the critics were longing for Trollope's lighter side, hoping for another *Framley Parsonage*. Curiously, *Is He Popenjoy?*, while investigating some dark matters and resembling the increasingly popular 'fast' fiction in extramarital infidelities (or near infidelities) and the sensation novel in its mystery of the legitimacy of an Italian-born heir, has none the less the unmistakably Barchesterian strains of small-town clerical infighting and local, country-style gossip.

Popenjoy *and* Ayala

One of the special features of *Is He Popenjoy?* lies in its satire of English mistrust of everything foreign. The dissolute and nasty Marquis of Brotherton, who has for years neglected his titled property and lived in Italy, returns home with an Italian wife, lately a widow, and with a child and supposed heir, Lord Popenjoy. The Marquis's mother, 'when she first heard of the Italian wife, went into hysterics'. Lord George, the scrupulously honest younger brother, though trying to be fair, 'mistrusted an Italian widow, because she was an Italian':

> It's a blot to the family—a terrible blot.'
> 'She is a lady of good family, a Marchesa,' said Mr. Knox.
> 'An Italian Marchesa!' said Lord George, with that infinite contempt which an English nobleman has for foreign nobility not of the highest order.

As for proof that his brother's marriage was legal, 'What evidence,' George asks, 'on which an Englishman might rely, could possibly be forthcoming from such a country as Italy!' As one of his sisters puts it, the whole mess 'comes of living in a godless country like Italy'.[8]

But the villainous Marquis at times makes very good sense; he believes his brother and sisters have turned against him 'because I have chosen to marry a foreigner. It is simply an instance of that pigheaded English blindness which makes us think that everything outside our own country is, or ought to be, given up to the devil. My sisters are very religious, and, I dare say, very good women. But they are quite willing to think that I and my wife ought to be damned because we talk Italian, and that my son ought to be disinherited because he was not baptised in an English church.' In conversation with his brother he says,

> 'I wonder why the deuce you never learned Italian!'
> 'We were never taught,' said Lord George.
> 'No; nobody in England ever is taught anything but Latin and Greek,—with the singular result, that after ten or a dozen years of learning not one in twenty knows a word of either language. That is our English idea of education. In after life a little French may be picked up, from necessity; but it is French of the worst kind. My wonder is that Englishmen can hold their own in the world at all.'
> 'They do,' said Lord George, to whom all this was ear-piercing blasphemy. The national conviction that an Englishman could thrash three Frenchmen, and if necessary eat them, was strong with him.
> 'Yes; there is a ludicrous strength even in their pig-headedness. But I always think that Frenchmen, Italians, and Prussians must, in dealing with us, be filled with infinite disgust. They must ever be saying, "Pig, pig, pig," beneath their breath, at every turn.'

'They don't dare to say it out loud,' said Lord George.

'They are too courteous, my dear fellow.'

Brotherton, callous and vengeful, is not altogether despicable; like Melmotte, he is in some ways admirable. Near the end he admits that he himself is not sure if his son is legally his heir: his adversaries, he acknowledges, 'had something to stand upon, but—damn it—they went about it in such a dirty way!'[9]

The most forceful investigator into the Popenjoy question is Henry Lovelace, the Dean of Brotherton, whose daughter, Mary, married to the younger son, stands to be the mother of future marquises should the Italian boy prove to be illegitimate. Lovelace is another figure embodying much of Trollope himself. Strong in his opinions, outspoken, frank, impulsive, at times loud, Lovelace is a man of immense energies, very 'active' and 'resolute in his work', and troublesome to his superior. Fond of parties and entertainments, he calls his son-in-law a fool for opposing his wife's waltzing ('He has no experience, no knowledge of the world'). The resemblances to Trollope even include his always jumping up out of his chair when news is brought him, and his often staying when in London at 'a hotel in Suffolk Street'—Garlant's. From the first he stubbornly refuses to believe in the Italian heir; in his zeal for his daughter's interests, he thinks of going to Italy himself to seek out evidence; he persists in spite of his own lawyer's investigation having pointed towards the boy's legitimacy. Like Archdeacon Grantly, the dean is, for a cleric, thoroughly 'worldly': when Mary seems not to want to trouble about the possibility of being the future Marchioness of Brotherton, her father tells her, 'That's nonsense. . . . Men, and women too, ought to look after their own interests. It is the only way in which progress can be made in the world.' When the Marquis insults his daughter, the dean, in spite of his cloth (the narrator observing that ordinarily 'It would probably be hard to extract a first blow from a whole bench of bishops') throws him into an empty fireplace grate, nearly killing him.* And when, at the end, news comes of the Marquis's death—the child having already died and the question of his legitimacy become irrelevant—the dean 'triumphs' exceedingly: 'I thank God that he is gone. I cannot bring myself to lie about it. I hate such lying. To me it is

---

* The near murder of the Marquis touches off proceedings reminiscent of Barchester: when the dean's enemies, especially the bishop's chaplain, the Slope-like Mr Groschut, try to get the bishop to interfere, the dean, very like Mr Crawley, says, 'In such a matter, I am amenable to the laws of the land, and am not, as I take it, amenable to any other authority.' In an interview he utterly overcomes the bishop, who later tells Groschut, 'I am almost inclined to think he was justified.' The chaplain, like Slope, is eventually exiled from the cathedral city, for playing 'not quite on the square with a young lady'.[10]

unmanly. . . . It is a grand thing to rise in the world. The ambition to do so is the very salt of the earth. It is the parent of all enterprise, and the cause of all improvement. They who know no such ambition are savages.' His own daughter is surprised at the 'pagan exaltation of her father at the death of his enemy', but the dean's words echo Trollope's own frequently expressed views.[11]

Part of the dean's pugnacious manner, we are told, lay in the fact that, being the son of a man who kept a livery stable, the dean 'had never ceased to be ashamed of the stable-yard'.[12] Trollope carried within himself always some of the secret shame of his early years and understood himself well enough to see at least part of his 'energetic' style as having its source in those terrible times. Indeed, numerous contemporary accounts of Trollope's social behaviour show his pugnacity abating not at all as he grew older. From the early days in Ireland, when the extroverted side of his personality had its first real opportunity to exercise itself, it had gradually taken on a legendary status. Of course he could no longer kick open desk drawers in search of hidden letters. (And yet Mrs Edward Ward recorded once seeing Trollope in the late 1870s at Lord Cowper's Panshanger estate, 'about to have a fight with a broad-shouldered rubicund trades-man. Anthony had divested himself of his coat and was shaking his fists in his opponent's face, as he danced around him.'[13]) Trollope's aggressive manner showed itself most frequently in conversation. Alfred Austin, a good friend, said that Trollope, 'though a delightful companion and brimming over with active intelligence, was . . . as unhelpful and impatient an arguer as I ever met'.[14] Frederick Locker-Lampson called him 'boisterous, but goodnaturedly so. He was abrupt in manners and speech; he was ebullient, and therefore he sometimes offended people. I suppose he was a wilful man, and we know that such men are always in the right; but he was a good fellow.'[15]

On 22 June Trollope left on a brief excursion to Iceland with John Burns, an old friend from the 1860s. Burns, later Lord Inverclyde, chairman of the Cunard Steamship Company, took a group of sixteen guests aboard his yacht *Mastiff* (the crew numbered thirty-two). Burns got Trollope to write a short account of the trip, which Burns then had privately printed by Virtue, *How the 'Mastiffs' Went to Iceland.* Trollope also produced a lengthy article, 'Iceland', for the *Fortnightly.* He was amused that even two British admirals, fellow guests, could not determine from recent and 'authoritative' charts whether Iceland extended beyond the Arctic Circle.[16]

Their first port of call was the sadly isolated island of St Kilda. Its handful of inhabitants, 'so many Robinson Crusoes', were at the moment desperate for a few fathoms of rope, which John Burns supplied. Trollope thought the place picturesque but not suitable for human habitation: 'I think it may be taken as a rule that no region can be of real value, the products of which must be eked out by charity from other regions.' He saw as most 'detrimental' the fact that the island had twelve marriageable young women but only two eligible young men. There being no spirits on the island, he gave brandy to a woman whose stomach was ill.[17]

At the Faroe Islands, like Iceland the property of Denmark, it seemed as though everyone were up in the middle of the night to meet the travellers; apparently the Governor was the only person in bed, from which he was 'extracted' to greet the guests. Their guide was the postmaster, who impressed Trollope by his command of English ('I doubt whether there are many English postmasters who could address a Faroite stranger in his own tongue, or even in Danish') and the fact that he looked 'singularly like Mr Gladstone'. Trollope 'should have liked to ask this gentleman what was his salary, and what his duties, and whether there ever came an inspector from the head office in Denmark to look after him'—whether there was any Anthony Trollope in his official life.

Reykjavik, clean and pleasing, prosperous in its way, was 'a dear little town, pervaded no doubt by a flavour of fish':

We are apt to think in London that we are the very centre and navel of the world. . . . but in so thinking we are led too frequently to believe that the people who are distant from us . . . must be very much behind us indeed. There are those Icelanders, with almost perpetual night during a great portion of the year, without a tree, living in holes for protection against the snow. . . . But . . . I did not think the people whom I saw to be at all unfortunate, and certainly in no degree barbarous.

As always, social facts fascinated Trollope: in Iceland, with its purported population of 90,000, everyone reads, everyone seems well clothed and comfortable; there are five newspapers, a college with 'learned professors . . . ripe scholars as regards the classics', but no commercial bank. He saw no poverty and no drunkenness; he visited one island given over entirely to the breeding of eider ducks, the source of 'those stuffy, fluffy, soft, slippery coverings which always fall off a German bed when an Englishman tries to sleep in it'.[18]

Trollope has great praise for Thora Pjetursson, the bishop's daughter, 'the Heroine of Reykjavik', who took the group around. She spoke English and was beautiful: 'One and all we lost our hearts to the bishop's daughter.'

At a formal dinner, Trollope, oldest of the company, sat with her on one side and the Governor on the other. To see the geysers, the visitors travelled some seventy rough miles, their party of sixteen augmented by five guides, two servants, a cook, and sixty-five ponies. Trollope found the geysers 'second-class' compared with those of New Zealand and the surrounding area 'curious . . . but not beautiful'.[19]

While Trollope and his party were in Iceland, the Eastern Question, which had continued to dominate foreign news for two years, came to a head. The Russians, who had in 1877 gone to war and defeated the Turks, were for imposing a treaty that would have extended Russian influence to the Mediterranean. Britain would not allow this, and moved Indian troops into Malta. But at the Congress of Berlin, June–July 1878, Disraeli had effected compromises whereby Russia was checked (in that the size of the new Bulgaria was smaller than Russia had wanted), and whereby Turkey, which was in effect given back Macedonia, maintained enough territory to remain part of Europe. Britain was given Cyprus. Disraeli, after what was probably his greatest triumph, would return home proclaiming 'Peace with honour'. When the *Mastiff* steamed into Wemyss Bay, Scotland, on 8 July, Trollope and his fellow passengers had been three weeks without news: 'We did not know whether we were or were not at war. Then we learned that the affairs at Berlin had straightened themselves, that the Russian had been smoothed and the Turk protected,—and that the Englishman who had lately bristled with so many arms was to be regarded as a peacemaker by the world at large.'[20] It was the kindest allusion, whatever its irony, that Trollope ever made to Disraeli.

Back in London, he had a flurry of things to do before going again to Switzerland and Germany for his holiday. He travelled down to Margate where his brother's wife's sister, Ellen Ternan, was now the wife of George Robinson, joint principal of the High School there. Trollope distributed the annual prizes, telling the boys that 'Rivalry is in itself a desirable thing'; that during his own schooldays 'we had plenty of flogging and no prizes'; 'I went to school when I was seven, and I left school when I was nineteen, and in all those years I don't think I ever saw a prize, and I'm sure I never got one!'[21] He conducted, with Frederic Ouvry, the annual audit of the books of the Royal Literary Fund; he finished the short text for Burns' book, wrote the *Fortnightly* article on Iceland and arranged for it to be privately printed as a pamphlet. He entertained Tom Trollope, who was in town, and was amused when his brother, reading *John Caldigate* as it appeared monthly in *Blackwood's Magazine*, asked him who the author was. [22]

Towards the end of July he travelled to the Black Forest where he met up with Rose, who had gone ahead. They went thence to Felsenegg, Switzerland, where he set steadily to work on *Ayala's Angel*. Felsenegg and Hollenthal had become favourite holiday places (Rose had gone there on her own the previous year, when Trollope was in South Africa). Their forests seemed to be especially fruitful sources of the kind of remote inspirational quiet Trollope savoured for 'castle-building'. In an article, 'A Walk in a Wood', published the following year in *Good Words*, he dilated on how for him the most difficult part of creating a novel was not the actual writing, but the 'thinking'. By this, he explained, he did not mean thinking about the 'entire plot' or overall story, since the larger incidents of his tales 'are fabricated to fit my story as it goes on, and not my story to fit the incidents'. (He mentions Lady Mason's confessing her forgery, Lizzie Eustace's stealing her own diamonds, and Mrs Proudie's dying of a heart attack as examples of large plot developments that had suddenly come upon him in the midst of writing.) Rather, the hard work of thinking was expended on the 'minute ramifications of tale-telling;—how this young lady should be made to behave herself with that young gentleman;—how this mother or that father would be affected by the ill conduct or the good of a son or a daughter'. Such thinking is best served by peaceful surroundings:

Bad noises, bad air, bad smells, bad light, an inconvenient attitude, ugly surroundings, little misfortunes that have lately been endured, little misfortunes that are soon to come, hunger and thirst, overeating and overdrinking, want of sleep or too much of it, a tight boot, a starched collar, are all inimical to thinking. . . . It is not the sorrows but the annoyances of life which impede. Were I told that the bank had broken in which my little all was kept for me I could sit down and write my love story . . . but to discover that I had given half a sovereign instead of sixpence to a cabman would render a great effort necessary before I could find the fitting words for a lover. These little lacerations of the spirit, not the deep wounds, make the difficulty. Of all the nuisances named, noises are the worst. . . . To think with a barrel organ within hearing is heroic.

Although he could do some thinking in a carriage—not in a railway car, though he could write in one—and more on horseback, and had even composed some 'little plots' on horseback waiting at the covert side, he much preferred to do the work while walking in a wood. It is best, he writes, to reject even the company of a dog, and to keep away from cottages, children, and chance wanderers, 'so much easier it is to speak than to think'. Solitary woods were becoming rarer in England, but the 'pure forests' of Switzerland and the Black Forest were the perfect 'hunting grounds' for thought.[23]

From Felsenegg he reported his regimen to George Eliot: 'Here we are on the top of a mountain, where I write for four hours a day, walk for four hours, eat for two, and sleep out the balance satisfactorily. I am beginning to think that the more a man can sleep the better for him. I can take a nap of nine hours each night without moving, in these latitudes.' From Hollenthal, having just finished *Ayala's Angel* with a burst of twenty-two days during each of which he produced exactly twelve pages or some 3,000 words per day, he wrote to Rusden, encouraging him in the writing of his histories of the colonies: '[It is] my conviction that in the fall of the leaf of a man's life nothing can make him happy but congenial work to do, or the reflection that congenial work has been well done.' He urges Rusden to get on with his work, not to wait till his evidence is complete. Accuracy is desirable, but a 'pleasing style' more so: 'dozens' of books on the colonies by well-informed persons have failed to find readers because their authors 'have not known how to write a book'. His own travel works are 'light' and 'inaccurate', but they have sold because 'I know the knack of writing a book'. Trollope often professed himself puzzled at his ability to do that which others, no matter how otherwise talented, could not. Like so many authors, he was constantly applied to for advice in writing and influence in getting works published, a situation he often found dismaying: 'the task of dealing with the Mss of other persons', he told Mary Holmes, 'is so painful,—the necessity of explaining to an aspirant that his or her aspirations must be disappointed is so grievous,—that I have often been tempted to say, that I would never again incur the punishment. I can hardly bring myself to tell a friend that he or she cannot do that which I by chance can do myself.'[24]

Trollope added a postscript to the letter to Rusden: 'Yesterday I completed my 80th tale;—not all what you would call novels, but of very various lengths.' The '80th tale', *Ayala's Angel*, would not be published until May 1881, when Chapman & Hall brought it out in three volumes (Trollope had unusual trouble selling the serial rights; they eventually went to the National Press Agency—which, apparently, never made use of the story).[25] *Ayala's Angel* was a virtuoso comic performance, the story of two orphans, Ayala and her sister, her rich uncle, his foolish son, his unattractive daughters, numerous suitors, and many others. Bright, witty, sparkling, gently satiric of everything from romantic love to money worship, from the marriage market to novel writing, the story represents a

1878

late flaring up of Trollope's lightest comic mode, perhaps the most sustained since *Barchester Towers*. The title itself mischievously reverses the Victorian notion of the woman as 'angel in the house', for this angel is not only a man, but a 'preternaturally ugly' man, whom Ayala twice refuses before realizing his 'angelic' qualities. One wonders if Trollope had Jane Austen's *Pride and Prejudice* in mind as the heroine slowly overcomes her prejudices against Jonathan Stubbs.[26] Reviewers would call Stubbs 'among Mr. Trollope's best male studies' and a sort of intelligent and witty Dobbin (from Thackeray's *Vanity Fair*) in the way his worth gradually impresses itself on those around him.[27]

Ayala's Angel presents a whole blaze of weddings, and the narrator begins the final chapter:

It may be doubted whether any reader [of this story],—unless he be someone specially gifted with a genius for statistics,—will have perceived how very many people have been made happy by matrimony. If marriage be the proper ending for a novel,—the only ending, as this writer takes it to be, which is not discordant,— surely no tale was ever so properly ended, or with so full a concord, as this one. Infinite trouble has been taken not only in arranging these marriages but in joining like to like,—so that, if not happiness, at any rate sympathetic unhappiness, might be produced.

The satire here turns gently on lovers, spouses, novel readers and novelists. And in spite of the presence of so many young lovers, foolish and witty, venal and generous, ugly and attractive, the best developed character—as in so many Trollope novels—is an older man, Sir Thomas Tringle, a wealthy City 'bullionaire'. Though he was a man who did not look kind, Sir Thomas is consistently kind to his niece Ayala: 'She was pretty, and though he was ugly himself he liked to look at things pretty.' But he is quickly angered; he speaks energetically, roughly, and wrathfully, with a gruff voice and in a 'burly authoritative way'; Sir Thomas is one of those men, no matter how accomplished in life—for he does know international finance—'whose original roughness does not altogether desert him, and who can on an occasion use it with a purpose. Such a one will occasionally surprise his latter-day associates by the sudden ferocity of his brow, by the hardness of his voice, and by apparently unaccustomed use of violent words. The man feels that he must fight, and, not having learned the practice of finer weapons, fights in this way. Unskilled with foils or rapier, he falls back upon the bludgeon with which his hand has not lost all its old familiarity.' 'I like to be plain,' he tells his sponging son-in-law, trying desperately to get the man to set up house on his own. 'This

[445]

might go on for ever if I didn't speak out.' 'Three weeks', he shouts at the top of his voice. Yet, as his daughter explains, even when he gets excited and 'flares up', even when 'he gets so fierce sometimes that we think he's going to eat everybody', in the end he 'has to come down, and he gets eaten worse than anybody else'. The fact is, she says, 'He is always so good-natured in the long run, and so generous. He can be very savage, but he would be sure to forgive.' He likes people to be afraid of him; on the other hand, as the narrator relates, 'Sir Thomas, rough as he was, had but a thin skin. . . . He was a soft-hearted man;—but there never was one less willing to endure interference in his own affairs.'[28] By the end, he is everybody's angel. And he is another version of Anthony Trollope.

Trollope went home and, having taken nearly a month off after completing *Ayala's Angel*, began, on 26 October, a short novel, *Cousin Henry*. He worked quickly, completing the two-volume work in six weeks. But writer's cramp had by now nearly paralysed his hand, and he dictated about one third of the novel to Florence Bland, Rose's niece, who for all practical purposes had been his adopted daughter since 1863. Trollope had sent her to school at Aix-la-Chapelle, Aachen, on the western border of the Rhine Province of Germany. She could spell, had a legible handwriting, and was evidently very patient. Now 23 years of age, she had, earlier in the year, begun to write out some of his letters. She would continue to serve as his amanuensis until the end, and in time would take down as much as two-thirds of some later manuscripts. Trollope's hand* and hers alternate according to no pattern: he would frequently begin a chapter, but give over after a page or paragraph. Sometimes the hands change in mid-paragraph, even in mid-sentence. Given Trollope's impatience, it must have been trying work for the young woman. According to one friend, Florence was forbidden to make the slightest suggestion or comment during the writing sessions, and on the one occasion when she did so, 'a whole chapter [was] consigned to the waste-paper basket'.[29] *Cousin Henry*, the novel with which she began assisting him, concerns various wills made by an old Welsh squire, and the next to last one leaves £4,000 to a beloved niece (the final will leaves his estate to her). Trollope himself at the time he began this story made his own will, and in it left Florence Bland £4,000—to be paid after his wife's death and only if

* Trollope's concern was with physical inability to write rather than with worry that printers would not be able to read his handwriting; like many others he relied upon, and marvelled at, the ability of printers to work from sloppy, all-but-illegible manuscripts. None the less he realized that his handwriting was becoming increasingly difficult to read; in the last year of his life he wrote to a relative: 'If you can read this at all I shall think very much of myself, and of you.'[30]

Florence were a spinster. In June 1882 Florence made her own will, in which she made Harry and Fred Trollope her heirs, since 'all the money I possess has been given to me by my uncle'. Perhaps Trollope gave her some of her fortune in advance.[31] The arrangement of dictating parts of his novels to her seems in no way to have affected his fiction.

Two weeks after completing *Cousin Henry*, he began, on 23 December 1878, a three-volume novel, *Marion Fay*, only to break off, after nine days. Most unusually, he was to allow two books, and seven months, to intervene before resuming this novel, which he did only the following August when again on holiday in Felsenegg and Hollenthal.

Mary Holmes, one of the few people with whom he would discuss in writing the relative merits of his books, died on 1 October. Trollope wrote to her niece, 'For the last 14 years I have been in the habit of hearing from her at great length, and of writing to her, I fear, with much less frequency. . . . I found her letters to be full of piety, good sense, and of most excellent literary criticism. She never spared me when,—as was very often the case,—she thought I had strayed either from truth to nature or from good sense in my writing. . . . I feel that her death has robbed me of a friend.'[32]

Two months later, on 30 November, death took one of his very closest friends, George Henry Lewes, the man he most admired among the *Cornhill* circle he met in 1860. Trollope attended the funeral at Highgate Cemetery on 4 December. At the suggestion of Lewes's son and George Eliot, Trollope wrote a memorial article on Lewes for the *Fortnightly Review*, the magazine of which Lewes, at Trollope's insistence, had been first editor. Feeling 'wholly ignorant of philosophic research' he enlisted Frederic Harrison to supply a long two-page analysis of Lewes's *Biographical History of Philosophy* for insertion within the ten-page article. Trollope's account is largely an appreciation of the person. He said, for example, 'To me personally Lewes was a great philosopher only because I was told so. When he would acquaint me with some newly found physical phenomenon, as that a frog could act just as well without his brains as with them,—I would take it all as gospel, though a gospel of which I had no part myself. When he would dilate on the perspicuity or the inaccuracy of this or the other philosopher . . . I would be careless as to his subject, though I loved his zeal. But though the philosopher was lost upon me, the humorist was to me a joy for ever.' Trollope's tribute closed: 'There was never a man so pleasant as he with whom to sit and talk vague literary gossip over a cup of coffee and a cigar. . . . there is no doubt . . . that he has left behind him here in London no pleasanter companion with whom to while away an hour.'[33] Trollope made no mention of George Eliot, doubtless more from consideration of her wishes than any squeamishness on his own part.

29

Extending the Range

WITH Lewes's death, Thackeray and the early 1860s were much on Trollope's mind, and in January 1879 he agreed to write the Thackeray volume for Macmillan's English Men of Letters series. He did so only after John Morley, the general editor of the series, got 'friendly assent' from Leslie Stephen, Minnie Thackeray's widower, and from Anne Thackeray Ritchie, the surviving daughter. Thackeray had enjoined his daughters not to permit a biography, but the English Men of Letters studies contained brief lives that served as introductions to writers' works.* Trollope named the end of March for delivery of the manuscript and began the book on 1 February. After six days' work, he told John Blackwood that he found it 'a terrible job. . . . There is absolutely nothing to say,—except washed out criticism. But it had to be done, and no one would do it so lovingly.'[1] He got bits of information and advice from Anne Thackeray (to whom he sent a questionnaire), William Howard Russell, George Smith, and others. Trollope finished the little 210-page book by 25 March, in seven and a half weeks.

Locked in a drawer of the very desk at which he sat working lay the manuscript of his *Autobiography*, which unhesitatingly placed Thackeray first among English novelists, named *Henry Esmond* 'the greatest novel in the English language', bracketed Colonel Newcome with Don Quixote, called Thackeray's style the purest, the most harmonious and the most lucid among novelists, and said that Thackeray himself was 'one of the most tender-hearted human beings I ever knew'.[2] But the English Men of Letters *Thackeray*, written three years later, turned out provocatively different. In spite of Trollope's intention to write 'lovingly', he totters uncertainly between adulation and fault-finding. In a brief biographical chapter he records how Thackeray's injunction against a biography had

---

* The English Men of Letters series volume on Trollope did not appear until 1928. Written by Hugh Walpole, it was generally considered a very inadequate treatment of its subject.

been occasioned by 'some fulsome biography', and says he will do no more than give 'such incidents and anecdotes of his life as will tell the reader perhaps all about him that a reader is entitled to ask'. Throughout the book Trollope was evidently trying desperately not to be 'fulsome'. This, coupled with his frankness, led to an excess of negative judgements and a constant qualification of praise, and the Thackeray that emerges is considerably flawed, both as writer and as man. On the one hand, he is in some respects almost saintly, a man of 'overflowing' charity and 'excessive' generosity, who went through the world 'doing good, and never wilfully inflicting a wound'. Nevertheless, Thackeray was 'unsteadfast, idle, changeable of purpose, aware of his own intellect but not trusting it'. Full as his works were of pathos, humour, and charity, 'they always seem to lack something that might have been there'.[3]

Trollope's Thackeray cannot recognize that he was meant to be a writer pure and simple. His bid for the Assistant Secretaryship of the Post Office in 1848, had it been successful, would have 'ruined' him. Equally wrong-headed was his hope to be Secretary of the English legation at Washington: 'There never was a man less fit for the Queen's coat.' Similarly Trollope dismisses Thackeray's candidacy in 1857 for a Parliamentary seat as a lark, and regards his near miss as fortunate: Thackeray looked on Parliament as a 'first-class club', and attempting to join it as simply 'the thing to do': 'He was too desultory for regular work,—full of thought, but too vague for practical questions. He could not have endured to sit for two or three hours at a time with his hat over his eyes, pretending to listen, as is the duty of a good legislator. He was a man intolerant of tedium, and in the best of times impatient of slow work.' Moreover, his political convictions were neither 'definite' nor 'accurate'.[4]

Trollope's account of the launch of the *Cornhill Magazine* and of the invitation to him to write the lead novel seemed also to imply criticism of Thackeray, who 'had himself intended to begin with one of his own great novels, but had put it off till it was too late'. Furthermore, Thackeray was not a 'good editor': he was not 'patient, scrupulous, judicious, [and] above all things hard-hearted'; he was too 'perfunctory', too 'unmethodical', and too kindly. He probably did not read the 'basketfuls of manuscripts with which he was deluged', but contented himself with reading the piteous appeals of the letters accompanying the manuscripts, the 'thorns', as he called them, in the editor's cushion.[5]

Trollope sees *Henry Esmond*, as he asserted in the obituary in 1864, as the summit of Thackeray's achievement; Trollope attributes its excellence to his having given more 'forethought' and 'elbow-grease of the mind' to this work. After *Esmond*, Trollope's greatest admiration was for the early *Barry Lyndon*, a preference in which he probably stood alone among his contemporaries. Trollope had also a special predilection for the ballads, burlesques, comic verses of Thackeray's early *Yellowplush Papers* days. Everything else gets qualified praise at best, including *Vanity Fair* ('the story is vague and wandering, clearly commenced without any idea of an ending'). The *Snob Papers* were better in small doses, 'more charming, more piquant, more apparently true, when they came out one after another in the periodical than they are now as collected together'. *Pendennis* and *The Newcomes* are marred in their construction, the sub-plots or 'digressions' not woven into the stories.[6] Indeed, in contrast to *Henry Esmond*, all the other novels are 'comparatively idle books', into which Thackeray had not put enough work.

Much of Trollope's book (and especially its last chapter) sets forth his own ideas about fictional 'realism' and style: novels may be realistic, or sublime, or ludicrous. Thackeray's manner was mainly realistic. Both the ludicrous and the sublime are in one respect easier than the realistic, in that 'they are not required to be true'. On the other hand, the realistic must not be 'true' either, 'but just so far removed from truth as to suit the erroneous idea of truth which the reader may be supposed to entertain'. Thus in dialogue the writer must 'mount somewhat above the ordinary conversational powers of such persons as are to be represented. . . . But he must by no means soar into correct phraseology.' Similarly, in nar-rative, 'The story of any incident, to be realistic, will admit neither of sesquipedalian grandeur nor of grotesque images' in its telling: 'The one gives an idea of romance, and the other of burlesque, to neither of which is truth supposed to appertain.' When desiring 'to soar', we try romance; when desiring to 'recreate ourselves with the easy and droll', we try burlesque. For the novelist, Trollope thinks the middle course is most powerful; we may delight in the burlesque, but the results are not much; the sublime had best be left to poetry. Thackeray's realistic dialogue, especially in *Esmond*, 'never disappoints'.[7]

In Trollope's view, a good style is 'easy, lucid, and grammatical'. The reader should not have to 'run backward over passages' to discover what the writer means (Trollope had late George Eliot, especially *Daniel Deronda*, in mind). 'Whatever Thackeray says, the reader cannot fail to understand; and whatever Thackeray attempts to communicate, he suc-ceeds in conveying.' As for grammar, unlike one or two who scorn this common ground of author and reader (by whom he meant Carlyle and Dickens), Thackeray 'quarrels with none of the laws'. In one particular of style Trollope feels Thackeray falls a bit short. Trollope believed that language should not call attention to itself: but *The Rambler* tastes of Johnson, *The Decline and Fall* of Gibbon; even 'the elephantine tread of *The Saturday*' is immediately recognizable. (Perhaps, Trollope offers, the nearest to the mark is Swift—'writing English and not writing Swift'.) Thackeray 'has a strong flavour of Thackeray', a 'certain affected familiarity' with the reader that works against the 'integrity' of some of the long novels; the reader is 'almost too much at home with his author'.[8] Trollope, than whom no one was ever more 'realistic' in these terms, whose style seems to some to be no style at all, whose narrator often achieves a balanced familiarity with his reader, appears to be talking about his own fiction in terms of Thackeray.

Knowingly or not, Trollope in his *Thackeray* produced an indirect apologia for his own career as writer. He was aware that he was largely setting forth his own theory of fiction, but he apparently missed many of the correlations with his own life. The book led to the understandable but damning inference that Trollope was claiming to have done many things better than the great man himself had. Never was anyone less idle, less given to working only 'in fits and starts' than Trollope. He was, if he was anything, energetic, punctual, methodical, precisely the opposite of the sometimes lazy, irregular, disorganized Thackeray that Trollope portrays. Everyone knew Trollope was able to work assiduously and full-time at the Post Office while regularly turning out successful novels in unprecedented numbers. Thackeray might have done so, had he been an early riser with a capability for grinding work and 'drilled to method', had he been, in short, more like Anthony Trollope. Parliament would have been a mistake for Thackeray, and his defeat was fortunate for letters; Trollope, the implication was, would have been able to manage a political career while continuing his writing; he could have sat through boring sessions of the House, and read through the tedious blue books; moreover his political ideas, unlike Thackeray's, were presumably 'definite' and 'accurate'. As an editor—albeit unsuccessful—Trollope had scrupulously read through the 'basketfuls of manuscripts'. (That he, like Thackeray, had found the thorns in the editorial cushion terrible, his *Editor's Tales* had admitted.) As for the actual writing of novels, the difficult 'living with his characters', the continual use of 'the elbow-grease of the mind', coupled with the cobbler's-wax-to-the-seat-of-the-pants approach, these constituted Trollope's regular *modus operandi*.

The charge that Trollope was putting himself forward at Thackeray's expense would have outraged him; he considered Thackeray as writer very much above him. But the disciple did not feel precluded from seeing the master as sometimes idle and disorganized. Trollope himself may have followed some of his own prescriptions for novel writing better than did Thackeray, but he thought Thackeray had a special genius. For himself Trollope would never claim more than a certain 'mechanical' genius that enabled him to work in so methodically productive a manner. He had good working habits; by native disposition and physical stamina he was able to manage two careers at once. Trollope seems to be saying that had Thackeray been built as was Trollope there would have been a stream of masterpieces.

Some of the reviews dismayed him. The severest ones Trollope never saw, as they appeared across the Atlantic. A. G. Sedgwick, in the New York *Nation*, protested that Trollope had unwittingly 'levelled down' Thackeray to himself: not having sufficient material on Thackeray, 'Mr. Trollope has thoughtfully filled in the outline here and there with some interesting details from his own career which further serve to bring out in a strong light the vices of Thackeray's nature'; indeed the work showed enough 'malicious ingenuity' as to have been written by an enemy. *Lippincott's Magazine* said that Trollope, 'feeling constrained to tell us so little about Thackeray, tells us a good deal about himself and his own experience as a literary man, until now and then he seems to forget whose life he is writing'; the review even questioned whether Trollope were not working off a grudge. The *Atlantic Monthly* called the work 'as entirely idle and valueless a disquisition as any we know'.[9]

The English reviews were more balanced. The *Spectator* thought Trollope did the job 'sensibly and well', and that, 'on the whole, he has brought out the chief characteristics of his author with considerable truth and precision'. T. H. S. Escott, in *Time*, found Trollope so generous and enthusiastic for Thackeray as to make the book 'hero worship with a vengeance', a portrayal of 'an impossible personage, a human creature infinitely too good for human nature's daily food'. The *Athenaeum* thought Trollope's biography in fifty pages 'more complete than many biographies in three volumes', affectionate but not fulsome; even the critical chapters 'increase our love and reverence' for the man.* T. H. Ward in the *Academy* said that although the book contained little that was stirring or original, and was too harsh on *Vanity Fair*, it was none the less 'sympathetic, admiring, and in the main probably right in its judgments of

---

* Trollope got a pleasant letter from Cardinal Manning (to whom he had sent a copy) saying, 'When the memories of your readers run back over your many works they will bear to you the witness you bear to Thackeray. And that is one of signal honour.'[10]

Thackeray's work'; Ward added that Trollope in some ways described 'the author of *Miss Mackenzie* and the *Eustace Diamonds*, and (for the matter of that) of some parts of this biography of Thackeray . . . to a nicety'. The *Westminster Review* thought the biographical portion 'excellent, and . . . mainly new', the critical portions 'somewhat capricious, and—a sore fault in the biographer—niggardly in his praise'. *Fraser's Magazine* judged the book an 'interesting study', informed by a 'jealous love' for Thackeray's memory, but remarked that Trollope's talk of Thackeray's 'idleness' is spoken 'with all the conscious strength of a man who takes Time by the forelock, does his so many hours of work daily, and has so many novels to the good, all put away in drawers and ready for use, according to the whisper of malicious gossip'.[11]

Some of the effects of the bad press lingered on. An especially harsh review in the *Pall Mall Gazette* said that 'the whole book is strewn from end to end with remarks that prove that though Mr. Trollope has written some extremely good novels himself he is naturally incapable of appreciating works like Thackeray's'; the reviewer also noted snidely of Trollope's remarks on Thackeray's earnings, 'It must be a source of satisfaction to Thackeray's children to be assured on Mr. Trollope's authority that the "comfortable income"—the precise figure is stated—which he left behind *was* "earned honestly, with the full approval of the world around him".'[12] Trollope wrote to Tom Taylor: 'I should have cared nothing for the article in the Pall Mall as a simple criticism. I have been too long at it, to be much moved by what the folk say of me, good or bad. But there were circumstances in this, connected with Annie, which made me unhappy.'[13] It was little help to know that Annie herself had supplied the figure (£750 per annum), and that, given Trollope's obsession with honesty, his words had been nothing more than his customary commonplace utterance with regard to making an honest livelihood, not meant for a moment to imply even the possibility of some other course in Thackeray's case. But Annie was upset by the book, and, it would seem, especially by the passage about earnings alluded to in the *Pall Mall*. In 1882 Trollope, dining at George Smith's, met Annie: 'We smiled at each other,' Trollope told Rose, 'and we had a thorough good talk. I am very glad because my memory of her father was wounded by the feeling of a quarrel.' Annie recorded in her diary, either of this meeting or a subsequent one, that Trollope came to see her and stood by the fireplace, 'very big and kind and made it up. . . . I said I'm so sorry I quarrelled with you. He said so am I my dear. I never saw dear Mr. Trollope again.'[14]

The reviewers, on the whole, had been giving Trollope's fiction poor notices ever since *Lady Anna*. For someone who followed reviews as closely as Trollope, this must have been troublesome. The publication, by Chapman & Hall, of *An Eye for An Eye* in January of 1879 brought no real change. Trollope had kept this short, tragic Irish novel lying in his desk drawer unpublished for eight years. It had been written in exactly four weeks in the autumn of 1870. In July 1878 he had agreed to £425 for book and serial rights, the latter to go to the *Whitehall Review*. Two years before that, in *An Autobiography*, he had said of the book, 'I look forward with some grim pleasantry to its publication . . . and to the declaration of the critics that it has been the work of a period of life at which the power of writing novels had passed from me.'[15] His prophecy was fulfilled.

One reviewer, however, dissented. Hutton said *An Eye for an Eye* 'will take a high place among Mr. Trollope's works'; he sensed that 'there is something in the atmosphere of Ireland which appears to rouse his imagination, and give force and simplicity to his pictures of life'; he said that as in all first-rate Trollope stories, there is really no villain: An Englishman, Fred Neville, a somewhat spoiled and self-indulgent young cavalry lieutenant, heir to an earldom, loves and makes pregnant Kate O'Hara, an Irish girl; yet, he had not intended her to be merely his mistress; he is later willing to enter into a morganatic marriage, the child of which would not succeed to the earldom; he is willing to surrender his aristocratic responsibilities to his younger brother,—he simply will not make Kate O'Hara a Countess of Scroope—having promised as much to his dying uncle, the former earl. Hutton observed: 'Mr. Trollope has hardly ever painted anything so striking as the mode in which the promise not to disgrace his house and name grows unconsciously and involuntarily in the young Lord Scroope's mind, till it takes all the life out of the more binding and far more sacred promise under the faith of which he has gained from Kate O'Hara all she has to give.' The so-called 'social obligations' of his order have overridden personal human obligations, but, Hutton insisted, Trollope manages it with great subtlety: although Lord Scroope, as his almost unsuspected pride of rank grows on him, cannot suppress a certain contempt for the girl who had yielded, he still does not want to desert her, will do anything short of making her his countess and the mother of future earls. Hutton also thought no 'truer or stronger' short sketch ever came from Trollope's pen than that of Father Marty, the priest closely implicated in the tragedy as adviser to Kate and her mother. The mother's murdering of Neville, 'expiated by hopeless madness', complements this short and 'classical' tale. Hutton, unaware of the early composition of the story, welcomed 'this flashing up of [Trollope's] higher power' of imagination, which 'has lately but too frequently lost itself in sands and marshes and all kinds of muddy fen-countries', most notably in *The Way We Live Now*. Trollope must have smiled: he was used to critics contradicting each other, but this time he had the 'grim pleasantry' of seeing most of them term this old novel a continuation of his late supposed decay; while the ever-clever Hutton, the critic he most respected, called it a return to his earlier manner and power. [16]

Meanwhile *John Caldigate*, the story of a young man who went to Australia to make his fortune, lived there with an adventuress, returned to England to marry his sweetheart only to be unjustly convicted of bigamy, was making its way (from April 1878 to June 1879), through the monthly pages of *Blackwood's Magazine*. As usual Blackwood was critical. He thought John Caldigate, 'the involuntary Don Giovanni . . . too cold [and] self satisfied', and wanted Trollope to make a few little alterations in proof to allay the hardness that 'chokes off the sympathy'. Trollope replied good-naturedly that he 'fully' agreed with the criticism: 'In such matters I generally know my own fault though I may have failed to avoid it,' and said that in correcting the press he would try to add 'something of tenderness' in him towards the heroine but could not attempt to 'alter the conduct of the story'. Later, when the novel was well into its sixth instalment, Blackwood requested an alteration in the way Caldigate pays money to the Australian 'rascals', his former mistress and his one-time gold-mine part-ner, who are blackmailing him. Trollope said that he would try to make some changes '*if I find anything feasible*; but I am bound to say that I have never found myself able to effect changes in the plot of a story. Small as the links are, one little thing hangs on another to such an extent that any change sets the whole narrative wrong.' Later, at the time of the twelfth instalment, Blackwood said that he had heard from Joseph Langford that the Garrick Club had declared that the Australian mistress could not have been a witness at the trial: 'You should have consulted Sir John Joram'— the fictional barrister in the story. Trollope answered that he had had 'an infinite amount of "bar" advice, having consulted quite a crowd of lawyers, including judges, ex attorney friends, and the like'. [17]

Alongside its 'sensational' subject of bigamy, *John Caldigate* provided an opportunity for another treatment of a more customary theme in Trollope, religious suppression of worldly, especially sexual, pleasures. Low-church people are again the culprits. The Bolton family, the heroine aside, is enveloped in evangelical gloom. The fanatical mother, half-mad in her religious rigour and jealousy of her daughter's love, is one of

Trollope's most frightening characters. Although Mrs Bolton views the voluntary celibacy advocated in the Church of Rome as 'abominable', yet, 'on behalf of her child, she desired seclusion from the world. . . . all sensual gratifications were wicked in her sight'; Mrs Bolton is convinced 'that this world is a world of woe; that wailing and suffering . . . is and should be the condition of mankind preparatory to eternal bliss'; even her dress matches her temper: she wears brown for the 'sad domesticities' of weekdays and a solemn 'funereal' black for Sundays ('There are women,' the narrator remarks, 'who seem always to be burying someone'). Trollope makes her so fierce a persecutor, so unnatural a mother, so extreme a religious puritan, as to nearly overstep himself. The narrator protests, somewhat perfunctorily, that in judging her one should allow for the sincerity of her convictions. In distinct contrast to Mrs Bolton, Daniel Caldigate, the hero's father, one of Trollope's 'old pagans', puts religious practitioners in their place when he tells a sanctimonious cleric who disapproves of the heroine's 'bigamous' loyalty to Caldigate: 'If you knew anything about her, I think you would refrain from threatening her with divine wrath; and as you know nothing about her, I regard such threats, coming from you, as impertinent, unmanly, inhuman, and blasphemous.'[18]

In *John Caldigate* Trollope looked back to the Post Office of his early days. Part of his purpose was once again to take on critics—popular newspapers, Members of Parliament, novelists ('the name of Charles Dickens will of course present itself to the reader who remembers the Circumlocution Office')—who would have the public believe that the average government clerk is 'indifferent' to his work: 'It is the nature of a man to appreciate his own work. . . . The policeman is ambitious of arresting everybody. The lawyer would rather make your will for you gratis than let you make your own. The General can believe in nothing but in well-trained troops.' Similarly, the postal employee charged with seeing to the proper daily changes in the franking stamps assures himself that 'so much of the civilisation of Europe' depends upon his doing his work accurately. Samuel Bagwax, a clerk in St Martin's-le-Grand, sets out to prove that the stamp on an envelope which formed a key piece of evidence in the bigamy conviction against John Caldigate had been manufactured and sent to the colonies at a date after that marked on the envelope. Bagwax, like Trollope himself, at least from his Irish days onwards, is a little 'too energetic' in his efforts, and wants desperately to be sent out to Sydney, in spite of resistance from the Postmaster-General. But then, even without the journey, he proves that the envelope had been fraudulently stamped in Sydney. At the close of the novel the Home Office rewards Bagwax's zeal by making the Postmaster-General send him to the colony for six months anyway, to set matters straight in the Sydney office. The Australian authorities of course did not want his interference, 'but he was treated with extreme courtesy by the Sydney officials, and was able to bring home with him a treasure in the shape of a newly-discovered manner of tying mail-bags. So that when the "Sydney Intelligencer" boasted that the great English professor who had come to instruct them all had gone home instructed, there was some truth in it.'[19] Trollope told Blackwood, 'There was a touch of downright love in the depicting of Bagwax. Was I not once a Bagwax myself?'[20]

The critical reception given *John Caldigate* in the press marked a decided turn upwards. Some reviewers remained negative: the *Examiner* thought the story represented the 'decadence' of a first-class novelist; *The Times* said it was 'a good novel expanded into a dull one'; and the *Athenaeum* found *Caldigate* an 'interesting story', but insisted, 'its art is neither specially elaborate nor very well sustained'. On the other hand, the *Academy* admired the 'careful delineation' of Caldigate himself and called the novel 'both masterly and judicious'. Hutton in the *Spectator* thought that this novel, along with the recently published *An Eye for An Eye*, had halted the 'falling-off' in Trollope's recent novels; the story was 'powerful', its heroine a 'great achievement'. The *Saturday Review* said that 'Trollope throws himself in the volumes before us with such zest and revival of power into all [aspects of bigamy], whether viewed on its legal, moral, domestic, or gossiping side—that, instead of regretting that he should have meddled with so questionable a topic now, we may rather wonder that he has not taken it up before.'[21]

John Caldigate returned Trollope to considerable critical favour; but his next published work, *Cousin Henry*, brought out by Chapman & Hall in October 1879, commanded positively rave notices, and from nearly all quarters. Trollope, as usual paying close attention to what was said in reviews, must have wondered how this short work—it had become a commonplace that Trollope needed the room of a large novel to develop his stories—drew nearly universal praise while his recent longer efforts had caused the same critics to think his hand had lost its skill. Since moving to Montagu Square in 1873, Trollope had written seven relatively long novels in a row (with the one exception of *Harry Heathcote*, a 'Christmas Story' so brief as to be practically a short story), but beginning with *Cousin Henry* in 1878 he would write a total of six short and three long novels over the remainder of his career. Moreover, *The Way We Live Now* (five-volume length) and *The Prime Minister* (four-volume length) were his last overlong novels; none of the later works would exceed three volumes. Age may have had something to do with the change to relatively shorter works. He had written *Cousin Henry* in six weeks the previous autumn, and had sold serial rights to Alexander Ireland for publication in provincial newspapers, the *Manchester Weekly Times* and the *North British Weekly Mail*; oddly, he had been willing to allow Ireland to select one among three titles, telling him he might call it, as planned, 'Cousin Henry', or 'Getting at a Secret', or 'Uncle Indefer's Will': 'The second is exactly apposite. My wife says that it sounds clap trap. The other two are quite appropriate.'[22] The serial appeared weekly from the beginning of March to the end of May 1879; Chapman & Hall, somewhat unusually, delayed publication of the book until the more propitious autumn season, when it appeared in two volumes. Trollope, perhaps weary of the argument, no longer insisted that short novels be packaged as one-volume works: *An Eye for Eye* and *Cousin Henry*, for example, are approximately the same length as *Harry Hotspur*, in connection with which he had forced the publisher to break up the type of the projected two-volume format.

Cousin Henry is a sustained study of an unattractive, neurotic character, Henry Jones, who becomes aware of a last-minute will by his late uncle that gives the property to his niece, Isabel Broderick. Henry cannot bring himself to disclose the will to the authorities, but neither does he hinder their investigation. For all his weaknesses, he is not altogether despicable: he suffers his doubts and guilt; moreover, the true heir and heroine, honest and decent, and loyal to her love for a young clergyman, is none the less somewhat hard and cold, 'imperious and inclined to domineer', a bit too aware of her moral and intellectual superiority over her cousin, and too desirous for 'martyrdom' in connection with the inheritance. The book is quintessentially Trollopian in seeming to espouse contradictory sides. Particularly dramatic in its quiet way is the moment when the search for the will goes forward while both Jones and Isabel are in the house. She retires to her room, finding it impossible to accompany the searchers, not wanting to appear to urge them on; Henry, having discovered the will in a volume of Jeremy Taylor's sermons, can't bring himself to hide it, or destroy it, or reveal its existence. Trollope's rendering of Henry's internal conflict throughout is a *tour de force*, the situation providing occasions for long, vacillating, dilemma-ridden interior monologues on his part, the kind that are the hallmark of so much of Trollope's story-telling.[23]

The novel impressed the critics with what they saw as its daring:

William Wallace, writing in the *Academy* said, 'No other novelist could have racked through two volumes' such a cowardly figure as Cousin Henry. *The Times* remarked that Trollope, having over the years described so many middle-class Englishmen, must be sorely puzzled 'to avoid plagiarizing from himself'; and yet his reputation is such that he can 'afford to risk hazardous experiments. No novice with sound literary instincts would have dared to stake his credit on [Trollope's] despicable "hero".' The *Athenaeum* proclaimed that 'from a less skilful pen so much ado about nothing would be intolerable'. The *Saturday* expressed the view that *Cousin Henry* 'is not a novel exactly, but rather a study, and a very able one'. The *Examiner* said that no author except Trollope could have succeeded in taking the over-familiar theme of a lost will and 'making us anxiously wonder from page to page . . . what phase Cousin Henry's weakness will next assume'. Trollope relished comments in the *Spectator* that seemed uncannily to complement his own on novel writing, in his book on Thackeray, and in the still unpublished *Autobiography*, about the falseness of the popular distinction between realistic and sensational fiction, about the need for lucid, understandable prose, and about the importance of 'character' over story or plot. This reviewer said that readers of *Cousin Henry* do not get tired 'despite the fact that we know, in a sense, just what is in store for us, or rather, we know what is not in store for us; no breathless astonishment, no curdling horror, no consuming curiosity. There may be, for aught we can say, as many murders, forgeries, abductions, foundlings, missing wills, in Mr. Trollope's novels as in any others; but they are not told about in a manner to alarm us. . . . His touch is eminently civilizing; everything, from the episodes to the sentences, moves without hitch or creak; we never have to read a paragraph twice, and we are never sorry to have read it once.'*[24] As far as these critics were concerned, Trollope seemed as much in vogue as ever.

The Trollopes spent a month's holiday in April 1879 at Lucas Collins's pleasant rectory in Lowick, Northamptonshire, from which place Trollope had hunted in days past with the Pytchley and the Fitzwilliam. He wrote

---

* The author of this appreciative review was Julian Hawthorne, staying in London at the time. By a pleasant coincidence Julian's review followed close upon Trollope's perceptive article about his father, 'The Genius of Nathaniel Hawthorne' in the *North American Review*. Having acknowledged Hawthorne's liking for his novels—'just as real as if some giant had hewn a great lump out of the earth and put it under a glass case'—Trollope demonstrates his own capability of appreciating fiction radically different from his own, novels filled with 'unutterable woe' and 'melancholy beyond compare', mysterious, sorrowful 'romances' that 'ennoble' the reader in a way his own 'mundane' works could not.[25]

to Collins: 'That I, who have belittled so many clergymen, should ever come to live in a parsonage! There will be a heaping of hot coals! . . . If the bishop should come that way, I will treat him as well as e'er a parson in the diocese. Shall I be required to preach? . . . I shall be quite disposed to give every one my blessing. . . . Ought I to affect dark garments? . . . Will it be right to be quite genial with the curate, or ought I to patronise a little? . . . If they take to address me as "The Rural Anthony," will it be all right?' For a while he and Rose were snowed in—'we could hardly get across the road to church.'[26] The secluded country holiday worked the same magic that Felsenegg and Hollenthal had of late done: on 8 April he began the novel that became *Dr Wortle's School*; he completed it on the 29th, writing with perfect regularity exactly twelve manuscript pages every day for twenty-two days—the exact numbers with which he had completed *Ayala's Angel* in the mountains the previous September.

On 16 July he offered Blackwood *Dr Wortle's School*, describing it as 'just the length of Nina Balatka' (it was in fact about a third longer), or *Ayala's Angel*, just the length of *Caldigate*. When, apparently for reasons of health, Blackwood didn't answer, Trollope wrote on 8 August telling him to not trouble himself about business, asking only for a 'simple line to tell me how you are'. On 4 September Blackwood showed interest in the shorter novel: although he felt *John Caldigate* was admirable he knew it did not 'tell' in the magazine. As so often Blackwood was a little gloomy about prospects: he was dismayed that *Nina Balatka* and *Linda Tressel* were 'absolute failures' as reprints. Trollope replied: 'I am grieved to hear what you say of J.C. I do not myself quite understand how the effect of a novel on a magazine is discovered,—not at least in one so established as the Maga. . . . But I am quite aware that you know your business. . . . As to my share of the work, I can only write my tale as well as I can; & leave the result to the public. When I am told that I have failed, I never fight the point: one attains a certain average of moderate success, & thanks the gods that the matter is not worse.' He reminded Blackwood that *Nina Balatka* and *Linda Tressel* were published, even as reprints, without his name.[27]

John Blackwood's illness became worse, and it was only on 24 October that Trollope heard from William Blackwood, the publisher's nephew, accepting the story for serialization at £200 (Chapman was to pay £300 for book rights). In the same letter young Blackwood requested permission to reprint an article, 'Whist at Our Club', from *Blackwood's* of May 1877. Trollope readily agreed but insisted on anonymity. The piece, which pokes fun at his own set of elderly whist players at the Garrick, is instructive since Trollope played whist there nearly every afternoon his schedule allowed; he formed part of a group of 'perhaps a dozen gentle-men, well stricken in years, who, having not much else to do in the afternoons, meet together and kill the hours between lunch and dinner'. Trollope says he subscribed to the notion, attributed to Talleyrand, that 'he who did not learn to play cards was preparing for himself a melancholy old age.' In Trollope's group, play was usually for shilling points, occasion-ally as much as a sovereign. Knowing the rules was pre-eminent—'Clay and Cavendish are in our hands at every turn'—and much 'scolding' about the rules enlivened play. One of the characters in the sketch, a soft-hearted but 'eager, excitable' man who, on sensing, wrongly, a mistake by his partner, flings down his cards, saying he 'couldn't play against three adversaries', and who is then accused of throwing his arms about 'like a demented windmill', may be a partial self-satire.[28]

Trollope now at last gave permission for using his name on the anonym-ous *Nina Balatka* and *Linda Tressel* 'if it will be of any service'. Trollope's letter was dated 28 October, and John Blackwood, his good friend of a dozen years, died the following day. Thereafter his dealings with the firm continued cordially under William Blackwood. (The following February Trollope got William into the Garrick: 'I think you will find the club a pleasant lounge when you are in town. A man with so many calls up to London as must come in your way now could hardly be comfortable without belonging to a first rate club.') William, like his uncle before him, indulged in critical analyses of Trollope's stories. Having read the opening chapters of *Dr Wortle's School* 'with great interest & amusement', he went on to praise the descriptions of Wortle, his wife and school, the bishop, and others; although at first alarmed to read that Mr and Mrs Peacocke were not man and wife, he found Trollope's 'explanation' satisfactory and unlikely to 'startle sensitive readers'.[29]

Like *Cousin Henry*, *Dr Wortle's School* is one of Trollope's best short novels; it incorporates his frequent narrative strategy of disclosing imme-diately the answer to any 'mystery', the effect of that mystery on various characters being the burden of the story—here its effect on Dr Wortle, rector of Bowick and headmaster of its private school. The mystery concerns Wortle's school assistant, Henry Peacocke, and his wife, who are living together even though her first husband has been discovered to be still alive. Trollope, reaching back to his 1862 visit to St Louis, makes Peacocke earlier an assistant to the Chancellor of the university there (in actual life that would have been Kate Field's old friend William Eliot). Peacocke had befriended a young woman, mistreated and abandoned by her drunken husband; and, on news of his death, had married her. When it later became known that the husband was not dead, Peacocke determined to continue as married; he returned to England and eventually became Wortle's assistant. When Wortle learns of the bigamy, he decides to stick by the couple. Wortle is another *alter ego* for Trollope. (T. H. S. Escott recognized this: 'Dr. Wortle has the same reputation as Trollope himself for blustering amiability, an imperious manner and a good heart'; and Harry Trollope, writing to Michael Sadleir in 1923, said that he was 'struck in reading *Dr. Wortle's School* with a likeness, not on all fours, between the Doctor and my father.'[30]) Wortle is generous, honest, 'manly'; but he is hot-headed, impetuous, impulsive; he likes to command. He stubbornly stands up to neighbours, parents of pupils, fellow clerics, the sensational press, and his bishop. Having sent Peacocke to America to discover if perhaps the first husband is finally dead, Wortle insists on keeping Mrs Peacocke at the school. If parents withdraw their children, let them. It makes him wonder 'whether the religion of the world is not more odious that its want of religion'. He keeps his sense of humour: explaining the situation to a student's father, he writes, 'More than twelve months ago I got an assistant named Peacocke, a clergyman, an Oxford man, formerly Fellow of Trinity. . . . He had gone as a Classical Professor to a college in the United States;—a rash thing to do, no doubt;—and had there married a widow, which was rasher still.' Wortle explains that he will not heed the bishop, who wants Mrs Peacocke to go into lodgings at a nearby town: 'You know what sort of lodgings she would get there among psalm-singing greengrocers who would tell her of her misfortune every day of her life.' (One thinks back to the great fun Trollope's mother had with the notion that a tablet to Allegra Byron in Harrow Church should 'lead the school boys into vice', or, as Trollope himself said in his gloss on her line, it 'should teach the boys to get bastards'.[31]) Wortle, the narrator insists, 'though a self-asserting and somewhat violent man, was thoroughly soft-hearted'. He adds, 'It would perhaps be unfair to raise a question whether he would have done as much, been so willing to sacrifice himself, for a plain woman. . . . Mrs. Peacocke was a very beautiful woman, and the Doctor was a man who thoroughly admired beauty. To say that Mrs. Wortle was jealous would be quite untrue. She liked to see her husband talking to a pretty woman, because he would be sure to be in a good humour and sure to make the best of himself. She loved to see him shine.'[32]

Trollope had to manage the Peacockes' situation 'so as to give no offence',[33] and in the end, the first husband is discovered to be conveniently dead at last, and the Peacockes, assisted by Wortle, are remarried in an 'interesting ceremony at London'. None the less, the book shows in its author an elasticity in regard to religious canons of behaviour, a kind of moral relativism that seems an extension of his usual tolerance and sympathy for so-called villains. The sympathy he aroused for jilts, weak gamblers, inconstant lovers, 'fallen' women like Carry Brattle, vacillating nothings like Cousin Henry, even dishonest tycoons like Melmotte, seems here to rise to a questioning of moral absolutes themselves. Wortle, we read, feels called on to say to all the world, 'I know that [the Peacockes] are not married. I know that their condition of life is opposed to the law of God and man. I know that she bears a name that is not, in truth, her own; but I think that the circumstances in this case are so strange, so peculiar, that they excuse a disregard even of the law of God and man.'[34] (One cannot help but feel that Trollope had Lewes and George Eliot in mind.) None of the critics argued with Trollope's handling of bigamy—one went so far as to find it 'bracing'—and *Dr Wortle's School* brought Trollope further good notices.[35]

On 21 November Trollope finally completed *Marion Fay* (the novel begun the previous December). The following June he unsuccessfully offered the serial rights to George Bentley for *Temple Bar* for £400, but about a year later he sold the rights for that price to Arthur Locker for the *Graphic*, where the novel appeared from December 1881 to June 1882. No record survives of how much Chapman & Hall paid for the book rights.

Marion Fay, though generally regarded as one of Trollope's least successful novels, has considerable biographical interest, being in part a reminiscence by the now elderly Trollope of the days of his young manhood. One sees the illnesses and deaths of Trollope's sisters Emily and Cecilia behind the main story, that of the young Lord Hampstead's frustrated love for Marion Fay, a girl of common birth who will not marry him because she knows she will die of consumption, the curse that had claimed so many of her family. The author's first-hand acquaintance with the disease is notable in lines such as those describing the early onset of Marion's condition: 'Occasionally there would rise to her cheeks a bright colour. . . . Occasionally there would be heard from her not a cough, but that little preparation for coughing which has become so painfully familiar to the ears of those whose fate it has been to see their beloved ones gradually fade from presumed health.' Having survived alone among her many siblings, Marion too at last succumbs, greatly strengthened and consoled by her religious faith—as had been the case with Cecilia Trollope. Marion's sad story is balanced by the happy, sometimes farcical accounts of the postal clerks in St Martin's-le-Grand, whereby Trollope revisits the days of his young manhood in the late 1830s. The office clerks—Roden, able and promising; Crocker, inept, always about to be dismissed; Geraghty and Bobbin, middling workers but always late for work and impatient to leave—all resonate with bits of Trollope's own career. Roden turns out to be an Italian duke, a revelation that eases his way towards marrying the daughter of an aristocrat. In some ways, such a development, no matter how much hinted at earlier in the story, seems out of place in Trollope's fictional world. Indeed, Roden's fellow clerk, the tuft-hunting Crocker, beside himself with joy that an associate of his should turn out to be a duke, says, 'It's a sort of thing that never happened before. . . . Did anybody ever read anything like it in a novel?'[36] Trollope may have found it no more to be wondered at than that a postal clerk should turn into a famous novelist.

The relatively short *Cousin Henry* drew good reviews, but *The Duke's Children*, concluding the Palliser series, seemed completely to restore Trollope's reputation with the critics, and to reverse the cool reception given four years earlier to the previous Palliser novel, *The Prime Minister*. The quarterly *Westminster Review* wrote: 'Those who fancied that Mr. Trollope had been falling off will be delighted to read "The Duke's Children," and to meet again their old friend the Duke of Omnium, the only duke whom all of us know. Mr. Trollope is upon old ground, and describes it with all the ease of his best days. The death of the Duchess so early in the tale will be a great shock to many worthy people, but even duchesses must die that novels may be written.' By the time that review appeared the book had already been warmly welcomed in the weeklies. The *Saturday* praised Trollope's presentation of the trials, at the hands of his children, of 'our old friend, now Duke of Omnium'; the *Athenaeum* congratulated Trollope on this 'successful' novel. The *Illustrated London News* found Trollope's representation of society very like what it actually was, and the novel 'all extremely interesting'. The *Spectator* wrote, 'No novelist of whom we have any knowledge seems to possess so sane a comprehension of the mode of life and thought of the British aristocracy as Mr. Trollope.' It lauded the young American heiress, Isabel Boncassen, saying that 'Her character, speech, and manners are so carefully and justly presented by Mr. Trollope, that few even of his most critical American readers would, we fancy, be inclined to raise objections to the portrait.' The reviewer pronounced the novel 'thoroughly readable and one of the most edifying that Mr. Trollope has yet produced'. In New York, the *Nation* called it 'one of Mr. Trollope's most successful novels'.37

The Duke of Omnium, formerly Plantagenet Palliser, the creation upon whom Trollope lavished most care, most 'elbow-grease of the mind', is at the centre of the book, a spot he had formerly shared with others, most notably with Lady Glencora. A widower now, his trials and sorrows at the hands of his three children are moving, and even sad. Both sons are rusticated from university; both incur gambling debts; the elder, Lord Silverbridge, decides to become a Tory, and wants to marry an American, Isabel Boncassen; the daughter, Mary, wants to marry a penniless Tory commoner, Frank Tregear. The Duke slowly relents, and the story closes with the two marriages, and also with the Duke returning—though in a modest role for a former Prime Minister—to political office. A muted comic spirit presides over this tale of his grudging acceptance of life as it is; Palliser may be mellowing, but will do so most gradually, and will always be a difficult man.

Much of the Duke's character continues to resemble Trollope's own. The polar opposite of the brash, loud, blustering Trollope, he none the less derives his apparent intractability and almost abnormal sensitivity from one aspect of Trollope's personality. The Duke also shares with Trollope an almost preternatural devotion to work: older now, his earlier ambition for decimal coinage still unrealized, and feeling rather useless, 'He knew that if anything could once again make him contented, it would be work', and at the close he becomes president of the council of the new Liberal cabinet. The Duke loves Cicero and Ovid, and as his son says of him—and as friends said of Trollope—he 'spouts Latin' at times. Moreover, in connection with the Duke's troubles with his children, the narrator remarks that had he been required to give in only with reference to the lovely Isabel Boncassen, he could have done so easily: 'There are men, who do not seem at first sight very susceptible to feminine attractions, who nevertheless are dominated by the grace of flounces, who succumb to petticoats unconsciously, and who are half in love with every woman merely for her womanhood. So it was with the Duke.'38 (The words echo those from the closing passage in *An Autobiography*: 'If the rustle of a woman's petticoat has ever stirred my blood . . .')39 And the woman whom the Duke accepts as daughter-in-law is an American, beautiful, witty, clever, lively. Isabel Boncassen is in many respects drawn from Kate Field. Like Kate in the 1870s, she is a huge success in London; she is a good conversationalist, can talk politics with great liveliness, and has unmarried men like Barrington Earl, Mr Warburton, and Mr Monk enraptured. Like so many of Trollope's young women she is incomparably more clever and quick-witted than the men who woo her. (In the early stages of Lord Silverbridge's bewildered courtship, when he asks her if she would accept the present of a ring if he offered it, she says, 'If you'll promise that you'll never offer me one, I'll promise that I'll take it when it comes.')[40] Henry James said that Trollope was 'evidently always more or less in love' with all his heroines, but this must have been especially the case with Isabel Boncassen.[41]

But another young woman, Lady Mabel Grex, is more prominent in the story than the American. Mabel and Tregear had once been in love, but she had told him that it wouldn't do, that they had not enough money to get married; he had quickly transferred his heart's allegiance; but Mabel, like almost all of Trollope's young women, cannot alter her heart's attachment; thereafter she had refused one offer after another; and then Lord Silverbridge, the Duke's son, rich, at least potentially, beyond calculation, had come along; she had 'laughed at him' and called him a boy, which he was, compared to her, though they were of the same age; she intended to 'spare him' once and then accept him; she planned to 'learn to love him'. But the American girl appeared in the mean time, and 'the prize had slipped from her through her own fault'.[42] Mabel remains passionately in love with Tregear till the end, and would be willing even to run off with him in disgrace.

Through Mabel Grex, Trollope again develops with sympathy and insight frustrations imposed upon women by society. She tells Tregear, 'because you are not a woman . . . you do not understand how women are trammelled. . . . Only think how a girl such as I am is placed; or indeed any girl. You, if you see a woman that you fancy, can pursue her, can win her and triumph, or lose her and gnaw your heart;—at any rate you can do something. You can tell her that you love her; can tell her so again and again even though she should scorn you. . . . What can a girl do?' She complains to Silverbridge of not being able to do the 'half mad things' that men can: 'We are dreadfully restricted. If you like champagne you can have a bucketful. I am obliged to pretend that I only want a very little. You can bet thousands. I must confine myself to gloves [small change]. You can flirt with any woman you please. I must wait till somebody comes,—and put up with it if nobody does come.' Lady Mabel understands that 'as an unmarried girl she was a burden', something her disagreeable old father, Lord Grex, keeps reminding her ('I don't see why the deuce you don't get married'). But when a girl like herself 'works hard' at getting a husband, 'everybody feels that they are sinning against their sex'. That she is particular about whom she would marry adds much to her problem: she is too bright, too quick for most young men, and they sense it. (Silverbridge worries that 'Lady Mabel as his wife would be his superior, and in some degree his master'.) She says, 'With nineteen men out of twenty, the idea of marrying them would convey the idea of hating them.' Most young men, in her view (and Trollope's), hardly know what they are doing in marrying; they 'seldom mean'; rather, 'they drift into matrimony'.[43] In her frustrated passion, Lady Mabel is one of Trollope's saddest and most powerful figures, and the equal of Lady Laura Kennedy from the Phineas books.

The Duke's Children, though without a formal farewell as in the closing pages of *The Last Chronicle*, brought the Palliser series to an end. Like the Barsetshire chronicles, the later series comprised six books; but the Palliser series was longer; it had begun with *Can You Forgive Her?*, the equivalent of a five-volume novel, and, except for *The Duke's Children*, the others had all exceeded the three-volume length; whereas the Barchester series had begun with *The Warden*, a one-volume novel, and the next three had been three-deckers. The first series had seen twelve and a half years elapse between publication of the first and last books, the later series nearly fifteen (owing largely to the relatively long delay in publishing *The Duke's Children*). Coincidentally, the time spans over which Trollope wrote the two series, from beginning *The Warden* to finishing *The Last Chronicle*, and from beginning *Can You Forgive Her?* until the finishing of *The Duke's Children*, were in both cases exactly thirteen years and two months.

Trollope placed his two series of novels at the head of his achievement; he thought *The Last Chronicle* his best single novel, and Palliser, Glencora, and Mr Crawley, in that order, his most realized characters. He had finished *The Duke's Children* in late 1876, and never seriously thought of reviving either series. In August 1881 he told Henry Howard, ex-Governor of Rhode Island, that he could not hope to bring back 'our old friends': 'Though I still go on writing, the new characters are much less troublesome than the old ones; and can be done without the infinite labour of reading back again and again my old works.' (In 1882 Trollope wrote for *Good Cheer*—the Christmas number of *Good Words*—'The Two Heroines of Plumplington', a short story set in Barsetshire, but in no sense Barchesterian, and embarrassingly thin.) Trollope explained to Howard that the two series 'are by no means distinct, lapping in under each other occasionally'. (The closest link between the two sequences is the old Duke of Omnium, who is prominent, though seldom in the absolute foreground, in both.) Trollope also told Howard, 'Of the others that I have written their name is legion; and it may be that a personage occasionally strays out of either of the two series into some loose volume. But if so, it is but a mistake.'[44] Of course this was ironic self-depreciation; readers of Trollope greet characters from one novel as they reappear unexpectedly in another with a pleasant sense of familiarity. Not only do characters from the series sometimes appear briefly in a 'loose' or independent novel—as when Lady Glencora plays a part in *The American Senator*—but characters from independent novels also show up in the series. The most important instance is Chaffanbrass, prominent in two earlier independent stories, *The Three Clerks* and *Orley Farm*, who takes a crucial role in *Phineas Redux*. Much slighter examples include Lord Grasslough and Lady Carbury, from *The Way We Live Now*, who are briefly mentioned in *The Duke's Children* and *The Prime Minister* respectively. Chaffanbrass represented also the phenomenon of the reappearance of characters within independent novels, as did Miss Todd, prominent in both *The Bertrams* and *Miss Mackenzie*; later examples include Lord Rufford, Lawrence Twentymen, and others from *The American Senator*, who are reintroduced—in passing—in *Ayala's Angel*. Such brief reappearances are often a source of quiet fun; certainly Trollope intended them to be little jokes for the initiated.

Early in 1880 Chapman & Hall, which was again in financial trouble, became a limited company, with Trollope as one of the directors (other directors included Sir Herbert Bruce Stanford, Spencer Walpole, and R. P. Harding, with Frederic Chapman as chairman). Shares to the amount of £116,160 were subscribed; and the company moved from 193 Piccadilly to 11 Henrietta Street, Covent Garden.[45] Both Trollope and Henry owned shares that Trollope watched closely over the next few years. One of the firm's great assets was the Dickens copyrights (another would be the Carlyle copyrights which the company would buy up the following year). The change to a limited company seems to have been connected with money troubles that for a while landed Chapman in the bankruptcy court. The problem, whatever it was, resulted in Chapman's having to resign from the Garrick Club, to which he had belonged since 1861; in 1881 Trollope tried, unsuccessfully, to get him readmitted ('The poor fellow', Trollope wrote to William Lethbridge, 'has paid to his creditors the money, and is most intent on regaining the club'). Whatever his doubts about some of Chapman's publishing practices, Trollope felt bound to the man who had published far more of his books than anyone else. Telling Rusden about becoming a company director, he said, 'Nothing more pernicious and damnable ever occurred, or more likely to break a man's heart. Twice a week I have to meet my brother directors & sit five hours a day. That I am half ruined is nothing to the trouble and annoyance and shame of such an employment. How could I have avoided it. . . . But I say to myself, "Nil conscire sibi" [To have no guilt at heart].'[46]

Since completing the much-interrupted *Marion Fay* in late November 1879, and through the first five months of 1880, Trollope worked hard at finishing a long-standing project, the 'magnum opus for my old age', a lengthy life of Cicero. He had dashed off *Thackeray* in seven weeks, but this was an altogether different matter. In 1851, reviewing Merivale's *History of the Romans*, a book he thought exalted Caesar unduly and denigrated Cicero unjustly, Trollope had developed an apology for Cicero. But it ran too long and had to be cut from the review as printed. By 1875, when he was reading Cicero in Australia, he had resolved to write a life of the great orator. By the end of 1876, he told Mary Holmes that he had just completed reading 'all Cicero's works from beginning to end'.*[47] In February and March 1877 he interrupted the writing of *John Caldigate* to produce for the *Fortnightly* two substantial articles, on Cicero as Politician and as Man of Letters.[48] By September 1879 he reported to Rusden that he had read most of Cicero's works for a second, many for a third time, and explained that he had undertaken the task because other commentators seemed so critical of the man; he added, 'If I live I shall finish the writing by the end of 1880. I shall then take a year for corrections. But what right has a man of 64 to speak of years in that way?' (The first sentence of the book indicates that Trollope had thought it might have had to be published—or 'burned'—posthumously.) In fact Trollope finished the book by the end of May 1880 (Rose, for the first time in many years, made a fair copy). He arranged in June that Chapman & Hall publish the book, in two volumes, at a selling price of 24s. with a royalty of 8s. 6d. per copy on the first 1,200 sold, the figure rising by a mere 6d. for copies beyond that number. This was a notable departure from his customary lump sum agreement, his only true royalty arrangement ever,

* Trollope worked from the French *Bibliothèque Latine-Française*, 178 vols. (Paris 1829–39), of which 36 comprised Cicero's works; the Cicero volumes—and about 50 of other authors—are annotated in Trollope's hand.

and the first since the half-profits agreement for *Barchester Towers* to tie basic payment to sales. He did not know how the book would sell, and was cautious not to overcharge his own company. (On 13 August Trollope wrote to fellow director R. P. Harding about proceeds from *The Duke's Children*: 'The Company loses £120 by the venture. I cannot allow that. It is the first account I have ever seen of one of my own books. . . . I will repay to the Company the amount lost, viz £120.' And on 9 November 1880 Trollope arranged a new agreement for *Ayala's Angel*, replacing one of a year earlier giving him £1,500 for the entire copyright, with one whereby Chapman & Hall paid only £750 for the book rights, the serial and foreign rights netting Trollope only an additional £300, a total reduction of £450.) *The Life of Cicero* was published in late November 1880. On no book had Trollope ever worked with such assiduity and at such length. He told Rusden, 'Oh, the work that I have done. The books I have referred to, and the volumes I have read!'[49] Trollope kept no working diary for the *Cicero*, but the reading, annotating, study, and writing had taken him, intermittently—for he continued to turn out novels at the same time— over four years.

It was claimed by some critics of Trollope's time (and later) that he treated Cicero as a London gentleman and judged him by the gentleman's standards:

What a man [Cicero] would have been for London life! How he would have enjoyed his club, picking up the news of the day from all lips, while he seemed to give it to all ears. How popular he would have been at the Carlton, and how men would have listened to him while every great or little crisis was discussed! How supreme he would have sat on the Treasury bench,—or how unanswerable, how fatal, how joyous when attacking the Government from the opposite seats! How crowded would have been his rack with invitations to dinner! How delighted would have been the middle-aged Countesses of the time to hold with him mild intellectual flirtations,—and the girls of the period, how proud to get his autograph, how much prouder to have touched the lips of the great orator with theirs! How the pages of the magazines would have run over with little essays from his pen![50]

On the other hand, Trollope insisted over and over again that Cicero, especially in his faults, be judged by Roman standards and not by nineteenth-century English standards. This, in fact, is the overreaching strategy of Trollope's 'apology'. To ignore this side of the book is to miss its (characteristically Trollopian) point. The references to the gentleman and the hypothetical Londoner are all made *mutatis mutandis*. With regard to Cicero's boasting, for example, Trollope urges readers to remember, 'that

Romans were not accustomed to be shamefaced in praising themselves'. Trollope accepts Cicero's own explanation for his false flattery, 'Sed quid agas. Sic vivitur,' words he translates—perhaps deliberately echoing his novel's title—as 'What would you have me do? It is thus we live now.' In his speech against Piso Cicero says that if he saw Piso and Gabinius crucified he would be delighted by both the punishment of their bodies and the ruin of their reputations; he prays for 'all evil' on Piso; and resorts to vilifying even his enemy's physical appearance, remarking that Piso came back from the provinces without his army or anything else except that 'old impudent face of his'. But, Trollope avers, abuse of enemies was an acceptable Roman custom, and, though he viewed this particular tirade as unworthy of Cicero, Trollope thought it 'full of life, and amusing as an expression of honest hatred'. (In his notes he says more sharply, 'There is something attractive in his absolute hatred of the man.') Trollope will not join with those who criticize Cicero for divorcing his wife of thirty years. Divorce, Trollope argues, was not the deadly thing it has become: 'All married Romans underwent divorce'; moreover, after her separation from Cicero, Terentia 'had the extreme honour of having married Sallust. . . . They say that she married twice again after Sallust's death, and that having lived nearly through the reign of Augustus she died at length at the age of a hundred and three. Divorce at any rate did not kill her.'[51]

Trollope, wittingly or not, tells much about himself in his commentary on Cicero. The conservatism and especially the honesty that Trollope posited in Cicero were very much his own. Similarly the common sense and moderation that Trollope thought central to Cicero paralleled Trollope's own. (Trollope's contemporaries, hostile as well as friendly, almost universally thought of him as 'commonsensical'.) Trollope's Cicero is not a man of absolutes; he is unlike, for example, the stern and stoical Cato, or one Zeno, who held any fault 'an unpardonable crime. To kill an old cock if you do not want it is as bad as to murder your father.' To such impossible virtue Trollope opposes Cicero's humanity and lack of fanaticism. Cicero, Trollope says, was 'too honest, too wise, too civilized, too modern' to live in accordance with the doctrine of any one special school of philosophy: 'He knew,—no one better,—that the pleasure of the world was pleasant, and that the ills are the reverse. . . . He avoided pain when it came near him, and did his best to have everything comfortable around him. He was so far an Epicurean,—as we all are. He did not despise death, or pain, or grief. He was a modern-minded man . . . of robust tendencies moral, healthy, and enduring. But he was anything but a philosopher in his life.' Trollope, who continually waged a fight against puritanical opposition to pleasure, notes that Cicero's defence of the 'irregular' Caelius was especially condemned for 'a passage which to my taste is the best in the whole piece', in which Cicero 'palliated' sensual pleasures, especially in the young; Trollope thinks any ladies reading the passage would like Cicero the better for it. Relishing the irony, he translates: 'If therefore you shall find one who can avert his eyes from all that is beautiful, who is charmed by no sweet smell, by no soft touch, by no rich flavour, who can turn a deaf ear to coaxing words,—I, indeed, and perhaps a few others may think that the gods have been good to such a one; but I doubt whether the world at large will not think that the gods have made him a sorry fellow.'[52]

Trollope, himself a reader of heroic dimensions, savours with evident satisfaction and identification Cicero's words on books: 'Other recreations do not belong to all seasons, nor to all ages, nor to all places. [Books] nourish our youth and delight our old age. They adorn our prosperity, and give a refuge and a solace to our troubles. They charm us at home, and they are not in our way when we are abroad. They go to bed with us. They travel about with us. They accompany us as we escape into the country.' Late in his second volume Trollope comments on Cicero's literary output, 'We are astonished at his fecundity and readiness. He was now nearly sixty-three, and, as he travels about the country he takes with him all the adjuncts necessary for the writing of treatises. . . . His "Topica" . . . he put together on board ship.'[53] Trollope, as productive and as ready to write anywhere as ever, was nearing 65 when he wrote these words.

Trollope probably watched the reviews of *The Life of Cicero* more closely than those of any of his works. (It was, he told a friend, a book he hoped 'would live'.[54]) The writer in the *St James's Gazette* was struck by Trollope's dealing with Cicero 'as if he were in the habit of meeting him at the Garrick', and praised the book as springing from admiration, though he criticized some of Trollope's defence of his subject as 'extenuation'. *The World* called *The Life of Cicero* 'a very characteristic, and in many respects, a thoroughly charming book', in which Cicero is treated 'in the same way that [Trollope] might [treat] his own Phineas Finn or Archdeacon Grantly'; Trollope wrote 'as if he had known the subject of his book intimately, and as if it were a duty of friendship to vindicate his memory'. The *Pall Mall* praised Trollope's 'sympathy and sound judgment' but faulted some of his scholarship. This Trollope accepted: 'I do not profess to be a scholar,—but simply one who has read enough of Latin literature, (and have sufficiently understood it,) to be able to tell my story.'[55]

Trollope could not help being concerned about the *Saturday Review*. A remark in its notice of *Dr Wortle's School* (saying that book was 'as happy in expression as Mr. Trollope usually is when he does not meddle with things too high for him') showed that 'they mean to be very heavy on the Cicero'. The reviewer, after praising the book for sound judgement, devotion to Cicero, a quiet natural style and skilful narration, concluded none the less that the book was 'superfluous': 'neither thorough, nor sustained, nor balanced, nor careful enough to hold its own among a crowd of competitors'. The *Daily News* said Trollope possessed 'a real love and admiration for his hero', but appeared 'neither to sympathize with nor to appreciate the society with which he is dealing'. The reviewer for *Truth* found nothing good in the book, decrying Trollope's alleged inaccuracy, ignorance of law, and lack of historical sense. When Charles Mackay protested to Trollope against what he thought was the injustice of such notices, Trollope wrote back: 'I fancy that we authors owe more to critics than any injustice we receive from them. I am sure that if any critic wanted to spite us, he could better do it by holding his tongue than by speaking evil of us.'[56] As Mackay was not a personal friend, Trollope was unwilling to enter closely into the matter; and while he certainly felt that critics were by and large good to him, he was sensitive to criticism, especially when he was accused of 'meddling with things too high for him'.

SOUTH HARTING

There is nothing to fear in death,—if you be wise. There is so much to fear in life, whether you be wise or foolish.

Letter of 23 January 1882

30

A Country Residence

WITH *The Life of Cicero* behind him, Trollope felt, even more than in 1876 after finishing *An Autobiography*, that he was 'ready to go'. Aside from the mental satisfaction, the completion of the *Cicero* also provided a good time to move back to the country, something he and Rose had been considering. She, with her predilection for gardening and growing vegetables, certainly preferred rural life. They thought that country air would be better for his health; Trollope was 65 but looked older; he had used his extraordinarily robust constitution to its limits and had worn himself down. Evidence indicates that he suffered from high blood-pressure, congested lungs, and shortness of breath. Trollope wrote to Tom, 'It will sometimes take a man more than 5 years to die. I thought I was going to die in Montagu Square when I came here. But it is not comfortable enough.'[1] One of the severest trials in London was the distraction of noises when trying to write:

I own that a brass band altogether incapacitates me. No sooner does the first note of the opening burst reach my ear, than I start up, fling down my pen, and cast my thoughts disregarded into the abyss of some chaos which is always there ready to receive them. . . . Here, in our quiet square, the beneficent police have done wonders for our tranquillity,—not, however, without creating for me personally a separate trouble in having to encounter the stern reproaches of the middle-aged leader of the band when he asks me in mingled German and English accents whether I do not think that he too as well as I,—he with all his comrades, and then he points to the nine stalwart, well-cropped, silent and sorrowing Teutons around him,—whether he and they should not be allowed to earn their bread as well as I. . . . I cannot make him understand that in earning my own bread I am a nuisance to no one. . . . I do feel, however, that this comparative peace within the heart of a huge city is purchased at the cost of many tears.[2]

And, of course, he himself had always loved country life more than city life, in spite of his addiction to clubs and dining out. By early May 1880 they had chosen a house called North End, at South Harting, a Sussex village on the Hampshire border. The house, of recent construction, was set in five cleared acres in a wooded estate of seventy acres.[3] He had his hesitations about moving, and a week before changing house, wrote to Harry: 'It makes me melancholy;—though I believe I shall be happier there than I am here. I dislike dinner parties and all going out.'[4]

The move came in early July, and the library was the major difficulty: having been two weeks in the house, he wrote to Harry, 'You may imagine what a trouble the library has been. . . . It is very much larger than the library in London, but still will not hold as many books. . . . If however I am in confusion with my books, I have got my wine into fine order, and have had iron bins put up in the cellar. We have the two horses, and a brougham, and a pony carriage. . . . We like the neighbors as far as we have seen them as yet.' To Mrs Meetkerke he wrote, 'Yes, we have changed our mode of life altogether. We have got a little cottage here, just big enough (or nearly so) to hold my books, with five acres and a cow and a dog and a cock and a hen. I have got seventeen years' lease, and therefore I hope to lay my bones here. Nevertheless I am as busy as would be one thirty years younger, in cutting out dead boughs, and putting up a paling here and a little gate there. We go to church and mean to be very good, and have maids to wait on us.'[5] That happy picture is confirmed by T. H. S. Escott's description of the house and Trollope's life there: he called the house 'among the best and prettiest buildings in the district', and described its 'long line of windows and doors open[ing] on a delightful lawn, with a background of copse, studded with Scotch firs and larches'. The walk from the garden gate to a hill on the South Downs was 'worthy of Windsor or Kensington'. Trollope tended the flowers in the greenhouse; he began to rise later than was his custom; he entertained neighbours, he took an active part in parish activities; for penny readings he secured the services of some of his well-known friends, including Sir Henry James and Millais.[6] His interest in local activities impressed the vicar of Harting, H. D. Gordon, who in his obituary of Trollope, described him as 'the life of our school manager meetings', and, perhaps with some pious exaggeration, paid tribute to his staunch churchmanship: 'He rarely, even when his health was failing, missed Sunday morning service, always punctual to the minute—an alert and reverent and audible worshipper, and a steady communicant.'[7]

Removal to the country did not deter Trollope from visiting London, on business or for occasional social engagements; the train journey (from Rogate, a mile and a half away, or from Petersfield, four and a half) took only a little over two hours, and he could, if necessary, stay the night at

Garlant's Hotel. He did offer to resign the treasurership of the Royal Literary Fund in his shame at forgetting an audit meeting three weeks after the move, 'amidst the terrible confusion of changing house', but he was persuaded not to do so. The Committee valued him, as they had shown the previous year, when they accommodated him after he threatened to resign over a practice he considered equivalent to having two presidents.[8]

Trollope's first writing in his new home was to complete a series, begun at Montagu Square, of eleven articles on London Tradesmen for the *Pall Mall Gazette*. In May 1880 George Smith had given the paper to his son-in-law, Henry Yates Thompson, a supporter of Gladstone; the change of proprietor caused the resignation of Frederick Greenwood—who had been editor from the first—and his replacement by John Morley. Trollope had not written for the *Pall Mall* since the 1860s and, while never one for much looking back, he must have been reminded of his heady days with George Smith. With Greenwood's departure, and the paper having taken a liberal turn, Trollope may have suggested he write something for it, or the idea may have come from Morley, for whom Trollope had recently done the *Thackeray*. Another such reminder came when, a year later, Leslie Stephen, editor of the *Cornhill*, mistakenly sent Trollope some proof. He wrote to George Smith that he wished it were his: 'It was 22 years since, or nearly, when I received the first proof for correction. And then, since that, there have been recollections so tender! Think of all the names that crowd upon me. And all the cheques!!! Alas,—that they can never be repeated!'[9]

Trollope had written only a handful of non-fiction articles in more than a decade. The 'London Tradesmen' sketches, along the line of the earlier clergymen and travellers series, were as good as anything he ever did in this line—light and deft, so different from the closely argued political essays of the 1860s. Easily written, they are easy to read. But he required some fresh first-hand experience for the material, and he commandeered a young relative, almost certainly his godson John Anthony Tilley,* to accompany him in the early hours of the morning to Billingsgate, Covent Garden, and Smithfield.

Trollope's interest in tradesmen sprang from his constant fascination

---

* Young Tilley, son of John Tilley and his third wife, recorded, 'I once wrote to ['Uncle Tony'] from my private school to tell him, with an eye to the main chance, that I had won second prize in a spelling bee, a form of entertainment then rather popular. He replied, sending me half a sovereign, but alleging, I still believe untruly, that in my letter to him I had spelt night with a k.'[10]

with how people make a living, from his long-standing hatred of advertising, and from his displeasure with large concerns driving the little man out of business. Overriding all was the persistent question of honesty in business. But here even honesty is treated lightly and ironically. Are plumbers, for example, who are supposed to be engaged in 'mending . . . those leakages among the leads, in conquering those fugitive smells, in stopping those pernicious runnings of water', really 'plotting some infernal hole among the roofs, or arranging for a catastrophe with the water-pipes' in preparation for future visits? If so, they are no different from barristers and cabinet ministers and bishops. Aren't solicitors at Lincoln's Inn continually preparing the way for fresh litigation? Yet the plumber's case remains especially suspect: 'It becomes a question to us whether it be possible that a plumber should go to heaven. But on thinking over all the conditions of his circumstances . . . we do not see why he should be debarred if barristers and Cabinet Ministers be allowed to enter. Sound undeviating honesty . . . is, as far as we can see, to be found exclusively among writers for the press.'[11]

This comparing of the plumber and the bishop, the mundane and the arcane, the ordinary and the supposedly special, calls to mind his own favourite comparison of the shoemaker and the novelist. Wine merchant, greengrocer, horse dealer, or writer, it comes to pretty much the same thing: they cannot overprice their products for fear 'they will be left with their goods or their knowledge unsold upon their hands'.[12]

But the star of the series is the tailor. Trollope, who was notorious for his rumpled look, largely the result of his vociferous gesturing and impatient careless movements, had none the less a nostalgic affection for tailors; they abound in his novels, frequently as minor figures, occasionally—Thomas Neefit in *Ralph the Heir* and Daniel Thwaite in *Lady Anna*—as principal characters. Londoners, Trollope says, like their tailors, but are in awe of them and dare not suggest that they charge too much lest the tailor intimate that the customer might prefer cheap 'reach-me-downs' from Tottenham Court Road. The tailor believes in his heart that among merchants and shopkeepers and artisans of all kinds he is the only just and honest man. Maybe he is right, for 'What is there in the world equal to a pair of well-fitting trousers?'[13] Whatever Trollope's contempt for dandies, he cannot help admiring the manner in which someone like Ferdinand Lopez (in *The Prime Minister*) manages always to look well dressed, who appears incapable by nature of being ill-dressed, who looks as though his smart clothes 'grew on him, as did his hair and his nails'.[14]

The Trollopes' first trip away from their new home was to attend his niece Beatrice Trollope's wedding in Paris. She had for many years lived partly in England and partly with her father in Rome, where he supported himself on a modest income from newspaper work for the London *Standard*. In 1876 she had become unofficially engaged to someone in the wine business, much to her father's distress (people, he wrote, heard from her that she was engaged, and 'they hear from the gentleman in question that he is *not* engaged'). The whole matter was quietly dropped, at least partly because of uncertainties about her marriage settlement. Bice had an income of £275, a legacy from her mother, but her father required that she contribute £200 of it to the household expenses. Especially when in England she was straitened for money, and in October 1878 she asked Anthony's advice on how to approach her father. Trollope told her he could write on her behalf, 'but it would make him *very* angry', and instead worded a letter for her to send to him. Tom replied that he could not allow her any more money, that if she wished to take the whole of her income and live elsewhere 'with some other persons', she might do so, in which case he and Frances would have to find a smaller house in Rome. She did not take her money, and a year later she became engaged, to everyone's satisfaction, to Charles Stuart-Wortley, an aspiring politician, the son of the late Recorder of London. 'I am very glad to hear your news,' Anthony wrote to her, 'and I wish you joy with all my heart,' and it was arranged that he meet Wortley. Tom was at first 'aggrieved', as he wrote to her, 'at Mr. Wortley having thought it superfluous to write to me'.[15] But Wortley then wrote to Tom, and plans went on smoothly. Harry Trollope was named one of the trustees of Bice's marriage settlement. A year later, when the wedding took place in the French capital on 16 August, 'Uncle Tony' was one of the witnesses, just as he had been one of the witnesses to Tom's marriage there in 1866.

Settled back again into Harting, Trollope began on 18 August a short two-volume novel, *Kept in the Dark*. It is the story of a young woman, Cecilia Holt, who somewhat foolishly—yet believably—conceals from the man she marries her former engagement; her secret, like Cousin Henry's, leads to guilt; and when the husband learns of it he becomes, almost in the manner of Louis Trevelyan, morbidly, obsessively jealous; he eventually deserts her—although Trollope tacks on a reconciliation at the end. The typically Trollopian ploy is that though the husband is clearly in the wrong, the wife is adamantly, stubbornly, unhelpfully angry. Trollope also used the story for another hit at what he regarded as misguided feminists in the person of one Francesca Altifiorla, an unkind busybody, who abets the break-up of the heroine's marriage. Trollope put the story by for six months, and then in May 1881 sold it to Isbister for serialization in *Good Words*. He sold the book rights to Chatto & Windus, an energetic firm that was challenging Chapman & Hall in the reissue market.

A slight work, *Kept in the Dark* remains one of Trollope's most neglected titles. But it carried one bright reminder of the past. Trollope had paid little attention to the illustrations of his fiction after Millais completed the drawings for *Phineas Finn* in 1869. He seems to have become resigned to the efforts of 'post-sixties' artists who illustrated his works, Henry Woods (*The Vicar of Bullhampton*), F. A. Fraser (*Ralph the Heir*), Francis Montague Holl (*Phineas Redux*), and, later, William Small (*Marion Fay*). All these artists worked in the so-called 'Graphic School' manner—most closely associated with Small—a style in which, as one authority put it, 'wash' is substituted for 'line', and, in an effort 'to appeal to a larger and less cultured public', 'art is turning to journalism, beauty to prettiness, sentiment to sentimentality'. Ruskin termed the new style 'Blottesque'. The very nadir in illustrations to Trollope was reached in the forty drawings to *The Way We Live Now* by an amateur artist named Lionel Grimston Fawkes. The stiff, awkward figures, contorted limbs, paw-like hands, and mongoloid-looking children positively deface the text. While the book was appearing in shilling parts, Mary Holmes complained to Trollope about the illustrations. He replied, 'What you say of illustrations is all true,—not strong enough in expression of disgust. But what can a writer do? I desire, of course, to put my books into as many hands as possible, and I take the best mode of doing so.'[16] But for *Kept in the Dark*, he persuaded the always busy Millais to provide one illustration (because of the artist's delays, it depicted a scene in the second rather than first number). The elegant drawing, showing Cecilia at her writing desk, was later used as frontispiece of the book edition, published in October 1882.

Lonely in the country, Trollope seems to have become closer to his son Harry, who had for years lived largely on the continent, where he pursued a desultory literary career. Trollope kept up a constant correspondence with Harry, loading the young man with advice and urging him on in his work: 'Make it as readable as possible,' he told Harry of a life of Bianconi that he was ghostwriting for Bianconi's daughter, Mrs Morgan John O'Connell; Trollope kept asking when it would be out. As for the £50 Harry was paid, 'It is at any rate good to earn something.' Harry's name ought to be included, if the book be good, on which question he must take his mother's advice, 'for she is never mistaken about a book being good or bad'.* (In fact Mrs O'Connell not only omitted Harry's name but said that 'save where the text will show the interposition of another hand, I have worked out and written all this book myself'.) For years Harry struggled with the *Corneille and Racine* volume for Blackwood's Foreign Classics for English Readers series, edited by Mrs Oliphant. When the book was commissioned in 1877 (doubtless through Trollope's influence with John Blackwood), Trollope urged Harry to get it out as one of the early entries in the series; Mrs Oliphant, who had given Harry the job against her will, told William Blackwood that Harry 'has an extremely *queer* look, and is anything but prepossessing and heaven forbid that he should have the Molière! [She did the Molière herself.] So far as I could make out he knows about the history of the French stage but nothing else. What a very odd creature to follow upon two generations of literature!' When Harry submitted the manuscript in 1880 she insisted on major revisions and freely made changes herself; 'I daresay the critics will be merciful to his father's son,' she told Blackwood. Trollope, much annoyed, wrote to Blackwood: 'I cannot but think that [Mrs Oliphant] has in some respect over-acted her part of Editor, having assumed an imperiousness which would have been very foreign to [Lucas] Collins or to your uncle. . . . Relieved from the superintendence of such an older critic as your uncle, she is I think a little without a guide.' When Harry translated G. Letourneau's *Sociology Based upon Ethology* for Chapman & Hall's Library of Contemporary Science (1881), Trollope gave him impossible advice about being 'very careful . . . in regard to style;—so as to soften as far as may be possible all awkwardness of phrase', and repeatedly urged him to be quick about submitting the manuscript for printing. When Harry was paid for the work, Trollope wrote him: 'I do not think that £60 is very magnificent pay for all your work, but still I congratulate you heartily on getting it.' Trollope also suggested that Harry was taking 'too long [a] time' with a dictionary-guidebook on Paris that Harry was preparing for Charles Dickens, jun.'s series. And again, while Harry was travelling about Normandy, working on another guidebook, this one for Isbister (and, in his father's opinion, not leaving sufficient postal addresses behind him—'I doubt much whether you will get this letter'), Trollope told him: 'Your fault always is in being somewhat too long a time,—not thinking

* It has recently been discovered that Rose Trollope, some half-dozen years after Anthony's death, wrote a story, 'The Legend of Holm Royde', which she submitted to *Blackwood's*; it was rejected.[17]

quite enough of the days as they run by; and in being a little too timid as to the work as you do it. . . . You will be over here in December [1881] and we shall be able to talk over the Norman book.'[18]

But in spite of the restrained impatience, Trollope often shows himself devoted and affectionate to his son. Upon the move to Harting, Trollope regretted terribly that Harry could not visit them during their first month: 'but I will put up with looking forward to your coming. Every day in August I shall think we are hardly used that does not see you.' Some months after Harry's first visit to Harting, Trollope wrote to him, on 21 December, 'I miss you most painfully. But I had expected that. I only hope that you may come back with the summer.' Then, becoming unusually confiding, he continued:

This is the longest day of the winter and I shall begin now to look for the lengthening days. Ah, me! How I used to look for the shortening days, when I was hunting, and had the first of November as a golden day before me for which my soul could long. I have now to look for the time when the green things in the garden may begin to shew themselves. But the expectation of green things in another garden prevents me from being sad.[19]

On the next day, 22 December, George Eliot died. Trollope wrote to Charles Lee Lewes, 'I did love her very dearly. That I admired her was a matter of course.' These two near-contemporaries (she was seven years younger) and friends had both achieved a wide readership and fame at about the same time—*Adam Bede* had appeared a year before the serialization of *Framley Parsonage* began—and each had warmly appreciated the other's quite different achievement. It was a shock as well as a sadness to hear of her death, just as he was planning to visit her and her new young husband, J. W. Cross. Trollope must have felt isolated and outmoded, since her passing left him alone remaining of the great mid-Victorian novelists: the Brontës, Thackeray, Mrs Gaskell, Dickens, had already gone; those now making a reputation were George Meredith, Hardy, Henry James. Young practitioners and theorists might view him as a relic of the past; but the weaving of fiction remained as necessary to him as food and drink. He would keep on writing, much as he had always done, since determining in May of 1856, to write for three hours a day, to keep his working diary before him, staring him in the face should he be delinquent. As he told Harry the day before George Eliot's death, 'I finished on Thursday the novel I was writing, and on Friday I began another.'[20]

The new story was *The Fixed Period*, a work altogether out of his line— futuristic fiction, a story set one hundred years later, in 1980. It was disappointing. The scientific advances it envisages are not very imagina-tive: steam bicycles, steam cricket bowling machines, telephones con-nected with invisible hairs. Trollope did show some perspicacity in making the most significant scientific advance an enormous gun, 'a 250-ton swiveller', a weapon so terrible it could wipe out an entire city with one firing. The embittered hero of the tale declares, 'It is an evil sign of the times . . . that the greatest inventions of the day should always take the shape of engines of destruction!' Some people say the gun is not even loaded; certainly it is used essentially as a threat: 'There are things so terrible,' says another character, 'that if you will only create a belief in them, that will suffice.[21] But the real focus of *The Fixed Period* is not science, but compulsory euthanasia, a subject prompted by Trollope's own growing concern with old age and death, a concern that the move to the country and the onset of his first winter there seem to have height-ened. Old men had always been something of a fictional speciality for Trollope, from Larry Macdermot in his very first novel, to Mr Harding, the old Duke of Omnium, and so on. But here the attention is most pointedly on ageing.

Trollope derived part of the idea for *The Fixed Period* from *The Old Law* (1618), a play by Massinger, Middleton, and Rowley, which he read in July 1876. The 'old law' would have men at 80 and women at 60 executed—'cut off as fruitless to the republic, and law shall finish what nature linger'd at'.[22] Trollope's story, set in the former British colony of Britannula, an island near New Zealand, concerns the efforts of the country's president, John Neverbend, to enforce its recently passed law of the 'Fixed Period': at age 67, old people—women equally with men—are to be taken to live in a college called the Necropolis ('The name had always been distasteful to me,' Neverbend remarks) and prepared for 'departing' before they reach the age of 68. The purpose of the law is the 'abolition of the miseries, weakness, and faineant imbecility of old age, by the prearranged ceasing to live of those who would otherwise become old'.[23] Neverbend, an 'enthusi-ast' obsessed with the scheme, does his best to implement the law, but before the first citizen is dispatched, England interferes by sending a man-of-war (named the HMS *John Bright*, after the 'demagogue' Trollope so disliked), equipped with the frightening great gun, to reannex the colony and carry Neverbend away to the mother country. Neverbend himself narrates the story, in the course of which he explains how he wrote the entire book on shipboard, working methodically for four hours every morning.

For all the grimness of the subject, Neverbend, so lacking in self-irony, is to some extent a figure of fun. (Most reviewers took the book as a sort of clumsy joke.) Neverbend is incensed to find that the law, which was passed easily enough, seems in practice so troublesome; he is driven nearly to distraction by the way people talk about the Fixed Period, as when they speak of his friend Crasweller, the first citizen 'deposited' in the college, as the first 'victim', someone 'locked up' in preparation for 'execution'. People charge Neverbend with being eager for 'polishing him off'. During the voyage back to England the ship's crew think Neverbend a 'bloody-minded cannibal'; he overhears a steward saying, 'He'd have killed that old fellow that came on board as sure as eggs if we hadn't got there just in time to prevent him.' Neverbend sees himself as a lonely pioneer for advanced thought; he likens himself to Socrates, Galileo, Hampden, and Washington, men who had done great things 'by constancy, in opposition to the wills and prejudices of the outside world'. Neverbend perceives that the scheme for a Fixed Period might have to be postponed for a century, or, at least that he should first preach it in the United States: 'No other republic would be strong enough to stand against those hydra-headed prejudices with which the ignorance of the world at large is fortified.'[24]

Despite his foolishness and lack of self awareness, Neverbend's ruminations reflect some of Trollope's own thinking on old age: Neverbend says: 'I look to my departure from this world with awe indeed, but still with satisfaction. But I cannot look with satisfaction to a condition of life in which, from my own imbecility, I must necessarily retrograde into selfishness. . . . I cannot but fear that a taint of that selfishness which I have hitherto avoided, but which will come if I allow myself to become old, may remain, and that it will be better for me that I should go hence while as yet my own poor wants are not altogether uppermost in my mind.'[25] Trollope in his letters over the last years of his life expressed a fear that he would fall into a mental or physical state in which he could not truly live, that is, could no longer work. Two days before finishing *The Fixed Period*, he told Henry Howard, 'I now am an old man, 66, and shall soon have come to the end of my tether.' Six months later, having indeed passed his sixty-sixth birthday, he told the same correspondent, 'I am nearly seventy years of age.' Tom Trollope said that he had had many conversations with Anthony about the desirability of 'quitting the scene' before one's mental powers were diminished or lost.[26] When Trollope finished *The Fixed Period* he would have had two years before arriving himself at the Britannulan 'fixed period' or sixty-eighth birthday. Lucas Collins told the story that when an eminent Queen's Counsel, an 'intimate friend' of

Trollope, referred to the book as a 'grim jest', Trollope 'stopped suddenly in his walk, and grasping the speaker's arm in his energetic fashion, exclaimed: "It's all true—I *mean* every word of it."'[27] It hardly needs remarking that such a comment, in the usual unhelpful way of authors on their own works, says little of Trollope's own beliefs, as the book seems at one time both to defend and, perhaps more frequently, to deride, euthanasia. Ironists invite ambiguity. (Sir William Osler, the eminent Canadian-born physician, later Regius Professor of Medicine at Oxford, in a speech on the occasion of his retirement from Johns Hopkins in 1905, made a humorous suggestion about endorsing Neverbend's ideas that brought down upon him violent attacks in the press.)[28]

With one of the aspects of Neverbend's project, cremation, Trollope was firmly in accord. In January 1874 Trollope had been one of sixteen prominent people at the home of Sir Henry Thompson, a distinguished physician and surgeon to Queen Victoria, who signed a document that brought into existence the Cremation Society of England: 'We . . . disapprove the present custom of burying the dead, and we desire to substitute some mode which shall rapidly resolve the body into its component elements, by a process which cannot offend the living, and shall render the remains perfectly innocuous. Until some better method is devised we desire to adopt that usually known as Cremation.' Other signatories included Shirley Brooks, Millais, Tenniel, T. Spencer Wells, and Alexander Strahan.[29] (Cremation became legal in 1884, largely through Thompson's efforts.) If Trollope wanted to help the cause of cremation in his book he certainly did not do so by associating it with compulsory euthanasia, a subject considered, as *The Times* said in a review of the book, 'essentially ghastly'.[30]

Trollope finished *The Fixed Period* on 28 February and, no longer leaving manuscripts quite so long in his drawer, wrote immediately to William Blackwood, offering the novel, 'the same length as Dr. Wortle, very unlike that in structure and method'. On 30 May Blackwood accepted the novel for serialization for £200 (a month later he agreed to pay £450 for both serial and book rights). Blackwood liked the 'novelty' and 'strangeness' of the story, and asked only that Trollope dispense with phrases containing the words 'God' and 'Lord' that might 'wound the feelings of strict people & bring down upon us a religious storm'. Trollope said that while returning proof he would 'endeavour to put out all the profanities'.[31] The novel appeared in *Blackwood's* from October 1881 to March 1882, with book publication in the latter month.

Trollope's last letter to Kate Field was written on 17 January 1881. She, having been a year back in the States, wrote from New York requesting information about George Eliot. Kate had written an article for the *New York Tribune* immediately on the novelist's death and apparently hoped to do something more ambitious. Trollope, as usual, throws cold water on her scheme: to her inquiry about the early acquaintance and relationship between George Eliot and Lewes, Trollope explained that, although he was 'very intimate' with her, she had never spoken to him about her life before they met. He observed, tentatively—though all the world knew it—that she and Lewes were together before the publication of *Adam Bede*. Trollope would assert only that George Eliot 'had lived down evil tongues before Lewes' death. She was asked to dine with Queen Victorias daughter. . . . I mention this because the English Royal family are awfully particular as to whom they see and do not see. That at any rate is true, because I saw her there.'* He closed with the discouraging comment, 'But in truth she was one whose private life should be left in privacy,—as may be said of all who have achieved fame by literary merits.'[32] Kate wrote nothing further on George Eliot. If Trollope had seen Kate's *New York Tribune* article he would have read, as part of her account of meeting George Eliot at the Villino Trollope in 1860, her description of 'the almost boyish enthusiasm and impulsive argumentation of Anthony Trollope, who is an admirable specimen of a frank and loyal Englishman'.[33]

Kate Field went her busy way, relatively well-off financially now. Some of her later causes, such as cremation, international copyright, the development of California wines (in the cause of temperate drinking), would have been much to Trollope's liking; some would have amused him, like her interest in the Mormons. He would probably have been less pleased with her enthusiasm for the annexation of Hawaii by the United States. Kate Field died from pneumonia, at Honolulu, on 19 May 1896.

The first winter in Sussex was particularly severe. On 24 January 1881 Trollope complained to Harry, 'There were 3 or 4 feet of snow and a white mist blinding every thing. When will it go away? We have had a week and not a grain has moved as yet. It is very melancholy.'[34] The harsh winter made an early holiday on the continent desirable, and on 15 March, he and

---

* Ada Strickland, a school friend of Bice Trollope's, who frequently visited 39 Montagu Square during the 1870s, wrote that Trollope was 'a favourite' with Edward VII when he was Prince of Wales; she recorded that at the Colonial Institute the Prince arranged to speak with Trollope (who on returning home told his family, 'Don't speak to us we have been in the presence of Royalty!'), and how on one occasion Trollope's short-sightedness kept him from recognizing the Prince as the latter was saying good evening to Trollope on the steps of the Turf Club.[35]

Rose and Florence left for a two-month visit to Italy and the Tom Trollopes. At Rome he met for the first time Edward Freeman, with whom, a dozen years earlier, he had done battle in the pages of the *Fortnightly* about the morality of fox-hunting. The distinguished Oxford scholar of modern history and the amateur classicist took to each other immediately. Field sports were forgotten. Freeman wrote, 'Mr. Trollope was quite willing to hear me talk about Mamilius, and I was more than willing to hear Mr. Trollope talk about Cicero. That was a subject on which he talked well and wisely, both on that day and at other times.' Freeman found Trollope's enthusiasm for Cicero such as to lead one to believe 'that his life had been given to Cicero and nothing else. It was a subject on which he would harangue, and harangue very well.' The two men disagreed about Palmerston, one of Trollope's heroes, and to Freeman a 'deceiver of the Liberal party'.[36]

The summer months at Harting were disturbed first by some unidentified but serious illness to Florence Bland. Writing on 25 June 1881, Trollope told Millais: 'we had to send for a surgeon up to London. . . . They put her under chloroform and did dreadful things to her. But they saved her life; and now she is convalescent.'[37] For nearly eight weeks he worked, without her assistance as amanuensis, on *Mr Scarborough's Family*.

Then on 15 July Bice Trollope, now Mrs Charles Stuart-Wortley, gave birth to a girl. Bice had an especially difficult and protracted delivery (her father, writing from Riga, Switzerland, told her mother-in-law that he 'had hoped that the strain of Indian and of Jewish blood in Bice would have ensured her an easy time'). But she developed severe puerperal fever. Trollope visited the Wortleys, but felt 'strangely in the way'. On returning home, he wrote to Mrs Stuart-Wortley, 'I cannot but feel that when you get this all may be over or she may be so much better as hardly to need that I should write. Poor dear girl! Nothing can be more sad than her state,— unless it be your sons, left with his little baby.' Anthony wrote to Tom about the dire prospects, and then soon had to write with the sad news that Bice, on 26 July, had died. Trollope also gave Tom 'a minute account of the arrangements at the funeral and at the grave'. To Lady Pollock Trollope wrote, 'Poor Bice's child is living, but is a delicate little girl. Is it to be wished that the poor motherless little baby should live?'[38] (The child, Beatrice Susan Theodosia Stuart-Wortley, lived until 1973.)

31

A Late Masterwork

AMID all this upheaval, Trollope had been intermittently writing *Mr Scarborough's Family*. Begun in Rome, continued in Florence on the way home, the novel was finished at Harting on 31 October 1881. It was to be his last major fiction. The seeds of the story can be found in the opening pages of *John Caldigate*: 'There were many institutions of his country which Mr. Caldigate hated with almost an inhuman hatred; but there were none more odious to him than that of entails, which institution he was wont to prove by many arguments to be the source of all the ignorance and all the poverty and all the troubles by which his country was afflicted.' Trollope did not make entail important to that novel; but in *Mr Scarborough's Family* he made it the central issue. Just prior to beginning *John Caldigate* he had read Middleton's *A Trick to Catch the Old One*, a play about disinheritance, about ingenious schemes of the disinherited, and about usurious creditors. Other parallels to *Mr Scarborough's Family* can be traced in Fletcher and Massinger's *The Elder Brother*—read by Trollope in July 1874—in which a father with two very different sons hopes to break the entail on his property and leave it to the younger son.[1]

Mr Scarborough's Family explores, with a thoroughness and depth that were to crown his achievement, two obsessive interests that run throughout Trollope's fiction from beginning to end: old age (particularly in men) and the law. These subjects he tackles with a cast of familiar yet enhanced types. Florence Mountjoy is devoted and loyal to her lover, and even more self-possessed and assertive than most of Trollope's heroines: she faces down her mother, her relations, and other suitors (she boldly tells one of these, 'I'm engaged to marry a gentleman whom I love with all my heart, and all my strength, and all my body.') Florence's successful lover, Harry Annesley, is another version of Trollope's hobbledehoy: handsome but unaware of it; hot-tempered, filled as yet with potential rather than accomplishment; eventually shone upon by fortune, more lucky in some ways than deserving. Mr Scarborough's sons provide superb

occasions for Trollope's never-ending examination into antagonisms between fathers and sons. The elder son, Mountjoy, a dissipated spendthrift,
is addicted to gambling; on the other hand, he is in his fashion unselfish
and open-handed. He is far more decent than his respectable younger
brother Augustus, who is selfish, calculating, and so greedy as to as much
as tell his father 'to die out of the way', and the sooner the better. The novel
offers another sad case of an unmarried ageing daughter, Dolly Grey,
whose life has been given to the care of her father, leaving her own
prospects bleak and lonely. Her father, John Grey, is Trollope's last
detailed study of a lawyer (his chambers are at Lincoln's Inn, of course).
Grey, scrupulously honest, and conscientious in handling Mr Scarborough's affairs, is finally driven to premature retirement by the vices
and frauds of his client. There is Peter Prosper, another 'old man' of 50,
frightened to death by his foolish attempt at marriage, the source of comic
scenes that deftly provide balance to the fearful ones of old Squire
Scarborough. Also strikingly present in the novel are such Trollopian
hallmarks as endlessly varying marriage proposal scenes (one taking place
in the presence of the girl's disapproving mother), and a generous infusion
of letters written by the characters. Miss Thoroughbung, the maiden lady
who scares off Mr Prosper, tells him that his letter withdrawing his offer of
marriage is 'very stupid. . . . If you want to write naturally you should
never copy a letter [i.e. make drafts and revisions],'[2] very much Trollope's
own view of writing, whether of letters, reports, or novels.

Mr Scarborough, the book's central figure, is near death, suffering
bravely from an incurable and painful disease, while doing battle with the
law. Thirty years earlier he had devised a scheme to enable him to
circumvent the laws of primogeniture and entail by marrying his wife
twice, once before and once after the birth of his first son. Dissatisfied with
the elder son's behaviour (his post-obit gambling debts would lose the
estate), he produces evidence of the second marriage, thereby displacing
Mountjoy as his heir; but when the second son proves even less worthy—
and after Mountjoy's money-lenders have been bought off cheaply—he
produces the evidence of the first marriage, reinstating the elder son,
contriving from his death-bed to have everything his own way. Scarborough is courteous and generous; he has 'a capacity for love and for
unselfishness which almost atones for his dishonesty'. There is no denying
his amorality in connection with the law. In lawyer Grey's view, Scarborough's 'intelligence is so high, and his principles so low, that there is no
scheme which he does not think that he cannot carry out against the
established laws of his country'. He has the ingenuity to tell a lie and stick

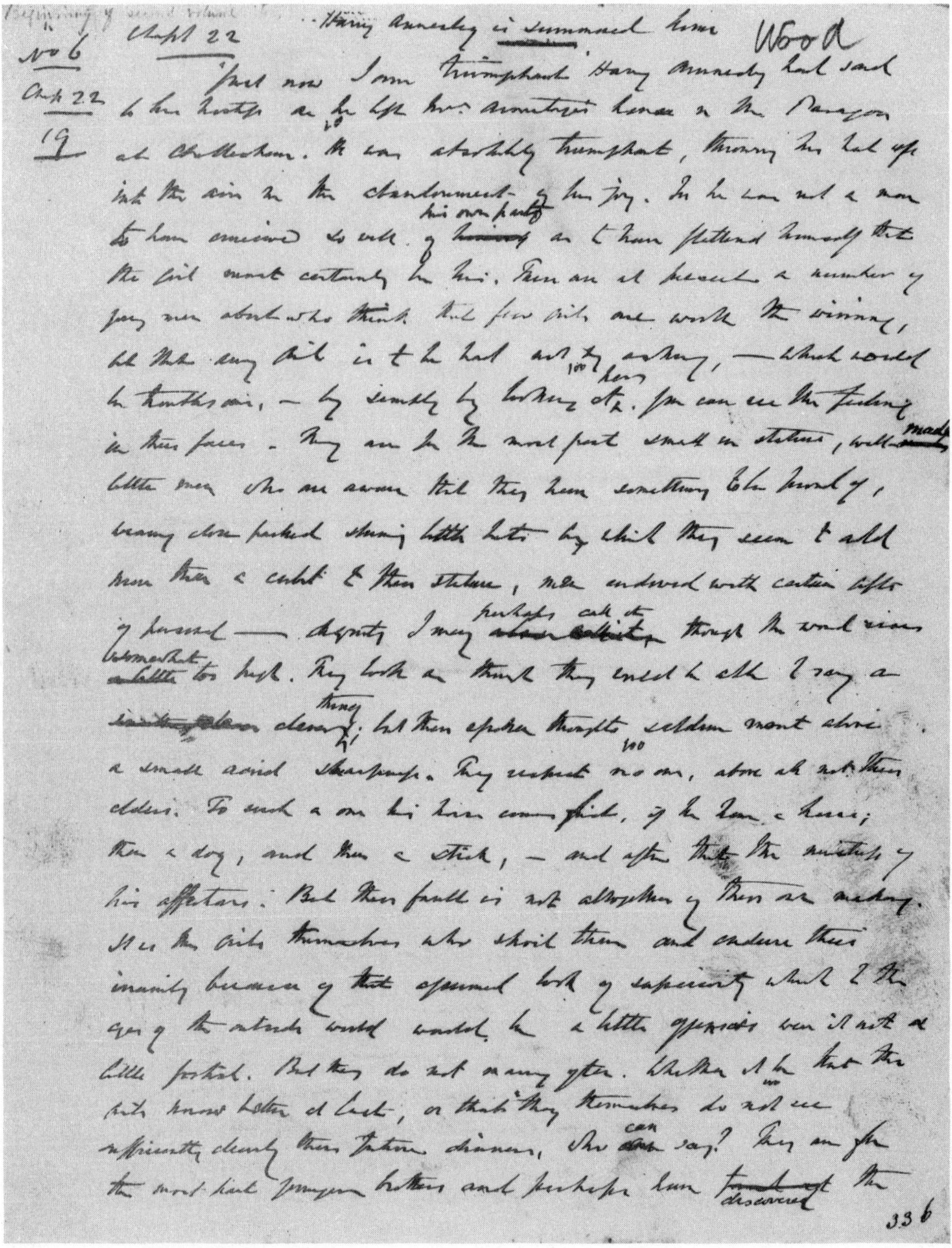

Manuscript page from *Mr. Scarborough's Family* (the beginning of Chapter 22, page 19 of instalment number six, written in June 1881). The name Wood at the top is the compositor's. Like almost all Trollope manuscript pages, it contains only minor revisions.

to it: 'It's a very great gift,' Scarborough boasts. He struggles not only to be stronger than the law but to be free from other conventionalities: 'All church-going propensities,—and these propensities in his estimate extended very widely,—he scorned from the very bottom of his heart.' Mountjoy says his father 'likes to show the world that he can bear his sufferings with a light heart, and is ready to die to-morrow without a pang or a regret. Who is the fellow who sent for a fellow to let him see how a Christian could die? I can fancy my father doing the same thing, only . . . he will bid you come and see a pagan depart in peace, and would be very unhappy if he thought that your dinner would be disturbed by the ceremony.' Mountjoy can say with little fear of contradiction, 'My father is the most singular man you ever came across.'[3]

The critics agreed: even those who disliked the book were awed by the 'Machiavellian' and 'Voltairian' personality of Scarborough. The *Academy* said 'Mr. Trollope has never given us two stronger or less commonplace characters than that terrible old pagan, John Scarborough, and his attorney, Grey. . . . the reader never wearies of them.' The *Saturday*, though it deemed the novel one of Trollope's failures, called Scarborough 'original, almost to incredibility . . . And yet . . . the story is so lifelike and so extremely readable that we lay it down with a pleasure largely leavened by regret.'[4] That Trollope, at this late stage in his career, could devise so striking and original a character as Scarborough in a brilliantly tangled yet balanced plot witnesses to growth rather than decay in his craft. But it was his last great effort. Nothing he wrote would rise to this level again.

Whatever else, he was still earning steadily. For *Mr Scarborough's Family*, a three-volume novel, Trollope was to receive a total of £1,000, £400 for serial rights in *All the Year Round*, and £600 for the book copyright from Chatto & Windus. The prices Trollope could command had certainly been declining. In order to understand the extent of the falling off properly, one must again keep in mind length, measured in units roughly equivalent to volumes of the traditional three-decker novel. During his best-paid years Trollope's novels were commanding between £600 and £640 per 'volume' for combined serial and book rights (payments for *The Claverings* and for *Phineas Finn* exceeded this average). He received £3,200 for *He Knew He Was Right* (agreement signed 1867), a 'five-volume' novel, and £2,500 for *The Eustace Diamonds* (1870) and *Phineas Redux* (1873), both 'four volumes'. This rate remained constant through *The Prime Minister* (1874), which again fetched £2,500 for four volumes, and stayed as high as £600 per volume with £1,800 paid for the three-volume *American Senator* (1875). A slight decline to £1,600 came with *Popenjoy* (January 1877), but *John Caldigate* (June 1877) again brought £1,800. The real dip came with *The Duke's Children* (1878), another three-volume novel, at £1,400, and finally *Mr Scarborough's Family* (serial agreement 1881, book agreement 1882) for which Trollope received £1,000. (*The Landleaguers* was to have fetched £600 for book rights, and although the serial rights agreement has not survived, it was very likely for £400.) On the other hand, £1,000—the same price George Smith had paid for the three-volume *Framley Parsonage* in Trollope's great leap forward in 1860—was still good money. (The price of £450 for late short novels like *The Fixed Period* was not so drastic a decline from the £600 to £700 of earlier days.)

Trollope's high-paying period had lasted some eighteen years, and he took the decline with good grace, thankful for, and still sometimes surprised at, his good fortune. In *An Autobiography* he totted up every pound, shilling, and penny earned by his writing up to *Caldigate*, the figures coming to exactly £68,959. 17s. 5d., a sum he called 'comfortable, but not splendid'.[5] (Eventually, his copyrights after *Caldigate* would bring nearly £10,000 additional.*) By this he did not mean to sound disappointed, for he did not rate his talent as 'splendid'. What he wanted credit for was hard work. He thought he had written more than 'any other living English author'.† He admits to 'making my boast as to quantity', but lays no claim 'to any literary excellence'. But while asserting that, obviously, 'quantity without quality is a vice and a misfortune', he insinuates at least a modest claim to quality. Still, the emphasis in the closing pages of *An Autobiography*, as throughout the book, is on 'persevering diligence' and 'constancy in labour'. '*Nulla dies sine lineâ*,' he says, quoting Pliny, no day without a line.[6]

In August 1881 Trollope agreed to write a book on Palmerston for Isbister, who was hoping to imitate the success of Macmillan's English Men of Letters with his own 'English Political Leaders' series. Long an admirer of

---

* Trollope's will, made 29 October 1878, was proved on 23 January 1883 and gave the gross value of his personal estate (exclusive of copyrights) at £25,892 19s. 3d. In 1897 the government, largely at the behest of Alfred Austin, then Poet Laureate, granted Rose Trollope a Civil List Pension of £100. Arthur James Balfour, First Lord of the Treasury under his uncle, Lord Salisbury, the Prime Minister, agreed to arrange for the pension, telling Austin in 1896, 'It would not be creditable to the country that the widow of one who has given such widespread pleasure should be wholly unassisted in her present straitened circumstances.' The next year Balfour was dismayed to find out, when it was apparently too late, that Mrs Trollope's tax return for 1896 showed an income of £538 from investments.[7]

† Mrs Margaret Oliphant (1828–97) eventually wrote some 120 books, but had not yet passed Trollope's total. He would have dismissed from consideration children's books, women's romances, and much working-class and detective fiction.

Palmerston, Trollope began writing the short book—214 pages—in November and finished it by 1 February 1882. (Rose made a fair copy, as she had with the Cicero, Trollope's non-fiction manuscripts being less clean.) Publication was promised for March, and he was annoyed at Isbister's proposed delay: 'It will . . . take you longer to print it than it did me to write it.' When it became clear that the difficulty had to do with payment, £200, Trollope told Isbister that he preferred immediate publication and deferred payment at four or even six months. After it was published, in June, Trollope was further annoyed to find the book spoken of in the *Daily News* as having been brought out under an 'editor', Barnett Smith. The mistake arose, Smith explained, from the fact that he was the 'originator of the Series', in the sense of having written the first volume, *Sir Robert Peel*.[8] (Trollope's was the second, and after the third, Lewis Sergent's *William Pitt*, the series lapsed.)

Trollope, novelist-like, begins his book *in medias res*, with the most dramatic phases of Palmerston's career, his bullying of Europe as Foreign Secretary, his Don Pacifico speech, his dismissal from office in 1851—largely through the influence of Prince Albert on Lord John Russell—and his triumphant return a few months later. That England agreed with Palmerston, that he was in 'perfect sympathy with those whom he was called upon to govern', is Trollope's argument. It was an elaboration of Matthew Arnold's dictum, 'Lord Palmerston was England'.[9] Trollope admits that Palmerston may have been occasionally 'rough' ('A man who will not be bullied will sometimes bully'), arrogant, boastful, speaking 'as though he were the only honest man concerned in the work'. Palmerston manifested 'a lust of personal power and a desire to rule from his desk in Downing Street as much of Europe as he could get into his hands'. Trollope recounts how a 'very triumphant and very jocund' Palmerston presided over what amounted to a victory dinner for Sir Charles Napier as he was leaving to assume command in the Crimea: 'It was not, perhaps, done in the best taste or with the most correct judgement. A triumphant banquet to a conquering hero should follow, and not precede, the victories to be celebrated.' Trollope gingerly side-steps the question of Palmerston's womanizing: 'He became so popular with the world generally that the world was afraid to be censorious or to inquire into him with prying eyes. The world called him "Cupid" when he was young, and the world said nothing of him more severe than that.'[10]

But for Trollope, Palmerston's failings did not add up to much when set against his patriotism, honesty, and his zest for work: during some fifty years Palmerston was:

always in Parliament, always in office, always at the oar. They offered to make him Lord-Lieutenant of Ireland, as they had also offered to make him Governor-General of India. But he laughed at the proposal. Not to be in the centre of everything,—at St. Stephen's, in Downing Street, in London where the Mayor and the Fishmongers held their banquets, ready for Greenwich dinners, ready for all attacks, for all explanations, for all discussions—was to him not to live. But he did live always, till at eighty-one he was taken to his rest, being at the moment Prime Minister of England.

It soon becomes evident that Trollope's Palmerston is very Trollopian. For all his achievements, 'he was by no means a man of genius, [and was] possessed of not more than ordinary gifts of talent. . . . He could work, requiring no rest, but only some change of employment. He shot, he raced, he hunted, he danced.' He did everything with 'a healthy energy'. A compeer like Guizot may have had greater thinking powers, but Palmerston had greater 'probity, truth, and industry'.[11]

Time and again *Palmerston* reads like someone's commentary on Trollope himself: Palmerston 'seldom rose to any specially exalted view of human nature. He saw all things from a common-sense point of view, with what we may call mundane eyes.' His enemies and critics asked, 'Who is this man who claims to be more hardworking and honester than any among us?' Peter Bayne is approvingly quoted (from an article in *Saint Pauls Magazine*), 'Perhaps no single word goes so far in the description of Lord Palmerston as the word "manly".' Trollope's book speaks continually of Palmerston's industry and perseverance, and how 'hard work was to him the first necessity of his existence'. Comments on Palmerston's writing and oratorical style, passages that seem to echo *An Autobiography* and *Thackeray* on novel writing, assert that Palmerston never 'arranged his words with studious care'; his prose may have lacked 'brightness and splendour', but it doesn't smell of 'polishing oil' or give the impression that some pruning of over-abundant words would improve it; his writing, neither showy nor self-conscious, simply makes its point, and convincingly. Trollope's book ends with words that reverberate with perhaps unconscious identification of author with subject: 'Some one has said that Palmerston, when at his greatest, was powerful and imperious only with a pen in his hand. . . . But it is thus that the official work of a man in office should be done. . . . The arbiter of the politics of Europe became like other arbiters, its bully. They who shall hereafter be desirous of saying severe words against him, must . . . confine themselves to this charge. Against his honesty, his industry and his courage we feel that no true word can be said.'[12]

Almost the only thing the reviewers liked about the book was Trollope's sympathy for his man. The *Academy* said, 'For those who know, [*Lord Palmerston*] is too long; for those who do not know, it is not long enough.' The *Saturday* saw the book as little more than Trollope's own remembered impressions of political events; it listed various errors of fact, like Trollope's misdating Palmerston's distrust of France on the Spanish marriage issue by ten years (to a time when Queen Isabella 'was six years old, and as yet safe from the shameless designs of Louis Philippe and Guizot'); such mistakes were the result of Trollope's 'indisposition to refer to authority for the verification of facts which seemed to be fresh in the writer's recollection'. From the *Saturday*, Trollope would have expected little better. But he was disappointed to read a similar complaint in the *Athenaeum*, concerning 'the bald and slipshod statement of facts about which the author's recollections were not exact, and which he has not taken the trouble to correct or amplify by consulting competent authorities'.[13]

32

An Old Man

A GREAT concern for Trollope at the beginning of 1882 was Harry's candidature for membership in the Athenaeum. The balloting was scheduled for February: 'What a twitter I shall be in,' he wrote to Harry, who was in France throughout the time, 'and how I shall tear my hair if they blackball you.' He spent the two weeks previous to the election in London, worrying and campaigning. He contacted various members of the Athenaeum, including Montague Hughes Cookson, whose law pupil Harry had been, and Lord Arthur Russell, asking them to underwrite Harry's nomination; he asked Millais to get some Royal Academicians to do the same. To Rose at Harting he wrote, 'They tell me that Harry is safe. Though in truth a man is never safe; but . . . many more have written their names on his card.' When the day finally arrived, 13 February, it ended, as Trollope told Harry, in 'a jolly triumph': 'I was awfully nervous. But when the balloting began the Secretary came to me and told me that you would certainly get in. . . . I remained there—as did Millais. . . . Nevertheless up to the end I was in a funk. . . . At a quarter to 7 a dozen men headed by the Secretary came to me and told me the result. . . . One blackball in 10 excludes,—but one in 50 would not have kept you out. I congratulate you with all my heart.' Harry, who had never done anything of note in the world of letters, who spent little time in London, who knew practically no members of the Athenaeum, was elected by the extraordinary margin of 204 votes to 4. The vote was clearly a tribute to Trollope. He promised to accompany Harry on his first appearance at the club: 'I think that you should buy a scarlet uniform and a white feather and spurs. . . . But if you feel too 'umble for that I will take you to that dragon the porter and when we have passed him we will go and have a modest mutton chop together. After the porter there are no dragons.'[1]

Another concern that brought Trollope to London was his health. A Petersfield doctor, Robert Shackleford Cross, had recently diagnosed him as having angina pectoris. 'I had a terrible verdict pronounced against me,' he told a friend, 'I am to eat and drink, and get up and sit down at my peril, and may drop dead at any moment.'² He went to see a London heart specialist, William Murrell, who practised at 38 Weymouth Street, just off Harley Street. Murrell was a young man, but already the leading authority on angina (he had published an article on 'Nitroglycerine as a Remedy for Angina Pectoris' in the *Lancet* in 1879—the drug is still the prescribed treatment). Trollope reported to Harry that Murrell 'pretends to know especially the inns [*sic*] and outs of Angina pectoris. He says that I have not a symtom of A.P. and that Cross is an old idiot. I am disposed to believe him.' A week later he told Harry that what Murrell said was 'mainly true', but that Cross was perhaps right in other things: 'I have got to be old, and nearly worn out by another disease,' a hernia.³ But his greatest distress came from asthma. Trollope apparently suffered not from bronchial asthma but from what came to be called cardiac asthma. The root of the problem is high blood-pressure, which loads the left side of the heart, congests the lungs, and brings on attacks of breathlessness, especially at night.⁴ Trollope often not only could not sleep, but could not continue lying down.

A strange aspect of the asthma was that it afflicted him more in his new country place at Harting than in London. About to visit Dr Murrell again in mid-April, he wrote to Mrs Meetkerke, 'What I fear is that I shall be told at last to live altogether in town,—or anywhere but here. I have taken a house and furnished it, and at my age it will be very mischievous to make another moving; and the more so as this place suits my wife.' The air at Harting, he told Harry, was 'too good' for his asthma, and he proposed that the two of them take a place in London: 'Can not we have three rooms between us, and some kind of servant for us (to ourselves). A small flat would be the thing if it is not too dear.'⁵

His ailments made him more conscious of death. He told Alfred Austin, 'I have been well,—off and on. That is I have been in the doctors hands and have had dreadful things threatened me,—angina pectoris and God knows what. But I do not believe them. Tom . . . writes as though a life indefinitely prolonged had allurements. Do you know Tennyson's "Two Voices"? Each voice speaks falsely. The small voice counsels death for wrong reasons; and the other, life by arguments equally fallacious. . . . There is nothing to fear in death,—if you be wise. There is so much to fear in life, whether you be wise or foolish. That should have been the line of argument.'⁶ He continued to worry about an incapacitating illness, now apparently a definite possibility. Lucas Collins said Trollope was 'fond of quoting, in the way of preference of a speedy to a lingering death, Lady Macbeth's words—"Stand not upon the order of your going, But go at once."'[7] Trollope told Tom that he thought 'the time has come upon me of which I have often spoken to you, in which I should know that it were better that I were dead.' He told Mrs Meetkerke, 'There is only one way out of the trouble that I see.'[8]

On the other hand, he tried to keep up his pace. Murrell prescribed palliatives, including chloral ('I take quarts of medicine, and mountains of pills,' he wrote to Tom[9]), and warned him not to over-work or over-exert himself. Mrs Meetkerke recorded that the injunction was useless: 'He was extraordinarily impatient and reckless of his own condition; would still dash out of railway-carriages before the stopping of the train, would hurry in and out of cabs, and give way in all things to his usual impetuosity.'[10] And, of course, writing, illness or no, went on as usual, though at a somewhat slower rate. He finished *Palmerston* on 1 February, reported to Isbister that he would spend two weeks checking through the manuscript, and then began a novel called *An Old Man's Love*, in 'one volume (or two)' as he noted uncharacteristically in his working diary. He wrote a modest average of six pages per day, with a few days off most weeks. He completed the story on 9 May. Once again, as in *Dr Wortle's School*, he put something of himself into the central figure. William Whittlestaff, the 'old man' of the title, is fifty, and he had fallen in love with the twenty-five-year-old Mary Lawrie, whom he has taken into his house after the death of her father and stepmother left her alone and penniless. She, not having heard for three years from her undeclared young lover, John Gordon, accepts Whittlestaff's offer of marriage, though she does so chiefly out of gratitude; then Gordon reappears, and Whittlestaff, after some struggle, surrenders her to the younger suitor. The Trollope-to-Whittlestaff transmutations are not difficult to see. As a young man Whittlestaff had tried to get an Oxford fellowship and to devote himself to literature: 'But the lad did not succeed . . . and neither father nor mother ever knew the amount of suffering which he endured thereby. He became plaintive and wrote poetry. . . . the sense of failure made him sad at heart. And his father, when he was in those straits, only laughed at him, not at all believing the assurances of his son's misery.' His engaged love jilts him (one thinks of Lily Dale and John Eames); he entertains half-serious thoughts of suicide; 'He took to his classics for consolation, and read the philosophy of Cicero, and the history of Livy, and the war chronicles of Caesar.' It is not surprising to find here something akin to Trollope's favourite analogy for his own novel writing: the classics did Whittlestaff good 'in the same way that the making of many shoes would have done him good had he been a shoemaker'.[11]

Moreover, 'No one ever considered that Mr. Whittlestaff as a young man was a fool or malicious; but people did think that he was reticent and honest. The inner traits of his character were very difficult to read.' That was because he affected 'a manner of speech which practice had now made habitual, but which he had originally adopted with the object of hiding his shamefacedness under the veil of a dashing manner. . . . His fellowship, his poetry, and his early love were all, to his thinking, causes of disgrace, which required to be buried deep within his own memory.' Although he 'boils over in anger', is 'pugnacious' and 'passionate' in his speech, and can be guilty of 'incivility' and 'want of courtesy', nevertheless he is inwardly all 'maundering softness'. Other people do not detect that 'vacillating softness' nor the struggle it cost him 'to learn to become stern and cruel'.[12] Mary Lawrie seems in no way like Kate Field, and the situations in the novel are entirely unlike his own and hers—either when Trollope was nearing his fifties or in the present. Doubtless his feelings for Kate, albeit disguised, perhaps half even from himself, were in some way the inspiration for the story. Trollope locked the manuscript of *An Old Man's Love* in his desk drawer where that of *An Autobiography* had lain since 1876.*

Within a week of completing *An Old Man's Love*, Trollope went to Ireland to collect material for a novel about the land agitation there. Always intractable, the Irish problem was at its worst. In 1877 the Home Rule movement, launched in 1870 by Isaac Butt (the barrister who had cross-examined Trollope in Tralee in 1848) to re-establish through lawful means an Irish Parliament, passed to the more aggressive leadership of Charles Parnell. The winter of 1878–9 was exceptionally disastrous for small farmers, the result of bad weather, poor crops, and slumping prices. Many tenants were evicted; another famine was feared. In Mayo, Galway, and other places in the West, demonstrations were held under the leadership of Michael Davitt, who in October 1879 founded the Land League, with Parnell as its president. The League comprised moderates and extremists, from Home Rulers agitating for reform by parliamentary action to Fenians seeking an independent republic through armed rebellion, along with distressed tenants of no particular political goal beyond the relief of their immediate problems. The 'Land War' took hold. In

---

* After Trollope's death, Harry, having arranged for the publication of the *Autobiography* with Blackwood, asked £500 for serial and book rights to *An Old Man's Love*, but the publisher paid only £225. This last published of Trollope's novels appeared in March 1884, after Trollope had been dead for 15 months.

September 1880 Captain Charles Boycott, a land agent at Lough Mask, Co. Mayo, was subjected to the ostracism that was to take its name from him. As evictions increased, so did retaliatory Irish 'outrages' against landowners, through vandalism, boycott, arson, and murder. The very rule of law seemed threatened. Gladstone, back in office since April 1880, found that once again the Irish problem would be a thorn in his side. As the 'war' grew more intense, the government passed a Coercion Bill, suspending the right of habeas corpus. But Gladstone, long sympathetic towards Ireland, then passed in August 1881 his second Land Act, providing the 'Three F's'—fixity of tenure, fair rents (to be established by a Land Commission), and free sale (the tenant's right to sell his improvements to a new tenant). But the League now wanted nothing less than tenant ownership, and the Land War, inflamed by Parnell's speeches, continued. The government reacted by imprisoning Parnell and other leaders and eventually outlawing the League itself. But with relative moderates like Parnell in prison, Irish violence ('Captain Moonlight') became still more prevalent, and after six months, in March 1882, the government released Parnell and eased the Coercion Laws in exchange for his promised efforts to temper the militants. The Chief Secretary for Ireland, W. E. Forster (a good friend of Trollope) resigned in protest. Then his successor, Lord Frederick Cavendish, was assassinated on his first day in Ireland, 6 May 1882, in Dublin's Phoenix Park, along with the Permanent Under-Secretary, Thomas Henry Burke. The deed was the work of a secret society, the Invincibles, and deplored by almost all Irishmen. The government reinstated even more lethal coercion measures. [13]

It was at this time, just after the Phoenix Park murders, that Trollope, taking Florence Bland with him, left to visit Ireland to gather first-hand information. His mind—like that of most Englishmen at the time—was already set: he considered the Fenians paid criminal assassins instigated by Irish-Americans, and he thought Parnell, who also enjoyed much American support, only a shade better; the Land League he deemed immoral, and inimical to that healthy closeness and mutual trust so often found—as he thought—between landlord and tenant. What troubled Trollope most in the Irish situation was the fact that the second Land Act, which he considered altogether unjust, was the work of the politician he most admired, Gladstone* (he attached some of the blame to John Bright's influence with Gladstone). [14]

---

* Trollope knew Gladstone only casually; when Gladstone had just taken office for the second time, Trollope wrote to him, on 2 May 1880, the two having attended the Royal Academy Banquet the day previous: 'May I venture to ask whether I have in aught offended you? For some years I

Trollope, having lived in Ireland for so many years and having closely followed political developments there for forty years, could have written his novel without stirring from Harting. (One can imagine Trollope reminding himself—or his listeners—that Gladstone had never been to Ireland until 1877 and then only for three weeks.) None the less, he believed that if he were to speak authoritatively, he must do so from recent experience. He probably also wanted to show himself that, ill health and age notwithstanding, he could still bang about the world. His conviction that his asthma would be less troublesome anywhere other than at Harting was an added enticement. He visited the scenes of the worst violence, in Cork, Limerick, Mayo, and Galway. At Cork he talked with Judge John O'Hagan, of the High Court of Justice and head of the Land Commission that Gladstone's bill had established to set fair rents; he also saw John Edward Vernon, Director of the Bank of Ireland and another member of O'Hagan's three-man Land Commission. He conferred with Charles Dalton Clifford Lloyd, Special Resident Magistrate for Killmallock, County Limerick. He visited various landowners, but as far as is known, had no contact with any member of the League. He also visited his old chief, Count Cornwall, still head of the Dublin Post Office. He sent Rose affectionate letters, mapping his progress, sharing his displeasure with Gladstone and Parnell; he reminisced about Clonmel—'We are just going to drive up to the slate quarries, where I remember going, you and I and the two Sankeys, nearly 40 years ago!!'—and inquired after her health and the house. 'How is the garden, and the cocks & hens, & especially the asparagus bed.'[15]

After four weeks in Ireland, he returned to Harting via London, and worked steadily on the novel. Tom and Fanny arrived at Harting on 1 August, but Anthony's asthma was especially bad during their stay. Wanting to get away from the air at Harting, he impatiently decided he needed more material for the book, and on 11 August left for another month's visit to Ireland, again taking Florence with him. He confined himself this time to Dublin, Kingstown, and Wicklow. From Glendalough, a scenic valley south of Dublin, he congratulated Rose on being in

have thought that you had, not unnaturally, forgotten me. But latterly,—and again yesterday,—I have been made to suppose that you purposely shunned me. Looking back over a long period I can fancy but one cause;—the offence I gave to a friend whom I believe you loved. . . . My sympathies are with you in all things; and as I want nothing from the Prime Minister, I can dare to endeavour to put you right if there be a mistake.' On the verso is written the outline of Gladstone's reply: 'Assure Mr T. there is not the smallest foundation for the apprehension he courteously expresses. I fear from what he says I must have been guilty of a rudeness quite unintentional and due only to the absorption of the present times, & I pray him to forgive it.'[16]

Switzerland while he was in this 'beastly place', beastly because someone else had taken their rooms: 'The rest of the house is abominable. It is very well that you did not come here. There would have been a kettle of fish! I grumble fearfully. The beggars I think would have brought you to an untimely end. However the brook still warbles just beneath our windows.' He had a bad attack of asthma, and left Glendalough for nearby Wooden Bridge; there he was entertained by Sir Charles Booth, 'a gin maker . . . [who] gave us the best dinner I ever ate'. He arranged to spend a night at the home of Sir Charles Stanley Monck, another of the Irish Land Commissioners. A week later he was able to consult with 'young Trevelyan'—George Otto Trevelyan, successor to the murdered Frederick Cavendish as Chief Secretary for Ireland. Trollope told him he doubted the government would be strong enough to invoke the new powers of trying and executing prisoners away from the scene of the crimes. Trevelyan 'blew me up, and told me that people did not know what they were talking about'.[17]

By mid-September, having returned first to London—where Tom came up to his bedroom at Garlant's to say goodbye—Trollope was back at Harting, working steadily on *The Landleaguers*. He incorporated into the novel all he could of recent developments in Ireland, drawing on some incidents almost as they happened, such as the massacre, in Galway, of five members of a peasant family called Joyce. (Trollope implies that the murders were the work of the Land League, although no evidence connected them with the League; rather, the fact that many of the murderers were named Joyce, and that they were quickly reported to the police, pointed to a local feud. In a letter to Lucas Collins, Trollope said he hoped the government would hang 'all the Joyces that are left'.[18]) *The Landleaguers*, set in Galway, near the town of Headford and the Mayo border, only a few miles from Lough Mask itself, was the most topical, the most overtly political of all his novels. Though cast in fictional form, it was, as one reviewer later said, more a political pamphlet than a novel.[19] The story concerns a decent Anglo Irish family victimized by Irish vandals and murderers. The sympathy with the Irish poor, so poignantly displayed in his very first novel nearly forty years earlier, found no voice here, as the focus is on the upright Protestant landowner Philip Jones, who is subjected to the destruction of his fields, boycott, and the murder of his young son. The prominence given to this boy of ten is altogether unusual (there is no child of comparable importance in all the rest of Trollope's fiction). Moreover the boy's conversion to Catholicism is unbelievable, and his murder atypically melodramatic for a Trollope novel. Not only is the story skewed, but the narrator continually instructs his readers in the rights and wrongs of the Irish situation, and at one point interrupts the story for a chapter-long essay, 'The State of Ireland', largely an attack on Gladstone's Land Act.[20]

The novelist in Trollope occasionally overcomes his overt political message. He makes Jones an honest landowner, though hardly pre-possessing, just but sullen, anxious to do no man an injustice, yet a little over-anxious to protect his own rights. Then too the Irish-American parliamentary reformer, Gerald O'Mahony—although the narrator frequently calls him 'ignorant of all political truths'—is amiable and 'thoroughly unselfish, and desirous of no violence'. Still, the novel lists heavily to a conservative, pro-English reading of events; the narrator implicitly seems to embrace the course of action recommended by the deeply prejudiced and embittered Black Tom Daly, master of the Galway Hounds (for the Land War has, ominously, put an end to hunting): 'Martial law with a regiment in each county, and a strong colonel to carry it out,—that is the only way of governing left us.' In the heroine Rachel O'Mahony, daughter of the radical politician, awkwardly connected to the main story by her love for Jones's elder son, there are fleeting reminders of Kate Field: Irish-American, she is independent, outspoken, frank; she enjoys the 'badinage of perfect equality' with her father and other men; she earns money by singing on the stage, and she moves without harm in the vulgar and slightly dangerous world of the London theatre. The narrator says she was as 'soft-hearted as any other girl. . . . She was loyal, affectionate, and dutiful. But there was missing to her a feminine weakness, which of all her gifts is the most valuable to an English woman, till she makes the mistake of bartering it away for women's rights.'[21]

Trollope was anxious to get *The Landleaguers* into print; for one thing, it was urgently topical; and the Land War was easing as he wrote. Bentley turned the story down for the *Temple Bar*, and Trollope arranged for its serialization in a weekly paper called *Life*. The instalments were scheduled to begin appearing on 16 November. He was willing to have the story commence before he had finished writing it, something he had not done since the hectic days of crowding the market in the 1860s. As it happened, he would not finish the novel.* On the morning of 3 November (the

---

* The unfinished *Landleaguers* was eventually published in three thin volumes in October 1883. Harry Trollope inserted a postscript saying that nothing was known of Trollope's intentions for the novel except that it was to end with two marriages and the hanging of the murderer of young Florian Jones.

evidence indicates), half-way through the forty-ninth of a planned sixty chapters of *The Landleaguers*, Trollope wrote, or rather dictated to Harry, who was staying with him in London, the last of his many millions of published words.[22]

The quantity of Trollope's accomplishment remains astonishing: forty-seven novels, five volumes of collected short stories, plus a handful of uncollected stories; four large travel books and the slight *Mastiffs*; three biographies, four collections of 'sketches' (hunting types, clergymen, travellers, tradesmen), an unpublished book of social criticism (*The New Zealander*), enough essays and reviews to fill three or four more volumes.[23] Of the forty-seven novels, twenty were the traditional three-volume length, nine were longer (the equivalent of four or five volumes), and twenty-three were shorter, one or two volumes. The great fecundity which Trollope so prided himself upon, occasionally rising to the nearly three novels a year that had so horrified the publisher in Paternoster Row, has often been held against his reputation, at least with critics. Certain reviewers believed that Trollope was writing too much as far back as 1857, before he had hit full stride. The Trollope reading public, on the other hand, along with many writers—Trollope has always been a writer's writer—have been grateful for the seemingly endless titles, that shelf in the British Museum groaning under their weight, that 'monument to British energy' as one reviewer had described it.

That readers would disagree about the relative merits of books amid so large a number is only natural. But the degree of difference of opinion about Trollope's novels is extraordinary. No one thinks that *Barnaby Rudge* is Dickens's greatest work, or *Philip* Thackeray's, or *Romola* George Eliot's,[24] but in Trollope's case there are people who rate, say, *Sir Harry Hotspur* as on a par with anything he ever wrote, while others dismiss it out of hand. Listing one's favourites among Trollope's many titles has long been a kind of endless game his readers play among themselves. It is true that from the first most people have over the years given pride of place to the six novels of the Barchester series, with special favour going to *Barchester Towers* (often thought of as Trollope's *Pride and Prejudice* in wide appeal) and to *The Last Chronicle*—many people's choice, and Trollope's own, for his single best novel. Among other Barchester titles, Trollope's contemporaries set great store by *Framley Parsonage*; later generations perhaps give the edge to *The Small House at Allington*. Next in popularity, and for many twentieth-century readers an even more sustained and realized achievement, has been the six-novel Palliser series, admired largely as a collective portrait of Plantagenet Palliser and Lady Glencora; among these books, in Trollope's day *The Eustace Diamonds* may have been the most admired; today the nod would go the Phineas novels or *The Duke's Children*. Among the 'independent' novels, *Orley Farm* stood out in Trollope's day, *The Way We Live Now* in ours. Other especially well-received works in Trollope's time were *The Three Clerks* and *Rachel Ray*; in the twentieth century, *Dr Wortle's School* and *Ayala's Angel*. But strong claims are made for *He Knew He Was Right* and *Is He Popenjoy?* One would have thought that with the winnowing of time some agreement would be nearer, but such is hardly the case, owing chiefly to Trollope's extraordinary evenness. The 'essential Trollope' was there from beginning to end, a fact attested to by the high critical regard that has settled upon his very first novel, *The Macdermots*, and upon *Mr Scarborough's Family*, finished about a year before his death. In nearly all of them, as George Bernard Shaw said, 'He delivered us from the marvels, senseless accidents, cat's-cradle plots of old romance, and gave us, to the best of his ability, a faithful picture of the daily life of the upper and middle classes.'[25] The *Saturday Review*, which had kept up an unbroken commentary, negative and positive, from 1857 till the end, said finally that only the 'stupid critic' would place Trollope in the second rank, that his characters 'will live in the memory of that very useful and much-abused creature, the general reader, and will help to keep alive Mr. Trollope's memory as one of the very first of English novelists'.[26] Trollope, as one of his most perceptive modern critics said, 'wrote better than he or his contemporaries realized, and . . . left behind him more novels of lasting value than any other writer in English'.[27]

Many of Trollope's contemporaries were puzzled or intrigued by the apparent incompatibility between the man they knew and the story-teller; other novelists—Thackeray, George Eliot, Dickens—did not give rise to similar questions. The contrast was especially surprising to those who knew him only slightly. In 1866 Lady Rose Fane, staying at Lord Houghton's estate, where Trollope was also a guest, wrote, 'I wish I had never seen Mr. Trollope. I think he is detestable—vulgar, noisy & domineering—a mixture of Dickens vulgarity & Mr. Burtons selfsufficiency—as unlike his books as possible.' But friends also remarked the contrast between author and his novels: James Bryce said that at first 'you were disappointed not to find so clever a writer more original', and even when, on further acquaintance he appeared more of a piece with his books, one still 'could never quite recognise in him the delineator of Lily

Dale'. Charles Lever, while denying high status to Trollope's books, was, none the less, 'always surprised that he could write them'. Frederic Harrison, describing Trollope's 'burly ubiquity and irrepressible energy in everything' as one of the 'marvels' of his generation, was mystified as to how 'such a colossus of blood and bone should spend his mornings, before we were out of bed, in analysing the hypersensitive conscience of an archdeacon, the secret confidences whispered between a prudent mamma and lovelorn young lady, or the subtle meanderings of Marie Goesler's heart'. W. P. Frith, an intimate of Trollope's, said, 'It would be impossible to imagine anything less like his novels than the author of them. The books, full of gentleness, grace, and refinement; the writer of them, bluff, loud, stormy, and contentious, neither a brilliant talker nor a good speaker.' Cecil Hay, referring to Trollope as 'Mr. Grizzly', speaks of him wonderingly as the 'pleasantest of romance writers, and gruffest and roughest of conversationalists'. William Dean Howells called him 'undoubtedly one of the finest of artists as well as the most Philistine of men'. It might even be that Trollope's loud, aggressive social manner cost him serious consideration for a peerage: in 1881 Lord Acton, an influential friend of Gladstone, wrote to Mary Gladstone, the Prime Minister's daughter, about having talked of 'bringing in outsiders'—Trollope and Morley—only to find that 'Trollope is condemned as noisy'.[28]

Most of Trollope's friends and acquaintance despaired of reconciling the man and the author of the books; they invariably qualified their assessments of Trollope as gruff, outspoken, and boisterous by referring to his proverbial honesty and loyalty: 'a kinder-hearted man and truer friend never lived' (Frith); 'a good fellow . . . [with] few jealousies and no rancours' (Lever); 'Crusty, quarrelsome, wrong-headed, prejudiced, obstinate, kind-hearted and thoroughly honest old Tony Trollope' (G. A. Sala); 'as good and staunch a friend as ever lived' (Wilkie Collins). A few insisted that they saw the author in the man, but offered little evidence. Locker-Lampson, for example, admitting that Trollope's friends and acquaintance often wondered how 'so commonplace a person' could have written such novels, could himself say only, 'I maintain that so honourable and interesting a man could not be commonplace.' T. H. S. Escott resorted to a simple assertion that style is the man, and that those who did not see the author in the 'unreserved friend' and 'candid, plain-speaking companion' were lacking in perception. Fred Chapman told Rosa Praed, an Australian novelist, that his wife fretted constantly after Trollope's death, saying 'she never loved any one so much—barring me. . . . He was a very good fellow, very kind. . . . I fancy you met him at our house; if so, and not knowing more of him, your impression would be that he was a rough boisterous man, and too uncouth for the society of ladies—He was the reverse, he was as tender hearted as a girl.'[29]

To some extent the dissimilarity between the man and the books does not matter. That the 'author' of a novel is a 'persona' or mask, a creation, like the story itself, quite distinct from the man who put pen to paper, has become a critical commonplace. Even less identifiable with the man who wrote is the narrator. Still, one expects to find some correspondences between the man and the story-teller. (Trollope himself would have vociferously insisted that he and the narrator were one.) In Trollope's case, the search for those correspondences is especially difficult because Trollope's own personality is so elusive. He is the demanding, sometimes bullying postal official; he is the loud, outspoken, abrupt, aggressive, occasionally discourteous social animal, and the successful, outspoken, opinionated, knowing, practical man of the world. At the same time he is the clumsy, unhappy, diffident boy and youth, the outsider coveting popularity; he is the still-shy, self-conscious, thin-skinned man, almost abnormally sensitive to the good opinions of others; he is the man with a quiet but decided streak of pessimism and melancholy, someone who never could but be amazed at how he had, as he said, fallen so wonderfully well on his feet after having come so close to failing utterly, and who silently feared all he had accomplished might slip away again.

It is easier to recognize the writer in Trollope's shy component, sensitive, slightly melancholic, tender-hearted to a fault; the man who enjoyed quiet talk and cigars with G. H. Lewes or Robert Bell in the small hours (it was generally groups that brought out the aggressiveness), acting the adviser to young authors or the paterfamilias to confiding young women, the man in whom, witnesses said, children delighted. This Anthony Trollope comes rather closer to the author of gentle, quiet, subtle fiction, and to the calm, fair-minded narrator who exists on such intimate terms with his readers as to make even his poor books somehow enjoyable to those who like this narrative voice; a narrator who, even when dealing with his most villainous characters, is drawn to them, is tolerant of their sins, always willing to look to circumstances and sympathize with human frailty.

But where to place the gruff, hard-boiled, shouting Anthony Trollope of anecdote and legend, the unhelpful arguer, the defender of commonplaces, the conversationalist who roared down his opponents? What has he to do with the novels? Perhaps this, that the gruffness, the apparent insistence on the commonplace, the shouting, the violent gesticulation, the belittling of his own accomplishment, the loud joking, the bullying, the almost physical attack he made upon all chores of work and play, the energetic absorption he gave to everything, these protected his inner vulnerable self. The most remarkable thing about this strategy—or act, or stance, or public persona—is that it fulfilled his need. It helped him to keep his balance, to prosper; it helped the other Trollope to continue his day-dreaming, his castle-building; it helped him to create yet another Trollope, the story-teller who wrote novels.

33

Last Days

TROLLOPE'S last weeks of conscious active life were characteristically filled with occupation and pleasure: with family, friends, a last visit to Somerset, and with his work as a writer. His chief concern as a family man was the education of his grandson, Frank Trollope, Fred's eldest child. On 4 September Fred wrote from Australia to confirm that he would send Frank to England in early 1883. Trollope had offered to take the boy into his house and send him to George Robinson's school at Margate. As for visiting England himself, Fred saw no hope. He now had six children, including two daughters, Frances Kathleen, and Effie, and he told his father how the very latest child, John Arthur—to be called Jack—'is like nobody else in the world if he is not like you, and he is so far a great deal bigger and stronger than any of the other children.'[1] Trollope probably never saw Fred's letter.*

On 2 October, Trollope and Harry took rooms at Garlant's Hotel; they rented the first and second floors, which included two bedrooms.

The next day Trollope wrote to Rose asking her to send him, in a registered package, the first six chapters of *The Landleaguers*; he had forgotten to bring them with him, and he wanted the printer for *Life* to get to work on them as soon as possible. He said that he would come back to Harting on Friday, and would bring fresh fish with him.

On 5 October he told her 'of course' they should attend the Lord Mayor's dinner at Mansion House on 26 October: 'Mind you carry a bottle of claret in your pocket and if you could take one of your fowls it would be a good thing.'

---

* Young Frank was sent to England in early 1883, despite Trollope's death. Fred, who eventually had eight children, died in 1910. In 1937 his third son, Frederic Farrand Trollope (1875–1957), inherited the family baronetcy.

In 1884 Harry Trollope married Ada Strickland, of Jersey, who had been in school at Aachen with Florence Bland. Harry and Ada had two children, Muriel Rose (1885–1953) and Thomas Anthony (1893–1931). Harry died in 1926, just past his 80th birthday.

Florence Bland, who never married, died in 1908. Rose Trollope died on 25 May 1917, aged 96.

Last Days

Back home at Harting, on 7 October, Saturday, he wrote somewhat peevishly, and laconically, to one G. N. Richardson, 'The Fraser's Magazine is I believe dead. At any rate I am not going to write a story for it.' (The magazine ceased publication with the October 1882 issue.)

On Tuesday, 10 October, up in London, he again visited Dr Murrell. 'There is nothing really to say,' he wrote to his wife, '—except that I am to see him again next week.' He suggested that Rose should take Harry's bedroom the night of the Lord Mayor's dinner. On that same day he made what turned out to be the last of many arrangements with many different publishers, a threefold agreement with Chatto & Windus for £600 apiece for the book rights to *Mr Scarborough's Family* and *The Landleaguers*, and £100 for a cheap edition of *Marion Fay*, subject to Chapman's permission. That evening Harry gave him and John Bannister (the stage name of Graham Showers) dinner at the Garrick.

On the 11th he met Fred Chapman, who agreed to the release of the *Marion Fay* rights to Chatto. He wrote to Rose, promising to bring home four pounds of coffee and some fish; and explained that Harry would be turned out of his room so that she might see 'what sort of place I live in'. If she disliked the idea of the Lord Mayor's dinner, they might cancel out of it. (They did so.) He sent his best love to Florence who was recovering from an illness. He and Harry dined at Goods. Harry had warned him that the wine was '*beastly*', and Anthony said he feared he would be 'taken ill and carried away in the middle' of the meal.

On the 13th he invited Browning to dine with him at the Garrick on Wednesday, 1 November.

On the 15th, from Harting, where he had gone for the weekend, he wrote to Mrs Jessie White Mario the disappointing news that Chapman & Hall would not take on an English translation of her life of Garibaldi.

Up in town again, he wrote to E. A. Freeman that he would make his planned visit to him in Somerset on Wednesday of the following week: 'I can, with due time, walk up anything,—only I cant sleep, walking or not walking. I cant write, as you see, because my hand is paralysed. I cant sit easily because of a huge truss I wear, and now has come this damnable asthma! But still I am very good to look at; and as I am not afraid to die, I am as happy as other people.'

On the 24th he told Rose, 'I start tomorrow to Somersetshire, and regret as I always do, that I have promised to go. But still I think it is better to go about. I had a bad night on Monday, rather.' He related how he had been looking in earnest for some more permanent London rooms than Garlant's Hotel: 'I am vacillating between Halfmoon Street and Victoria Street, the

first furnished, & the second not so.' He had also visited his old friend
General Edward Hamley, sympathizing with Hamley's disgust at receiv-
ing so little credit for his part in the defeat of Arabi Pasha's rebellion in
Egypt.[2]

On the 25th he went to Freeman's house, at Somerlease near Wells.
Late that afternoon, Freeman took him, in the company of the (Catholic)
Bishop of Clifton, over some of the hills between Wells and Wedmore.
Trollope enjoyed the scenery, but had trouble with mud and stiles.

On the next day he was shown Wells and Glastonbury. Trollope allowed
that Barsetshire was Somerset, but denied that Barchester was Wells.
Winchester, where he had gone to school, was Barchester, and St Cross
had been the original for Hiram's Hospital. Freeman argued that Wells
and other places had helped to supply ideas for Barchester. Were not
towers, for example, more a feature of Wells than of Winchester? and was
not the notion of old woolcombers taken from Wells? No. 'Barset was
Somerset, but Barchester was Winchester, not Wells.' He had never even
heard of the Wells woolcombers.[3]

On the evening of 27 October Trollope arrived back in London, and
from the Athenaeum wrote to Cardinal Newman thanking him for an
asthma remedy, the inhaling of smoke from burning saltpetre paper,
which Newman had sent him through Lord Emly: 'I will at once try it. . . .
I fear that it will not be efficacious, because no smoking, or nothing that
touches my throat, is of any avail. . . . May I be allowed to take this
opportunity also of telling your Eminence how great has been the pleasure
which I have received from understanding that you have occasionally read
and been amused by some of my novels. It is when I hear that such men as
yourself have been gratified that I feel that I have not worked altogether in
vain; but there is no man as to whom I can say that his good opinion would
give me such intense gratification as your own.'[4]

On the same day, in his last traced letter, Trollope wrote to Lord Emly,
'I can hardly tell you the amount of pleasure which I have received from
the Cardinal's opinions of my novels.' (Newman answered Trollope the
next day, thanking him for the kind sentiments, and saying that he read
many of Trollope's novels 'again and again'.[5])

On 1 November Trollope had a 'big dinner' at the Garrick for Browning
and other guests.

On 2 November he dined, along with Freeman, at the home of
Alexander Macmillan in Tooting. Freeman said that Trollope 'talked as
well and heartily as usual'.[6]

On Friday, 3 November, according to a story that is undocumented but which Harry or some other knowledgeable source may have related to Trollope's biographer, Trollope was disturbed during the afternoon by a German street band playing outside his window at Garlant's Hotel in Suffolk Street, and got himself excited while engaging in an altercation with the leader. (That this sounds suspiciously like Trollope's own account of such troubles a few years earlier in Montagu Square need not necessarily invalidate the story; another version says an organ-grinder was the culprit.[7])

That evening Trollope dined with John Tilley (again a widower, the third Mrs Tilley having died in 1880) and his daughter Edith at Tilley's house in St George's Square. After dinner the party retired to the drawing-room where Edith read aloud from a current best-selling comic novel, F. Anstey's *Vice Versa*. For a while 'Uncle Tony roared as usual', and then suddenly Tilley and Edith realized that as they were laughing he was silent. Trollope had had a stroke.[8]

Trollope's seizure paralysed his right side, almost completely impairing his powers of reason and of speech. He was in the hands of William Murrell, the heart specialist whom he had been seeing, Sir William Jenner, Physician in Ordinary to the Queen, who had been called in as consultant, and Sir Richard Quain, his regular London physician and a close friend. (Rose for a while was dissatisfied with Jenner.) In the following weeks, Murrell and Jenner issued a dozen bulletins in *The Times* on his condition. For the first ten days the announcements were optimistic: the doctors said that though the seizure had 'largely overpowered his mental faculties', he was 'improving' and, later, 'decidedly better'. On 10 November they said, 'He now is able to walk and also to use the right arm a little. . . . he sleeps well, and his nights are quiet.' By the 14th they said he was 'better . . . except that the power of speech has not yet returned'. On the 16th Trollope was reported as 'making slow, but sure progress towards recovery'.[9] The bulletins then ceased for two weeks.

Mrs Meetkerke recorded that for a time the Suffolk Street doors 'were besieged with anxiously inquiring visitors'.[10] He was removed to a nursing home, not many blocks away, at 34 Welbeck Street. Harry wrote to Tom in Rome that although the doctors still thought his 'ultimate recovery' assured, he himself was alarmed at his father's attempting to get out of the carriage while being carried to the nursing home, and at other 'unreasonable' actions, such as wanting to get undressed in the dining-room.[11]

On 2 December Murrell and Jenner resumed their bulletins, saying that their patient had 'lost strength'. Millais, who went to see Trollope frequently, wrote to William Howard Russell that there was 'little hope':

'he is rarely conscious and has only been able to utter one word since the attack—"No".'[12] On 5 December the doctors said his condition was 'undoubtedly critical', and on 6 December they reported him 'lying in critical condition' and 'unconscious'.[13]

Trollope died at 6 p.m. on Wednesday, 6 December 1882, at 34 Welbeck Street. The relatively small funeral was on Saturday, 9 December. Millais, Browning, G. W. Rusden, Frederic Chapman, Francis Charles Lawley, and Charles Stuart-Wortley were among the friends who accompanied the hearse, which left Welbeck Street at 12 noon. At one o'clock Trollope's body was laid in the ground, not far from Thackeray's grave, in Kensal Green Cemetery.

NOTES

Place of publication is London, unless otherwise stated.

LIST OF SHORT TITLES USED IN THE NOTES

An Autobiography	Anthony Trollope, *An Autobiography*, ed. Frederick Page (Oxford, 1950)
Escott	T. H. S. Escott, *Anthony Trollope: His Work, Associates, and Literary Originals* (1913)
FET	Frances Eleanor Trollope, *A Memoir of Frances Trollope* [*Frances Trollope: Her Life and Literary Work*], 2 vols. (1895)
Garnett Letters	*The Garnett Letters*, ed. Cecilia Payne-Gaposchkin [privately printed] (1979)
Heineman	Helen Heineman, *Mrs Trollope: The Triumphant Feminine in the Nineteenth Century* (Athens, Ohio, 1979)
Letters	*The Letters of Anthony Trollope*, 2 vols., ed. N. John Hall (Stanford, Calif., 1983)
NCF	*Nineteenth-Century Fiction*
Parrish Collection	The Morris L. Parrish Collection of Victorian Novelists, Princeton University Library, Princeton NJ
Sadleir, *Bibliography*	Michael Sadleir, *Trollope: A Bibliography* (1928)
Smalley	Donald Smalley, ed., *Trollope: The Critical Heritage* (1969)
Super, *Post Office*	R. H. Super, *Trollope in the Post Office* (Ann Arbor, Mich., 1981)
TAT	Thomas Adolphus Trollope, *What I Remember*, 3 vols. (1887–9)
Taylor Collection	The Robert H. Taylor Collection, Princeton University Library, Princeton, NJ
Whiting	Lilian Whiting, *Kate Field: A Record* (Boston, 1899)

CHAPTER 1: GENTLE ORIGINS

1. *The Prime Minister*, ch. 1; see also *Doctor Thorne*, where the title character is well aware of 'the advantage held by men who have grandfathers over those who have none, or none worth talking about' (ch. 2).
2. M. N. Trollope, *A Memoir of the Family of Trollope* (1897), 49–72, 92–4; Burke's *Peerage* and *Landed Gentry*.
3. *Victoria County History of Hertfordshire*, ed. W. Page, (1912), iii. 267–9.
4. He first matriculated at St John's College, Cambridge, and was admitted as a scholar in 1792; doubtless he was waiting for a place on the foundation of New College. His father had also been admitted to the Middle Temple, 20 Nov. 1784. J. Venn, *Alumni Cantabrigienses*, pt. 2, vol. vi (Cambridge, 1954), p. 234; *Register of Admissions to the Honourable Society of the Middle Temple* (1949), ii. 417; *Records of the Honorable Society of Lincoln's Inn* (1896), ii. 26.

5. Information about income and property from Heineman, p. 262, nn. 14 and 20, using Revd Anthony's will and Thomas Anthony's marriage settlement (Public Record Office Prob. 11/1453; Gloucestershire Records Office, D34/9/94).
6. TAT i. 57–8.
7. Heineman, 261, n. 5.
8. Mary Gresley is the heroine of a short story by that name; Lord Alfred Gresley is a character in *Sir Harry Hotspur of Humblethwaite*.
9. FET i. 28.
10. TAT i. 19.
11. Heineman, 7.
12. FET i. 26.
13. *An Autobiography*, 20.
14. MS Taylor Collection; Michael Sadleir, *Trollope: A Commentary*, 3rd edn. (Oxford, 1961), 41–2.
15. MS Taylor Collection; Sadleir, 42–3.
16. FET i. 23; Heineman, 10, 263, n. 21.
17. MS Taylor Collection; Heineman, 12, 13.
18. MS Taylor Collection; Heineman, 14.
19. MS Taylor Collection; Sadleir, 49.
20. MS Taylor Collection; Heineman, 14, 16.
21. *An Autobiography*, 20.
22. Heineman, 13–15.
23. Ibid., 16, 263, n. 36.
24. TAT i. 16–17.
25. *An Autobiography*, 22.
26. St George's Church Parish Register, Greater London Record Office.
27. Heineman, 17.
28. *An Autobiography*, 2.

CHAPTER 2: HARROW DAY BOY

1. Heineman, p. 264, n. 5.
2. TAT i. 72.
3. Heineman, 21–3.
4. *A History of the County of Middlesex*, ed. J. S. Cockburn and T. F. T. Baker (1971), iv. 212–13.
5. TAT i. 63–6.
6. *Gentleman's Magazine*, 88 (1818), 560; and 89 (1819), 634.
7. TAT i. 68.
8. *Orley Farm*, ch. 1.
9. *An Autobiography*, 57.
10. FET i. 47–8.
11. 'The National Gallery', *Saint James's Magazine*, 2 (Sept. 1861), 166.
12. TAT i. 14–16, 57–60.
13. *An Autobiography*, 14.
14. TAT i. 58.
15. Ibid. 13–14.
16. Ibid. 88.

17. Charles Merivale, *Autobiography of Dean Merivale*, ed. Judith Anne Merivale (1899), 31.
18. N. John Hall, *Salmagundi: Byron, Allegra, and the Trollope Family* (Pittsburgh, 1975), 67.
19. *History of the County of Middlesex*, iv. 212.
20. TAT i. 93.
21. Michael Sadleir, *Trollope: A Commentary*, 3rd edn. (1961), 57–8.
22. FET i. 92.
23. Hall, *Salmagundi*, 71–2.
24. Harrow School Admission Register, Vaughan Library, Harrow School; *Harrow School Register, 1800–1911*, ed. Dauglish and Stephenson, 87.
25. *An Autobiography*, 2.
26. *Harrow School*, ed. E. W. Howson and G. T. Warner (1898), 67–8; E. D. Laborde, *Harrow School: Yesterday and Today* (1948), 46–8; see Richard Poate Stebbins, 'Trollope at Harrow School', *The Trollopian*, 1 (Summer 1945), 35–44.
27. TAT i. 78.
28. TAT i. 73.
29. Laborde, *Harrow School*, 182.
30. Saba Holland, *A Memoir of the Reverend Sydney Smith* (1855), i. 6–7; see John Chandos, *Boys Together: English Public Schools 1800–1864* (New Haven, Conn., 1984), 37.
31. 'Thoughts of an Outsider: Public Schools', *Cornhill Magazine*, 27 (Mar. 1873), 287; Chandos, *Boys Together*, 31.
32. Sir William Gregory, *An Autobiography*, ed. Lady Gregory (1894), 36.
33. *An Autobiography*, 4.
34. Sir G. F. Duckett, *Anecdotal Reminiscences of an Octo-Nonogenarian* (Kendal, 1895), 6.
35. *An Autobiography*, 4.
36. Charles Merivale, *Autobiography*, 26.
37. *An Autobiography*, 5–6.
38. Heineman, 27 ff.
39. Ibid. 37–8.
40. FET i. 73; Heineman, 30 ff.; Frances Trollope MS Journal, University of Illinois Library.
41. FET i. 52.
42. *The Friendships of Mary Russell Mitford as Recorded in Letters from Her Literary Correspondences*, ed. Alfred Guy L'Estrange (1882), i. 168–9; Heineman, 39.
43. FET i. 76–7.

CHAPTER 3: WYKEHAMIST

1. Winchester records show Anthony elected in the summer of 1826 and admitted on 14 April 1827; he left sometime in the summer of 1830; information supplied by P. J. Gwyn, College Archivist.
2. FET i. 95.
3. *An Autobiography*, 8.
4. *The Bertrams*, ch. 1.

5. 'Public Schools', *Fortnightly Review*, 2 (1 Oct. 1865), 476–8.
6. TAT i. 138–9.
7. 'Public Schools', 478–9.
8. *An Autobiography*, 18.
9. TAT i. 115–17.
10. FET i. 78.
11. *An Autobiography*, 11–12, 3.
12. Heineman, 43–5.
13. Ibid. 47–8.
14. Harriet Garnett to Julia Pertz, 12 Dec. 1827, *Garnett Letters*, 156–7; Heineman, 48.
15. Frances Trollope to Julia Pertz, 26 Dec. 1827, *Garnett Letters*, 157; Heineman, 49.
16. Frances Trollope to Harriet Garnett, 7 Dec. 1828, *Garnett Letters*, 164; Heineman, 50; Frances Trollope to Charles Wilkes, 14 Feb. 1828, quoted in Heineman, 50; FET i. 105ff.
17. Heineman, 52–3; Mrs Trollope, *Domestic Manners of the Americans* (1832), chs. 3 and 4.
18. FET i. 113.
19. Cincinnati *Gazette*, 28 Mar. 1828; quoted in Heineman, 52–3.
20. Heineman, 52–7.
21. Frances Trollope to Harriet Garnett, 7 Dec. 1828, *Garnett Letters*, 163; Heineman, 63.
22. Quoted in Heineman, 273–4, n. 16.
23. Frances Trollope to Julia Pertz, 22 Aug. 1831, *Garnett Letters*, 176; Heineman, 66.
24. *An Autobiography*, 7.
25. Heineman, 65ff.; *Garnett Letters*, 175–7; FET i. 125–6.
26. FET i. 129.
27. *An Autobiography*, 9–10.
28. Escott, 16.
29. *An Autobiography*, 42–3.

CHAPTER 4: HARROW WEALD

1. *An Autobiography*, 10.
2. TAT ii. 213.
3. FET i. 144.
4. *An Autobiography*, 9, 2–3.
5. *Orley Farm*, ch. 12.
6. *An Autobiography*, 14.
7. TAT i. 297.
8. *An Autobiography*, 14.
9. Ibid. 13, 12.
10. TAT i. 240.
11. *An Autobiography*, 15.
12. TAT i. 87.
13. *An Autobiography*, 14–15.

14. *John Caldigate*, chs. 1, 3.
15. *Mr Scarborough's Family*, ch. 58.
16. *The Bertrams*, ch. 3.
17. *The Small House at Allington*, ch. 17.
18. *The Way We Live Now*, ch. 81.
19. *The American Senator*, ch. 36.
20. *The Duke's Children*, ch. 20.
21. *The Prime Minister*, ch. 70.
22. *Can You Forgive Her?*, ch. 29.
23. *Phineas Finn: The Irish Member*, ch. 53; see Donald D. Stone, 'Prodigals and Prodigies: Trollope's Notes as a Son and Father', *Victorian Perspectives*, ed. John Clubbe and Jerome Meckier (1989), 42–67.
24. *Framley Parsonage*, ch. 36.
25. *The Last Chronicle of Barset*, chs. 12, 40, 4, 9.
26. *An Autobiography*, 11–12.
27. Sir William Gregory, *An Autobiography*, ed. Lady Gregory (1894), 30.
28. N. John Hall, *Salmagundi: Byron, Allegra, and the Trollope Family* (Pittsburgh, 1975), 68.
29. E. W. Howson and G. T. Warner (eds.), *Harrow School* (1898), 80; *An Autobiography*, 12–13; Gregory, *Autobiography*, 35.
30. John Chandos, *Boys Together: English Public Schools 1800–1864* (New Haven, Conn., 1984), 142.
31. TAT i. 225–6.

CHAPTER 5: A FAMOUS MOTHER

1. FET i. 127.
2. Frances Trollope to Julia Pertz, 12 Mar. 1830, *Garnett Letters*, 171; Heineman, 70.
3. FET i. 130–1.
4. Frances Trollope to Julia Pertz, 22 Aug. 1831, *Garnett Letters*, 176; Heineman, 74.
5. *The Friendships of Mary Russell Mitford as Recorded in Letters from her Literary Correspondences*, ed. Alfred Guy L'Estrange (1882), i. 226–8.
6. FET i. 132; *A History of the County of Middlesex*, ed. J. S. Cockburn and T. F. T. Baker (1971), iv. 228ff.; Heineman, 75.
7. Thomas Anthony Trollope *et al.* to Lord Northwick, 17 Dec. 1830 (MS GLC), quoted in Heineman, 75.
8. *History of the County of Middlesex*, iv. 230.
9. Heineman, 76.
10. FET i. 136, 139.
11. Ibid. 145.
12. TAT i. 295, 190.
13. FET i. 147, 140–1, 149.
14. Ibid. 136, 150–1.
15. *Quarterly Review*, 47 (Mar. 1832), 39ff.; *Edinburgh Review*, 110 (July 1832), 481ff.; *Athenaeum*, 231 (1832), 204–6.

16. Frances Trollope to Julia Pertz, 22 Mar. 1832, *Garnett Letters*, 182–3; Heineman, 100–1.
17. FET i. 159, 155.
18. Heineman, 100, 103; Michael Sadleir, *Trollope: A Commentary*, 3rd edn. (1961), 89; FET i. 170–1.
19. *An Autobiography*, 16–17.
20. Sir William Gregory, *An Autobiography*, ed. Lady Gregory (1894), 35.
21. *An Autobiography*, 17.
22. Ibid. 18.
23. *Fortnightly Review*, 2 (1 Oct. 1865), 482–3.
24. *Platonis Dialogi Selecti*, 4 vols., ed. Ludwig Friedrich Heindorf (Berlin, 1802–10), i. 121–83. University of California Los Angeles Library. I am indebted to Professor G. W. Pigman III of the California Institute of Technology for assistance in assessing this book and Trollope's annotations to the text.
25. Cf. Robin Waterfield, Introduction to 'Hippias Major' in *Early Socratic Dialogues* (1987), 213–28.
26. *An Autobiography*, 18–19; Percy M. Thornton, *Harrow School and its Surroundings* (1885), 250.
27. Escott, 29; FET i. 180ff.
28. Susan L. Humphreys, 'Trollope on the Sublime and Beautiful', *Nineteenth-Century Fiction*, 33 (Sept. 1978), 194–214.
29. *An Autobiography*, 17.
30. Frances Trollope to Julia Pertz, n.d., quoted in Heineman, 111–12.
31. Northwick to Quilton, 24 Nov. 1833 (MS GLC), quoted in Heineman, 112.
32. Frances Trollope to Julia Pertz, 13 July 1834, *Garnett Letters*, 196; Heineman, 112.
33. FET i. 170; *An Autobiography*, 25.
34. Heineman, 113–14; *An Autobiography*, 25ff.
35. Quilton to Northwick, 26 Apr. 1834 (MS GLC), quoted in Heineman, 115.
36. TAT i. 245.
37. *An Autobiography*, 27–9.
38. Ibid. 28–9.
39. FET i. 224–7; Escott, 18–19.
40. *An Autobiography*, 28ff., 34.

CHAPTER 6: ST MARTIN'S-LE-GRAND

1. *An Autobiography*, 34–5.
2. TAT i. 250.
3. *London Tradesmen* (1927), 1.
4. Super, *Post Office*, 2.
5. *An Autobiography*, 35–7.
6. Ibid. 37.
7. Super, *Post Office*, 1, 107–8, n. 2.
8. *An Autobiography*, 35–41.
9. Escott, 19.
10. N. John Hall, *Salmagundi: Byron, Allegra, and the Trollope Family* (Pittsburgh, 1975), 57, 63, 75.

11. *An Autobiography*, 168–9.
12. Ibid. 44, 45, 46, 49–50.
13. FET i. 228–30, 252; TAT i. 295, 262–3.
14. *An Autobiography*, 53.
15. *The Last Chronicle of Barset*, ch. 45.
16. *Phineas Redux*, chs. 47, 56.
17. *An Autobiography*, 53, 35, 54.
18. Ibid. 48–9.
19. *The Three Clerks*, ch. 18.
20. *Phineas Finn: The Irish Member*, ch. 21.
21. *Saturday Review*, 19 (4 Mar. 1865), 263–4; Smalley, 216.
22. *An Autobiography*, 51–2.
23. Escott, 27.
24. 'A Poet of the Actual', review of James Pope Hennessy, *Anthony Trollope*, in *The New Yorker*, 1 Apr. 1972, 104.
25. *The Small House at Allington*, ch. 51.
26. *An Autobiography*, 47–8.
27. *The Three Clerks*, chs. 17, 27.
28. *Letters*, i. 5.
29. *The Small House at Allington*, ch. 21.
30. *The Three Clerks*, ch. 17.
31. Margaret Oliphant, *Autobiography and Letters* (New York, 1899), 246.
32. *The Small House at Allington*, chs. 4, 14.
33. TAT i. 294–5; Heineman, 134.
34. *One Fault*, quoted in Heineman, 189–90.
35. *An Autobiography*, 31–2.
36. TAT i. 298.
37. *Letters*, i. 2.
38. *The Bertrams*, ch. 30.
39. TAT i. 299.
40. *The Bertrams*, ch. 28.
41. FET i. 260ff.; *An Autobiography*, 57.
42. *An Autobiography*, 54–7.
43. *Travelling Sketches* (1866), 44–5.
44. FET i. 283.
45. Frances Trollope to Julia Pertz, 26 Jan. 1838, *Garnett Letters*, 207; Heineman, 154.
46. FET i. 291, 300; TAT ii. 6; *Garnett Letters*, 211.
47. TAT i. 355–6.
48. FET i. 311ff.
49. Frances Trollope to Julia Pertz, *Garnett Letters*, 210; Escott, 33.
50. TAT ii. 69.
51. *Letters*, i. 9.
52. TAT i. 369–74.
53. *Letters*, i. 9.
54. FET i. 314.
55. *An Autobiography*, 50.

56. Edmund Yates, *Recollections and Experiences* (1884), i. 96–9; Super, *Post Office*, 3.
57. *An Autobiography*, 44–6.
58. Super, *Post Office*, 3–4.
59. *An Autobiography*, 46–7; R. H. Super wonders if this is a fictionalized version of an incident in which Trollope was accused of improperly recording a £3 note found in a newspaper in the post (Super, *Post Office*, 5).
60. *Marion Fay*, chs. 7, 23.
61. *Dublin University Magazine*, 46 (1855), 421.

CHAPTER 7: ASPIRATIONS

1. *Fraser's Magazine*, 17 (1838), 79 ff.; Heineman, 151–2.
2. *New Monthly Magazine*, 55 (Mar. 1839), 417.
3. *An Autobiography*, 33, 24, 22.
4. FET ii. 261.
5. *Letters*, i. 3.
6. Ibid. 1.
7. *An Autobiography*, 53, 43.
8. Ibid. 53.
9. Escott, 24.
10. *Letters*, Appendix A, ii. 1021–8.
11. Ibid., Appendix B, ii. 1029–32.
12. *An Editor's Tales* (1870), 150 ff.; *An Autobiography*, 337.
13. *An Editor's Tales*, 206–13.
14. *An Autobiography*, 1, 365.
15. Ibid. 34, 1.
16. *Ayala's Angel*, ch. 20.
17. *Orley Farm*, ch. 3.
18. *Framley Parsonage*, ch. 42.
19. *Travelling Sketches* (1866), 46–7.
20. *An Autobiography*, 60.
21. Ibid. 57 ff.; Super, *Post Office*, 10.
22. *An Autobiography*, 58, 61.

CHAPTER 8: BANAGHER AND GOOD FORTUNE

1. *An Autobiography*, 59. MS travel diaries, Parrish Collection; these six diaries make it possible to determine Trollope's whereabouts almost every working day of his postal career, from the time of his arrival in Ireland until his retirement in 1867; they will not be cited in subsequent notes unless for some unusual content.
2. *An Autobiography*, 60.
3. Ibid. 62–3.
4. John Hynes, 'Anthony Trollope's Creative "Culture-Shock": Banagher, 1841', *Éire–Ireland*, 23 (Fall 1986), 124–31.
5. House of Commons, Parliamentary Papers, 1860, LXII. 129–45.
6. *An Autobiography*, 65–6; Super, *Post Office*, 12, 110, n. 23.
7. *An Autobiography*, 66–8.

8. *Lotta Schmidt: And Other Stories* (1867), 143 ff.
9. *An Autobiography*, 63.
10. Ibid. 72–3.
11. *Letters*, ii. 645.
12. *An Autobiography*, 65.
13. *North America*, ed. Donald Smalley and Bradford Allen Booth (New York, 1951), 526–7.
14. *An Autobiography*, 63–4, 68.
15. *Tales of All Countries* (1861), 51 ff.
16. *Framley Parsonage*, ch. 31.
17. *Reminiscences of Rotherham & District in the Early Part of the Present Century*, repr. from the *Rotherham Advertiser* (Rotherham, 1891), 118–19, 8–9.
18. 'Mr. Trollope's Father-in-Law', *Three Banks Review* (Edinburgh and London), 66 (June 1965), 25–38.
19. Rotherham census return of 1841; Richard Mullen, *Anthony Trollope: A Victorian in His World* (1990), 130–1.
20. *Sheffield Mercury*, 27 Nov. 1841, 7.
21. *Sheffield and Rotherham Independent*, 17 Dec. 1842.
22. Henry Brackenbury, *Some Memories of My Spare Time* (1909), 49.
23. *The George Eliot Letters*, ed. Gordon S. Haight (New Haven, Conn., 1978), viii. 282.
24. *Letters*, i. 496.
25. *An Autobiography*, 73, 68.
26. *Doctor Thorne*, ch. 7.
27. *Letters*, i. 64.
28. *Orley Farm*, ch. 33.
29. *Can You Forgive Her?*, ch. 11.
30. *Ralph the Heir*, ch. 56.
31. *An Eye for an Eye*, ch. 3.
32. *Letters*, i. 145–6.
33. TAT ii. 76–9.
34. *An Autobiography*, 72.

CHAPTER 9: MARRIAGE AND AUTHORSHIP

1. *An Autobiography*, 69.
2. Ibid. 70–1.
3. R. J. Kelly, 'Trollope in Ireland', *Irish Book Lover*, July–Aug. 1931, 110.
4. Edward Bradley ('Cuthbert Bede'), 'Some Recollections of Mr Anthony Trollope', *Graphic*, 26 (23 Dec. 1882), 707.
5. *An Autobiography*, 42, 135, 71.
6. Ibid. 68, 71.
7. Rose Trollope's MS chronology, University of Illinois.
8. TAT ii. 79–81.
9. FET ii. 39.
10. Rose Trollope's MS chronology, Illinois.
11. *The Bertrams*, ch. 30.

12. *Letters*, i. 11.
13. Super, *Post Office*, 16.
14. James Pope Hennessy, *Anthony Trollope* (Boston, 1971), 114–15; Carlyle, *Oliver Cromwell's Letters and Speeches*, Part V, *Campaign in Ireland* [May 1650].
15. Escott, 44–5; House of Commons, Parliamentary Papers, 1857, IV. 360.
16. Pope Hennessy, *Anthony Trollope*, 116.
17. *An Autobiography*, 96.
18. *Letters*, ii. 967.
19. Baptismal register, Church of St Mary, Clonmel; MS family records, Illinois.
20. *An Autobiography*, 74.
21. *Letters*, i. 11–12.
22. John Sutherland, *Victorian Novelists and Publishers* (1976), 45.
23. *Letters*, i. 12. Trollope's many agreements with publishers are kept in the Bodleian Library, Oxford (MS Don. c. 9; MS Don. c. 10; MS Don. c. 10*). Their dates, prices, and other terms are given in Sadleir, *Bibliography* and, most of them, in the Trollope *Letters*. The agreements will not be further cited in this work.
24. Michael Sadleir, *Trollope: A Commentary*, 3rd edn. (1961), 148.
25. T. J. Wise and J. A. Symington, *The Brontës: Their Lives, Friendships and Correspondence* (Oxford, 1932), ii. 154; cf. Winifred Gérin, *Charlotte Brontë* (1967), 339–40.
26. *Correspondence of Henry Taylor*, ed. Edward Dowden (1888), 297–8.
27. Escott, 49 ff.; see Robert Tracy, '"The Unnatural Ruin": Trollope and Nineteenth-Century Irish Fiction', *Nineteenth-Century Fiction*, 37 (Dec. 1982), 358 ff.
28. Trollope's Commonplace Book, *Letters*, ii. 1021 ff.
29. *An Autobiography*, 70–1.
30. Kelly, 'Trollope in Ireland', *Irish Book Lover*, 111.
31. *The Macdermots of Ballycloran*, ch. 5.
32. Ibid., ch. 1.
33. See R. C. Terry, *Anthony Trollope: The Artist in Hiding* (1977), 181 ff.
34. Lance Tingay, 'The Publication of Trollope's First Novel', *TLS*, 30 Mar. 1956, 200–1; Gérin, *Charlotte Brontë*, 349–50; and Gordon S. Haight, *George Eliot* (New York, 1968), 313 ff.
35. *An Autobiography*, 75.
36. *Critic*, 5 (1 May 1847), 344, Smalley, 546; *Douglas Jerrold's Shilling Magazine*, 5 (June 1847), 566, Smalley, 551; *Howitt's Journal*, 1 (19 June 1847), 350, Smalley, 550; *Spectator*, 20 (8 May 1847), 449, Smalley, 547; *Athenaeum*, 15 May 1847, 517, Smalley, 548; *John Bull*, 27 (22 May 1847), 327, Smalley, 549.
37. *Letters*, i. 13–15.
38. John Sutherland, 'Henry Colburn Publisher', *Publishing History*, 19 (1986), 59 ff.; Mrs Oliphant, *Annals of a Publishing House* (1897), ii. 349.
39. *Letters*, i. 16.
40. Essay originally published in the New York *Century Magazine*, NS 4 (July 1883), 385–95, and republished, with alterations, in *Partial Portraits* (1888), 97–133; repr. in *The Trollope Critics*, ed. N. John Hall (1981), 1–20 [p. 14 quoted here].
41. *The Prime Minister*, ch. 13; *The Belton Estate*, ch. 17.
42. *The Kellys and the O'Kellys*, chs. 11, 29.

43. *An Autobiography*, 64.
44. Ibid. 76; *Athenaeum*, 15 July 1848, 701, Smalley, 553; *Douglas Jerrold's Weekly Newspaper*, 22 July 1848, 941, Smalley, 554; *Sharpe's London Magazine*, 7 (Aug. 1848), 118–21, Smalley, 556.
45. *The Times*, 7 Sept. 1848, 6, Smalley, 557.
46. *An Autobiography*, 78–9; *Letters*, i. 17–18.
47. TAT i. 258–9.
48. *Tralee Chronicle*, 31 Mar. 1849.
49. *Kerry Evening Post*, 28 July 1849.
50. Justin McCarthy, *Reminiscences* (New York, 1900), i. 372.
51. Escott, 59.
52. *Castle Richmond*, ch. 35.
53. Super, *Post Office*, 17–18.
54. Ibid. 20.
55. *Thackeray Letters*, ed. Gordon N. Ray (Cambridge, Mass., 1945), ii. 427.
56. *Thackeray* (1879), 34–6.
57. Super, *Post Office*, 17.
58. *Castle Richmond*, chs. 24, 30.

CHAPTER 10: CONSERVATIVE LIBERAL

1. *Letters*, i. 17.
2. *An Autobiography*, 80–1.
3. *Memoirs of the Marchioness Rochejaquelein* (Edinburgh, 1827), vol. v, *Constable's Miscellany*, 15.
4. *An Autobiography*, 80–1.
5. Escott, 52.
6. *An Autobiography*, 291.
7. 'Trollope's Letters to the *Examiner*', ed. Helen Garlinghause King, *Princeton University Library Chronicle*, 26 (Winter 1965), 72–6.
8. *An Autobiography*, 82–4.
9. *Examiner* letters, King, *Princeton University Library Chronicle*, 76–101.
10. *An Autobiography*, 84.
11. *Castle Richmond*, ch. 7.
12. Ibid., chs. 37, 33.
13. Ibid., ch. 31.
14. FET ii. 91–2, 106ff., 140ff.
15. *Letters*, i. 18–19.
16. Ibid. 22. MS Taylor Collection.
17. Harriet Garnett to Julia Pertz, 12 Aug. 1849 and 26 May 1850, quoted in Heineman, 237, 238.
18. *Letters*, i. 20–2.
19. Ibid. 18–19.
20. FET ii. 153ff., 161ff.
21. *Letters*, i. 19.
22. *Spectator*, 15 Aug. 1846, 787; *Athenaeum*, 29 Aug. 1846, 885.
23. TAT ii. 167.
24. *Letters*, i. 39.

25. *Doctor Thorne*, ch. 32.
26. *The Last Chronicle of Barset*, ch. 17.
27. *Barchester Towers*, ch. 4.
28. *The Kellys and the O'Kellys*, ch. 38.
29. *Castle Richmond*, chs. 12, 10, 19.
30. *The Kellys and the O'Kellys*, ch. 38.
31. *Castle Richmond*, ch. 37.
32. *Letters*, i. 25.
33. *The Warden*, ch. 16.
34. *An Autobiography*, 86–7.
35. Ibid. 85–6; *Letters*, i. 26–7.
36. *The Noble Jilt*, ed. Michael Sadleir (1923), 22, 34.
37. *The Eustace Diamonds*, ch. 52.
38. *An Autobiography*, 101–2; *Letters*, i. 22–3.
39. 'Merivale's History of the Romans', *Dublin University Magazine*, 37 (May 1851), 611–24.
40. *Letters*, i. 25–6.
41. *An Autobiography*, 101–2.
42. Hansard, 3rd ser., CXIV (1851), 106.
43. *Morning Advertiser*, 1 May 1851.
44. *Letters*, i. 22–5.
45. Muriel R. Trollope, 'What I Was Told', *Trollopian*, 2 (Mar. 1948), 226.

CHAPTER 11: THE WEST COUNTRY AND *THE WARDEN*

1. *An Autobiography*, 87 ff.
2. Ibid. 88, 97.
3. J. G. Uren, 'My Early Recollections of the Post Office in the West of England', *Blackfriars*, 9 (July–Dec. 1889), 157–8.
4. Anonymous, 'Anthony Trollope as a Post Office Surveyor', *St Martin's-le-Grand*, 14 (Oct. 1904), 453–4.
5. Uren, 'My Early Recollections', 158–9.
6. *The Small House at Allington*, ch. 60.
7. *He Knew He Was Right*, ch. 18.
8. *Framley Parsonage*, ch. 5.
9. *The American Senator*, ch. 34.
10. Super, *Post Office*, 25–9; *Letters*, i. 28–9; Jean Young Farrugia, *The Letter Box: A History of Post Office Pillar and Wall Boxes* (Fontwell, Sussex, 1969), 25 ff., 122; Philip Stevens, 'Anthony Trollope and the Jersey Postal Service', *Bulletin de la Société Jersiane* (1980), 421–33; Philip Stevens, 'Anthony Trollope and the Guernsey Postal Service', *Transactions of La Société Guernesiaise* (1981), 103–6.
11. *He Knew He Was Right*, ch. 8.
12. *Letters*, i. 31 ff.
13. Ibid. 30 ff.
14. Rose Trollope's MS chronology, Illinois.
15. Escott, 133.
16. MS letter of 12 Apr. 1923, Parrish Collection.

17. Inga-Stina Ekeblad, 'Anthony Trollope's Copy of the 1647 Beaumont and Fletcher Folio', *Notes and Queries*, NS 6 (Apr. 1959), 153–5.
18. *An Autobiography*, 91–6.
19. Ibid. 96.
20. *Letters*, i. 34–8.
21. Super, *Post Office*, 29–30.
22. John Sutherland, *Victorian Novelists and Publishers* (1976), 5.
23. *Letters*, i. 38–9.
24. *An Autobiography*, 93–5; Ralph Arnold, *The Whiston Matter* (1961); R. B. Martin, *Enter Rumor: Four Early Victorian Scandals* (1962), 137–84.
25. *Spectator*, 28 (6 Jan. 1855), 22–8, Smalley, 32; *Examiner*, 6 Jan. 1855, 5, Smalley, 30–1; *Athenaeum*, 27 Jan. 1855, 107–8, Smalley, 34–5; *Leader*, 17 Feb. 1855, 164–5, Smalley, 36–8.
26. *An Autobiography*, 98.
27. *Letters*, i. 40.
28. 'Ranke's *History of the Popes*', *Edinburgh Review*, 145 (Oct. 1840), 228.
29. *Letters*, i. 29.
30. *The Warden*, ch. 15.
31. *The New Zealander*, ed. N. John Hall (Oxford, 1972), 43, 46.
32. Ibid. 14, 26, 27, 16–18, 25.
33. Ibid. 174–5.
34. *Letters*, i. 40. The argument for placing this letter of 27 March in 1856 rests on the presumption, suggested to me in private correspondence by R. H. Super, that Trollope's mention of 'the MS. of which I spoke to you when in London' refers to a recent visit to London, 26–31 January 1856; if the date were 1855, it would have to refer back to July. The 1856 dating presumes that Michael Sadleir misdated two letters (both since destroyed), this one and that of Joseph Cauvin's report, 2 April (both 1855 in *Commentary*); the 1856 dating also allows for more time for the writing of *The New Zealander* (about a year), rather than the mere six weeks that the 1855 dating implies; moreover, one can argue that it was somewhat unlikely that Trollope would have spent a year revising the text of a book so resoundingly rejected by the publisher's reader. On the other hand, the evidence for the 1856 dating is not conclusive, and the manuscript, all of it in fair copy (except a late chapter on Art dated March 1856), bears signs of four different paginations, indicative of what for Trollope was a most unusual amount of revision. Other internal evidence could suit either date.
35. *Letters*, i. 42.
36. House of Commons, Parliamentary Papers, 1854–5, XI. 431–532.
37. 'The Civil Service', *Dublin University Magazine*, 46 (Oct. 1855), 409–26.

CHAPTER 12: *BARCHESTER TOWERS* AND SUCCESS

1. *An Autobiography*, 103.
2. Ibid. 119. The working diaries for most of Trollope's novels are in the Bodleian Library. The Chronology in the *Letters* draws extensively on them for the dates on which Trollope began and finished; large interruptions are also noted. The diaries will not be further cited in this work.
3. *Letters*, i. 44.

4. TAT i. 357–8.
5. *Letters*, i. 45–6.
6. Ibid. 47.
7. Ibid. 51–2; *An Autobiography*, 362.
8. *An Autobiography*, 105–6.
9. *Can You Forgive Her?*, ch. 25.
10. *An Autobiography*, 107; N. John Hall, 'Seeing Trollope's *An Autobiography* through the Press: The Correspondence of William Blackwood and Henry Merivale Trollope', *Princeton University Library Chronicle*, 47 (Winter 1986), 206–7.
11. *Letters*, i. 52, 54.
12. Smalley, headnote, 50; *An Autobiography*, 99–100.
13. *Letters*, i. 116–17.
14. *Partial Portraits* (1888), repr. in *The Trollope Critics*, ed. N. John Hall (1981), 12.
15. *The Times*, 13 Aug. 1857, 5, Smalley, 51.
16. *An Autobiography*, 93.
17. *Leader*, 23 May 1857, 497, Smalley, 43–4; *Westminster Review*, 68 (Oct. 1857), 594–6, Smalley, 53; *Athenaeum*, 30 May 1857, 689–90, Smalley, 45; *Saturday Review*, 3 (30 May 1857), 503–4, Smalley, 47–8.
18. Gordon N. Ray, *Thackeray: The Age of Wisdom* (New York, 1958), 304; *Roundabout Papers*, No. 14 'Small-beer Chronicle', *Cornhill Magazine*, 4 (July 1861), 123; see David Skilton, *Trollope and His Contemporaries* (1972), 53 ff.
19. *The Letters and Diaries of John Henry Newman*, ed. C. S. Dessain (1968), xviii. 482.
20. *An Autobiography*, 104.
21. See James R. Kincaid, *The Novels of Anthony Trollope* (Oxford, 1977), 113.
22. *Barchester Towers*, ch. 33.
23. Ibid., ch. 11.
24. Ibid., ch. 45.
25. *Saturday Review*, 20 (19 Aug. 1865), 240–2, Smalley, 241.
26. *Thackeray*, 185–6.
27. See Andrew Wright, *Anthony Trollope: Dream and Art* (1983), 37 ff.; P. D. Edwards, *Anthony Trollope: His Art and Scope* (St Lucia, Queensland, 1977), 16 ff.
28. *Partial Portraits*, repr. in *The Trollope Critics*, 11; cf. Kincaid, *The Novels of Anthony Trollope*, 37–8, and W. P. Ker, *On Modern Literature*, ed. Terence Spencer and James Sutherland (Oxford, 1955), 136–46; repr. in *The Trollope Critics*, 26–33.
29. *Letters*, ii. 548; cf. 773.
30. *An Autobiography*, 107.
31. *Letters*, i. 58–9.
32. Ibid. 59.
33. *An Autobiography*, 109–10.
34. Ibid. 110–11.
35. *The Way We Live Now*, ch. 89.
36. *An Autobiography*, 111.
37. Ibid. 111–12.

38. *The Three Clerks*, ch. 11.
39. *An Autobiography*, 111.
40. *Leader*, 19 Dec. 1857, 1318, Smalley, 62; *Saturday Review*, 4 (5 Dec. 1857), 517–18, Smalley, 56–7.
41. TAT ii. 188; *Thackeray Letters*, iv. 158–9.
42. *Athenaeum*, 26 Dec. 1857, 1621, Smalley, 63; *Saturday Review*, 4 (5 Dec. 1857), 517–18, Smalley, 57–8; *Doctor Thorne*, chs. 45, 46.
43. *Saturday Review*, 5 (12 June 1858), 618–19, Smalley, 77.

CHAPTER 13: EGYPT AND THE HOLY LAND

1. *An Autobiography*, 116–17; *Letters*, i. 62.
2. *Letters*, i. 63–4.
3. *An Autobiography*, 118.
4. *Letters*, i. 65.
5. *An Autobiography*, 123–4.
6. Escott, 123–4.
7. *Letters*, i. 74–5; see Super, *Post Office*, 34–7.
8. *Bentley's Quarterly Review*, 1 (July 1859), 456–62, Smalley, 100; *Athenaeum*, 26 Mar. 1859, 420, Smalley, 92.
9. *The Bertrams*, chs. 38, 39.
10. Ibid., ch. 6.
11. Ibid., ch. 9.
12. *Letters*, i. 71–3; Super, *Post Office*, 37.
13. *The Bertrams*, ch. 38.
14. *An Autobiography*, 125.
15. *Tales of All Countries* (1861), 79 ff.
16. *An Autobiography*, 115.
17. *Leader*, 29 May 1858, 519–20, Smalley, 69–70.
18. *An Autobiography*, 126.
19. Figures from Dr Chester W. Topp of Cleveland, Ohio, based on his collection. See also Lance Tingay, 'Trollope's Popularity: A Statistical Approach', *Nineteenth-Century Fiction*, 11 (1956), 223–9; Tingay similarly places *Doctor Thorne* first on the list of titles frequently reprinted during Trollope's lifetime.
20. *Leader*, 29 May 1858, 519–20, Smalley, 69; *Harper's Magazine*, 17 (Sept. 1858), 693, Smalley, 79.
21. *Australia*, ed. P. D. Edwards and R. B. Joyce (St Lucia, Queensland, 1967), 441.
22. *Doctor Thorne*, chs. 1, 15, 2, 18, 4.
23. Ibid., ch. 3.
24. *Letters*, ii. 1005; i. 73–4.
25. *Saturday Review*, 5 (12 June 1858), 618–19, Smalley, 75; *National Review*, 7 (Oct. 1858), 416–35, Smalley, 87–8; *Spectator*, 32 (19 Mar. 1859), 328–9, Smalley, 91.
26. *An Autobiography*, 122, 127.
27. Ibid. 127.
28. *Letters*, i. 148, 85–6; R. C. Terry, 'Three Lost Chapters of Anthony Trollope's First Novel', *Nineteenth-Century Fiction*, 27 (June 1972), 71–80.

CHAPTER 14: THE WEST INDIES

1. Anonymous, *St Martin's-le-Grand*, 12 (1902), 131–40, repr. in R. C. Terry, *A Trollope Chronology* (1989), 148–56.
2. *The West Indies and the Spanish Main* (New York, 1860), 7; 'The Journey to Panama', *Lotta Schmidt: And Other Stories* (1867), 364 ff.
3. *The West Indies and the Spanish Main*, 12.
4. Super, *Post Office*, 38 ff.
5. *An Autobiography*, 127–8.
6. TAT i. 259–60.
7. The stories from the earlier trip included 'An Unprotected Female among the Pyramids', 'George Walker at Suez', 'A Ride Across Palestine' (reprinted as 'The Banks of the Jordan'), and 'John Bull on the Guadalquivir'; those from the West Indies journey included 'Miss Sarah Jack of Spanish Town, Jamaica', 'The Courtship of Susan Bell', 'Aaron Trow', 'Returning Home', and 'The Journey to Panama'; for details of reprintings, see Sadleir, *Bibliography*, 36, 49–50, 86–7.
8. *Letters*, i. 80–1.
9. *An Autobiography*, 129.
10. *Letters*, i. 81.
11. *The West Indies and the Spanish Main*, 5–11.
12. Ibid. 15–17, 19, 48, 25, 44.
13. Ibid. 52–6, 285 ff.
14. Ibid. 64 ff., 182.
15. Ibid. 65, 75–86.
16. Ibid. 132–6.
17. Ibid. 167.
18. Ibid. 240–7.
19. Super, *Post Office*, 41.
20. *The West Indies and the Spanish Main*, 249–65.
21. Muriel R. Trollope, 'What I Was Told', *Trollopian*, 2 (Mar. 1948), 232.
22. *Thackeray* (1879), 60.
23. *Thackeray Letters*, ed. Gordon N. Ray (Cambridge, Mass., 1945), iv. 262–3.
24. *The West Indies and the Spanish Main*, 270–1, 276–7.
25. Ibid. 321.
26. Ibid. 368 ff.
27. *Tales of All Countries*, Second Series (1863), 1 ff.; see Donald D. Stone, Introduction, Arno Press edn. (New York, 1981).
28. *The West Indies and the Spanish Main*, 381 ff.
29. *Letters*, i. 95, 329; N. John Hall, 'Trollope's Letters to Harriet and Mary Knower', *Princeton University Library Chronicle*, 43 (Autumn 1981), 23–37.
30. *An Autobiography*, 128.
31. Super, *Post Office*, 43–4; *Letters*, i. 87–8.
32. *The Bertrams*, chs. 33, 47.
33. Ibid., chs. 7, 10, 8, 12.
34. *Letters*, i. 111; ii. 933.
35. *The Bertrams*, ch. 38.
36. Ibid., chs. 18, 26.

37. *The George Eliot Letters*, ed. Gordon S. Haight (New Haven, Conn., 1955), iv. 81–2, 266.

CHAPTER 15: WALTHAM HOUSE AND THE *CORNHILL*

1. *An Autobiography*, 132–4.
2. W. F. Pollock, *Personal Remembrances* (1887), ii. 149–50.
3. *Letters*, i. 83.
4. *An Autobiography*, 130.
5. *The Times*, 6 Jan. 1860, 4, and 18 Jan. 1860, 12.
6. *The West Indies and the Spanish Main* (New York, 1860), 14.
7. *The Times*, 23 May 1859, 12, Smalley, 103.
8. *An Autobiography*, 130.
9. Ibid. 264.
10. *The Letters of George Meredith*, ed. C. L. Cline (Oxford, 1970), i. 39; see also Guinevere L. Greist, *Mudie's Circulating Library* (Bloomington/London, 1970), 140 ff.
11. John Sutherland, *Victorian Novelists and Publishers* (1976), 26–7; BL Add. MS 46595, p. 421.
12. *Letters*, i. 86–7.
13. Rose Trollope's MS chronology, Illinois; *Harper's Magazine* published only two more stories, 'The O'Conors of Castle Conor', and 'La Mère Bauche', and did not issue the latter until 1868.
14. *Letters*, i. 89–90; Sutherland, *Publishers*, 142; 'Some Letters of Whitwell Elwin', *TLS*, 25 Sept. 1953, 630.
15. *Letters*, i. 91.
16. Gordon N. Ray, *Thackeray: The Age of Wisdom* (New York, 1958), 295.
17. *Thackeray* (1879), 52.
18. *An Autobiography*, 141–2; *Thackeray*, 51.
19. *An Autobiography*, 142.
20. Ibid. 138–9.
21. John Blackie, *Bradfield: 1850–1975*, privately printed (Bradfield, 1976), 1.
22. Anthony Trollope, 'Public Schools', *Fortnightly Review*, 2 (1 Oct. 1865), 481 ff.
23. Blackie, *Bradfield*, 9; *The George Eliot Letters*, ed. Gordon S. Haight (New Haven, Conn., 1955), iii. 362, 426.
24. A. F. Leach, *History of Bradfield College* (1900), 116.
25. *Letters*, ii. 894.
26. Muriel R. Trollope, 'What I Was Told', *The Trollopian*, 2 (Mar. 1948), 230; Muriel Trollope gives Barney's surname as Fitzpatrick; Pope Hennessy says it was MacIntyre (p. 75); the 1861 census calls him Smith, and gives his age as 63 (*Letters*, i. 215 n.).
27. *An Autobiography*, 271–3.
28. *Letters*, i. 93–5.
29. [Leonard Huxley], *The House of Smith, Elder* [privately printed] (1923), 100; George Smith, 'Our Birth and Parentage', *Cornhill Magazine*, 10 [3rd ser.] (Jan. 1901), 9.
30. *Daily News*, 22 Dec. 1859, 5; *Illustrated Times*, quoted in *Athenaeum* advertisement, 7 Jan. 1860, 25.

31. *Thackeray Letters*, ed. Gordon N. Ray (Cambridge, Mass., 1945), iv. 169–70.
32. Smith, 'Our Birth and Parentage', 8.
33. MS Huntington Library, quoted in Ray, *Thackeray: The Age of Wisdom*, 303–4; *Thackeray Letters*, iv. 236.
34. *Letters of the Brownings to George Barrett*, ed. Paul Landis (1958), 247–8; *The Letters of Mrs Gaskell*, ed. J. A. V. Chapple and Arthur Pollard (Manchester, 1966), 602.
35. *Saturday Review*, 11 (4 May 1861), 451–2, Smalley, 121; *Sharpe's London Magazine*, 19 (July 1861), 103–5, Smalley, 129–32.
36. *Thackeray*, 52.
37. *An Autobiography*, 142–3, 154.

CHAPTER 16: LITERARY LONDON

1. *George Smith: A Memoir with Some Pages of Autobiography*, privately printed (1902), 106 ff.; Gordon S. Haight, *George Eliot* (New York, 1968), 356.
2. Escott, 132.
3. G. A. Sala, *Things I Have Seen and People I Have Known* (1894), 30–1.
4. Smith, *Memoir*, 120; Leonard Huxley, *House of Smith, Elder* (1923), 104; see also, Gordon N. Ray, *Thackeray: The Age of Wisdom*, (New York, 1958), 299.
5. *New York Times*, 26 May 1860, 2; Huxley, *House of Smith, Elder*, 105; 'Newspaper Gossip', *Saturday Review*, 23 June 1860, 799–800; *An Autobiography*, Appendix I, 370–1.
6. 'On Screens in Dining-Rooms', *Cornhill Magazine*, 2 (Aug. 1860), 252–6; *Letters*, i. 111; *An Autobiography*, 371.
7. *Letters*, i. 157.
8. *An Autobiography*, 147 ff.
9. *Letters*, i. 111, 118.
10. *An Autobiography*, 152.
11. *The George Eliot Letters*, ed. Gordon S. Haight (New Haven, Conn., 1955, 1978), iii. 360, viii. 297, iv. 59.
12. N. John Hall, *Trollope and His Illustrators* (1980), 8–9.
13. *The Warden*, ch. 14.
14. *Letters*, i. 97, 104, 111; *An Autobiography*, 148–50.
15. *An Autobiography*, 155–6.
16. *Spectator*, 33 (19 May 1860), 477, Smalley, 115; *Athenaeum*, 19 May 1860, 681, Smalley, 111; *Saturday Review*, 9 (19 May 1860), 643–4, Smalley, 113–14. See also P. D. Edwards, *Notes and Queries*, NS 15 (Nov. 1968), 419–20.
17. *Letters*, i. 364.
18. *An Autobiography*, 143–4.
19. Ibid. 141.
20. *Letters*, i. 102–3; *An Autobiography*, 161.
21. *Letters*, i. 116–17.
22. Ibid. 123, 127–9; *Thackeray* (1879), 55; *Thackeray Letters*, ed. Gordon N. Ray (Cambridge, Mass., 1945), iv. 208.
23. *Letters*, i. 141.
24. Ibid. 120–1.
25. Whiting, 66, 69, 72, 74, 94, 96, 100–1, 107, 132.

26. Whiting, 123.
27. *An Autobiography*, 316.
28. *Letters*, i. 127.
29. *Is He Popenjoy?*, ch. 32.
30. *Letters*, i. 137–8.
31. *An Autobiography*, 160.
32. *Letters*, i. 134.
33. *Orley Farm*, ch. 63.
34. Taylor Collection.
35. *An Autobiography*, 167.
36. *Saint James's Magazine*, 2 (Sept. 1861), 163–76.
37. W. F. Pollock, *Personal Remembrances* (1887), ii. 149–50; *An Autobiography*, 157, 270.
38. *Letters*, i. 146, 220; [W. Lucas Collins], review of *An Autobiography*, *Blackwood's Magazine*, 134 (Nov. 1883), 591; George Smith, autobiographical typescript, National Library of Scotland, 24–5; *Thackeray and His Daughter: The Letters and Journals of Anne Thackeray Ritchie*, ed. Hester Thackeray Ritchie (New York, 1924), 137; Michael Sadleir, *Trollope: A Commentary*, 3rd edn. (1961), 202; [John Morley and Mrs Humphry Ward] *Macmillan's Magazine*, 49 (Nov. 1883), 55–6.
39. *Can You Forgive Her?*, chs. 16, 17.
40. *An Autobiography*, 170–2; *Letters*, i. 398 n.; ii. 574; i. 204; Evangeline Bradhurst, 'Anthony Trollope—The Hunting Man', *Essex Review*, 38 (1928), 186–7; Smith, autobiographical typescript, 25.
41. [Cecilia Meetkerke], 'Last Reminiscences of Anthony Trollope', *Temple Bar*, 70 (Jan. 1884), 130.
42. *The Correspondence of John Lothrop Motley*, ed. George William Curtis (1889), i. 227, 229.
43. *An Autobiography*, 160; *Letters*, i. 147.
44. *An Autobiography*, 151.
45. *Letters*, ii. 942, 944.
46. *Report of the Anniversary of 1861*, 27; *An Autobiography*, 212–14; see also Bradford A. Booth, 'Trollope and the Royal Literary Fund', *NCF*, 7 (Dec. 1952), 208–16; R. H. Super, 'Trollope at the Royal Literary Fund', *NCF*, 37 (Dec. 1982), 316–28; Nigel Cross, *The Royal Literary Fund 1790–1918* (1984), 10–24.
47. *The West Indies and the Spanish Main* (New York, 1960), 380.
48. Quoted in Super, *Post Office*, 52.
49. *Thackeray Letters*, iv. 363.
50. 'The Civil Service as a Profession', *Cornhill Magazine*, 3 (Feb. 1861), 214–28; *Letters*, i. 138.
51. *An Autobiography*, 134; Super, *Post Office*, 51–2.
52. *An Autobiography*, 162–3; Super, *Post Office*, 58, 59.
53. *North America*, ed. Donald Smalley and Bradford Allen Booth (New York, 1951), 3–4; *An Autobiography*, 161.

CHAPTER 17: NORTH AMERICA

1. 'Mr and Mrs J. T. Fields', *Atlantic Monthly*, 116 (July 1915), 24.

2. *North America*, 19, 5; FET ii. 164.
3. *North America*, 23, 24, 26–7.
4. Quoted in Horace Elisha Scudder, *James Russell Lowell: A Biography* (Boston, 1901), ii. 82–4.
5. Quoted in James C. Austin, *Fields of 'The Atlantic Monthly'* (San Marino, Calif., 1953), 215.
6. *An Autobiography*, 144; *Letters*, i. 96–7.
7. *North America*, 232.
8. *An Autobiography*, 164; *North America*, 122, 37–8.
9. *North America*, 95, 126, 136–7, 151–2.
10. Ibid. 140, 163.
11. Ibid. 154–5, 157–8.
12. Ibid. 173, 175–80.
13. Ibid. 191, 193, 195.
14. Ibid. 207–8.
15. Ibid. 209–11, 178.
16. Ibid. 212.
17. *Letters*, i. 195.
18. *North America*, 198–201; *Harper's New Monthly Magazine*, 25 (July 1862), 262–4.
19. Whiting, 129–32.
20. *Letters*, i. 161.
21. *North America*, 223–30.
22. Ibid. 233–4, 243, 248–50, 255.
23. TAT i. 164.
24. *North America*, 239–41.
25. *Letters*, i. 161.
26. *North America*, 303.
27. Ibid. 305, 311, 317.
28. Ibid. 339–41.
29. Ibid. 331 ff.
30. Ibid. 424 ff.
31. Ibid. 313.
32. *Letters*, i. 168–9, 170–1, 173.
33. *North America*, 312, 369, 372–4.
34. Ibid. 380–1.
35. Ibid. 392–3, 395.
36. Ibid. 405.
37. *Letters*, i. 174–5.
38. Whiting, 190 ff.
39. *North America*, 447–8.
40. Ibid. 398–9.
41. *Lotta Schmidt: And Other Stories* (1867), 319 ff.
42. *North America*, 463.
43. Ibid. 526–7.
44. Ibid. 493 ff.
45. Ibid. 463–4, 357, 521, 354, 359–61.

46. *North America*, 266.
47. *Saturday Review*, 13 (31 May 1862), 625–6; *British Quarterly Review*, 36 (Oct. 1862), 477; *Athenaeum*, 24 May 1862, 685–7; *Spectator*, 7 June 1862, 635–7; *Cornhill Magazine*, 6 (July 1862), 105–7.
48. *An Autobiography*, 164.
49. *Letters*, i. 191 ff.
50. Ibid. i. 192, 193 ff.
51. Super, *Post Office*, 59.

CHAPTER 18: ALMOST A NATIONAL INSTITUTION

1. *Illustrated London News*, 139 (10 Aug. 1861), 148; *Saturday Review*, 19 (4 Mar. 1865), 263, Smalley, 216; *Westminster Review*, 95 (July 1871), 574–5, Smalley, 138–9.
2. *The Struggles of Brown, Jones, and Robinson*, chs. 5, 10.
3. *An Autobiography*, 161.
4. *Saturday Review*, 7 Dec. 1861, 587; *Spectator*, 18 Jan. 1862, 80.
5. Candidates' Book, Garrick Club Library.
6. *An Autobiography*, 157–9.
7. 'My Tour in Holland', *Cornhill Magazine*, 6 (Nov. 1862), 616–22.
8. *The George Eliot Letters*, ed. Gordon S. Haight (New Haven, Conn., 1955), iv. 8–9.
9. *Dublin University Magazine*, 61 (Apr. 1863), 437, Smalley, 165; *National Review*, 16 (Jan. 1863), 27–40, Smalley, 171; *London Review*, 5 (18 Oct. 1862), 344–5, Smalley, 152; *The Times*, 26 Dec. 1862, 5, Smalley, 161; *London Review*, 5 (8 Nov. 1862), 405–7, Smalley, 156; *Examiner*, 25 Oct. 1862, 677–8, Smalley, 154; *Saturday Review*, 14 (11 Oct. 1862), 444–5, Smalley 143–4; *Spectator*, 33 (11 Oct. 1862), 1136–8, Smalley, 146–51; *Cornhill Magazine*, 6 (Nov. 1862), 702–4, Smalley, 157.
10. *Orley Farm*, ch. 45.
11. *An Autobiography*, 166–7, 227.
12. Ibid. 167 ff.
13. *Letters*, ii. 715.
14. Ibid. ii. 596; i. 179–80.
15. *An Autobiography*, 178.
16. *The Small House at Allington*, chs. 23, 55.
17. *An Autobiography*, 178–9; *London Review*, 8 (7 May 1864), 494–6, Smalley, 203; *Spectator*, 37 (9 Apr. 1864), 421–3, Smalley, 198; *Athenaeum*, 26 Mar. 1864, 437–8, Smalley, 194–5; *Illustrated London News*, 44 (16 Apr. 1864), 375, Smalley, 202; *Saturday Review*, 17 (14 May 1864), 595–6, Smalley, 208.
18. Donald D. Stone, Introduction, *Tales of All Countries*, Second Series (Arno, New York, 1981), [5–6].
19. *Spectator*, 7 Mar. 1863, 20–1; *Saturday Review*, 28 Feb. 1863, 276–8.
20. *Tales of All Countries*, Second Series (1863), 132 ff., 195.
21. Patricia Thomas Srebrnik, *Alexander Strahan: Victorian Publisher* (Ann Arbor, Mich., 1986), 29 ff.
22. John Hollingshead, *My Lifetime* (1895), i. 178.

23. *The Letters of Sydney Smith*, ed. Nowell C. Smith (Oxford, 1953), ii. 442; Srebrnik, *Strahan*, 17.
24. Letters, i. 178.
25. *An Autobiography*, 186–8.
26. *Good Words* announcement reproduced in *An Autobiography*, 187.
27. *The Record*, 13 Apr. 1863, 4.
28. Srebrnik, *Strahan*, 62–3.
29. Ibid. 64.
30. Published in Robert Lee Wolff, *Nineteenth-Century Fiction: A Bibliographical Catalogue* (New York, 1985), iv. 205.
31. *Letters*, i. 222–4.
32. *An Autobiography*, 188.
33. *Rachel Ray*, chs. 9, 1.
34. *Letters*, i. 221.
35. Ibid. 220.
36. Reproduced in N. John Hall, *Trollope and His Illustrators* (1980), 74, and on the cover of OUP's 1988 World's Classics edition of the novel.
37. *Letters*, i. 238.
38. *George Eliot Letters*, iv. 110–11; *Letters*, i. 238.
39. *Athenaeum*, 17 Oct. 1863, 492–4, Smalley, 180; *The Times*, 25 Dec. 1863, 4, Smalley, 190; *Saturday Review*, 16 (24 Oct. 1863), 554–5, Smalley, 184–5.
40. *Letters*, i. 78; O. A. Sherrard, *Two Victorian Girls: With Extracts from the Hall Diaries*, ed. A. R. Mills (1966), 277; [Anonymous] *The Notebooks of a Spinster Lady: 1878–1903* (1919), 74–5.
41. *Saturday Review*, 9 Dec. 1882, 755–6.
42. *The Way We Live Now*, ch. 27.
43. MS letter to Michael Sadleir, 9 Oct, 1926, Parrish Collection.
44. *Letters*, ii. 606, 644, 753.
45. *Letters*, i. 235; *Athenaeum*, 10 Oct. 1863, 469; *Letters*, i. 254; ii. 1037 (Appendix D); FET ii. 301–2; Heineman, 255.
46. *Letters*, i. 244–5.
47. *Cornhill Magazine*, 9 (Feb. 1864), 134–7; cf. *An Autobiography*, 185–6.
48. *Letters*, i. 271.
49. Ibid. 241.
50. *An Autobiography*, 363, 197.
51. *George Smith: A Memoir with Some Pages of Autobiography*, privately printed (1902), 122–3.
52. *Lotta Schmidt: And Other Stories*, 253; *Orley Farm*, ch. 67.
53. *Letters*, i. 255–6 and n.
54. *An Autobiography*, 278–9.
55. *Letters*, i. 259–60, 260–1, 272–8, 279–81.
56. Super, *Post Office*, 68–9.
57. R. J. W., 'Early Post Office Days', *St Martin's-le-Grand*, 6 (July 1896), 295; *Letters*, i. 345–6.
58. *An Autobiography*, 277–8.
59. Nigel Cross, *The Royal Literary Fund 1790–1918* (1984), 10ff.; *Letters*, i. 257; ii. 707.

60. *Letters*, ii. 756.
61. *An Autobiography*, 158–60; *Letters*, ii. 621, 920.
62. Michael Sadleir, *Trollope: A Commentary*, 3rd edn. (1961), 333; one of the girls, later Mrs Reginald Smith, told the story in the same words to Gordon Ray; she also gave an identical account to Bradford Booth, recorded in 'They Knew Trollope', *Trollopian*, 2 (Sept. 1947), 118–19.
63. *Letters*, i. 271, 285; ii. 682; i. 101; ii. 675; *Illustrated Review*, 15 May 1871, 487 ff.
64. *An Autobiography*, 197–8; Andrew Wright, *Anthony Trollope: Dream and Art* (1983), 128 ff.; Robert M. Polhemus, *The Changing World of Anthony Trollope* (Berkeley and Los Angeles, 1968), 113 ff.; Arthur Pollard, *Anthony Trollope* (1978), 124.
65. *An Autobiography*, 188.
66. *London Review*, 10 (8 Apr. 1865), 387, Smalley, 228; *Reader*, 3 (27 May 1865), 596, Smalley, 229; *Westminster Review*, 84 (July 1865), 282–5, Smalley, 231; *The Times*, 23 Aug. 1865, 13, Smalley, 238; *Saturday Review*, 19 (4 Mar. 1865), 263–5, Smalley, 215–18.
67. *Letters*, i. 319.
68. *Nation*, 1 (13 July 1865), 51–2, Smalley, 236–7.

CHAPTER 19: PALLISERS AND PERIODICALS

1. *An Autobiography*, 175.
2. *Can You Forgive Her?*, ch. 11.
3. *An Autobiography*, 180.
4. Ibid. 180–1.
5. *Can You Forgive Her?*, ch. 22.
6. *Letters*, i. 316; *An Autobiography*, 182–3.
7. Frederic G. Kitton, *Dickens and His Illustrators* (1899), 113.
8. *An Autobiography*, 248–9.
9. *Letters*, i. 267–8.
10. Ibid. 230–1.
11. See *The Collected Works of Walter Bagehot*, ed. Norman St John-Stevas (1986), xiv. 407–19. Evidence of Bagehot's involvement in the setting up of the *Fortnightly* from Eliza Bagehot's unpublished diary, Dec. 1864 (MS Lord St John).
12. Escott, 173–4; *The Wellesley Index to Victorian Periodicals*, ed. Walter Houghton (Toronto, 1972), ii. 173–83.
13. *The George Eliot Letters*, ed. Gordon S. Haight (New Haven, Conn., 1955), iv. 169, 172; *Letters*, i. 288–9.
14. *An Autobiography*, 192.
15. *Fortnightly Review*, 1 (1 July 1865), 491 ff.
16. *Saturday Review*, 25 Mar. 1865, 362; *Athenaeum*, 27 May 1865, 732.
17. *An Autobiography*, 189–91.
18. *Letters*, i. 304–5.
19. *Fortnightly Review*, 1 (1 June 1865), 129 ff.
20. *Fortnightly Review*, 1 (15 July 1865), 633–5.
21. *Thomas Carlyle: Letters to His Wife*, ed. Trudy Bliss (Cambridge, Mass. 1953), 381; *George Eliot Letters*, viii. 287; *Letters*, i. 258.
22. *Fortnightly Review*, 2 (15 Aug. 1865), 82–90.

23. Ibid. 2 (15 Oct. 1865), 613–26.
24. Ibid. 3 (15 Jan. 1866), 650–2.
25. Ibid. 4 (1 Apr. 1866), 510–12.
26. Ibid. 5 (15 May 1866), 126–8; 5 (1 June 1866), 251–4; 5 (15 June 1866), 381–415; 2 (15 Sept. 1865), 379–80.
27. Ibid. NS 1 (1 Feb. 1867), 252–5.
28. 'George Henry Lewes', [obituary], *Fortnightly*, NS 25 (1 Jan. 1879), 21; Preface to *Essays from 'Good Words'* (1868), quoted in Houghton, *Wellesley Index*, ii. 175.
29. *An Autobiography*, 190–1.
30. *Letters*, i. 353–4.
31. *Macmillan's Magazine*, 49 (Nov. 1883), 55–6 (written with Mrs Humphry Ward); 'In and Out of Society', *Life*, 14 Dec. 1882, 1037.
32. 'What Does Ireland Want?', *Saint Pauls Magazine*, 5 (Dec. 1869), 296; 'Mr. Gladstone's Irish Land Bill', *Saint Pauls Magazine*, 5 (Mar. 1870), 621.
33. *He Knew He Was Right*, ch. 55.
34. Michael St John Packe, *The Life of John Stuart Mill* (New York, 1954), 478–9.
35. *An Autobiography*, 190; *Letters*, i. 359–60.
36. Patricia Thomas Srebrnik, *Alexander Strahan: Victorian Publisher* (Ann Arbor, Mich., 1986), 204.
37. *An Autobiography*, 198 ff.
38. *Pall Mall Gazette*, 27 July 1865, 3–4.
39. Ruth apRoberts, Introduction, *Clergymen of the Church of England* (Leicester, 1974), 35–6.
40. 'Gossip about a Newspaper', *St James's Gazette*, 16 Oct. 1883, 5–6.
41. *Pall Mall Gazette*, 10 May 1865, 3–4.
42. *Letters*, i. 301.
43. *Hunting Sketches* (1865), 72, 94, 13–18.
44. *Letters*, i. 299, 301–2.
45. *Travelling Sketches* (1866), 3–4, 24–6, 79–80, 107–12.
46. *Letters*, i. 306–7.
47. See Ada Nisbet, *Dickens and Ellen Ternan* (Berkeley, 1952), and Michael Slater, *Dickens and Women* (1983), 202–17.
48. TAT iii. 41; Rose Trollope's MS chronology, Illinois; Thomas Adolphus Trollope family MS letters (courtesy Robert A. Cecil).
49. *An Autobiography*, 326; *North America*, 132.
50. Rose Trollope's MS chronology, Illinois.
51. *An Autobiography*, 204–6.
52. 'On Anonymous Literature', *Fortnightly Review*, 1 (1 July 1865), 491.
53. *Letters*, i. 334–6.
54. Ibid. 337–8.
55. Ibid. 351.
56. *An Autobiography*, 335. See James Gindin, Introduction, *Nina Balatka* (Arno, New York, 1981).
57. *Nina Balatka*, ch. 2.
58. *Rachel Ray*, chs. 24, 25.
59. *South Africa*, ed. J. H. Davidson (Cape Town, 1973), 35.
60. *Nina Balatka*, chs. 8, 2, 5, 6.

61. *Letters*, ii. 541.
62. *Spectator*, 40 (23 Mar. 1867), 329–30, Smalley, 268; *Examiner*, 11 May 1867, 293–4, Smalley, 270; *Athenaeum*, 2 Mar. 1867, 288, Smalley, 266; *London Review*, 14 (2 Mar. 1867), 266–7, Smalley, 267.
63. [W. H. Pollock], 'Anthony Trollope', *Harper's New Monthly Magazine*, 66 (May 1883), 907.
64. *An Autobiography*, 196.
65. *The Belton Estate*, chs. 3, 4, 13, 32.
66. *Athenaeum*, 3 Feb. 1866, 166, Smalley, 262; *Saturday Review*, 21 (3 Feb. 1866), 140–2, Smalley, 263; *Nation*, 2 (4 Jan. 1866), 21–2, Smalley, 254–8.
67. Thomas Carlyle, *Letters and Memorials of Jane Welsh Carlyle*, ed. J. A. Froude (New York, 1883) ii. 227.

CHAPTER 20: FAREWELLS AND *SAINT PAULS MAGAZINE*

1. *Letters*, i. 325.
2. Ibid. 327, 328–9, 331, 332.
3. *Clergymen of the Church of England* (1866), 26–30.
4. Ibid. 33, 35 ff.
5. Ibid. 43 ff.
6. Ibid. 62 ff.
7. Ibid. 97.
8. Ibid. 105–16.
9. Ibid. 124 ff. See Ruth apRoberts, Introduction, *Clergymen of the Church of England* (Leicester, 1974), 35–7.
10. *An Autobiography*, 201.
11. See apRoberts, Introduction, 38 ff.
12. *Contemporary Review*, 2 (June 1866), 240–62.
13. *Guardian*, 6 June 1866, 602; 18 July 1866, 748.
14. *Pall Mall Gazette*, 20 July 1866, 9; 24 July 1866, 3–4.
15. *The Last Chronicle of Barset*, ch. 81.
16. John Wellwood, *Norman Macleod* (Edinburgh and London, 1897), 118, and Donald Macleod, *Memoir of Norman Macleod* (1876), ch. 18; cited in Patricia Thomas Srebrnik, *Alexander Strahan: Victorian Publisher* (Ann Arbor, Mich., 1986), 81.
17. *Fortnightly Review*, 3 (15 Jan. 1866), 529–38.
18. *Saturday Review*, 3 Feb. 1866, 131–3; *Pall Mall Gazette*, 5 Feb. 1866, 3; *Saturday Review*, 13 May 1865, 563–4; *Pall Mall Gazette*, 15 May 1865, 9–10.
19. *Letters*, i. 347.
20. *An Autobiography*, 275; [W. H. Pollock], 'Anthony Trollope', *Harper's New Monthly Magazine*, 66 (May 1883), 909; [Cecilia Meetkerke], 'Anthony Trollope', *Blackwood's Magazine*, 133 (Feb. 1883), 317; Augustus Hare, *The Story of My Life* (1896–1900), v. 300; *Last Chronicle of Barset* MS, Beinecke Library, Yale University.
21. *Letters*, i. 342, 353.
22. *Saturday Review*, 11 (4 May 1861), 451–2, Smalley, 123; *Dublin University Magazine*, 59 (Apr. 1862), 405–6, Smalley, 136.

23. *An Autobiography*, 275–6.
24. *Letters*, i. 348, 350, 352, 355.
25. *Spectator*, 40 (13 July 1867), 778–80, Smalley, 291–2; *London Review*, 15 (20 July 1867), 81, Smalley, 299; *Athenaeum*, 3 Aug. 1867, 141, Smalley, 302; *Blackwood's Magazine*, 102 (Sept. 1867), 277–8, Smalley, 303–4.
26. *An Autobiography*, 274.
27. *The Last Chronicle of Barset*, chs. 1, 77.
28. Ibid., ch. 70.
29. Royal Literary Fund's *Annual Report* for 1867, 27–9.
30. *Letters*, i. 379, 382; Escott, 307.
31. *Letters*, i. 372.
32. *An Autobiography*, 336.
33. *Letters*, i. 372–3.
34. Ibid. 375, 384.
35. Ibid. 387–90.
36. *Linda Tressel*, chs. 1, 9, 6, 14.
37. *An Autobiography*, 284.
38. *Letters*, i. 357–8; see Patricia Thomas Srebrnik, 'Trollope, James Virtue, and *Saint Pauls Magazine*', *Nineteenth-Century Fiction*, 37 (Dec. 1982), 443–63; and John Sutherland, Introduction, *Writings for Saint Paul's Magazine* (Arno, New York, 1981).
39. *Letters*, i. 361–2, 366.
40. *An Autobiography*, 321.
41. New York *Nation*, 18 June 1868; repr. in *Henry James: Literary Criticism*, ed. Leon Edel and Mark Wilson ([Library of America] New York, 1984), 1326–30.
42. 'Anthony Trollope', New York *Century Magazine*, NS 4 (July 1883), 385–95; repr. in *Partial Portraits* (1888) with slight alterations, including the substitution of 'usual' in the phrase 'complete appreciation of the real'.
43. *An Autobiography*, 205–6.
44. *Harper's New Monthly Magazine*, 66 (May 1883), 912.
45. *Letters*, i. 477–8; ii. 540–2.
46. *An Autobiography*, 285–6; *Letters*, i. 378, 387; my thanks to Malcolm Warner for his assessment of the title-page drawing.
47. See Srebrnik, 'Trollope, James Virtue and *Saint Pauls*', 456, n. 35; *Bookseller*, 1 May 1868, 336.
48. *Saint Pauls Magazine*, 1 (Oct. 1867), 1–7.
49. *An Autobiography*, 317, 321.
50. *Letters*, i. 368–9.
51. Ibid. 392.
52. *An Autobiography*, 279–82.
53. *Letters*, ii. 396.
54. *The George Eliot Letters*, ed. Gordon S. Haight (New Haven, Conn., 1955), iv. 392.
55. *An Autobiography*, 271.
56. *Letters*, i. 393; *Spectator*, 2 Nov. 1867, 1219.
57. 'Gossip about a Newspaper', *St James's Gazette*, 16 Oct. 1883, 5–6; *An Autobiography*, 198–203.

58. *Examiner*, 20 July 1867, 452–3, Smalley, 297.
59. *Letters*, i. 399, 447, 408, 492–3, 464, 459–60.
60. Ibid. 442, 418, 399–400, 445, 424, 450, 419.

CHAPTER 21: WASHINGTON AND BEVERLEY

1. *Letters*, i. 416, 419; see Super, *Post Office*, 73 ff.
2. *Letters*, i. 423.
3. Ibid. 397; Charles Kent, *The Dickens Dinner* [1867], 23–5.
4. *The Letters of Charles Dickens*, ed. Walter Dexter (1938), iii. 645.
5. *Letters*, i. 426, 436, 427–8, 435, 436; *An Autobiography*, 308.
6. *An Autobiography*, 308–12.
7. *Phineas Redux*, ch. 2.
8. *Letters*, i. 432; cf. *The New Zealander*, 70 ff.; TAT i. 374 ff.; Rose Trollope's MS chronology, Illinois.
9. *Letters*, i. 429, 449; Whiting, 183.
10. Whiting, 183.
11. *Letters*, i. 433, 437–8.
12. Ibid. 438–9, 448.
13. Ibid. 440.
14. Ibid. 449.
15. Henry Brackenbury, *Some Memories of My Spare Time* (1909), 50–1.
16. *Letters*, ii. 946.
17. *Athenaeum*, 2 May 1868, 623–4; *Letters*, i. 450–1; Joyce Marlow, *The Uncrowned Queen of Ireland* (1975), 23.
18. *Letters*, i. 434.
19. *The Times*, 7 June 1920, 17.
20. Quoted in Michael Sadleir, *Things Past* (1944), 90.
21. *Can You Forgive Her?*, ch. 45.
22. *An Autobiography*, 296–7.
23. Arthur Pollard, *Trollope's Political Novels* (Hull, 1968), 4–5.
24. *Letters*, i. 452; *An Autobiography*, 298; the fullest account of Trollope's election bid at Beverley is in John Halperin, *Trollope and Politics* (1977), ch. 5, 'The Real Thing', 112–50; see also Pollard, *Political Novels*, and Lance O. Tingay, 'Trollope and the Beverley Election', *Nineteenth-Century Fiction*, 5 (June 1950), 23–37.
25. Robert Blake, *Disraeli* (New York, 1967), 450 ff., 473.
26. *An Autobiography*, 300.
27. TAT ii. 128–9.
28. *An Autobiography*, 300.
29. *Beverley Recorder*, 31 Oct. 1868, repr. in Tingay, 'Beverley Election', 26–7.
30. Ibid., repr. in Tingay, 'Beverley Election', 25–6.
31. *Hull and Eastern Counties Herald, Election Supplement*, 3 Nov. 1868, repr. in Tingay, 'Beverley Election', 28.
32. *Letters*, i. 453.
33. *An Autobiography*, 301.
34. *The Duke's Children*, ch. 55.
35. Charles Dickens, 'In Memoriam', *Cornhill Magazine*, 9 (Feb. 1864), 130.

36. *An Autobiography*, 300 ff.
37. Escott, 249–50.
38. *Beverley Recorder*, 14 Nov. 1868, repr. in Tingay, 'Beverley Election', 32.
39. *An Autobiography*, 301.
40. *Beverley Recorder*, 14 Nov. 1868, repr. in Tingay, 'Beverley Election', 30–1.
41. *Beverley Recorder*, 21 Nov. 1868, *Hull News*, 18 Nov. 1869, and 21 Nov. 1868, repr. in Tingay, 'Beverley Election', 32 ff.
42. *Beverley Recorder*, 21 Nov. 1868; reproduced in Frederick Page edn. of *An Autobiography*, 304.
43. *Letters*, i. 454.
44. *Escott*, 247.
45. House of Commons, Parliamentary Papers, 1868–9, XLVIII. 415–523; *Copy of the Minutes of Evidence taken at the Trial of the Beverley Election Petition* (1869), House of Commons, 18 Mar. 1869.
46. *Letters*, i. 480.
47. Halperin, *Trollope and Politics*, 115; Pollard, *Political Novels*, 3.
48. *Beverley Guardian*, 4 Sept. 1869, repr. in Tingay, 'Beverley Election', 36–7; *Report of the Commissioners appointed to inquire into the Suggestion of Corrupt Practices at the last election . . . the Borough of Beverley* 1870; Parliamentary Papers, 1868–9, XV. No. 90; and election expenses, Parliamentary Papers, 1868–9, XVII. No. 424, 11, 58.
49. *An Autobiography*, 305–6.
50. *Ralph the Heir*, ch. 51.
51. *An Autobiography*, 343.
52. *Ralph the Heir*, chs. 20, 21.
53. Information brought to my attention by John Sutherland.
54. *Ralph the Heir*, chs. 40, 51.
55. Escott, 170–1.
56. *Spectator*, 44 (15 Apr. 1871), 450–3, Smalley, 350; *The Times*, 17 Apr. 1871, 6, Smalley, 351.
57. *An Autobiography*, 343.

CHAPTER 22: OTHER POLITICS

1. *An Autobiography*, 326; P. D. Edwards, *Anthony Trollope's Son in Australia* (St Lucia, Queensland, 1982), 4.
2. *Letters*, i. 266–7; ii. 945; i. 479, 483–4; *An Autobiography*, 325.
3. *Letters*, i. 465; *An Autobiography*, 276–7. See Robert H. Taylor's Introduction to the play (Princeton, NJ, 1952, repr. Arno, New York, 1981).
4. *An Autobiography*, 317.
5. *Phineas Finn: The Irish Member*, ch. 18.
6. Ibid., chs. 20, 58.
7. *An Autobiography*, 295–6.
8. *Spectator*, 42 (20 Mar. 1869), 356–7, Smalley, 309; *Saturday Review*, 27 (27 Mar. 1869), 431–2, Smalley, 314–18.
9. *Daily Telegraph*, 31 Mar. 1869, 4; *Letters*, i. 468.
10. *An Autobiography*, 357–8; *Letters*, ii. 692–3.
11. *T. P.'s & Cassell's Weekly*, 5 June 1926, 199–200; Justin McCarthy, *Reminiscences*

(New York, 1900), i. 373–4; Michael Sadleir, *Trollope: A Commentary*, 3rd edn. (1961), 418; John Halperin, *Trollope and Politics* (1977), 82–3, drawing on unpublished Princeton dissertation of Barry A. Bartrum.

12. From *Partial Portraits*, repr. in *The Trollope Critics*, ed. N. John Hall (1981), 16.
13. See P. D. Edwards, 'Trollope and the Reviewers', *Notes and Queries*, NS 15 (Nov. 1968), 420.
14. *An Autobiography*, 321–2.
15. *He Knew He Was Right*, chs. 7, 4, 43.
16. *Spectator*, 42 (12 June 1869), 706–8, Smalley, 324–8; *The Times*, 26 Aug. 1869, 4, Smalley, 329–31; *British Quarterly Review*, 50 (July 1869), 263–4, Smalley, 333; *Saturday Review*, 27 (5 June 1869), 751–3, Smalley, 323.
17. *Can You Forgive Her?*, ch. 11.
18. *North America*, 264–5.
19. *Letters*, ii. 633.
20. *Four Lectures* (1938), 68–88.
21. 'The Journey to Panama', *The Victoria Regia* (1861); 'Miss Ophelia Gledd', *A Welcome* (1863). The stories were reprinted in *Lotta Schmidt: And Other Stories* (1867).
22. *He Knew He Was Right*, chs. 16, 5, 4.
23. Ibid., chs. 51, 16, 25.
24. *The Belton Estate*, chs. 7, 8.
25. See note 1 to ch. 81 in P. D. Edwards' edition of the novel (St Lucia, Queensland, 1974) on the most famous of Mrs Linton's articles, 'The Girl of the Period', *Saturday Review*, 14 Mar. 1868, published just as Trollope was writing this part of *He Knew He Was Right*. See also Vineta Colby, *The Singular Anomaly* (1971) on the sensation it caused.
26. *He Knew He Was Right*, chs. 77, 55, 81, 56.
27. John Sutherland, *Is He Popenjoy?* (Oxford, World's Classics, 1986), Appendix, ii. 313 ff.
28. *Is He Popenjoy?*, chs. 17, 60.
29. *Letters*, i. 508–9; Whiting, 211 ff., 414, 276.
30. *An Autobiography*, 194–5; *Fortnightly Review*, NS 5 (1 June 1869), 748–50.
31. E. A. Freeman, 'The Morality of Field Sports', *Fortnightly Review*, NS 6 (1 Oct. 1869), 353–85; Trollope's 'Mr. Freeman on the Morality of Hunting', *Fortnightly Review*, NS 6 (1 Dec. 1869), 616–25; *An Autobiography*, 194–6.
32. *Saturday Review*, 11 Dec. 1869, 760–1; *Daily Telegraph*, 18 and 19 Dec. 1869; Ruskin's letter appeared 15 Jan. 1870, repr. in *The Complete Works of John Ruskin*, ed. E. T. Cook and Alexander Wedderburn (1908), xxxiv. 498.
33. *Letters*, i. 414, 460, 466.
34. John Sutherland, *The Longman Companion to Victorian Fiction* (1989), 241.
35. *An Autobiography*, 328.
36. *Saint Pauls Magazine*, 4 (July 1869), 466–81.
37. *Letters*, i. 491, 424.
38. *Four Lectures*, 94 ff.
39. *Letters*, i. 483.
40. A. K. H. Boyd, *Twenty-Five Years of St Andrews* (1892), i. 100–1.

41. *World*, 24 Feb. 1892, 19.
42. *Letters*, i. 494–5; Patricia Thomas Srebrnik, 'Trollope, James Virtue, and *Saint Pauls Magazine*', *Nineteenth-Century Fiction*, 37 (Dec. 1982), 457 ff.
43. Patricia Thomas Srebrnik, *Alexander Strahan: Victorian Publisher* (Ann Arbor, Mich., 1986), 107.
44. *An Autobiography*, 285–9.
45. *An Editor's Tales* (1870), 19, 104, 137–8, 53–4, 77, 71, 81.
46. James Payn, *Some Literary Recollections* (1884), 172–3.
47. *Saint Pauls Magazine*, 1 (Jan. 1868), 419–24; John Sutherland in notes to the Penguin edition of *Phineas Finn* (1972) mentions an outbreak of garrottings in the West End in the early 1860s, the victims including an MP on his way to the Reform Club (p. 736).
48. 'Mr. Disraeli and the Mint', *Saint Pauls Magazine*, 4 (May 1869), 192–7.
49. *Letters*, i. 512, 520–1; Robert Blake, *Disraeli* (New York, 1967), 517, 519, 733. See Robert L. Patten, *Charles Dickens and His Publishers* (Oxford, 1978), esp. 215 ff.
50. 'Mr. Disraeli and the Dukes', *Saint Pauls Magazine*, 6 (Aug. 1870), 447–51.
51. *An Autobiography*, 260.
52. *Letters*, ii. 646.
53. *The Wellesley Index of Victorian Periodicals* (Toronto, 1979), iii. 362 ff.; Srebrnik, 'Trollope, James Virtue, and *Saint Pauls Magazine*', 460–1; Srebrnik, *Alexander Strahan*, 116–17.
54. *Letters*, i. 496.
55. 'Ancient Classics for English Readers', *Saint Pauls Magazine*, 5 (Mar. 1870), 664–8.
56. *An Autobiography*, 338–9; *Letters*, i. 503–7, 510, 517.
57. *Letters*, i. 496 n.
58. *The Commentaries of Caesar* (1870), 6–7, 25–7, 158–9.
59. *An Autobiography*, 339; R. H. Super in correspondence with me has argued plausibly that Trollope misread Merivale's abbreviation for 'Commentaries' as 'comic'.
60. *Athenaeum*, 11 June 1870, 771.
61. Michael Sadleir, *Trollope: A Commentary*, 3rd edn. (1961), 310.
62. 'Formosa', *Saint Pauls Magazine*, 5 (Oct. 1869), 75–80.
63. *Letters*, i. 523–4.
64. *John Caldigate*, ch. 5.
65. *An Eye for an Eye*, chs. 3, 21.
66. *Athenaeum*, 30 Apr. 1870, 574; *Saturday Review*, 29 (4 May 1870), 646–7, Smalley, 335–7; *The Times*, 3 June 1870, 4, Smalley, 338.
67. *An Autobiography*, 335–7; *Letters*, i. 532–3.
68. *The Times*, 16 Nov. 1870, 4, Smalley, 339; *Athenaeum*, 19 Nov. 1870, 654, Smalley, 340; *Spectator*, 43 (26 Nov. 1870), 1415–16, Smalley, 341–2; *Saturday Review*, 30 (10 Dec. 1870), 753–5, Smalley, 345.
69. See Gordon N. Ray, 'Trollope at Full Length', *Huntington Library Quarterly*, 31 (Aug. 1968), 321, and John Halperin, introduction to Arno Press edn. of the novel (1981).
70. *An Autobiography*, 335.
71. *The Times*, 16 Nov. 1870, 4, Smalley, 339; *Sun*, 15 Dec. 1870, 2; *Letters*, i. 535.

72. 'Charles Dickens', *Saint Pauls Magazine*, 6 (July 1870), 370–5.
73. David A. Roos, 'Dickens at the Royal Academy of Arts', *Dickensian*, 73 (May 1977), 103–4.
74. *Dublin Review*, 71 (Oct 1872), 393–430, Smalley, 361–4.

CHAPTER 23: AUSTRALIA AND NEW ZEALAND

1. *An Autobiography*, 341.
2. *Letters*, ii. 544–5.
3. *An Autobiography*, 271, 342–3.
4. *Letters*, ii. 548.
5. Ibid. 546; *The George Eliot Letters*, ed. Gordon S. Haight (New Haven, Conn., 1955, 1978), v. 143; ix. 15.
6. Frederic Harrison, *Studies in Early Victorian Literature* (1895), 185–6; [John Morley and Mrs Humphry Ward], 'Anthony Trollope', *Macmillan's Magazine*, 49 (Nov. 1883), 54; Escott, 184–5.
7. *Brisbane Courier* (16 Sept. 1871) and *Sydney Punch* (Oct. 1871); Marcie Muir, *Trollope in Australia* (Adelaide, 1949), 25, 27; 'Trollope's Itinerary', Appendix I, *Australia*, ed. P. D. Edwards and R. B. Joyce (St Lucia, Queensland, 1967), 746 ff.; this edition cited throughout this chapter.
8. MS diary fragment, Houghton Library, Harvard University.
9. *Letters*, ii. 693.
10. Gordon N. Ray, 'Trollope at Full Length', *Huntington Library Quarterly*, 31 (Aug. 1968), 320–1.
11. *Harry Heathcote of Gangoil: A Tale of Australian Bush Life*, ch. 6.
12. *Australia*, 309.
13. Ibid. 313–14.
14. Gordon Clavering Trollope, 'Trollope in Australia', *Sydney Bulletin*, 2 Apr. 1930; quoted in R. C. Terry, *Trollope: Interviews and Recollections* (1987), 180.
15. *Australia*, 597–8, 296, 527.
16. Ibid. 95, 645–6, 596; Muir, *Trollope in Australia*, 68–9, quoting D. C. Cowen, *Australasian*, 8 June 1927; MS diary fragment, Houghton Library (on Miss Scott).
17. *Australia*, 318, 392.
18. Ibid. 121, 124, 299 and n.; Appendix 3, pp. 765 ff.; Muir, *Trollope in Australia*, 22–3.
19. *Australia*, 640, 240, 242–3.
20. Ibid. 496–502, 511–12.
21. Ibid. 569, 582–3, 586.
22. MS Princeton University Library; see Bradford Booth, 'Trollope, Reade, and "Shilly-Shally"', *Trollopian*, 1 (Mar. 1947), 45–54, and 2 (June 1947), 43–51.
23. *Letters*, ii. 558–9, 561–2, 1012.
24. John Hollingshead, *Gaiety Chronicles* (1898), 211.
25. *Letters*, ii. 1013.
26. Ibid. 575; typescript, with MS of the play, Princeton University Library; John Coleman, *Charles Reade As I Knew Him* (1903), 325–6.
27. Booth, 'Trollope, Reade, and "Shilly-Shally"', pt. 1, pp. 49–51.
28. *Australia and New Zealand* (1873), ii. 322, 457.
29. Ibid. 403, 417, 425–6, 322, 394; see Alan Bell, *Sydney Smith* (Oxford, 1980), 198.

30. *Australia and New Zealand*, ii. 463–4, 422.
31. Ibid. 335–6, 475–6; Mair's *Reminiscences*, quoted in *With Anthony Trollope in New Zealand*, ed. A. H. Reed (Wellington, 1969), 149.
32. *Australia and New Zealand*, ii. 561, 471–3.
33. *Australia*, 105, 109, 474–5, 112–13.
34. Ibid. 147, 375–6, 54–5.
35. Ibid. 59, 311.
36. *Letters*, ii. 562.
37. *Australia*, 347.
38. *Letters*, ii. 581.
39. *An Autobiography*, 350.
40. Ibid. 350–1.
41. *The George Eliot Letters*, v. 351, 357.
42. *An Autobiography*, 325.
43. Ibid. 345.
44. Ibid. 344.
45. *The Eustace Diamonds*, ch. 3.
46. *Spectator*, 45 (26 Oct. 1872), 1365–6, Smalley, 372–3; *Saturday Review*, 34 (16 Nov. 1872), 637–8, Smalley, 376.
47. *An Autobiography*, 227–9, 256–7, 344.
48. *Saturday Review*, 34 (16 Nov. 1872), 637, Smalley, 376; *The Times*, 30 Oct. 1872, 4, Smalley, 374.
49. *The Letters of Edward FitzGerald*, ed. A. M. and A. B. Terhune (Princeton, NJ, 1980), iii. 427.
50. Escott, 280.

CHAPTER 24: *THE WAY WE LIVE NOW*

1. *Letters*, ii. 580–1, 579.
2. *An Autobiography*, 353.
3. *The Way We Live Now*, ch. 88.
4. Richard H. Grossman and Andrew Wright, 'Anthony Trollope's Libraries', *Nineteenth-Century Fiction*, 31 (June 1976), 48 ff.
5. Escott, 306.
6. See John A. Sutherland, 'Trollope at Work on *The Way We Live Now*', *Nineteenth-Century Fiction*, 37 (Dec. 1982), 478–81.
7. *An Autobiography*, 353.
8. John Sutherland, Introduction, World's Classics edn. (Oxford, 1982), xvi–xx.
9. Ibid. xxiii–xxiv.
10. *An Autobiography*, 355.
11. *The Way We Live Now*, chs. 2, 89.
12. Ibid., ch. 85.
13. Ibid., chs. 60, 78, 79.
14. Ibid., ch. 43.
15. See Christopher Herbert, *Trollope and Comic Pleasure* (Chicago, 1987), 175 ff., and P. D. Edwards, *Anthony Trollope: His Art and Scope* (St Lucia, Queensland, 1977), 182–3.
16. *The Way We Live Now*, ch. 55.

17. *An Autobiography*, 353–4.
18. *Athenaeum*, 26 June 1875, 851, Smalley, 396; *Spectator*, 48 (26 June 1875), 825–6, Smalley, 397; *Saturday Review*, 40 (17 July 1875), 88–9, Smalley, 401; *Examiner*, 28 Aug. 1875, 384–5, Smalley, 412; *Nation*, 20–1 (2 Sept. 1875), 153–4, Smalley, 413; *Westminster Review*, NS 48 (Oct. 1875), 529–30, Smalley, 415.
19. *The Times*, 24 Aug. 1875, 4, Smalley, 407 (Lady Barker attribution in David Skilton, *Trollope and His Contemporaries* [1972], 162).
20. *The Times*, 11 Aug. 1875, 4.
21. Whiting, 298–9, 285; *Letters*, i. 448 n.
22. *Letters*, ii. 589.
23. Ibid. 591.
24. Whiting, 311.
25. *An Autobiography*, 316.
26. *Mark Twain in Eruption*, ed. Bernard De Voto (1940), 332–3.
27. *Letters*, ii. 599.
28. *An Autobiography*, 350–1.
29. Arthur Waugh, *A Hundred Years of Publishing* (1930), 87.
30. *The Amberley Papers*, ed. Bertrand and Patricia Russell (1938), ii. 27.
31. Quoted in George Somes Layard, *A Great 'Punch' Editor: Being the Life, Letters, and Diaries of Shirley Brooks* (1907), 526.
32. Frederick Locker-Lampson, *My Confidences* (1896), 331–3.
33. Quoted in Robert Ashley, *Wilkie Collins* (New York, 1952), 105.
34. *Word Portraits of Famous Writers*, ed. Mabel E. Wotton (1887), 313–16.
35. *The World*, 24 Feb. 1892, 19.
36. N. John Hall, 'Letters of Thomas Adolphus Trollope to Henry Merivale Trollope, 1882–1892', *University of Pennsylvania Library Chronicle*, 39 (Spring 1973), 116.

CHAPTER 25: PALLISERS AGAIN

1. *An Autobiography*, 347.
2. *Saturday Review*, 37 (9 May 1874), 598–9, Smalley, 387.
3. *Letters*, ii. 565, 569.
4. *An Autobiography*, 345.
5. *Letters*, ii. 600.
6. *An Autobiography*, 317–18.
7. *Phineas Redux*, chs. 51, 33.
8. *Hull and Eastern Counties Herald*, 3 Nov. 1868; Pollard, *Political Novels*, 7.
9. *Phineas Redux*, ch. 32.
10. *An Autobiography*, 319–20.
11. *Phineas Redux*, ch. 67.
12. Ibid., chs. 48, 54, 62, 63.
13. *Spectator*, 47 (3 Jan. 1874), 15–17, Smalley, 380–1.
14. *Phineas Redux*, chs. 24, 25, 31.
15. *Spectator*, 47 (3 Jan. 1874), 15–17, Smalley, 378.
16. 'Phases of Fiction', *Collected Essays* (1966), ii. 57, 62; originally published in the *Bookman*, 1929.
17. *An Autobiography*, 357–60.
18. *The Prime Minister*, chs. 50, 27, 51, 56.

19. *An Autobiography*, 360–1.
20. *The Prime Minister*, ch. 68.
21. Julian Hawthorne, *Confessions and Criticisms* (Boston, 1887), 140–3.
22. *An Autobiography*, 360.
23. *Spectator*, 49 (22 July 1876), 922–3, Smalley, 420–2; *Saturday Review*, 42 (14 Oct. 1876), 481–2, Smalley, 426.
24. *The Letters of Edward FitzGerald*, ed. A. M. and A. B. Terhune (Princeton, NJ, 1980), iv. 144.
25. Ibid. iii. 403, 427, 458; iv. 9, 133.
26. *Jubilee Edition* of Tolstoy's works, XLII. 302; XLVI. 68, 71; XLVIII. 63–4. My thanks to Amy Mandelker and Richard Gustafson.

CHAPTER 26 : *AN AUTOBIOGRAPHY*

1. *Letters*, ii. 642.
2. Ibid. 651–4.
3. *The Tireless Traveler: Twenty Letters to the Liverpool Mercury*, ed. Bradford Allen Booth (Berkeley, Calif., 1941), 48, 62–3, 66–7, 72.
4. *Letters*, ii. 659.
5. Quoted in Edwards and Joyce, Introduction, *Australia*, 36.
6. *Tireless Traveler*, 89–91, 79, 99, 79 ff., 123–4, 126.
7. Ibid. 189–90.
8. *Letters*, ii. 657–9.
9. Ibid. ii. 677–9; see P. D. Edwards, *Anthony Trollope's Son in Australia* (St Lucia, Queensland, 1982), 10 ff.
10. *An Autobiography*, 348.
11. *Sydney Bulletin*, 2 Apr. 1930, quoted in R. C. Terry, *Trollope: Interviews and Recollections* (1987), 180.
12. *Letters*, ii. 679.
13. *Tireless Traveler*, 209.
14. Ibid. 209 and n., 212, 213, 217, 219, 221.
15. *Letters*, ii. 675.
16. *John Caldigate*, ch. 5.
17. *Henry James Letters*, ed. Leon Edel (1974–5), i. 486; ii. 94; *Partial Portraits* (1888), repr. in *The Trollope Critics*, ed. N. John Hall (1981), 2.
18. *Letters*, ii. 557, 671, 691–2.
19. Ibid. 664, 670.
20. Ibid. 673, 679–80.
21. *An Autobiography*, 1, 107, 365–6.
22. *Letters*, ii. 685–6.
23. N. John Hall, 'Seeing Trollope's *An Autobiography* through the Press', *Princeton University Library Chronicle*, 47 (Winter 1986), 197.
24. The passages were restored in the Frederick Page edition of the book, pp. 153, 255–6, 316. *An Autobiography* was printed not from Trollope's manuscript, but from a copy (later destroyed) that Harry made of it. Frederick Page, correcting the first edition against the manuscript, discovered 544 departures from the manuscript—misreadings of Trollope's hand, omissions of single words and groups of words, compressions of words and phrases, transpositions of words and

groups of words, insertions of words and phrases, changes of words, grammatical changes, factual errors. Some of the corruptions were relatively minor, such as changing 'bring down on my head . . .' to 'bring down upon my head . . .' Others were serious, such as the substitution of 'French prig' for 'female prig' in Trollope's characterization of Lily Dale in *The Small House at Allington*, or saying that Archdeacon Grantly in *The Last Chronicle of Barset* was very real 'in his victory' instead of 'at his rectory' ('Seeing *An Autobiography* through the Press', 200–1, 205–6).

25. *Westminster Review*, NS 60 (July 1881), 283, Smalley, 481; *Saturday Review*, 9 Dec. 1882, 755; *The Times*, 13 Oct. 1883, 10, 14 Oct. 1883, 8; *Athenaeum*, 13 Oct. 1883, 457–9; *Spectator*, 56 (20 Oct. 1883), 1343–4 and (27 Oct. 1883), 1373–4; *Saturday Review*, 20 Oct. 1883, 505–6; *Fortnightly Review*, NS 34 (Dec. 1883), 86–7; *Morning Post*, 13 Oct. 1883, 2; *Daily Telegraph*, 13 Oct. 1883, 3.

26. *The Private Papers of Henry Ryecroft* (1903), 213. The view that *An Autobiography* played a major role in diminishing Trollope's reputation was fostered by Michael Sadleir, who did so much to bring Trollope before the public from the 1920s to the 1950s. Sadleir wrote in his Introduction to the 1923 World's Classics edition of the book that it 'made its posthumous appearance, extinguished its author's good name for a quarter of a century, and vanished'. In Sadleir's important and influential *Trollope: A Commentary* (1927), he elaborated on the same point: 'A few months after [Trollope's] death his *Autobiography* appeared, and from beyond the grave he flung in the face of fashionable criticism the aggressive horse-sense of his views on life and book-making.' This caused 'malevolent hostility' and an overwhelming 'tempest of reaction' against his work and ideas (p. 363). Many commentators picked up this notion, including, for example, Frank O'Connor, who wrote that the 'senile fatuity' of Trollope's *Autobiography* caused his reputation to collapse (*The Mirror in the Roadway: A Study of the Modern Novel* [New York, 1956], 165).

27. *Letters*, ii. 691.

28. Ibid. 644, 673, 760.

29. *An Autobiography*, 351–2; Richard Francis Ball and Tresham Gilbey, *The Essex Foxhounds* (1896), 270–1.

30. *Letters*, ii. 614–20.

31. Edmund Yates, *Recollections and Experiences* (1884), i. 237; Gordon N. Ray, *Thackeray: The Age of Wisdom* (New York, 1958), 273.

32. *Letters*, ii. 696; *An Autobiography*, 150; Yates, *Recollections*, i. 237.

33. *An Autobiography*, 215–16.

34. Ibid. 366–7; Elizabeth R. Epperly, *Anthony Trollope's Notes on Old Drama* (University of Victoria ELS Monograph No. 42, 1988), 13 ff.; that which follows draws upon this useful and thorough work on the subject. See also Christopher Herbert, *Trollope and Comic Pleasure* (Chicago, 1987) for Trollope's possible use of old drama in his own fiction.

35. Epperly, *Notes on Old Drama*, 113–19.

36. Ibid. 115–22.

37. Ibid. 49, 104, 93.

38. Ibid. 93, 79–80, 41.

39. Ibid. 75, 63, 60, 98, 108, 110, 89.

40. *Letters*, ii. 1033–4 (Appendix C).
41. *An Autobiography*, 366.
42. See Andrew Wright, 'Trollope Revises Trollope', *Trollope Centenary Essays*, ed. John Halperin (1982), 121 ff.
43. Bodleian MS. Don. c. 10*.
44. *Letters*, ii. 924, 928, 954.
45. Ibid. 699–700.
46. *The Bulgarian Horrors and the Question of the East* (1876), 62, 53.
47. *Letters*, ii. 696.
48. *Pall Mall Gazette*, 8 Dec. 1876, 8; Florence E. Hardy, *The Early Life of Thomas Hardy, 1840–1891* (New York, 1928), 148.

CHAPTER 27: SOUTH AFRICA

1. See Robert H. Taylor, Introduction, *The American Senator* (Arno, New York, 1981).
2. Mrs Gerald Porter, *Annals of a Publishing House: John Blackwood* [vol. iii of *William Blackwood and His Sons*] (1898), 317; see *Letters*, ii. 722–3.
3. *The American Senator*, chs. 12, 55, 66, 28.
4. *Letters*, ii. 702, 710.
5. *Examiner*, 21 July 1877, 916–17, Smalley, 430; *The Times*, 10 Aug. 1877, 3, Smalley, 432.
6. *The American Senator*, chs. 12, 42, 51.
7. Ibid., chs. 77, 78.
8. *Letters*, ii. 701.
9. *Athenaeum*, 16 June 1877, 766–7, Smalley, 428; *Saturday Review*, 43 (30 June 1877), 803–4, Smalley, 429; *The Times*, 10 Aug. 1877, 3, Smalley, 431; *Academy*, 12 (24 Nov. 1877), 487–8, Smalley, 435; *Spectator*, 51 (31 Aug. 1878), 1101–2, Smalley, 436; *Nation*, 25 (23 Aug. 1877), 122–3, Smalley, 433; *Examiner*, 21 July 1877, 916–17, Smalley, 430.
10. *Letters*, ii. 729.
11. *South Africa*, ed. J. H. Davidson (Cape Town, 1973), 76.
12. *Letters*, ii. 730, 731.
13. *South Africa*, 77, 83.
14. Ibid. 84.
15. *Letters*, ii. 735.
16. See 'Kafir Land', *Fortnightly Review*, NS 23 (Feb. 1878), 196–7; *South Africa*, 160–1 and n.
17. *South Africa*, 212.
18. Frances Sarah Colenso, *Letters from Natal*, ed. Wyn Rees (Pietermaritzburg, 1958), 337–8.
19. *South Africa*, 241–4.
20. Ibid. 235, 231–2, 226, 228.
21. Ibid. 434, 444–5.
22. Ibid. 245, 248, 251; *Letters*, ii. 736.
23. *Letters*, ii. 739.
24. *South Africa*, 279 ff., 286–92, 324.

25. H. Rider Haggard, *The Days of My Life* (1926), i. 136–7; Davidson, *South Africa*, Editor's Introduction, 8, 24, n. 47.
26. *The Fixed Period*, ch. 5; see Davidson, *South Africa*, Appendix F, 495.
27. *Letters*, ii. 740.
28. *South Africa*, 485, and Editor's Introduction, 9.
29. Ibid. 334; *Letters*, ii. 742.
30. *South Africa*, 370, 373, 360, 368–9.
31. Ibid. 452, 398.
32. Ibid. 408.
33. *Letters*, ii. 740.
34. *South Africa*, 109.
35. MS Parrish Collection.
36. *South Africa*, 452 ff.
37. *Examiner*, 2 Mar. 1878, 271–2; *Saturday Review*, 23 Feb. 1878, 241–3; *New York Tribune*, 4 Mar. 1878, 6; *Letters*, ii. 763.
38. *South Africa*, Appendix A, 471; *Letters*, ii. 826.
39. MS Taylor Collection.

CHAPTER 28: *POPENJOY AND AYALA*

1. *Letters*, i. 405, 407; ii. 760.
2. Ibid. ii. 835.
3. Ibid. 714, 708–9.
4. Whiting, 350–3, 358–9.
5. *Letters*, ii. 770–2.
6. *Dublin University Magazine*, 4 (Oct. 1879), 436–42, Smalley, 458; see John Sutherland, Introduction, *Is He Popenjoy?* (Oxford, World's Classics, 1986), viii–ix.
7. *Academy*, 8 June 1878, 505, Smalley, 440; *Saturday Review*, 45 (1 June 1878), 695–6, Smalley, 440; *The Times*, 14 Sept. 1878, 4, Smalley, 443; *Spectator*, 51 (5 Oct. 1878), 1243–4, Smalley, 444.
8. *Is He Popenjoy?*, chs. 6, 14, 23.
9. Ibid., chs. 30, 36, 53.
10. Ibid., chs. 44, 56.
11. Ibid., chs. 1, 28, 14, 16, 41, 61.
12. Ibid., ch. 63.
13. Mrs E. M. Ward, *Memories of Ninety Years*, ed. Isabel G. McAlister (1924), 147.
14. *The Autobiography of Alfred Austin* (1911), i. 166.
15. Frederick Locker-Lampson, *My Confidences* (1896), 331.
16. 'Iceland', *Fortnightly Review*, NS 24 (Aug. 1878), 176.
17. *How the 'Mastiffs' Went to Iceland* (1878), 5–11.
18. 'Iceland', 179, 177, 182; *How the 'Mastiffs' Went to Iceland*, 13–14, 24–5.
19. 'Iceland', 179, 184–5; *How the 'Mastiffs' Went to Iceland*, 30 ff., 40–1.
20. *How the 'Mastiffs' Went to Iceland*, 45–6.
21. *Keble's Margate & Ramsgate Gazette*, 13 July 1878; *Thanet Guardian*, 20 July 1878, 4.
22. *Letters*, ii. 783.
23. 'A Walk in a Wood', *Good Words*, 20 (Sept. 1879), 595 ff.

24. *Letters*, ii. 785, 790–1, 636.
25. Sadleir, *Bibliography*, 183.
26. See Robert Tracy, *Trollope's Later Novels* (Berkeley, Calif., 1978), 244–51, and Andrew Wright, *Anthony Trollope: Dream and Art* (1983), 141–7.
27. *The Times*, 16 July 1881, 5, Smalley, 486; *Saturday Review*, 51 (11 June 1881), 756–7, Smalley, 484.
28. *Ayala's Angel*, chs. 64, 5, 13, 14, 58.
29. [Cecilia Meetkerke], 'Anthony Trollope', *Blackwood's Magazine*, 133 (Feb. 1883), 317.
30. *Letters*, ii. 939.
31. Richard Mullen, *Anthony Trollope: A Victorian in his World* (1990), 646–7; Mullen points out that on her death in 1908—while Rose was still alive—her estate, something over £4,000, went to Harry and Fred (660).
32. *Letters*, ii. 793–4.
33. 'George Henry Lewes', *Fortnightly Review*, NS 25 (1 Jan. 1879), 15–24.

CHAPTER 29: EXTENDING THE RANGE

1. *Letters*, ii. 815.
2. *An Autobiography*, 243, 185–6.
3. *Thackeray* (1879), 2, 61, 19–20.
4. Ibid. 34–6, 48–9.
5. Ibid. 52–5
6. Ibid. 122–3, 95, 79, 111.
7. Ibid. 184–8.
8. Ibid. 196–201.
9. *Nation*, 21 Aug. 1879, 127; *Lippincott's Magazine*, Sept. 1879, 387–9; *Atlantic Monthly*, Aug. 1879, 267; see Robert A. Colby, 'Trollope as Thackerayan', *Dickens Studies Annual*, 11 (1983), 266–8.
10. *Letters*, ii. 831.
11. *Spectator*, 52 (6 Sept. 1879), 1130–2; *Time*, 1 (Aug. 1879), 628; *Athenaeum*, 14 June 1879, 749–50; *Academy*, 15 (21 June 1879), 533; *Westminster Review*, NS 56 (July 1879), 258; *Fraser's Magazine*, NS 20 (Aug. 1879), 264–7.
12. *Pall Mall Gazette*, 18 Oct. 1879, 12.
13. *Letters*, ii. 854–5.
14. Ibid. 947; journal quoted in Winifred Gérin, *Anne Thackeray Ritchie: A Biography* (Oxford, 1981), 193.
15. *An Autobiography*, 273.
16. *Spectator*, 52 (15 Feb. 1879), 210–11, Smalley, 445–8.
17. *Letters*, ii. 749–51, 789, 814–15.
18. *John Caldigate*, chs. 18, 45, 46, 44.
19. Ibid., chs. 47, 64.
20. *Letters*, ii. 815.
21. *Examiner*, 2 Aug. 1879, 1000, Smalley, 454; *The Times*, 8 Aug. 1879, 3, Smalley, 455; *Athenaeum*, 14 June 1879, 755, Smalley, 450; *Academy*, 16 (5 July 1879), 5, Smalley, 451; *Spectator*, 52 (19 July 1879), 916–17, Smalley, 452; *Saturday Review*, 48 (16 Aug. 1879), 216–17, Smalley, 456.
22. *Letters*, ii. 805.

23. See J. Hillis Miller, Introduction, *Cousin Henry* (Arno, New York, 1981).
24. *Academy*, 16 (1 Nov. 1879), 316, Smalley, 465; *The Times*, 6 Nov. 1879, 6, Smalley, 466; *Athenaeum*, 18 Oct. 1879, 495, Smalley, 460; *Saturday Review*, 48 (25 Oct. 1879), 515–16, Smalley, 464; *Examiner*, 25 Oct. 1879, 1382, Smalley, 462–3; *Spectator*, 52 (18 Oct. 1879), 1319–21, Smalley, 461.
25. *North American Review*, 129 (Sept. 1879), 203–22; *An Autobiography*, 144–5; Hawthorne's tribute had come in a letter to James T. Fields, who published extracts from it in 1871 and 1872.
26. *Letters*, ii. 822–3, 827.
27. Ibid. 834, 836, 839, 840–1.
28. *Blackwood's Magazine*, 121 (May 1877), 597–604; repr. in *Tales from 'Blackwood'*, NS 12 (1881).
29. *Letters*, ii. 847, 856, 859.
30. Escott, 303; MS letter of 12 Apr. 1923, Parrish Collection.
31. N. John Hall, *Salmagundi: Byron, Allegra, and the Trollope Family* (Pittsburgh, 1975), 72.
32. *Dr Wortle's School*, chs. 11, 12, 13.
33. *Letters*, ii. 860.
34. *Dr Wortle's School*, ch. 9; Ruth apRoberts discusses Trollope and Situation Ethics in *The Moral Trollope* (1971); see especially ch. 2.
35. The *Critic* (New York), 12 Feb. 1881, 35, Smalley, 476.
36. *Marion Fay*, chs. 24, 46.
37. *Westminster Review*, NS 58 (Oct 1880), 574, Smalley, 474; *Saturday Review*, 49 (12 June 1880), 767–8, Smalley, 468; *Athenaeum*, 29 May 1880, 694, Smalley, 467; *Illustrated London News*, 76 (26 June 1880), 622, Smalley, 472; *Spectator*, 53 (12 June 1880), 754–5, Smalley, 470–1; *Nation*, 31 (19 Aug. 1880), 138–9, Smalley, 473.
38. *The Duke's Children*, ch. 74.
39. *An Autobiography*, 365–6.
40. *The Duke's Children*, ch. 39.
41. *Partial Portraits* (1888), repr. in *The Trollope Critics*, ed. N. John Hall (1981), 13, 16.
42. *The Duke's Children*, chs. 20, 77.
43. Ibid., chs. 10, 35, 20, 31.
44. *Letters*, ii. 920, 903.
45. Ibid. 807; Arthur Waugh, *A Hundred Years of Publishing* (1930), 180ff.
46. *Letters*, ii. 905, 867; quotation from Horace, *Epistles* I. i. 61.
47. *Letters*, ii. 702.
48. *Fortnightly Review*, NS 21 (Apr. 1877), 495–515, and NS 22 (Sept. 1877), 401–22.
49. *Letters*, ii. 842, 880, 867.
50. *The Life of Cicero* (1880), i. 37–8, 176; ii. 133–4, 46–7.
51. Ibid. i. 176; ii. 133–4, 46–7 (MS note dated 22 Oct. 1876, Parrish Collection); ii. 169–70. See apRoberts, *The Moral Trollope*, ch. 3.
52. *The Life of Cicero*, i. 231; ii. 337, 37–8.
53. Ibid. i. 50–1; ii. 226.
54. [John Morley and Mrs Humphry Ward], 'Anthony Trollope', *Macmillan's Magazine*, 49 (Nov. 1883), 56.

55. *St James's Gazette*, 7 Jan. 1881, 12–13; *The World*, 10 Jan. 1881, 19; *Pall Mall Gazette*, 10 Jan. 1881, 11–12; *Letters*, ii. 891.
56. *Letters*, ii. 895, 911; *Saturday Review*, 22 Jan. 1881, 122, and 26 Feb. 1881, 279–80; *Daily News*, 6 Jan. 1881, 6; *Truth*, 3 Feb. 1881, 159.

CHAPTER 30: A COUNTRY RESIDENCE

1. *Letters*, ii. 870.
2. 'A Walk in a Wood', *Good Words*, 20 (Sept. 1879), 596.
3. The house and 70 acres were sold in 1886 for £5,000; information from Lady Faber, recent owner of the house.
4. *Letters*, ii. 874.
5. Ibid. 875–7.
6. Escott, 299–300.
7. *Publishers' Circular*, 25 (18 Dec. 1882), 1515–16.
8. *Letters*, ii. 877–8, 816–18.
9. Ibid. 909.
10. Sir John Tilley, *London to Tokyo* (1942), 8.
11. *London Tradesmen* (1928), 32–9.
12. Ibid. 16.
13. Ibid. 1–11.
14. *The Prime Minister*, ch. 1.
15. T. A. Trollope family letters, courtesy Robert A. Cecil; *Letters*, ii. 797, 844.
16. Forrest Reid, *Illustrators of the Eighteen Sixties* (1928), 216; *Letters*, ii. 613; see N. John Hall, *Trollope and His Illustrators* (1980), 140–9.
17. Richard Mullen, *Anthony Trollope: A Victorian in His World* (1990), 658.
18. *Letters*, ii. 737, 744, 739, 746, 856n., 857, 871, 874, 899, 918, 925, 930.
19. Ibid. 874, 886.
20. Ibid. 886–7.
21. *The Fixed Period*, ch. 8.
22. Quoted in Robert Tracy, *Trollope's Later Novels* (Berkeley, Calif., 1978), 285.
23. *The Fixed Period*, ch. 6.
24. Ibid., chs. 2, 12, 4, 11, 12.
25. Ibid., ch. 6.
26. *Letters*, ii. 903, 920, 1037 (Appendix D).
27. [Review of *An Autobiography*], *Blackwood's Magazine*, 134 (Nov. 1883), 594.
28. See David Skilton, '*The Fixed Period*: Anthony Trollope's Novel of 1980', *Studies in the Literary Imagination* 6 (Fall 1973), 49–50; Harvey Cushing, *The Life of Sir William Osler*, (Oxford, 1925), i. 664–70.
29. MS, Cremation Society of Great Britain; *Letters*, i. 409.
30. *The Times*, 12 Apr. 1882, 3; see Skilton, 'Anthony Trollope's Novel of 1980', 48.
31. *Letters*, ii. 904, 908, 923–4.
32. Ibid. 892.
33. Quoted in Whiting, 396.
34. *Letters*, ii. 895.
35. MS Letter, Parrish Collection, Ada Strickland Trollope to Michael Sadleir, 9 Oct. 1926.
36. *Macmillan's Magazine*, 47 (Jan. 1883), 237–9.

37. *Letters*, ii. 911.
38. T. A. Trollope family letters, courtesy Robert A. Cecil; *Letters*, ii. 917, 919.

CHAPTER 31: A LATE MASTERWORK

1. *John Caldigate*, ch. 1. See Robert Tracy, *Trollope's Later Novels* (Berkeley, Calif., 1978), 305 ff.; Christopher Herbert, *Trollope and Comic Pleasure* (Chicago, 1987), 124 ff.; and Elizabeth R. Epperly, *Anthony Trollope's Notes on Old Drama* (University of Victoria ELS Monograph No. 42, 1988), Appendix B, 134 ff.
2. *Mr Scarborough's Family*, chs. 31, 50.
3. Ibid., chs. 54, 8, 21, 41.
4. *Academy*, 23 (19 May 1883), 344, Smalley, 514; *Saturday Review*, 55 (19 May 1883), 642–3, Smalley, 515.
5. *An Autobiography*, 363 ff.
6. Ibid. 362–5.
7. Yale MS letters of 2 Dec. 1896 and 4 Aug. 1897; House of Commons, Parliamentary Papers, 1897, LII. 130.
8. *Letters*, ii. 945, 961, 969, 973, 974.
9. 'My Countrymen', *Cornhill Magazine*, 13 (Feb. 1866), 153–72; repr. in *Friendship's Garland* (1871).
10. *Lord Palmerston* (1882), 200, 4, 53, 118, 10.
11. Ibid. 8–9, 95.
12. Ibid. 46, 209, 212, 210, 213–14.
13. *Academy*, 22 (5 Aug. 1882), 98–9; *Saturday Review*, 5 Aug. 1882, 182–3; *Athenaeum*, 16 Sept. 1882, 367.

CHAPTER 32: AN OLD MAN

1. *Letters*, ii. 932, 945, 947, 948, 950.
2. [Cecilia Meetkerke], 'Last Reminiscences of Anthony Trollope', *Temple Bar*, 70 (Jan. 1884), 133–4.
3. *Letters*, ii. 938–9, 941.
4. My thanks to Dr John G. Weir of St Andrews, Scotland, for this assessment of Trollope's illness.
5. *Letters*, ii. 959, 957.
6. Ibid. 942.
7. *Blackwood's Magazine*, 134 (Nov. 1883), 594.
8. *Letters*, ii. 936, 959.
9. Ibid. 970.
10. Meetkerke, 'Last Reminiscences', 134.
11. *An Old Man's Love*, ch. 2.
12. Ibid., chs. 2, 11, 18.
13. T. W. Moody, 'Fenianism, Home Rule and the Land War', *The Course of Irish History*, ed. T. W. Moody and F. X. Martin (Cork, 1967), 275 ff.; Robert Tracy, Introduction, *The Landleaguers* (Arno, New York, 1981).
14. *Letters*, ii. 963, 978, 984.
15. Ibid. 962–6.
16. Ibid. 864–5.
17. Ibid. 978, 980, 985.

18. Ibid. 985.
19. *Spectator*, 56 (15 Dec. 1883), 1627, Smalley, 518.
20. *The Landleaguers*, ch. 41.
21. Ibid., chs. 5, 23, 7, 18.
22. MS of *The Landleaguers*, Taylor Collection.
23. The Arno Press *Selected Works* (1981) added three titles to the Trollope bibliography, *Miscellaneous Essays and Reviews*, ed. Michael Y. Mason, *Writings for Saint Paul's Magazine*, ed. John Sutherland, and *Collected Short Stories*, ed. Susan L. Humphreys.
24. Cf. Bradford A. Booth, *Anthony Trollope: Aspects of His Life and Art* (1958), 229 ff.
25. Quoted from the *Pall Mall Gazette* by Michael Holroyd, 'George Bernard Shaw, Cub Reviewer', *New York Times Book Review*, 18 Sept. 1988, 38.
26. *Saturday Review*, 54 (9 Dec. 1882), 755–6.
27. Gordon N. Ray, 'Trollope at Full Length', *Huntington Library Quarterly*, 31 (Aug. 1968), 334.
28. Weigall MSS, Kent County Archives, and *Letters*, i. 321 n.; James Bryce, *Studies in Contemporary Biography* (New York, 1903), 118–19, 126–7; Edmund Downey, *Charles Lever: His Life in His Letters* (Edinburgh, 1906), ii. 227; Frederic Harrison, *Studies in Early Victorian Literature* (1895), 223; W. P. Frith, *My Autobiography and Reminiscences* (1887), ii. 335; Cecil Hay, *The Club and Dining Room* (1870), i. 236; Howells, *My Literary Passions* (New York, 1895), 247; *Letters of Lord Acton to Mary Gladstone*, ed. Herbert Paul (1904), 164.
29. Sala's remarks inscribed in a copy of Trollope's *Autobiography*, reproduced in Frederick Page edn., xix; Collins quoted in Robert Ashley, *Wilkie Collins* (New York, 1952), 105; Frederick Locker-Lampson, *My Confidences* (1896), 331–2; T. H. S. Escott, 'A Novelist of the Day', *Time*, 1 (Aug. 1879), 627; MS, Murray–Prior Papers: Oxley OM 54–1, letter of 12 Dec. 1882 (University of Queensland).

CHAPTER 33: LAST DAYS

1. *Letters*, ii. 982–3.
2. Ibid. 986–91.
3. [E. A. Freeman], 'Anthony Trollope', *Macmillan's Magazine*, 47 (June 1883), 239.
4. *Letters*, ii. 991–3.
5. Ibid. 993; *The Letters and Diaries of John Henry Newman*, ed. C. S. Dessain and Thomas Gornall (Oxford, 1977), xxxi. 97*–98*.
6. Freeman, 'Trollope', 240.
7. Michael Sadleir, *Trollope: A Commentary*, 3rd edn. (1961), 331; Arthur Waugh, *A Hundred Years of Publishing* (1930), 87.
8. Sir John Tilley, *London To Tokyo* (1942), 8.
9. *The Times*, 6 Nov. 1882, 9; 8 Nov. 1882, 9; 11 Nov. 1882, 10; 14 Nov. 1882, 9; 16 Nov. 1882, 9.
10. [Cecilia Meetkerke], 'Last Reminiscences' of Anthony Trollope, *Temple Bar*, 70 (Jan. 1884), 134.
11. *Letters*, Appendix D, ii. 1036.
12. J. B. Atkins, *The Life of William Howard Russell* (1911), ii. 316–17.
13. *The Times*, 6 Dec. 1882, 9.

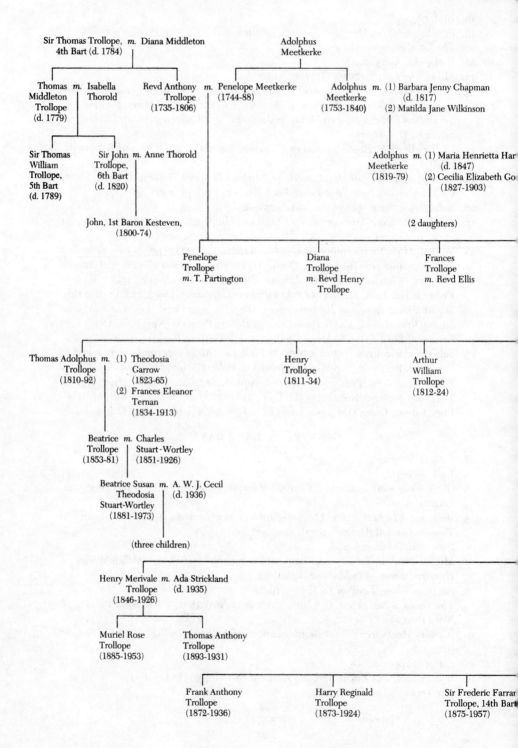

FAMILY TREE

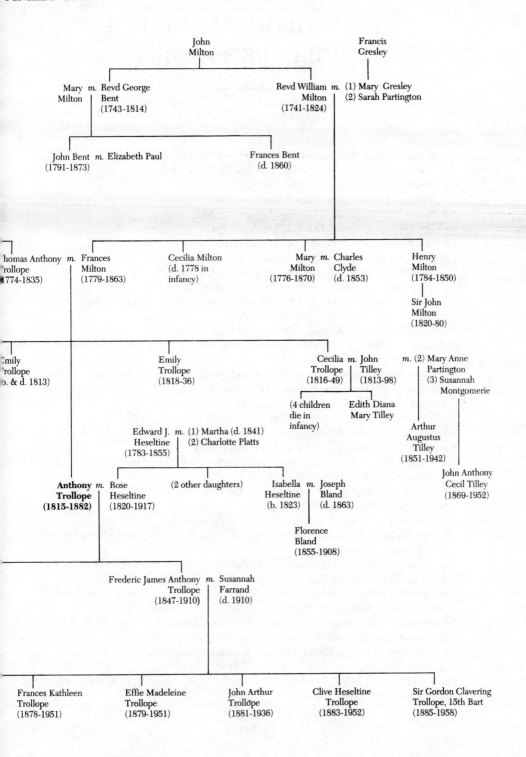

John
Milton

Francis
Gresley

Mary *m.* Revd George
Milton Bent
(1743-1814)

Revd William *m.* (1) Mary Gresley
Milton (2) Sarah Partington
(1741-1824)

John Bent *m.* Elizabeth Paul
(1791-1873)

Frances Bent
(d. 1860)

Thomas Anthony *m.* Frances
Trollope Milton
(1774-1835) (1779-1863)

Cecilia Milton
(d. 1778 in
infancy)

Mary *m.* Charles
Milton Clyde
(1776-1870) (d. 1853)

Henry
Milton
(1784-1850)

Sir John
Milton
(1820-80)

Emily
Trollope
b. & d. 1813)

Emily
Trollope
(1818-36)

Cecilia *m.* John
Trollope Tilley
(1816-49) (1813-98)

m. (2) Mary Anne
Partington
(3) Susannah
Montgomerie

(4 children
die in
infancy)

Edith Diana
Mary Tilley

Arthur
Augustus
Tilley
(1851-1942)

Edward J. *m.* (1) Martha (d. 1841)
Heseltine (2) Charlotte Platts
(1783-1855)

John Anthony
Cecil Tilley
(1869-1952)

Anthony *m.* Rose
Trollope Heseltine
(1815-1882) (1820-1917)

(2 other daughters)

Isabella *m.* Joseph
Heseltine Bland
(b. 1823) (d. 1863)

Florence
Bland
(1855-1908)

Frederic James Anthony *m.* Susannah
Trollope Farrand
(1847-1910) (d. 1910)

Frances Kathleen
Trollope
(1878-1951)

Effie Madeleine
Trollope
(1879-1951)

John Arthur
Trollope
(1881-1936)

Clive Heseltine
Trollope
(1883-1952)

Sir Gordon Clavering
Trollope, 15th Bart
(1885-1958)

CHRONOLOGICAL LIST OF
TROLLOPE'S WORKS

The Macdermots of Ballycloran, 3 vols., London: Newby, 1847.

The Kellys and the O'Kellys, 3 vols., London: Colburn, 1848.

La Vendée, 3 vols., London: Colburn, 1850.

The Warden, London: Longman, 1855.

Barchester Towers, 3 vols., London: Longman, 1857.

The Three Clerks, 3 vols., London: Bentley, 1858.

Doctor Thorne, 3 vols., London: Chapman & Hall, 1858.

The Bertrams, 3 vols., London: Chapman & Hall, 1859.

The West Indies and the Spanish Main, London: Chapman & Hall, 1859.

Castle Richmond, 3 vols., London: Chapman & Hall, 1860.

Framley Parsonage, 3 vols., London: Smith, Elder, 1861. Serialized in the Cornhill Magazine, Jan. 1860–Apr. 1861.

Tales of All Countries, London: Chapman & Hall, 1861.

Orley Farm, 2 vols., London: Chapman & Hall, 1862. Serialized in monthly shilling parts, Mar. 1861–Oct. 1862.

The Struggles of Brown, Jones, and Robinson By One of the Firm, New York: Harper, 1862 [pirated edition; first authorized edn., London: Smith, Elder, 1870]. Serialized in the Cornhill Magazine, Aug. 1861–Mar. 1862.

North America, 2 vols., London: Chapman & Hall, 1862.

Tales of All Countries, Second Series, London: Chapman & Hall, 1863.

Rachel Ray, 2 vols., London: Chapman & Hall, 1863.

The Small House at Allington, 2 vols., London: Smith, Elder, 1864. Serialized in the Cornhill Magazine, Sept. 1862–Apr. 1864.

Can You Forgive Her?, 2 vols., London: Chapman & Hall, 1865. Serialized in monthly shilling parts, Jan. 1864–Aug. 1865.

Miss Mackenzie, 2 vols., London: Chapman & Hall, 1865.

Hunting Sketches, London: Chapman & Hall, 1865. Essays reprinted from the Pall Mall Gazette, Feb.–Mar. 1865.

The Belton Estate, 3 vols., London: Chapman & Hall, 1866. Serialized in the Fortnightly Review, 15 May 1865–1 Jan. 1866.

Travelling Sketches, London: Chapman & Hall, 1866. Essays reprinted from the Pall Mall Gazette, Aug.–Sept. 1865.

Clergymen of the Church of England, London: Chapman & Hall, 1866. Essays reprinted from the Pall Mall Gazette, Nov. 1865–Jan. 1866.

Nina Balatka, 2 vols., Edinburgh and London: Blackwood, 1867. Serialized in Blackwood's Magazine, July 1866–Jan. 1867.

The Claverings, 2 vols., London: Smith, Elder, 1867. Serialized in the Cornhill Magazine, Feb. 1866–May 1867.

Chronological List of Trollope's Works

The Last Chronicle of Barset, 2 vols., London: Smith, Elder, 1867. Serialized in weekly sixpenny parts, 1 Dec. 1866–6 July 1867.

Lotta Schmidt: And Other Stories, London: Strahan, 1867.

Linda Tressel, 2 vols., Edinburgh and London: Blackwood, 1868. Serialized in *Blackwood's Magazine*, Oct. 1867–May 1868.

Phineas Finn: The Irish Member, 2 vols., London: Virtue, 1869. Serialized in *Saint Pauls Magazine*, Oct. 1867–May 1869.

Did He Steal It? A Comedy in Three Acts, London [privately printed by Virtue], 1869.

He Knew He Was Right, 2 vols., London: Strahan, 1869. Serialized in weekly sixpenny parts, 17 Oct. 1868–22 May 1869.

The Vicar of Bullhampton, London: Bradbury, Evans, 1870. Serialized in monthly shilling numbers, July 1869–May 1870.

An Editor's Tales, London: Strahan, 1870.

The Commentaries of Caesar, Edinburgh and London: Blackwood, 1870.

Sir Harry Hotspur of Humblethwaite, London: Hurst & Blackett, 1871. Serialized in *Macmillan's Magazine*, May–Dec. 1870.

Ralph the Heir, 3 vols., London: Hurst & Blackett, 1871. Serialized in monthly numbers and simultaneously as supplement to *Saint Pauls Magazine*, Jan. 1870–July 1871.

The Golden Lion of Granpere, London: Tinsley, 1872. Serialized in *Good Words*, Jan.–Aug. 1872.

The Eustace Diamonds, 3 vols., London: Chapman & Hall, 1873. Serialized in the *Fortnightly Review*, July 1871–Feb. 1873.

Australia and New Zealand, 2 vols., London: Chapman & Hall, 1873.

Phineas Redux, 2 vols., London: Chapman & Hall, 1874. Serialized in the *Graphic*, 19 July 1873–10 Jan. 1874.

Lady Anna, 2 vols., London: Chapman & Hall, 1874. Serialized in the *Fortnightly Review*, Apr. 1873–Apr. 1874.

Harry Heathcote of Gangoil: A Tale of Australian Bush Life, London: Sampson Low, 1874. Published in the *Graphic*, 25 Dec. 1873.

The Way We Live Now, 2 vols., London: Chapman & Hall, 1875. Serialized in monthly shilling parts, Feb. 1874–Sept. 1875.

The Prime Minister, 4 vols., London: Chapman & Hall, 1876. Serialized in monthly shilling parts, Nov. 1875–June 1876.

The American Senator, 3 vols., London: Chapman & Hall, 1877. Serialized in *Temple Bar*, May 1876–July 1877.

South Africa, 2 vols., London: Chapman & Hall, 1878.

Is He Popenjoy?, 3 vols., London: Chapman & Hall, 1878. Serialized in *All the Year Round*, 13 Oct. 1877–13 July 1878.

How the 'Mastiffs' Went to Iceland, London: Virtue, 1878.

An Eye for an Eye, 2 vols., London: Chapman & Hall, 1879. Serialized in the *Whitehall Review*, 24 Aug. 1878–1 Feb. 1879.

Thackeray, London: Macmillan, 1879.

John Caldigate, 3 vols., London: Chapman & Hall, 1879. Serialized in *Blackwood's Magazine*, Apr. 1878–June 1879.

Cousin Henry, 2 vols., London: Chapman & Hall, 1879. Serialized in the *Manchester Weekly Times* and the *North British Weekly Mail*, 8 Mar.–24 May 1879.

The Duke's Children, 3 vols., London: Chapman & Hall, 1880. Serialized in *All the Year Round*, 4 Oct. 1879–14 July 1880.

The Life of Cicero, 2 vols., London: Chapman & Hall, 1880.

Dr Wortle's School, 2 vols., London: Chapman & Hall, 1881. Serialized in *Blackwood's Magazine*, May–Dec. 1880.

Ayala's Angel, 3 vols., London: Chapman & Hall, 1881.

Why Frau Frohmann Raised Her Prices: And Other Stories, London: Isbister, 1882.

Lord Palmerston, London: Isbister, 1882.

Kept in the Dark, 2 vols., London: Chatto & Windus, 1882. Serialized in *Good Words*, May–Dec. 1882.

Marion Fay, 3 vols., London: Chapman & Hall, 1882. Serialized in the *Graphic*, 3 Dec. 1881–3 June 1882.

The Fixed Period, 2 vols., Edinburgh and London: Blackwood, 1882. Serialized in *Blackwood's Magazine*, Oct. 1881–Mar. 1882.

Mr Scarborough's Family, 3 vols., London: Chatto & Windus, 1883. Serialized in *All the Year Round*, 27 May 1882–16 June 1883.

The Landleaguers, 3 vols., London: Chatto & Windus, 1883. Serialized in *Life*, 16 Nov. 1882–4 Oct. 1883.

An Autobiography, 2 vols., Edinburgh and London: Blackwood, 1883.

An Old Man's Love, 2 vols., Edinburgh and London: Blackwood, 1884.

The Noble Jilt, London: Constable, 1923 [written 1850].

London Tradesmen, London: Mathews and Marrot, 1927 [essays reprinted from the *Pall Mall Gazette*, 10 July 1880–7 Sept. 1880].

The New Zealander, Oxford: The Clarendon Press, 1972 [written 1855–6].

Miscellaneous Essays and Reviews, New York: Arno Press, 1981 [essays published in various magazines, 1851–81].

Writings for Saint Paul's Magazine, New York: Arno Press, 1981 [essays published 1867–70].

Collected Short Stories, New York: Arno Press, 1981 [miscellaneous short stories published 1866–82].

INDEX

Index

Bell, Robert, 202, 216, 219–20, 244, 263, 270, 303, 309
Bell, Mrs Robert, 303
Bell Telephone Co., 436
Bent family, 5
Bent, Frances (Fanny), 5, 46, 338
Bent, George, 5
Bent, Revd George, 5
Bent, Mrs George (Mary Milton), 5
Bent, John, 5
Bentinck, George, 219
Bentley, George, 404, 410, 436, 464
Bentley, Richard, 53, 68, 97, 102, 155, 159, 169
Bentley's Quarterly Review, 161
Bermuda, 130, 180
Bessborough, Frederick George Brabazon Ponsonby, Earl of, 44
Beverley Recorder, 324, 327–8
Beverley, Yorks., 322–32 *passim*, 394, 395
Bianconi, Charles, 95, 482
Birch, Peregrine, 60
Birtwhistle, J. B., 326, 330
Blackwood, John: and AT's experiment in anonymity, 286–7, 289, 304–5, 308; *Ancient Classics for English Readers*, 355–7; declines *Eustace Diamonds*, 348; death, 462; other references, 109, 333, 349, 377, 413, 421, 425, 458, 461, 483
Blackwood, William, 411 n., 461, 462, 487, 501 n.
Blackwood's Edinburgh Magazine, 41, 286, 287, 301, 412, 456, 487
Bland, Florence Nightingale: taken into the Trollope household, 256–7; becomes AT's amanuensis, 446; serious illness, 489; twice accompanies AT to Ireland, 502–3; death, 511 n.; other references, 405 n., 418, 512
Bland, Joseph, 256
Bland, Mrs Joseph (Isabella Heseltine), 96, 256
Blaze de Bury, Mme Marie Pauline Rose, *All for Greed*, 310
Blessington, Marguerite Gardiner, Countess of, 109
Blewitt, Octavian, 263
Bloemfontein, Orange Free State, 429, 432
Blue Mountain Peak, Jamaica, 174
Blumenthal, Jacques, 216
Boccaccio, Giovanni, 69
Bodichon, Madame, 184
Boehm, Joseph Edgar, 258
Boers, Dutch, 431–2
Booth, Sir Charles, 504
Boston, 225, 226–7, 232, 238–9; Boston Public Library, 232
Bothnia, SS, 406, 407, 408

Boucicault, Dion: *Formosa*, 357
Boyd, A. K. H., 349
Brackenbury, Sir Henry, 320
Bradbury & Evans, 347, 357
Braddon, Mary Elizabeth, 338
Bradfield College, 194
Bradlaugh, Charles, 389
Brand, John Henry, 432
Bright, John, 149, 327, 336–7, 485
Brisbane Courier, 364, 403
Bristol, 125, 148
British Guiana, 172, 173, 175
British Quarterly Review, 240, 338
Bronson, Mrs Katherine Colman DeKay, 407, 419
Brontë, Anne: *Agnes Grey*, 97
Brontë, Charlotte, 85, 97, 208, 352, 484; *Jane Eyre*, 199 n., 378; *Villette*, 199 n.
Brontë, Emily, 484; *Wuthering Heights*, 97
Brooks, Shirley, 244, 391, 414, 487
Broughton, Rhoda, 321; *Not Wisely But Too Well*, 321
Browne, Hablot Knight, 268–9
Browning, Elizabeth Barrett, 157, 197, 210, 310; *Aurora Leigh*, 418 n.
Browning, Robert, 157, 202, 210, 219, 363, 389, 512, 513, 515; *The Ring and the Book*, 418
Bruges, Château d'Hondt, 46–7, 52
Bryce, James, 507
Buchanan, Robert, 355
Buckle, Henry Thomas, 239
Buffalo, NY, 227, 228
Bulwer, Sir Henry, 426
Bulwer, Lady Rosina (later Lady Lytton), 63, 64
Burgers, Thomas, 426, 430
Burgoyne, Sir John Fox, 201
Burke, Edmund: *Philosophical Enquiry into the Origins of Our Ideas of the Sublime and the Beautiful*, 44–5
Burke, Thomas Henry, 502
Burne-Jones, Edward, 363
Burns, John (later Lord Inverclyde), 440
Burns, Robert, 139
Butler, Dr George, 15, 17, 20
Butt, Isaac, 107–8, 501
Buxton, Charles, 279, 322; *Ideas of the Day on Policy*, 275–6
Byron, Allegra, 16, 51
Byron, George Gordon, 6th Baron, 16, 51, 139; *Childe Harold*, 418; *The Siege of Corinth*, 418 n.

Caesar, Julius, 121–2, 356
Cairo, 162; Shepheard's Hotel, Cairo, 162
Cairo, Illinois, 237

Index

Index

Index

Index

Index

[569]

Index

Lloyd, Charles Dalton Clifford, 503
Locker, Arthur, 393–4, 464
Locker-Lampson, Frederick, 219, 391, 508
Lockhart, John Gibson, 40; *Adam Blair*, 70
London Review, 208–9, 246, 249, 266, 289, 300
Long, George, 356
Longfellow, Henry Wadsworth, 239, 241; *The Courtship of Miles Standish*, 418 n.; *Evangeline*, 418 n.; *Hiawatha*, 418 n.; *The Skeleton in Armor*, 418 n.
Longley, Revd Charles Thomas (later Archbishop of Canterbury), 17, 41, 43, 44, 387
Longman, Thomas, 353–4, 435
Longman, William, 133–4, 139–40, 145–7, 153–4
Lothrop, Dr Samuel Kirkland, 241
Louisville, Kentucky, 237
Lovel, Edward, 355
Lowell, James Russell, 226, 239, 242
Lowell, Mass., 232
Lowick, Northants, 413, 460–1
Lowndes, William Selby, 377
Lucan, 415
Lunt, George, 210
Lytton, Edward George Lytton Bulwer, 69–70, 98, 102, 266, 310, 415; *Godolphin*, 69; *The Last Days of Pompeii*, 69; *The New Timon*, 418 n.
Lytton, Edward Robert Bulwer, 1st Earl of Lytton ('Owen Meredith'), *Lucille*, 418 n.

Maberly, Col. William Leader, 64–6, 76, 77, 82, 108–9, 128–9
Macaulay, Thomas Babington, 136, 310, 365; *Essays*, 365; *History of England*, 146
McCarthy, Justin, 108
McClellan, Gen. George B., 234
MacDonald, George, 314
Mackay, Charles, 474
Mackay, William, 404
Macleod, Donald, 419
Macleod, Revd Norman, 251–4, 296, 308
Macmillan, Alexander, 359, 513
Macmillan's English Men of Letters series, 449
Macmillan's Magazine, 359
Macquoid, Mrs Katherine Sarah, 355
Macready, William Charles: *Reminiscences*, 408–9, 413
Magog, Canada, 227
Maine, Sir Henry, 168–9
Mair, Capt. Gilbert, 373
Mallow, Co. Cork, 109, 117
Malta, 130, 159, 163–4
Manchester Weekly Times, 459

Manners, Lord John James Robert, 262, 421 n.
Manning, Henry Edward, Cardinal, 19, 453 n.
Maori peoples, 371–3
Mario, Mrs Jessie White, 512
Marrable, Frederick, 258
Marryat, Capt. Frederick, 28 n., 102
Marsh, Mrs Anne, 102
Marston, John, 41; *History of Antonio and Mellida*, 417
Martin, Baron Samuel, 328
Martineau, Harriet, 28 n.
Marylebone Workhouse, 53, 72
Mason, James, 233
Massinger, Philip, 415; *The Elder Brother* (with Fletcher), 490; *The Fatal Dowry*, 416–17; *The Old Law*, 485
Mastiff (yacht), 440–2
Maxwell, John, 201
Maxwell, the Hon. Marmaduke, 324–9 *passim*
Meetkerke family, 3–4
Meetkerke, Adolphus, 12, 40
Meetkerke, 1st Mrs Adolphus (Barbara Jenny Chapman), 12
Meetkerke, 2nd Mrs Adolphus (Matilda Jane Wilkinson), 12
Meetkerke, Mrs Adolphus (Cecilia Elizabeth Gore), 12, 298, 478, 499, 500, 514
Melbourne Argus, 403
Melbourne Club, 376
Melbourne, William Lamb, Viscount, 48
Meredith, George, 149, 189–90, 271, 279, 484; *The Ordeal of Richard Feverel*, 189–90
Mérimé, Prosper, 21
Merivale family, 13
Merivale, Revd Charles, 16, 357; *History of the Romans*, 121–2, 133, 355, 356, 357, 470
Merivale, Herman, 270
Merivale, John Lewis, 60–1, 91, 121, 134
Merrimac, 177
Metastasio, Pietro Antonio, 69
Metternich, Prince, and Princess Melanie, 60
Michelangelo, 215
Middleton, Thomas, 415; *A Game at Chess*, 417; *A Trick to Catch the Old One*, 490; *Your Five Gallants*, 417
Mill, John Stuart, 278–9, 340, 384
Millais, John Everett: AT meets, 202; illustrates AT's novels, 13 n., 203–4, 213–14, 249, 254–5, 269, 300, 308–9, 482; intimate friend, 214–15, 216, 331, 404–5, 478, 498, 514–15; *Parables of Our Lord*,

Index

254–5; other references, 219, 244, 251, 414, 487
Miller, Cincinnatus Hiner ('Joachim'), 389
Mills, William, 36, 37
Milltown Malbay, Co. Clare, 95
Milman family, 40
Milman, Lady Frances, 13
Milman, Revd Henry, 13, 40
Milman, Hugh Miles, 367
Milman, Sir William, 13
Milnes, Monckton, *see* Houghton, Richard
Milton, Henry (AT's uncle), 5, 6–7, 46, 48, 54, 96, 322
Milton, John (the poet), 51, 139; *Lycidas*, 69, 139 n.; *Paradise Lost*, 418
Milton, John (AT's great-grandfather), 4–5
Milton, Revd William (AT's grandfather), 5–6, 12, 21
Milton, 1st Mrs William (Mary Gresley, AT's grandmother), 5
Milton, 2nd Mrs William (Sarah Partington), 6
Milwaukee, 227–8
Mitford, Mary Russell, 13, 38–9, 42
Moher, Cliffs of, Co. Clare, 95
Molteno, Sir John Charles, 425–6
Monck, Sir Charles Stanley, 504
Montagu Square, London, 383, 477
Montrose, James Graham, 4th Duke of, 311
Morison, James Cotter, 271
Morley, John, 217, 277–9, 346, 449, 479, 508
Morning Advertiser, 123, 371 n.
Morning Post, 412
Morris, Mowbray, 362
Mortray, New South Wales, 364–5, 404–6
Motley, John Lothrop, 219, 239
Mousehole, Cornwall, 126
Mozley, Tom, 388
Mudie, Charles Edward: Mudie's Lending Library, 188–90
Müller, Karl Otfried, 72
Mulock, Dinah (Mrs Craik), 251, 355
Murray, John (the elder), 40, 45, 68
Murray, John (the younger), 120
Murrell, Dr William, 499, 500, 512, 514

Napier, Sir Charles, 495
Naples, 402
Napoleon I, 356
Napoleon III, 356, 385
Nase-ed-din, Shah of Persia, 385
Nashoba, Tenn., 26–7
Nation, New York, 266, 290, 388, 425, 453, 466
National Gallery, 215
National Press Agency, 444
National Review, 169, 245–7, 270

Nebraska, SS, 376
New College, Oxford, 4, 5, 11, 22, 31
New Granada, 172, 177, 180
New Guinea, 404
New Monthly Magazine, 67
New Poor Law, 113
New South Wales Select Parliamentary Committee, 367
'New Weekly' (proposed magazine), 269–70
New York City, 229–30
New York Times, 201
New Zealand, 371–3
Newby, Thomas Cautley, 97, 101
Newcastle, Henry Pelham Clinton, 4th Duke of, 138
Newman, John Henry, Cardinal, 150, 513
Newport, Rhode Island, 225–6
Niagara Falls, 38, 181, 227
Nineteenth Century, 271
North American Review, 460 n.
North British Daily Mail, 402
North British Weekly Mail, 459
Northcote, Sir Stafford, 141, 155
Northumberland Street, London, 53
Northwick, John Rushout, 2nd Baron, 11, 12, 39, 45–6
Nott, Dr George Frederick, 14
Nubar Bey (later Nubar Pasha), 160–1
Nuremberg, 130, 285
Nuwara Elliya, Ceylon, 403

O'Brien, Smith, 111
O'Connell, Daniel, 103
O'Connell, Mrs Morgan John, 482–3
O'Hagan, Judge John, 503
O'Neil, Henry Nelson, 244, 309, 311, 377
O'Neill, Hugh Dubh, 95
O'Reilly, Mary, 106–8
O'Shea, Mrs Katherine (*née* Wood, 'Kitty'), 217 n.
Okey sisters, 63–4
Old Square, Lincoln's Inn, 4, 31–2, 491
Oliphant, Laurence, 208, 219
Oliphant, Mrs Margaret, 57, 301, 483, 494 n.
Once A Week, 347
Orley Farm School, 213
Osborne, Revd Sidney Godolphin, 112
Osler, Sir William, 487
Ouseley, Sir William, 178
Ouvry, Frederic, 442
Ovid, 415
Owen, Robert: New Harmony Settlement, 26, 27

Paget, Sir James, 409
Pakington, Sir John, 327

[571]

Index

Index

St Helier, Jersey, 127–8
St James's Gazette, 473
St James's Magazine, 215
St John's College, Cambridge, 4
St John's College, Oxford, 5
St Kilda, 441
St Louis, 236–7
Saint Pauls Magazine, 306–15 *passim*, 318, 320, 350–5, 363, 394
St Peter Port, Guernsey, 128
St Thomas, Virgin Islands, 172, 176, 177, 181–2
Sala, George Augustus Henry, 200, 202, 508
Salisbury, 125, 131
Sallust, 415
Salt Lake City, Utah, 376
San Francisco, 406
San José, Costa Rica, 177–9
Sand, George: *L'Uscoque*, 70
Sanford, Cordelia Riddle, 209
Sanford, Milton, 209–10
Santa Marta, New Granada, 177
Sarony, Napoleon (photographer), 319
Saturday Review, 55, 149, 151, 157–8, 168–9, 197, 201, 205, 240, 243, 244, 246, 249, 250, 256, 266, 297, 298, 299, 339, 346, 357, 358, 359, 378–9, 387–8, 393, 400–1, 412, 424, 433, 437, 452, 458, 460, 465, 474, 493, 497, 507
Saunders, John, 355
Schlegel, Augustus Wilhelm von, 72; *Dramatic Art and Literature*, 69
Scotland, Church of, 251–3
Scott, Clement, 371
Scott, Miss, 367
Scott, Sir Walter, 51, 139, 208, 348, 349, 435; *Ivanhoe*, 51, 378; *Old Mortality*, 378; *Waverley*, 205
Scudamore, Frank Ives, 260
Sedgwick, A. G., 453
Selwyn, Bishop George, 372
Sergent, Lewis, 495
Seville, 164
Seward, William Henry, 234
Sewell, Revd James Edwards, 413
Sewell, Mrs Elizabeth: *Rose of Cheriton*, 276–7
Seymour, Henry Danby, 270
Seymour, Indiana, 237–8
Shaftesbury, Anthony Ashley Cooper, 7th Earl of, 420
Shakespeare, 51, 365, 415; *All's Well that Ends Well*, 416; *As You Like It*, 416; *Hamlet*, 139 n., 416; *Henry IV*, 70, 416; *Julius Caesar*, 416; *King Lear*, 416; *Love's Labour's Lost*, 416; *Macbeth*, 139 n., 416,

500; *Measure for Measure*, 416; *The Merchant of Venice*, 416; *A Midsummer Night's Dream*, 416; *Much Ado about Nothing*, 416; *Richard II*, 70; *Richard III*, 416; *Romeo and Juliet*, 416; *The Tempest*, 416; *Twelfth Night*, 416
Shand, Alexander Innes, 412
Sharpe's London Magazine, 104, 197
Shaw, George Bernard, 507
Shelley, Adolphus, 76
Shelley, Mary, 26
Shelley, Percy Bysshe, 139; *The Revolt of Islam*, 418 n.
Shepstone, Sir Theophilus, 428, 429–30
Sibthorp, Col. Charles de Laet Waldo, 123
Sidney, Sir Philip: *Arcadia*, 415
Sismondi, J. C. L. Sismonde de, 21, 72; *Literature of the South*, 69
Slidell, John, 233
Small, William, 482
Smalley, George, 388, 433
Smith, Albert, 202
Smith, Barnett, 495
Smith, Elder and Co., 190–2, 208, 258, 291, 300, 435
Smith, George: publishes AT in *Cornhill Magazine*, 190–2, 196–9, 203–4, 212, 223, 243–4, 249, 259; and in *Pall Mall Gazette*, 280–3, 370; insists on 'delicacy', 207–8; publishes *Last Chronicle*, 291–2, 299–300; declines collected edition, 313–14; hospitality to and friendship for AT, 199–202, 209, 259, 264–5; AT sponsors for Garrick, 282; other references, 147 n., 203–4, 206, 217, 218, 251, 285–6, 291–2, 310, 354, 370, 435, 449, 479; *see also* Smith, Elder and Co.
Smith, Mrs George (Elizabeth Blakeway), 217
Smith, Godwin, *The Civil War in America*, 276
Smith, Sydney, 18–19, 251 n., 310, 372
Smith, W. H., 313, 435
Somerset, 125, 513
South Africa, 421, 425–34
Southey, Robert, 42, 139
Spain, 130
Spanish Town, Jamaica, 174
Spectator, 101, 135, 169, 204, 241, 244, 249, 250, 288, 336, 338, 359, 378, 387, 397, 400, 425, 437, 453, 458, 460, 465–6
Spedding, James, 330 n.
Spenser, Edmund, 139; *Faerie Queene*, 418
Stanford, Sir Herbert Bruce, 469
Stanhope, Philip Henry, 5th Earl, 262, 263, 302, 316, 409

[573]

Index

Index

Index

Index

Wales, 125, 126, 129

Wallace, William, 460

Walpole, Hugh, 449

Walpole, Spencer Horatio, 469

Waltham House, Waltham Cross, 188, 194, 216–18, 242, 362, 377

Ward, Mrs Edward, 440

Ward, Mrs Humphry, 217

Ward, T. H., 453–4

Waring, Charles, 270–1

Washington, DC, 233–6, 238, 317–19 *passim*

Washington, George, 356

Watkins, Herbert, 265

Webster and Rowley: *The Thracian Wonder*, 417

Wedderburn, W. T., 129

Wells, 513

Wells, T. Spencer, 487

West Indies, 130, 171–82 *passim*, 274

West Point Military Academy, 229

Western Australia, 366, 369–70, 404

Westminster, Hugh Lupus Grosvenor, 1st Duke of, 420

Westminster Review, 149, 243, 266, 388, 411, 454, 465

Whately, Revd Richard, 31

Whewell, William, 310

White Mountains, Vermont, 227

Whitehall Review, 455

Whiteside, James, 120

Whiting, Lilian, 345

Whiting, the Misses, 407

Whittaker, George, 38–9, 42

Wilberforce, Samuel (Bishop of Oxford), 262

Wilkes, Charles, 29

Wilkes, Capt. Charles, 233, 234

Wilkins, William, 215

Wiltshire, 125

Winchester, 125, 148, 513

Winchester College, 4, 5, 11, 21–2, 23–5, 29–31, 43, 435

Women's Rights, 339–45, 467–8

Wood, Lady (Emma Caroline Michell), 217; *Sorrow on the Sea*, 321

Woods, Henry, 482

Woolf, Virginia, 397

Worcester, 125, 148

Wordworth, Christopher (Bishop of Lincoln), 19

Wordsworth, William, 32, 139; *The Excursion*, 418 n.

World, 473

Wright, Frances, 21, 26–7; *Views of Society and Manners in America*, 21

Yates, Edmund, 162, 200–1, 222, 349 n., 391–2, 414

York Street, Portman Square, 61

Yosemite, 406

Young, Brigham, 376

Zulu people, 421, 427–8, 434

[581]

THE WORLD'S CLASSICS

A Select List

SERGEI AKSAKOV: A Russian Gentleman
Translated by J. D. Duff
Edited by Edward Crankshaw

A Russian Schoolboy
Translated by J. D. Duff
Introduction by John Bayley

HANS ANDERSEN: Fairy Tales
Translated by L. W. Kingsland
Introduction by Naomi Lewis
Illustrated by Vilhelm Pedersen and Lorenz Frølich

LUDOVICO ARIOSTO: Orlando Furioso
Translated by Guido Waldman

ARISTOTLE: The Nicomachean Ethics
Translated by David Ross

JANE AUSTEN: Emma
Edited by James Kinsley and David Lodge

ROBERT BAGE: Hermsprong
Edited by Peter Faulkner

R. D. BLACKMORE: Lorna Doone
Edited by Sally Shuttleworth

MARY ELIZABETH BRADDON: Lady Audley's Secret
Edited by David Skilton

CHARLOTTE BRONTË: Jane Eyre
Edited by Margaret Smith

EMILY BRONTË: Wuthering Heights
Edited by Ian Jack

DANIEL DEFOE: Colonel Jack
Edited by Samuel Holt Monk and David Roberts

THOMAS DE QUINCEY:
The Confessions of an English Opium-Eater
Edited by Grevel Lindop

CHARLES DICKENS: Christmas Books
Edited by Ruth Glancy

Oliver Twist
Edited by Kathleen Tillotson

BENJAMIN DISRAELI: Coningsby
Edited by Sheila M. Smith

FËDOR DOSTOEVSKY: Crime and Punishment
Translated by Jessie Coulson
Introduction by John Jones

ARTHUR CONAN DOYLE:
Sherlock Holmes: Selected Stories
Introduction by S. C. Roberts

ALEXANDRE DUMAS *fils*:
La Dame aux Camélias
Translated by David Coward

MARIA EDGEWORTH: Castle Rackrent
Edited by George Watson

GEORGE ELIOT: Daniel Deronda
Edited by Graham Handley

Felix Holt, The Radical
Edited by Fred C. Thompson

JOHN MEADE FALKNER: The Nebuly Coat
Edited by Christopher Hawtree

MICHELANGELO: Life, Letters, and Poetry
Translated by George Bull with Peter Porter

MOLIÈRE: Don Juan and Other Plays
Translated by George Graveley and Ian Maclean

GEORGE MOORE: Esther Waters
Edited by David Skilton

JOHN HENRY NEWMAN: Loss and Gain
Edited by Alan G. Hill

MARGARET OLIPHANT:
A Beleaguered City and Other Stories
Edited by Merryn Williams

OVID: Metamorphoses
Translated by A. D. Melville
Introduction and Notes by E. J. Kenney

THOMAS LOVE PEACOCK: Headlong Hall and Gryll Grange
Edited by Michael Baron and Michael Slater

EDGAR ALLAN POE: Selected Tales
Edited by Julian Symons

JEAN RACINE: Britannicus, Phaedra, Athaliah
Translated by C. H. Sisson

ANN RADCLIFFE: The Italian
Edited by Frederick Garber

PAUL SALZMAN (Ed.):
An Anthology of Elizabethan Prose Fiction

SIR WALTER SCOTT: The Heart of Midlothian
Edited by Claire Lamont

IZAAK WALTON and CHARLES COTTON:
The Compleat Angler
Edited by John Buxton
Introduction by John Buchan

MRS HUMPHREY WARD: Robert Elsmere
Edited by Rosemary Ashton

OSCAR WILDE: Complete Shorter Fiction
Edited by Isobel Murray

The Picture of Dorian Gray
Edited by Isobel Murray

MARY WOLLSTONECRAFT:
Mary *and* The Wrongs of Woman
Edited by Gary Kelly

ÉMILE ZOLA:
The Attack on the Mill and other stories
Translated by Douglas Parmeé

A complete list of Oxford Paperbacks, including The World's Classics, OPUS, Past Masters, Oxford Authors, Oxford Shakespeare, and Oxford Paperback Reference, is available in the UK from the Arts and Reference Publicity Department (RS), Oxford University Press, Walton Street, Oxford OX2 6DP.

In the USA, complete lists are available from the Paperbacks Marketing Manager, Oxford University Press, 200 Madison Avenue, New York, NY 10016.

Oxford Paperbacks are available from all good bookshops. In case of difficulty, customers in the UK can order direct from Oxford University Press Bookshop, Freepost, 116 High Street, Oxford, OX1 4BR, enclosing full payment. Please add 10 per cent of published price for postage and packing.